Lecture Notes in Computer Science   12571

Services Science

Subline of Lectures Notes in Computer Science

More information about this subseries at http://www.springer.com/series/7408

Eleanna Kafeza · Boualem Benatallah ·
Fabio Martinelli · Hakim Hacid ·
Athman Bouguettaya · Hamid Motahari (Eds.)

Service-Oriented Computing

18th International Conference, ICSOC 2020
Dubai, United Arab Emirates, December 14–17, 2020
Proceedings

 Springer

Editors
Eleanna Kafeza 📵
Zayed University
Dubai, United Arab Emirates

Fabio Martinelli
IIT National Research Council C.N.R.
Pisa, Italy

Athman Bouguettaya 📵
University of Sydney
Darlington, NSW, Australia

Boualem Benatallah
University of New South Wales
Sydney, NSW, Australia

Hakim Hacid 📵
Zayed University
Dubai, United Arab Emirates

Hamid Motahari
Ernst & Young AI Lab
San Jose, CA, USA

ISSN 0302-9743   ISSN 1611-3349   (electronic)
Lecture Notes in Computer Science
ISBN 978-3-030-65309-5   ISBN 978-3-030-65310-1   (eBook)
https://doi.org/10.1007/978-3-030-65310-1

LNCS Sublibrary: SL2 – Programming and Software Engineering

This Springer imprint is published by the registered company Springer Nature Switzerland AG
The registered company address is: Gewerbestrasse 11, 6330 Cham, Switzerland

Preface

Welcome to the proceedings of the 18th International Conference on Service-Oriented Computing (ICSOC 2020). ICSOC 2020 took place virtually, during December 14–17, 2020. Its aim is to bring together academics, industry researchers, developers, and practitioners to report and share ground-breaking work in the area of Service Oriented Computing (SOC). The objective of ICSOC 2020 was to foster cross-community scientific excellence by gathering experts from various disciplines, such as Web services, business-process management, distributed systems, mobile computing, cloud/edge/fog computing, security/privacy and trust for services, cyber-physical systems, Internet of Things (IoT), scientific workflows, services science, data science and services, and software engineering. This edition of ICSOC built upon a history of successful series of previous editions in Toulouse (France), Hangzhou (Zhejiang, China), Malaga (Spain), Banff (Alberta, Canada), Goa (India), Paris (France), Berlin (Germany), Shanghai (China), Paphos (Cyprus), San Francisco (California, USA), Stockholm (Sweden), Sydney (Australia), Vienna (Austria), Chicago (USA), Amsterdam (The Netherlands), New York (USA), and Trento (Italy).

The conference attracted papers co-authored by researchers, practitioners, and academics from different countries. We received 137 research and industry paper submissions from countries across all continents. Each paper submission was carefully reviewed by at least five members of the Program Committee (PC), followed by discussions moderated by a senior PC member who made a recommendation in the form of a meta-review. The PC consisted of 179 world-class experts in service-oriented computing and related areas (161 PC members and 18 Senior PC members). Based on the recommendations, and the discussions, 26 papers were accepted (23 research papers and 3 industry papers) making the acceptance rate 18.9% for full papers. We also selected 16 short papers (11.6%). A vision track was introduced this year which attracted 10 submissions. The committee rejected all the submissions as they were not visionary. This track will be reconducted in the next edition to give the community a forum for expressing futuristic ideas that can drive and guide ongoing research efforts.

The program we assembled is reflective of the breadth and depth of the research and applications of SOC, organized into four main focus areas:

- Focus Area-1: Service Oriented Technology Trends
- Focus Area-2: Blockchain Technologies
- Focus Area-3: Industry 4.0 Technologies
- Focus Area-4: Smart services, Smart data and Smart applications

Contributions discuss different topics including, but not limited to, service-oriented engineering, run-time service operations and management, security, privacy and trust for services, data science and services, Internet of Things (IoT), and services in organizations, business, and society. Furthermore, the program includes key notes from distinguished speakers.

In addition to the technical program consisting of the keynote talks, the main research track, the industry track, the PhD symposium, and the demo session, the scope of ICSOC 2020 was broadened by different workshops.

In addition, special thanks are due to the members of the Senior PC, the International PC, and the external reviewers for a rigorous and robust reviewing process. The ICSOC 2020 Organizing Committee is also grateful to the workshop organizers for their great efforts to help promote SOC research to broader domains. We are also grateful to Zayed University, UAE, for supporting the organization of the event, and the technical support for ensuring a successful online event. We would also like to acknowledge all the members of the Organizing Committee and all who contributed to make ICSOC 2020 a successful event. We also acknowledge the prompt and professional support from Springer, the publisher these proceedings in printed and electronic volumes as part of the *Lecture Notes in Computer Science* series. Most importantly, we would like to thank all authors and participants of ICSOC 2020 for their insightful work and discussions.

We expect that the ideas that have emerged in ICSOC 2020 will result in the development of further innovations for the benefit of scientific, industrial, and social communities.

November 2020

Eleanna Kafeza
Boualem Benatallah
Fabio Martinelli
Hakim Hacid
Athman Bouguettaya
Hamid Motahari

Organization

Committees

Honorary Chairs

Zakaria Maamar   Zayed University, UAE
Jianwei Yin   Zhejiang University, China

General Co-chairs

Hakim Hacid   Zayed University, UAE
Athman Bouguettaya   The University of Sydney, Australia

Program Co-chairs

Eleana Kafeza   Zayed University, UAE
Boualem Benatallah   UNSW, Australia
Fabio Martinelli   Institute of Informatics and Telematics, CNR, Italy

Industrial Track Co-chairs

Hamid Motahari   EY AI Lab, USA
Shengbo Guo   Facebook, USA

Workshop Co-chairs

Fatma Outay   Zayed University, UAE
Helen Paik   UNSW, Australia
Amira Alloum   Huawei, France

Special Sessions/Area Co-chairs

Tetsuya Yoshida   Nara Women's University, Japan
Brahim Medjahed   University of Michigan, USA

Tutorial/Panel Co-chairs

Salima Benbernou   Université de Paris, France
Patrick C. K. Hung   Ontario Tech University, Canada
Reda Bouadjenek   Deakin University, Australia

Demonstrations Co-chairs

Amin Beheshti   Macquarie University, Australia
Xumin Liu   RIT, USA
Abderrahmane Maaradji   Université de Paris, France

PhD Symposium Co-chairs

Mohamad Badra	Zayed University, UAE
Marinella Petrocchi	Institute of Informatics and Telematics, CNR, Italy

Sponsorship Co-chairs

Huwida Said	Zayed University, UAE
Emad Bataineh	Zayed University, UAE
Haseena Al Katheeri	Zayed University, UAE

Finance Chair

Bernd J. Krämer	FernUniversität in Hagen, Germany

Local Arrangement Co-chairs

Andrew Leonce	Zayed University, UAE
Chandrashekaran Nagarajan	Zayed University, UAE

Publication Chair

Hakim Hacid	Zayed University, UAE

Publicity Co-chairs

Noura Faci	Claude Bernard Lyon 1 University, France
Guilherme Horta Travassos	COPPE/Federal University of Rio de Janeiro, Brazil
Hai Dong	RMIT, Australia

Website Co-chairs

Emir Ugljanin	State University of Novi Pazar, Serbia
Emerson Bautista	Zayed University, UAE

ICSOC Steering Committee Representative

Jian Yang	Macquarie University, Australia

Program Committee

Senior Program Committee Members

Aditya Ghose	University of Wollongong, Australia
Canal Carlos	University of Malaga, Spain
Casati Fabio	University of Trento, Italy
De Paoli Flavio	University of Milano-Bicocca, Italy
Dustdar Schahram	TU Wien, Austria
Farouk Toumani	LIMOS, France
Michael Q. Sheng	Macquarie University, Australia
Mohand-Said Hacid	Claude Bernard Lyon 1 University, France
Mohamed Adel Serhani	UAEU, UAE

Pautasso Cesare	University of Lugano, Switzerland
Pernici Barbara	Politecnico di Milano, Italy
Rossi Gustavo	UNLP, Argentina
Ruiz-Cortés Antonio	University of Seville, Spain
Tai Stefan	TU Berlin, Germany
Weske Mathias	HPI, University of Potsdam, Germany
Yang Jian	Macquarie University, Australia
Zakaria Maamar	Zayed University, UAE
Zhang Liang	Fudan University, China

Program Committee Members

Abdelkarim Erradi	Qatar University, Qatar
Afonso Fereira	University of Toulouse, France
Alessandro Aldini	University of Urbino, Italy
Alex Norta	Tallinn University of Technology, Estonia
Alvaro Arenas	IE Business School, Spain
Amin Beheshti	Macquarie University, Australia
Anne Ngu	Texas State University, USA
Antonio Brogi	University of Pisa, Italy
Antonio Bucchiarone	Fondazione Bruno Kessler, Italy
Antonio Ruiz-Cortés	University of Seville, Spain
Anup Kumar Kalia	IBM T. J. Watson Research Center, USA
Armin Haller	The Australian National University, Australia
Aviv Segev	University of South Alabama, USA
Barbara Pernici	Politecnico di Milano, Italy
Belatreche Ladjel	ISAE-ENSMA, France
Brahim Medjahed	University of Michigan, USA
Bruno Defude	Télécom Sud Paris, France
Carlos E. Cuesta	Rey Juan Carlos University, Spain
Cesare Pautasso	University of Lugano, Switzerland
Chihab Hanachi	IRIT Laboratory, Toulouse 1, France
Christian Zirpins	Karlsruhe University of Applied Sciences, Germany
Christoph Bussler	Google, Inc., USA
Colette Roland	Universite Paris1 Panthéon Sorbonne, France
Cristina Cabanillas	Vienna University of Economics and Business, Austria
Daniela Grigori	Paris Dauphine University, France
Dimka Karastoyanova	University of Groningen, The Netherlands
Diptikalyan Saha	IBM Research, India
Djamal Benslimane	Claude Bernard Lyon 1 University, France
Ejub Kajan	State University of Novi Pazar, Serbia
Ernesto Pimentel	University of Malaga, Spain
Fabio Casati	University of Trento, Italy
Faouzi Ben Charrada	University of Tunis El Manar, Tunisia
Flavio De Paoli	University of Milano-Bicocca, Italy
Floriano Zini	Free University of Bozen-Bolzano, Italy

Lin Chen (Liana)	IBM Research, USA
Lina Yao	UNSW, Australia
Lionel Seinturier	University of Lille, France
Luca Foschini	University of Bologna, Italy
Luciano Baresi	Politecnico di Milano, Italy
Manfred Reichert	Ulm University, Germany
Manuel Lama	University of Santiago de Compostela, Spain
Marcelo Fantinato	University of São Paulo, Brazil
Marco Aiello	University of Stuttgart, Germany
Marcos Baez	LIRIS Lyon, France
Marin Litoiu	York University, Canada
Marios-Eleftherios Fokaefs	École Polytechnique Montréal, Canada
Maja Vukovi	IBM, USA
Massimo Mecella	Sapienza Università di Roma, Italy
Mathias Weske	HPI, University of Potsdam, Germany
Matthias Weidlich	Humboldt-Universität zu Berlin, Germany
Maude Manouvrier	University of Paris Dauphine, France
Michael Mrissa	InnoRenew CoE, University of Primorska, Slovenia
Mingxue Wang	Huawei Ireland Research Center, Ireland
Moez Ben Haj Hmida	National Engineering School of Tunis (ENIT), Tunisia
Mohammad Allahbakhsh	University of Mashhad, Iran
Mohamed Graiet	ISIMM, Tunisia
Mohamed Mohamed	IBM Almaden Research Center, USA
Mohamed Sellami	Télécom SudParis, France
Monica Vitali	Politecnico di Milano, Italy
N. D. Gangadhar	M. S. Ramaiah University of Applied Sciences, India
Nanjangud C. Narendra	Ericsson Research, India
Naouel Moha	UQAM, Canada
Nawal Guermouche	Université de Toulouse, France
Nirmit Desai	IBM T. J. Watson Research Center, USA
Noura Faci	Claude Bernard Lyon 1 University, CNRS, France
Olaf Zimmermann	University of Applied Sciences of Eastern Switzerland (HSR FHO), Switzerland
Olivier Perrin	Lorraine University, France
Omar Boucelma	Aix-Marseille University, France
Onyeka Ezenwoye	Augusta University, USA
Pablo Fernandez	University of Seville, Spain
Pascal Poizat	Université Paris Nanterre, LIP6, France
Pedro Álvarez	University of Zaragoza, Spain
Philippe Lalanda	UGA, France
Philippe Massonet	CETIC, Belgium
Pierluigi Plebani	Politecnico di Milano, Italy
Pooyan Jamshidi	University of South Carolina, USA
Qi Yu	Rochester Institute of Technology, USA
Qiang He	Swinburne University of Technology, Australia
Marouane Kessentini	University of Michigan, USA

Raffaela Mirandola	Politecnico di Milano, Italy
Richard Hull	IBM Research, USA
Rik Eshuis	Eindhoven University of Technology, The Netherlands
Salima Benbernou	Université Paris Descartes, France
Sami Bhiri	Télécom SudParis, France
Sami Yangui	LAAS, France
Sanjay Chaudhary	Ahmedabad University, India
Sergey Smirnov	SAP, Germany
Shiping Chen	CSIRO, Australia
Shuiguang Deng	Zhejiang University, China
Sira Yongchareon	Auckland University of Technology, New Zealand
Sokratis Katsikas	Norwegian University of Science and Technology, Norway
Stefan Schulte	TU Wien, Austria
Stefan Tai	TU Berlin, Germany
Stefanie Rinderle-Ma	University of Vienna, Austria
Sumaira Sultan Minhas	Fatima Jinnah Women University, Pakistan
Surya Nepal	CSIRO, Australia
Talal H. Noor	Taibah University, Saudi Arabia
Thais Batista	UFRN, Brazil
Tommi Mikkonen	University of Helsinki, Finland
Uwe Zdun	University of Vienna, Austria
Walid Gaaloul	Télécom SudParis, France
Walter Binder	University of Lugano, Switzerland
Weiliang Zhao	Macquarie University, Australia
Wing-Kwong Chan	The City University of Hong Kong, Hong Kong
Wolfgang Reisig	Humboldt-Universität zu Berlin, Germany
Xiang Fu	Hofstra, USA
Xianzhi Wang	University of Technology Sydney, Australia
Xuanzhe Liu	Peking University, China
Xumin Liu	Rochester Institute of Technology, USA
Yan Wang	Macquarie University, Australia
Yehia Taher	University of Versailles-St-Quentin-en-Yvelines, France
Ying Li	Zhejiang University, China
Yucong Duan	Hainan University, China
Zhangbing Zhou	China University of Geosciences (Beijing), China.
Zhiyong Feng	Tianjin University, China
Zhongjie Wang	Harbin Institute of Technology, China

External Reviewers

| Davide Micale | University of Catania, Italy |
| José Javier Berrocal Olmeda | University of Extremadura, Spain |

Vasileios Karagiannis	TU Wien, Austria
Pietro Biondi	University of Catania, Italy
Mahsa Hadian	Polytechnique Montreal, Canada
Mohammadreza Rasolroveicy	Polytechnique Montreal, Canada

A Tribute to Florian Daniel's Contributions to Service-Oriented Computing

Marcos Baez, Boualem Benatallah, Cinzia Cappiello, Fabio Casati

Florian's friends and colleagues

Florian Daniel left us abruptly at the age of 42. He left a void that can not be filled, memories and teachings that will stay with us friends, colleagues, and students forever. Florian is remembered as an active and prolific member of the ICSOC community, contributing to the advancement of key areas of service-oriented computing, and shaping the minds of a new generation of researchers. While it is impossible to condense the impact of a creative, intelligent, and wonderful person like Florian in a few paragraphs, we try to highlight his main contributions in the following.

Florian's research in software-oriented computing is marked by the exploration into a diversity of topics that led to fundamental, practical, and seminal work that benefited the IC-SOC community and beyond.

This exploration started with contributions to service composition and orchestration, building on the technological foundation of distributed computing. His research contributed with techniques, algorithms, and tools to leverage service interactions to derive service dependencies, protocols, and ultimately service compositions [4, 5, 22, 26]. It helped cement the work on service composition [21] and highlight core concerns and open questions.

In business process management, his work contributed most notably to process intelligence, modeling, and compliance. In process intelligence, he focused on the challenges of low-quality data, introducing the concept of uncertain key indicators, as well as models and tools to address this problem [26, 24]. The research on process modeling produced modeling languages (e.g., extensions of BPMN or BPEL) and runtime environments for project-centered learning [8], resource lifecycle management [3], user interface orchestration [18, 17], wireless sensor networks [6], and

Fig. 1 Florian with friends and colleagues at ICSOC 2009, Stockholm

crowdsourcing [30]. In terms business compliance, it addressed the practical and conceptual challenges in designing, executing, and evaluating compliance with regulations governing business process, contributing with concepts [29, 28], techniques and algorithms [27, 26], and tools [12].

His work also looked at challenges and opportunities that emerge at the intersection of processes and crowdsourcing. It advanced the knowledge in this area with contributions ranging from surveys that brought understanding to the notion of crowdsourcing processes [20] and associated quality attributes [15] to new approaches in the modeling and execution of crowdsourcing processes that seamlessly integrate with common BPM practice [30]. This line of research also extended to relevant application areas, such as leveraging crowdsourcing for data mining [23] and activity matching in BPM [25].

In his continuous exploration for new avenues for service-oriented computing, his most recent work investigated the feasibility of leveraging blockchain, and particularly smart contracts, to enable a blockchain-based, service-oriented computing paradigm [14]. This work and its follow-up [19] are already motivating promising research in this area.

Another important line of research that he pursued with passion had to do with assisting the development of software-enabled services. Besides fundamental contributions to the engineering of service-oriented systems, this produced seminal work in Mashups, UI-computing, and lately chatbot development. The work on mashups contributed with one of the first mashup frameworks, a universal integration approach for data, application logic and UIs [11], domain-specific mashups [7], and a complete, conceptual tool suite for the development of custom mashup platforms [31]. The experience gained in mashups, led Florian to propose a paradigm shift in end-user programming, moving away from APIs and Web Services to software artefact end-users truly knew: the graphical interface. This motivated his work on UI-oriented computing [10, 13], where the goal was to provide a development environment where end users would leverage existing UI components and data directly from rendered UIs to build their solutions, without going through APIs and services. Perhaps the final materialization of this A Tribute to Florian Daniel's Contributions to Service-Oriented Computing idea can be seen in his latest work on deriving chatbots directly from software artefacts, allowing users to engage in dialogs directly with databases [16] and websites [1, 9], leading to the definition of chatbot integration as an emerging new problem [2].

Last but not least, Florian represents and embodies the spirit of what the ICSOC community – and the research community in general – should be. Deep technical competences, humbleness, enthusiasm, uncompromising professional integrity, focus on topics that matter, and most importantly a natural propensity to help others in any way possible, always with a smile and a positive, constructive, make-you-feel-good attitude. Let's all remember the lessons he gave us by example to make our community a great place to be.

References

1. Baez, M., Daniel, F., Casati, F.: Conversational web interaction: proposal of a dialog-based natural language interaction paradigm for the web. In: Følstad, A., et al. (eds.) CONVERSATIONS 2019. LNCS, vol. 11970, pp. 94–110. Springer, Cham (2020). https://doi.org/10.1007/978-3-030-39540-7_7
2. Baez, M., Daniel, F., Casati, F., Benatallah, B.: Chatbot integration in few patterns. IEEE Internet Comput. (2020)
3. Báez, M., et al.: Gelee: cooperative lifecycle management for (composite) artifacts. In: Baresi, L., Chi, C.H., Suzuki, J. (eds.) ServiceWave 2009, ICSOC 2009. LNCS, vol 5900, pp. 645–646. Springer, Heidelberg (2009). https://doi.org/10.1007/978-3-642-10383-4_50
4. Basu, S., Casati, F., Daniel, F.: Web service dependency discovery tool for SOA management. In: IEEE International Conference on Services Computing (SCC 2007), pp. 684–685. IEEE (2007)
5. Basu, S., Casati, F., Daniel, F.: Toward web service dependency discovery for SOA management. In: 2008 IEEE International Conference on Services Computing, vol. 2, pp. 422–429. IEEE (2008)
6. Casati, F., et al.: Towards business processes orchestrating the physical enterprise with wireless sensor networks. In: 2012 34th International Conference on Software Engineering (ICSE), pp. 1357–1360. IEEE (2012)
7. Casati, F., et al.: Developing mashup tools for end-users: on the importance of the application domain. Int. J. Next-Gener. Comput. 3(2) (2012)
8. Ceri, S., Daniel, F., Matera, M., Raffio, A.: Providing flexible process support to project-centered learning. IEEE Trans. Knowl. Data Eng. 21(6), 894–909 (2008)
9. Chittò, P., Baez, M., Daniel, F., Benatallah, B.: Automatic generation of chatbots for conversational web browsing. arXiv preprint https://arxiv.org/abs/2008.12097 (2020)
10. Daniel, F.: Live, personal data integration through ui-oriented computing. In: Cimiano, P., Frasincar, F., Houben, G.J., Schwabem D. (eds.) ICWE 2015. LNCS, vol. 9114, pp. 479–497. Springer, Cham (2015). https://doi.org/10.1007/978-3-319-19890-3_31
11. Daniel, F., Casati, F., Benatallah, B., Shan, M.C.: Hosted universal composition: models, languages and infrastructure in mashArt. In: Laender, A.H.F., Castano, S., Dayal, U., Casati, F.,

de Oliveira J.P.M. (eds.) ER 2009. LNCS, vol. 5829, pp. 428–443. Springer, Heidelberg (2009). https://doi.org/10.1007/978-3-642-04840-1_32.

12. Daniel, F., et al.: Business compliance governance in service-oriented architectures. In: 2009 International Conference on Advanced Information Networking and Applications, pp. 113–120. IEEE (2009)

13. Daniel, F., Furlan, A.: The interactive API (iAPI). In: Sheng, Q.Z., Kjeldskov, J. (eds.) ICWE 2013. LNCS, vol 8295, pp. 3–15. Springer, Cham (2013). https://doi.org/10.1007/978-3-319-04244-2_2

14. Daniel, F., Guida, L.: A service-oriented perspective on blockchain smart contracts. IEEE Internet Comput. 23(1), 46–53 (2019)

15. Daniel, F., Kucherbaev, P., Cappiello, C., Benatallah, B., Allahbakhsh, M.: Quality control in crowdsourcing: a survey of quality attributes, assessment techniques, and assurance actions. ACM Comput. Surv. (CSUR) 51(1), 1–40 (2018)

16. Daniel, F., Matera, M., Zaccaria, V., Dell'Orto, A.: Toward truly personal chatbots: on the development of custom conversational assistants. In: Proceedings of the 1st International Workshop on Software Engineering for Cognitive Services, pp. 31–36 (2018)

17. Daniel, F., Soi, S., Tranquillini, S., Casati, F., Heng, C., Yan, L.: From people to services to UI: distributed orchestration of user interfaces . In: Hull, R., Mendling, J., Tai, S. (eds.) BPM 2010. LNCS, vol. 6336, pp. 310–326 (2010). Springer, Heidelberg. https://doi.org/10.1007/978-3-642-15618-2_22

18. Daniel, F., Soi, S., Tranquillini, S., Casati, F., Heng, C., Yan, L.: Distributed orchestration of user interfaces. Inf. Syst. 37(6), 539–556 (2012)

19. Falazi, G., Breitenbücher, U., Daniel, F., Lamparelli, A., Leymann, F., Yussupov, V.: Smart contract invocation protocol (SCIP): a protocol for the uniform integration of heterogeneous blockchain smart contracts. In: Dustdar, S., Yu, E., Salinesi, C., Rieu, D., Pant, V. (eds.) CAiSE 2020. LNCS, vol. 12127, pp. 134–149. Springer, Cham (2020). https://doi.org/10.1007/978-3-030-49435-3_9

20. Kucherbaev, P., Daniel, F., Tranquillini, S., Marchese, M.: Crowdsourcing processes: a survey of approaches and opportunities. IEEE Internet Comput. 20(2), 50–56 (2015)

21. Lemos, A.L., Daniel, F., Benatallah, B.: Web service composition: a survey of techniques and tools. ACM Comput. Surv. (CSUR) 48(3), 1–41 (2015)

22. Musaraj, K., Yoshida, T., Daniel, F., Hacid, M.S., Casati, F., Benatallah, B.: Message correlation and web service protocol mining from inaccurate logs. In: 2010 IEEE International Conference on Web Services, pp. 259–266. IEEE (2010)

23. Rodríguez, C., Daniel, F., Casati, F.: Mining and quality assessment of mashup model patterns with the crowd: a feasibility study. ACM Trans. Internet Technol. (TOIT) 16(3), 1–27 (2016)

24. Rodriguez, C., Daniel, F., Casati, F., Cappiello, C.: Toward uncertain business intelligence: the case of key indicators. IEEE Internet Comput. 14(4), 32–40 (2010)

25. Rodríguez, C., Klinkmüller, C., Weber, I., Daniel, F., Casati, F.: Activity matching with human intelligence. In: La Rosa, M., Loos, P., Pastor, O. (eds.) BPM 2016. LNBIP, vol. 260, pp. 124–140. Springer, Cham (2016). https://doi.org/10.1007/978-3-319-45468-9_8

26. Rodríguez, C., Schleicher, D., Daniel, F., Casati, F., Leymann, F., Wagner, S.: Soaenabled compliance management: instrumenting, assessing, and analyzing service based business processes. SOCA 7(4), 275–292 (2013)

27. Rodríguez, C., Silveira, P., Daniel, F., Casati, F.: Analyzing compliance of service-based business processes for root-cause analysis and prediction. In: Daniel, F., Facca, F.M. (eds.) ICWE 2010. LNCS, vol. 6385, pp. 277–288. Springer, Heidelberg (2010). https://doi.org/10.1007/978-3-642-16985-4_25

28. Silveira, P., et al.: Aiding compliance governance in service-based business processes. In: Handbook of Research on Service-Oriented Systems and Non-Functional Properties: Future Directions, pp. 524–548. IGI Global (2012)
29. Silveira, P., et al.: On the design of compliance governance dashboards for effective compliance and audit management. In: Dan, A., Gittler, F., Toumani, F. (eds.) ServiceWave 2009, ICSOC 2009. LNCS, vol. 6275, pp. 208–217. Springer, Heidelberg (2009). https://doi.org/10.1007/978-3-642-16132-2_20
30. Tranquillini, S., Daniel, F., Kucherbaev, P., Casati, F.: Modeling, enacting, and integrating custom crowdsourcing processes. ACM Trans. Web (TWEB) 9(2), 1–43 (2015)
31. Yu, J., Benatallah, B., Casati, F., Daniel, F.: Understanding mashup development. IEEE Internet Comput. 12(5), 44–52 (2008)

Contents

Machine Learning for Service Oriented Computing

Smart Data and Smart Services

Service Oriented Technology Trends

Industry Papers

Microservices

Optimal Evolution Planning and Execution for Multi-version Coexisting Microservice Systems

Xiang He$^{(\boxtimes)}$, Zhiying Tu, Lei Liu, Xiaofei Xu, and Zhongjie Wang

School of Computer Science and Technology, Harbin Institute of Technology,
Harbin, China
september_hx@outlook.com, liulei@stu.hit.edu.cn,
{tzy_hit,xiaofei,rainy}@hit.edu.cn

Abstract. A microservice-based system is composed of a set of microservices that are developed and deployed independently for agile DevOps. Intensive and iterative adaptations/upgrades of microservices are essential for such systems to adapt to user requirement changes, and as a consequence, result in the phenomenon of "multi-version microservice coexistence" in a system. Besides traditional API-based functional dependencies between different microservices, there appear complicated dependencies between different versions of difference microservices. The complicated dependencies dramatically deteriorate the maintainability of microservice systems, especially when systems evolve to adapt to user requirement changes. To meet this challenge, a version dependency model is proposed for describing the complex dependencies between different versions of microservices, and a greedy-based optimization algorithm is developed for generating an optimal evolution plan. A programming framework (MF4MS) and cloud-edge based infrastructure (MI4MS) are implemented to facilitate microservice systems to automatically execute the evolution plan. Experiments show that the proposed approach performs well to cope with self-adaptation in the situation where complicated version dependencies exist.

Keywords: Microservice systems · Multi-version coexistence · Version dependency · Self adaptation · User requirement changes

1 Introduction

As business logics become more and more sophisticated in ubiquitous computing scenarios like smart city [4], both container technology and microservice architecture pattern gain much more attentions because of their advantage on continuous delivery and agile DevOps nowadays [7]. Independent development and deployment of microservices lead to complex dependencies between them. Since microservices communicate with each other through APIs, there are call dependencies between them, which can be represented as a service dependency

© Springer Nature Switzerland AG 2020
E. Kafeza et al. (Eds.): ICSOC 2020, LNCS 12571, pp. 3–18, 2020.
https://doi.org/10.1007/978-3-030-65310-1_1

graph (SDG) [10]. Once a microservice is upgraded to a new version, the call dependencies may change, and other microservices that depend on it may fail to invoke its APIs due to incompatibility caused by the upgrade. Considering the situation that some users would keep requesting specific older versions, microservices developers should not update all microservice instances that have been deployed in the system. As a consequence, there might be multiple versions of individual microservices that are co-deployed together in the system, which is called `multi-version coexisting`. Further, `version dependency` occurs, which implies the dependencies between different versions of different microservices in multi-version coexisting system. A simple example is shown in Fig. 1(a).

Due to the enormous amount of users and services in the scenarios of edge computing, there are lots of changes in user requirements, which leads to the decline of Quality of Service (QoS). Since the multi-version coexisting leads to an increase in version dependency complexity, it is a challenge to react to the user requirement changes with version dependency in such a scenario. The service system should evolve itself automatically to adapt to the user requirement changes. So that, it can keep the QoS stable with the consideration of version dependency in cloud-edge environments [15], as shown in Fig. 1(b).

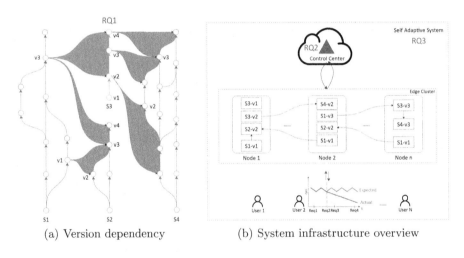

(a) Version dependency   (b) System infrastructure overview

Fig. 1. Introduction for multi-version coexisting microservice system

In this paper, we consider three research questions (RQs) on multi-version coexisting microservice system evolution in cloud-edge environment:

RQ1 **How to model the version dependency between microservices?**
Due to the independent version trees of each microservice, the version dependency changes over time, and it is essential for the service system to model the version dependency at runtime. Moreover, the existing approaches of describing the call dependency by the SDG cannot cope with the iterative development of microservices. Microservices should extend their version dependency dynamically when compatible upgrades happen.

RQ2 **How to generate an optimal evolution plan with version dependency?** To satisfy changing user requirements, the cost of the evolution plan should be concerned since each feasible evolution plan has a specific cost, like the monetary cost, service downtime, etc. An optimal evolution plan should be generated in a limited time with the consideration of the version dependency.

RQ3 **How to execute the evolution plan automatically with version dependency?** Due to the complexity of the multi-version coexisting microservice system, the system should be self-adaptive [17], which means it should have the ability to monitor the runtime state of the system, decide when and how to evolve the system and execute the plan automatically. The correctness of request routing should be ensured and the version dependency should be satisfied in the multi-version coexisting microservice system during evolution.

The main contributions and innovations are as follows:

- A model named Version Dependency Model (VDM) was proposed for describing the version dependency for RQ1, which copes well with the iterative deployment. A programming framework MF4MS was also implemented to integrate the version dependency into source code, which enables multi-version coexistence and automatic dependency analysis before deployment.
- A greedy based algorithm was presented to find the optimal evolution plan with the consideration of the version dependency for RQ2. It aims to find a feasible solution to improve the QoS with the changes in user requirements. The constraints of computing resources and version dependency are concerned.
- An infrastructure MI4MS based on the MAPK-E reference model [8] was developed for RQ3. It adopts the MAPK-E model and enables the self-adaptation to user requirement changes with version dependency. The correctness of request routing and the version dependency can be satisfied according to the collaborative work between MI4MS and MF4MS.

Experiments were conducted at different scenarios that are common in the real world, and the experiments are conducted in real cloud-edge environment. The results show that our approach performs well according to user requirement changes with version dependency, and the QoS keeps stable, meanwhile.

The rest of this paper is organized as follows. Section 2 introduces the related work. Section 3 describes the VDM. Section 4 details the optimal problem. Section 5 presents the programming framework and infrastructure. Section 6 shows the experiments. Section 7 concludes the paper and explores future works.

2 Related Work

The problems in the multi-version coexistence, evolution plan generating, and self-adaptive service system have been researched in recent years, and some solutions were proposed.

For the multi-version coexistence, the work [16] explored autonomic version management in the microservice system. It considered versioning both at application and company level to ensure the self-healing ability. The work [13] presented APP-bisect, which can analyze the dependencies between services and find the best coexisting patterns to solve the performance problems. The work [11] proposed a solution named VMAMVS to analyze the dependencies between microservices, monitor the system, and visualize the dependencies. The work [2] extended the microservice architecture. The clients and microservices in the system can request for the specific version of microservices in the multi-version coexisting system. The work [12] erased the gap between different versions of the same service by adding adaptor dynamically. Though the work [3] allowed to deploy services with dependencies automatically, the multi-version coexistence was missing. Although the microservices dependencies are concerned in these works, they focus less on the self-adaptive evolution according to the user requirement changes.

In terms of the evolution plan generating, the work [5] evaluated three algorithms for fog service replacement considering resource usage, service spread, and latency. The work [6] proposed a optimization policy for service placement to improve network usage and service latency. However, call dependency is immutable in current works, which is the opposite of the real world. And user requirement changes are not taken into account. Thus, algorithms should be extended for the challenge with call dependency and user requirement changes.

For the self-adaptive service system, the work [9] developed MiCADO for supporting horizontal scalability by an orchestration layer according to the network traffic. The work [14] applied the MAPE-K model to automatically optimize the deployment according to the performance. The work [1] presented Kubow for automated management of applications. However, the user requirement changes are not concerned in those works, and the version dependency is overlooked.

In summary, current studies need to be extended for self-adaptation with variable version dependency between microservices according to user requirement changes, and it is urgent to solve the problem since the problem is ubiquitous in the real world.

3   Version Dependency Model

Considering the service dependency graph can only describe the call dependencies between APIs of specific versions of microservices, which is not suitable to iterative development with changing service dependencies, we propose the version dependency model based on the service dependency graph.

Definition 1 (Service). A service is defined as $s =< \mathcal{I}, c, m, v >, s \in S$, where S denotes the service set:

- $\mathcal{I} = \{i_1, ..., i_n\}$ is a set of functional interfaces offered by s. Each interface is denoted by $i_j =< f_j, l_j, d_j^{in}, d_j^{out} >$, where f_j is the functionality that s can offer via i_j and is in the form of unstructured texts describing the functional semantics; l_j describes the constraint on quality attributes that i_j offers; d_j^{in} and d_j^{out} are estimated sizes of i_j's input and output parameters (unit: KB).

- c is the computing resource requirement level of s. The execution of a service requires many types of computing resources such as CPU, RAM, hard disk storage, and network bandwidth.
- m is the maximum number of users which can be concurrently served by s.
- $v =< MAJOR, MINOR, PATCH >$ is the version number of s. The Semantic Version is adopted: MAJOR changes when incompatible API change happens, MINOR changes when adding functionality in a backward-compatible manner, and PATCH changes when making backward compatible bug fixes [1].

Definition 2 (Dependency Categories). There are three kinds of dependency for every service in the microservice system: $\mathcal{P} = \{p_v, p_i, p_f\}$, where

- $p_v(s, i, v) =< s, i, V >$ stands for calling the specific interface i of service s with versions V, where $V = \{v_1, v_2, ..., v_n\}$;
- $p_i(s, i, L) =< s, i, L >$ stands for calling the specific interface i of service s with SLAs L, where $L = \{l_1, l_2, ..., l_n\}$;
- $p_f(f, L) =< f, L >$ stands for calling any API of function f with SLAs L;

For the traditional service dependency graph, the API invoking is usually hardcoded, such as the OpenFeign[2]. Without the code modification, the dependency between microservices can not be changed if the called microservices are upgraded due to bug fixes, which can not adapt to iterative development. With these three kinds of API calls, the service system can route the requests flexibly.

Definition 3 (Version dependency Model). The model is described as $VDM = \{< s, v, P > | s \in S\}$, where $P = \{p_1, p_2, ..., p_n\}, p_i \in \mathbf{P}$ stands for the calling of the dependency set of service s with version v.

The traditional call dependency in most microservice frameworks like Spring Cloud can be described as service name and APIs. Once some microservices are upgraded to new versions with incompatible changes, other services depend on them need to be modified in code level, which increases the burden on developers. What's worse, the developers must be careful about the versions of the services in the system for correctness of requests routing. Coping VDM with MF4MS detailed in Sect. 5 allows changing the dependencies without code modification or rebooting instances at runtime.

VDM extends the traditional SVG with flexible version dependencies between services by p_v. It allows the multiple version dependencies description of the same microservice, which allows the system to re-direct the requests to the compatible versions. Besides the traditional call dependency, VDM provides other two new dependency descriptions p_i and p_f. p_i is used when trying to request the APIs of a service with specific SLAs. The system can automatically route the requests with p_i to the instances with the target SLAs even there are frequent upgrades for

---

[1] https://semver.org/.
[2] https://spring.io/projects/spring-cloud-openfeign.

the microservices. p_f allows the developers request the APIs by functionality and expected SLAs, and it further decouples the dependencies between microservices. With p_f, the service system can re-direct the requests to the instances with the best SLAs and performance. And the developers do not need to modify the source code during the independent iterative development of different microservices.

4 Optimization Algorithm with Version Dependency

To keep QoS stable when user requirements change, the algorithm needs to generate an optimal plan considering the version dependency and other constraints. In this paper, the average response time is our main concern.

4.1 Problem Definition

Definition 4 (User Requirement). A user Requirement is defined as $d = <u, p, loc, t>$ where u is the user, t is the time when d is raised by u, loc is the location of u at the time t, and p is the Requirement description, where $p \in \mathcal{P}$. The Requirement set is described as D, where $d \in D$.

Definition 5 (Server Node). A server node $e = <type, c, loc>$ where $type \in \{ES, CS\}$ is the type of e (ES: an edge server, CS: a cloud server), c is the total computing resources e can offer for service instances deployed on it (defined by Key-Value pairs, same as Definition 1), and loc is e's geographic location (defined by latitude and longitude). The connection between two nodes e_i, e_j, are described by bandwidth (in Mb/s) and time delay (in milliseconds). E stands for the set of the server node, $e \in E$.

Definition 6 (Microservice Instance). A microservice instance $\tau(s) = <s, e>, \tau(s) \in \mathcal{T}$, where s is the service that τ belongs to, e is the server node on which $\tau(s)$ is deployed.

Definition 7 (Direction State). A direction state $r(d) \in \mathcal{DS}$ of a user requirement d records a mapping between a service request in d and a microservice instance that is selected to fulfill the request. $r = <\tau(s), i>$, where i is the corresponding interface.

Definition 8 (Deployment State). Deployment state of a service system at time t is denoted by $\Theta(t) = <S(t), E(t), \mathcal{T}(t), D(t), \mathcal{DS}(t)>$, where the five components are the sets of services, cloud/edge server nodes, deployed instances, user requirements, and user requirement direction states, at time t, respectively.

Definition 9 (Evolution operations). There are three evolution operations, i.e., Switch, Add, and Remove. $\mathcal{OP} = \{\text{Switch}, \text{Add}, \text{Remove}\}$.

- Switch$(d, \tau_i(s_m), i_j \tau_j(s_n), i_k)$ is to switch a user requirement d from interface i_j of service s_m's instance τ_i to the interface i_k of service s's instance τ_j. It is possible that $m = n$ or $j = k$.

– Add$(\tau(s), e)$ is to create a new instance τ of a service s on server node e;
– Remove$(\tau(s))$ is to stop an existing instance τ of a service s.

Problem Definition. A service system evolves from time t to $t + \delta$ by a set of operations $OP = \{op|op \in \mathcal{OP}\}$, and the δ denotes the time interval from the last evolution:

$$\Theta(t) \xrightarrow{OP} \Theta(t + \delta) \tag{1}$$

Furthermore, to minimize the average response time and evolution cost, the optimization problem is described as Eq. 2a, where the $rt(.)$ means the response time defined as the sum of the delay and the transfer time of in/out data:

$$min(\frac{\sum_d^D rt(d)}{|D|}), \ min(\sum_{op}^{OP} cost(op)) \tag{2a}$$

$$s.t. \begin{cases} Q(\tau(s)) >= Q(d_j), & \forall d_j \in D(t + \theta) \\ \sum_{\tau \ on \ e_k} r(\tau) <= r_{max}(e_k), & \forall e_k \in E(t + \delta) \\ 1 \le ns(\tau) \le ns_{max}(\tau), & \forall \tau \in T(t + \delta) \end{cases} \tag{2b}$$

The first constraint assures that the quality level that each user requirement expected to get from service can be satisfied by the selected service instance. The second constraint makes sure that the total computing resources that all instances consume on one server node do not exceed the maximal resource offering of the node. The number of users that have been allocated to one service instance cannot exceed the maximal user number that the instance can serve concurrently,and it is assured by the last constraint. It should be noticed that the version dependency should be taken into consideration.

4.2   Optimal Evolution Algorithm

Due to the unknown future, it is impossible that to calculate the $\mathcal{DS}$ in the next status during the optimal plan generation. Thus, the algorithm consists of two phases: the planning phase and the running phase. The former focuses on providing new service placement and routing rules during planning, and the latter concentrates on the requests routing at runtime.

For the planning phase, the output of the algorithm is the deployment changes, which consists of Add and Remove operations, and a set of rules to help to route the requests. The rules describe what service should be used to serve a call with dependency $p \in \mathcal{P}$. A greedy based algorithm is proposed as Algorithm 1.

The basic idea of this algorithm is trying to provide the lowest average response time with as little cost as possible for each edge node. The service serves most requirements with less resources are chosen by the ratio, as shown on line 6–10. It is worth pointing out that the $getMetDemands$ function considers the compatibility of versions with MINOR and PATCH version changes. After that, line 11 calls the $buildMiniSvcTree$ to construct the service tree with version dependency. A breadth-first strategy is used to solve the dependencies of the given services. For each dependency of every service, the services in the given set will be used if

---

Algorithm 1. The greedy based algorithm at planning phase

Require: Last system deployment status os
Ensure: Deployment changes and routing rules
1: $S \leftarrow getServices(os)$, $N \leftarrow getNodes(os)$, $D \leftarrow getDemands(os)$
2: $unDeployedSvc = \emptyset$, $rules = \emptyset$
3: $ns \leftarrow createEmptyDelopStatus()$
4: **for** n in N **do**
5:     $D_n \leftarrow getNodeDemands(D, n)$, $S_n = \emptyset$
6:     **while** $size(D_n) \neq 0$ **do**
7:         $s \leftarrow pickOneService(D_n, S)$
8:         $D_s \leftarrow getMetDemands(D_n, s)$
9:         $S_n = S_n \cup \{s\}$, $D_n = D_n \setminus D_s$
10:    **end while**
11:    $T_s \leftarrow buildMiniSvcTree(S_n, S)$
12:    $rules \leftarrow rules \cup getRules(T_s)$
13:    $S_n \leftarrow getAllServices(T_s)$
14:    $instSizeMap \leftarrow calcInstNum(S_n, D_n)$
15:    **while** $(s \leftarrow getNextSvc(T_s)) \neq null$ **do**
16:        **if** $deployInsts(ns, n, s, instSizeMap[s]) = true$ **then**
17:            $S_n \leftarrow S_n \setminus \{s\}$
18:        **end if**
19:        $T_s \leftarrow T_s \setminus \{s\}$
20:    **end while**
21:    $unDeployedSvc \leftarrow unDeployedSvc \cup S_n$
22: **end for**
23: **for** s in $unDeployedSvc$ **do**
24:    **if** $otherNodesCanSupply(s) = false$ **then**
25:        $deployOnMostCloseNode(s, ns)$
26:    **end if**
27: **end for**
28: **return** $calcDiff(ns, os)$, $rules$

---

they satisfy the dependency, or the service that meets most of the requirements is selected. The routing rules are also returned as tree's edges.

On line 14, $calcInstNum$ calculates how many instances are needed considering user capabilities of services and the count of requirements. It should be noticed that the call coefficient is considered because when calling one service, it can invoke other services several times instead of once, and the coefficient presents how many times the dependency is called when calling the API. The coefficient is calculated with the call history obtained in Sect. 5 on average.

When deploying instances on line 15–20, $getNextSvc$ is used to pick up one service without parent node in the tree, and it serves more requirements with lowest resource usage. If the edge node has no sufficient resources for deploying new instances, the existing instances on other nodes with enough user capabilities are used instead of deploying new one, otherwise creating new instances on the closest node with enough resources, as shown on line 23–27.

For the running phase, the routing rules generated in the planning phase are used. With the routing rules that describe which service is used to satisfy for each $p \in \mathcal{P}$, the instance with enough user capabilities on the closest server node to the requester is selected for each request.

5 Infrastructure and Programming Framework with Version Dependency

To empower the system with self-adaptation, the MAPE-K model is adopted. However, without a specific programming framework, the system can not analyze the version dependency and deal with the multi-version coexistence. Both the infrastructure MI4MS and programming framework MF4MS based on Java and Spring Cloud are implemented for self-adaptation.

5.1 Overview

The MI4MS aims to empower the microservices with the help of the MAPE-K model. Therefore, the system can automatically detect the user requirement changes, generate the evolution plan, and execute the plan automatically. As shown in Fig. 2, there are five main components in the MI4MS:

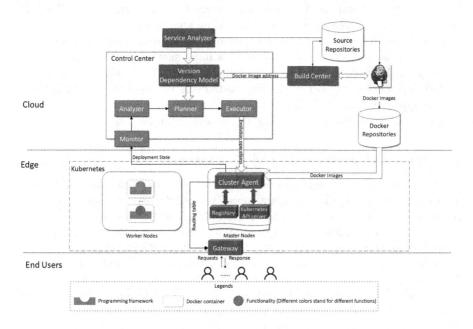

Fig. 2. Overview of the MI4MS

- `Control Center`: It is the essential part of MI4MS that controls the entire service system. It implements the self-adaption control loop, which monitors the system at runtime, analyzes current QoS of system, generates an evolution plan with the algorithms in Sect. 4.2, and executes the plan.
- `Service Analyzer`: It aims to analyze the source code of the microservices integrated with MF4MS to obtain the service information defined in Definition 1 and extract the dependencies of the service. It works with the `Control Center` to build the version dependency model described in Sect. 5.2.
- `Cluster Agent`: It is responsible for fetc.hing the deployment status about the edge cluster defined in Definition 6 with the help of Kubernetes API Server[3] and Microservice Registry Server[4], and passing it to the `Control Center`. Moreover, it accepts the evolution operations from the `Control Center` and executes them as detailed in Sect. 5.4.
- `Gateway`: It aims to route all the requests from the service instances and users with unified form defined in Definition 2. It copes with the `Cluster Agent` to perform the request routing in a multi-version coexisting microservice system, as shown in Sect. 5.3. The request history is also cached for calculating the QoS and the call coefficient in `Control Center`.
- `Build Center`: It is responsible for packaging the microservices from source code and building the dockers automatically with Maven[5] and Jenkins[6].

At the beginning of every time window, the `Control Center` fetc.hes the latest deployment state and request history for QoS analyzing and call coefficient calculating at the monitoring step. After analyzing, an evolution plan is generated and executed, and the control loop waits for the next execution.

The programming framework MF4MS is implemented based on the annotation in Java. MF4MS takes the responsibility to integrate the microservices with version dependency support, including loading the version dependency description in `application.yaml` files detailed in Sect. 5.2 and sending the requests with version dependency to other instances detailed in Sect. 5.3.

5.2   Version Dependency Model Generation

For the developers, the microservice needs to be integrated with MF4MS at the source code level. The configuration of version dependency should be integrated into configuration file `application.yaml`, and three kinds of dependencies defined in Definition 2 are supported, as shown in Fig. 3(a). For the functionality and SLAs description of each API, the `MFuncDescription` annotation is needed, as shown in (1) of Fig. 3(b), and developers should annotate each API function in every controller with it. For other information like the resource usage, max user capabilities of services, and source code repository should be included in the service description when the service enters the system.

---

[3] https://kubernetes.io/docs/concepts/overview/components/#kube-apiserver.
[4] https://microservices.io/patterns/service-registry.html.
[5] https://maven.apache.org/.
[6] https://www.jenkins.io/.

Once a new service enters the system, the `Control Center` sends the source code repository of the new service to the `Service Analyzer` to analyze the service of every version. The tags of the source code are used to distinguish different versions of the same service. By analyzing each tag of the given repository at the source code level with JavaParser, the `Service Analyzer` extracts the service information and the version dependency of every version from controller classes and configuration file, and returns the result to `Control Center`. Then the results are saved to the version dependency model, and the `Build Center` is called when no docker image exists for the new service.

```
mvf4ms:
   version: 1.0.1                       @Controller
   dependencies:                        public class MainController {
    - name: dependency1
      dependence:                            private Logger logger = LogManager.getLogger(this);
       - id: navigation
         serviceName: SampleGaoDe            @PostMapping(path = "/taxi")
         patternUrl: /navigation             @ResponseBody
         versions:                           @MFuncDescription(value = "taxi", level = 1)   (1)
          - 1.1.1                            public MResponse weather(
          - 1.2.2                                @RequestBody MResponse params, HttpServletRequest request) {
       - id: weather
         function: weather                       MResponse p = new MResponse();
         slas:                                   MResponse response =
          - 2                                        MVerRequestUtils.request("weather", p, RequestMethod.POST, request);
       - id: pay
         function: pay                           // ...                                          (2)
         slas:
          - 2                                     return response;
          - 3                                 }
                                        }
```

(a) MF4MS configuration   (b) Controller example with MF4MS

Fig. 3. An example of the MF4MS integration

5.3 Version Dependency Based Requesting

The `Gateway` and `Cluster Agent` work together to route requests with version dependency. For all the requests from both instances and users, the developers need to use the `MVerRequestUtils.request` provided by MF4MS to send a request with a unique dependency id defined in the configuration file, as shown in (2) of Fig. 3(b). Since the data formatting between different APIs is not our primary concern, the `MResponse` type, which is a key-value map, is provided to hold all the parameters or return values.

The requests are sent to the `Gateway` by `MVerRequestUtils.request` for redirecting with version dependency. When there is no routing cache in `Gateway` for the requester, the `Cluster Agent` is called. The `Cluster Agent` finds an instance with the running phase algorithm detailed in Sect. 4.2 and returns the URL to the `Gateway`. After that, the `Gateway` re-directs the request according to the routing info and caches the info.

5.4 Version Coexistence Evolution Plan Executing

There are three kinds of operations: `Switch`, `Add`, and `Remove`. For `Switch` operation, the `Control Center` sends the routing rules to the `Cluster Agent`. All the caches in `Gateway` are deleted and all the requests need to be re-directed by the `Cluster Agent` with the new rules. To execute the `Add` and `Remove`, the `Control Center` sends the operations to the `Cluster Agent`, and the operations are transformed to API calls to Kubernetes API Server since it provides convenient APIs for managing the dockers. The Blue Green Deployment is adopted here to erase the service down time during evolution.

6   Experiments

6.1   Experiment Setup

The experiments wre conducted in a proto system. Five 8vCPU and 16 GB RAM AWS EC2 instances with Kubernetes 1.18.2 were used as the edge cluster. The delay between each other was less than 1ms, and the bandwidth was 1000Mb/s. Other two AWS EC2 instances ware used as the cloud servers. The `Control Center`, `Service Analyzer`, and `Build Center` were deployed on the cloud server. `Cluster Agent` was deployed on the master node of the edge cluster, and `Gateway` was deployed on every edge server.

There were two service sets that we created according to the taxi, shopping, payment scenarios in the real world. The set 1 contained 6 services, and each service had 0–2 dependencies. There were no more than two layers of dependency, i.e., service A depends on service B, and service B has no dependency. The set 2 extended service set 1. It contained 4 new services, and each of them had at least three layers of dependency. In both service set 1 and 2, every service had 2–3 APIs, and the size of input and output data ranged from 1 to 20 KB. For each service, they had 2–3 versions, and the dependencies of different versions of the same service differed from other versions. Thus, service set 2 had more complex version dependency than set 1. All three kinds of dependency methods were included in set 1 and 2. The max user number ranged from 100 to 300.

For the users, there were 2000 simulated users in the system, and they were evenly distributed around five edge servers. All the users sent their requests to the `Gateway` on the closest server node every 5–10 seconds. The average response time and the count of failed user requirements were used as the evaluation indicators. The service availability was also adopted to evaluate the performance of the system, which is calculated by service down time divides running time. Only the affected services were included during the calculation of the service availability.

Since existing algorithms are not suitable for this problem, the performance of the solution is evaluated in two common scenarios from the real world.

6.2   Scenario 1: Service Upgrade

Scenario 1 was simulated according to the service upgrade situation, which is one of the most common scenario in the real world, with service set 1 and 2. It was simulated by dividing users into three groups: upgrading requirements just after new version releases, upgrading in 5–10 min after the new release, and keeping the old version. The time window of the control loop was set to 5 min, and the experiments 1 and 2 were conducted with service set 1 and 2 respectively. The results are shown in Fig. 4(a), Fig. 4(b), and Table 1.

The results show that after detecting failed requirements, the system evolved itself and kept QoS stable with both simple and complex version dependency. The QoS of both the scenario with simple dependencies (service set 1) and scenario with complex dependencies (service set 2) were improved after the evolution since there were no failed user requirements and average response time was stable. It should be noticed that the average response time increased first then decreased during evolution. The reason is the recalculation of routing info requires sending requests from `Gateway` to `Cluster Agent`, which increases the average response time. After caching the routing info, the average response time decreases. The service availability in Table 1 also shows the system works well with the user requirement changes in the multi-version coexisting system.

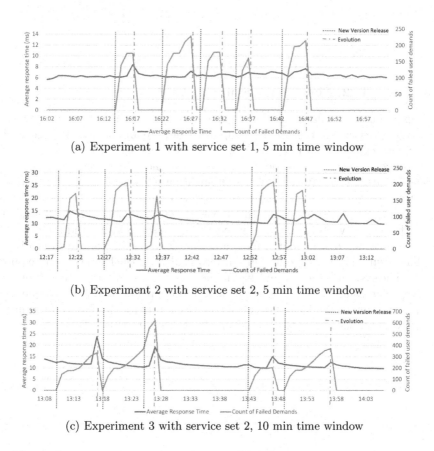

(a) Experiment 1 with service set 1, 5 min time window

(b) Experiment 2 with service set 2, 5 min time window

(c) Experiment 3 with service set 2, 10 min time window

Fig. 4. Average response time and count of failed requirements in scenario 1

To study the effect of different time windows, experiment 3 was conducted with a 10 min time window. Experiment 3 had the same settings to experiment 2, including the time of service upgrades and user settings, except the time window size. The results in Fig. 4(c) and Table 1 show that the service availability decreases a lot since the system needs more time to discover the unsatisfied requirements with a bigger time window than with a smaller one. However, the bigger time window leads to less system evolution. There were 4 times of evolution in experiment 3 while 5 times in experiment 2, which means the other users in the system are less affected by the fluctuations in average response time.

Table 1. Service availability of experiment 1, 2, and 3

Experiment	Service down time in total (minute)	Service availability (%)
1	3.0	95
2	2.5	95.83
3	28	53.33

6.3 Scenario 2: New User Requirements

This experiment simulates another common scenario in the real world: new services are released after users come up with new requirements. This scenario differs with experiments 1, 2, and 3 because the users ask for new requirements that the system can not provide. After the appearance of new requirements, new services that can satisfy the new requirements are released in a random time. Experiments 4 and 5 were conducted with service set 1 and 2, and the time window was set to 5 min. Since the service availability is severely affected by when the new services released, only the average response time and the count of failed requirements are adopted for evaluation. The results are shown in Fig. 5.

The results show that our solution also evolved itself for new user requirements. The system responsed quickly in one time window after the release of new services that could satisfy the unmet user requirements with both simple and complex version dependencies between services automatically. New user requirements were satisfied after the evolution, which keeps the QoS stable.

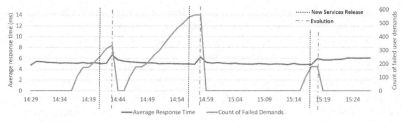

(a) Experiment 4 with service set 1, 5 min time window

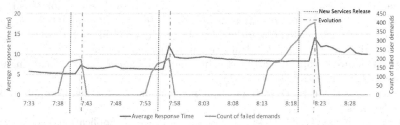

(b) Experiment 5 with service set 2, 5 min time window

Fig. 5. Average response time and failed requirements number in scenario 2

7 Conclusion

In this paper, we proposed the version dependency model for describing the complex dependency between microservices. A programming framework MF4MS and a self-adaptive system infrastructure MI4MS with a greedy based evolution algorithm were implemented for satisfying the user requirement changes automatically with version dependency. The performance of the system was evaluated in two common scenarios. The results show that MF4MS performs well with complex version dependency and keeps the QoS stable.

The future work includes detecting the lack of function due to new requirements and evolving the system to fill in the functional holes automatically.

Acknowledgement. Research in this paper is partially supported by the National Key Research and Development Program of China (No 2018YFB1402500), the National Science Foundation of China (61772155, 61832014, 61832004, 61802089, 61472106).

References

1. Aderaldo, C.M., Mendonça, N.C., Schmerl, B., Garlan, D.: Kubow: an architecture-based self-adaptation service for cloud native applications. In: Proceedings of the 13th European Conference on Software Architecture - Volume 2, ECSA 2019, pp. 42–45. Association for Computing Machinery (2019)
2. Akbulut, A., Perros, H.G.: Software versioning with microservices through the api gateway design pattern. In: 2019 9th International Conference on Advanced Computer Information Technologies (ACIT), pp. 289–292 (2019)

3. Gabbrielli, M., Giallorenzo, S., Guidi, C., Mauro, J., Montesi, F.: Self-reconfiguring microservices. In: Ábrahám, E., Bonsangue, M., Johnsen, E.B. (eds.) Theory and Practice of Formal Methods. LNCS, vol. 9660, pp. 194–210. Springer, Cham (2016). https://doi.org/10.1007/978-3-319-30734-3_14

4. Gaur, A., Scotney, B., Parr, G., McClean, S.: Smart city architecture and its applications based on iot. Procedia Comput. Sci. **52**, 1089–1094 (2015)

5. Guerrero, C., Lera, I., Juiz, C.: Evaluation and efficiency comparison of evolutionary algorithms for service placement optimization in fog architectures. Future Gener. Comput. Syst. **97**, 131–144 (2019)

6. Guerrero, C., Lera, I., Juiz, C.: A lightweight decentralized service placement policy for performance optimization in fog computing. J. Ambient Intell. Humaniz. Comput. **10**, 2435–2452 (2019). https://doi.org/10.1007/s12652-018-0914-0

7. Kang, H., Le, M., Tao, S.: Container and microservice driven design for cloud infrastructure devops. In: 2016 IEEE International Conference on Cloud Engineering (IC2E), pp. 202–211. IEEE (2016)

8. Kephart, J.O., Chess, D.M.: The vision of autonomic computing. Computer **36**(1), 41–50 (2003)

9. Kiss, T., et al.: MiCADO-microservice-based cloud application-level dynamic orchestrator. Future Gener. Comput. Syst. **94**, 937–946 (2019)

10. Ma, S., Fan, C., Chuang, Y., Lee, W., Lee, S., Hsueh, N.: Using service dependency graph to analyze and test microservices. In: 2018 IEEE 42nd Annual Computer Software and Applications Conference (COMPSAC), vol. 02, pp. 81–86 (2018)

11. Ma, S., Liu, I., Chen, C., Lin, J., Hsueh, N.: Version-based microservice analysis, monitoring, and visualization. In: 2019 26th Asia-Pacific Software Engineering Conference (APSEC), pp. 165–172 (2019)

12. Paques, H., Liu, L., Pu, C.: Adaptation space: a design framework for adaptive web services. Int. J. Web Serv. Res. (IJWSR) **1**(3), 1–24 (2004)

13. Rajagopalan, S., Jamjoom, H.: App-bisect: autonomous healing for microservice-based apps. In: 7th {USENIX} Workshop on Hot Topics in Cloud Computing (HotCloud 2015) (2015)

14. Sampaio, A.R., Rubin, J., Beschastnikh, I., Rosa, N.S.: Improving microservice-based applications with runtime placement adaptation. J. Internet Serv. Appl. **10**(1), 4 (2019). https://doi.org/10.1186/s13174-019-0104-0

15. Satyanarayanan, M.: The emergence of edge computing. Computer **50**(1), 30–39 (2017)

16. Wang, Y.: Towards service discovery and autonomic version management in self-healing microservices architecture. In: Proceedings of the 13th European Conference on Software Architecture - Volume 2, ECSA 2019, 9p. 63–66. Association for Computing Machinery, New York (2019)

17. Weyns, D.: Software engineering of self-adaptive systems: An organised tour and future challenges (2017)

Topology-Aware Continuous Experimentation in Microservice-Based Applications

Gerald Schermann[1]([✉]), Fábio Oliveira[2], Erik Wittern[3], and Philipp Leitner[4]

[1] Software Evolution and Architecture Lab, University of Zurich, Zurich, Switzerland
schermann@ifi.uzh.ch
[2] IBM T. J. Watson Research Center, Yorktown Heights, NY, USA
[3] IBM, Hybrid Cloud Integration, Hamburg, Germany
[4] Chalmers | University of Gothenburg, Gothenburg, Sweden

Abstract. Continuous experiments, including practices such as canary releases or A/B testing, test new functionality on a small fraction of the user base in production environments. Monitoring data collected on different versions of a service is essential for decision-making on whether to continue or abort experiments. Existing approaches for decision-making rely on service-level metrics in isolation, ignoring that new functionality might introduce changes affecting other services or the overall application's health state. Keeping track of these changes in applications comprising dozens or hundreds of services is challenging. We propose a holistic approach implemented as a research prototype to identify, visualize, and rank topological changes from distributed tracing data. We devise three ranking heuristics assessing how the changes impact the experiment's outcome and the application's health state. An evaluation on two case study scenarios shows that a hybrid heuristic based on structural analysis and a simple root-cause examination outperforms other heuristics in terms of ranking quality.

1 Introduction

The ever-increasing need for rapidly delivering code changes to fix problems, satisfy new requirements, and ultimately survive in a highly-competitive, software-driven market has been fueling the adoption of *DevOps* practices [2] by many companies. DevOps promotes the *continuous deployment* [13] of code to production, breaking the traditional barrier between development and operations teams and establishing a set of software development methodologies heavily based on tools to automate software builds, tests, configuration, and deployment. To further increase development agility, companies are frequently following a *microservice-based* [10] software architecture style. Microservice-based architectures are an evolution of the idea of service-oriented architectures [5,20], in which applications comprise a multitude of distributed services.

The agility facilitated by DevOps practices and microservice-based architectures enables companies to perform *continuous experiments* [16], which test the

© Springer Nature Switzerland AG 2020
E. Kafeza et al. (Eds.): ICSOC 2020, LNCS 12571, pp. 19–35, 2020.
https://doi.org/10.1007/978-3-030-65310-1_2

functionality and performance of new versions of application components under production load. A common embodiment of continuous experimentation is to perform *canary releases* [6]. In this practice, which resembles testing in production, one compares the test version (the "canary") of a microservice against the current version (the baseline) with respect to performance and correctness. Initially, the canary is exposed to requests of a small portion of users. If its performance and correctness remains acceptable, it is gradually exposed to more users until it replaces the baseline. If it fails to perform as expected at any time, all traffic is shifted to the baseline and the canary is terminated. Crucially, determining the health of a canary requires (1) collecting and storing the metrics of interest, and (2) comparatively analyzing the baseline and canary metrics.

Previous work [3,18] on assessing the outcome of continuous experiments considers the microservice under test in isolation, focusing on service-level metrics alone. These approaches ignore the fundamental principle that microservices communicate with each other and that these interactions affect the overall application behavior. For example, performance issues in a canary version of a service propagate delays (e.g., higher response times) within the network and when solely judging on isolated service-level metrics, multiple services could appear to misbehave. Given the scale of modern microservice-based applications compounded by a myriad of possible inter-service dependency patterns, identifying the root cause of such issues is challenging, especially when multiple microservices are under experimentation, e.g., running multiple canaries simultaneously.

We contend that continuous experimentation in microservice-based applications must consider the topology underlying all inter-service calls so as to allow developers to evaluate new versions holistically as opposed to in isolation. Out of dozens or even hundreds of identified (topological) changes it is crucial to assess those in detail that cause effects on the application's health state. Therefore, we propose an approach to not only identify and visualize changes between baseline and canary versions, but also heuristics to rank these changes based on their potential impact with the ultimate goal to guide developers when assessing continuous experiments. We implemented our approach as a research prototype that supports analyses in the context of multiple experiments running in parallel. Our approach starts with inferring *interaction graphs* for both the baseline and canary versions from distributed traces collected from microservice-based applications. We then compare these interaction graphs to identify topological changes, and rank these changes. A visual frontend allows developers to review specific changes and associated quality metrics (e.g., response times).

In summary, this paper makes the following contributions: (1) a characterization of topological changes that occur in microservice-based applications; (2) a general approach for ranking those observed changes; (3) three concrete ranking heuristics as embodiments of this approach; (4) a proof-of-concept implementation; and (5) an evaluation of the quality of the produced rankings.

Our evaluation shows that a heuristic combining principles of both structural analysis and performance analysis performs best across our evaluation scenarios.

2   Related Work

Previous research has empirically assessed continuous experimentation practices and challenges [15,16]. These works analyze reports on continuous experimentation practices by selected companies [8,17], and also present data collected more broadly using interviews and surveys. They find that software architectures based on components that can be deployed and operated independently (e.g., microservices) are essential for continuous experimentation, but also attest that root-cause analysis of observed problems is challenging. Our work attempts to address these challenges by considering the interactions in which updated services participate.

Multiple methods and systems have been proposed for continuous experimentation. *Kraken* is a system proposed by Facebook [19] for traffic routing between services, servers, or even data centers to identify performance bottlenecks using actual user traffic. *Bifrost* [14] formalizes continuous experiments consisting of multiple phases. Experiments that are specified in a domain-specific language are automatically executed by a middleware using smart traffic routing. The *MACI* framework [4] for management, scalable execution, and interactive analysis presents an alternative way to express experiments integrating recurring tasks around experiment documentation and management, scaling, and data analysis with the goal of reducing specification efforts.

The work by Sambasivan et al. [11] is the closest to our approach. It compares distributed traces to diagnose performance changes, distinguishing between *structural* changes and ones in *response-time*. While Sambasivan et al. assume similar workloads for the variants, our approach focuses on the topology and on experimentation settings to assign only a small fraction of users to experimental variants. Due to our set of change types, the comparison between the experimentation variants is more fine-grained in our approach. This does also apply for comparing our approach with Kiali[1], a tool that helps observing services within service meshes such as Istio[2]. While Kiali provides some basic health assessment, our approach dives deeper by not only analyzing topological differences but also ranking them to guide developers assessing the overall application's health state.

Ates et al. [1] proposed *Pythia*, a framework making use of distributed tracing to automatically enable instrumentation such as logs or performance counters on those layers (e.g., application, operating system) that are needed to diagnose performance problems. Santana et al. [12] investigates how syscall monitoring in combination with a proxying approach can be used to obtain and inject tracing-related meta-information with the goal to avoid code changes in the application to propagate trace information. Our work relies on distributed traces collected by the Istio service mesh using Envoy[3] proxies in combination with Zipkin[4] to infer topologies of microservice-based applications.

---

[1] https://kiali.io/.
[2] https://istio.io/.
[3] https://www.envoyproxy.io/.
[4] https://zipkin.io/.

3   Characterizing Change Types

In the following, we characterize recurring change types we identified when comparing service topologies. For this purpose, we derive formal representations of microservice-based applications and service-interaction graphs that frame our basis to define topological change types.

3.1   Microservice-Based Application

A microservice-based application $\mathcal{A}$ consists of a set of interacting services $\mathcal{A} = \{s_1, s_2, \ldots, s_n\}$. Services are available in different versions, e.g., stable version 1 of the *frontend* service and a new experimental canary version 2 depicted in Fig. 1 (Left). For a service $s_i \in \mathcal{A}$ this is represented as a tuple $\mathcal{VS}_i = \langle s_{i,1}, s_{i,2}, \ldots, s_{i,m} \rangle$, where $s_{i,1} \ldots s_{i,m}$ are the corresponding versions j of service s_i with $1 \leq j \leq m$. Note that Fig. 1 (Left) not only represents our running example, but also depicts a topological difference which we will cover in detail in later sections when we revisit this example.

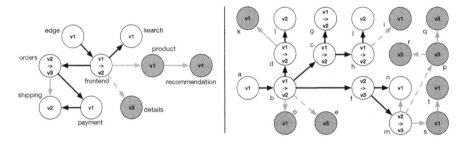

Fig. 1. Topological difference graphs of microservice-based sample applications. Left: running example (scenario 1). Right: scenario 2. Green depicts added functionality or calls, red depicts removed functionality or calls, and yellow depicts service version updates. (Color figure online)

In the context of continuous experiments a microservice-based application is available in multiple *variants* $\mathcal{VA} = \langle va_1, \ldots, va_p \rangle$ at the same time. An application variant comprises a combination of services $\langle s_i, \ldots, s_k \rangle$ with $i \leq j \leq k$ and $s_j \in \mathcal{A}$. For each of those services $s_j \in \mathcal{A}$ a concrete version u with $s_{j,u} \in \mathcal{VS}_j$ is selected. In Fig. 1, the *baseline* variant of the application includes version 1 of *frontend*, while the *canary* variant includes the new version 2 of *frontend*.

3.2   Interaction Graph

In a microservice-based application, version j of a service s_i interacts with other services by calling one or more of their endpoints. In our model, this interaction is represented by a directed graph $G = \langle V, E \rangle$ in which V and E denote sets of vertices and edges respectively. Every service $s_{i,j}$ of an application corresponds to a vertex $v \in V$ in the graph, referring to version j of $s_i \in \mathcal{A}$, where $s_{i,j} \in \mathcal{VS}_i$. A directed edge $e = s_{i,j} \rightarrow s_{u,v}$, where $e \in E$, represents a call from a service $s_{i,j}$ (subsequently named *caller*) to another service $s_{u,v}$ (*callee*).

3.3   Topological Change Types

The presented formal model allows us to construct interaction graphs for every application variant and to compare them. Comparing interaction graphs of two or more variants reveals changes at the topological level. For example, in Fig. 1, when the canary version 2 of *frontend* is deployed, we observe that a new service (*product*) is required while the *details* service is no longer called.

In the following, we characterize typical change types that surface in the evolution of microservice-based applications. When comparing interaction graphs G_1 and G_2, every such change type appears as a certain pattern involving a subset of the vertices. We distinguish two categories of change types: *fundamental* and *composed*, where a *composed* change type is a combination of multiple *fundamental* change types.

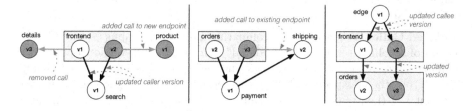

Fig. 2. Topological change types demonstrated on sample application (excerpt). Left: add call to new service, removed call, and updated caller version. Center: add call to existing endpoint. Right: updated callee version and updated version.

Fundamental Change Types. Fundamental change types involve calling newly added services (or service endpoints), calling endpoints of existing services, or removing calls to service endpoints.

Calling a New Endpoint. This change type represents new functionality manifesting as a call to a new resource, such as a service or a service endpoint that was added. In both interaction graphs G_1 and G_2 there exists a vertex (or node) representing a service a, but in different service versions: i in case of G_1 (i.e., $s_{a,i}$), and j in case of G_2 (i.e., $s_{a,j}$). The interaction graph G_2 contains an edge $e \in E$ with $e = s_{a,j} \rightarrow s_{u,v}$ calling a service u in version v that does not exist in graph G_1. Figure 2 (left) depicts this change type in our running example. The *frontend* service of the *canary* variant (version 2) calls a newly added *product* service that does not exist in the *baseline* variant (version 1).

Calling an Existing Endpoint. This change type characterizes reusing functionality, i.e., a new call to an existing service endpoint is made. There are again two nodes in the interaction graphs representing the same service a, but in different service versions: $s_{a,i}$ in G_1 and $s_{a,j}$ in G_2. Graph G_2 contains an edge $e \in E$ with $e = s_{a,j} \rightarrow s_{u,v}$ denoting a call to service u that also exists in graph G_1; thus, $s_{u,v}$ is represented by a vertex $v \in V$ of G_1. However, there is no direct interaction (no edge) between $s_{a,i}$ and $s_{u,v}$ in G_1. Figure 2 (center) shows this change type in which the *canary* variant of *orders* (version 3) calls *shipping*. The *shipping* service is also part of the *baseline* variant involving version 2 of *orders*, but there is no direct interaction between *orders* and *shipping*.

Removing a Service Call. This change type represents the inverse of the previous one. A previously used resource is no longer used. Revisiting the previous change type, this time the interaction graph G_1 contains an edge $e \in E$ with $e = s_{a,i} \rightarrow s_{u,v}$ representing a call to a service u, but no equivalent edge between $s_{a,j}$ and $s_{u,v}$ exists in G_2. However, the service u might still be used in G_2 by other services. Figure 2 (left) represents this change type between the *canary* variant of *frontend* (version 2) which no longer calls *details*.

Composed Change Types. These change types are constructed from fundamental change types and denote updated caller version, updated callee version, and updated version.

Updated Caller Version. When comparing interaction graphs G_1 and G_2, the version of a calling service a is "updated". This caller-side version update is a combination of *removing a service call* and *calling an existing endpoint* change types. From the perspective of G_2, the service $s_{a,i}$ no longer calls a service endpoint $s_{u,v}$ (i.e., removed service call), but the same service a of the updated service version ($i \rightarrow j$) is adding a call to $s_{u,v}$ (i.e., calling an existing service endpoint). Figure 2 (left) depicts an example. In the canary, the *frontend* service is updated to version 2, and both version 1 and version 2 call the *search* service.

Updated Callee Version. This change type represents the case of a version change in the service that is called. This callee-side version update combines *removing a service call* and *calling a new endpoint* change types. From the perspective of G_2, the service $s_{a,i}$ no longer calls a service $s_{u,v}$ (i.e., removed service call), but the same service $s_{a,i}$ calls a new version x of service u (update: $v \rightarrow x$, i.e., calling a new endpoint), hence there exists an edge $e = s_{a,i} \rightarrow s_{u,x}$. Figure 2 (right) exemplifies this change type when the version of *frontend* that is called by *edge* is updated from version 1 (*baseline*) to version 2 (*canary*).

Updated Version. This change type is a combination of *updated caller version* and *updated callee version* change types. There exists a service a and service u in both interaction graphs G_1 and G_2. In G_1, there is an edge $e_1 = s_{a,i} \rightarrow s_{u,v}$, and in G_2, there is an edge $e_2 = s_{a,j} \rightarrow s_{u,x}$. Hence, in G_1 the interaction happens between versions i and v of the services a and u, and in G_2 between versions j and x. From the perspective of G_2, both the caller and the callee versions are updated. Figure 2 (right) shows this pattern between *frontend* and *orders*. While for the *baseline*, version 1 of *frontend* calls version 2 of *orders*, in the *canary*, version 2 of *frontend* requires version 3 of *orders*.

4   Ranking Identified Changes

This section covers (1) the construction of the graph-based topological differences, (2) a generic algorithm that traverses these differences to produce a ranking of identified changes, and (3) three embodiments of this algorithm in the form of heuristics to assess the impact of the changes identified.

4.1   Constructing the Topological Difference

Our approach relies on distributed traces of a microservice-based application to (1) infer interaction graphs for each variant of the experiment and to (2) construct a graph-based topological difference resulting from their comparison.

Inferring Interaction Graphs. Distributed tracing is a technique used to collect information about calls between microservices. A *trace* is a set of data about the sequence of all inter-service calls resulting from a top-level action performed by an end user. Each call is associated with timestamped events corresponding to sending the request, receiving the request, sending the response, and receiving the response. In our approach, a developer needs to specify the application variants of interest, i.e., versions of services for baseline and canary and the experiment start time. Given the inputs, we then divide collected distributed traces of baseline and canary variants into clusters, where each cluster contains multiple interaction graphs (as defined in Sect. 3) with the same *root request*. A *root request* is a service call made to an edge service of the application, which in turn triggers other inter-service calls within the application, forming an interaction graph. In each cluster we also compute statistics on metrics for each inter-service call, namely, duration, timeouts, retries, and errors.

Comparing Interaction Graphs. The next step is to compare corresponding baseline and canary clusters of interaction graphs to identify topological changes based on the types described in Sect. 3.3. Once the changes and their types are identified, the graphs are merged into a single graph forming an "extended" topological difference (e.g., Fig. 1). The topological difference contains all the changes identified, their assigned type, and further statistics that were captured during the interaction graph's construction. Due to the merge, the difference graph contains also those structures (services and their interactions) that are common to the graphs under comparison. Doing so preserves the "big picture" and enables detailed analyses on the entire service network.

4.2   Traversing the Topological Difference

Once the graph-based topological difference is built, we execute a two-phase graph-traversal algorithm, consisting of the *annotation* and the *extraction* phases.

Basic Algorithm. In a first step, all vertices (or nodes) in the graph without *outbound* calls are visited (and marked as such). Then, the algorithm visits those vertices calling service endpoints that have been flagged as visited, marking them as visited again. This process is repeated until all nodes in the graph are visited.

Annotation Phase. In our approach, every node in the graph-based topological difference has an associated state $\mathcal{T}$, which is used to store any information to reason about, and ultimately rank changes. In the *annotation* phase, these states are set to hold information required for the concrete implementation of the ranking algorithm (i.e., heuristic). During a node's visit, a wide range of information is available, including the involved endpoint, outgoing calls and their change types, statistics (for either one or for both variants) that were computed during the construction of the interaction graphs, and any other queryable monitoring information (e.g., from Prometheus[5]). It depends on the concrete implementation of a heuristic which information is used and how it is combined.

Extraction Phase. In this phase, every node is revisited with the goal to *extract* a score $\mathcal{S}$ for each interaction (i.e., outgoing edge). Due to the nature of our change types, an interaction in the topological difference graph could comprise two edges in the source interaction graphs. The scoring happens on the change type level: edges belonging to the same change are merged. Edges that are common (without any change) in both source interaction graphs are treated as a special change type. The idea of the extraction phase is to rely on the state information gained in the annotation phase and to transform it into scalar values. Formally, this scoring function has the type signature $score : change \rightarrow int$.

Ranking. Once scores for all edges in the difference graph are computed, the scores are sorted in descending order and ranks from 1 to k are assigned, where k is the number of edges in the graph-based topological difference. The edge achieving the highest score is ranked on position 1. Equal scores leading to tied ranks are possible, even though they appear rarely.

In the following we will cover three specific embodiments of our algorithm. Starting with the *Subtree Complexity* heuristic, followed by the *Response Time Analysis* heuristic, we will cover their joint variant, the *Hybrid* heuristic.

4.3   Subtree Complexity Heuristic

This heuristic analyzes sub-structures of a topological difference and considers uncertainty in the context of experiments.

Concept. The graph structure is broken down into multiple subtrees (see Fig. 3 for an example). The fundamental idea of this heuristic is that the more complex the structure of the (sub-)tree is, the more likely it contains changes that affect the outcome of the experiment and the application's health state.

Initially, every node a has an assigned state of $\mathcal{T}_a = 0$. Whenever a node a is visited during the algorithm's annotation phase, its state $\mathcal{T}_a$ is set to $\mathcal{T}_a = \sum_1^n \mathcal{T}_i + p_{a,i}$ being $1 \leq i \leq n$ the (child) nodes of the outgoing calls of a. Thus, the state values $\mathcal{T}_i$ of called nodes i are summed up and weights $p_{a,i}$ representing individual *propagation* factors for these calls are added. During the *extraction* phase, for every interaction of a node a with a node i, the score for this edge e is computed as follows: $\mathcal{S}_e = \mathcal{T}_i + c_{a,i}$. Thus, the score is built from the state value $\mathcal{T}_i$ of the node (i.e., service) that is being called and an individual *scoring* factor $c_{a,i}$ for the edge.

---

[5] https://prometheus.io/.

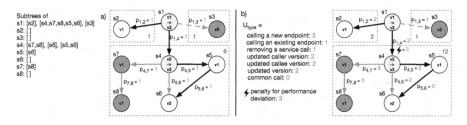

Fig. 3. Example of (topmost) subtrees in a topological difference. **a)** Basic subtree complexity (ST) in blue (i.e., counting the number of edges in a subtree). Service $s1$ has three subtrees. The state value of $s4$ is 5 (3 subtrees, 5 edges in total). Thus, the extracted score for the edge between $s1$ and $s4$ is $5 + 1 = 6$. **b)** Extended subtree (ST Ext) in blue, propagation values $p_{a,i}$ based on U_{type} values assigned to change types. Extracted score for the edge between $s1$ and $s4$ is $10 + 2 + 3 = 15$. (3 represents the performance penalty). (Color figure online)

The distinction between *propagation* and *scoring* factors serve the following purposes. The propagation factor directly influences the state values of the nodes (and thus the individual scores) when walking up the tree. This is useful if severe issues within a subtree are detected that should be reflected in the ranking of the changes. The scoring factor only influences individual scores, e.g., a single change. It allows expressing fine-grained differences among the changes. Depending on how propagation and scoring factors are chosen, the subtree complexity heuristic allows for multiple variations. Within the scope of this paper, we focus on two variations: *Subtree* and *Subtree Extended*.

Subtree (ST). This standard variant of the heuristic analyzes the structural complexity of the difference graph by counting the number of edges within subtrees. Propagation and scoring factors $p_{a,i}$ and $c_{a,i}$ are set to 1 for all edges independent of their change types. Figure 3a depicts an example in blue.

Extended (ST Ext). This variation introduces the concept of *uncertainty*. Calling entirely new services compared to calling a new version of an existing service leads to a different degree of uncertainty when assessing the application's health state. For the former, no information to compare to (i.e., previous calls or historical metrics) exists, while for the latter calls to the new version can be compared with previous calls. Deviations in metrics, such as response times or error rates, can be considered. Similarly, when a new call to an existing endpoint is made, even though a direct comparison on the interaction-level is not possible, there are still metrics available that are associated to the called service allowing an assessment whether this added call introduces unwanted effects. In our approach, we built upon these subtle differences in uncertainty for the identified change types and assign a weight U_{type} to each of them.

For the *extended subtree* heuristic, instead of the number of edges, the uncertainty values U_{type} associated to the individual edges' change types are summed up within a subtree. Hence, individual propagation factors $p_{a,i} = U_{type}$ are set to the uncertainty value of the edge's change type. Figure 3b depicts an example.

The rationale for this is to emphasize the uncertainty of subtrees involving many changes. Scoring factors are defined as $c_{a,i} = U_{type} + P$. Similar to the propagation factors we use the uncertainty values U_{type} and we introduce penalties P that are added to those interactions for which deviations are measured, e.g., significant changes in response times. This mechanism allows us to account for performance issues without running in depth root-cause analyses. Penalization applies to all interactions for which direct comparisons between the variants on the edge-level are possible, i.e., composed change types and common calls.

4.4   Response Time Analysis Heuristic

This heuristic tries to identify services and changes that have caused performance issues by incorporating the notion of uncertainty.

Concept. The intuition here is that in case of performance deviations (e.g., response time) spotted at a node, the node's surrounding changes that·add additional calls (e.g., *calling a new endpoint*, or *calling an existing endpoint*) are potential sources of these deviations. This heuristic focuses on the overall response time (i.e., how long did the called endpoint take to respond) extracted from tracing data. However, the concept can be extended to incorporate other metrics that have similar cascading effects. Further, note that these performance comparisons are only possible for specific change types, namely composed change types and common calls.

The state T_a of a node a is extended to keep track of deviations and their potential sources while traversing the graph. It involves *flag*, a counter that keeps track how often a node is considered as the source of a deviation, a map *deviations* that stores which outgoing call (i.e., key) causes how much deviation (i.e., value, in milliseconds), and a list *source* keeping track which child caused the deviation. Algorithm 1 illustrates the analysis executed for every outgoing call in the *annotation* phase when visiting a node a.

Algorithm 1: Response Time Analysis

Input: node, child, call
if *call.hasDeviation()* :
    node.state.*addSource*(child)
    if *len(child.state.deviations)* == *0* :
        node.state.*addDeviation*(call=call,deviation=call.deviation)
        child.state.flag := 1
    else:
        flagSources(child)
        total := *sum*(child.state.deviations)
        node.state.*addDeviation*(call=call, deviation=*max*(call.deviation, total))
        if *call.deviation > total* :
            inc(child.state.flag)
            for *c in child.calls* :
                if *c.type in [call_new_endpoint, call_existing_endpoint]* :
                    inc(c.target.state.flag)
                    child.state.*addSource*(c.target)

In case of a deviation, the called child is added as a source. If there are no stored deviations for the child node, then the deviation is added to the node's state, and the child's state *flag* counter is set to 1. If there are deviations, the recursive function *flagSources* walks through all the stored sources that might caused the deviation on the child's side and increases their *flag* counters. In the next step, the sum of all stored deviations (i.e., *total*) is calculated and the deviation is added to the node's state. If the call's deviation is higher than the total sum of deviations on the child's side, then it is likely that a change introduced this new deviation. Therefore, the child's *flag* counter is increased and the child's surrounding changes are analyzed. This involves all of the child's outgoing edges with *calling a new endpoint* and *calling an existing endpoint* change types. The target nodes of these edges are added as potential sources and their flag counters are increased.

By using different *scoring* factors in the heuristic's *extraction* phase we distinguish two variations: RTA and RTA Ext. The *annotation* phase (i.e., flagging) described in Algorithm 1 is the same for both variations.

Response Time Analysis (RTA). In the *extraction* phase, for every outgoing call of a node a to a child node i, the score for an edge e is defined as $S_e = T_{i.flag}$. The resulting score corresponds to the final value of the child node's *flag*. Consequently, those services with the highest flag counts are ranked first.

Extended (RTA Ext). For this variation we revisit the concept of uncertainty and reuse weights U_{type} as scoring factors. Again, the rationale is that those interactions with high uncertainty for a change should have higher scores. To have a mechanism to balance between *flag* and *uncertainty* values, we introduce a *penalty* constant C. The scoring function for an edge e is defined as $S_e = T_{i.flag} * C + U_{type}$.

4.5 Hybrid Heuristic

More complex (sub-)structures are more likely to contain changes that could cause problems. This is the strength of the subtree complexity heuristic. However, in case of performance deviations, the response time analysis heuristic provides more detailed analyses to identify the origin of problems. The goal of the hybrid heuristic is to combine the strengths of both, structural and performance analyses. The underlying mechanics of both heuristics remain untouched for the hybrid heuristic. During the algorithm's annotation phase, both the structural and the performance analyses are conducted. The extraction phase shapes how the individual results of the heuristics are transformed into a single result. We distinguish two variants: **Hybrid (HYB)** and **Extended (HYB Ext)**.

Both variants use the *extended subtree* heuristic (ST Ext) to determine state values T_i. To determine state *flag* values, the standard variant of the heuristic uses *standard RTA*, while the extend hybrid variant uses *extended RTA*. Consequently, the scoring function for an edge e is defined as $S_e = T_i + U_{type} + T_{i.flag} * C$, being C the penalty constant established in RTA Ext, which is set to 1 in the case of the standard hybrid variant.

5   Ranking Quality Evaluation

To demonstrate our (formal) approach we developed a research prototype with the goal to assist developers on experiment health assessment and decision-making. The paper's online appendix[6] provides screenshots of the user interface (also depicting those two scenarios), source code of the heuristics, and a comprehensive replication package.

We evaluated the quality of the produced rankings on two concrete scenarios: (1) revisiting the running example, and (2) dealing with multiple breaking changes. Before we dive into details of the ranking quality evaluation, we briefly describe our evaluation's setup.

5.1   Setup

The setup involves a description of the method we used to assess the quality of the produced rankings, how we calibrated the parameters the heuristics are operating on, and how we generated the distributed tracing data.

Method. Normalized discounted cumulative gain (nDCG) [7] is a measure of ranking quality, widely used in information retrieval. Based on a graded *relevance* scale of documents in the result list of search-engine queries, DCG (or its normalized variant nDCG) assesses the usefulness (i.e., the gain) of a document based on its position in the result list. The gain of each document is summed up from top to bottom in the ranking, having the gain of each result discounted the lower the rank, which has the consequence that highly relevant documents ranked at lower positions are penalized. The DCG accumulated at a particular rank position p is defined as $DCG_p = \sum_{i=1}^{p}(rel_i/log_2(i+1))$.

rel_i is the relevance of the document at position i. Instead of documents we rank identified changes. In order to use DCG, the authors assessed the relevance of every single change of our two scenarios. In total, including sub-scenarios, 6 relevance assessments were conducted rating changes on a scale from 0 (not relevant) to 4 (highly relevant). We use a normalized DCG (nDCG) producing relative values on the interval 0.0 to 1.0, this allows for result comparison across scenarios. 1.0 is the maximum value representing a ranking with the most relevant changes on the top positions. As tied ranks are possible (e.g., changes with the same score and rank as resulting from a heuristic), we applied the nDCG adaption proposed by McSherry and Najork [9] considering average gains at tied positions.

Calibration. To calibrate the heuristics we followed an iterative exploratory parameter optimization procedure across all scenarios. For nDCG we considered the top $3, 5, 7$, and 10 positions of the ranking to be compared. For the penalties P and C used in the heuristics' scoring functions we iterated through values $1, 3, 5, 7$, and 10. We tested four different mappings of *uncertainty* values to change types U_{type}. Based on more than 9000 calibration results, we determined that

---

[6] https://github.com/sealuzh/topology-experimentation-appendix.

$P = C = 3$ and an uncertainty mapping U_{type} (i.e., *change type → uncertainty*) of {'calling new endpoint': 3, 'calling existing endpoint': 1, 'removing call': 1, 'updated caller version': 2, 'updated callee version': 2, 'updated version': 2, 'common call': 0} yielded the most promising results. We determined the nDCG for the top 5 positions to allow comparison across scenarios of different sizes.

Tracing Data. We implemented the two evaluation scenarios as microservice-based applications running on top of a Kubernetes cluster in the IBM Cloud. The Istio service mesh was in place to handle experiment traffic routing between the application's variants along with a Zipkin installation keeping track of service interactions. For every (sub-) scenario 1000 requests were generated.

5.2   Scenario 1: Revisiting the Sample Application

As a first scenario we use the example application shown in Fig. 1. Contrary to the next scenario, we do not cover a specific evaluation aspect here. However, this scenario involves all of the change types we identified, hence making it a useful baseline to assess the proposed heuristics.

Scenario. This scenario involves two sub-scenarios: *basic* and *delayed*. *Basic* executes the baseline variant of the application without modification, the canary variant involves added functionality and updated service versions. The *delayed* sub-scenario introduces a delay of $100ms$ at the *payment* service for the *canary* variant. This reflects an abnormally behaving *orders* service in the *canary* that multiplies the traffic towards the *payment* service causing it to overload, resulting in higher response times.

Relevance. For the basic scenario, the added calls to *product* and the updated versions of *frontend* and *orders* were classified as highly relevant (i.e., a relevance score of 4). For the delayed scenario, in addition, the call between *payment* and *orders* is classified as highly relevant. Relevance ratings for all scenarios are listed in our online appendix.

Table 1. $nDCG_5$ scores for all variations of the three heuristics across all evaluation scenarios. Scenario 1 with sub-scenarios basic and delayed (in the canary variant). Scenario 2 with four sub-scenarios: basic, a delay involving service j (canary), a delay involving service s (canary), and a combination of both delays (canary).

| | Scenario 1 | | Scenario 2 | | | |
Heuristic	Basic	Delay	Basic	Delay j	Delay s	Combined
ST	0.89	0.93	0.91	0.83	0.87	0.76
ST Ext.	0.96	0.93	0.99	0.85	0.91	0.77
RTA	0.76	0.87	0.64	0.91	0.82	0.90
RTA Ext.	0.93	0.95	0.73	0.91	0.83	0.91
HYB	0.98	0.96	1.00	0.85	0.92	0.81
HYB Ext.	0.96	0.98	0.96	0.93	0.92	0.87

Results. Table 1 (Scenario 1) shows the nDCG scores of the three heuristics in their 6 variations for the *basic* and the *delayed* sub-scenarios. Scores are color-coded, the higher the score, the more intense the background color. The *hybrid* variations outperform the other heuristics, though some other approaches achieve high scores as well. *RTA* produces good results for the *delayed* sub-scenario. However, it only captures the "relevance" of the delayed fragments and ignores the high relevance of the added functionality. This is simply because there are no performance issues associated with these changes. The addition of *uncertainty* for the *RTA Ext* variant helps to compensate this flaw and leads to stronger scores for both sub-scenarios. Moreover, penalizing as a scoring factor turns out to have positive effects on the delayed sub-scenario. However, the standard *HYB* variant without penalties performs slightly better, though only by a whisker, e.g., by 0.005 on the combined score of both sub-scenarios for *HYB* and *HYB Ext*.

5.3   Scenario 2: Breaking Changes

The goal of the second scenario is to identify how the heuristics behave when dealing with more complex, cascading changes resulting in multiple version updates. This represents deployment scenarios and experiments dealing with multiple breaking API changes. Figure 1 (right) depicts its topological differ-ence in which b is the experiment's target service.

Scenario. We split into multiple sub-scenarios involving simulated performance issues in the *canary* variant. In addition to the *basic* scenario, which contains multiple version updates and new services, we added two specific performance deviations: a delay at service h when calling service j (100 ms), and a delay at service s (200 ms) simulating a more complex request processing compared to the removed service pairs p, q, and r. As a fourth sub-scenario, we combined these two delays, making them active at the same time.

Relevance. For the *basic* sub-scenario, the version updates between b and c, b and f, f and m, and the added functionality for m calling s are rated as highly relevant. The delayed variants emphasize the changes introducing performance deviations.

Results. Similar to the running example, on average across all sub-scenarios, the *hybrid* heuristics perform best (see Table 1, Scenario 2). Some individual results on sub-scenarios provide valuable insights into the single heuristics' strengths and weaknesses. Keeping the *basic* results aside, *RTA* (in both variations) achieves an average nDCG score of 0.88, only topped by *HYB Ext*, which naturally inherited *RTA* functionality, with a score of 0.91. For the *basic* sub-scenario, the standard *HYB* performs best, almost reporting the perfect ranking with a score of 0.996, immediately followed by *ST Ext* with *uncertainty* involved (as propagation and scoring factor). Remarkably, the standard version of *ST* achieves a score of 0.91, also due to the fact that changes rated with high relevance are particularly "up high in the tree" (e.g., between b and f, and b and c) in this scenario. This enables this simple heuristic to come close to the best rankings.

5.4   Discussion

Combining the nDCG scores across all evaluation scenarios yields the highest (average) score of 0.94 for *HYB Ext*, a heuristic involving both uncertainty and a penalty mechanism in the scoring function. Interestingly, when diving deeper and distinguishing between (1) all basic scenarios and (2) all scenarios involving introduced performance issues we observe *HYB Ext* being not ranked first for both (1) and (2). Despite being superior for performance cases (2) with an average score of 0.93 and a gap of 0.03 to the second-best heuristic (i.e., *RTA Ext*), it is ranked third for non-performance cases, lacking a score of 0.03 to its leading standard *HYB* counterpart without penalty mechanism. As the performance cases dominate – 4 versus 2 non-performance cases – *HYB Ext* clearly benefits from the evaluation setup. This result is an indication that it would make sense to let developers or release engineers using our proposed tooling toggle between multiple (selected) heuristics which provide insights onto the application's state from different angles.

6   Limitations

One limitation of our approach is that the ranking quality evaluation was conducted on traces for self-generated scenarios. We mitigated this threat by covering two complex scenarios and combined them with sub-scenarios including simulated performance issues. A more thorough evaluation based on multiple real cases is desirable, and part of our future research. A further threat involves the relevance classification conducted by the authors of this paper. We classified all changes for all sub-scenarios on a scale from not relevant (0) to highly relevant (4). As the relevance is used as baseline for nDCG, these ratings have a direct effect on the resulting scores. Our online replication package allows inspecting how results change when relevance ratings are adjusted. Another threat involves the parameter calibration for the heuristics, which has a strong influence on the results. We mitigated this threat by performing thorough calibration runs with different parameter settings across all covered scenarios.

One limitation regarding the heuristics is that *RTA* variations only account for changes that impact the response time negatively. We focus on the total response time, ignoring that individual changes can have both positive and negative effects. However, our heuristics can be extended to cover this case as well.

Our evaluation focused solely on the ranking quality and left aside questions on how our approach would perform on industry-scale applications. We conducted a performance evaluation on the heuristic's execution behavior on self-generated difference graphs of multiple sizes and with various characteristics. First results are promising and show that the heuristics are able to cope with graphs consisting of thousands of nodes within seconds. However, detailed analysis are, also due to space reasons, out of scope for this paper and an evaluation on real instead of self-generated graphs is subject of future work.

7 Conclusion

We proposed an approach that analyzes request traces captured from distributed tracing systems to identify changes of microservice-based applications in the context of continuous experiments. Using heuristics, we rank these identified changes according to their potential impact on the experiment and the application's health state, with the goal of supporting decisions on whether to continue or abort the experiment. While previous work on experiment health assessment considers the services under test in isolation, which could skew the assessment as certain effects are left out, we focus on the topological level. We characterized a set of recurring topological change types consisting of fundamental patterns and more complex composed variants. We proposed three heuristics that operate on top of these characterized changes taking the concept of *uncertainty* into account. Our evaluation conducted on two case study scenarios demonstrated that the rankings produced by the heuristics are promising and could be a valuable resource for experiment health assessments. An comprehensive evaluation on how our approach performs on industry-scale applications is subject of future work.

References

1. Ates, E., et al.: An automated, cross-layer instrumentation framework for diagnosing performance problems in distributed applications. In: Proceedings of the ACM Symposium on Cloud Computing, SoCC 2019 (2019)
2. Bass, L., Weber, I., Zhu, L.: DevOps: A Software Architect's Perspective. Addison-Wesley Professional, Boston (2015). ISBN 0134049845
3. Davidovic, S., Beyer, B.: Canary analysis service. ACM Queue **16**(1) (2018). https://dl.acm.org/doi/10.1145/3190566
4. Froemmgen, A., Stohr, D., Koldehofe, B., Rizk, A.: Don't repeat yourself: seamless execution and analysis of extensive network experiments. In: Proceedings of the 14th International Conference on emerging Networking EXperiments and Technologies (CoNEXT 2018) (2018)
5. Huhns, M.N., Singh, M.P.: Service-oriented computing: key concepts and principles. IEEE Internet Comput. **9**(1), 75–81 (2005)
6. Humble, J., Farley, D.: Continuous Delivery: Reliable Software Releases Through Build, Test, and Deployment Automation. Addison-Wesley Professional, Bostan (2010). ISBN 0321601912
7. Järvelin, K., Kekäläinen, J.: Cumulated gain-based evaluation of IR techniques. ACM Trans. Inf. Syst. **20**(4), 422–446 (2002)
8. Kevic, K., Murphy, B., Williams, L., Beckmann, J.: Characterizing experimentation in continuous deployment: a case study on bing. In: Proceedings of the 39th International Conference on Software Engineering: Software Engineering in Practice Track, ICSE-SEIP 2017, pp. 123–132 (2017)
9. McSherry, F., Najork, M.: Computing information retrieval performance measures efficiently in the presence of tied scores. In: Macdonald, C., Ounis, I., Plachouras, V., Ruthven, I., White, R.W. (eds.) ECIR 2008. LNCS, vol. 4956, pp. 414–421. Springer, Heidelberg (2008). https://doi.org/10.1007/978-3-540-78646-7_38
10. Newman, S.: Building Microservices, 1st edn. O'Reilly Media Inc., Newton (2015)

11. Sambasivan, R.R., et al.: Diagnosing performance changes by comparing request flows. In: Proceedings of the 8th USENIX Conference on Networked Systems Design and Implementation, NSDI 2011 (2011)
12. Santana, M., Sampaio, A., Andrade, M., Rosa, N.S.: Transparent tracing of microservice-based applications. In: Proceedings of the 34th ACM/SIGAPP Symposium on Applied Computing, SAC 2019 (2019)
13. Savor, T., Douglas, M., Gentili, M., Williams, L., Beck, K., Stumm, M.: Continuous deployment at Facebook and OANDA. In: Proceedings of the 38th International Conference on Software Engineering Companion, ICSE 2016, pp. 21–30, New York, NY, USA. ACM (2016)
14. Schermann, G., Schöni, D., Leitner, P., Gall, H.C.: Bifrost: supporting continuous deployment with automated enactment of multi-phase live testing strategies. In: Proceedings of the 17th International Middleware Conference, Middleware 2016, pp. 12:1–12:14, New York, NY, USA. ACM (2016)
15. Schermann, G., Cito, J., Leitner, P.: Continuous experimentation: challenges, implementation techniques, and current research. IEEE Softw. 35(2), 26–31 (2018)
16. Schermann, G., Cito, J., Leitner, P., Zdun, U., Gall, H.C.: We're doing it live: a multi-method empirical study on continuous experimentation. Inf. Softw. Technol. 99, 41–57 (2018)
17. Tang, C., et al.: Holistic configuration management at Facebook. In: Proceedings of the 25th Symposium on Operating Systems Principles (SOSP), pp. 328–343, New York, NY, USA. ACM (2015)
18. Tarvo, A., Sweeney, P.F., Mitchell, N., Rajan, V., Arnold, M., Baldini, I.: CanaryAdvisor: a statistical-based tool for canary testing (Demo). In: Proceedings of the 2015 International Symposium on Software Testing and Analysis (ISSTA), pp. 418–422, New York, NY, USA. ACM (2015)
19. Veeraraghavan, K., et al.: Kraken: leveraging live traffic tests to identify and resolve resource utilization bottlenecks in large scale web services. In: Proceedings of the 12th USENIX Conference on Operating Systems Design and Implementation, OSDI 2016 (2016)
20. Xiao, Z., Wijegunaratne, I., Qiang, X.: Reflections on SOA and microservices. In: 4th International Conference on Enterprise Systems (ES) (2016)

Charting Microservices to Support Services' Developers: The Anaximander Approach

Sébastien Mosser[1(✉)], Jean-Philippe Caissy[1], Florian Juroszek[1,2], Florian Vouters[1,3], and Naouel Moha[1]

[1] Université du Québec à Montréal (UQAM), Montréal, Canada
{mosser.sebastien,caissy.jean-philippe,juroszek.florian, vouters.florian,moha.naouel}@uqam.ca
[2] Université Côte d'Azur (UCA), Sophia Antipolis, France
florian.juroszek@univ-cotedazur.fr
[3] Centre des Études Supérieures Industrielles (exia.CESI), Toulouse, France
florian.vouters@viacesi.fr

Abstract. Microservice architectures have gained popularity in the last ten years, based on their intrinsic capabilities of implementing scalable software architectures. However, understanding a microservice architecture is still a challenging task for software architects. Current state-of-the-art approaches addressing this challenge focus on exhaustive solutions, working in an all-or-nothing way. These all-or-nothing solutions rely on heuristics to create one *map* of a given architecture, using static and/or dynamic analysis of the existing source code. This is not compatible with the classical approaches used in software comprehension, that relies on the exploration of a program in an incremental way. In this paper, we leverage the *exploration* metaphor and describes the ANAXIMANDER approach to support the incremental definition of a map that suits the needs of the architect exploring an architecture. Using probes working at different levels of abstraction and precision, one can incrementally chart a map representing the architecture and leverage the map by querying it. We applied the ANAXIMANDER approach to six reference microservice architecture published by major actors from the state-of-practice.

Keywords: Microservice architecture · Software comprehension · Software composition

1 Introduction

Microservices are gaining momentum to support the development of complex service architecture. Relying on the promising principles of domain-driven design [12], microservices architectures provide an excellent answer to tame the challenge of developing scalable service-based systems. Such architectures are

© Springer Nature Switzerland AG 2020
E. Kafeza et al. (Eds.): ICSOC 2020, LNCS 12571, pp. 36–44, 2020.
https://doi.org/10.1007/978-3-030-65310-1_3

decomposed into a set of independent microservices, each of these being dedicated to a given domain. The communication between services is delegated to reliable communication paradigms, such as messages buses [2]. From a software engineering point of view, micro-services triggers several maintainability issues, *e.g.,*, how to maintain and evolve such systems.

Table 1. Size and technology heterogeneity for each reference architecture

Id.	Ref. architecture [1]	Technologies				Size		
		Lang.	DBs	Mess.	Depl.	#Files	#LoCs	#Serv.
S1	HipsterShop	5	1	2	2	163	38,934	10
S2	SockShop	3	4	2	9	222	19,014	8
S3	eShopOnContainers	1	7	5	3	1,585	143,356	8
S4	Vert.x MS Blueprint	1	7	2	1	218	18,881	9
S5	Shopping Cart	1	7	2	1	396	70,045	8
S6	Robot shop	4	3	2	1	120	6,341	7
Total for all arch.		*5*	*5*	*6*	*11*	*2,704*	*296,580*	*50*

In 2020, Assunçãao *et al.* described a variability challenge related to microservice engineering [1], where they identified six references open-source microservice architectures. These reference systems (see Sect. 4) demonstrate the high level of variability related to microservices development (Table 1). This level of heterogeneity is intrinsic to microservices architectures, and it is necessary to support developers and architects who have to maintain such systems. Reverse-engineering approaches typically support this task [9]. However, in the very case of microservices architecture, the quest for a fully-automated tool that can reverse-engineer any microservice architecture is pointless by design. On the one hand, static code analysis approaches will quickly reach a limit considering the flexibility offered to the developers by the existing technologies, and the upcoming frameworks that are not yet invented. On the other hand, dynamic approaches (*e.g.*, analyzing traces of execution) are fragile *w.r.t.* the scenarios used as input to capture the dynamic traces.

Instead of targeting an ultra-high-definition description of the architecture, we propose here to define an incremental and iterative way of creating such a description. The key idea is to consider such a description as a map, and leverage the way cartographers addressed the creation of maps in the early days of our civilization. We named our approach after ANAXIMANDER, a Greek philosopher known to have produced the first map of the world. Based on a source code audit of the reference architectures, we propose in this paper to describe an incremental approach to support developers and architects who maintain microservice architecture.

2   Related Work

Haitzer and Zdun [4] present a *Domain-Specific Language* (DSL) to abstract an application's architecture in a semi-autonomous way. This approach emphasizes that working incrementally is essential. Granchelli *et al.* [3] present an approach to recover the architecture of microservice systems called MicroART from a GitHub repository and a reference to the container engine managing the application. This approach differs from ours by using a monitoring tool such as tcpdump to capture the communication log between services without taking into account the architecture deployment artifacts. Kleehaus *et al.* [6] provides a tool called *MICROLYZE* to recover the infrastructure in real-time of a microservice architecture. Similar to our approach, *MICROLYZE* uses both automatic and manual processes to gather information. Ma *et al.* [8] propose another approach to generate service dependency graphs automatically. Those graphs are used to analyze and visualize the dependencies between the microservices deployed for the application. Their solutions allow them to select specific test cases in order to run regression tests on the application. Ma *et al.* explore similar monitoring solutions [7] to leverage annotation in Java source code. Those annotations are used to help build service dependency graphs.

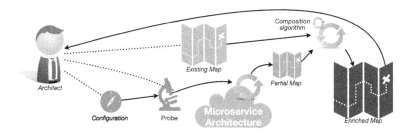

Fig. 1. Overview of the ANAXIMANDER approach

Leveraging the cartography metaphor, all the approaches described in this can be seen as exploration campaigns of the architecture, trying to create a complete map out of a single exploration. The maps are dedicated to a single objective (*e.g.*, non-regression testing) and cannot inter-operate with each other. Moreover, the amount of information produced is very detailed, and it might overwhelm an architect, preventing the approach to answer the architect's questions.

3   The Anaximander approach

Taking a different point of view, the key concepts of ANAXIMANDER are the definition of *(i) partial maps*, obtained as the result of the execution of *(ii) exploration probes* applied to the system. This approach tackles by design the heterogeneity of micro-services architectures (see Sect. 4), and is complementary of the approaches already existing in the state-of-the-art that can be considered as *exploration probes*. We describe in Fig. 1 the approach for a software architect, that relies on the classical *extract - abstract - present* paradigm [10] used in reverse engineering. The architect selects a *probe* among the one available off the shelf, and execute it on the architecture. A probe can rely on static analysis, or dynamic traces. As a result of its exploration, a probe returns a partial map, *i.e.*, the information gathered by the probe. The obtained partial map is then composed with the already existing one (if any), to enrich the knowledge (*e.g.*, adding new information, correcting errors).

3.1 Modelling the Map as a Graph

We define an architecture *map* as a typical graph $g = (V, E) \in \mathcal{G}$, where $V = \{v_1, \ldots, v_i\} \in \mathcal{V}^i$ is a set of vertices and $E = \{e_1, \ldots, e_j\} \in \mathcal{E}^j$ a set of edges. A vertex v is defined as an vertex identifier, a type, and a set of associated properties P. An edge e is defined as a pair of source and target vertex identifiers, a type, and a set of properties. A property p is a simple key-value pair. To support the efficient manipulation of the maps, we rely on two constraints that need to hold in a given map: *(i)* vertex uniqueness and *(ii)* edge uniqueness.

To manipulate the map and support its enrichment, we leverage the classical *match and merge* algorithm [5]. Each graph element (*i.e.*, graphs, vertices and edges) defines an *equivalence relation* (denoted as $\equiv$) for matching purpose (*e.g.*, two nodes are considered equivalent when they have the same identifier), and a *merge* function (denoted as $\oplus$) to merge two elements identified as equivalent. Thus, enriching an existing map m with the result of a probe m' is simply to compute $m'' = m \oplus m'$. To correct an error, we rely on the opposite operation *remove* (denoted as $\ominus$), where the following law holds: $m = (m \oplus m') \ominus m'$.

3.2 Modelling Probes as Functions

Exploration probes are the software artifacts used to produce the partial maps. According to the heterogeneity of the technologies involved in microservices architectures, it is unrealistic to develop a polyglot framework supporting the state-of-practice as well as anticipating any upcoming technological trends. As a consequence, we decided to model a probe as a black-box function $p : conf \rightarrow \mathcal{G}$, taking as input its configuration, and producing as output a map, in a textual format. Adding or removing information to the map relies on the $\oplus$ and $\ominus$ operators previously described, *e.g.*, $m_{t+1} = m_t \oplus p(configuration)$.

The immediate advantage of this black-box representation is that it unifies the outcome of each exploration while supporting the designers of probes to use the most appropriate technologies for their very own probes. For example, a static analysis of Go source code will leverage the compiler capabilities directly embedded inside the Go language, where a probe dedicated to analyzing Spring Boot Java services will leverage the reflexivity API available in Java to analyze the developed artifacts. Dynamic analysis can leverage classical formal models such as the *Knowledge Discovery Metamodel* [11], an international standard promoted by the OMG to support software modernization. To tame this heterogeneity and consider all the probes as equals from the architect point of view, it is possible to wrap each probe into an image (*e.g.*, using Docker or Singularity container technologies). The image will contain all the necessary software dependencies (*e.g.*, executable, compiler, libraries, frameworks) for a given probe, and hide this complexity to the architect into a black-box approach. It emphasizes the idea of probes' black-box representation, where the internal implementation details are hidden inside the container. The probes library available off-the-shelf is then a set of turn-key images ready to be used by the architect, and creating a new probe is as simple as publishing a new image inside the library.

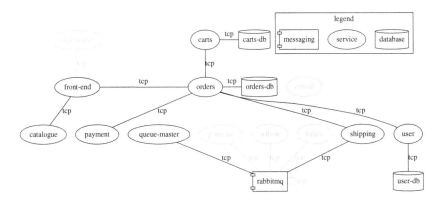

Fig. 2. ANAXIMANDER map obtained dynamically using WeaveScope (m_i)

4   Exploring a Reference Architecture

In this section, we validate the ANAXIMANDER approach based on the reference architectures used to express the requirements. The source code of the probes is available on the project repository[1]. For the sake of concision, it is not possible to provide here an in-depth analysis of each of the reference architecture. Instead, we focus on a single one (S2, *SockShop*[13]), as it is built as a demonstration showcase by a tool vendor (WeaveWorks), medium-sized concerning the five others, a representative in terms of heterogeneity (three languages for service development, three databases technologies, two messaging framework and nine deployment technologies), and involves 8 services.

As a starting point, we transformed the dynamic map provided by the tool vendor into an ANAXIMANDER artifact (Fig. 2). This first map m_i is the composition of three different information: *(i)* the server that host the services, *(ii)* the TCP connections that exist between the services and *(iii)* the kind of service

---

[1] https://github.com/ace-design/anaximander-microservices.

(*i.e.*, database, messaging, service). For the sake of readability, we only kept the two last ones in the paper version of the map. As the map is obtained by listening to a runtime infrastructure, it contains noise, *i.e.*, existing containers in the deployment infrastructure that are not related to the business logic (*e.g.*, edge-router, consul).

To remove the noise, we use a probe dedicated to extracting services from a Kubernetes descriptor. This probe extracts from the deployment descriptors the services into a map m_k, but cannot infer their interconnection. This is where the composition of multiple probes provided by ANAXIMANDER is helpful: to date, our most useful map is $m_0 = m_i \ominus (m_i \ominus m_k)$, *i.e.*, the map containing all the discovered interconnection in m_i, without the infrastructure noise ($m_i \ominus m_k$).

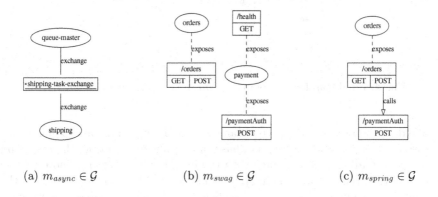

(a) $m_{async} \in \mathcal{G}$ (b) $m_{swag} \in \mathcal{G}$ (c) $m_{spring} \in \mathcal{G}$

Fig. 3. Partial maps used to explore S2 with probes (RabbitMQ, Swagger, Spring)

Based on this initial map, we can start the incremental exploration of the infrastructure. First, we want to understand the interconnection that uses asynchronous messages (*e.g.*, RabbitMQ exchange topics) in this architecture. A query to m_0 to know all the services exchanging data with RabbitMQ returns two services: queue-master and shipping. It means that if the message bus suffers an outage, only the shipping infrastructure will be impacted. To improve the precision of the map concerning asynchronous communications, we use a source code analysis probe to identify the exchange topics from the source code, obtaining a map m_{async} (Fig. 3a).

A critical part of the architecture is the payment of orders, so we decide to explore the interconnection that exists between the payment and order services. Without more information, we assume that both services communicate using an HTTP REST protocol. We first use a probe dedicated to Swagger contracts identification, identifying the routes exposed by each service (m_{swag}, Fig. 3b). Then, we use a probe that performs a static analysis of the order service to identify the control-flow of its Spring implementation (m_{spring}, Fig. 3c). As there is no other connection between order and payment, we can use this information to correct our initial map, and erase the technical `tcp` link that exists between the two services and use the proper control-flow instead.

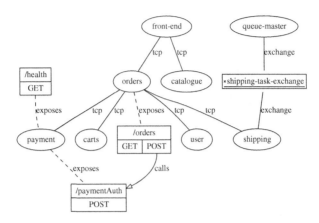

Fig. 4. Final map for S2, composing m_i, m_k, m_{async}, m_{swag} & m_{spring}

We describe in Fig. 4 the map obtained after these preliminary explorations. We used a query to identify the databases and remove them from the map, and then compose all the partial maps with the initial one to obtain a more precise picture of the architecture. The map is still shadowed for some services, but the amount of information inside it was sufficient to answer the questions we were asking about the architecture.

An immediate threat to validity is related to the lack of validation outside of the six reference architectures used to defined ANAXIMANDER. This is emphasized by the difficulty of collecting open-source microservice architecture, as this paradigm is used to implement business-driven logic. However, we mitigate this threat by the fact that the six architectures were highly heterogeneous, using different coding styles and technologies, and therefore representative of microservice development. Moreover, the representativity of these architectures is emphasized by their selection for a variability study by Asunçãao *et al.*

5   Conclusions and Perspectives

In this paper, we described a novel approach named ANAXIMANDER to support microservice architecture maintenance, leveraging the idea of gathering incomplete information about the architecture and composing this incomplete information with the existing ones to enrich the knowledge of the architect incrementally. This approach complements the state-of-the-art ones, which try to create ultra-precise maps by focusing on particular technological choices, where ANAXIMANDER support a more flexible way of creating such maps. The need for ANAXIMANDER emerged after a careful audit of six references architectures.

This work opens an interesting perspective concerning uncertainty. As the map created by ANAXIMANDER is imprecise by design and aims to be refined iteratively, finding a way to model such imprecision (*e.g.*, with goal modelling from the requirements engineering community) will help the architect during the exploration of the system.

Acknowledgments. This research has been supported by the Natural Sciences and Engineering Research Council of Canada (NSERC), *Université du Québec à Montréal* (UQAM), and the Inria - *Équipe Associée* program.

References

1. Assunção, W.K.G., Krüger, J., Mendonça, W.D.F.: Variability management meets microservices: six challenges of re-engineering microservice-based webshops. In: 24rd International Systems and Software Product Line Conference, SPLC, Montreal, Canada. ACM (2020). https://variability-challenges.github.io/
2. Garg, N.: Apache Kafka. Packt Publishing Ltd., Birmingham (2013)
3. Granchelli, G., Cardarelli, M., Francesco, P.D., Malavolta, I., Iovino, L., Salle, A.D.: Towards recovering the software architecture of microservice-based systems. In: 2017 IEEE International Conference on Software Architecture Workshops (ICSAW), pp. 46–53, April 2017. https://doi.org/10.1109/ICSAW.2017.48
4. Haitzer, T., Zdun, U.: DSL-based support for semi-automated architectural component model abstraction throughout the software lifecycle. In: Proceedings of the 8th International ACM SIGSOFT Conference on Quality of Software Architectures, QoSA 2012, pp. 61–70.Association for Computing Machinery, New York (2012). https://doi.org/10.1145/2304696.2304709
5. Kienzle, J., Mussbacher, G., Combemale, B., DeAntoni, J.: A unifying framework for homogeneous model composition. Softw. Syst. Model. **18**(5), 3005–3023 (2019). https://doi.org/10.1007/s10270-018-00707-8
6. Kleehaus, M., Uludağ, Ö., Schäfer, P., Matthes, F.: MICROLYZE: a framework for recovering the software architecture in microservice-based environments. In: Mendling, J., Mouratidis, H. (eds.) CAiSE 2018. LNBIP, vol. 317, pp. 148–162. Springer, Cham (2018). https://doi.org/10.1007/978-3-319-92901-9_14
7. Ma, S., Liu, I., Chen, C., Lin, J., Hsueh, N.: Version-based microservice analysis, monitoring, and visualization. In: 2019 26th Asia-Pacific Software Engineering Conference (APSEC), pp. 165–172, December 2019. https://doi.org/10.1109/APSEC48747.2019.00031. iSSN 2640-0715
8. Ma, S.P., Fan, C.Y., Chuang, Y., Liu, I.H., Lan, C.W.: Graph-based and scenario-driven microservice analysis, retrieval, and testing. Future Gener. Comput. Syst. **100**, 724–735 (2019). http://www.sciencedirect.com/science/article/pii/S0167739X19302614
9. Müller, H.A., Jahnke, J.H., Smith, D.B., Storey, M.A., Tilley, S.R., Wong, K.: Reverse engineering: a roadmap. In: Proceedings of the Conference on The Future of Software Engineering, ICSE 2000, pp. 47–60. Association for Computing Machinery, New York (2000)
10. Müller, H.A., Tilley, S.R., Wong, K.: Understanding software systems using reverse engineering technology perspectives from the Rigi project. In: Proceedings of the 1993 Conference of the Centre for Advanced Studies on Collaborative Research: Software Engineering, CASCON 1993, vol. 1, pp. 217–226 (1993)

11. OMG: Knowledge Discovery Metamodel 1.4. Technical report, OMG (2016)
12. Vernon, V.: Implementing Domain-Driven Design. Addison-Wesley Professional, Boston (2013)
13. Weaveworks: SockShop, a generic microservices application (2020). https://github.com/microservices-demo. Accessed 27 May 2020

Fast Replica of Polyglot Persistence in Microservice Architectures for Fog Computing

Michele Cantarutti, Pierluigi Plebani, and Mattia Salnitri[✉]

Politecnico di Milano, Milan, Italy
michele1.cantarutti@mail.polimi.it,
{pierluigi.plebani,mattia.salnitri}@polimi.it

Abstract. Aiming to break the software monoliths that traditional approaches usually produce as artifacts, solutions that are based on microservices consist of heterogeneous and independent software platforms to manage applications and data. In this scenario, the term polyglot persistence has been introduced to characterize software solutions where the involved microservices rely on different data storage technologies. Especially in Fog Computing where data are expected to efficiently flow among nodes – usually from the edge to the cloud – the polyglot persistence could have a negative impact since a combination of data replication and transformation is required. The goal of this paper is to study the challenges in data management in Fog Computing when microservices are adopted, and to present a solution which combines the advantages of the physical copy approach performed by network file systems to provide a fast data movement and the ability of the logical copy approach to transform the data. The resulting mix is demonstrated to reduce the time of creating the replica up to 70%.

Keywords: Efficient data management · Data movement

1 Introduction

The microservice architectural style is more and more adopted in software solutions due to its ability, among the others, to deal with scalability and ease of maintenance. As discussed in [13], seven main principles constitute the fundamentals of microservice architectures: fine-grained interface, business-driven development, cloud-native design, polyglot programming and persistence, lightweight containers, decentralized continuous delivery, and DevOps lean.

Polyglot programming and the persistence principle aim to enable the production of a software solution as a composition of several independent modules, developed by independent teams, and based on different technologies. This way, developers can break the classical monolithic solutions and use the most suitable technology for a given specific task, without the need to agree on a specific platform. The polyglot principle is in line with the need to get rid of the "one-size

© Springer Nature Switzerland AG 2020
E. Kafeza et al. (Eds.): ICSOC 2020, LNCS 12571, pp. 45–55, 2020.
https://doi.org/10.1007/978-3-030-65310-1_4

fits all" approach [11]. Thus, a microservice-based solution could involve a set of different DBMSs which could even rely on different models: e.g., relational DB, noSQL. This is also important when data to be managed by software solutions come from legacy systems but we want to exploit as much as possible new programming and storage paradigms to properly manage those data. As a consequence, mechanisms are required to keep the alignment of different data stores in the different nodes in which microservices are running.

The literature already proposes some solutions for the alignment of data stored in heterogeneous environments which are ready to be adopted also in a microservice architecture. Conversely, such solutions become no longer useful when considering the deployment of microservices along the continuum between the cloud and the edge, i.e., Fog Computing, which introduces additional requirements in terms of velocity, polyglot persistence, data transformation, and partial replication. In fact, Fog Computing [6], a paradigm for managing distributed systems where nodes, called fog nodes, live in the continuum between the cloud and the edge, implies: (i) a dynamic environment where fog nodes could easily join and leave the system, and (ii) a continuous data movement among different nodes which – due to the polyglot persistence principle – could be based on different storage technologies. In this context, providing a fast access to the data needed by a microservice is fundamental and it can be obtained by locating the required data closer to where the computation is running.

The goal of this paper is twofold. First, to investigate how the adoption of microservices affects software solutions in Fog Computing with respect to data management. As discussed in the paper, an efficient and flexible replica mechanism is fundamental and the current approaches – such as physical and logical copy [10] – either are not able to satisfy all the requirements of Fog Computing or the time required to create the replica is not acceptable. Second, this paper proposes a solution to efficiently ensure the creation of replicas on the nodes which are able to cope with the dynamism of the system and the heterogeneity of the technologies involved. As demonstrated by the performed tests, the proposed solution is comparable to traditional approaches for small databases but outperforms them up to 70% when the size of the database becomes significant.

The rest of the paper is organized as follows. Section 2 motivates the requirements for replica mechanisms in Fog Computing. Section 3 introduces the proposed solution, of which the evaluation results are presented in Sect. 4. Finally, Sect. 5 discusses related work and Sect. 6 concludes the paper.

2 Background and Motivation

Fog Computing has recently emerged as a paradigm for improving the performance of applications where data are generated on the edge but, due to the limited capacity in terms of computation and memory, they are processed on the cloud [2]. As the network can introduce a significant latency, the processing performed on the cloud may experience an unacceptable delay. For this reason, Fog Computing aims to create a synergy among resources on the edge, resources on the cloud, and even resources that connect the edge and the cloud, where all these nodes are generically referred to as fog nodes.

In this context, mechanisms for enabling data and computation movements hold a primary role. When possible, computation should be moved closer to where data are generated. As not all computation is possible on edge nodes due to their limited capacity, the data resulting from the initial analysis – which are less than the generated ones anyway – should be sent or replicated to cloud nodes. Moreover, especially when considering dynamic contexts, a fog node could unpredictably join or leave the system. Hence, when a node is part of the system, it can be a source of data or a place in which the computation can be executed. Thus, it has to access the data to be processed which could be other than the data that the node itself is generating.

Data generated at the sensing layer must, therefore, be replicated for the computation layer, usually organized according to a microservice architecture. Several challenges must be addressed concerning the creation and the management of the database replicas in Fog Computing. **R1:** *fast creation*: when a fog node joins the system, a secondary database should be quickly made available to the newly deployed microservices. **R2:** *polyglot persistence*: fog nodes could be based on heterogeneous storage technologies. **R3:** *partial replication*: for privacy issues or to reduce the amount of data to be transferred, the secondary database could contain a projection or a selection of data stored in the primary database. **R4:** *data transformation*: before moving to the secondary database, data could be transformed for privacy, security, or optimization reasons.

It is worth noticing that the resources available on fog nodes may vary from few cores and few megabytes of RAM and storage for nodes closer to the edge, to powerful nodes when considering the cloud. For this reason, the solution must be lightweight to be deployed in all configurations.

3   Fast Replica for Fog Computing

The replication mechanism proposed to satisfy the requirements introduced above is based on dynamic replication. Thus, secondary databases are added dynamically after the deployment of the primary database [12]. Static replication, where all secondary copies are deployed at the same time of the primary copy, is indeed not an option in our context, as in Fog Computing all fog nodes are not known in advance, as they could change dynamically.

The initial load phase of a database is considered in this paper. Such a phase is required every time a microservice is deployed on a fog node. Depending on the type of analysis and the amount of data generated by the sensing layer, it might happen that the replica creation could require to move a significant amount of data. In the literature [10], (see Fig. 1) two options are commonly considered: i) *logical copy*, which refers to the mechanism of extracting data from the primary copy and importing them onto the secondary copy using queries; and ii) *physical copy*, which refers to directly transferring files containing the DBMS data, from machine to machine, at filesystem level.

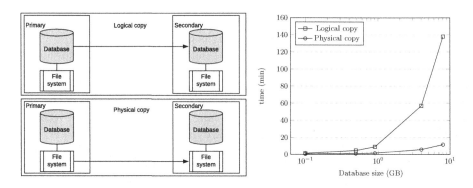

Fig. 1. Comparison of physical and remote copy.

The physical copy is a very fast process (actually the fastest according to our tests) but it only addresses R1. In fact, only full replication can be achieved as a physical copy is obtained by copying the entire data directory of the database onto a remote machine. For the same reason, data cannot be transformed (e.g., anonymized) during the replication process. Indeed, it is not possible to distinguish between columns, rows, or tables at the filesystem level. Finally, a physical copy cannot be used in a heterogeneous setup with different DBMSs, since the data directory, copied onto a remote machine, will be readable only by a DBMS that uses the same technology of the primary one. An adopted workaround to allow a polyglot environment with physical copy, consists of a primary node where data are stored in all the different database technologies that might be needed. When a replica is required, the physical copy of the database with the needed technology is performed. However, this approach is extremely space consuming, so it is not an acceptable solution, especially when considering fog nodes.

When it comes to logical copy, it allows filtering and transforming the data since, once rows are extracted from the primary copy, they can be filtered or transformed before they are sent to the secondary copy (R3, R4), so also different database technologies can be involved (R2). The main drawback of the logical copy concerns the time required to complete the copy on the secondary node. Indeed, as shown in Fig. 1, the performed tests show that the logical copy always requires more time than the physical one and, with an increasing size of the database to be replicated, the replica time has an exponential trend which makes this approach not suitable.

We propose a *hybrid approach* (see Fig. 2) to perform the initial load, that exploits the flexibility of the logical copy while maintaining the higher speed of the physical copy. The hybrid approach consists of four phases:

1. *Temporary node creation.* A DBMS (of the same technology as the technology of the secondary database) is deployed on a temporary node near the primary node (or, if possible, on the same node).
2. *Local logical copy.* The (partition of the) database to be replicated is copied into the new DBMS by using a logical copy. This allows to filter and to

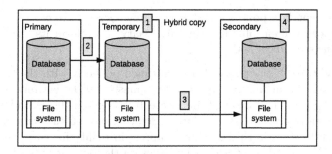

Fig. 2. Proposed hybrid approach

transform the data, and to translate the queries for a DBMS that is different from the primary DBMS. This operation takes less time than it would take to perform remotely onto the secondary node since it is performed on a node that is near (or local to) the primary node. The logical copy is performed by reading the primary copy and it does not need to lock the primary copy.

3. *Remote physical copy.* The newly created database is moved to the secondary machine by using a physical copy which has been demonstrated to be fast.
4. *Finalization.* The secondary DBMS is started on the secondary node, where it can access the newly copied database. The temporary node can be destroyed.

The overhead of this approach is given by the time necessary to deploy the temporary machine and create extra resources (e.g., a temporary DBMS). However, some technologies (e.g., Docker and Kubernetes) allow to deploy these necessary resources in a few tens of seconds, which is a negligible amount of time if compared to the overall benefit provided by the proposed approach. Similarly, the overhead given by the transmission of data between the primary database and the temporary one is negligible since the temporary machine should be created near the primary one (or be connected with a fast network connection).

It is worth noting that the usage of a temporary node is a valid approach in Fog Computing. For nodes located in a cloud environment, the overhead of the creation of a temporary node is negligible, due to the virtually unlimited resources available. Edge nodes, are typically IoT devices which produce data, that are stored in fog nodes. In this case, the temporary node will be created in fog nodes where resources, even if limited, are usually higher than IoT devices and the overhead will have a limited, and temporary, impact on the system.

Better performance can be achieved by starting the third phase (i.e., the remote physical copy) during the second phase (i.e., the local logical copy), without waiting for the second phase to finish. Using this variation, data is copied onto the secondary node while it is being written on the temporary node.

This variation (named *overlapped hybrid approach*) introduces three cases:

No Overlap. If the third phase (i.e., moving the temporary replica to the secondary node) is performed after the second one has finished, then the overlap will be minimum, that is, null. In this case, the total necessary time to create a copy on the secondary node is equal to the time necessary to create a local copy on the temporary node plus the time necessary to perform its entire physical copy onto the secondary node.

Perfect Overlap. If the physical copy is timed perfectly with the logical copy, the overlap will be maximum, and the two phases will be entirely overlapped. In this case, the total necessary time to create a copy on the secondary node is equal to the time necessary to perform a logical copy on the temporary node. This is an ideal scenario that does not happen in reality for two main reasons. First of all, the logical copy creates new files on the temporary node, while the physical copy copies them on the secondary node, and these two processes may follow different orders. Secondly, the exact times needed for logical and physical copies are unpredictable in a Fog Computing environment. Therefore, it is not possible to time the beginning of the physical copy perfectly so that its end coincides with the end of the logical copy.

Partial Overlap. The best obtainable degree of overlap is a partial overlap. The best strategy in order to maximize the overlapping of the two phases is to run the process of the physical copy twice. Keeping in mind that the physical copy is faster than the logical one, the first execution of the physical copy should be timed so as to finish approximately when the logical copy finishes. As soon as the logical copy ends, the second execution of the physical copy should start. This maximizes the amount of raw data copied by the first physical copy leaving to the second run of the physical copy only a small portion of the data. Transactions performed during the first physical copy may lead to integrity problems in the secondary node, because files are physically copied from the temporary node to the secondary one, while writes are occurring on the temporary node. This is not a problem, as the data is initially not accessed on the secondary node. Therefore, just before the second physical copy, the alignment between the primary and temporary node is suspended, and then the second physical copy to align and restore the integrity of the data on the secondary node is performed. Immediately after that, the alignment between the primary copy and the secondary copy starts. All the transactions performed after the beginning of the second physical copy will be propagated to the secondary copy.

3.1 Implementation Details

The proposed hybrid approach (both with and without overlap) has been implemented adopting the most common tools used to deploy and run microservices (i.e., Docker and Kubernetes) as well as existing software (i.e., SymmetricDS) that is able to provide a logical copy.

More in detail, Docker[1] allows to create isolated virtual environments known as *containers*, in which applications can be run. Containers are very lightweight: they use less space and they also take less time to start up compared to other virtualization tools. As a result, Docker allows to: (i) deal with fog heterogeneity,

---

[1] https://www.docker.com.

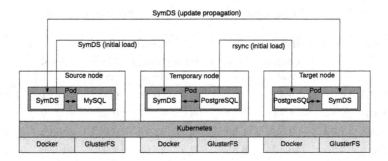

Fig. 3. Architecture of the approach

as applications are containerized and they do not need to rely on the specific hardware of the host machine; (ii) deal with fog dynamicity, as applications can be started in a fast and practical way.

To coordinate multiple nodes, orchestrator tools, such as Kubernetes[2], are involved. More specifically, Kubernetes is an open-source container-orchestration system for automating deployment, scaling and management of containerized applications in distributed systems that, amongst others, supports Docker containers. It provides a container-centric management environment, that orchestrates computing, networking, and storage infrastructure.

In a Fog environment, a *Kubernetes Node* is a worker machine, and it may be a virtual machine or a physical machine that corresponds to a node, a.k.a., Fog node. A set of Kubernetes Nodes makes up a *Kubernetes cluster*. A Kubernetes cluster corresponds to a set of fog nodes. Each microservice can be containerized and, therefore, it belongs to a single Docker container. A *Kubernetes Pod* is a group of containers with shared network and storage, that are always co-scheduled and co-located.

Finally, SymmetricDS[3] is an open source software package for database replication. It performs a type of replication known as transaction replication [5] as opposed to statement replication [5] . This means that the secondary copies do not receive SQL statements to apply, but rather only the changes produced by SQL statements, known as *writesets*. As it is built on top of JDBC, SymmetricDS supports a wide range of databases and it can automatically translate between different SQL dialects. Moreover, SymmetricDS supports filtered replication (to allow replication of specific tables, columns or rows) and it supports data transformation (which allows to anonymize or pseudonymize data before it is replicated).

Figure 3 shows the architecture for the implementation proposed in this paper. The lower part consists of Docker service, and GlusterFS service[4], a network filesystem we used for the creation of persistent volume where DBMS data is stored. Both services are installed in every fog node, that provide the

---

[2] https://kubernetes.io.

[3] https://www.symmetricds.org.

[4] https://www.gluster.org/.

Table 1. Replica time (in min) for the different approaches

DB Size	Physical	Hybrid			Overlap			Logical
		Logical local	Physical remote	Total	Logical local	Physical remote	Total	
100 MB	0.5	0.45	0.5	1.95	0.48	0.43	1.91	1.27
490 MB	0.87	1.78	0.87	3.65	1.77	0.52	3.29	4.62
900 MB	1.52	3.55	1.52	6.07	3.42	0.6	5.02	9.03
4 GB	5.85	16.32	5.85	22.9	16.65	1.9	19.55	56.93
8 GB	11.57	34.82	11.57	47.39	34.47	2.38	37.85	137.98

primitives for the management of containers. On top of it, Kubernetes provides the infrastructure that groups Fog nodes into a cluster. Kubernetes manages the resources provided by Docker and GlusterFS.

Kubernetes works as a central authority. This makes the scheduling of the resources very efficient since containers, being lightweight, are fast to start (generally less than 5 s).

4 Evaluation

To evaluate the proposed approach we compare the time needed to a create a new replica with traditional approaches, i.e., physical and logical copy, with the time required by the proposed approaches, i.e., the hybrid and overlapped hybrid copy. To obtain reliable results, primary databases of different sizes are considered to check how the results change as the size of the primary database grew. Moreover, to mitigate the influence of the network, the tests were repeated 5 times in each configuration, on different days and different times of the day.

Evaluation Setup and Execution. Three nodes were used to simulate the Fog nodes: two in the same physical location (Zurich - Switzerland) and one remote (Miami - USA). The nodes in Zurich were local to each other for the reasons explained in Sect. 3. We chose the location of the third node purposely at a great distance from the other two, to simulate a geographically distributed deployment of the Fog nodes, where the connection could be affected by great variations of performance. The three nodes are hosted in cloud resources and share similar characteristics: the two nodes in Zurich have 1 single-core CPU and 4 GB of RAM, while the node in Miami has 1 single-core CPU and 2 GB of RAM.

In order to produce significant results, OLTP-Bench[5] was used to populate the primary database with sample data. We used this benchmark defined by the Transaction Processing Performance Council (TPC) [4] as it emulates transactions of real databases mimicking new observations of the sensing layer.

---

[5] https://github.com/oltpbenchmark/oltpbench.

Results. Table 1 shows the results of the conducted tests. Here, the logical and physical copy represent, respectively, the upper and lower bound.

Hybrid and overlapped approaches are decomposed in two execution times:

- Logical local: the execution time of the logical copy in the temporary node.
- Physical remote: the execution time of the physical copy from the temporary machine to the secondary node.

The difference between the observed total time and the time to perform both the logical local copy and the remote physical one is related to the rescheduling time needed to bootstrap the third node.

The results clearly highlight that the proposed approaches have a lower execution time that the classical one (logical copy). Such a difference is up to 73% in case of a 8 GB database with the overlap method. The tests show that the time of the traditional approach grows over twice as faster than that of our proposed approaches. However, the hybrid approaches are advantageous only beyond a certain size of the database. Indeed, when the database is small, the traditional approach of the remote logical copy is faster.

5   Related Work

Database replication has been extensively studied in the literature and, as discussed in this section, there are solutions which inspired the proposed approach but that also have limitations which hamper their adoption in Fog Computing.

Among these approaches most of them propose a middleware. Since [3] offers a read-one/write-all approach, its proposed solution requires a lock of the primary copy, thus reducing the efficiency of the replica creation. The middleware proposed in [1] is based on a scheduler accepting transactions from users which will be sent to replicas with a distributed conflict aware approach. Such an approach parses SQL statements while users must declare at each transaction which tables are being modified. This approach permits to fine tune the amount of transactions to be sent on each DBMS, however, it does not support polyglot persistence. MIDDLE-R [9] is a middleware mainly focused on granting consistency among the copies, but it is unable to deal with dynamic environments, as it only considers systems with a fixed number of nodes. Moreover, it is unable to recover nodes after they crash, and, when nodes are falsely suspected to have crashed, they are forced to commit suicide regardless. In [8], authors propose a middleware to distribute requests based on the locality of the data and, therefore, increasing the likelihood of using the cache of the DBMS. However, this approach is based on static replication and static content, and so it does not support updates on the replica, but it rather focuses on the distribution of content. Finally, [7] compares some peer-to-peer solutions, where data storage and processing are distributed across completely autonomous peers. These solutions support a write-anywhere approach, and, consequently, they require reconciliation algorithms to fix the divergences that arise among the replicas. In dynamic environments where data is continuously updated, this can drain a lot of computational power from the nodes. Also, most of these solutions are based on a weak type of replication, known as passive replication, where a piece of data is specifically replicated only after the user tries to access it.

6   Conclusion

Due to the provided flexibility and scalability, the microservice architectural style represents a good approach to developing applications according to the Fog Computing paradigm. Nevertheless, the dynamicity of fog nodes requires a data management that is able to quickly react to the re-deployments that may occur to satisfy the quality of service that the applications have to ensure. In particular, this paper has identified the need for mechanisms able to quickly create replicas. As the typical physical copy does not provide the proper support for fog environments and the logical copy is too slow, this paper proposes a hybrid approach that is able to exploit both the advantages of the classical solutions. The performed tests demonstrated how the hybrid approach can save up to 70% of the time usually required to create replicas for an almost 10 GB database.

References

1. Amza, C., Cox, A.L., Zwaenepoel, W.: A comparative evaluation of transparent scaling techniques for dynamic content servers. In: Proceedings of ICDE 2005, pp. 230–241 (2005)
2. Bonomi, F., Milito, R., Zhu, J., Addepalli, S.: Fog computing and its role in the Internet of Things. In: Proceedings of MCC 2012, pp. 13–16. ACM (2012)
3. Cecchet, E.: C-JDBC: a middleware framework for database clustering. IEEE Data Eng. Bull. **27**(2), 19–26 (2004)
4. Difallah, D.E., Pavlo, A., Curino, C., Cudre-Mauroux, P.: OLTP-bench: an extensible testbed for benchmarking relational databases. VLDB **7**, 277–288 (2014)
5. Cecchet, E., Candea, G., Ailamaki, A.: Middleware-based database replication: the gaps between theory and practice. In: Proceedings of the 2008 ACM SIGMOD International Conference on Management of Data, SIGMOD 2008, pp. 739–752 (2008)
6. IEEE: IEEE Standard for Adoption of OpenFog Reference Architecture for Fog Computing. IEEE STD 1934–2018, pp. 1–176, August 2018
7. Martins, V., Pacitti, E., Valduriez, P.: Survey of data replication in P2P systems. Technical Report RR-6083, INRIA (2006)
8. Pai, V.S., et al.: Locality-aware request distribution in cluster-based network servers. ACM SIGPLAN Not. **33**(11), 205–216 (1998)
9. Patiño-Martinez, M., Jiménez-Peris, R., Kemme, B., Alonso, G.: MIDDLE-R: Consistent database replication at the middleware level. ACM Trans. Comput. Syst. (TOCS) **23**(4), 375–423 (2005)
10. Plattner, C., Alonso, G., Özsu, M.T.: Extending DBMSs with satellite databases. The VLDB J. **17**(4), 657–682 (2008). https://doi.org/10.1007/s00778-006-0026-x
11. Stonebraker, M., Cetintemel, U.: "One size fits all": an idea whose time has come and gone. In: Proceedings of ICDE 2005, pp. 2–11 (2005)

12. Tos, U., Mokadem, R., Hameurlain, A., Ayav, T., Bora, S.: Dynamic replication strategies in data grid systems: a survey. J. Supercomput. **71**(11), 4116–4140 (2015). https://doi.org/10.1007/s11227-015-1508-7
13. Zimmermann, O.: Microservices tenets. Comput. Sci. Res. Dev. **32**(11), 301–310 (2016). https://doi.org/10.1007/s00450-016-0337-0

On Discovering Data Preparation Modules Using Examples

Khalid Belhajjame[(✉)]

PSL, Universití Paris-Dauphine, LAMSADE, Paris, France
khalid.belhajjame@dauphine.fr

Abstract. A major issue that arises when designing data-analysis pipelines is that of identifying the services (or what we refer to as modules in this paper) that are suitable for performing data preparation steps, which represents 80% of the modules that compose data analysis workflows. Such modules are ubiquitous and are used to perform, amongst other things, operations such as record retrieval, format transformation, data combination to name a few. To assist scientists in the task of discovering suitable modules, we examine, in this paper, a solution that utilizes semantic annotations describing the inputs and outputs of modules together with data examples that characterize modules' behavior as ingredients for the discovery of data preparation modules. The discovery strategy that we devised is iterative in that it allows scientists to explore existing modules by providing feedback on data examples.

1 Introduction

Despite the impressive body of work in data management on data preparation tasks, it is recognized that there is not a single generic one-shop-stop solution that can be utilized by the scientists to prepare their data prior their analysis. Instead, data preparation tasks are numerous, can be difficult to generalize (e.g., data cleansing, data integration), and tends to vary depending on the processing tasks at hand, but also on the semantic domains and the format of the data subject to processing. As a result, scientists tend to develop their own program/script using their favorite language, e.g., Python, R or Perl, to prepare their data. This operation is time-consuming and recurrent since sometimes the scientist has to redevelop data preparation scripts that s/he has previously performed on the same or similar data.

To overcome the above problem, a number of researchers have been calling for the creation of repositories dedicated to data preparation modules with the view to save the time scientists spend on data preparation to allow them to focus their effort on the analysis tasks. Examples of such repositories are BigGo-rilla[1], an ecosystem for data preparation and integration, Bio.Tools[2], a catalogue

---

[1] https://www.biggorilla.org.

[2] https://bio.tools.

© Springer Nature Switzerland AG 2020
E. Kafeza et al. (Eds.): ICSOC 2020, LNCS 12571, pp. 56–65, 2020.
https://doi.org/10.1007/978-3-030-65310-1_5

which provides access to, amongst other things, services for the preparation of bioinformatics data, and Galaxy tools[3].

In this paper, we set out to examine the problem of querying data preparation modules. Specifically, the objective is to locate a module that can be perform a data preparation task at hand, if such a module exists. Semantic annotations can be used to reach this objective [9]. A module is semantically annotated by associating it to concepts from ontologies. Different facets of the module can be described using semantic annotations, e.g., input and output parameters, task and quality of service (QoS). In practice, however, we observe that most of semantic annotations that are available are confined to the description of the domain of input and output parameters of modules. Annotations specifying the behavior of the module, as to the task it performs, are rarely specified. Indeed, the number of modules that are semantically described with concepts that describe the behavior of the module lags well behind the number of modules that are semantically annotated in terms of the domains of the input and output parameters, e.g., in BioTools. Even when they are available, annotations that describe the behavior of the module tend to give a general idea of the task that the module implements, and fall short in describing the specifics of its behavior. For example, the modules in BioTools, which is a registry that provides information about data preparation modules, are described using terms such as *merging* and *retrieving*. While such terms provide a *rough* idea of what a module does, they do not provide the user with sufficient information to determine if a it is suitable for the data preparation at hand. The failure in crisply describing the behavior of scientific modules should not be attributed to the designers of task ontologies. Indeed, designing an ontology that captures precisely the behavior of modules, without increasing the difficulty that the human annotators who use such ontologies may face thereby compromising the usability of the ontology, is challenging.

To overcome this issue, we examine in this paper a solution that utilizes semantic annotations describing the inputs and outputs of modules together with data examples that characterize modules' behavior as ingredients for the discovery of data preparation modules. Given a module m, a data example provides concrete values of inputs that are consumed by m as well as the corresponding output values that are delivered as a result. Data examples are constructed by harvesting the retrospective provenance of modules' executions. They provide an intuitive means for users to understand the module behavior: the user does not need to examine the source code of the module, which is often not available, or the semantic annotations, which require the user to be familiar with the domain ontology used for annotation. Moreover, they are amenable to describing the behavior of a module in a precise, yet concise, manner. It has been shown in [2] that data examples are an effective means for characterizing and understanding the behavior of modules. We show in this paper that data examples can also be used to effectively and efficiently discover modules that are able to perform a data preparation task of interest.

---

[3] https://galaxyproject.org/tools.

Fig. 1. Data example.

It is worth noting that a number of systems have been developed recently to facilitate data preparation tasks, including Trifacta[4], NADEEF [3], Tamer [8] and VADA [6]. These systems come with a number of functionalities that covers, amongst other things, format transformation, data deduplication and data repair. They are primarily targeted for end-users (be they domain expert or not), who would like to use a GUI to clean a single tabular dataset (mainly in relational form or CSV). In our work, we target scientists who wish to *programatically* process one or multiple datasets, in any format (relational, CSV, text, JSON, etc).

The paper is structured as follows. We start by introducing background information regarding data examples and how they are generated for characterizing modules based on retrospective provenance of modules' executions (in Sect. 2). We go on to present our solution for module discovery (in Sect. 3), and close the paper (in Sect. 4).

2   Background

For the purposes of this paper, we define a data-preparation module by the pair: $m = \langle id, name \rangle$, where id is the module identifier and $name$ its name. A module m is associated with two ordered sets $inputs(m)$ and $outputs(m)$, representing its input and output parameters, respectively. A parameter p of a module m is characterized by a structural type, $str(i)$, and a semantic type, $sem(i)$. The former specifies the structural data type of the parameter, e.g., $String$ or $Integer$, whereas the latter specifies the semantic domain of the parameter using a concept, e.g., $Protein$, that belongs to a domain ontology [5].

A data example δ that is used to describe the behavior a module m can be defined by a pair: $\delta = \langle I, O \rangle$, where: $I = \{\langle i, ins_i \rangle\}$ and $O = \{\langle o, ins_o \rangle\}$. i (resp. o) is an input (resp. output) parameter of m, and ins_i and ins_o are parameter values. δ specifies that the invocation of the module m using the instances in I to feed its input parameters, produces the output values in O. We use in what follows $\Delta(m)$ to denote the set of data examples that are used to describe the behavior of a module m.

Example 1. *To illustrate how data examples can be used to understand a module behavior, consider the module* GetRecord, *which has one input and one output. Figure 1 illustrates an input instance that is consumed by* GetRecord *and*

---

[4] www.trifacta.com.

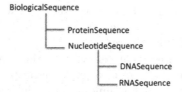

Fig. 2. Fragment of the myGrid Ontology.

the corresponding value obtained as a result of the module invocation. By exam-
ining such a data example, a domain expert will be able to understand that the
GetRecord *module retrieves the protein record that corresponds to the accession*
number given as input.

2.1 Data Example Generation

Enumerating all possible data examples that can be used to describe a given
module may be expensive or impossible since the domains of input and output
parameters can be large or infinite. Moreover, data examples derived in such a
manner may be redundant in the sense that multiple data examples are likely
to describe the same behavior of the module. A solution that can be used is to
create data examples that cover the classes of behavior of the module in question,
and then construct data examples that cover the classes identified. When the
modules are white boxes, then their specification can be utilized to specify the
classes of behavior and generate the data examples that cover each class (see e.g.,
[1]). If, on the other hand, the modules are black boxes and their specification is
not accessible, then a heuristic such as the one described in [2] can be utilized.
To make our paper self-contained, we will describe the solution presented in [2]
for generating data examples. We stress, however, that our approach for module
discovery is not confined to modules described using the approach presented in
[2]. Instead, it can be applied to potentially any module repository where the
modules are described using data examples that are annotated with semantic
domain concepts.

Using the solution proposed in [2], to construct data examples that characterize the behavior of a module m, the domain of its input i is divided into partitions,
$p_1, p_2, \ldots, p_n$. The partitioning is performed in a way to cover all classes of behavior of m. For each partition p_i, a data example δ is constructed such that the
value of the input parameter in δ belongs to the partition p_i. A source of information that is used for partitioning is the semantic annotations used to describe
module parameters. Indeed, the input and output parameters of many scientific
modules are annotated using concepts from domain ontologies [7]. In its simple
form, an ontology can be viewed as a hierarchy of concepts. For example, Fig. 2
illustrates a fragment of the myGrid domain ontology used for annotating the
inputs and output parameters of bioinformatics modules [4]. The concepts are
connected together using the subsumption relationship, e.g., ProteinSequence

is a sub-concept of `BiologicalSequence`, which we write using the following notation: `ProtSequence ⊑ BioSequence`. Such a hierarchy of concepts can be used to partition the domain of parameters.

To generate data examples that characterize the behavior of a module m, m is probed using input instances from a pool, the instances of which cover the concepts of the ontology used for annotations. The retrospective provenance obtained as a result of the module' executions are then used to construct data examples. In doing so, only module executions that terminates without issues (that is without raising any exception) are utilized to construct data examples for m. For more details on this operation, the reader is referred to [2].

3 Module Discovery

To discover a module, a user can provide data examples that characterize the module s/he had in mind. However, specifying data examples that characterize the desired module can be time-consuming, since the user needs to construct the data examples by hand. We present in this section a method that allows users to discover modules by simply providing feedback on a list of data examples they are presented with.

3.1 Feedback-Based Discovery of Scientific Modules

To identify the modules that meet his/her needs, the user starts by specifying the semantic domains and the structural types of the inputs and outputs of the modules s/he wishes to locate. The modules with inputs and outputs that are compatible with the specified semantic domains and structural types are then located. Consider, for example, that the user is interested in locating a module that consumes input values that belong to the semantic domain c_i and structural type t_i, and produces output values that belong to the semantic domain c_o and structural type t_o. A module m meets such a query if it has an input (resp. output) with a semantic domain and structural type that are equivalent to or subsumed by c_i and t_i (resp. c_o and t_o). Specifically, the set of modules that meet those criteria can be specified by the following set comprehension:

$$\{\text{m s.t. } (\exists\, i \in \text{inputs}(m), (\text{sem}(i) \sqsubseteq c_i) \wedge (\text{str}(i) \sqsubseteq t_i))$$
$$\wedge\, (\exists\, o \in \text{outputs}(m), (\text{sem}(o) \sqsubseteq c_o) \wedge (\text{str}(o) \sqsubseteq t_o))\}$$

It is likely that not all the modules retrieved based on the semantic domain of input and output parameters perform the task that is expected by the user. Because of this, we refer to such modules using the term *candidate modules.*

To identify the candidate module(s) that perform the task expected by the user, the data examples characterizing candidate modules are displayed to the user. The user then examines the data examples and specifies the ones that meet the expectations, and the ones that do not. To do so, the user provides feedback instances. A feedback instance `uf` is used to annotate a data example, and can be defined by the following pair $\text{uf} = \langle \delta, \text{expected} \rangle$, where δ denotes the data

	Data examples		User feedback	
	protein name	accession	expected	unexpected
δ_1	Chorion protein S36	CH36_CERCA	X	
δ_2	Zinc metalloproteinase	VMDM_VIRST		X

Fig. 3. Data examples and user feedback.

example annotated by the feedback instance uf, and expected is a boolean that is true if δ is expected, i.e., compatible with the requirements of the user who supplied uf, and false, if it is unexpected.

3.2 Incremental Ranking of Candidate Modules

The discovery strategy we have just described can be effective when the number of candidate modules and the number of data examples characterizing each candidate are small. If the number of candidate modules to be annotated and/or the number of data examples used for their characterization are large, then the user may need to provide a large amount of feedback before locating the desired module among the candidates. Moreover, there is no guarantee that the set of candidates is complete in the sense that it contains a module that implements the behavior that meets user requirements. Therefore, the user may have to annotate a (possibly) large number of data examples only to find out that none of the candidates meet the requirements. Because of the above limitations, we set out to develop a second discovery strategy with the following properties:

1. **Ranking candidate modules**: Instead of simply labeling candidate modules as suitable or not to user requirements, they are ranked based on metrics that are estimated given the feedback supplied by the user, to measure their fitness to requirements. In the absence of candidates that meet the exact requirements of users, ranking allows the user to identify the modules that best meet the requirements among the candidate modules.
2. **Incrementality**: The user does not have to provide feedback annotating every data example characterizing the candidate modules before being presented with the modules that best meet the requirements. Instead, given feedback supplied by the user to annotate a subset of the data examples, the candidate modules are ranked and the obtained list of candidates is shown to the user. The list of candidates is incrementally revisited as more feedback instances are supplied by the user.
3. **Learning feedback**: To reduce the cost in terms of the amount of feedback that the user needs to provide to locate suitable modules, new feedback instances annotating data examples that the user did not examine are inferred based on existing feedback that the user supplied to annotate other data examples.

Ranking Candidate Modules. To be able to rank candidate modules, we adapt the notions of precision and recall [10] that are used in information retrieval, to estimate the fitness of a module to user requirements based on the feedback supplied by the user. Consider that the user provided the feedback instances UF to annotate some (not necessarily all) data examples that characterize the candidate modules. We define the precision of a candidate module, m, relative to the feedback instances in UF as the ratio of the number of true positives of m given UF to the sum of true positives and false positives of m given the feedback instances in UF. That is:

$$\text{precision}(\text{m}, \text{UF}) = \frac{|\text{tp}(\text{m}, \text{UF})|}{|\text{tp}(\text{m}, \text{UF}) + \text{fp}(\text{m}, \text{UF})|}$$

where tp(m, UF) (resp. fp(m, UF)) is the set of data examples describing the module m, and that are annotated as expected (resp. unexpected) by feedback instances in UF, i.e:

$$\text{tp}(\text{m}, \text{UF}) = \{\delta \in \Delta(\text{m}) \text{ s.t. } \langle \delta, \text{true} \rangle \in \text{UF}\}$$
$$\text{fp}(\text{m}, \text{UF}) = \{\delta \in \Delta(\text{m}) \text{ s.t. } \langle \delta, \text{false} \rangle \in \text{UF}\}$$

Ranking based on precision only may not be enough: a module may be associated with the maximum precision of 1, i.e., all its data examples are true positives, and yet it may not implement all the classes of behavior expected by the user. Recall can be used to identify such modules. The recall of a module m relative to the feedback instances in UF can be defined as the ratio of the number of true positives of m given UF to the sum of true positives and false negatives of m given the feedback instances in UF. That is:

$$\text{recall}(\text{m}, \text{UF}) = \frac{|\text{tp}(\text{m}, \text{UF})|}{|\text{tp}(\text{m}, \text{UF}) + \text{fn}(\text{m}, \text{UF})|}$$

where fn(m, UF) denotes the false negatives of m given the feedback instances in UF. To illustrate what we mean by a false negative data example, consider δ' a data example that is the user annotated as expected. δ' is a false negative for the module m if when invoked using the input values specified by nδ', the module m returns output values that are different from the output values specified by δ'.

$$\text{fn}(\text{m}, \text{UF}) = \{\delta \text{ s.t., } < \delta, \text{true} > \in \text{UF} \wedge \text{ not } \text{match}(\text{invocation}(\text{m}, \delta.\text{I}).\text{O}, \delta.\text{O})\}$$

where invocation(m, δ.I).O denotes the output values delivered by the module m when it is invoked using the input values specified by the data example δ.

match(invocation(m, δ.I).O, δ.O) is a boolean that is true if the output values delivered by the invocation of the module m are the same as the output values specified by the data example δ.

To rank candidate modules, we use the F-score, which combines precision and recall using the harmonic mean as illustrated below. The module associated with the highest F-measure is the candidate that best meets user requirements given the feedback instances in UF.

$$F(\text{m}, \text{UF}) = \frac{2 \times \text{precision}(\text{m}, \text{UF}) \times \text{recall}(\text{m}, \text{UF})}{\text{precision}(\text{m}, \text{UF}) + \text{recall}(\text{m}, \text{UF})}$$

Learning Feedback. Notice that the method for identifying false negatives of candidate modules that we have just described can be computationally expensive. In particular, every candidate module m may need to be invoked using all data examples that are not used to characterize m and that are labeled as expected by the user, i.e., the data examples in expected(UF) − tp(m, UF).

To overcome the above problem, we adopt an approach that not only reduces the number of times a candidate module needs to be invoked (using known expected data examples) to identify false negatives, but also allows learning new feedback instances that the user would give on unannotated data examples based on existing feedback instances. To illustrate the approach we adopt for this purpose, consider the candidate module getAccession and getAccessionOfSimilarProtein (see Fig. 3). These two modules consume a protein name and output a protein accession, and are characterized by one data example each because the concepts ProteinName and ProteinAccession are leaf nodes in the ontology used for annotation. The feedback supplied by the user to annotate the data examples δ_1 and δ_2 illustrated in Fig. 3 shows that δ_1 is expected and δ_2 is unexpected. Therefore, δ_1 is a true positive for the module getAccession, and δ_2 is a false positive for the module getAccessionOfSimilarProtein. Now, to know whether δ_1 is a false negative for the module getAccessionOfSimilarProtein, we will need to invoke getAccessionOfSimilarProtein using the input value specified in δ_1, i.e., Chorion protein S36.

Intuition Behind Feedback Learning. Using the solution that we adopt, we do not need to invoke getAccessionOfSimilarProtein. To do so, we slightly modify the process by which data examples are constructed to cover the partitions of input parameters presented in [2] and overviewed in Sect. 2.1. Specifically, when selecting input values for data examples to cover a given partition, i.e., semantic domain, c, the same input value v (in c) is used in all those data examples. For example, using this method, the data examples used to characterize the two modules getAccession and getAccessionOfSimilarProtein will have the same input value. Figure 4 illustrates the data examples δ_1 and δ_3 specified using this method to characterize such modules.

Consider that the user supplies the feedback instance annotating the data example δ_1 as expected (see Fig. 4). Given this feedback instance, we do not have to invoke the module getAccessionOfSimilarProtein using the input value specified in δ_1 to know if δ_1 is a false negative for getAccessionOfSimilarProtein. Indeed, the data example δ_3 shows that the output produced by getAccessionOfSimilarProtein using the same input value as that used in δ_1. Given that the output values of δ_1 and δ_3 are different, we can make the following inferences: i) δ_1 is a false negative for getAccessionOfSimilarProtein, moreover, ii) δ_3 is unexpected, and is, therefore, a false positive for getAccessionOfSimilarProtein. This last inference can be made because the modules that we consider are deterministic. Therefore, the fact that δ_1 is expected implies that δ_3 is unexpected. Note that if δ_3 had

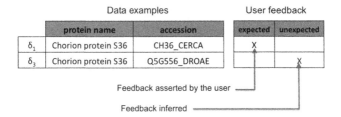

Fig. 4. Example illustrating feedback inference.

the same output value as δ_1, then we would have inferred that δ_3 is expected and is, therefore, a true positive for `getAccessionForSimilarProtein`.

4 Concluding Remarks

To assess the performance of the discovery strategy described in the previous section, we ran an experiment to identify the amount of feedback required to detect the modules that are relevant to users' needs. We also examined the error in the F-score estimates computed for candidate modules based on user feedback. To perform a systematic sweep of the parameters of the experiment, we use a synthetic dataset that we created for this purpose. We also used real-world bioinformatic modules.

The result of this experiment showed that users can effectively discover scientific modules using a small number of feedback instances. A particularly interesting result that we empirically showed is that the number of feedback instances that the user needs to provide to identify the module that meets the requirement, and more generally a ranking that meets his/her expectations, is small even in the cases where the number of data examples describing the behavior of the modules is large.

References

1. Alexe, B., Cate, B.T., Kolaitis, P.G., Tan, W.C.: Characterizing schema mappings via data examples. ACM Trans. Database Syst. **36**(4), 23:1–23:48 (2011)
2. Belhajjame, K.: Annotating the behavior of scientific modules using data examples: a practical approach. In: EDBT, pp. 726–737. OpenProceedings.org (2014)
3. Ebaid, A., et al.: NADEEF: a generalized data cleaning system. PVLDB **6**(12), 1218–1221 (2013)
4. Goble, C., et al.: BioCatalogue: a curated web service registry for the life science community. In: Microsoft eScience Conference (2008)
5. Gruber, T.: Ontology. In: Encyclopedia of Database Systems (2009)
6. Konstantinou, N., et al.: The VADA architecture for cost-effective data wrangling. In: SIGMOD Conference, pp. 1599–1602. ACM (2017)
7. Kuropka, D., Tröger, P., Staab, S., Weske, M. (eds.): Semantic Service Provisioning. Springer, Heidelberg (2008). https://doi.org/10.1007/978-3-540-78617-7

8. Stonebraker, M., et al.: Data curation at scale: the data tamer system. In: CIDR (2013). www.cidrdb.org
9. Studer, R., Grimm, S., Abecker, A. (eds.): Semantic Web Services, Concepts, Technologies, and Applications. Springer, Berlin (2007). https://doi.org/10.1007/3-540-70894-4
10. van Rijsbergen, C.J.: Information Retrieval. Butterworth, London (1979)

Internet of Things

Accelerate Personalized IoT Service Provision by Cloud-Aided Edge Reinforcement Learning: A Case Study on Smart Lighting

Jun Na$^{(\boxtimes)}$, Handuo Zhang, Xin Deng, Bin Zhang$^{(\boxtimes)}$, and Ziyi Ye

Software College, Northeastern University, Shenyang, China
{najun,zhangbin}@mail.neu.edu.cn

Abstract. To enhance the intelligence of IoT devices, offloading suffi-cient learning and inferencing down to the edge environment is promising. However, there are two main challenges for applying the cloud generated model in the edge environment. On the one hand, the input may vary on dimensions or cover different situations that the cloud hasn't met. On the other hand, the model's output might not satisfy the given user's personalized preference. To make full use of the cloud generated model in the edge environment for accelerating personalized service provision, we propose cloud-aided edge learning. Unlike current federated learning and transfer learning, we focus on knowledge fusion in edge decision making and try to build the supplement/correction model. We take the person-alized service provision in a smart lighting system as an example, design and implement the related deep reinforcement learning model, and take experiments based on the data generated on the open software DAILux to show our approach's effectiveness and performance.

Keywords: Edge intelligence · Edge-cloud collaborated learning · Personalized service provision · Smart lighting · Deep Reinforcement Learning (DRL)

1 Introduction

The Internet of Things (IoT) [3,20] enables all kinds of real-world objects (includ-ing human beings) to be connected to the cyber world. Considering the char-acteristics of human-in-the-loop, providing personalized IoT services efficiently and transparently turns to be essential. Recently, applying machine learning to speed up personalization becomes a promising way[22,36], which can extract useful knowledge from interactions happening in the physical world to produce proper reactions.

To process the continuously generated IoT data efficiently, it needs a pow-erful data center with enough storage and computing resources. Although cloud computing is an excellent platform to handle the enormous IoT data, push-ing all the raw data to the cloud is inefficient in response latency, network

© Springer Nature Switzerland AG 2020
E. Kafeza et al. (Eds.): ICSOC 2020, LNCS 12571, pp. 69–84, 2020.
https://doi.org/10.1007/978-3-030-65310-1_6

bandwidth cost, and possible privacy concerns [8,23]. To solve these problems, edge computing [28], also known as fog computing [4], is becoming the right solution and get more attention in both research and industry domain. By offloading sufficient training and inferencing down to the edge environment, edge intelligence would be enhanced to satisfy users' personalized needs more efficiently while protecting privacy [19,27,32,37]. Combining both cloud computing and edge computing advantages to offer flexible edge-cloud collaboration gets more attention [5,27,36].

Existing studies usually focus on the underlying mechanisms of edge-cloud collaboration. However, there are more challenges to accelerate personalized service provision through deep learning. For example, data achieved by the edge node might be different from the generic dataset used to generate the global model. It does not only refer to the differences in input dimensions but also other situations occurring in the edge environment. Besides, different preferences among edge nodes may cause conflicts during knowledge fusing [17,24].

To solve the above problems, we focus on reducing the edge computation cost as much as possible by making full use of the global model and only learn to deal with the inapplicable parts. Since the successful application of Deep Reinforcement Learning (DRL) [6,9,16,30] in playing Atari and Go games, we adopt DRL to realize efficient online learning. Taking the example of offering comfortable, personalized illumination in a smart lighting system, we designed and implemented the corresponding algorithms, generated data based on an open software platform, DIALux, and tested our approaches' effect. The main contributions of this paper are as follows.

- We propose a cloud-aided edge reinforcement learning framework that supports downloading the global consensus model from the cloud center and fuses it into the edge learning process.
- To enhance the efficiency and effect by applying the downloaded pre-trained model, we put forward two integration strategies, i.e., input expansion strategy and output correction strategy.
- We conduct a case study on smart lighting as an example and present the proposed approach's effects.

2   Background and Related Work

2.1   Edge-Cloud Collaboration

Among most current studies, virtualizing the resources and services over WAN networks is the shared premises to combine cloud computing and edge computing. Researches such as Pcloud [11], CoTware [1], FocusStack [2], etc. emphasize to virtualize resources of individual devices, edge nodes and cloud to build a distributed resource pool for supporting resource-limited front-end devices. While, SpanEdge [26], CloudPath [21], ECHO [25], etc. focus on the data stream processing across different layers seamlessly.

These works establish an elastic data analysis environment. However, most of them pay attention to leveraging resources on higher layers along the path from front-end devices to cloud with fewer considerations on how these analysis results will reflect behaviors provided on the front layers. Moreover, as presented in several works [28,29,34], most existing studies lack information sharing among multiple stakeholders, while the sharing may help these edge nodes to make smarter decisions. Thus, it is still challenging to support more diversified, personalized, and delay-sensitive system behaviors in the edge environment.

2.2   Schemes for Edge-Cloud Collaborated Model Training

At present, research on improving computing power and effects based on edge-cloud collaboration is still in its early stages [34]. There are three primary schemes for edge-cloud collaborated training models.

1) Gradient sharing: Reduce the transmission size of a single model by compressing the gradient, so that the model update results are transmitted frequently and multiple times to make up for the lack of computing power of edge nodes [10,12]. The training effect in the network is independent of the same and distributed data. As a result, the sharing effect of multi-edges in heterogeneous networks with different data sets cannot be guaranteed.
2) Parameter sharing: The edge side conducts preliminary training of the model and transmits the parameters to the parameter server. The parameter aggregation method in the cloud improves the accuracy of the edge side model [15,18]. This scheme can reduce the transmission volume. It also protects the privacy and improves model accuracy, but in scenarios with high personalization requirements, parameter aggregation still has challenges.
3) Data sharing: When it is necessary to collect the original data and perform parameter aggregation or train directly on the parameter server, noise can be added to the data on the edge side or privacy leakage can be reduced by preprocessing [35]. Simultaneously, there are some methods to study how to enhance the processing capabilities of edge nodes through algorithms or model hardware [14,31].

Existing work focuses more on improving the efficiency of data analysis and model training and protecting privacy. However, the issue of how to improve the personalized intelligence at the edge through the edge-cloud collaboration still needs further studies.

2.3   Fast Personalization by Federated Reinforcement Learning

Personalization aims to understand user behavior and adapting to it, which is crucial for gaming, personal assistants, dialogue managers, etc. It is often time consuming, so a critical challenge of personalization is how to adapt to a new situation quickly. To make robots quickly adapt to the new environment by sharing their experiences, Liu et al. [17] proposed the Lifelong Federated Reinforcement

Learning (LFRL) architecture. Each robot learns to avoid some new types of obstacles in the new environment through reinforcement learning. After obtaining a private Q-network model, the robot will upgrade this model by fusing with models submitted by other robots through federated learning. This work assumed all agents make the same decision when they meet the same type of obstacle. However, different agents might prefer to make other decisions to adapt to their current behavior. Zhou et al. [38] proposed a similar federated reinforcement learning framework by building a Multilayer Perception (MLP) to compute a global Q-network output with all Q-network results. It also doesn't consider to enable agents to make personalized decisions.

Nadiger et al. [22] pay attention to personalization in the context of gaming. They propose an overall architecture, including the grouping policy, the learning policy, and the federation policy. By putting forward the grouping policy, this approach can avoid the risk of adding irrelevant samples, which may increase the personalization time while guaranteeing the model quality. Unlike the above works, this approach solves the problem resulting from conflict samples by only allowing similar agents to share data samples. However, as reinforcement learning is a typical online learning algorithm, considering the latency of generating a new shared model, directly updating the private model weights might overwrite some new knowledge learned during the shared model updating.

To solve these problems, we propose cloud-aided edge learning to fuse shared knowledge gained at the cloud to the edge. Unlike existing studies, we try to avoid training the whole shared model by only focusing on different situations to reduce edge computation as much as possible.

3   System Model for Cloud-Aided Edge Reinforcement Learning

3.1   Basic Ideas of the Cloud-Aided Edge Reinforcement Learning

To provide satisfactory personalized services, it requires capturing users' personalized explicit or implicit requirements by self-learning. Besides, considering the influences from the external environment and the users' changing preferences, the system should be able to adapt to these new situations to provide better services. We propose a hybrid framework focusing on how to realize and improve the self-learning and adaptive ability of an edge system. Figure 1 shows the proposed edge-cloud collaborative framework.

We focus on two key aspects to achieve smarter automation, learning, and adaptation.

1) How to share knowledge among different edge nodes with cloud assistance: Single edge environments always face the data sparsity problem. For example, lack of various states of weather, season, and system deployment. It is necessary to share knowledge among different edge systems, which will enable an edge system to make more smart decisions by taking advantage of the situations shared by others that haven't already appeared but might happen in

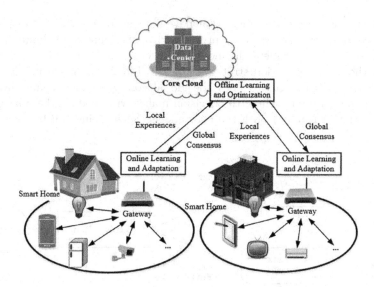

Fig. 1. The overview of collaboration for learning and adaptation in smart home systems between the edge node and the cloud.

the future. The offline learning part in Fig. 1 is in charge of sharing knowledge among different edge nodes by parameter sharing.

2) How to utilize the historical experiences/knowledge generated on cloud in making real-time decisions on edge nodes efficiently: Learning performed on cloud is based on the historical data. Therefore, the resulting knowledge usually reflects past situations that may be outdated in current states. An appropriate mechanism is needed to integrate such historical experiences with fast rules of the local environment to improve the accuracy of reactions generated by an edge decision-maker. The online learning part in Fig. 1 aims to enhance real-time decision making by applying consensus achieved through offline learning on the cloud.

3.2 Knowledge Fusion Strategies on Edge Nodes

As mentioned above, data achieved by the edge node might be different from the generic dataset used to generate the pre-trained model, including differences in either input dimensions or situations occurring in the edge environment. Besides, different preferences among edge nodes may also be different from each other. To cope with such various problems, we propose two knowledge fusion strategies to accelerate edge personalized decision making, i.e., input expansion and output correction.

The Input Expansion Strategy. As the global model and the local model are trained based on different data samples, there may be some special states emerging in the edge environment that have not met by the cloud. In this case, the global consensus model only captures part of the knowledge about the edge environment. To complement the model to provide more accurate decisions, we propose the input expansion strategy shown in Fig. 2. As shown in Fig. 2, the current state will be sent to both the global consensus model and the local private model as input. Then, the decision-maker will produce the final action by integrating outputs of both the two models. Such fusing can be realized as follows.

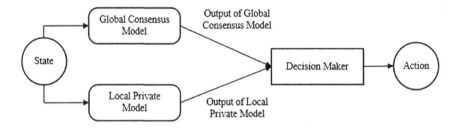

Fig. 2. The input expansion strategy.

$$H(x) = \sum_{i=1}^{N} w_i * h_i(x) \tag{1}$$

where, w_i is the weight of the output $h_i(x)$, and N is the total number of models participate in fusing.

Under the edge-cloud collaboration framework, both the global and the local model might have some information not learned by the counterpart model. So the setting of weights needs to balance the advantages of both parties. Assuming that the accuracy of both parties is the same, the weights of the two are the same, and the advantages of both parties can be guaranteed to be balanced. While, if they have different degrees of accuracy, it is necessary to ensure that the model with higher accuracy has a higher weight. For reinforcement-learning, we define accuracy as the proportion of decisions resulted in a reward greater than zero in all decisions. With this in mind, we define the following equation to compute the weight w_i based on the corresponding accuracy Acc_i.

$$w_i = \frac{Acc_i}{\sum_{i=1}^{N} Acc_i} \tag{2}$$

Considering the simplest situation that there are only one global model and one local model, the value of N is 2.

On this basis, suppose the accuracy of the private model is Acc_{edge}, and the accuracy of the global model is Acc_{cloud}. The corresponding model output value formula is

$$H(x) = \frac{Acc_{edge}}{Acc_{edge} + Acc_{cloud}} * h_{edge}(x)$$
$$+ \frac{Acc_{cloud}}{Acc_{edge} + Acc_{cloud}} * h_{cloud}(x) \tag{3}$$

Initially, the edge model has just started training and is still in the process of exploration. At this time, the accuracy of the local model should be set to 0 while the weight of the cloud model should be set to 1. After training for a while, as the accuracy of the edge model improves, its weight, i.e. the value of $Acc_{edge}/(Acc_{edge} + Acc_{cloud})$ will gradually increase.

The Output Correction Strategy. Because the global consensus model is achieved by integrating, it contains user consensus with similar characteristics. However, when the model is delivered to a given edge environment, it may not be able to meet the preference of a specific user. To satisfy users' personalized usage habits and requirements, we need to modify the output of the global model properly. To this end, we take the output of the global model as an additional input in training the local personalized model, as shown in Fig. 3.

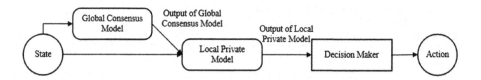

Fig. 3. The output correction strategy.

The corresponding algorithm is shown in Algorithm 1, which both accelerates the training of the local model but also improves the effectiveness of the decision making. Here, we only consider revising the final decision generated by the global model.

4 Reinforcement Learning for Providing Personalized Illuminance in Smart Lighting

Lighting plays a significant role in our daily lives. Generally, lighting includes the use of both natural illumination in the form of daylight and electric illumination provided by various light sources. Together with the flourishing of IoT, a new generation of LED lighting systems are emerging, i.e., LED-based intelligent lighting systems where LEDs are integrated with sensors and actuators to have intelligence. For example, Philips Hue is a wireless lighting product, which can cooperate with a range of smart devices such as Amazon Echo, Apple HomeKit, Google Home, etc. to provide a convenient and comfortable way for occupants to control and experience light.

Algorithm 1. Collaborative algorithm by adjusting cloud model's output.

Require:

  The environment state, $S = < Bright1, Bright2, Distance, Time >$;

  User's operation on the light, $I_{control}$

  The globel model, $Model1$

Ensure:

  The adjustment action to the light, $Action$;

1: Set the training episode to n;

2: **for** $i = 1$ to n **do**

3:   Achieve the initial state S;

4:   Set the max adjustment time to m;

5:   **for** $j = 1$ to m **do**

6:     Input S to $Model1$ and get the output $o1$;

7:     Combine S and $o1$ to a new state S^-;

8:     Input the state S^- into the local model $Model2$. Train the model and get the output $Action$;

9:     Perform the generated $Action$;

10:     Achieve the next state $S^{'}$;

11:     Achieve use's operation $I_{control}$;

12:     Compute the $Reward$ based on $I_{control}$;

13:     Perform related iterative formula or loss function to optimize $Model2$.

14:     Update the state to the next iteration, $S = S^{'}$;

15:   **end for**

16: **end for**

To enhance the quality of user experience, light control strategies need to be more flexible and automatic. Thus, AI and data-mining technologies are widely adopted to seek useful information on resident behavior and the state of the environment for generating satisfactory reactions [7,13,24,33]. These approaches are usually storing and analyzing the continuous human-system interactions during the non-stop system running. Considering the successful application of DRL, we adopt DRL to realize personalized illuminance setting.

According to the definition of reinforcement learning, we use a quadruple $< S, A, P, R >$ to represent a reinforcement learning model, where S represents an environmental state, A represents an action, P represents a state transition probability, and R represents a reward value.

In reinforcement learning, the state comes from the agent's observation of the environment. We suppose there are four sensors around a light, which are two light sensors, one ultrasonic sensor, and one infrared sensor. Generally, the infrared sensor is usually used to determine whether there is a person or not to turn on or turn off the light. Thus, we only use the other three sensors to construct the current state. Specifically, we define the state as a 4-tuple $< B_feeling, B_nature, Distance, Time >$. We get the synthesized brightness (i.e., B_light) and natural light (i.e., B_nature) by the two light sensors. The distance data (i.e., $Distance$) is obtained by the ultrasonic sensor and the $Time$ is when constructing the state values.

For an LED, the action represents the adjustment of the lamp output by the model. For simplicity, we only consider the brightness in this paper. There should be two kinds of actions. One is a determined value of brightness or a predefined gear. The other is one of the operations up, down, and hold.

Reinforcement learning needs to construct reward functions for training the model. To achieve higher user satisfaction, we define the reward function as follows.

$$r = \alpha * R_{positive} + \sum \gamma^i * R_{positive} + I_{control} * R_{negative} \qquad (4)$$

When the user moved to another place or the sunlight intensity changed, the algorithm should generate a proper illuminance and set the light accordingly. Whether the user adjusts the light manually after running the automated setting is used as the feedback for training a DQN. In the above equation, $R_{negative}$ is the negative feedback, which is collected if the user adjusts the light manually after an automated adaptation. In other words, the algorithm didn't find a satisfactory brightness for the user. Similarly, if the user didn't take any action after an automated adaptation, it means the algorithm meets users expect. α is the times that there is no user adjustment during an episode. γ is the reward decay rate to decrease the reward if there is no manual adjustment. i is the continuous times without manual adjustment in an episode, and $I_{control}$ is the number of manually adaptions.

5 Experiments

5.1 Dataset

We use the open software DIALux to generate a dataset for simulating the training and decision making procedure. DIALux is a lighting design software, which is a useful lighting calculation software. It can use all the lamps and lanterns provided by the lamp manufacturers and add sunlight to the scene according to actual calculation requirements. We set a 5.4 m * 3.6 m room in DIALux with a window, a variable power lamp placed on a table in the center of the room, as shown in Fig. 4. The light is 1.8 m away from the window and 0.85 m away from the ground. Taking the height of 0.85 m above the ground as the daily working plane, people can obtain the light intensity of each point on the working plane under different power under the influence of the current sunlight.

When we set the present time is 8 am, Fig. 5 shows the brightness in the room. The red point is the position of the light, and the blue line at the bottom is the window's position. We can find that light intensity around the lamp is about 300 lux, while the light intensity near the window is about 1367 lux. Different conditions of the room can be obtained by adjusting the power of the table lamp and the sunlight. Based on this basic dataset, we generate sequences to simulate interaction procedures between different users and lamps under various environments.

Fig. 4. Data collection environment setting in DAILux.

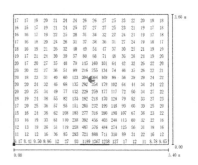

Fig. 5. Brightness value in the room. (Color figure online)

5.2 Experimental Setup

To verify the effectiveness and performance of the proposed approach, we build a three-layer neural network, an input layer, a fully connected layer and an output layer, in which four neuron activation functions are set to Relu in the input and the fully connected layer. Three neurons are set in the output layer, and the activation function is linear. The distance, current sunlight intensity, and current table light intensity are used as input of the neural network. The three output values represent increasing the lamp power, decreasing the lamp power, and keeping the power unchanged. The lamp power is adjusted through the decision output of the neural network.

We ran the experiments on a PC with an Intel Core i7-7700HQ and 16G RAM. DQN, the algorithm of the input expansion strategy, and the algorithm of output correction strategy were used for experiments. Each algorithm trained 50 episodes, and each episode carried out 600 network interactions with humans. It is known that people work in comfortable environments with an illumination of about 300 lux. If the comprehensive illumination near the lamp does not reach 290 lux or more than 320 lux, the network will receive a negative reward of −1. Otherwise, it will receive a positive reward of 1. Adjust the network through the reward value obtained, and the upper limit of the positive reward obtained is 600. Initially, we apply the same network to train both the global model and the local private model.

5.3 Experimental Results

Lab1: Comparison on Working in the Same Environment. First, we compared the rewards of the proposed two strategies and a pure DQN model. In this experiment, we train a DQN model as the global model and then fuse it with a new private model which is start training from scratch. The results are shown in Fig. 6.

We can find that using these three algorithms all quickly obtain a higher reward value. However, the reward value obtained by using pure DQN and training 50 episodes alone does not exceed 400. It means there are still some wrong decisions in these episodes, which result in a low reward. To get a higher reward, we need more episodes to train the model. On the contrary, both the input expansion strategy and output correction strategy can get a high reward in a short episode. The output correction strategy is better than the input expansion strategy from the perspective of speed and stability. It's because the global model is achieved in the same environment as the private model. Thus, the global model output can reach high rewards in most of the cases in the edge environment. However, as initialization of the local model in the input expansion strategy might bring more influences.

Lab2: Comparison on Satisfying Different Preferences. To compare the performance of the two proposed knowledge fusion strategies, we first train the global model with a target brightness between 290–320lux. At the same time, the user in the local environment prefers the illumination between 350–380lux. The results are shown in Fig. 7. From the results, we can see both strategies can get a high reward quickly compared with using pure DQN, as shown in Fig. 6, even though the global model is trained to get a different target brightness.

Lab3: Comparison on Training in Different Environments. To test the performance for fusing models trained in a different environment, we train a global model in the environment of around 8 am. Then, we try to fuse this model by the proposed two fusion strategies to adapt to the environment of 8 pm. Figure 8 shows the accordingly results. It can be seen from the experimental results that using the global model to perform auxiliary training on edge, both the two strategies can achieve perfect results. In the output correction strategy, the edge node needs to be adjusted briefly to adapt to the current night environment. However, the input expansion strategy can get a higher reward in the initial states.

5.4 Quantitative Comparison of the Performance of Different Algorithms

We set the condition that if the algorithm gets a reward which greater than 450 within five consecutive episodes, it is stable enough to adapt to the environment. Then, by running the above experiments, we collect the time cost, average training time, and memory size, as shown in Table 1.

We can clearly find that the average iterations of only using DQN, which is nearly ten times using either of the proposed strategies. In the latter two groups of experiments, we can see the output correction strategy requires less time than the input expansion strategy. While, from the perspective of memory occupation, our strategies need a little more memory than only using DQN as we need to load the global model.

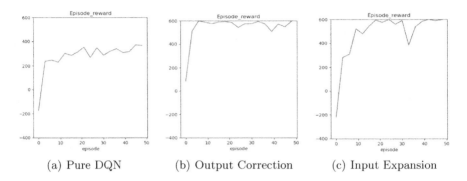

(a) Pure DQN   (b) Output Correction   (c) Input Expansion

Fig. 6. Rewards comparison for applying models trained in the same environment.

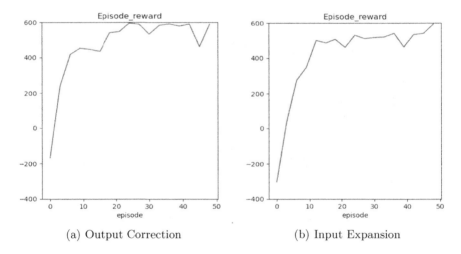

(a) Output Correction   (b) Input Expansion

Fig. 7. Rewards comparison for applying models trained for satisfying different preferences.

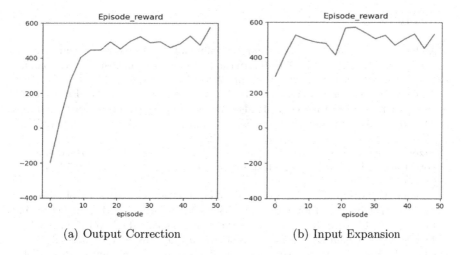

(a) Output Correction   (b) Input Expansion

Fig. 8. Rewards comparison for applying models trained in different environments.

Table 1. Quantitative comparison of performance of different algorithms.

Experiment	Strategy	Average iterations	Time for training	Memory occupation
Lab 1	DQN	186	6 m10 s	0.2281 GB
	Output correction	10	28 s	0.2301 GB
	Input expansion	24	1 m19 s	0.2296 GB
Lab 2	Output correction	19	56 s	0.2303 GB
	Input expansion	24	1 m13 s	0.2303 GB
Lab 2	Output correction	14	41 s	0.2310 GB
	Input expansion	14	52 s	0.2307 GB

6   Conclusion

In this paper, we propose a cloud-aided edge reinforcement learning framework and introduce two edge knowledge fusion strategies. As shown in the experiments, the proposed approach can accelerate personalized service provision while do not increase the memory occupation obviously. We present a case study on applying the method in providing personalized illuminance services. The proposed framework and strategies are also suitable for other applications. In our future work, we will focus on identifying and describing the features of different edge environments, which would better enhance the inference accuracy.

References

1. Al-Jaroodi, J., Mohamed, N., Jawhar, I., Mahmoud, S.: CoTWare: a cloud of things middleware. In: 2017 IEEE 37th International Conference on Distributed Computing Systems Workshops (ICDCSW), pp. 214–219. IEEE (2017)
2. Amento, B., Balasubramanian, B., Hall, R.J., Joshi, K., Jung, G., Purdy, K.H.: FocusStack: orchestrating edge clouds using location-based focus of attention. In: 2016 IEEE/ACM Symposium on Edge Computing (SEC), pp. 179–191. IEEE (2016)
3. Atzori, L., Iera, A., Morabito, G.: Understanding the Internet of Things: definition, potentials, and societal role of a fast evolving paradigm. Ad Hoc Netw. **56**, 122–140 (2017)
4. Bonomi, F., Milito, R., Natarajan, P., Zhu, J.: Fog computing: a platform for Internet of Things and analytics. In: Bessis, N., Dobre, C. (eds.) Big Data and Internet of Things: A Roadmap for Smart Environments. SCI, vol. 546, pp. 169–186. Springer, Cham (2014). https://doi.org/10.1007/978-3-319-05029-4_7
5. Chen, J., Ran, X.: Deep learning with edge computing: a review. Proc. IEEE **107**(8), 1655–1674 (2019)
6. Cheng, Z., Zhao, Q., Wang, F., Jiang, Y., Xia, L., Ding, J.: Satisfaction based q-learning for integrated lighting and blind control. Energy Build. **127**, 43–55 (2016)
7. Cheuque, C., Baeza, F., Marquez, G., Calderon, J.: Towards to responsive web services for smart home led control with Raspberry Pi: a first approach. In: 2015 34th International Conference of the Chilean Computer Science Society (SCCC), pp. 1–4. IEEE (2015)
8. Corcoran, P., Datta, S.K.: Mobile-edge computing and the Internet of Things for consumers: extending cloud computing and services to the edge of the network. IEEE Consum. Electron. Mag. **5**(4), 73–74 (2016)
9. Fu, Q., Hu, L., Wu, H., Hu, F., Hu, W., Chen, J.: A Sarsa-based adaptive controller for building energy conservation. J. Comput. Methods Sci. Eng. **18**(2), 329–338 (2018)
10. Hardy, C., Le Merrer, E., Sericola, B.: Distributed deep learning on edge-devices: feasibility via adaptive compression. In: 2017 IEEE 16th International Symposium on Network Computing and Applications (NCA), pp. 1–8. IEEE (2017)
11. Jang, M., Schwan, K., Bhardwaj, K., Gavrilovska, A., Avasthi, A.: Personal clouds: sharing and integrating networked resources to enhance end user experiences. In: IEEE INFOCOM 2014-IEEE Conference on Computer Communications, pp. 2220–2228. IEEE (2014)
12. Kairouz, P., et al.: Advances and open problems in federated learning. arXiv preprint arXiv:1912.04977 (2019)
13. Kandasamy, N.K., Karunagaran, G., Spanos, C., Tseng, K.J., Soong, B.H.: Smart lighting system using ANN-IMC for personalized lighting control and daylight harvesting. Build. Environ. **139**, 170–180 (2018)
14. Lee, J., Tang, H., Park, J.: Energy efficient canny edge detector for advanced mobile vision applications. IEEE Trans. Circ. Syst. Video Technol. **28**(4), 1037–1046 (2016)
15. Li, H., Ota, K., Dong, M.: Learning IoT in edge: deep learning for the Internet of Things with edge computing. IEEE Netw. **32**(1), 96–101 (2018)
16. Li, H., Wei, T., Ren, A., Zhu, Q., Wang, Y.: Deep reinforcement learning: framework, applications, and embedded implementations. In: 2017 IEEE/ACM International Conference on Computer-Aided Design (ICCAD), pp. 847–854. IEEE (2017)

17. Liu, B., Wang, L., Liu, M.: Lifelong federated reinforcement learning: a learning architecture for navigation in cloud robotic systems. IEEE Robot. Autom. Lett. **4**(4), 4555–4562 (2019)
18. Lu, S., Yao, Y., Shi, W.: Collaborative learning on the edges: a case study on connected vehicles. In: 2nd {USENIX} Workshop on Hot Topics in Edge Computing (HotEdge 19) (2019)
19. Mahdavinejad, M.S., Rezvan, M., Barekatain, M., Adibi, P., Barnaghi, P., Sheth, A.P.: Machine learning for Internet of Things data analysis: a survey. Digit. Commun. Netw. **4**(3), 161–175 (2018)
20. Mattern, F., Floerkemeier, C.: From the Internet of computers to the Internet of Things. In: Sachs, K., Petrov, I., Guerrero, P. (eds.) From Active Data Management to Event-Based Systems and More. LNCS, vol. 6462, pp. 242–259. Springer, Heidelberg (2010). https://doi.org/10.1007/978-3-642-17226-7_15
21. Mortazavi, S.H., Salehe, M., Gomes, C.S., Phillips, C., de Lara, E.: Cloudpath: a multi-tier cloud computing framework. In: Proceedings of the Second ACM/IEEE Symposium on Edge Computing, pp. 1–13 (2017)
22. Nadiger, C., Kumar, A., Abdelhak, S.: Federated reinforcement learning for fast personalization. In: 2019 IEEE Second International Conference on Artificial Intelligence and Knowledge Engineering (AIKE), pp. 123–127. IEEE (2019)
23. Osia, S.A., et al.: A hybrid deep learning architecture for privacy-preserving mobile analytics. IEEE Internet Things J. **7**, 4505–4518 (2020)
24. Paulauskaite-Taraseviciene, A., Morkevicius, N., Janaviciute, A., Liutkevicius, A., Vrubliauskas, A., Kazanavicius, E.: The usage of artificial neural networks for intelligent lighting control based on resident's behavioural pattern. Elektronika ir Elektrotechnika **21**(2), 72–79 (2015)
25. Ravindra, P., Khochare, A., Reddy, S.P., Sharma, S., Varshney, P., Simmhan, Y.: ECHO: an adaptive orchestration Platform for hybrid Dataflows across cloud and edge. In: Maximilien, M., Vallecillo, A., Wang, J., Oriol, M. (eds.) ICSOC 2017. LNCS, vol. 10601, pp. 395–410. Springer, Cham (2017). https://doi.org/10.1007/978-3-319-69035-3_28
26. Sajjad, H.P., Danniswara, K., Al-Shishtawy, A., Vlassov, V.: SpanEdge: towards unifying stream processing over central and near-the-edge data centers. In: 2016 IEEE/ACM Symposium on Edge Computing (SEC), pp. 168–178. IEEE (2016)
27. Samie, F., Bauer, L., Henkel, J.: From cloud down to things: an overview of machine learning in Internet of Things. IEEE Internet Things J. **6**(3), 4921–4934 (2019)
28. Shi, W., Cao, J., Zhang, Q., Li, Y., Xu, L.: Edge computing: vision and challenges. IEEE Internet Things J. **3**(5), 637–646 (2016)
29. Stojkoska, B.L.R., Trivodaliev, K.V.: A review of Internet of Things for smart home: challenges and solutions. J. Clean. Prod. **140**, 1454–1464 (2017)
30. Wei, T., Wang, Y., Zhu, Q.: Deep reinforcement learning for building HVAC control. In: Proceedings of the 54th Annual Design Automation Conference 2017, pp. 1–6 (2017)
31. Xu, Q., Varadarajan, S., Chakrabarti, C., Karam, L.J.: A distributed canny edge detector: algorithm and FPGA implementation. IEEE Trans. Image Process. **23**(7), 2944–2960 (2014)
32. Yazici, M.T., Basurra, S., Gaber, M.M.: Edge machine learning: enabling smart Internet of Things applications. Big Data Cogn. Comput. **2**(3), 26 (2018)
33. Yu, T., Kuki, Y., Matsushita, G., Maehara, D., Sampei, S., Sakaguchi, K.: Design and implementation of lighting control system using battery-less wireless human detection sensor networks. IEICE Trans. Commun. **E100-B**(6), 974–985 (2016)

34. Zhang, Q., Zhang, Q., Shi, W., Zhong, H.: Distributed collaborative execution on the edges and its application to amber alerts. IEEE Internet Things J. **5**(5), 3580–3593 (2018)
35. Zhang, T., He, Z., Lee, R.B.: Privacy-preserving machine learning through data obfuscation. arXiv preprint arXiv:1807.01860 (2018)
36. Zhang, X., Qiao, M., Liu, L., Xu, Y., Shi, W.: Collaborative cloud-edge computation for personalized driving behavior modeling. In: Proceedings of the 4th ACM/IEEE Symposium on Edge Computing, pp. 209–221 (2019)
37. Zhang, Y., Ma, X., Zhang, J., Hossain, M.S., Muhammad, G., Amin, S.U.: Edge intelligence in the cognitive Internet of Things: improving sensitivity and interactivity. IEEE Netw. **33**(3), 58–64 (2019)
38. Zhuo, H.H., Feng, W., Xu, Q., Yang, Q., Lin, Y.: Federated reinforcement learning. arXiv:1901.08277 (2019)

A Game-Based Secure Trading of Big Data and IoT Services: Blockchain as a Two-Sided Market

Ahmed Saleh Bataineh[1], Jamal Bentahar[1], Omar Abdel Wahab[2(✉)],
Rabeb Mizouni[3], and Gaith Rjoub[1]

[1] CIISE Department, Concordia University, Montreal, Canada
{ah_batai,bentahar,g_rjoub}@encs.concordia.ca
[2] Université du Québec en Outaouais, Gatineau, QC, Canada
omar.abdulwahab@uqo.ca
[3] Khalifa University of Science and Technology, Abu Dhabi, UAE
rabeb.mizouni@ku.ac.ae

Abstract. The blockchain technology has recently proved to be an efficient solution for guaranteeing the security of data transactions in data
trading scenarios. The benefits of the blockchain in this domain have been
shown to span over several crucial security and privacy aspects such as
verifying the identities of data providers, detecting and preventing malicious data consumers, and regulating the trust relationships between
the data trading parties. However, the cost and economic aspects of
using this solution such as the pricing of mining process have not been
addressed yet. In fact, using the blockchain entails high operational costs
and puts both the data providers and miners in a continuous dilemma
between delivering high-quality security services and adding supplementary costs. In addition, the mining leader requires an efficient mechanism to select the tasks from the mining pool and determine the needed
computational resources for each particular task in order to maximize
its payoff. Motivated by these two points, we propose in this paper a
novel game theoretical model based on the two-sided market approach
that exhibits a mix of cooperative and competitive strategies between
the (blockchain) miners and data providers. The game helps both the
data providers and miners determine the monetary reward and computational resources respectively. Simulations conducted on a real-world
dataset show promising potential of the proposed solution in terms of
achieving total surpluses for all involved parties, i.e., data providers,
data consumers and miners.

Keywords: Game-based trading · Big data · IoT · Blockchain ·
Two-sided market

1 Introduction

Blockchain technology has lately emerged as a revolutionary paradigm for
addressing the challenges of finding trustworthy third-parties and guaranteeing

© Springer Nature Switzerland AG 2020
E. Kafeza et al. (Eds.): ICSOC 2020, LNCS 12571, pp. 85–100, 2020.
https://doi.org/10.1007/978-3-030-65310-1_7

the privacy and security of data trading transactaions in critical domains such as Internet of Things (IoT), data analytics, mobile crowd-sensing, and machine learning. Interestingly, recent statistics estimate that the data contained in the blockchain ledger is expected to worth up to 20% of the global big data market and to generate up to 100 billion in annual income to the data market that already hit \$203 billion dollar of revenue at the end of 2019 [6,9]. In the context of data trading using blockchain, three players are to be considered: miners, data providers and data consumers. Miners are responsible for supervising and regulating the execution of what is known as *smart contracts*. A Smart contract is a self-executing computer program that states and organizes the agreed terms of a certain data transaction such as the desired quality of service clauses and secure payment mechanism between the data providers and data consumers. Processing smart contacts by miners entails high (mining) operational costs and processing time, which might negatively affect the execution time of real-time and delay-critical applications such as IoT and data analytics. In the literature, there is lack of attention on the business model that would enable data trading over blockchain where the main stream research in the general context of data focuses on developing mechanisms of data resource management such as [14–16]. Several challenging issues are yet to be addressed, in particular, assigning optimal amount of computational units to the mining tasks, sustaining optimal payoffs to involved players and serving data requests on time. In this work, our objective is to provide a novel contribution to the data trading over blockchain through proposing a game-theoretic-based business model that helps regulate the secure data trading of IoT and big data analytics services. In particular, we aim to address the following two substantial research challenges: 1) how should the blockchain node distribute the computational resources of the mining process among the data providers in such a way to maximize its payoff; and 2) how should the data providers decide on the optimal monetary reward that needs to be given to the miners versus their service in such a way to guarantee optimal execution time of their transactions while avoiding over-payments.

1.1 Motivating Example

We provide in Fig. 1 a motivating example to better clarify the research gap in the literature and highlight the need of our solution. As explained in the figure, data consumers request to run real-time data analytics on an edge IoT server. Following the blockchain technology, the request is deployed as a smart contract which includes clauses that regulate the relationships between the data consumers and the edge IoT server in terms of data quality, data size and processing speed. The execution of the smart contract is supervised and executed by the blockchain node, which manages the mining process and the mining computational units. Smart contracts vary in their terms, and hence they differ in their executions in terms of execution time and required resources. For instance, in Fig. 1, the hospital server is exposed to more privacy threatens as it stores patients data, which requires more computational units from the blockchain node to authenticate only trusted consumers. This creates the need for a distributing mechanism that determines the optimal amount of resources for each smart contract. However, the absence of such a mechanism might assign more resources to less profitable contracts.

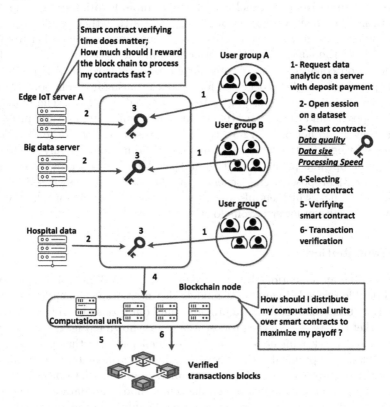

Fig. 1. Motivating scenario: run real time data analytics procedures on Edge IoT server using the blockchain technology.

1.2 Related Work and Problem Statement

The state-of-the-art proposals focus on deploying verification approaches into the blockchain technology in order to tackle the privacy and security issues such as preserving the anonymity of the data providers, and preventing impersonation attacks and colluding miners. For instance, the approaches proposed in [18,22] leverage the blockchain technology to address the problem of user location impersonation and re-identification attacks respectively in a crowd-sensing context. The approaches proposed in [8,11] aim to increase the engagement of the crowd system participants through capitalizing on the anonymous and reliable interaction features provided by the blockchain technology.

The proposals [10,13,19,20] propose game theoretical foundations in the context of mobile blockchain supported by edge computing services. The interactions between miners and edge computing nodes are modeled using Stackelberg games and auctions to derive an optimal price for the proof-of-work for offloading allocation tasks. The main limitation of such games is that they result in putting the miners into an aggressive competition situation between each other from one side, and with the edge computing services from the other side. This leads to less efficient outcomes in terms of total surpluses for all these parties. In [21], the authors propose to deploy blockchain for big data sharing in a collaborative edge environment. Similar works have also been proposed in [12,23]. The aforementioned proposals, and the state-of-the-art in general suffer from several problems. In fact, they 1) do not explain how the mining resources should be distributed over the existing smart contracts and miners; 2) do not provide any mechanism to derive the optimal payment that should be given by data providers to miners); and/or 3) propose pricing schemes for the mining process based on pure competitive games, which entails an aggressive competition among the involved parties and results in lower payoffs for them.

1.3   Contribution

To address the aforementioned issues, we extend the work in [3,4] by proposing a novel double two-sided game that models the interactions among the involved parties (i.e., blockchain node, data providers and data consumers) using the two-sided market theory [17]. In the proposed game, as shown in Fig. 2, both the data providers and blockchain node act as a two-sided platform that gets on board two market sides. Specifically, the blockchain node intermediates the interactions between the data providers and data consumers, while the data providers intermediate the interactions between the blockchain node and data consumers. As shown in the figure, the data providers either 1) subsidize the blockchain node by a higher portion of revenue to motivate it to supply more mining computational units, which results in attracting more data consumers and increasing the revenue; or 2) subsidize the data consumers by more data computational units, which increases the consumers' demand and hence contributes in attracting the blockchain node. Similar strategies are set up to the blockchain node as shown in Fig. 2b. The proposed game combines both strategies as two separate games. The solution of the games helps derive the equilibrium in terms of shared revenue among the blockchain node and data providers and amount of mining resources that each smart contract should be assigned with.

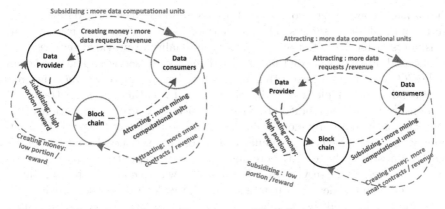

Data provider as two-sided market   Blockchain as two-sided market

Fig. 2. Proposed model: a double two-sided market game

2 Proposed Model for Secure Trading of Data

2.1 Model Description: A Double Two-Sided Game Formulation

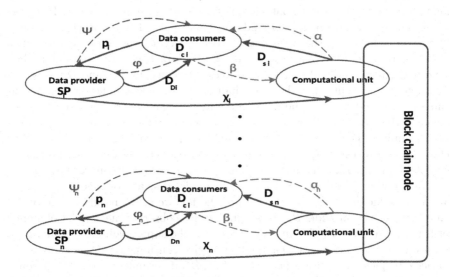

Fig. 3. Double two-sided game

The proposed secure data trading model, depicted in Fig. 3, consists of three entities: Data Service Consumers (SC), Big Data Service Providers (SP) and Blockchain node (BC) that consists of a network of miners. In our solution, a certain big data service provider SP_i receives a monetary value of P_i per a data service consumer's access to its services. The service provider SP_i provides both the data and computing resources that are required to execute the data analytics duties of the data consumers. The interactions between data providers and data consumers include negotiating the data type, quality of provided services, payments, and all the associated terms of delivered data services. The blockchain node BC is in charge of executing the transactions of smart contracts in order to append a correct block into the blockchain. Executing smart contracts will also ensure the sustainability of consumers' access security, verification of the identities of the data providers and consumers, protection of the privacy of data providers and enforcement of quality control of data services. In our model, the blockchain node seeks to distribute and allocate its computing resources for the mining process among service providers in such a way to maximize its own payoff.

The Consumers' demand on data service i provided by a service provider SP_i is denoted by D_{c_i} and the computing resources allocated by service i to run the data analytics duties of its consumers is donated by D_{D_i}. D_{D_i} is measured in terms of the throughput per second of executing the data requests. The relationship between consumers' demand D_{c_i} and supplying service i is modeled using the two-sided market theory [17] as cross-group externalities ϕ and ψ. Here, ψ represents the increase in the number of data consumers obtained when some new computing and storage resources are added to D_{D_i}. ϕ represents the amount of profit that the data service provider earns when one more new consumer is added to D_{c_i}. Similarly, the computing resources allocated by the blockchain node to regulate the smart contracts of service i is denoted by D_{s_i}. The relationship between consumers' demand and the supply of the blockchain node is likewise modeled using the two-sided market theory as cross-group externalities α and β. Here, α represents the increasing of data consumers obtained when some new computing and storage resources are added to D_{s_i} and β represents the amount of benefits that the blockchain node earns when one more new consumers are added to D_{c_i}. The parameters α, β, ϕ, and ψ are dependant on the service i. However, the variable i is omitted from the notations of these parameters to simplify the equations when the service i is understood from the context. Thus, instead of using α_i for instance, α will be used. The same simplification is applied for the other parameters that appear as exponents in our equations.

The interaction between SP and BC is modeled as a two-stage game, where BC acts as the game leader and SP are the followers. In the first stage of the game, each service provider SP_i providing service i observes the amount of money returns χ_i requested by BC in order to adjust the supply volume of computing resources and the price to be charged to service consumers SC_i consuming the service i. In quest of the price specified by SP_i, BC determines the optimal amount of computing resources D_{s_i} that should be supplied to handle the smart contracts between SP_i and SC_i. The model forms a closed loop of dependencies that involves subsidizing techniques from the two-sided market theory. Thus, SP_i may chose to subsidize BC by an extra amount of payment that exceeds the contribution of BC. The objective is to keep an optimal level of D_{s_i} that maximizes the return revenues $P_i * D_{c_i}$. Alternatively, BC may subsidize SP_i with a low portion of the resulting revenue to keep an optimal level of P_i. The different parameters and symbols used in our proposed solution are summarized in Table 1.

2.2   Players Demands and Utility Functions

The consumer's demand and supply are modeled using the Cobb-Douglas function, which have the ability to represent the elasticity of the computing and storage resources supply (D_{s_i}, D_{D_i}) and its variations depending on the user's demand. These demand functions are defined as per Eqs. (1), (2), and (3). By substituting Eqs. (2) and (3) into Eq. (1), we can express the consumer's demand as a function of χ_i and P_i as described in Eq. (4).

$$D_{c_i} = k_1 P_i^{-\gamma} D_{s_i}^{\alpha} D_{D_i}^{\psi} \tag{1}$$

$$D_{s_i} = k_2 (\chi_i P_i D_{c_i})^{\beta} \tag{2}$$

$$D_{D_i} = k_3 (P_i D_{c_i})^{\phi} \tag{3}$$

Table 1. Model parameters

Model parameters	Descriptions
SP_i	Service provider providing service i
BC	A blockchain node
SC_i	Consumers of service i
D_{c_i}	SC_i's demand
D_{D_i}	IT-infrastructure supply to handle requests of SC_i
D_{s_i}	IT-infrastructure supply to handle smart contracts between SP_i and SC_i
P_i	Service i's price
χ_i	Portion of revenue required by BC from SP_i
α	The Network effects (externality) on D_{c_i} by D_{s_i}
β	The Network effects (externality) on D_{s_i} by D_{c_i}
ψ	The Network effects (externality) on D_{c_i} by D_{D_i}
ϕ	The Network effects (externality) on D_{s_i} by D_{c_i}
γ	D_{c_i}'s elasticity with respect to P_i
k_1, k_2, and k_3	Constant multipliers
f_c	Associated costs per smart contract
f_s	Associated costs per service request by a consumer
π_i	SP_i's payoff
π	Blockchain node's payoff
a_1	$= -\gamma + \alpha\beta + \phi\psi$
a_2	$= \alpha\beta$
a_3	$= 1/(1 - \alpha\beta - \psi\phi)$

$$D_{c_i} = (k_1 k_2^\alpha k_3^\psi P_i^{a_1} \chi_i^{a_2})^{a_3} \tag{4}$$

Each big data service provider SP_i is subject to a fixed cost f_s per each consumer access. SP_i aims to maximize its payoff as described in Eq. (5).

$$\pi_i = ((P_i)(1 - \chi_i) - f_s)D_{c_i} \tag{5}$$

The blockchain node BC is subject to a fixed cost f_c per each smart contract between SP_i and a data consumer. As a rational agent, the blockchain node seeks to maximize its payoff as given in Eq. (6).

$$\pi = (P_i \chi_i - f_c)D_{c_i} \tag{6}$$

2.3   Game Equilibrium

The equilibrium of the above-described game is solved using a backward induction methodology. Specifically, the followers' (data service providers) sub-game is solved first to obtain their optimal response P_i^* to the service consumers. The leader's (blockchain node) sub-game is then computed to obtain the optimal χ_i^*. The game equilibrium is stated in Theorem 1.

Theorem 1. *Under the assumption validated in [4] stating that the cross-group externalities are not too week and not too strong, $(0.1 < \alpha\beta < 0.8)$ and $(0.1 < \phi\psi < 0.8)$, The equilibrium of our double two-sided game is given by the best responses of the different players as follows:*

1. The best response of the data service provider SP_i is given by:

$$P_i^* = \frac{a_1 a_3 f_s}{(a_1 a_3 - 1)(\chi_i^* - 1)} \tag{7}$$

$$if: \quad 1 < (1/a_1 a_3)$$

2. The best response of the Blockchain node with respect to a service i is given by:

$$\chi_i^* = \frac{a_2 a_3 f_c}{(a_2 a_3 + 1)P_i^*} \tag{8}$$

Proof. From Eq. (5) of the data service provider's payoff, using log for both sides of the equation, we obtain:

$$\log \pi_i = \log(P_i(1 - \chi_i) - f_s) + \log D_{c_i} \tag{9}$$

Then, the optimal price P_i^* is defined by $\partial \pi_i / \partial P_i = 0$ as follows:

$$\frac{1}{\pi_i} \times \frac{\partial \pi_i}{\partial P_i} = \frac{1 - \chi_i}{P_i(1 - \chi_i) - f_s} + \frac{1}{D_{c_i}} \times \frac{\partial D_{c_i}}{\partial P_i} = 0 \tag{10}$$

By deriving Eq. (4) with respect to P_i, then:

$$\frac{\partial D_{c_i}}{\partial P_i} = a_1 a_3 D_{c_i} P_i^{-1} \tag{11}$$

By substituting Eq. (11) into Eq. (10), we get:

$$P_i = \frac{a_1 a_3 f_s}{(a_1 a_3 - 1)(\chi_i - 1)} \tag{12}$$

Since $P_i > 0$, $fs > 0$, $((\chi_i - 1) < 1)$ then $(a_1 a_3/(a_1 a_3 - 1) < 0)$, so the condition. By considering the acceptable range for γ analysed in [5], $0.2 < \gamma < 0.3$ then $\partial \pi_i/\partial P_i > 0$ when $P_i < (a_1 a_3 f_s)/((a_1 a_3 - 1)(\chi_i - 1))$ and $\partial \pi_i/\partial P_i < 0$ when $P_i > (a_1 a_3 f_s)/((a_1 a_3 - 1)(\chi_i - 1))$. Consequently, P_i is the best response.

For the second result of the theorem, we consider and take the log for both sides of the equation of the blockchain node's payoff (Eq. (6)) and obtain:

$$\log \pi = \log(P_i \chi_i - f_c) + \log D_{c_i} \tag{13}$$

Then, the optimal χ_i^* is defined by $\partial \pi/\partial \chi_i = 0$ as follows:

$$\frac{1}{\pi} \times \frac{\partial \pi}{\partial \chi_i} = \frac{P_i}{P_i \chi_i - f_c} + \frac{1}{D_{c_i}} \times \frac{\partial D_{c_i}}{\partial \chi_i} = 0 \tag{14}$$

By deriving Eq. (4) with respect to χ_i, we get:

$$\frac{\partial D_{c_i}}{\partial \chi_i} = a_2 a_3 D_{c_i} \chi_i^{-1} \tag{15}$$

By substituting Eq. (15) into Eq. (14), then:

$$\chi_i = \frac{a_2 a_3 f_c}{(a_2 a_3 + 1) P_i} \tag{16}$$

$\partial \pi/\partial \chi_i > 0$ when $\chi_i < (a_2 a_3 f_c)((a_2 a_3 + 1) P_i)$ and $\partial \pi/\partial \chi_i < 0$ when $\chi_i > (a_2 a_3 f_c)((a_2 a_3 + 1) P_i)$. Consequently, χ_i is the best response, so the theorem.

3   Simulation and Empirical Analysis

3.1   Simulation Setup

Our simulation analysis is grounded on statistical observations from big data and IoT services from the AWS marketplace [2], BMR [1]—the annual statistical report that publishes the revenues, payoffs and market growth of the the AWS marketplace—and a real-world dataset from Google [7]. The price, P_i, of the data service is chosen from the interval $[0.2, 3.2]$ USD/hour, following the price distribution of 150 data and IoT services from the AWS marketplace. According to [1], Amazon Web services (AWS) received 30 billion USD in revenue with a net income of approx. 12 billion. The gap between the gross and net revenues is caused by the marginal operating costs which made up approx. 60% of revenue. The operating costs represents in our model the costs associated with the smart contracts f_c and service requests initiated by data consumers f_s. The Google dataset [7] records statistics on the execution of big data requests executed on

Google-powered virtual machines, which are similar to the instances of Amazon cloud infrastructure (EC2). According to these statistics, each virtual machine takes on average 1.42 to 10 s to complete a data processing request (with a mean of 5.71 s and standard deviation of 4.29 s). The instances and their average computational power are respectively represented in our model by D_{s_i} and the externality factor α. Adding a compute instance has a direct impact on the increase of the consumers' demand between 0.1 to 0.7 data request per second. By following the mathematically proved result in [4] that the cross-group externalities should not be neither too weak nor too strong, the cross-group externalities should be bounded by $0.1 < \alpha\beta < 0.8$. Hence, the externality factor β would range from $0.1/\alpha$ to $0.8/\alpha$. We follow those estimations and set up the cross-group externalities ϕ and ψ in the same range of α and β. The price elasticity γ is set to 0.15, which is similar to the sensitivity of mobile/telecommunication services price estimated in the literature [5]. The simulation takes the aforementioned parameters as inputs, and then calculates the optimal shared revenue χ_i from each service i according to Eq. (8) in Theorem 1. Moreover, the simulation inputs meet the theoretical condition $(1 < 1/a_1a_3)$ in Theorem 1. Thus, by substituting the real ranges of the simulation parameters, the mathematical term representing the strength of total externalities (a_3) is greater than zero (i.e $\alpha\beta + \phi\psi < 1$). Hence, we demonstrate our three dimensional results in three sets of criteria: 1) week externalities $(0.1 < \alpha\beta < 0.4, 0.1 < \phi\psi < 0.4)$; 2) strong externalities of $\alpha\beta$ - weak externalities of $\phi\psi$ $(0.4 < \alpha\beta < 0.7, 0.1 < \phi\psi < 0.2)$; and 3) strong externalities of $\phi\psi$ - weak externalities of $\alpha\beta$ $(0.1 < \alpha\beta < 0.2, 0.4 < \phi\psi < 0.7)$.

3.2   Shared Revenues and Computational Costs over Externalities

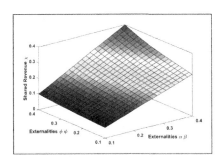 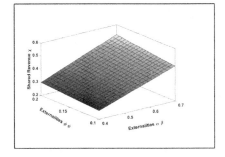

Fig. 4. Shared revenue over week externalities

Fig. 5. Shared revenue over strong externalities $\alpha\beta$

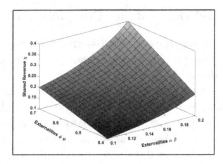

Fig. 6. Shared revenue over strong externalities $\phi\psi$

In this section, we study the impact of the cross group externalitie metrics $(\alpha\beta)$ and $(\phi\psi)$ on the shared revenue χ_i among data providers and blockchain node. In Fig. 4, we study the percentage of shared revenue received by the blockchain node for a weak level of externalities between, on one side the data providers and blockchain node, and on the other side the data consumers. In Figs. 5 and 6, we study the shared revenue for a stronger level of externalities $\alpha\beta$ and $\phi\psi$ respectively. As shown in these figures, the blockchain node receives a higher percentage of revenue as the externality factors $\alpha\beta$ and $\phi\psi$ become stronger. Another important observation is that the average of shared revenues increases at a higher pace over the blockchain node externalities with data consumers $(\alpha\beta)$ than that over data provider and data consumers $(\phi\psi)$. This behavior is clearly observed in Fig. 5 which shows that the shared revenue reaches 60% over strong externalities of $\alpha\beta$ versus a maximum of 40% over strong externalities of $\phi\psi$ as shown in Fig. 6. This behavior is interpreted as follows. The demand of data consumers is positively impacted when its externalities with the blockchain node $(\alpha\beta)$ become stronger. Consequently, the data providers entice the blockchain node by a higher portion χ_i of revenues to supply more computational units with the aim of increasing the consumers' demand and hence the total revenue. Nonetheless, the blockchain node faces higher operating costs by increasing its supply of mining computational units. Consequently, it would ask for a higher portion of revenue. Moreover, the consumers' demand is positively impacted as its externalities with data provider become stronger. Thus, the data providers would face higher operating costs when they add more computational units in an attempt to increase the consumers' demand. This forces the blockchain node to subsidize data providers with a lower portion χ_i of revenue to sustain a higher level D_{c_i} of consumers' demand. In general, increasing the consumers' demand adds more computational cost on the blockchain node, which leads to increasing the portion of blockchain node as the externalities among the data provider and data consumers become stronger. This explains the slower increase pace of shared revenues over the externalities $\phi\psi$ compared to the externalities $\alpha\beta$.

3.3 Data Consumers' Demand and Computational Unit Supply

In this section, we study the impact of cross-group externalities among all the involved parties (i.e., data providers, blockchain node, and data consumers) on the data consumers' demand. As shown on Figs. 7, 8 and 9, the consumers' demand is higher under a weak level of externalities than the strong level. Those observed results are interpreted as follows. A higher externality level among the market players incurs a higher cost for the two-sided market platform to get the market players on board. Specifically, under a strong level of externalities among the blockchain node and data consumers $\alpha\beta$, data providers either (1) subsidize the blockchain node with a higher portion of revenue to attract more data consumers (as discussed in Sect. 3.2); or (2) subsidize the data consumers by supplying higher amounts of data computational units, which in turns, leads to incentivizing the blockchain node. However, data providers cannot ultimately subsidize data consumers due to their mutual cross-group externalities ($\phi\psi$). To study this phenomenon, we show in Figs. 10 and 11 the amount of data computational units supplied by data providers as well as the number of data consumers attracted over the externalities $\phi\psi$ respectively. As shown in Fig. 10, the amount of supplied computational units increases under weak externalities ($\phi\psi \in [0.1 - 0.4]$) and gradually decreases as the cross-group externalities become stronger (i.e., $\phi\psi \in [0.4 - 0.8]$). However, as shown in Fig. 11, the number of attracted data consumers exponentially decreases over the whole range of externalities. This implies that the subsidizing technique becomes costly as the externalities become stronger. For instance, data providers attract 2×10^5 data consumers by providing 20 data computational units at an externality level of 0.2, while they attract a number of data consumers that is 0.1×10^5 less by providing the same amount of data computational units but with a higher externality level of 0.5. In both cases (i.e., subsidizing data consumers and data providers), the data providers would undergo higher costs. Similarly, under a strong level of externalities between data providers and data consumers, the blockchain node subsidizes either the data providers (by asking lower portion of revenues) or the data consumers (by supplying a higher amount of computational units), which entails higher costs for both cases. Similarly, the blockchain node cannot ultimately subsidize the data consumers due to their mutual cross-group externalities represented by $\alpha\beta$. Similar observations are depicted in Fig. 12 in terms of mining computational units over $\alpha\beta$.

3.4 Data Providers and Blockchain Payoffs

In this section, we investigate the impact of externalities on the payoff of the data providers and blockchain node. Figure 13 shows the payoff of data providers under weak externalities, while Figs. 14 and 15 depict providers' payoff under strong externalities $\alpha\beta$ and $\phi\psi$ respectively. As illustrated in these figures, the data providers' payoff gradually decreases as the externalities increase. The reason behind this increasing is that the overall demand of consumers decreases while computational costs and asked shared revenue increase over externalities

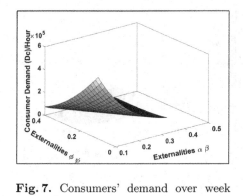

Fig. 7. Consumers' demand over week externalities

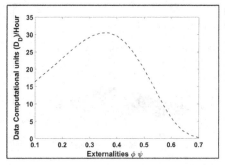

Fig. 8. Consumers' demand over strong externalities $\alpha\beta$

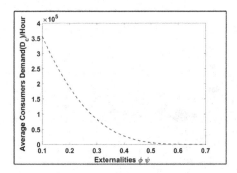

Fig. 9. Consumers' demand over strong externalities $\phi\psi$

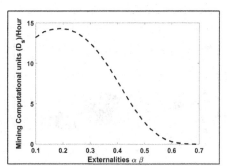

Fig. 10. Data computational units over $\phi\psi$

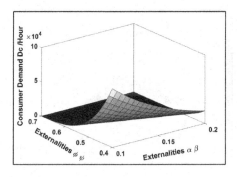

Fig. 11. Number of attracted consumers over $\phi\psi$

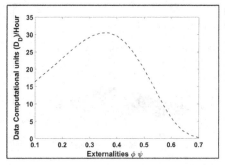

Fig. 12. Mining computational units over $\alpha\beta$

as discussed in Sects. 3.2 and 3.3. Similarly, the payoff of the blockchain node decreases under externalities as shown Figs. 16, 17 and 18.

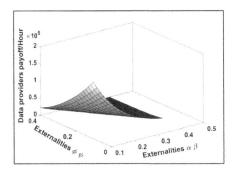

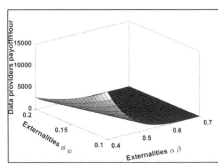

Fig. 13. Data providers payoff over weak externalities

Fig. 14. Data providers payoff over strong externalities $\alpha\beta$

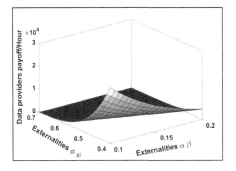

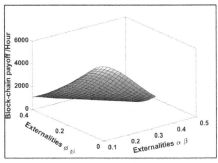

Fig. 15. Data providers payoff over strong externalities $\phi\psi$

Fig. 16. Blockchain payoff over weak externalities

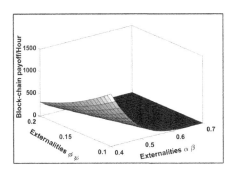

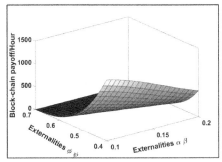

Fig. 17. Blockchain payoff over strong externalities $\alpha\beta$

Fig. 18. Blockchain payoff over strong externalities $\phi\psi$

4 Conclusion

In this work, we proposed a new game-based business model for data trading over blockchain. The problem is formulated as a double two-sided game that solved the problem of maximizing the players' payoff by optimally distributing the mining computational powers over smart contracts. Technically, the game considered the smart contract characteristics as well as the impact of the mining computational units on the data service and consumers' demand. The theoretical and simulation results proved the efficiency of the proposed game.

References

1. DMR Amazon statistical report 2018. https://expandedramblings.com/index.php/downloads/dmr-amazon-web-services-report/. Accessed 31 Jan 2019
2. Amazon: IoT and big data services in Amazon market places. https://aws.amazon.com/marketplace/search?page=1&category=96c2cd16-fe69-4b1899cc-e016c61e820c. Accessed 19 Nov 2019
3. Bataineh, A.S., Mizouni, R., Barachi, M.E., Bentahar, J.: Monetizing personal data: a two-sided market approach. Procedia Comput. Sci. **83**, 472–479 (2016)
4. Bataineh, A.S., Mizouni, R., Bentahar, J., Barachi, M.E.: Toward monetizing personal data: a two-sided market analysis. Future Gener. Comput. Syst. **111**, 435–459 (2020)
5. Danaher, P.J.: Optimal pricing of new subscription services: analysis of a market experiment. Mark. Sci. **21**(2), 119–138 (2002)
6. Fedak, V.: Blockchain and big data: the match made in heavens (2018). https://towardsdatascience.com/blockchain-and-big-data-the-match-made-in-heavens-337887a0ce73. Accessed 02 Jan 2019
7. Google: Google cluster data. https://github.com/google/cluster-data. Accessed 19 July 2019
8. Hu, J., Yang, K., Wang, K., Zhang, K.: A blockchain-based reward mechanism for mobile crowdsensing. IEEE Trans. Comput. Soc. Syst. **7**(1), 178–191 (2020)
9. Jiao, Y., Wang, P., Feng, S., Niyato, D.: Profit maximization mechanism and data management for data analytics services. IEEE Internet of Things J. **5**(3), 2001–2014 (2018)
10. Jiao, Y., Wang, P., Niyato, D., Xiong, Z.: Social welfare maximization auction in edge computing resource allocation for mobile blockchain. In: 2018 IEEE International Conference on Communications (ICC), pp. 1–6 (2018). https://doi.org/10.1109/ICC.2018.8422632
11. Kadadha, M., Otrok, H., Mizouni, R., Singh, S., Ouali, A.: Sensechain: a blockchain-based crowdsensing framework for multiple requesters and multiple workers. Future Gener. Comput. Syst. **105**, 650–664 (2020)
12. Liu, Z., et al.: A survey on blockchain: a game theoretical perspective. IEEE Access **7**, 47615–47643 (2019). https://doi.org/10.1109/ACCESS.2019.2909924
13. Luong, N.C., Xiong, Z., Wang, P., Niyato, D.: Optimal auction for edge computing resource management in mobile blockchain networks: a deep learning approach. In: 2018 IEEE International Conference on Communications (ICC), pp. 1–6 (2018)
14. Rjoub, G., Bentahar, J., Abdel Wahab, O., Saleh Bataineh, A.: Deep and reinforcement learning for automated task scheduling in large-scale cloud computing systems. Concurr. Comput. Pract. Exper. (2020)
15. Rjoub, G., Bentahar, J., Wahab, O.A.: Bigtrustscheduling: trust-aware big data task scheduling approach in cloud computing environments. Future Gener. Comput. Syst. **110**, 1079–1097 (2020)

16. Rjoub, G., Bentahar, J., Wahab, O.A., Bataineh, A.: Deep smart scheduling: a deep learning approach for automated big data scheduling over the cloud. In: 7th International Conference on Future Internet of Things and Cloud (FiCloud), pp. 189–196 (2019)
17. Rochet, J., Tirole, J.: Platform competition in two-sided markets. J. Eur. Econ. Assoc. **1**(4), 990–1029 (2003)
18. Wang, J., Li, M., He, Y., Li, H., Xiao, K., Wang, C.: A blockchain based privacy-preserving incentive mechanism in crowdsensing applications. IEEE Access **6**, 17545–17556 (2018)
19. Xiong, Z., Feng, S., Wang, W., Niyato, D., Wang, P., Han, Z.: Cloud/fog computing resource management and pricing for blockchain networks. IEEE Internet of Things J. **6**(3), 4585–4600 (2019). https://doi.org/10.1109/JIOT.2018.2871706
20. Xiong, Z., Feng, S., Niyato, D., Wang, P., Han, Z.: Optimal pricing-based edge computing resource management in mobile blockchain. In: 2018 IEEE International Conference on Communications (ICC), pp. 1–6. IEEE (2018)
21. Xu, C., et al.: Making big data open in edges: a resource-efficient blockchain-based approach. IEEE Trans. Parallel Distrib. Syst. **30**(4), 870–882 (2019). https://doi.org/10.1109/TPDS.2018.2871449
22. Yang, M., Zhu, T., Liang, K., Zhou, W., Deng, R.H.: A blockchain-based location privacy-preserving crowdsensing system. Future Gener. Comput. Syst. **94**, 408–418 (2019)
23. Yang, R., Yu, F.R., Si, P., Yang, Z., Zhang, Y.: Integrated blockchain and edge computing systems: a survey, some research issues and challenges. IEEE Commun. Surv. Tutor. **21**(2), 1508–1532 (2019). https://doi.org/10.1109/COMST.2019.2894727

A Dynamic Cost Model to Minimize Energy Consumption and Processing Time for IoT Tasks in a Mobile Edge Computing Environment

João Luiz Grave Gross[✉], Kassiano José Matteussi, Julio C. S. dos Anjos, and Cláudio Fernando Resin Geyer

Institute of Informatics, Federal University of Rio Grande do Sul,
Porto Alegre, RS 91509–900, Brazil
{jlggross,kjmatteussi,jcsanjos,geyer}@inf.ufrgs.br
https://www.inf.ufrgs.br/

Abstract. The rapid growth of IoT devices and applications with data-intensive processing has led to energy consumption and latency concerns. These applications tend to offload task processing to remote Data Centers in the Cloud, distant from end-users, increasing communication latency and energy costs. In such a context, this work proposes a dynamic cost model to minimize energy consumption and total elapsed time for IoT devices in Mobile Edge Computing environments. The solution presents a Time and Energy Minimization Scheduler (TEMS) that executes the cost model, validated through simulation, which resulted in a reduction in energy consumption by up to 51.61% and in task completion time by up to 86.65%.

Keywords: Mobile Edge Computing · Internet of Things · Cost minimization model · Energy consumption · Scheduling algorithm

1 Introduction

Billions of smart devices can now connect to the Internet in the form of *Internet of Things* (IoT) and applications have evolved, especially those used in artificial intelligence and computer vision, and require high computing power [7,8]. For these applications, IoT devices usually rely on task processing offload to remote *Cloud Computing* (CC) Data Centers, far away from the end-user, to boost processing time and reduce battery energy consumption. This results in higher latency, which became inefficient for high distributed scenarios [1].

Mobile Edge Computing (MEC) is a suitable alternative to CC, as it provides low latency and better QoS to end-users [3]. It relies on top of high-speed mobile networks such as 5G to allow fast and stable connectivity for mobile devices and users. But energy consumption remains an open issue [6,9], because most IoT devices run on batteries with limited energy capacity and need to handle

© Springer Nature Switzerland AG 2020
E. Kafeza et al. (Eds.): ICSOC 2020, LNCS 12571, pp. 101–109, 2020.
https://doi.org/10.1007/978-3-030-65310-1_8

lots of data, which is energy-consuming. Thus, reducing energy consumption in networks with IoT devices is a goal worth exploring.

This work tackles these issues by proposing a dynamic cost model to minimize energy consumption and task processing time for IoT devices in MEC environments. Also, we propose the TEMS scheduling algorithm that implements the dynamic cost minimization model, which calculates the cost of different allocation options and chooses one that yields the lesser cost for the execution of tasks. Finally, the efficiency of TEMS is evaluated through simulation.[1]

The main contributions of this work are i) we evaluate tasks with different profiles such as critical tasks (with a deadline) and non-critical tasks (without a deadline) in a variety of case scenarios; ii) Our methodology covers a considerable number of energy and time metrics for task processing and data transmissions, including the accounting of CPU cores idle energy; iii) The model uses a DVFS technique aiming to optimize CPU cores processing time and energy consumption; iv) Our model considers three possible processing sites, including processing in the IoT device itself, in a local MEC server and in a remote Data Center from CC; v) We develop and adapt experiments based on a well-defined simulation tool for scenarios with IoT devices, MEC servers, and CC Data Centers.

2   Dynamic Cost Minimization Model

In this section, we introduce a detailed view of our dynamic cost minimization model. Figure 1 presents the architecture design of the system decoupled in three layers, following a bottom-up approach:

- **IoT Layer (L1)**: Composed of IoT devices, which generate the application tasks. They run on batteries and have limited processing power.
- **MEC Layer (L2)**: Composed of MEC servers with a limited number of CPU cores and mid-range processing power. They are close to the end-users, providing small communication delays.
- **CC Layer (L3)**: Composed of Data Centers from CC. They are far located from the end-users, and geographically distributed, with high processing power and high network latency.

For the system we assume set D to be the mobile IoT devices, S the local MEC servers, W the wireless communication channels and A the tasks. Each task A_i is represented by a tuple $A_i = (C_i, s_i, d_i, t_i)$, where $i \in A$.

For each task A_i, C_i represents the number of CPU cycles required for its complete execution. s_i and d_i represent, respectively, the source code and data entry sizes. t_i represents the deadline of the task, which is the maximum time to complete its execution. Tasks can be normal or critical if the deadline is positive.

Also, for every task scheduled to MEC or CC, a wireless channel is associated, which is represented by set H. If a task i is associated with a channel w, then $h_i = w$, otherwise $h_i = 0$ for computation in the IoT device, where h_i is an element of H. Every $h_i \in W \cup 0$.

---

[1] MEC Simulator available at https://github.com/jlggross/MEC-simulator.

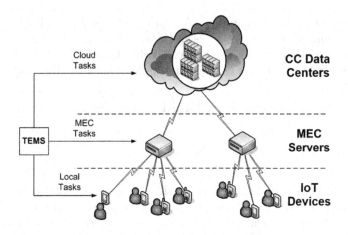

Fig. 1. System architecture and task allocation policies.

2.1 Local Computing in the IoT Device

Each mobile device $j \in D$ has one or more CPU cores, which is given by $PL_j = \{pl_{j,1}, pl_{j,2}, ..., pl_{j,n}\}$. We compute *idle* energy for vacant CPU cores, and dynamic energy ($E_{i,local}$) for occupied ones. Each core has an operating frequency ($f_{local,j,k}$), an effective commutative capacitance ($C_{local,j,k}$) [11], and a voltage supply ($V_{local,j,k}$). Each task i has a total number of CPU cycles (CT_i) for its execution.

The total execution time [11] (Eq. 1), dynamic power (Eq. 2), and dynamic energy consume [5] (Eq. 3) can be calculated as:

$$T_{i,local} = \frac{CT_i}{f_{local,j,k}} \tag{1}$$

$$P_{i,local} = C_{local,j,k} * V_{local,j,k}^2 * f_{local,j,k} \tag{2}$$

$$E_{i,local} = P_{i,local} * T_{i,local} \tag{3}$$

The lesser cost for the system, that provides a better relationship between battery energy consumption and latency, can be expressed by:

$$Cost_{i,local} = u_{localT} * T_{i,local,total} + u_{localE} * E_{i,local} \tag{4}$$

In Eq. 4 u_{localT} and $u_{localE} \in [0,1]$, and $u_{localT} + u_{localE} = 1$. As mentioned in [10] these coefficients are used to represent the weight of time and energy, and work as a trade-off to prioritize the minimization of one of the costs.

2.2 Local Computing in the MEC Server

Every local MEC servers has multiple CPU cores, which is given by $PS_j = \{ps_{j,1}, ps_{j,2}, ..., ps_{j,n}\}$. A $ps_{j,k}$ core has an operating frequency ($f_{mec,j,k}$), an effective commutative capacitance $(C_{mec,j,k})$, and a supply voltage $(V_{mec,j,k})$. Communications between IoT devices and local servers that use the same wireless channel cause mutual interference between each other (I_i). In this case, the data transfer rate $(r_i(h_i))$ attenuates according to *Shannon's formula* [11]:

$$r_i(h_i) = W * \log_2 \left(1 + \frac{p_m * g_{j,m}}{N + I_i} \right) \tag{5}$$

$$I_i = \sum_{n \in A|\{i\}:h_n=h_i} p_{m'} * g_{j',m'} \tag{6}$$

For Eq. 5, W is the channel bandwidth, $g_{j,m}$ is the channel gain between a mobile device m and a local server j. The variable p_m is the transmission power of m when offloading task i to j. N is the power of the thermal noise of the wireless channel, and h_n the wireless channel for task n.

The time required to send data and source code, and download results from an IoT device to a local server are shown below. Also, the total time accounts for these two times plus the task execution time $T_{i,mec}$, calculated the same way as for the IoT devices.

$$T_{i,mec-up}(h_i) = \frac{s_i + d_i}{r_i(h_i)} \tag{7}$$

$$T_{i,mec-down}(h_i) = \frac{d_i'}{r_i(h_i)} \tag{8}$$

$$T_{i,mec,total} = T_{i,mec-up}(h_i) + T_{i,mec} + T_{i,mec-down}(h_i) \tag{9}$$

The energy consumed by the data transmissions is calculated by the transmission power $(p_{wireless})$ times the elapsed time $(T_{i,mec-up}(h_i)$ or $T_{i,mec-down}(h_i))$, resulting in $E_{i,mec-up}(h_i)$ and $E_{i,mec-down}(h_i)$, respectively. Finally, the dynamic energy consumed $(E_{i,mec})$ is calculated as $P_{i,mec} * T_{i,mec}$, and the total dynamic energy consumption is given by:

$$E_{i,mec,total} = E_{i,mec-up}(h_i) + E_{i,mec} + E_{i,mec-down}(h_i) \tag{10}$$

The cost equation for the local server is expressed as follows:

$$Cost_{i,mec} = u_{mecT} * T_{i,mec,total} + u_{mecE} * E_{i,mec,total} \tag{11}$$

2.3   Remote Computing in the Cloud

CC is assumed to have unlimited resources, which is why cores are not distinguished, and *idle* energy not computed. The CC Data Center formulas are very similar from the MEC server formulas, but with some more components such as time spent $(T_{i,cloud-up}$ and $T_{i,cloud-down})$ and energy $(E_{i,cloud-up}$ and $E_{i,cloud-down})$ consumed for transmissions between MEC and CC layers.

$$T_{i,cloud,total} = T_{i,mec-up}(h_i) + T_{i,cloud-up} + T_{i,cloud}$$
$$+ T_{i,cloud-down} + T_{i,mec-down}(h_i) \qquad (12)$$

$$E_{i,cloud,total} = E_{i,mec-up}(h_i) + E_{i,cloud-up} + E_{i,cloud}$$
$$+ E_{i,cloud-down} + E_{i,mec-down}(h_i) \qquad (13)$$

Finally, the cost to run a single task i in CC is given by:

$$Cost_{i,cloud} = u_{cloudT} * T_{i,cloud,total} + u_{cloudE} * E_{i,cloud,total} \qquad (14)$$

2.4   System Dynamic Cost Minimization Equation

For every task i the minimum cost is chosen between all three allocation options, one from each layer. The total system cost is equal the sum of all task costs and idle energy costs.

$$Cost_i = min(Cost_{i,local}, Cost_{i,mec}, Cost_{i,cloud}) \qquad (15)$$

$$Cost_{system} = \sum_{i=1}^{A} Cost_i + E_{local,idle} + E_{mec,idle} \qquad (16)$$

3   Time and Energy Minimization Scheduler (TEMS)

The TEMS heuristic scheduling algorithm executes the dynamic cost minimization model with reduced computational cost. It has complexity $O(n^2)$.

Algorithm 1: Time and Energy Minimization Scheduler (TEMS)

   Result: Task mapping to the processing nodes
1 **execute** Step 1 - Collection of system information and initialization
2 **repeat**
3 | **execute** Step 2 - Task allocation
4 | **execute** Step 3 - Task conclusion monitor
5 | **execute** Step 4 - New tasks and device battery level monitor
6 **until** *user decides to keep running*;

In Algorithm 1 are presented the steps of TEMS. Step 1 defines the sets of the IoT devices, MEC servers, communication channels, and battery levels of the IoT devices. A *Lower Safety Limit* (LSL) is set for the battery capacity, which may not be reached, preventing the device to run out of energy. The algorithm collects the number of CPU nodes available in each IoT device and MEC server, their operating frequencies, and supply voltages.

In step 2, TEMS classifies the tasks between critical and non-critical. Critical tasks are ordered by deadline and scheduled to the CPU with the minimum total elapsed time. Then normal tasks are scheduled to the CPU with lesser total cost.

In step 3, tasks are monitored for their completion status, and when completed, the CPU core resources are released and made available for other allocations in step 2. The battery level check is performed for the IoT devices. Task cancellation may occur if the elapsed time is higher than the deadline or if the IoT device runs out of battery.

Finally, in step 4, the battery level from each IoT device is collected, as well as newly created tasks. Execution continues as long as tasks are being created.

4 Evaluation

This section explains the simulation details and the different experimental scenarios used. The simulated environment was designed with low, mid-range and high processing power devices for IoT, MEC and CC layers, respectively. For IoT devices we chose Arduino Mega 2560, with five operating frequencies and corresponding supply voltages. The MEC servers were simulated on top of 5 Raspberry Pi 4 Model B boards, each board with a Quad-core Cortex-A72 1.5 GHz (ARM v8) 64-bit, summing a total of 20 CPU cores per server. The CPU cores have three operating frequencies and corresponding supply voltages. For CC it was chosen Data Centers with *Intel Xeon Cascade Lake* processors of 2.8 GHz per CPU core, reaching up to 3.9 GHz with *Turbo Boost* on. The network throughput was configured to achieve up to 1 Gbps speed and latencies to 5ms, for both 5G and fiber optics communications [2]. Moreover, two vehicular applications were defined [4], one with high processing workload and high task creation time (Application 1), and another with low processing workload and low task creation time (Application 2).

a. Number of MEC servers: This experiment used Application 1 in two different scenarios. Both with 500 tasks distributed to 100 IoT devices, but one with only a single MEC server (case 1, plot 1) and the second with two MEC servers (case 2, plot 2). Figure 2 shows the results for the execution of Application 1.

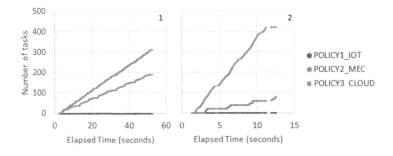

Fig. 2. Task allocation for Application 1.

The energy and time coefficients were set, respectively, as 4/5 and 1/5, that is, a high weight was given to the energy consumed so that it could be minimized. In Fig. 2, from plot 1 to plot 2, the increase in the number of MEC servers made fewer tasks be to allocated in the CC layer, reducing total energy consumed for case 2. Compared to another scenario with the same characteristics, but without MEC servers, the reduction in energy consumption for case 1 was 42.51%, while for case 2 it was 44.71%. Thus, the use of MEC servers helps the system to lower the total energy consumed.

b. Impact on different energy and time coefficients: This experiment used Application 2 in four different scenarios. Each case with 500 tasks, 100 IoT devices, and one MEC server. The energy coefficients were set to 1/5, 2/5, 3/5, 4/5 and the time coefficients to 4/5, 3/5, 2/5 and 1/5.

Table 1. Costs for Application 2, varying the cost coefficients for energy and time.

Case	E_{Coeff}	T_{Coeff}	Cost	E_{Total}	T_{Total}	Policy
$C1$	1/5	4/5	0.01859	0.14550	0.03336	MEC
$C2$	2/5	3/5	0.02597	0.14276	0.03469	MEC
$C3$	3/5	2/5	0.03318	0.14276	0.03469	MEC
$C4$	4/5	1/5	0.03544	0.07040	0.25000	IoT

The lowest calculated cost was the same for cases 2 and 3, with MEC as an offloading option. Case 1 had the lowest calculated cost among all coefficient pairs. In these three cases the time coefficient had high values, and MEC was chosen because task execution got the lowest processing times. For case 4, the allocation took place on the IoT device itself. Now, energy had a high-value coefficient, which made the scheduler choose the policy that provided the lowest energy cost, reducing total cost. In case 4 energy consumption reduced up to 51.61% compared to the other cases. To reduce task completion time, coefficients from cases 1, 2 and 3 are better, with a reduction of up to 86.65% compared to case 4 (Table 1).

c. Impact of input data size: As the size of data entry increases from 3.6MB to 3.6GB, the calculated costs progresses in the MEC and CC allocation policies. The cost to execute in the IoT devices remains the same, as no data transmissions are carried out. When data entry scales, allocation policies that require data transmissions become very costly, and allocation on the device itself becomes increasingly advantageous. We observed that with more tasks with less data per task it is possible to reduce energy and time by up to 29% compared to a scenario with fewer tasks and lots of data per task. With this approach less time is spent waiting for data transmission to end, maximizing CPU usage in the MEC servers.

d. IoT device battery consumption: Battery should stay in healthy levels to avoid reaching the LSL threshold, avoiding the device to be unavailable for processing. Also, adequate task processing workloads may help save battery, extending the operation time of the IoT device.

e. Deadline for critical tasks: Very low deadlines made tasks to be canceled because any given policy could execute the task in a feasible time. Therefore, the deadline must be properly configured for at least one of the allocation policies to have enough time to process and conclude the task correctly.

f. Impact on using the DVFS technique: With DVFS activated, the total energy consumption decreased by 13.74%, while the total time increased by 28.32% in comparison with DVFS off. This demonstrates the effectiveness of the proposed model, and the scheduling algorithm in minimizing total energy consumption. Although the whole time may have been longer in the approach with DVFS, it is no problem because the tasks were completed within the time limit imposed by the deadline.

5 Conclusion

In an environment with accelerated generation of large volumes of data and mobile devices connected to the Internet with restricted QoS requirements and battery limitations, energy and time reduction are mostly needed. The TEMS scheduler could choose the best allocation options in the system, reducing both energy consumption and elapsed time. Experiments show that the adequate adjustment of the cost coefficients were essential for the final cost perceived by the scheduling algorithm. Adequate coefficients allowed the energy in the system to be reduced by up to 51.61% or the total times to be reduced by up to 86.65%, ending critical tasks before deadline. The system has become more sustainable and the user experience has not been affected.

The use of MEC servers helped extend the battery life of the IoT devices and made task execution more agile. Also, using the DVFS technique brought interesting results, helping to reduce the overall energy consumption. Major contributions are the TEMS algorithm, the addition of data transmissions to the model, accounting for idle costs, calculating transmission rate interference, use of the DVFS technique, and the interaction with the CC layer to provide resources whenever the local network becomes saturated.

As future works, we can relate the improvement of the system cost model, with the insertion of new variables and new experiments to explore applications in new scenarios such as industry, healthcare, aviation, mining, among others.

Acknowledgment. This study was financed in part by the Coordenação de Aperfeiçoamento de Pessoal de Nível Superior - Brasil (CAPES) - Finance Code 001. PROPESQ-UFRGS and by projects: "GREEN-CLOUD: Computação em Cloud com Computação Sustentável" (#162551-0000 488-9) and SmartSent (#172551-0001 195-3) from FAPERGS, PNPD Capes, and CNPq Brazil, program PRONEX 122014.

References

1. Aijaz, A.: Towards 5G-enabled tactile internet: radio resource allocation for haptic communications. In: 2016 IEEE Wireless Communications and Networking Conference Workshops, pp. 145–150 (2016)
2. Gupta, A., Jha, R.K.: A survey of 5G network: architecture and emerging technologies. IEEE Access **3**, 1206–1232 (2015)
3. Haouari, F., Faraj, R.: Fog computing potentials, applications, and challenges. In: 2018 International Conference on Computer and Applications, pp. 399–406 (2018)
4. Jansson, J.: Collision avoidance theory with application to automotive collision mitigation. Ph.D. thesis (2005)
5. Liu, Y., Yang, H., Dick, R.P.: Thermal vs energy optimization for DVFS-enabled processors in embedded systems. In: 8th International Symposium on Quality Electronic Design, pp. 204–209 (2007)
6. Matteussi, K.J., Geyer, C.F.R., Xavier, M.G., Rose, C.A.F.D.: Understanding and minimizing disk contention effects for data-intensive processing in virtualized systems. In: 2018 International Conference on High Performance Computing Simulation (HPCS), pp. 901–908 (2018). https://doi.org/10.1109/HPCS.2018.00144
7. Matteussi, K.J., Zanchetta, B.F., Bertoncello, G., Dos Santos, J.D.D., Dos Anjos, J.C.S., Geyer, C.F.R.: Analysis and performance evaluation of deep learning on big data. In: 2019 IEEE Symposium on Computers and Communications (ISCC), pp. 1–6 (2019). https://doi.org/10.1109/ISCC47284.2019.8969762
8. Ravindranath, L., Bahl, P.: Glimpse: continuous, real-time object recognition on mobile devices. In: Proceedings of the 13th ACM Conference on Embedded Networked Sensor Systems, pp. 155–168 (2015)
9. Sarangi, S.R., Goel, S., Singh, B.: Energy efficient scheduling in IoT networks. In: Proceedings of the 33rd Annual ACM Symposium on Applied Computing, pp. 733–740 (2018)
10. Wang, C., Dong, C., Qin, J.: Energy-efficient offloading policy for resource allocation in distributed mobile edge computing. In: 2018 IEEE Symposium on Computers and Communications, pp. 366–372 (2018)
11. Yu, H., Wang, Q., Guo, S.: Energy-efficient task offloading and resource scheduling for mobile edge computing. In: 2018 IEEE International Conference on Networking, Architecture and Storage, pp. 1–4 (2018)

Automated SLA Negotiation in a Dynamic IoT Environment - A Metaheuristic Approach

Fan Li[(✉)] and Siobhán Clarke[(✉)]

Trinity College Dublin, College Green, Dublin, Ireland
{fali,Siobhan.Clarke}@scss.tcd.ie

Abstract. In the Internet of Things (IoT), billions of physical devices, distributed over a large geographic area, provide a near real-time state of the world. By adopting a service-oriented paradigm, the capabilities of mobile or static devices can be abstracted as IoT services and delivered to users in a demand-driven way. In service environments, a particular service provisioning tends to be specified in a service level agreement (SLA), which can be further used to monitor and guarantee the quality of service (QoS). Automatic SLA negotiation can be used to resolve possible conflicts between trading parties, but existing SLA negotiation approaches do not consider the characteristics of an IoT environment. In this paper, we present an automated negotiation strategy for multi-round bilateral negotiation that caters for the level of dynamicity in an IoT environment. The negotiation strategy makes concessions based on the artificial bee colony (ABC) optimization algorithm. The simulation results demonstrate that our proposal provides a better balance between success rate and negotiation utility, compared to other approaches.

Keywords: Internet of Things · SLA · Automatic negotiation · WS-Agreement Negotiation · Artificial bee colony optimization

1 Introduction

The Internet of Things (IoT) envisions a large number of physical objects, connecting over the Internet to provide a near real-time state of the world. By adopting the Service-Oriented Architecture (SOA), a device's capabilities or measurements can be abstracted as services [6] and delivered to applications in a demand-driven way. For mission-critical IoT applications, Service Level Agreements (SLA) are widely used as a contract-like concept to assure the obligations and guarantees of involved parties [5], but the scale of the IoT makes human intervention infeasible for SLA negotiation. An automated, dynamic negotiation process is needed for trading parties to express their preference and resolve possible conflicts. However, existing negotiation strategies may be insufficient for IoT SLA negotiation because they do not consider the characteristics of the IoT environment. Compared to web and cloud services, the negotiable scope of services

© Springer Nature Switzerland AG 2020
E. Kafeza et al. (Eds.): ICSOC 2020, LNCS 12571, pp. 110–120, 2020.
https://doi.org/10.1007/978-3-030-65310-1_9

in the IoT is likely to be more diversified when mobile devices and reconfigurable resources are considered. IoT services also exhibit time-varying QoS levels [12] that may be caused by unpredictable workload, an unstable wireless network, and device malfunction. QoS variability may impact a service provider's negotiation boundaries or negotiation preferences, which further affects negotiation efficiency.

In this paper, we propose a negotiation strategy for multi-round bilateral negotiation, which uses a bio-inspired negotiation tactic to dynamically adjust concessions based on the opponent's behaviour. As resources in the IoT environment are geographically distributed, we assume a negotiation system is deployed on a set of edge devices, which negotiate with service providers for consumers. These edge devices are referred to as negotiation gateways. Providers publish their SLA-supported services to a nearby gateway in the form of SLA templates (SLAT), and wait for negotiation requests. SLATs are partially completed agreements filling default values relating to negotiable SLA terms that the providers are expecting to offer, and the constraints that restrict the values of those negotiable terms. Gateways select candidate service providers by matching a request with registered templates, and send the negotiation request to the candidate service providers to start a bilateral negotiation [10].

In the remainder of this paper, Sect. 2 summarizes related work on SLA negotiation in related field. Section 3 describes the negotiation strategy that uses artificial bee colony optimization to adjust offerings. Section 4 details the experimental setup and evaluation results. Section 5 concludes the paper with a discussion about future research directions.

2   Related Work

Generally, a negotiation strategy is a mathematical model used to evaluate proposals and make decisions [15]. Faratin et al. proposed three types of negotiation tactics agents can employ during a negotiation process: time-dependent, resource-dependent, and behavior-dependent [4]. They concluded that there is a tradeoff between the number of successful deals and the utility gained. To increase negotiation utility, Fharna et al. proposed a policy-based negotiation strategy where agents dynamically adapt decision functions during the negotiation process to comply with an opponent's preferences according to performance observations [18]. However, this adaptation may be inefficient when the strategy adopted by the counterpart is unknown. To balance the success rate and utility for negotiations with incomplete information, Zheng et al. [16] proposed a game-theory based strategy that combines the concession and tradeoff tactics to resolve possible conflicts. However, this does not guarantee a solution will be found when one exists. To optimize negotiation behaviour, some approaches use machine learning techniques and metaheuristic algorithms to learn opponents' negotiation models. Faratin et al. used fuzzy similarity to approximate an opponent's preference, and a hill-climbing algorithm detects a tradeoff offer that might be acceptable by the counterpart [3]. Coehoorn et al. assumed that the opponent employs a time-dependent tactic, and adopted kernel density estimation to estimate the opponent's negotiation preference [2]. Narayanan *et al.* used a Markov chain to model bilateral negotiations among agents, and Bayesian learning for agents to learn the optimal strategy [11]. Sim *et al.* combined Bayesian learning with genetic algorithms (GA) to search for the optimal strategy [13]. Carbonneau *et al.* created a three-layer neural network that exploits information from past counteroffers to predict opponent's future proposals [1]. The drawbacks of these strategies are that they are computationally expensive for multi-issue negotiation, and their assumptions ignore the dynamicity of the opponent's behaviour. When using metaheuristic algorithms, the common disadvantage is the multiple negotiation rounds that are required to find the final solution. Also, GA needs a coding mechanism to transform each possible offer to a real number, which is complex for multivariable problems.

3   Negotiation Strategy

The bilateral negotiation session begins when a negotiation gateway sends the consumer's preferred values as the initial offer to a candidate service provider. The purpose of the negotiation is to reach an agreement that has the best possible utility through a bargaining process. In each round, negotiating parties perform their own negotiation strategies to evaluate a received offer and make decisions about whether to accept/reject the offer or propose a counteroffer. A *Negotiation Offer* proposed by a service provider p to a gateway g at time t is defined as $x^t_{p \to g}$, the value of negotiable term j offered in $x^t_{p \to g}$ is noted by $x^t_{p \to g}[j]$. Each negotiable term j ($j \in 1, ..., k$) has a *negotiation space* noted by Ω^g_j, which is the collection of possible values of term j. In a competitive market, providers may regard some negotiation spaces as business sensitive data and may not be willing to disclose them to the negotiation opponent, which means the negotiation may occur under an assumption of incomplete information.

To measure an offer's satisfaction level, each negotiable term j in the offer is normalized and evaluated by gateways using a score value V^g_j ($V^g_j \in [0,1]$). A higher score represents a higher satisfaction. In our previous work, we have identified four types of negotiable terms for IoT services and defined the scoring functions V^g_j targeting each type [9]. In this paper we assume consumers will not clearly specify their preferences on each negotiable term, the average utility is used to quantitatively measure the negotiation utility of a received offer $x^t_{p \to g}$:

$$U^g(x^t_{p \to g}) = \frac{1}{k} \sum_{j=1}^{k} V^g(x^t_{p \to g}[j]) \tag{1}$$

Each time a gateway g receives one or more counteroffers $X^t_{p \to g}$ from provider p, it evaluates the offers using Eq. 1 and selects the offer with the highest utility $x^t_{p \to g}$ to make decisions (i.e., accept/reject an offer or propose a counter offer). The decision-making process is controlled by WS-Agreement Negotiation's (WSAN) offer state transition model [14]. The WSAN-based decision-making model has been discussed in our previous publication [9]. However, in this paper we use a modified ABC-based negotiation tactic to generate new counteroffers rather than using the context-based tactic.

Algorithm 1. Gateway: Perform ABC-based Tactics

Input: Solutions $F[10]$, received offer of last round $x_{p \to g}^{tr-1}$, the number of current round r, loop limit $Loop_{max}$, request req, similarity factor α, best solution F_{best}

Output: The vector of updated negotiable terms F_{best}

1: $\alpha \leftarrow$ updateSimilarityFactor(r)
2: **if** $F[n]$ **is** null **then** Initialize solutions and bees
3: Evaluation of solutions (α, req, $x_{p \to g}^{tr-1}$)
4: cycle $\leftarrow 0$
5: **while** cycle $\leq Loop_{max}$ **do**
6:     Employed bees phase(α, req, $x_{p \to g}^{tr-1}$, $F[n]$)
7:     $P_r \leftarrow$ Calculate selection probabilities(α, $F[n]$)
8:     **If** $Random(0,1) < P_r$ **then** Onlooker bees phase(α, req, $x_{p \to g}^{tr-1}$, $F[n]$)
9:     **if any** $F[i].T_r > Tr_{max}$ **then** Scout bee phase (req, $x_{p \to g}^{tr-1}$, F_{best}, $F[i]$)
10:     Evaluation of solutions (α, req, $x_{p \to g}^{tr-1}$)
11:     $F_{best} \leftarrow$ memorizeBestSolution($F[n]$)
12: **end while**

The main goal of designing a negotiation tactic is to find the best possible agreement for a specific request that not only satisfies all the user's constraints but also maximizes the utility. However, if both parties are only concerned with their individual utility and ignore the opponent's preference, it is harder to reach an agreement. Automatic negotiation with incomplete information can be modeled as an optimization problem, which tries to find a solution that has the highest possible utility for both parties from all feasible solutions under the partially known negotiation constraints. The Artificial Bee Colony Optimisation (ABC) algorithm is simple and accurate when addressing multivariable problems [7], and we use a modified version to seek a win-win solution from the solution domain. ABC abstracts solutions as food sources and searching for them is performed by three types of specialized bees: scout bees, employed bees, and onlooker bees [17]. They work cooperatively to find a food source with maximum fitness. Algorithm 1 shows how negotiation gateways use the modified ABC to update the expectations of negotiable terms. Different combinations of negotiable terms make up the solution domain. A possible solution is modeled as the position of a food source, which is evaluated by a fitness function. The ABC-based negotiation tactic defines each food source as $F = \{position, bee_e, bee_o, fit, T_r\}$. $position$ is a k-dimension vector $\vec{V_i} = (v_{i,1}, v_{i,2}, ..., v_{i,k})$ representing a possible solution, which contains the expected values of negotiable terms ($i \in [1,n]$, n is the number of food sources, k is the number of negotiable terms), bee_e and bee_o are the associated employed bee and onlooker bee respectively, fit is the fitness value and T_r is the number of times that a solution has been exploited. Initially, ten solutions are generated based on a user's most preferred values and the first received counter offer $x_{p \rightarrow g}^{t_1}$(Line 2). The elements in initial position vector $\vec{V_i}$ are computed using Eq. 2:

$$v_{i,j} = \text{Min}\{\text{Max}\{N \left(\frac{v_{prf,j} + x_{p \rightarrow g}^{t_1}[j]}{2}, \left| v_{prf,j} - x_{p \rightarrow g}^{t_1}[j] \right| \right), min_j\}, max_j\} \quad (2)$$

where $N(\cdot)$ denotes a Gaussian distribution with mean $(v_{prf,j} + x_{p \rightarrow g}^{t_1}[j])/2$ and variance $\left| v_{prf,j} - x_{p \rightarrow g}^{t_1}[j] \right|$, $v_{prf,j}$ is the user's most preferred term value j. max_j and min_j are the upper and lower boundaries of the term's negotiation space j. Gaussian distributed values are used rather than randomly distributed values as in the standard ABC to avoid too many concessions in the early stage when the maximum number of iterations is limited. The standard ABC algorithm usually has thousands of iterations, which introduces latency. Reducing the number of iterations reduces the solution accuracy, but decreases computation complexity. To make the algorithm more lightweight, in each round, the maximum number of loops (Line 5) is defined as:

$$Loop_{max} = 2(mt + r) \quad (3)$$

where 2 is the scale factor, r is the current round number, mt is a constant positive integer, representing the minimum times a solution can be exploited initially. The sum of mt and r is the limit of exploitation times as the negotiation processes. Equation 3 shows that more loops is introduced when r is increasing.

Through the next repeated cycles, the ten solutions are modified by the searching processes of different bees (Line 6–9) and evaluated according to a fitness function (Line 10). The particular mechanism for finding a win-win solution is that each solution is evaluated by its utility and the absolute cosine similarity between the current solution and the counteroffer proposed by the opponent. The fitness function of solution $\vec{V_i}$ is defined as:

$$fit(\vec{V_i}) = \begin{cases} 0, & U^g(\vec{V_i}^{\,t}) > U^g(\vec{V_i}^{\,t-1}) \\ (1 - \alpha) \times U^g(\vec{V_i}^{\,t}) + \alpha \times sim(\vec{V_i'}, \vec{S'}), & \text{otherwise.} \end{cases} \quad (4)$$

where $U^g(\vec{V_i}^{\,t})$ is $\vec{V_i}$'s utility at time t (Eq. 1). $\vec{S'}$ is the normalized[1] vector of an opponent's expectation, extracted from the optimal counteroffer of the last round $x_{p \rightarrow g}^{t_{r-1}}$. $\vec{V_i'}$ is the normalized $\vec{V_i}$. α is the similarity factor for the weight of making concessions ($\alpha \in (0,1)$), which gradually increases from C_0 to C_1:

$$\alpha = C_0 + C_1 \frac{e^{\beta \hat{r}} - 1}{e^\beta - 1}, (0 < C_0 + C_1 < 1) \quad (5)$$

where $\hat{r}$ is the ratio of the current round to the maximum negotiation round. β is an integer that controls the change rate of α ($|\beta| < 10$). A negative β means

---

[1] The values of terms are normalized using the score functions V_j^g defined in [9].

α increases quickly at the start but gets slower as the negotiation proceeds, while positive β does the opposite. The negotiation is more conservative when β is positive. Equation 4 and Eq. 5 show that the fitness evaluating criteria weight dynamically changes as the negotiation proceeds. The fitness is set to zero when the solution has higher utility than the last proposal since the solution is likely to be rejected by the opponent. The fitness function illustrates why more iterations are needed as the rounds increase (Eq. 3). This avoids conservatism in the early stage, and increases the chance of finding a better solution that has higher utility when the concession rate increases. In the repeated iteration, the searching process is performed in three phases: employed bee phase (Line 6), onlooker bee phase (Line 8), and scout bee phase (Line 9), as follows:

Employed Bee Phase: Each employed bee searches for a new solution depending on the current one $\vec{V_i}$ and another random one $\vec{V_m}$ ($k \in \{1,...,n\}, k \neq i$). For all elements $v_{i,j}$ in $\vec{V_i}$, new values are generated as follows [17]:

$$v'_{i,j} = \text{Min}\{\text{Max}\{v_{i,j} + [2Random(0,1) - 1](v_{i,j} - v_{m,j}), min_j\}, max_j\} \quad (6)$$

where $v_{m,j}$ is the value of term j in $\vec{V_m}$ ($j \in \{1,...,k\}$), $Random(0,1)$ is a uniformly distributed random number (range $[0,1]$). If the new solution $\vec{V'_i}$ has a higher fitness, it replaces the old $\vec{V_i}$. Otherwise the solution exploitation time increases by 1.

Onlooker Bee Phase: After an employed bee completes its searching process, the current solution's information is shared with the associated onlooker bee, which decides whether to exploit it based on the probability computed by fitness:

$$Prob(F_i) = \frac{fit(F_i)}{\underset{l \in n}{\text{Max}}\{fit(F_l)\}} \quad (7)$$

Considering the iterations limit, maximum fitness is used as the denominator instead of the sum of fitness defined in standard ABC to increase the chance of discovering a better solution. Based on the probability and Roulette-wheel selection mechanism, the onlooker bee may further modify the current solution by following the same searching process defined in the employed bee phase.

Modified Scout Bee Phase: After all the onlooker bees are distributed, the solution whose exploitation time reaches the limit is exhausted, and the corresponding employed bees turn into scout bees to find a new solution. In classic ABC, the scout bee randomly chooses a solution that satisfies the boundary constraint (Eq. 9). However, when the number of iterations is limited, a more efficient searching mechanism that accelerates the convergence process is needed. Inspired by the bare bones particle swarm algorithm [8], here, a Gaussian barebone searching equation uses the global best solution and received counteroffer. For all elements $v_{i,j}$ in $\vec{V_i}$, new values are generated as follows:

$$v_{i,j} = \text{Min}\{\text{Max}\{N\left(\frac{v_{best,j} + x_{p \to g}^{tr-1}[j]}{2}, |v_{best,j} - x_{p \to g}^{tr-1}[j]|\right), min_j\}, max_j\} \quad (8)$$

where $v_{best,j}$ is the global best solution's term j. Solution $\vec{V_i'}$ is further compared with the random solution (Eq. 9) to select the solution with the higher fitness.

$$v_{i,j} = min_j + Random(0,1)(max_j - min_j) \tag{9}$$

4   Evaluation

4.1   Experimental Setup

In the simulation experiment, there are two types of providers: static and mobile. Mobile providers are more likely to provide a service that can satisfy the spatial requirement, while static providers have a limited negotiation space for the spatial feature. The price for a mobile service linearly depends on the standard Euclidean distance between the current offering and the requested properties; while the price for a static service is restricted by a range if the price is negotiable (PIN), or a static value if it is non-negotiable (PNN). The service providers are classified based on the service level they can provide: high-performance (HP) services, moderate-performance (MP) services, and low-performance (LP) services. The intersection degree of negotiation space between negotiating parties is set to 0.7, 0.4 and 0.2 for HP, MP and LP providers respectively. We assume the simulation environment is a rectangular area where latitude varies from 53.33385 to 53.35556, and longitude varies from -6.27963 to -6.23328. Static HP providers have six service instances uniformly distributed in the area, while MP and LP providers have four and two service instances respectively. For mobile providers, the probability of satisfying a user's spatial requirement is set to 0.9, 0.5, 0.2 for HP, MP and LP providers. If the requested location is not acceptable, a mobile provider offers a random location within 1 km around the requested location.

In our scenario, a service consumer is randomly distributed in the simulation area, and requests a hazardous gas monitoring service. Negotiation on price, sample rate, accuracy, availability and response time is needed to satisfy its requirements. Two test cases simulate different environments: (i) In test case A, one mobile provider (MP) and one static provider (MP-PNN) are the negotiation candidates (i.e., resource-limited environment); (ii) In test case B, six mobile providers (LP, MP, and HP) and six static providers (LP-PIN, LP-PNN, MPPIN, MP-PNN, HP-PIN, HP-PNN) are the negotiation candidates (i.e., resource-rich environment). To reduce chance variation, we repeated the experiment 100 times under each test case. In each trial, each requested term's negotiation constraint is randomly generated based on a pre-defined range. The ABC-based tactic's parameters are set as $C_0 = 0$, $C_1 = 0.9$, $mt = 5$, $\beta = 1$. This experiment is implemented with Java using Eclipse Mars IDE.

4.2   Result

Two metrics are used to evaluate the performance of the ABC-based negotiation strategy (ABC): average negotiation utility and success rate. The negotiation utility is the utility of the acceptable offer used to create the final SLA, which is computed by Eq. 1. We compare the performance against other four tactics, which demonstrate a good balance between utility and success rate: the game theory-based strategy for cloud service negotiation (UMC) [16], the behavior-dependent relative tit for tat tactic (BDR), the time-dependent linear tactic (TDL) and the resource-dependent patient tactic (RDP) [4]. In the experiment, providers play the TDL tactic while the gateway plays the five different tactics.

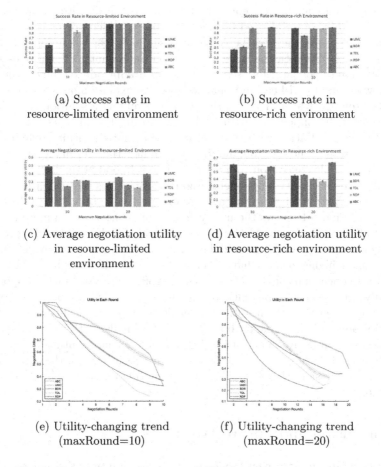

(a) Success rate in resource-limited environment

(b) Success rate in resource-rich environment

(c) Average negotiation utility in resource-limited environment

(d) Average negotiation utility in resource-rich environment

(e) Utility-changing trend (maxRound=10)

(f) Utility-changing trend (maxRound=20)

Fig. 1. Negotiation performance of ABC-based negotiation strategy

The results in Fig. 1 show the average negotiation utility and success rate using different negotiation tactics when the maximum negotiation round R increases. When R is set to 10, ABC and UMC outperform other tactics in utility in a resource-rich environment. When the available resources are limited, ABC has moderate utility, lower than UMC and BDR, but it maintains a much higher success rate. Figure 1e shows the utility-changing trend of solutions under this situation. Each graph shows the mean utility observed in each round with the error band representing the standard errors. ABC concedes more in the early negotiation rounds but becomes more conservative as the negotiation proceeds. Once the negotiation deadline approaches, it becomes more inclined to concede again, trying to reach an agreement with the service provider. ABC controls the balance between success rate and negotiation utility by dynamically changing fitness values and restricting the number of search iterations. From Eq. 4 and Eq. 5, when $C_0 = 0$, $C_1 = 0.9$, the fitness value in the early negotiation rounds mainly depends on the solution's utility. Equation 3 shows that fewer iterations are allowed during the process, which prevents ABC from being too greedy. As the negotiation proceeds, the fitness value depends more on the similarity between the detected solution and counter offer proposed by the negotiation opponent. More search iterations are introduced during the process, allowing employed bees and onlooker bees to explore more solutions than the earlier rounds, which increases the chance of finding a solution more likely to be accepted by opponents, without losing too much utility. This process is similar to the negotiation with the tradeoff tactic that the utility remains at a similar level from round 3 to round 6. In the final negotiation round, ABC makes the largest possible concession to maximize the likelihood of the last offer being accepted by the negotiation opponent. Figure 1 also shows that when R is set to 20, ABC demonstrates better and more stable performance in both utility and success rate. Figure 1f shows the utility change of solutions when more interactions are allowed. Similarly, ABC makes concessions in the early/ending rounds but is more conservative in the middle rounds than other tactics, which means it maintains a higher utility than other approaches. Although both ABC and BDR adjust concessions based on recent counteroffers proposed by the opponent, BDR only imitates the opponent's behaviour, while ABC combines the opponent's counteroffer with the negotiation deadline and its self utility to search for a win-win solution acceptable for both parties. This makes ABC more adaptable to the negotiation environment, achieving higher negotiation utility than BDR. Also, the irregular utility change in each round makes it hard for the opponent to predict the concession, therefore the risk of accepting an offer with lower utility is reduced.

5   Conclusion and Future Work

To enable an agreement-driven service provisioning, a negotiation component is necessary to resolve possible conflicts on service properties between the trading parties. In this paper, we proposed a metaheuristic negotiation strategy that uses the artificial bee colony algorithm to find a win-win solution through a bargaining process. The proposed strategy demonstrates better and more stable performance in terms of utility and success rate compared to the other four popular approaches. This strategy can be used for SLA negotiation with incomplete information, specially when the user does not specify any negotiation preference in the request. However, this strategy may be trapped into the current optimum for several rounds when the constraint on negotiation deadline is loose. In future work, we will modify the searching equations and possibly, add an opponent behaviour learning mechanism to overcome this problem.

Acknowledgment. This work was funded by Science Foundation Ireland (SFI) under grant 13/IA/1885.

References

1. Carbonneau, R., Kersten, G.E., Vahidov, R.: Predicting opponent's moves in electronic negotiations using neural networks. Expert Syst. Appl. **34**(2), 1266–1273 (2008)
2. Coehoorn, R.M., Jennings, N.R.: Learning on opponent's preferences to make effective multi-issue negotiation trade-offs. In: Proceedings of the 6th International Conference on Electronic Commerce. ACM (2004)
3. Faratin, P., Sierra, C., Jennings, N.R.: Using similarity criteria to make issue trade-offs in automated negotiations. Artif. Intell. **142**(2), 205–237 (2002)
4. Faratin, P., Sierra, C., Jennings, N.R.: Negotiation decision functions for autonomous agents. Robot. Auton. Syst. **24**(3–4), 159–182 (1998)
5. Grubitzsch, P., Braun, I., Fichtl, H., Springer, T., Hara, T., Schill, A.: ML-SLA: multi-level service level agreements for highly flexible IoT services. In: 2017 IEEE International Congress on Internet of Things (ICIOT). IEEE (2017)
6. Kantarci, B., Mouftah, H.T.: Sensing services in cloud-centric Internet of Things: a survey, taxonomy and challenges. In: 2015 IEEE International Conference on Communication Workshop (ICCW). IEEE (2015)
7. Karaboga, D., Akay, B.: A comparative study of artificial bee colony algorithm. Appl. Math. Comput. **214**(1), 108–132 (2009)
8. Kennedy, J.: Bare bones particle swarms. In: Proceedings of the 2003 IEEE Swarm Intelligence Symposium, SIS 2003 (Cat. No. 03EX706). IEEE (2003)
9. Li, F., Clarke, S.: A context-based strategy for SLA negotiation in the IoT environment. In: 2019 IEEE International Conference on Pervasive Computing and Communications Workshops (PerCom Workshops). IEEE (2019)
10. Li, F., Palade, A., Clarke, S.: A model for distributed service level agreement negotiation in Internet of Things. In: Yangui, S., Bouassida Rodriguez, I., Drira, K., Tari, Z. (eds.) ICSOC 2019. LNCS, vol. 11895, pp. 71–85. Springer, Cham (2019). https://doi.org/10.1007/978-3-030-33702-5_7
11. Narayanan, V., Jennings, N.R.: Learning to negotiate optimally in non-stationary environments. In: Klusch, M., Rovatsos, M., Payne, T.R. (eds.) CIA 2006. LNCS (LNAI), vol. 4149, pp. 288–300. Springer, Heidelberg (2006). https://doi.org/10.1007/11839354_21
12. Shao, R., Mao, H., Jiang, J.: Time-aware and location-based personalized collaborative recommendation for IoT services. In: 2019 IEEE 43rd Annual Computer Software and Applications Conference (COMPSAC), vol. 1. IEEE (2019)
13. Sim, K.M., Guo, Y., Shi, B.: BLGAN: Bayesian learning and genetic algorithm for supporting negotiation with incomplete information. IEEE Trans. Syst. Man Cybern. Part B (Cybern.) **39**(1), 198–211 (2009)
14. Waeldrich, O., et al.: WS-Agreement Negotiation Version 1.0 (2011)
15. Yao, Y., Ma, L.: Automated negotiation for web services. In: 11th IEEE Singapore International Conference on Communication Systems, ICCS 2008. IEEE (2008)

16. Zheng, X., Martin, P., Brohman, K., Da, X.L.: Cloud service negotiation in Internet of Things environment: a mixed approach. IEEE Trans. Ind. Inform. **10**(2), 1506–1515 (2014)

17. Zhou, X., Wu, Z., Wang, H., Rahnamayan, S.: Gaussian bare-bones artificial bee colony algorithm. Soft Comput. **20**(3), 907–924 (2014). https://doi.org/10.1007/s00500-014-1549-5

18. Zulkernine, F.H., Martin, P.: An adaptive and intelligent SLA negotiation system for web services. IEEE Trans. Serv. Comput. **4**(1), 31–43 (2011)

PATRIoT: A Data Sharing Platform for IoT Using a Service-Oriented Approach Based on Blockchain

Faiza Loukil[1]([⊠]), Chirine Ghedira-Guegan[2], and Aïcha-Nabila Benharkat[3]

[1] University of Lyon, University Jean Moulin Lyon 3, CNRS, LIRIS, Lyon, France
faiza.loukil@liris.cnrs.fr

[2] iaelyon School of Management, University of Lyon, University Jean Moulin Lyon 3, CNRS, LIRIS, Lyon, France
chirine.ghedira-guegan@univ-lyon3.fr

[3] University of Lyon, INSALyon, CNRS, LIRIS, Lyon, France
nabila.benharkat@insa-lyon.fr

Abstract. The Internet of Things has emerged as a paradigm in a variety of application domains where several parties share data to tackle specific tasks. However, these IoT data can be sensitive and the data subject wish not share them with other competitor organizations without retaining some level of control. Thus, a privacy-preserving, user-centric, and transparent solution is needed to deal with the challenges of IoT data sharing, such as the loss of control over the shared data, the trust need in data consumer infrastructure, and the lack of transparency in terms of data handling. Therefore, we propose PATRIoT, a privacy-preserving PlATfoRm for IoT data sharing using a service-oriented approach. The latter is proposed based on the blockchain technology, which enforces privacy requirement compliance according to the General Data Protection Regulation. For validation purposes, we deploy the proposed solution on a private Ethereum blockchain and give the performance evaluation.

Keywords: Privacy · IoT · Blockchain technology · Data sharing

1 Introduction

The Internet of Things (IoT) is a paradigm that improves delivering advanced services in a wide range of application domains. Indeed, multiple devices collect, exchange, store, and process a large amount of fine-granularity and high-frequency data in every aspect of life [4]. However, these smart devices have limited memory and storage capabilities, so they collect and send IoT data to consumers' external platforms to be stored and analyzed. Indeed, these external platforms receive these IoT data and use them to personalize services, optimize decision-making processes, and predict future trends. However, the produced IoT data are generally rich in sensitive data and their analysis allows data consumers

© Springer Nature Switzerland AG 2020
E. Kafeza et al. (Eds.): ICSOC 2020, LNCS 12571, pp. 121–129, 2020.
https://doi.org/10.1007/978-3-030-65310-1_10

to deduce personal behaviors, habits and preferences of data subjects.[1] Indeed, collecting data in IoT applications increases the data subject's worries about the potential uses of these data. Hence, centralizing the storage and analysis of a huge amount of data poses significant issues in terms of data subject privacy, such as the loss of control over the externalized data, the need to trust the consumer platforms, and the lack of data handling transparency. To overcome the aforementioned issues, various legislative bodies have enacted privacy legislation, such as the General Data Protection Regulation (GDPR) [9] in Europe that gives data subjects rights to be informed how their personal information are handled by consumers. However, a user-centric and transparent solution for ensuring that these rights are respected in the IoT domain is still missing.

Motivated by the limited computing capabilities of smart devices, the sensitive feature of IoT data, and the increasing privacy legislation pressure, we propose PATRIoT, a preserving privacy PlATfoRm for IoT data sharing while adapting a service-oriented approach based on the blockchain technology. PATRIoT provides a set of services, generic enough to be applied to a large variety of IoT applications. These services can be deployed over a given architecture to make applications aware of users' privacy requirements, such as data purpose, disclosure, and retention. The components of PATRIoT are built around the semantic description of data (e.g., data sensitivity level, data purpose, etc.) without storing personal data. Furthermore, the reason behind the blockchain technology use is its immutable nature secured by a peer-to-peer network. It hosts smart contracts which contain conditions to trigger and actions to execute if the conditions are satisfied. In our case, the conditions represent the preferences and requirements of the data subjects concerning their IoT data privacy that need to be respected by consumers. Thus, the smart contract use prevents any attempt to violate privacy by ensuring that the shared data are handled as expected during their lifecycle.

This paper is organized as follows. Section 2 analyses existing solutions that studied the privacy-preserving issue in the IoT domain. Section 3 describes the proposed system model. Experiments and results are detailed in Sect. 4. Finally, Sect. 5 concludes the paper and presents some future endeavors.

2   Related Work

Early attempts to incorporate blockchain technology into IoT proposed new blockchain systems. For instance, Dorri et al. [8] proposed a custom blockchain, where the home gateways hold the role of the miners. Such a solution is hard to be deployed since they require a "critical mass". As it seems relevant to new IoT solutions, it is worth building on existing technologies to be compatible with already available libraries and wallets. More recent attempts are using blockchain and smart contracts to provide security and access control for IoT. Novo [11] proposed an IoT access control system with gateway nodes, which are responsible for handling resource requests by taking into consideration the policies stored in the

---

[1] Data subject: any person whose personal data are being collected, held or processed.

blockchain. For their part, Zhang et al. [12] proposed a smart contract-based access control system while an IoT gateway handles resource requests. These solutions encoded statically in smart contracts the actions a specific consumer can perform to a particular IoT device/data. Furthermore, the blockchain technology is also used in the healthcare field. For instance, Dagher et al. [7] proposed a blockchain-based framework for secure access to medical records by several parties, while preserving the patients' privacy. However, this work cannot perform data erasure, since it stored some personal data in the blockchain. To overcome this issue, an off-chain distributed database can be used to store the shared IoT data to guarantee data subjects' right to be forgotten as required by the GDPR.

3   System Model Overview

Despite the increasing legislation pressure, several privacy requirements have been less addressed in the IoT domain. Using a service-oriented approach to address the GDPR compliance makes it easier to the data consumers to build new applications or change existing applications while ensuring the enforcement of the data subject privacy thanks to smart contracts. For this purpose, we propose the system model that is depicted in Fig. 1. It consists of five involved parties, namely data producer, blockchain and smart contract, PATRIoT platform, distributed database, and data consumer. The PATRIoT platform aims at providing an environment that allows data subjects to easily exercise their rights defined by GDPR and assisting data consumers to meet the GDPR requirements using a privacy ontology and the blockchain technology. To this end, PATRIoT has been designed to be an IoT data sharing platform while adapting a service-oriented approach that provides several components including the privacy preference matching service and the privacy policy compliance service.

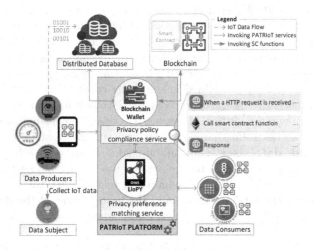

Fig. 1. System model

In the rest of this section, we first outline the proposed model core components, then describe the IoT data sharing process.

3.1 Core Components Description

Figure 1 depicts the model components, which we describe hereafter:

Data producer: it is an IoT device equipped with sensing and communication capabilities that allow it to collect data, communicate with other devices, or connect to the Internet. In this work, a mobile phone can provide a user-friendly environment for data subjects in order to control their shared data and manage their privacy preferences thanks to the privacy preference matching service.

Privacy preference matching service: it is responsible for matching the data subjects' and data consumers' privacy requirements that are served as inputs, then generating a common privacy policy, as an output. This privacy policy consists of several rules that specify why, when, how, to whom and for how long the requested IoT data are handled. To ensure privacy preference matching, the PATRIoT platform adopted the data privacy ontology, called LIoPY and the reasoning process that we have previously proposed in [10]. Indeed, LIoPY ontology models the privacy requirements in the IoT environment and the common privacy policy that will be enforced by the blockchain and smart contracts.

Blockchain and smart contract: blockchain is responsible for transparency, integrity, non-repudiation, and validity of the data handling operations. Moreover, it hosts a privacy policy as a set of self-enforcing and machine-readable rules using smart contracts [6]. Therefore, we propose IoTDataSharing, a smart contract that aims at addressing the data subject's control enforcement over the shared data and assisting the data consumers to meet the fundamental GDPR requirements. The predefined smart contract's functions can be invoked by the data producers and consumers by means of the privacy policy compliance service.

Privacy policy compliance service: it is responsible for exposing the functionality of the deployed smart contract as an application REST interface for simpler external application interaction with the blockchain. Both POST and GET methods are provided to push transactions and query for transactions on the blockchain. These methods can invoke the smart contract's functions. Indeed, this service ensures that the data sharing management works properly according to the access authorizations defined in the smart contract while eliminating the data producers' needs to interact directly with the blockchain due to their limited memory and storage capabilities. Moreover, it verifies the consumer's permissions before allowing access to the shared data that are stored in distributed databases.

Distributed database: it is an off-chain database, used to store the IoT data. It is a peer-to-peer storage system used to overcome the expensive cost of storing IoT data on the blockchain and to guarantee the right to be forgotten defined by the GDPR. Thus, only the hash pointer of the data location is exchanged by the blockchain's transactions between the data producers and the data consumers.

Data consumer: it can be a medical application, an energy substation, or a traffic routing station that can use the privacy preference matching service

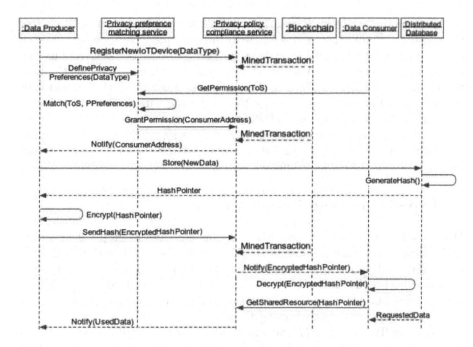

Fig. 2. The process for IoT data sharing using the PATRIoT platform. Assume that actors have established a blockchain address prior to this process.

to request data subjects' consents and the privacy policy compliance service to handle the requested data transparently and unambiguously.

For more details, we refer the reader to a full description that is available on.[2]

3.2 Blockchain-Based IoT Data Sharing Process

Figure 2 depicts the process of sharing IoT data between data producers and consumers using the PATRIoT platform while logging the established communication on the blockchain. This process begins by registering a new data producer using the RegisterNewIoTDevice function to store the producer's blockchain address and its sensed data type on the IoTDataSharing smart contract. Once the privacy preferences are defined, the data consumer asks for getting permission by specifying its terms of service, such as the requested data type, why, to whom, and for how long the data are used. Then, the privacy preference matching service matches the received terms of service with the data subject's privacy preferences, off-chain. In case of a match, the service uses the Grant-Permission function to add the consumer's blockchain address to the authorized consumers' list stored in the smart contract that notifies the producer of the new consumer. When the data producer collects new data, it sends them to the distributed database that generates a hash pointer of the file location and

---

[2] https://www.dropbox.com/s/levxfzid1s3o50b/PATRIoT.pdf?dl=0.

returns it to the producer. The latter encrypts the received hash pointer using the consumer's public key and sends it to the consumer. Once mined, the consumer receives the transaction, retrieves the encrypted hash pointer, and uses its private key to decrypt the hash pointer. When the consumer obtains the hash pointer of the file location, it uses the GetSharedResource function provided by the privacy policy compliance service to retrieve the data from the distributed database or invoke one of the IoTDataSharing smart contract functions to handle the data. By using the privacy policy compliance service, the data subject is periodically informed how the data are handled and can easily add or revoke authorization to the data consumers.

4   Experiments and Result Analysis

Due to a lack of space, we only show in this section the proposal feasibility by implementing smart contracts, but the entire proposal is designed for a service-oriented architecture deployment. As Ethereum is currently the most common blockchain platform for the development of smart contracts [6], we implemented our smart contract using the Solidity language [1] and deployed it to the Ethereum test network using Ganache [2]. Therefore, we created a test system using Truffle development framework [3], used InterPlanetary File System (IPFS) [5] as an off-chain distributed database, and deployed the PATRIoT services to Swarm that is a Docker orchestration tool.

4.1   Computation Time Cost

In order to measure the performance of our solution, we conducted some experiments to compute the computational time cost of both addFile and updateFile functions defined on the IoTDataSharing smart contract. Thus, we performed add file operation by adding random file contents for 100 repetitions. We measured the required time to off-chain compute the file content's hash and execute the addFile function (see Fig. 3a) and the updateFile function (see Fig. 3b) by making several tests while increasing the file size from 1KB to 2MB. We observe that the processing time of updating an existing file that varies from 95 to 180 ms is less than the processing time of adding a new file that varies from 257 to 390 ms.

4.2   Cost Overhead

To evaluate the PATRIoT efficiency, we conducted an experiment to measure the gas[3] used by a transaction to invoke one of the IoTDataSharing smart contract's functions, namely addFile, updateFile, addConsumer, and removeConsumer.

Table 1 illustrates the average gas usage and cost per invoked function. We observe that the gas used by a transaction changed depending on the function. This can be explained by the fact that functions that require more computational resources cost more gas than functions that require few computational resources.

---

[3] gas: it is a measure unit of the cost necessary to perform a transaction on the network.

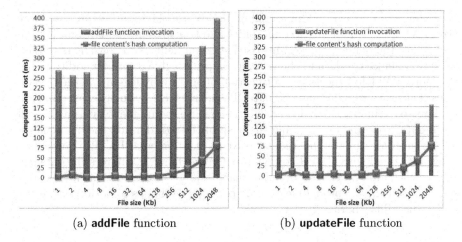

(a) **addFile** function   (b) **updateFile** function

Fig. 3. Average processing time of two functions with different file size

Table 1. Cost overhead

Invoked function	Average *Gas* Usage (*gas*)		Average *Gas* Cost (USD)
	File size = 1KB	File size = 2MB	
addFile	471959	471959	3,00
updateFile	28946	28946	0,18
addConsumer	332429	332429	2,11
removeConsumer	23456	23456	0,15

Moreover, we used in this experiment two file sizes, namely 1KB and 2MB. We deduce that the *gas* used by the transactions is independent of the file size. This can be explained by the fact that the functions only used the file content's hash whose bit length is fixed and equal to 32 bits. Thus, the file size has no impact on the cost overhead of our proposal. Indeed, this latter can be used in case of files with a huge amount of data without increasing the cost overhead.

Table 1 also illustrates the average gas cost of the four smart contract's functions. Currently, 1 *gas* costs about 20 Gwei (i.e., $20 * 10^{-9}$ Ether) and the exchange rate is about 318 USD for 1 Ether at the time of writing. Thus, we compute the *gas* cost by multiplying the used *gas* by the *gas* price for each function. Therefore, we can deduce that our solution is not a cost-expensive one.

After evaluating the performance, we analyze below the legal compliance.

4.3 PATRIoT Platform in Legislation Context: GDPR Compliance

PATRIoT aims at achieving the GDPR compliance by meeting several privacy requirements. First, PATRIoT meets the consent requirement by using the IoT-DataSharing smart contract that offers to the data subjects the ability to manage their consents by easily adding, modifying, and revoking authorizations. Moreover, PATRIoT establishes accountability and transparency of data sharing process. Thus, the defined blockchain-based solution helps data consumers to automate compliance checks and allows for a comprehensible record for auditing. Furthermore, PATRIoT meets the notification obligation by logging all the transactions that prove who has handled data. Thus, any privacy violation attempts can be detected. Finally, PATRIoT meets the erasure requirement by using the off-chain data store and only storing the hash of the IoT data on the blockchain.

By meeting the aforementioned privacy requirements, PATRIoT addresses areas associated with GDPR compliance. On one hand, it enforces the data subject's ownership and control over the shared data. On the other hand, it can be seen as a consumer's proof of legislation compliance thanks to both transparency and auditability characteristics.

5   Conclusion

In recent years, several researchers have agreed that the blockchain technology can be used to improve the data subject privacy in the IoT domain while being GDPR compliant. In this context, we proposed PATRIoT, an IoT data sharing platform for preserving privacy using a service-oriented approach based on blockchain. Indeed, we proposed a smart contract that ensures that the shared data will be handled as expected. Besides, we relied on off-chain database use to store the shared IoT data. In our future work, we aim at continuing research in the use of blockchain to meet other privacy legislative standards by deploying a Blockchain as a Service to be available for all actors in different domains.

References

1. Solidity language (2014). https://solidity.readthedocs.io/en/develop/. Accessed 20 Aug 2020
2. Ganache: Personal blockchain for ethereum development (2016). https://www.trufflesuite.com/ganache. Accessed 20 Aug 2020
3. Truffle: Ethereum development framework (2016). https://github.com/trufflesuite/truffle. Accessed 20 Aug 2020
4. Atzori, L., Iera, A., Morabito, G.: The Internet of Things: a survey. Comput. Netw. **54**(15), 2787–2805 (2010)
5. Benet, J.: IPFS-content addressed, versioned, P2P file system (2014)
6. Buterin, V., et al.: A next-generation smart contract and decentralized application platform. White paper (2014)
7. Dagher, G.G., Mohler, J., Milojkovic, M., Marella, P.B.: Ancile: Privacy-preserving framework for access control and interoperability of electronic health records using blockchain technology. Sustain. Cities Soc. **39**, 283–297 (2018)
8. Dorri, A., Kanhere, S.S., Jurdak, R., Gauravaram, P.: Blockchain for IoT security and privacy: the case study of a smart home, pp. 618–623 (2017)

9. GDPR: Regulation (EU) 2016/679 of the European parliament and of the council of 27 April 2016 on the protection of natural persons with regard to the processing of personal data and on the free movement of such data, and repealing directive 95/46. Off. J. Eur. Union (OJ) **59**, 1–88 (2016)

10. Loukil, F., Ghedira-Guegan, C., Boukadi, K., Benharkat, A.N.: LIoPY: a legal compliant ontology to preserve privacy for the Internet of Things. In: 2018 IEEE 42nd Annual Computer Software and Applications Conference (COMPSAC), pp. 701–706. IEEE (2018)

11. Novo, O.: Blockchain meets IoT: an architecture for scalable access management in IoT. IEEE Internet of Things J. **5**(2), 1184–1195 (2018)

12. Zhang, Y., Kasahara, S., Shen, Y., Jiang, X., Wan, J.: Smart contract-based access control for the Internet of things. IEEE Internet of Things J. **6**(2), 1594–1605 (2018)

Services at the Edge

Energy Minimization for Cloud Services with Stochastic Requests

Shuang Wang[1,2(✉)], Quan Z. Sheng[2], Xiaoping Li[1], Adnan Mahmood[2], and Yang Zhang[2,3]

[1] Southeast University, Nanjing, Jiangsu, China
{wangshuang,xpli}@seu.edu.cn
[2] Macquarie University, Sydney, Australia
{michael.sheng,adnan.mahmood}@mq.edu.au
[3] Wuhan University, Wuhan, Hubei, China
yangz10@whu.edu.cn

Abstract. Energy optimization for cloud computing services has gained a considerable momentum over the recent years. Unfortunately, minimizing energy consumption of cloud services has its own unique research problems and challenges. More specifically, it is difficult to select suitable servers for cloud service systems to minimize energy consumption due to the heterogeneity of servers in cloud centers. In this paper, the energy minimization problem is considered for cloud systems with stochastic service requests and system availability constraints where the stochastic cloud service requests are constrained by deadlines. An energy minimization algorithm is proposed to select the most suitable servers to achieve the energy efficiency of cloud services. Our intensive experimental studies based on both simulated and real cloud instances show the proposed algorithm is much more effective with acceptable CPU utilization, saving up to 61.95% energy consumption, than the existing algorithms.

Keywords: Energy minimization · Cloud service · Service request · Quality of Service · Rejection probability · System availability

1 Introduction

Energy optimization is not only important for protecting environments because it mitigates the carbon emission, but also indispensable for the cloud providers since it reduces the electricity consumption. It is estimated that 70 billion kilowatt-hours of electricity, i.e., about 1.8% of the total electricity consumption of the United States, is consumed in 2014 alone for cloud services [11]. According to the International Energy Agency's New Policies Scenario, which takes account of existing and planned government policies, the world primary energy demand is projected to be increased by 37% between 2012 and 2040 [23]. Energy consumption is directly proportional to power consumption. To reduce power consumption in computing systems, there are in general two approaches:

© Springer Nature Switzerland AG 2020
E. Kafeza et al. (Eds.): ICSOC 2020, LNCS 12571, pp. 133–148, 2020.
https://doi.org/10.1007/978-3-030-65310-1_11

(a) *thermal-aware hardware design* and (b) *power-aware software design* [20]. The thermal-aware hardware design approaches are related to hardware devices, while on the contrary, the power-aware software design approaches involve computing systems, including operating system-level power management, compiler-level power management, application-level power management, and cross-layer adaptations [20]. Our work falls largely as one of the power-aware software design methods.

In this paper, we take into consideration of the energy consumption minimization problem for stochastic requests with deadlines. Service requests arrive at the cloud centers both stochastically and dynamically while servers are heterogeneous in nature with different configurations. Dealing with stochastically arriving requests and heterogeneous servers in cloud service systems is a complex problem in its own essence [8,22]. The power consumption of servers and the response time of service requests are typically negatively correlated. If the service rate of servers is higher, more power is consumed and the service requests are processed quicker, thereby leading to a smaller response time. In addition, it is hard to evaluate the energy consumption with different service rates of servers in cloud systems. Server selection is a NP-hard problem. This is further complicated when selecting optimal number of servers from the cloud centers to minimize the energy consumption, with the needs to satisfy the deadlines of service requests and the system availability [15] (which defines the probability that requests can be processed) constraints of the selected servers. The major contributions of this work are as the following:

- We develop a novel cloud service system model that is based on the *queuing theory* to deal with the stochastic property of the cloud service requests. The model enables the efficient server selection by considering i) service request arrival rates, ii) service rates of the cloud servers, iii) deadlines of the service requests, and iv) the system availability constraints.
- The energy consumption of a cloud service system is measured by the power consumption of the servers based on their response time of the service requests, which is calculated by a proposed *energy evaluation* (EE) algorithm. We further develop an *energy minimization* (EM) algorithm to select suitable servers to minimize the energy consumption while meeting the service request deadlines and system availability constraints.
- We conduct extensive experimental studies using both simulated and real-life cloud instances and the results show the effectiveness of our proposed approach on energy optimization of cloud services.

The rest of the paper is organized as follows. In Sect. 2, we discuss the related work and in Sect. 3, we detail the model and formulate the research problem. The energy optimization algorithms are presented in Sect. 4. Finally, the experimental results are reported in Sect. 5, followed by conclusions and future research directions in Sect. 6.

2   Related Work

Energy consumption is closely related to power consumption. A stochastic activity network model was constructed to evaluate the power consumption and performance of servers in cloud computing [3]. By allocating the power to the servers, the overall quality of service (QoS) of the servers in the data center was optimized [7]. A heuristic algorithm was presented to minimize the energy consumption on the condition of location constraint of nodes [21]. A brownout-based approximate Markov Decision Process approach was proposed to improve trade-offs between energy saving and discount offered to service users [22]. The key novelty was to reduce the cumulative power by the dynamic voltage scaling [1]. A Constrained Markov Decision Process model was built for power management in web server clusters [18]. The energy consumption was minimized by optimizing the power consumption of different servers in [1, 7, 18] while the deadline constraint of service requests was not considered. In this paper, we consider the stochastic service requests with deadline constraint and the suitable servers are selected to minimize the energy consumption. The dynamic property of the queue capacity makes the energy consumption minimization problem different from the existing problems tackled in [1, 7, 18].

Low energy consumption and high service performance (e.g., response time, reliability and service level agreement) are usually negatively correlated. Higher performance implies less response time and faster service rates while lower energy implies lower allocated power which results in slower service rates and longer response time. A suitable queuing model was built to satisfy the conflicting objectives of high performance and low power consumption in [10]. Mobile devices were modeled as a semi-Markov decision process to achieve a good balance between the application execution time and power consumption [2]. The balance between higher performance and lower energy was studied in [2,10]. In [19], two novel adaptive energy-aware algorithms were proposed to achieve energy efficiency while minimizing SLA (service-level agreement) violation rate in cloud data centers. When balancing the performance and energy consumption, the queue capacity in [2,10] is determined while in our paper, the queue capacity changes dynamically with different servers.

Energy minimization with heterogeneous cloud servers has been studied in [6,8,14]. When the servers are heterogeneous, the server sequence has to be certain for performance analysis since different server sequences lead to different results. The heterogeneity of servers make problem more difficult. In this paper, heterogeneous servers in cloud service systems are considered with deadline constraint, which is not handled in the existing works [6,8,14].

3   Cloud Service System Model and Problem Description

In this section, the cloud service system model is constructed and then the research problem is formally defined.

3.1 Cloud Service System Model

When service requests arrive, cloud providers offer suitable servers to deal with the requests while minimizing the energy consumption. The arrival rate of the service requests is assumed to follow a Poisson distribution with parameter λ [9]. Let us assume that there are N heterogeneous servers in the cloud service system and the number of selected servers is n $(n \leq N)$. According to our recent work [15], the service rates of the servers, which are the speed of requests processed by the servers, are assumed to follow exponential rates with $\mu_1, \cdots, \mu_N$. The deadline of service requests is denoted as D which implies that requests are processed before the arriving time plus D. All requests have the same D. The rejection probability is assumed to be P_R and the system availability is ξ.

The model of the cloud service system can be constructed, as illustrated in Fig. 1. Once the service requests arrive at the cloud system, a dedicated server is firstly selected to process these requests. If more requests arrive, requests wait in the queue. Due to the deadline constraint, the maximum number of service requests is computed by the selected server and if the system availability is satisfied, no more server will be selected. Requests are executed by the selected servers. Otherwise, more servers will be considered by iteration in order to meet the requirement of the system availability.

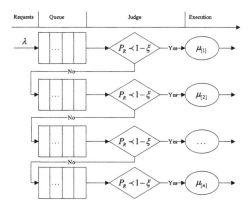

Fig. 1. Cloud service system model based on the queuing theory.

The queuing theory [13] is adopted in terms of the stochastic property of the cloud service requests. $R_{[i]}(i \in \{1, \cdots, n\})$ is the maximum queue length when the server with service rates $\mu_{[i]}$ is selected to process requests. $R_{[i]}$ is determined in terms of comparing the response time of requests processed by service rate with $\mu_{[i]}$ to the deadlines. $\{0, 1, \cdots, i, \cdots, \sum_{j=1}^{n} R_{[j]} + n\}$ is the state space where i is the number of service requests in the system. According to the system model in Fig. 1, states $\{0, 1, \cdots, 1 + R_{[1]}\}$ correspond to the first selected server with service rate $\mu_{[1]}$. States $\{\sum_{j=1}^{i-1} R_{[j]} + i, \cdots, \sum_{j=1}^{i} R_{[j]} + i\}$ correspond to the ith

selected server with service rate $\mu_{[i]}$. When $1 - \xi \leq P_{\sum_{i=1}^{n} R_{[i]}+n}$, no new server will be selected. According to the stochastic property of requests and servers, the cloud service system is a Markov process. For the first selected server, the arrival rate of requests is λ while the arrival rate of next selected servers is the rejection probability that requests cannot be processed by the previous selected server by the arrival rate λ. The state transition process is shown in Fig. 2.

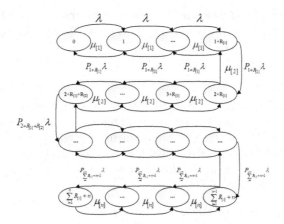

Fig. 2. State transition process.

According to the state transition process described in Fig. 2, the input rate of requests is equal to the output rate of requests for each state. Denote $P_i (i \in \{0, 1, \cdots, 1 + R_{[1]}\})$ as the steady state probability for state i. Therefore, the balance equations for the first server are:

$$\lambda P_0 = \mu_{[1]} P_1 \tag{1}$$

$$(\lambda + \mu_{[1]}) P_1 = \lambda P_0 + \mu_{[1]} P_2 \tag{2}$$

$$\cdots$$

$$\lambda P_{R_{[1]}} = \mu_{[1]} P_{1+R_{[1]}} \tag{3}$$

In addition, the steady state probabilities $P_0, P_1, \cdots, P_{1+R_{[1]}}$ satisfy

$$\sum_{i=1}^{1+R_{[1]}} P_i = 1 \tag{4}$$

$\rho_{[1]}$ is denoted as $\frac{\lambda}{\mu_{[1]}}$. According to Eq. (1), Eq. (2) and Eq. (3), it is obtained

$$P_1 = \rho_{[1]} P_0 \tag{5}$$

$$P_2 = \rho_{[1]}^2 P_0 \tag{6}$$

$$\cdots$$

$$P_{1+R_{[1]}} = \rho_{[1]}^{1+R_{[1]}} P_0 \tag{7}$$

P_0 is calculated in terms of Eq. (4), (5), (6) and (7):

$$P_0 = \begin{cases} \dfrac{1 - \rho_{[1]}}{1 - \rho_{[1]}^{R_{[1]}+2}} & \rho_{[1]} \neq 1 \\[4mm] \dfrac{1}{2 + R_{[1]}} & \rho_{[1]} = 1 \end{cases} \tag{8}$$

The steady state probabilities in different states are calculated according to Eq. (5), (6), (7) and (8). Based on the steady state probabilities, the rejection probability $P_{r_{[1]}}$ is calculated using:

$$P_{r_{[1]}} = P_{1+R_{[1]}} \tag{9}$$

The rejection probability $P_{r_{[1]}}$ is related to the system availability ξ. When the nth server is selected, it should meet the requirement of the system availability ξ, which implies that $P_{r_{[n]}} \leqslant 1 - \xi$. For minimizing the energy consumption, when a server is selected, the rejection probability $P_{r_{[1]}}$ should be as small as possible so that more service requests can be processed. The relationship between $P_{r_{[1]}}$ and $R_{[1]}$ can been proved in Theorem 1.

Theorem 1. $P_{r_{[1]}}$ decreases with the increase of $R_{[1]}$.

Proof. According to (8), $P_{r_{[1]}} = \dfrac{(1-\rho_{[1]})\rho_{[1]}^{1+R_{[1]}}}{1-\rho_{[1]}^{2+R_{[1]}}}$. The derivative of $P_{r_{[1]}}$ is calculated as

$$\frac{DP_{r_{[1]}}}{DR_{[1]}} = \frac{((1 - \rho_{[1]})\rho_{[1]}^{1+R_{[1]}})'(1 - \rho_{[1]}^{2+R_{[1]}}) - (1 - \rho_{[1]}^{2+R_{[1]}})'((1 - \rho_{[1]})\rho_{[1]}^{1+R_{[1]}})}{(1 - \rho_{[1]}^{2+R_{[1]}})^2}$$

$$= \frac{((1 - \rho_{[1]})\rho_{[1]}^{1+R_{[1]}})\ln \rho_{[1]}(1 - \rho_{[1]}^{2+R_{[1]}}) + \rho_{[1]}^{2+R_{[1]}}\ln \rho_{[1]}(1 - \rho_{[1]})\rho_{[1]}^{1+R_{[1]}}}{(1 - \rho_{[1]}^{2+R_{[1]}})^2}$$

$$= \frac{((1 - \rho_{[1]})\rho_{[1]}^{1+R_{[1]}})\ln \rho_{[1]}}{(1 - \rho_{[1]}^{2+R_{[1]}})^2} \tag{10}$$

When $0 < \rho_{[1]} < 1$, it is easy to calculate that only $\ln \rho_{[1]} < 0$ which results in $\frac{DP_{r_{[1]}}}{DR_{[1]}} < 0$. $P_{r_{[1]}}$ decreases with the increase of $R_{[1]}$. When $\rho_{[1]} = 1$, according to Eq. (5), (6), (7) and (8), the steady state probabilities are the same for all states. $P_{r_{[1]}}$ decreases with the increase of the number of states which results from the increase of $R_{[1]}$. When $\rho_{[1]} > 1$, only $1 - \rho_{[1]} < 0$. $\frac{DP_{r_{[1]}}}{DR_{[1]}} < 0$. Therefore, $P_{r_{[1]}}$ decreases with the increase of $R_{[1]}$. ∎

Based on the steady state probabilities, it is easy to calculate the number of requests in the cloud service system. The number of service requests $L_{[1]}$ in the system is

$$L_{[1]} = \sum_{i=0}^{1+R_{[1]}} i \times P_i \qquad (11)$$

Based on $L_{[1]}$, the response time of requests is determined. The response time of requests $T_{r_{[1]}}$ is determined based on the Little theorem [5]:

$$T_{r_{[1]}} = \frac{L_{[1]}}{\lambda(1 - P_{r_{[1]}})} \qquad (12)$$

If $T_{r_{[1]}} \leq D$, compared $P_{r_{[1]}}$ to $1 - \xi$, $R_{[1]}$ is calculated. With the ξ (system availability) and D (service requests deadline) constraints, servers are selected to minimize the energy consumption in a cloud system. When the next server is selected, the arrival rate of requests changes with the current rejection probability $P_{r_{[i]}}$. Similar to the first selected server, the balance equations for the ith selected server are obtained. The steady state probabilities are computed in terms of the balance equations. The rejection probability $P_{r_{[i]}}$ and the expected response time of requests are calculated by using Eq. (9) and (12).

Energy consumption is measured by the power consumption of servers based on the response time of requests. According to [8], the power consumption of a server is determined by $W = wCV^2\eta$, where w is the switching activity, C the electrical capacitance, V the supply voltage and η the clock frequency. For any physical server with a service rate $\mu_{[i]}$, $\mu_{[i]} \propto \eta$ and $\eta \propto V^\phi$ with $0 < \phi \leq 1$. $\eta \propto V^\phi$ implies $V \propto \eta^{1/\phi}$. According to [17], $\mu_{[i]} \propto \eta$ and $V \propto \eta$ imply $W_{[i]} \propto \mu_{[i]}^\alpha$ where $\alpha = 1 + 2/\phi \geq 3$, i.e., P can be represented by $\kappa\mu_{[i]}^\alpha$ where κ is a constant:

$$W_{[i]} = \kappa\mu_{[i]}^\alpha + W^*. \qquad (13)$$

W^* is the static power consumption.

3.2   Problem Description

Since the number of servers are dynamic, the expected energy consumption is calculated in terms of the expected response time of service requests, the power consumption of servers, and the probability of states calculated by the corresponding servers. The total number of service rates should be not less than λ to balance the system. Otherwise, the system could break down. The energy consumption minimization problem is therefore formally described as follows:

$$\min E = (1 - P_{r_{[1]}})W_{[1]}T_{r_{[1]}} + \sum_{i=2}^{n} \prod_{j=1}^{i-1} P_{r_{[j]}}(1 - P_{r_{[i]}})W_{[i]}T_{r_{[i]}} \qquad (14)$$

$$\lambda \leq \sum_{i=1}^{n} \mu_{[i]} \qquad (15)$$

$$1 - \xi \leq P_{\sum_{i=1}^{n} R_{[i]} + n} \qquad (16)$$

$$T_{r_{[i]}} \leq D \quad i \in \{1, 2, \cdots, n\} \qquad (17)$$

$$n \leq N \qquad (18)$$

According to Eq. (12), we can have $T_{r_{[i]}} = \frac{L_{[i]}}{\lambda(1-P_{r_{[i]}})}$. Therefore, the following equation is obtained:

$$
\begin{aligned}
E &= (1 - P_{r_{[1]}})W_{[1]}T_{r_{[1]}} + \sum_{i=2}^{n}\prod_{j=1}^{i-1} P_{r_{[j]}}(1 - P_{r_{[i]}})W_{[i]}T_{r_{[i]}} \\
&= (1 - P_{r_{[1]}})W_{[1]}\frac{L_{[1]}}{\lambda(1 - P_{r_{[1]}})} + \sum_{i=2}^{n}\prod_{j=1}^{i-1} P_{r_{[j]}}(1 - P_{r_{[i]}})W_{[i]}\frac{L_{[j]}}{P_{r_{[j]}}\lambda(1 - P_{r_{[i]}})} \\
&= \sum_{i=1}^{n}\frac{W_{[i]}L_{[i]}}{\lambda}
\end{aligned}
\tag{19}
$$

Therefore, Eq. (14) is transformed equivalently into $E = \sum_{i=1}^{n}\frac{W_{[i]}L_{[i]}}{\lambda}$.

4   Energy Minimization Algorithm

Energy minimization is closely related to the response time of service requests, the number of servers and the power consumption in a cloud service system. To solve the problem, different servers are selected to satisfy the deadline constraint and minimize the energy consumption. The number of service requests waiting in the cloud system is determined by the selected servers. The queue capacity is determined firstly by considering the deadline constraint D and the system availability ξ by Algorithm 1 according to which the energy consumption is evaluated. After energy evaluation, selected servers are determined to minimize the energy consumption in Algorithm 2.

The Energy Evaluation (EE) algorithm (see Algorithm 1) is proposed to evaluate the energy consumption of a selected server. μ is assumed as the service rate of the selected server. With the increase of R, the response time of service increases while the rejection probability decreases gradually. With the deadline D and the system availability ξ constraints, the queue capacity R is determined (lines 3–6). The number of requests in the cloud service system is computed (line 7) and the power consumption for the selected server is calculated (line 8). The energy consumption E is evaluated (line 9). The time complexity of Algorithm 1 is determined by the queue length R.

Different servers are selected to minimize the energy consumption in the cloud service system by Algorithm 2. E^{o} is the energy consumption vector for the selected servers and P_{r}^{o} is the rejection probability vector for the selected servers. $U = \{\mu_1, \cdots, \mu_N\}$ is the server set. E is the energy consumption vector for servers. E_{sum} is the total energy for the selected servers. The arrival rates of service requests for the next server is determined by the current rejection probability in terms of Fig. 2. During the server selection procedure, N servers are evaluated firstly (lines 5–6). Since the rejection probability in the cloud service system and the energy consumption have different ranges and units, we employ a min-max normalization. We use E' and P_{r}' to denote the values of E^{o} and P_{r}^{o} after min-max normalization, respectively (line 9). When selecting

---

Algorithm 1: Energy Evaluation (EE) Algorithm

    Input: μ, ξ

1 **begin**

2     $R \leftarrow 0$, $T_r \leftarrow 0$, $P_R \leftarrow 1$;

3   **while** $T_r < D \& P_R > 1 - \xi$ **do**

4        $R \leftarrow R + 1$;

5   Calculate T_r by Eq. (12) and μ;   /* Response time calculation*/

          Calculate P_R by Eq. (9);   /* Rejection probability calculation*/

6   Calculate L by R and μ;   /*The number of requests calculation*/

       Calculate W by Eq. (13);   /*Power consumption calculation*/

       $E \leftarrow \frac{LW}{\lambda}$;   /*Energy consumption evaluation*/

7 **return** R, P_R, E.

---

more servers, the rejection probability of the system decreases while the energy consumption increases. We denote $r = \frac{P_r{'}}{E'}$ as the selection metric (line 9). A server with the min (r) value is selected to minimize energy consumption (lines 10–11). With the constraint of system availability ξ, different servers are selected and the number of servers n is determined (lines 3–13). The nth server is compared with the rest servers to minimize the energy consumption further because one of the rest servers may be better than the last selected server with the system availability ξ and deadline D constraints (lines 15–24). The time complexity of Algorithm 2 is $O(NR)$.

5 Experiments

In the proposed EM algorithm, there are five system parameters and we will first present our experiments to calibrate the parameters using simulated cloud instances. We then present experimental results to compare the proposed EM algorithm against three existing algorithms using both simulated and real-life instances. All compared algorithms are coded in MATLAB and un on an Intel Core i7-4770 PC (CPU@3.20 GHz, RAM@8 GBytes).

5.1 Parameter Calibration

For energy minimization in a cloud service system, the commonly tested parameters are: the total number of servers in a cloud service system N, the service rates of the N heterogeneous servers, the service request arrival rate λ, the request deadline D, and the system availability ξ. To statistically analyze the effects of the system parameters on the proposed algorithm framework, we calibrate these parameters over randomly generated test instances.

    Since the values of the calibrated parameters should be as close as possible to real scenarios, we set the parameter configurations according to the Alicloud[1]

---

[1] https://github.com/alibaba/clusterdata.

Algorithm 2: Energy Minimization (EM) Algorithm

Input: U, λ, ξ

1 **begin**

2      $E^o \leftarrow \mathbf{0}$, $\mathbf{P}_r^o \leftarrow \mathbf{0}$, $U_s \leftarrow \emptyset$;

3   **while** $P_R > 1 - \xi$ **do**

4          $E \leftarrow \mathbf{0}$, $\mathbf{P}_r \leftarrow \mathbf{0}$, $r \leftarrow \mathbf{0}$, $E_{sum} \leftarrow 0$;

5   **for** $i = 1$ **to** N **do**

6              $[R, E_i, \mathbf{P}_{r\,i}] \leftarrow EE(\mu_i, \xi)$;   /*Energy evaluation*/

7          $r_{min} \leftarrow 10$, $\mathbf{P}_r{}' \leftarrow \mathbf{0}$, $E' \leftarrow 0$;

8   **for** $i = 1$ **to** N **do**

9              $E_i' \leftarrow \frac{E_i - \min(E)}{\max(E) - \min(E)}$, $\mathbf{P}_r{}'_i \leftarrow \frac{\mathbf{P}_{r\,i} - \min(\mathbf{P}_r)}{\max(\mathbf{P}_r) - \min(\mathbf{P}_r)}$,
             $r_i \leftarrow \frac{\mathbf{P}_r{}'_i}{E_i'}$;   /*Normalization*/

10   **if** $r_i \leqslant r_{min}$ **then**

11                  $r_{min} \leftarrow r_i$, $k \leftarrow i$;   /*the ith server selection*/

12          $U \leftarrow U - \mu_k$, $U_S \leftarrow U_S \cup \mu_k$, $n \leftarrow n + 1$, $N \leftarrow N - 1$;

13          $P_R \leftarrow \mathbf{P}_{r\,k}$, $P_{ri}^o \leftarrow \mathbf{P}_{r\,k}$, $E_i^o \leftarrow \mathbf{E}_k$, $E_{sum} \leftarrow E_{sum} + \mathbf{E}_k$;

14   /*Last server determination*/;

15   **for** $i = 1$ **to** N **do**

16          $R \leftarrow 1$, $T_R \leftarrow 0$;

17   **if** $n > 1$ **then**

18              $P_R \leftarrow P_{r(n-1)}^o$;

19   **else**

20              $P_{ri}^o \leftarrow 1$;

21          $[R, E_1, P_R] \leftarrow EE(\mu_i, \xi)$;   /*Energy evaluation*/

22      $E' \leftarrow E_n^o$;

23   **if** $E_1 < E'$ **then**

24          $E_{sum} \leftarrow E_{sum} - E' + E_1$, $E' \leftarrow E_1$, $P_{rn}^o \leftarrow P_R$, $U_{Sn} \leftarrow \mu_i$;

25 **return** R, E_{sum}.

---

as: $N \in \{10, 20, 30, 40\}$, $\lambda \in \{\{1, \ldots, 20\}, \{21, \ldots, 40\}, \{41, \ldots, 60\}, \{61, \ldots, 80\}\}$(per second), $D \in \{0.2, 0.4, 0.6, 0.8, 1\}$(second), $\xi \in \{0.55, 0.65, .75, 0.85, 0.95\}$. The maximum service rate of cloud servers is assumed to be $\mu \in \{10, 20, 30, 40\}$(per second). The service rates of heterogeneous servers are determined by $\mu_i = \frac{i\mu}{N}(i \in \{1, \cdots, N\})$. Therefore, there are $4 \times 4 \times 5 \times 5 \times 4 = 1,600$ parameter combinations in total. Five instances are generated randomly for each arrival rate λ, i.e., five instances are generated for each combination, that is, $1,600 \times 5 = 8,000$ instances in total are tested for calibrating the parameters combinations.

Th experimental results are analyzed by using the multi-factor analysis of variance (ANOVA) statistical technique [15]. Three main hypotheses (normality, homoscedasticity, and independence of the residuals) are checked from the residuals of the experiments. All three hypotheses can be accepted by considering the well-known robustness of the ANOVA technique. The resulting p-values

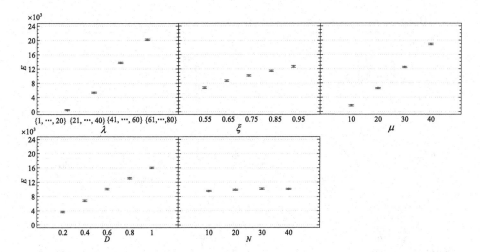

Fig. 3. Means plot of the five studied parameters with 95% confidence level Tukey HSD intervals.

are less than 0.05, meaning that all studied factors have a significant impact on the response variables at the 95% confidence level within ANOVA.

The means plot of the five studied factors on the total energy consumption E with 95% HSD (Tukey's Honest Significance Differences) intervals is shown in Fig. 3 and we can observe that:

- λ has a great influence on energy consumption E. With an increase in the upper bound of λ, E increases with statistically significant differences. E becomes minimum when λ takes values from $\{1, \ldots, 20\}$. The reason lies in that fewer arriving service requests can be processed by servers with small service rates, which consumes few energy.
- ξ greatly influences energy consumption. E increases with the increase of ξ. The differences are statistically significant. E becomes the minimum when ξ=0.55. The reason lies in that a higher ξ implies less rejection probability which requires more servers.
- Similarly, μ has a great impact on E. E takes the minimum value when $\mu = 10$ because a bigger μ implies more power consumption.
- D has a great influence on E. With an increase in D, the energy E increases. A bigger D results in an increase in the response time of requests for servers.
- Though the statistical differences of N on E are insignificant, which implies that the number of servers are satisfied with the stochastic requests, E becomes maximum when N equals 30.

5.2   Algorithm Comparison

During server selection, the FS (Fastest Server) policy always selects the fastest server while the Random policy selects servers randomly when the system availability is not satisfied. To minimize the energy consumption, the rejected requests

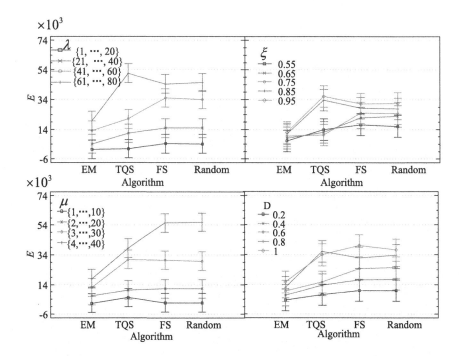

Fig. 4. The mean plots of the interactions between each parameter and the four compared algorithms.

that current server cannot process will be executed by the next selected servers while in the traditional queuing system (TQS) $M/M/N/N + R$ [13], it implies that service requests are processed immediately when there are idle servers. In our experiments, we compare EM with these three methods.

Algorithm Comparison over Simulated Instances. Since there are no benchmark instances for the considered problem, we first compare the four algorithms across simulated instances. Based on the calibrated results in Sect. 5.1, the system parameters $N=10$ and other parameters are the same as Sect. 5.1. Five instances are randomly generated for each of the 400 combinations, i.e., 2,000 instances are tested on each of the four algorithms. The results are shown in Fig. 4.

From Fig. 4, we can see that when the arrival rate λ takes a value from $\{61, \ldots, 80\}$, EM obtains the smallest E while TQS obtains the largest. FS and Random perform similarly. In other words, with an increase in service requests arrival rate λ, EM becomes more effective than the other three algorithms.

With an increase in ξ from 0.55 to 0.95, EM always results in the smallest E whereas TQS becomes the largest. FS is always worse than Random with a larger E. The higher values of ξ demonstrate the superiority of E. Random has the largest E which is similar to FS. The energy on TQS is smaller than FS. EM

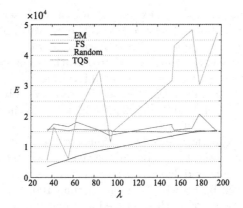

Fig. 5. Algorithm comparison over real instances.

is much more robust than the other three algorithms, i.e., with an increase in μ, the performance of EM fluctuates less than the other three. Similarly, with an increase of D, FS obtains the largest E, while EM gets the smallest E. Random is a littler larger than TQS.

Table 1. Algorithm comparison

	EM	TQS	FS	Random
E	9,398.28	21,220.6	24,705.0	24,659.6
CPU time	0.0043	0.0003	0.0023	0.0021

To further compare the algorithms, the average performance on effectiveness (the average energy consumption) and efficiency (CPU time) are shown in Table 1. According to Table 1, we can observe that EM obtains the smallest E, 9,398.28, followed by 21,220.6 of TQS. FS obtains the largest E 24,705 and for Random, it is 24,659.6. Comparing to TQS, FS, and Random, EM can save up to 61.95% energy consumption. Although EM has the longest CPU time of 0.0043 s, it is still comparable to the other three algorithms and acceptable in practice.

Algorithm Comparison over Real Instances. To evaluate the performance in real systems, the real production Cluster-trace-v2018[2] published by the Alibaba Group is analyzed, which contains eight-day sample data from one of the production clusters. By analyzing the *start_time*[3] of requests [15], the arriving time interval is obtained which implies that the arrival rates are Poisson distributed. According to *start_time* and *end_time*[4], the execution times of

---

[2] https://www.aliyun.com.
[3] http://clusterdata2018pubcn.oss-cn-beijing.aliyuncs.com/batch_task.tar.gz.
[4] http://clusterdata2018pubcn.oss-cn-beijing.aliyuncs.com/batch_instance.tar.gz.

all servers are calculated and the execution time of each server is exponential with different arrival rates and service rates. The arrival rate λ is analyzed by different types of service requests. The service rates $\mu_{[i]}$ $(i \in \{1, \ldots, N\})$ are evaluated by different types of servers. Similar to the simulated instances, D, ξ are set to 0.2, 0.95 respectively because the information on these parameters is not available in the real instances. The service rates are obtained with $\{14.5, 15.4, 16.9, 17.4, 18.5, 19.4, 20.4, 21.3, 22.8, 23.9\}$ [15] and the number of servers is already known, i.e., $N = 10$.

Figure 5 shows the performance of the four compared algorithms. It can be observed that our proposed EM algorithm always obtains the smallest values as λ increases. FS, Random and TQS fluctuate as λ is less than 100. TQS is worse than Random followed by FS when λ is bigger than 100.

From the experiments on both simulated and real instances, we can observe the similar results in terms of algorithm performance. Our proposed EM algorithm always achieves the best performance on energy consumption.

6   Conclusion

Energy optimization of cloud computing services has been a key challenge due to their unique characteristics such as dynamic and stochastic service requests and heterogeneous cloud servers. In this paper, we present a novel approach to minimize the energy consumption by selecting appropriate cloud servers with the consideration of the service request deadline and system availability constraints. In particular, we develop a new cloud service system model based on the queuing theory to deal with stochastic service requests. An energy minimization (EM) algorithm is proposed to select the most suitable servers to achieve the energy efficiency while satisfying service request deadlines and system availability constraints. Our experimental studies show that the EM algorithm saves up to 61.95% energy consumption than the other algorithms. Ongoing work will focus on further improving our model by relaxing some constraints, e.g., the Poisson distribution of service requests.

References

1. Bilal, K., Fayyaz, A., Khan, S.U., Usman, S.: Power-aware resource allocation in computer clusters using dynamic threshold voltage scaling and dynamic voltage scaling: comparison and analysis. Cluster Comput. **18**(2), 865–888 (2015). https://doi.org/10.1007/s10586-015-0437-9
2. Chen, S., Wang, Y., Pedram, M.: A semi-Markovian decision process based control method for offloading tasks from mobile devices to the cloud. In: 2013 IEEE Global Communications Conference (GLOBECOM), pp. 2885–2890. IEEE (2013)
3. Entezari-Maleki, R., Sousa, L., Movaghar, A.: Performance and power modeling and evaluation of virtualized servers in IaaS clouds. Inf. Sci. **394–395**, 106–122 (2017)

4. Gerards, M.E.T., Hurink, J.L., Hölzenspies, P.K.F.: A survey of offline algorithms for energy minimization under deadline constraints. J. Sched. **19**(1), 3–19 (2016). https://doi.org/10.1007/s10951-015-0463-8

5. Gross, D., Harris, C.M.: Fundamentals of Queueing Theory. Wiley, New York (2008)

6. Khazaei, H., Ic, J., Ic, V.B., Mohammadi, N.B.: Modeling the performance of heterogeneous IaaS cloud centers. In: IEEE International Conference on Distributed Computing Systems Workshops, pp. 232–237. Philadelphia, PA, USA (2013)

7. Li, K.: Optimal power allocation among multiple heterogeneous servers in a data center. Sustain. Comput. Inf. Syst. **2**, 13–22 (2012)

8. Li, K.: Improving multicore server performance and reducing energy consumption by workload dependent dynamic power management. IEEE Trans. Cloud Comput. **4**(2), 122–137 (2016)

9. Mei, J., Li, K., Li, K.: Customer-satisfaction-aware optimal multiserver configuration for profit maximization in cloud computing. IEEE Trans. Sustain. Comput. **2**(1), 17–29 (2017)

10. Mitrani, I.: Managing performance and power consumption in a server farm. Ann. Oper. Res. **202**(1), 121–134 (2013)

11. Shehabi, A., et al.: United states data center energy usage report. Technical report, Lawrence Berkeley National Lab. (LBNL), Berkeley, CA (United States) (2016)

12. Tarello, A., Sun, J., Zafer, M., Modiano, E.: Minimum energy transmission scheduling subject to deadline constraints. In: Third International Symposium on Modeling and Optimization in Mobile, Ad Hoc, and Wireless Networks (WiOpt 2005), pp. 67–76. IEEE (2005)

13. Tijms, H.C.: A First Course in Stochastic Models. Wiley, Amsterdam (2004)

14. Tirdad, A., Grassmann, W.K., Tavakoli, J.: Optimal policies of M(t)/M/C/C queues with two different levels of servers. Eur. J. Oper. Res. **249**(3), 1124–1130 (2016)

15. Wang, S., Li, X., Ruiz, R.: Performance analysis for heterogeneous cloud servers using queueing theory. IEEE Trans. Comput. **69**(4), 563–576 (2020)

16. Wu, C.M., Chang, R.S., Chan, H.Y.: A green energy-efficient scheduling algorithm using the DVFS technique for cloud datacenters. Future Gener. Comput. Syst. **37**, 141–147 (2014)

17. Zhai, B., Blaauw, D., Sylvester, D., Flautner, K.: Theoretical and practical limits of dynamic voltage scaling. In: Design Automation Conference. Proceedings, pp. 868–873 (2004)

18. Zheng, X., Yu, C.: Markov model based power management in server clusters. In: IEEE/ACM Intl Conference on Green Computing and Communications and International Conference on Cyber, Physical and Social Computing (2010)

19. Zhou, Z., et al.: Minimizing SLA violation and power consumption in cloud data centers using adaptive energy-aware algorithms. Future Gener. Comput. Syst. **86**, 836–850 (2018)

20. Zomaya, A.Y., Lee, Y.C.: Energy-Efficient Distributed Computing Systems. Wiley, New York (2012)

21. Cong, X., Zi, L., Shuang, K.: Energy-aware and location-constrained virtual network embedding in enterprise network. In: Liu, X., et al. (eds.) ICSOC 2018. LNCS, vol. 11434, pp. 41–52. Springer, Cham (2019). https://doi.org/10.1007/978-3-030-17642-6_4

22. Xu, M., Buyya, R.: Energy efficient scheduling of application components via brownout and approximate Markov decision process. In: Maximilien, M., Vallecillo, A., Wang, J., Oriol, M. (eds.) ICSOC 2017. LNCS, vol. 10601, pp. 206–220. Springer, Cham (2017). https://doi.org/10.1007/978-3-319-69035-3_14
23. Sieminski, A., et al.: International energy outlook. Energy Inf. Admin. (EIA) **18** (2014)

Scalable Joint Optimization of Placement and Parallelism of Data Stream Processing Applications on Cloud-Edge Infrastructure

Felipe Rodrigo de Souza[1(✉)], Alexandre Da Silva Veith[2],
Marcos Dias de Assunção[1], and Eddy Caron[1]

[1] Univ Lyon, EnsL, UCBL, CNRS, Inria, LIP, 69342 LYON Cedex 07, France
`felipe-rodrigo.de-souza@ens-lyon.fr`
[2] University of Toronto, Toronto, Canada

Abstract. The Internet of Things has enabled many application scenarios where a large number of connected devices generate unbounded streams of data, often processed by data stream processing frameworks deployed in the cloud. Edge computing enables offloading processing from the cloud and placing it close to where the data is generated, whereby reducing both the time to process data events and deployment costs. However, edge resources are more computationally constrained than their cloud counterparts. This gives rise to two interrelated issues, namely deciding on the parallelism of processing tasks (a.k.a. operators) and their mapping onto available resources. In this work, we formulate the scenario of operator placement and parallelism as an optimal mixed integer linear programming problem. To overcome the issue of scalability with the optimal model, we devise a resource selection technique that reduces the number of resources evaluated during placement and parallelization decisions. Experimental results using discrete-event simulation demonstrate that the proposed model coupled with the resource selection technique is 94% faster than solving the optimal model alone, and it produces solutions that are only 12% worse than the optimal, yet it performs better than state-of-the-art approaches.

Keywords: Data stream processing · Operator placement · Operator parallelism · End-to-end latency · Edge computing

1 Introduction

A Data Stream Processing (DSP) application is often structured as a directed graph whose *vertices* represent data sources, operators that execute a function over incoming data, and data sinks; and *edges* that define the data interdependencies between operators [4]. DSP applications are often deployed in the cloud to explore the large number of available resources and benefit from its pay-as-you-go business model. The growth of the Internet of Things (IoT) has led to

© Springer Nature Switzerland AG 2020
E. Kafeza et al. (Eds.): ICSOC 2020, LNCS 12571, pp. 149–164, 2020.
https://doi.org/10.1007/978-3-030-65310-1_12

scenarios where geo-distributed resources at the edge of the network act both as data sources and actuators or consumers of processed data. Streaming all this data to a cloud through the Internet, and sometimes back, takes time and quickly becomes costly [4].

Exploration of computing resources from both the cloud and the Internet edges is called as *cloud-edge infrastructure*. This paradigm combines cloud, micro datacenters, and IoT devices and can minimize the impact of network communication on the latency of DSP applications. An inherent problem, however, relies upon deciding how much and which parts of a DSP application to offload from the cloud to resources elsewhere. This problem, commonly known as *operator placement* and shown to be NP-Hard [2], consists in finding a set of resources to host operators while meeting the application requirements. The search space can be large depending on the size and heterogeneity of the infrastructure.

When offloading operators from the cloud, the DSP framework needs to adjust the operators' parallelism and hence decide how to create the number of operator instances to achieve a target throughput. The operator placement needs to address two interrelated issues, namely deciding on the number of instances for each operator and finding the set of resources to host the instances; while guaranteeing performance metrics such as application throughput and end-to-end latency. As an additional level of complexity, the deployment of DSP applications in public infrastructure, such as a cloud, incurs monetary costs, which must be considered when deciding on where to place each DSP operator and how many replicas to create.

This work describes the Cloud-Edge Stream Model (CES), an extension of an optimal Mixed Integer Linear Programming (MILP) model introduced in our previous work [16] for the problem of determining the degree of parallelism and placement of DSP applications onto cloud-edge infrastructure. The model is enhanced with a heuristic that improves its scalability. We devise a solution for estimating the number of replicas, and the processing and bandwidth requirements of each operator to respect a given throughput and minimize the application end-to-end latency and deployment costs. The contributions of this work are therefore: (i) it presents a MILP model for the joint-optimization of operator parallelism and placement on cloud-edge infrastructure to minimize the data transfer time and the application deployment costs (Sect. 2); (ii) it introduces a resource selection technique to improve the system scalability (Sect. 3); and (iii) it evaluates the model and the resource selection technique against traditional and state-of-the-art solutions (Sect. 4).

2   Proposed Model

This section introduces preliminaries, the placement problem and CES.

2.1   System Model

This work considers a three-layered cloud-edge infrastructure, as depicted in Fig. 1, where each layer contains multiple sites. The *IoT* layer contains numerous geo-distributed computational constrained resources, therefore, often acting as source or sinks, but with non negligible computational capacity to support some DSP operators. *Micro Datacenters (MDs)* provide geo-distributed resources (*e.g.*, routers, gateways, and micro datacenters), but with less stringent computational constraints than those in the IoT layer. The *cloud* comprises high-end servers with fewer resource constraints [13].

The three-layered cloud-edge infrastructure is represented as a graph $\mathcal{G}^I = \langle \mathcal{R}, \mathcal{P} \rangle$, where $\mathcal{R}$ is the set of computing resources of all layers ($\mathcal{R}^{IoT} \cup \mathcal{R}^{MD} \cup \mathcal{R}^{cloud}$), and $\mathcal{P}$ is the set of network interconnections between computing resources. Each $k \in \mathcal{R}$ has CPU (CPU_k) and memory (Mem_k) capacities, given respectively in $100 \times num\_of\_cores$, and bytes. The processing speed of a resource (V_k) is its CPU clock in GHz. Similar to existing work [9], the network has a single interconnection between a pair of computing resources k and l, and the bandwidth of this interconnection is given by $Bw_{k,l}$ and its latency is $Lat_{k,l}$.

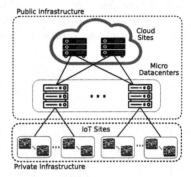

Fig. 1. Target infrastructure.

The application graph specified by a user is a directed graph $\mathcal{G}^A = \langle \mathcal{O}, \mathcal{E} \rangle$, where $\mathcal{O}$ represents data source(s) $Source^{\mathcal{O}}$, data sink(s) $Sink^{\mathcal{O}}$ and transformation operators $Trans^{\mathcal{O}}$, and $\mathcal{E}$ represents the streams between operators, which are unbounded sequences of data (*e.g.*, messages, packets, tuples, file chunks) [4]. The application graph contains at least one data source and one data sink. Each operator $j \in \mathcal{O}$ is the tuple $\langle S^j, C^j, \mathcal{U}^j, AR^j \rangle$, where S^j is the selectivity (message discarding percentage), C^j is the data transformation factor (how much it increases/decreases the size of arriving messages), $\mathcal{U}^j$ is the set of upstream operators directly connected to j, and AR^j is the input rate in Bps that arrives at the operator. When operator j is a data source (*i.e.*, $j \in Source^{\mathcal{O}}$) its input rate is the amount of data ingested into the application since $\mathcal{U}^j = \emptyset$. Otherwise, AR^j is recursively computed as:

$$AR^j = \sum_{i \in \mathcal{U}^j} \rho^{i \rightarrow j} \times DR^i \tag{1}$$

where $\rho^{i \rightarrow j}$ is the probability that operator i will send an output message to operator j, capturing how operator i distributes its output stream among its downstream operators. DR^i is the departure rate of operator i after applying selectivity S^i and the data transformation factor C^i to the input stream:

$$DR^i = AR^i \times (1 - S^i) \times C^i \tag{2}$$

A physical representation of the application graph is created when operators are placed onto available resources as depicted in Fig. 2. Operators placed within the same host communicate directly whereas inter-resource communication is done via the *Data Transfer Service*. Messages that arrive at a computing resource are received by the *Dispatching Service*, which then forwards them to the destination operator within the computing resource. This service also passes messages to the Data Transfer Service when inter-resource communication is required. Each operator comprises an internal queue and a processing element, which are treated as a single software unit when determining the operator properties (*e.g.*, selectivity and data transformation factor), and its CPU and memory requirements. Moreover, an operator may demand more CPU than what a single resource can offer. In this case, multiple operator replicas are created in a way that each individual replica fits a computing resource.

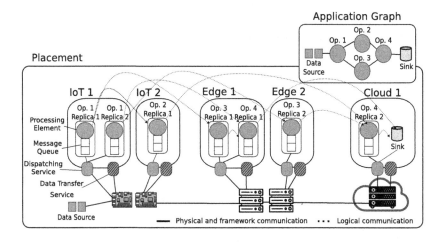

Fig. 2. Application graph adjusted to the computing resource capacities (placement).

The quality of a placement is guaranteed by meeting the application requirements. The CPU and memory requirements of each operator j for processing its incoming byte stream are expressed as Req_{cpu}^j and Req_{mem}^j and they are obtained by profiling the operator on a reference resource [1]. Ref_{cpu}^j, Ref_{mem}^j and Ref_{data}^j refers to the reference CPU, memory and processed data of operator j, respectively. Since CPU and memory cannot be freely fractioned, the reference values are rounded up and combined with AR^j of j in order to compute Req_{cpu}^j and Req_{mem}^j that handle the arriving data stream:

$$Req_{cpu}^j = \left\lceil \frac{Ref_{cpu}^j \times AR^j}{Ref_{data}^j} \right\rceil \quad \text{and} \quad Req_{mem}^j = \left\lceil \frac{Ref_{mem}^j \times AR^j}{Ref_{data}^j} \right\rceil \quad (3)$$

2.2 Problem Formulation

The problem is modeled as a MILP with variables $x(j,l)$ and $f(i,k \rightarrow j,l)$. Variable $x(j,l)$ accounts for the amount of bytes that a replica of operator j can process on resource l, whereas variable $f(i,k \rightarrow j,l)$ corresponds to the number of bytes that operator replica i on resource k sends to downstream operator replica j deployed on resource l.

The data ingestion rate in sources is constant and stable. Hence, it is possible to compute CPU and memory requirements recursively to the entire application to handle the expected load. Placing an application onto computing resources incurs a cost. This cost is derived from Amazon Fargate's pricing scheme[1]. The cost of using one unit of CPU and storing one byte in memory at resource l is given by $C_{cpu}(l)$ and $C_{mem}(l)$, respectively. While the cost of transferring a byte over the network from resource k to l is denoted by $C_{bw}(k,l)$.

As cloud-edge infrastructure comprises heterogeneous resources, the model applies a coefficient $\Omega_l = Ref_V^j / V_l$ to adapt the operator requirements to resource l. Ref_V^j is the reference processing speed of the resource for operator j, and V_l is the clock speed of resource l. The computational cost is given by:

$$CC = \sum_{l \in \mathcal{R}} \sum_{j \in \mathcal{O}} \frac{C_{cpu}(l) \times \frac{\frac{Req_{cpu}^j}{\Omega_l} \times \beta \times x(j,l)}{AR^j}}{\max C_{cpu}(l)} + \frac{C_{mem}(l) \times \frac{Req_{mem}^j \times x(j,l)}{AR^j}}{\max C_{mem}(l)} \qquad (4)$$

where $\max C_{cpu}(l)$ and $\max C_{mem}(l)$ are the cost of using all the CPU and memory capacity of resource l. The CPU and memory costs are normalized using their maximum amounts resulting in values between 0 and 1. β refers to a safety margin to each replica requirements aiming to a steady safe system. This margin relies on Queueing Theory premises to avoid an operator reaching the CPU limits of a given computing resource, which requires a higher queuing time.

The network cost NC is computed as:

$$NC = \sum_{p \in \mathcal{P}} \sum_{a,b \in p} \sum_{j \in \mathcal{O}} \sum_{i \in \mathcal{U}^j} \frac{C_{bw}(a,b) \times f(i, p_s \to j, p_d)}{\max C_{bw}(a,b)} \qquad (5)$$

where a,b is a link that represents one hop of path p, and a,b can belong to multiple paths. The resources at the extremities of path p hosting replicas i and j are given by p_s and p_d, respectively. NC is normalized by $\max C_{bw}(a,b)$, the cost of using all the bandwidth available between resources a and b.

The Aggregate Data Transfer Time (ATT) sums up the network latency of a link and the time to transfer all the data crossing it, and is normalized by the time it takes to send an amount of data that fills up the link capacity:

$$ATT = \sum_{p \in \mathcal{P}} \sum_{k,l \in p} \sum_{j \in \mathcal{O}} \sum_{i \in \mathcal{U}^j} \frac{f(i, p_s \to j, p_d) \times (Lat_{k,l} + \frac{1}{Bw_{k,l}})}{Lat_{k,l} + 1} \qquad (6)$$

The multi-objective function aims at minimizing the data transfer time and the application deployment costs:

$$\min : ATT + CC + NC \qquad (7)$$

The objective function is subject to:

---

[1] https://aws.amazon.com/fargate/pricing.

Physical Constraints: The requirements of each operator replica j on resource l are a function of $x(j,l)$; *i.e.*, a fraction of the byte rate operator j should process (AR^j) with a safety margin (β). The processing requirements of all replicas deployed on l must not exceed its processing capacity, as follows:

$$CPU_l \geq \sum_{j \in \mathcal{O}} \frac{\frac{Req^j_{cpu}}{\Omega_l} \times \beta \times x(j,l)}{AR^j} \quad \text{and} \quad Mem_l \geq \sum_{j \in \mathcal{O}} \frac{Req^j_{mem} \times x(j,l)}{AR^j} \tag{8}$$

To guarantee that the amount of data crossing every link a, b must not exceed its bandwidth capacity:

$$\sum_{j \in \mathcal{O}} \sum_{i \in \mathcal{U}^j} f(i, p_s \rightarrow j, p_d) \leq Bw_{a,b} \qquad \forall a, b \in p; \forall p \in \mathcal{P} \tag{9}$$

Processing Constraint: The amount of data processed by all replicas of j must be equal to the byte arrival rate of j:

$$AR^j = \sum_{l \in \mathcal{R}} x(j,l) \qquad \forall j \in \mathcal{O} \tag{10}$$

Flow Constraints: Except for *sources* and *sinks*, it is possible to create one replica of operator j per resource, although the actual number of replicas, the processing requirements, and the interconnecting streams are decided within the model. The amount of data that flows from all replicas of i to all the replicas of j is equal to the departure rate of upstream i to j:

$$DR^i \times \rho^{i \rightarrow j} = \sum_{k \in \mathcal{R}} \sum_{l \in \mathcal{R}} f(i, k \rightarrow j, l) \qquad \forall j \in \mathcal{O}; \forall i \in \mathcal{U}^j \tag{11}$$

Likewise, the amount of data flowing from one replica of i can be distributed among all replicas of j:

$$x(i,k) \times (1 - S^i) \times C^i \times \rho^{i \rightarrow j} = \sum_{l \in \mathcal{R}} f(i, k \rightarrow j, l) \tag{12}$$

$$\forall k \in \mathcal{R}; \forall j \in \mathcal{O}; \forall i \in \mathcal{U}^j$$

On the other end of the flow, the amount of data arriving at each replica j of operator i, must be equal to the amount of data processed in $x(j,l)$:

$$\sum_{i \in \mathcal{U}^j} \sum_{k \in \mathcal{R}} f(i, k \rightarrow j, l) = x(j,l) \qquad \forall j \in \mathcal{O}; \forall l \in \mathcal{R} \tag{13}$$

Domain Constraints: The placement k of sources and sinks is fixed and provided in the deployment requirements. Variables $x(j,l)$ and $f(i, k \rightarrow j, l)$ represent respectively the amount of data processed by j in l, and the amount of data sent by replica i in k to replica j in l. Therefore the domain of these variables is a real value greater than zero:

$$x(j,l) = AR^j \qquad \forall j \in Source^{\mathcal{O}} \cup Sink^{\mathcal{O}}; \forall l \in \mathcal{R} \tag{14}$$

$$x(j,l) \geq 0 \qquad \forall j \in Trans^{\mathcal{O}}; \forall l \in \mathcal{R} \tag{15}$$

$$f(i, k \rightarrow j, l) \geq 0 \qquad \forall k, l \in \mathcal{R}; j \in \mathcal{O}; i \in \mathcal{U}^j \tag{16}$$

3   Resource Selection Technique

The three-layered cloud-edge infrastructure may contain thousands of computing resources resulting in an enormous combinatorial search space when finding an optimal operator placement. This work therefore proposes a pruning technique that reduces the number of evaluated resources and finds a sub-optimal solution under feasible time. The proposed solution extends the *worst fit* sorting heuristic from Taneja *et al.* [17] by applying a resource selection technique to reduce the number of considered computing resources when deploying operators.

The resource selection technique starts by identifying promising sites in each layer from which to obtain computing resources. Following a bottom-up approach, it selects all IoT sites where data sources and data sinks are placed. Then, based on the location of the selected IoT sites, it picks the MD site with the shortest latency to each IoT site plus the MD sites where there are data sources and data sinks placed. Last, the cloud sites are chosen considering their latency-closeness to the selected MD sites as well as those with data sources and data sinks. After selecting sites from each layer, the function *GetResources* (Algorithm 1) is called for each layer.

As depicted in Algorithm 1, *GetResources* has as input the layer name, the vector of selected sites in the layer and the set of operators. First, it calls *GetResourcesOnSites*, to get al.l computing resources from the selected sites, sorted by CPU and memory in a worst-fit fashion (line 3). Second, it selects resources that host sources or sinks (lines 4–7). Third, CPU and memory requirements from the operators that are neither sources or sinks are summed to *ReqCPU* and *ReqMem*, respectively (line 9). When the evaluated layer is *IoT*, *ReqCPU* and *ReqMem* are used to select a subset of computing resources whose combined capacity meets the requirements (lines 18–21). For each operator of the other two layers, the function selects a worst-fit resource that supports the operator requirements. Since the goal is just to select candidate resources and not a deployment placement, if there is no resource fit, it ignores the operator and moves to the next one (lines 11–16). At last, the combination of resources evaluated by the model contains those selected in each layer.

4   Performance Evaluation

This section describes the experimental setup, the price model for computing resources, and performance evaluation results.

4.1   Experimental Setup

We perform an evaluation in two steps as follows. First CES is compared against a combination of itself with the resource selection technique, hereafter called CES-RS, to evaluate the effects that the resource pruning has on the quality of solutions and on resolution time. Second, we compare CES-RS against state-of-the-art solutions. The evaluations differ in the number of resources in the

---

Algorithm 1: Resource selection technique.

---

1 **Function** *GetResources(layer, Sites, $\mathcal{O}$)*
2      $Selected \leftarrow \{\}, ReqCPU \leftarrow 0, ReqMem \leftarrow 0$
3      $Resources \leftarrow$ **GetResourcesOnSites** *(Sites)*
4   **foreach** $j \in (Source^{\mathcal{O}} \cup Sink^{\mathcal{O}})$ **do**
5   **if** *j.placement* $\in$ *Resources* **then**
6              $Selected \leftarrow Selected \cup j.placement$
7              $Resources \leftarrow Resources - j.placement$
8   **foreach** $j \in (\mathcal{O} - (Source^{\mathcal{O}} \cup Sink^{\mathcal{O}}))$ **do**
9          $ReqCPU \leftarrow ReqCPU + CPU_j, ReqMem \leftarrow ReqMem + Mem_j$
10   **if** $layer ! = IoT$ **then**
11   **foreach** $r \in Resources$ **do**
12   **if** $CPU_r \geq CPU_j$ **and** $Mem_r \geq Mem_j$ **then**
13                     $selected \leftarrow selected \cup r$
14                     $Resources \leftarrow Resources - r$
15   **break**
16   Sort $(Resources)$
17   **if** $layer == IoT$ **then**
18   **foreach** $r \in Resources$ **do**
19   **if** $CPU_r \leq ReqCPU$ **or** $Mem_r \leq ReqMem$ **then**
20                 $Selected \leftarrow Selected \cup r$
21                 $ReqCPU \leftarrow ReqCPU - CPU_r, ReqMem \leftarrow ReqMem - Mem_r$
22   **else**
23   **break**
24   **return** *Selected*

---

infrastructure and the solutions evaluated. Both evaluations are performed via discrete-event simulation using a framework built on OMNET++ to model and simulate DSP applications. We resort to simulation as it offers a controllable and repeatable environment. The model is solved using CPLEX v12.9.0.

The infrastructure comprises three layers with an IoT site, one MD and one cloud. The resource capacity was modeled according to the characteristics of the layer in which a resource is located, and intrinsic characteristics of DSP applications. IoT resources are modeled as Raspberry Pi's 3 (*i.e.*, 1 GB of RAM, 4 CPU cores at 1,2 GHz). As DSP applications are often CPU and memory intensive, the selected MD and cloud resources should be optimized for such cases. The offerings for MD infrastructure are still fairly recent and, although there is a lack of consensus surrounding what the MD is composed of, existing work highlights that the options are more limited than those of the cloud, with more general-purpose resources. In an attempt to use resources similar to those available on Amazon EC2, MD resources are modeled as general purpose t2.2xlarge machines (*i.e.*, 32 GB of RAM, 8 CPU cores at 3.0 GHz), and cloud servers are high-performance C5.metal machines (*i.e.*, 192 GB of RAM, 96 CPU cores at

3.6 GHz). Resources within a site communicate via a LAN, whereas IoTs, MDs, and cloud are interconnected by single WAN path. The LAN has a bandwidth of 100 Mbps and 0.8 ms latency. The WAN bandwidth is 10 Gbps and is shared on the path from the IoT to the MD or to the cloud, and the latency from IoT is 20 ms and 90 ms to the MD and cloud, respectively. The latency values are based on those obtained by empirical experiments carried out by *Hu et al.* [9].

Existing work evaluated application graphs of several orders and interconnection probabilities, usually assessing up to 3 different graphs [4,7,8,10]. To evaluate CES and CES-RS we crafted five graphs to mimic the behaviour of large DSP applications using a built-in-house python library. The graphs have varying shapes and data replication factors for each operator as depicted in Fig. 3. The applications have 25 operators, often more than what is considered in the literature [18]. They also have multiple sources, sinks and paths, similar to previous work by *Liu and Buyya* [10]. As the present work focuses on IoT scenarios, the sources are placed on IoT resources, and sinks are uniformly and randomly distributed across layers as they can be actuators – except for one sink responsible for data storage, which is placed on the cloud.

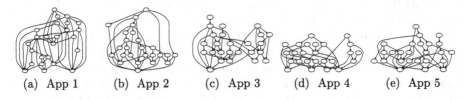

(a) App 1   (b) App 2   (c) App 3   (d) App 4   (e) App 5

Fig. 3. Application graphs used in the evaluation.

The operator properties were based on the RIoTBench IoT application benchmark [15]. RIoTBench offers 27 operators common to IoT applications and 4 datasets with IoT data. The CITY dataset is used with 380 byte messages collected every 12 s containing environmental information (temperature, humidity, air quality) from 7 cities across 3 continents. It has a peak rate of 5000 tuples/s, which in the experiments is continuous and divided among sources. The remaining properties are drawn from the values in Table 1.

We consider that Ref_{cpu}^{j}, Ref_{data}^{j}, the arrival byte rate AR^j, probability that an upstream operator i sends data to j $\rho^{i \to j}$, selectivity S^j, and data transformation pattern C^j, are average values obtained via application profiling, using techniques proposed in existing work [1]. With Ref_{cpu}^{j} and Ref_{data}^{j} we are able to compute requirements for each operator To create a worst case scenario in terms of load, $\rho^{i \to j}$ is set to 1 for all streams in the application request. As the model creates multiple replicas, $\rho^{i \to j}$ gets divided among instances of operator j, hence creating variations on the arrival rate of downstream operators during runtime. The operator processing requirements estimated by the model may not be enough to handle the actual load during certain periods, so resulting in large operator queues. To circumvent this issue we add a small safety margin, the β

Table 1. Operator properties in the application graphs.

Property	Value	Unit
Selectivity	0–20	%
Data transformation pattern	70–130	%
Reference CPU	1–26	CPU units
Reference memory	1–27300000	Bytes
Reference data	38–2394000	Bytes

factor, as mentioned in Sect. 2.2, which is a percentage increase in the application requirements estimated by the proposed model. A β too high results in expensive over-provisioning. After multiple empirical evaluations, β was set to 10% of each replica requirement.

Price Model: The price of using resources is derived from Amazon AWS services, considering the US East Virginia location. The CPU and memory prices are computed based on the AWS Fargate Pricing[2] under a 24/7 execution. Regarding the network, we consider a Direct Connection[3] between the IoT site and the AWS infrastructure. Direct Connections are offered under two options, 1 GB/s and 10 GB/s. As DSP applications generate large amounts of data, we consider the 10 GB/s offer. The data sent from the IoT to AWS infrastructure uses AWS IoT Core[4]. Connections between operators on the edge or on IoT resources to the cloud use Private Links[5]. Amazon provides the values for CPU, memory and network as, respectively, fraction of a vCPU, GB and Gbps, but in our formulation the values for the same metrics are computed in CPU units ($100 * num\_cores$), bytes and Mbps. The values provided by Amazon converted to the scale used in our formulation are presented in Table 2. As the environment combines both public and private infrastructure, deployment costs are applied only to MD and cloud resources, the network between these two, and the network between these two and IoT resources. As IoT resources are on the same private network infrastructure, the communication between IoT resources is free.

Evaluated Approaches and Metrics: Five different configurations of deployment requests are submitted for each application. The reported values for each application are averages of these five executions. Each deployment request has a different placement for sources and sinks with sources always on IoT resources and at least one sink in the cloud. The operator properties such as selectivity and data transformation pattern vary across configurations.

The performance of DSP applications is usually measured considering two main metrics, namely *throughput*, which is the processing rate, in bytes/s, of all sinks in the application; and *end-to-end latency*, which is the average time

---

[2] https://aws.amazon.com/fargate/.

[3] https://aws.amazon.com/directconnect/.

[4] https://aws.amazon.com/iot-core/.

[5] https://aws.amazon.com/privatelink/.

Table 2. Computing and network costs.

Resource	Unit	Cost
CPU	CPU/month	$0.291456
Memory	Byte/month	$3.2004e−09
Direct link IoT to AWS	10 GB link/Month	$1620
Link IoT to AWS	Connection/Month	$0.003456
	KB	$0.0000002
Communication IoT to cloud, IoT to MD, and MD to cloud	GB	$7.2 + 0.01 per GB

span from when a message is generated until it reaches a sink. The MILP model takes the throughput into account in the constraints, and the end-to-end latency indirectly by optimizing the Aggregate Data Transfer Time.

4.2   Resolution Time Versus Solution Quality

Here we evaluate how much the quality of a solution is sacrificed by reducing the search space. The simulation, which runs for 220 s, considers 100 IoT devices, a MD with 50 resources and a cloud with 50 resources. The throughput is the same in all scenarios since it is guaranteed as a model constraint.

Figure 4 shows the end-to-end latency and deployment costs under CES and CES-RS. There are some variations regarding the end-to-end latency both on CES and on CES-RS. Since CES-RS aims to reduce the search space, it might be counter intuitive to see cases where the resource selection with less options obtains better end-to-end latency, such as in App3. However, the objective function considers both latency and execution costs as optimisation metrics. As CES searches to strike a balance between cost and end-to-end latency, the average deployment costs obtained with CES-RS for App 3 (Fig. 4(b)) are higher. This behavior happens because under the limited search space, CES-RS finds suboptimal solutions, where the best trade-off resulted in better end-to-end latency. To do so, it needed to use more edge or cloud devices, which incurs higher computational and network costs.

As CES considers the whole search space, it explores more options and yields better results. Despite reduced search space CES-RS can produce very similar results – in the worst case yielding an end-to-end latency $\simeq$ 12% worse, and deployment costs $\simeq$ 12% higher. The resolution time (Fig. 5), clearly shows that CES considering the whole infrastructure faces scalability issues. Despite producing results that sometimes are worse than those achieved under CES, CES-RS can obtain a solution up to $\simeq$ 94% faster. CES-RS would yield even more similar results on a larger infrastructure because their search space is limited by the application size and requirements rather then by the infrastructure size.

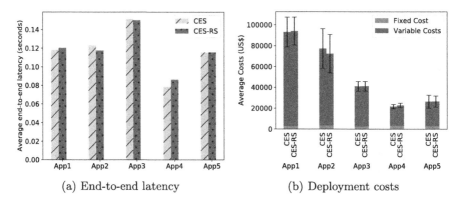

(a) End-to-end latency   (b) Deployment costs

Fig. 4. End-to-end latency and deployment costs under CES and CES-RS.

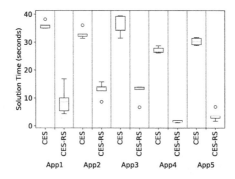

Fig. 5. Resolution time to obtain a deployment solution.

4.3   Comparing CES-RS Against the State-of-the-Art

CES-RS is compared against two state-of-the-art approaches, namely *Cloud-Only* and *Taneja's Cloud-Edge Placement (TCEP)*. Cloud-Only applies a random walk considering only cloud resources, and TCEP is the work proposed by Taneja *et al.* [17], where all resources (IoT, MD and cloud) are sorted accordingly with their capacities, and for each operator it s elects a resource from the middle of the sorted list. This experiment was executed during 120 s and considered 400 IoT devices, 100 resources on the MD and 100 resources on the cloud.

Figure 6 shows the throughput and end-to-end latency for all solutions, with averages for each application. Since CES-RS guarantees a maximum throughput through a constraint, on the best case the other approaches would achieve the same values, and this can be observed on App3, App4 and App5. But under App1 and App2 Cloud-Only struggles because these applications perform a lot of data replication, thus producing large volumes of data. The large volume of messages generated by App1 and App2 has an even bigger effect on the end-to-end latency for Cloud-Only. When compared to Cloud-Only, TCEP provided better results, but still $\simeq 80\%$ worse than the results provided by CES-RS. CES-

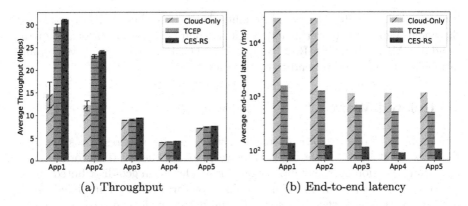

(a) Throughput   (b) End-to-end latency

Fig. 6. Throughput and latency under CES-RS and state-of-the-art solutions.

RS achieves low values because, different from Cloud-Only and TCEP, it creates several replicas, being able to better explore the IoT resources considering their computational capacities and even further reducing the amount of data that is send through the internet, facing less network congestion.

Figure 7 contains the costs results. Beyond better end-to-end latency, CES-RS provides better computational costs. The reason that makes CES-RS achieve computational costs at least $\simeq 6\%$ better than the traditional approaches is the creation of replicas. The considered cost model, accounts for an IoT infrastructure without deployment costs, making such devices very attractive for deployment. Since IoT devices have constrained computational capacity, it is hard to deploy on such devices. Due to CES, CES-RS breaks an operator into several small replicas, allowing the use of IoT resources.

Regarding network costs, CES-RS provides cheaper deployments on most cases except on App4 and App5. In these two applications, IoT resources support the operators' requirements without creating operator replicas allowing TCEP to exploit it and result in fewer data transfers. TCEP has higher computational costs

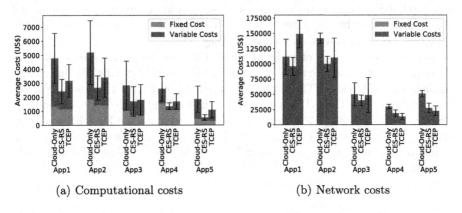

(a) Computational costs   (b) Network costs

Fig. 7. Computational and network costs under CES-RS and state-of-the-art solutions.

because it cannot split operators into multiple replicas, thus resulting in placing the whole operator on powerful and expensive computing resources located on the cloud or a MD. When CES-RS is compared to TCEP, it achieves a lower computational cost and a shorter end-to-end latency.

5   Related Work

The problem of placing DSP dataflows onto heterogeneous resources has been shown to be at least NP-Hard [2]. Moreover, most of the existing work neglects the communication overhead [6], although it is relevant in geo-distributed infrastructure [9]. Likewise, the considered applications are often oversimplified, ignoring operator patterns such as selectivity and data transformation [14].

Effort has been made on modeling the operator placement on cloud-edge infrastructure, including sub-optimal solutions [5,17], heuristic-based approaches [12,19], while others focus on end-to-end latency neglecting throughput, application deployment costs, and other performance metrics when estimating the operator placement [3,4]. Existing work also explores Network Function Virtualization (NFV) for placing *IoT* application service chains across fog infrastructure [11]. Solutions for profiling DSP operators are also available [1]. The present work addresses operator placement and parallelism across cloud-edge infrastructure considering computing and communication constraints by modeling the scenario as a MILP problem and offering a solution for reducing the search space.

6   Conclusion

This work presented CES, a MILP model for the operator placement and parallelism of DSP applications that optimizes the end-to-end latency and deployment costs. CES combines profiling information with the computed amount of data that each operator should process whereby obtaining their processing requirements to handle the arriving load and achieve maximum throughput. The model creates multiple lightweight replicas to offload operators from the cloud to the edge, thus obtaining lower end-to-end latency.

To overcome the issue of scalability with CES, we devise a resource selection technique that reduces the number of resources evaluated during placement and parallelization decisions. The proposed model coupled with the resource selection technique (*i.e.*, CES-RS) is 94% faster than solving CES alone, it produces solutions that are only 12% worse than those achieved under CES and performs better than traditional and state-of-the-art approaches. As a future work we intent to apply the proposed model along with its heuristic to a real-world scenario.

References

1. Arkian, H., Pierre, G., Tordsson, J., Elmroth, E.: An experiment-driven performance model of stream processing operators in Fog computing environments. In: ACM/SIGAPP Symposium on Applied Computing (SAC 2019), Brno, Czech Republic, March 2020
2. Benoit, A., Dobrila, A., Nicod, J.M., Philippe, L.: Scheduling linear chain streaming applications on heterogeneous systems with failures. Future Gener. Comput. Syst. **29**(5), 1140–1151 (2013)
3. Canali, C., Lancellotti, R.: GASP: genetic algorithms for service placement in fog computing systems. Algorithms **12**(10), 201 (2019)
4. Cardellini, V., Lo Presti, F., Nardelli, M., Russo Russo, G.: Optimal operator deployment and replication for elastic distributed data stream processing. Concurrency Comput. Pract. Experience **30**(9), e4334 (2018)
5. Chen, W., Paik, I., Li, Z.: Cost-aware streaming workflow allocation on geo-distributed data centers. IEEE Trans. Comput. **66**, 256–271 (2017)
6. Cheng, B., Papageorgiou, A., Bauer, M.: Geelytics: enabling on-demand edge analytics over scoped data sources. In: 2016 IEEE International Congress on Big Data (BigData Congress) (2016)
7. Gedik, B., Schneider, S., Hirzel, M., Wu, K.L.: Elastic scaling for data stream processing. IEEE Trans. Parallel Distrib. Syst. **25**(6), 1447–1463 (2013)
8. Hiessl, T., Karagiannis, V., Hochreiner, C., Schulte, S., Nardelli, M.: Optimal placement of stream processing operators in the fog. In: 2019 IEEE 3rd International Conference on Fog and Edge Computing (ICFEC), pp. 1–10. IEEE (2019)
9. Hu, W., et al.: Quantifying the impact of edge computing on mobile applications. In: Proceedings of the 7th ACM SIGOPS Asia-Pacific Workshop on Systems, p. 5. ACM (2016)
10. Liu, X., Buyya, R.: Performance-oriented deployment of streaming applications on cloud. IEEE Trans. Big Data **5**(1), 46–59 (2019)
11. Nguyen, D.T., Pham, C., Nguyen, K.K., Cheriet, M.: Placement and chaining for run-time IoT service deployment in edge-cloud. IEEE Trans. Netw. Serv. Manage. **17**, 459–472 (2019)
12. Peng, Q., Xia, Y., Wang, Y., Wu, C., Luo, X., Lee, J.: Joint operator scaling and placement for distributed stream processing applications in edge computing. In: Yangui, S., Bouassida Rodriguez, I., Drira, K., Tari, Z. (eds.) ICSOC 2019. LNCS, vol. 11895, pp. 461–476. Springer, Cham (2019). https://doi.org/10.1007/978-3-030-33702-5_36
13. Puthal, D., Obaidat, M.S., Nanda, P., Prasad, M., Mohanty, S.P., Zomaya, A.Y.: Secure and sustainable load balancing of edge data centers in fog computing. IEEE Commun. Mag. **56**(5), 60–65 (2018)
14. Sajjad, H.P., Danniswara, K., Al-Shishtawy, A., Vlassov, V.: Spanedge: towards unifying stream processing over central and near-the-edge data centers. In: 2016 IEEE/ACM Symposium on Edge Computing, October 2016
15. Shukla, A., Chaturvedi, S., Simmhan, Y.: Riotbench: a real-time iot benchmark for distributed stream processing platforms. corr abs/1701.08530 (2017). arxiv. org/abs/1701.08530 (2017)
16. de Souza, F.R., da Silva Veith, A., Dias de Assunção, M., Caron, E.: An optimal model for optimizing the placement and parallelism of data stream processing applications on cloud-edge computing. In: 32nd IEEE International Symposium on Computer Architecture and High Performance Computing. IEEE (2020, in press)

17. Taneja, M., Davy, A.: Resource aware placement of iot application modules in fog-cloud computing paradigm. In: IFIP/IEEE Symposium on Integrated Network and Service Management (IM), May 2017
18. Zeuch, S., et al.: Analyzing efficient stream processing on modern hardware. Proc. VLDB Endow. **12**(5), 516–530 (2019)
19. Zhang, S., Liu, C., Wang, J., Yang, Z., Han, Y., Li, X.: Latency-aware deployment of IoT services in a cloud-edge environment. In: Yangui, S., Bouassida Rodriguez, I., Drira, K., Tari, Z. (eds.) ICSOC 2019. LNCS, vol. 11895, pp. 231–236. Springer, Cham (2019). https://doi.org/10.1007/978-3-030-33702-5_17

Impact of Service- and Cloud-Based Dynamic Routing Architectures on System Reliability

Amirali Amiri[1(✉)], Uwe Zdun[1], Georg Simhandl[1], and André van Hoorn[2]

[1] University of Vienna, Vienna, Austria
{Amirali.Amiri,Uwe.Zdun,Georg.Simhandl}@univie.ac.at
[2] University of Stuttgart, Stuttgart, Germany
van.hoorn@informatik.uni-stuttgart.de

Abstract. Various kinds of dynamic routing architectures are used in today's service- and cloud-based architectures, including sidecar-based routing, routing through a central entity such as an event store, or architectures with multiple dynamic routers. We propose an analytical model of request loss during router and service crashes, as well as an empirical validation of that model. The comparison of the empirical data to the predicted values by our model shows a low enough and converging error rate for using the model during system architecting. Our model predicts that, having the same crash probability, decentralized routing results in losing a higher number of requests in comparison to more centralized approaches. To the best of our knowledge, our study is the first to empirically study the reliability trade-off in such architectural decisions.

1 Introduction

Many distributed system architecture patterns [3,10,15] have been suggested for dynamic routing [8]. Some dynamic routing architectures require a single dynamic request routing decision, e.g., when using load balancing. More complex request routing decisions or combinations of decisions, such as routing to the right branch of a company or checking for compliance to privacy regulations, often require multiple runtime checks during one sequence of requests.

In our prior work [1], we studied representative service- and cloud-based system architecture patterns for dynamic request routing. A typical cloud native architecture pattern is the *sidecar* pattern [10,12] in which the sidecar of each service handles incoming and outgoing traffic [6]. In contrast, a *central entity*, e.g., an API Gateway, an event streaming platform [15], or any kind of central service bus [3], can be used to process the request routing decisions. These two extremes are often combined and multiple routers are used; this is called *dynamic routers*

This work was supported by FWF (Austrian Science Fund), project ADDCompliance: I 2885-N33; FFG (Austrian Research Promotion Agency), project DECO no. 846707; Baden-Württemberg Stiftung, project ORCAS.

E. Kafeza et al. (Eds.): ICSOC 2020, LNCS 12571, pp. 165–174, 2020.
https://doi.org/10.1007/978-3-030-65310-1_13

in this paper. Consider an API Gateway, two event streaming platforms, and a number of sidecars, all making routing decisions in a cloud-based architecture.

At present, the impacts of such architectures and their different configurations on system reliability have not been studied. More is known about other qualities relevant for this decision. For instance, our prior work [1] has shown that more distributed approaches for dynamic data routing offer a better performance compared to more centralized solutions. As reliability is a core consideration in service and cloud architectures [14], a reasonably accurate failure prediction for the feasible architecture design options in a certain design situation would help architects to better design system architectures considering quality trade-offs.

RQ1: *What is the impact of choosing a dynamic routing architecture, in particular central entity, sidecar-based, or dynamic routers, on system reliability?*

RQ2: *How can we predict this impact when making architectural design decisions regarding system reliability?*

We model request loss during router and service crashes in an analytical model based on Bernoulli processes; request loss is used as the externally visible metric indicating the severity of the crashes' impacts. The model abstracts central entities, dynamic routers, and sidecars in a common router abstraction. To validate our analytical model, we designed an experiment in which we studied 36 representative experimental cases (i.e., different experiment configurations) for the three kinds of architectures Our results show that the error is constantly reduced with a higher number of experimental runs, converging at a prediction error of 8.1%. Given the common target prediction accuracy of up to 30% in the cloud performance domain [11] these results are more than reasonable. Our model predicts and our experiment confirms that more decentralized routing results in losing a higher number of requests than more centralized approaches.

2   Related Work and Background

2.1   Related Work

Architecture-Based Reliability Prediction. To predict the reliability of a system and to identify reliability-critical elements of its system architecture, various approaches such as fault tree analysis or methods based on a continuous time Markov chain have been proposed [17]. Architecture-based approaches, like ours, are often based on the observation that the reliability of a system does not only depend on the reliability of each component but also on the probabilistic distribution of the utilization of its components, e.g., a Markov model [4].

Empirical Reliability or Resilience Assessment. Today many software organizations use large-scale experimentation in production systems to assess the reliability of their systems, which is called chaos/resilience engineering [2]. A crucial aspect in resilience assessment of software systems is efficiency [13]. To reduce the number of experiments needed, knowledge about the relationship of resilience patterns, anti-patterns, suitable fault injections, and the system's architecture can be exploited to generate experiments [18].

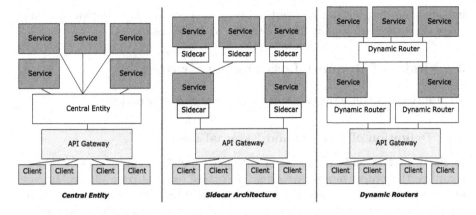

Fig. 1. Dynamic routing architecture patterns (adapted from [1])

Service-Specific Reliability Studies. Some related works introduce service-specific reliability models, e.g., Wang et al. [19] propose a discrete time Markov chain model for analyzing system reliability based on constituent services. Grassi and Patella [7] propose an approach for reliability prediction that considers the decentralized and autonomous nature of services. However, none of these approaches studies and compares major architecture patterns in service and cloud architectures; they are based on a very generic model about the notion of service.

2.2 Background: Dynamic Routing Architecture Patterns

Central Entity (CE). In a CE architecture, as shown in Fig. 1, the *central entity* manages all request flow decisions. One benefit of this architecture is that it is easy to manage, understand, and change as all control logic regarding request flow is implemented in one component. However, this introduces the drawback that the design of the internals of the *central entity* component is a complex task. CE can be implemented utilizing an API Gateway, an event store, an event streaming platform [15], or a service bus [3].

Sidecar Architecture (SA). Figure 1 presents an SA example. Sidecars [6,10, 12] offer benefits whenever decisions need to be made structurally close to the service logic. One advantage of this architecture is that, in comparison to the *central entity* service, it is usually easier to implement *sidecars* since they require less complex logic to control the request flow; however, it is not always possible to add *sidecars*, e.g., when services are off-the-shelf products.

Dynamic Routers (DR). Figure 1 shows a specific dynamic router [8] configuration. One benefit of using DR is that *dynamic routers* can use local information regarding request routing amongst their connected services. For instance, if a set of services are dependent on one another as steps of processing a request, DR can be used to facilitate the dynamic routing; nonetheless, *dynamic routers* introduce an implementation overhead regarding control logic, deployment and so on since they are usually distributed on multiple hosts.

3   Model of Request Loss During Crashes

We use the common term *router* for all request flow control logic.

3.1   Definition of Internal and External Loss

In Fig. 1 *routers* and *services* send *internal requests* amongst one another to complete the processing of one *external request* received from *clients*. In case of a crash, *external requests* will not be processed fully. We define external and internal loss as the number of lost *external* and *internal requests*, respectively.

Internal Loss. In case of a crash, per each external loss, the internal loss is the total number of *internal requests* (IR_T) minus the ones that have been executed. Let IL_c, EL_c and n_c^{exec} be the internal and external loss, and the number of executed *internal requests* for the crash of a *component c*:

$$IL_c = EL_c \cdot (IR_T - n_c^{exec}) \tag{1}$$

Note that IR_T and n_c^{exec} need to be parameterized based on the application. An example of this parameterization is given in Sect. 4.

External Loss. Let d_c be the expected average downtime after a *component c* crashes and cf the incoming call frequency, i.e., the frequency at which *external requests* are received. Then, the *external loss* per crash of each *component c* is:

$$EL_c = d_c \cdot cf \tag{2}$$

3.2   Bernoulli Process to Model Request Loss

In this section, we model request loss based on Bernoulli processes [17]. We only model the crash of *routers* and *services* in Fig. 1 because we assume an *API Gateway* is stable and reliable. Moreover, a crash of a *Client* results in *external requests* not being generated; as a result, *external requests* are not lost. Hence, from now on, we use the common term *components* for all *routers* and *services*.

Number of Crash Tests. During T, all *components* can crash with certain failure distributions. Here, T should be interpreted as the time interval in which these failure distributions are observed (e.g., failure distributions of a day or a week). We model this behavior by checking for a crash of any of the system's *components* every crash interval CI. That is, our model "knows" about crashes in discrete time intervals only, as it would be the case, e.g., if the Heartbeat pattern [9] is used for checking system health. Let n_{crash} be the number of times we check for a crash of *components* during T, i.e., the number of crash tests:

$$n_{crash} = \lfloor \frac{T}{CI} \rfloor \tag{3}$$

Expected Number of Crashes. Each crash test is a Bernoulli trial in which success is defined as *"component* crashed". Assuming $CI > d_c$ (justifiable because when a component crashes it cannot crash again) all n_{crash} crash tests of a *component* c are independent. The binomial distribution of each Bernoulli process gives us the number of successes. Let P_c be the crash probability of a *component* c every time we check for a crash and $E[C_c]$ the expected number of its crashes, i.e., the expected value of its binomial distribution during T:

$$E[C_c] = n_{crash} \cdot P_c \tag{4}$$

Total Internal and External Loss. The total *internal loss* (IL_T) is the sum of internal loss per crash of each *component*. Let C be the set of all *components* that can crash, i.e., *routers* and *services*. Using Eqs. (1) to (4):

$$IL_T = \sum_{c \in C} E[C_c] \cdot IL_c = \lfloor \frac{T}{CI} \rfloor \cdot cf \cdot \sum_{c \in C} P_c \cdot d_c \cdot (IR_T - n_c^{exec}) \tag{5}$$

The total *external loss* (EL_T) is the sum of external loss per crash of each *component*. Using Eqs. (2) to (4):

$$EL_T = \sum_{c \in C} E[C_c] \cdot EL_c = \lfloor \frac{T}{CI} \rfloor \cdot cf \cdot \sum_{c \in C} P_c \cdot d_c \tag{6}$$

Total Number of Crashes. The total number of crashes (C_T) is the sum of the expected number of crashes of each *component*. Using Eqs. (3) and (4):

$$C_T = \sum_{c \in C} E[C_c] = \lfloor \frac{T}{CI} \rfloor \cdot \sum_{c \in C} P_c \tag{7}$$

4 Empirical Validation

4.1 Experimental Planning

Goals. We aim to empirically validate our model's accuracy with regard to the number of crashes as well as the total *external* and *internal loss* represented by Eqs. (5) and (6). We realized these architectures using a prototypical implementation, instantiated and ran them in a cloud infrastructure, measured the empirical results, and compared the results with our model.

Technical Details. We used a private cloud with three physical nodes, each having two identical Intel® Xeon® E5-2680 CPUs. On top of the cloud nodes we installed Virtual Machines (VMs) with eight CPU cores and 60 GB system memory running Ubuntu Server 18.04.01 LTS. Docker containerization is used to run the cloud services which are implemented in Node.js. We utilized five desktop computers to generate load, each hosting an Intel®Core™i3-2120T CPU @ 2.60 GHz, 8 GB of system memory which run Ubuntu 18.10. They generate load using Apache JMeter which sends HTTP version 1.1 requests to the cloud nodes.

Specific Model Formulae. In our example configurations each *service* receives an *internal requests*, processes it and sends it back either to a *router* or the *API gateway*, so we can calculate IR_T based on the number of services (n_{serv}):

$$IR_T = 2n_{serv} + 1 \tag{8}$$

In order to calculate n_c^{exec}, we need to differentiate between *service* and *router* crashes. In case of a *service* crash, all *internal requests* up until the last *router* will be executed. Let $s_{crashed}$ be the label number of the crashed *service*:

$$n_c^{exec} = 2s_{crashed} - 1 \tag{9}$$

In case of a *router* crash, we need to know the allocation of routers (A) which is a set indicating the number of directly linked *services* of each *router*. Let $r_{crashed}$ be the label number of the crashed *router*:

$$n_c^{exec} = 2 \sum_{r=1}^{r_{crashed}} A_{r-1} \tag{10}$$

Experimental Cases. We chose different levels for cf and n_{serv} to study their effects on IL_T. We selected cf based on a study of related works, e.g., [5,16], as 10, 25, 50, and 100 requests per second. Based on our experience and a survey on existing cloud applications in the literature and industry [1], the number of cloud services which are directly dependent on each other in a call sequence is usually rather low. As a result, we chose 3, 5, and 10 as values for n_{serv}. We simulated a node crash by separately generating a random number for each cloud component. If the generated random number for a component was below its crash probability, we stopped the component's Docker container and started it again after a time interval $d = 3$ s. We chose $T = 10$ min, during which we checked for a crash for all components simultaneously every $CI = 15$ seconds resulting in $n_{crash} = 40$ (Eq. (3)). Each component had a uniform crash probability of 0.5%; akin to the related works we chose a relatively high crash probability to have a high enough likelihood to observe a few crashes during T.

Data Set Preparation. For each experimental case, we instantiated the architectures and ran the experiment for exactly ten minutes (excluding setup time). We studied three architectures, three levels of n_{serv} and four levels of cf, resulting in a total of 36 experimental cases; therefore, a single run of our experiment takes exactly six hours (36×10 min) of runtime. Since our model revolves around expected values in a Bernoulli process, we repeated this process 200 times (1200 h of runtime) and report the arithmetic mean of the results[1].

4.2   Results

Experimental Results Analysis. Based on Eq. (5), IL_T is a model element that incorporates crashes of all *components* and it includes all model views,

---

[1] The data of this study is published as an open access data set for supporting replicability: https://zenodo.org/record/4008041, doi:10.5281/zenodo.4008041.

e.g., architecture configurations, expected average downtime, etc. Therefore, we conduct our analysis mainly based on IL_T. It can be observed from Table 1 that when we keep n_{serv} constant, increasing cf results in a rise of EL_T (predicted by Eq. (6)) in all cases, which leads to a higher value of IL_T (Eq. (5)).

Table 1. Results of the model and the experiment

Arch.	n_{serv}	cf	C_T	EL_T	IL_T	C_T	EL_T	IL_T	$\sigma(IL_T)$
			Model			Experiment			
CE	3	10	0.800	24.000	114.000	0.760	23.395	98.960	118.552
		25	0.800	60.000	285.000	0.620	47.435	228.975	292.389
		50	0.800	120.000	570.000	0.705	106.370	480.235	608.635
		100	0.800	240.000	1140.000	0.725	218.130	1045.000	1216.765
	5	10	1.200	36.000	246.000	1.165	36.405	236.575	236.536
		25	1.200	90.000	615.000	1.110	85.400	608.040	574.267
		50	1.200	180.000	1230.000	1.115	172.085	1155.550	1173.295
		100	1.200	360.000	2460.000	1.040	317.585	2223.655	2101.272
	10	10	2.200	66.000	786.000	1.920	62.000	720.190	616.778
		25	2.200	165.000	1965.000	2.125	171.290	2063.305	1711.931
		50	2.200	330.000	3930.000	2.160	344.765	4223.665	3458.119
		100	2.200	660.000	7860.000	1.960	590.665	6853.500	6567.047
DR	3	10	1.200	36.000	162.000	1.075	32.505	153.045	175.952
		25	1.200	90.000	405.000	1.225	92.745	452.160	466.814
		50	1.200	180.000	810.000	1.225	182.595	882.695	916.540
		100	1.200	360.000	1620.000	1.130	328.925	1477.405	1470.332
	5	10	1.600	48.000	306.000	1.670	51.995	319.210	301.989
		25	1.600	120.000	765.000	1.760	135.105	816.895	686.709
		50	1.600	240.000	1530.000	1.790	270.540	1597.535	1324.199
		100	1.600	480.000	3060.000	1.635	490.990	2909.115	2353.168
	10	10	2.600	78.000	930.000	2.525	82.255	921.610	495.543
		25	2.600	195.000	2325.000	2.355	187.715	2181.590	1275.035
		50	2.600	390.000	4650.000	2.205	345.350	4043.070	2508.002
		100	2.600	780.000	9300.000	2.375	741.870	8544.700	5022.780
SA	3	10	1.200	36.000	162.000	1.140	34.910	170.265	186.911
		25	1.200	90.000	405.000	1.230	93.265	435.685	452.190
		50	1.200	180.000	810.000	1.215	181.305	883.510	911.088
		100	1.200	360.000	1620.000	1.185	345.950	1634.850	1844.829
	5	10	2.000	60.000	390.000	1.795	55.745	350.055	244.898
		25	2.000	150.000	975.000	1.795	138.910	891.525	647.402
		50	2.000	300.000	1950.000	1.715	261.740	1716.095	1284.733
		100	2.000	600.000	3900.000	1.790	528.420	3385.240	2633.592
	10	10	4.000	120.000	1380.000	3.900	127.715	1443.040	773.632
		25	4.000	300.000	3450.000	3.745	306.745	3477.305	1979.270
		50	4.000	600.000	6900.000	3.860	617.375	7140.655	4262.114
		100	4.000	1200.000	13800.000	3.870	1232.770	14072.910	8287.361

Table 2. Prediction error of experimental runs

Number of Runs	$C_T\,(\%)$	$EL_T\,(\%)$	$IL_T\,(\%)$
50	12.919	12.307	13.946
100	9.416	8.492	9.593
150	8.326	7.426	8.731
200	8.081	7.097	8.105

Since in our experiment, we instantiated the DR architecture with three dynamic routers, it is interesting to consider the experimental case of $n_{serv} = 3$. In this case, SA and DR have the same number of components, i.e., routers and services. Note that SA uses a *sidecar* per each cloud service; as a result with $n_{serv} = 3$, we will also have three *sidecars*. The difference between the two architectures in this experimental case is that in DR *dynamic routers* are placed on a different VM than their directly linked services, but in SA *sidecars* are placed on the same VM as their corresponding cloud services. For this reason, it can be observed that the reported values for SA and DR closely resemble each other when we have different values of cf but keep n_{serv} constant at three. Considering the cases with five or ten cloud services, we almost always observe higher IL_T when we change the architecture from a CE to a DR or from a DR to an SA but keep the same configurations, i.e., constant n_{serv} and cf. It is because in our experiment, CE has only one control logic component (the *central entity*), DR has three (*dynamic routers*), and SA has n_{serv} (*sidecars*). Consequently, the number of crashes corresponding to control logic components goes up from CE to DR and then to SA. This increases C_T, which results in losing more requests.

5　Discussion and Conclusions

Evaluation of the Prediction Error. We measure the prediction error by calculating the Mean Absolute Percentage Error (MAPE) [17]. Let $model_i$ and $empirical_i$ be the result of the model, and the measured empirical data for experimental case i, respectively. n_{case} is the number of cases (36 in this study).

$$MAPE = \frac{100\%}{n_{case}} \cdot \sum_{i=1}^{n_{case}} \left| \frac{model_i - empirical_i}{empirical_i} \right| \qquad (11)$$

Table 2 reports prediction error measurements of our model for a different number of runs. As the table shows, with a higher number of experimental runs the prediction error is reduced, which indicates a converging error rate. After 200 runs, the final prediction error regarding IL_T is 8.1%. As mentioned before, the common target prediction accuracy in the cloud performance domain is 30% [11].

Threats to Validity. While injecting crashes is a commonly taken approach (see Sect. 2.1), a threat remains that measuring internal and external loss based on these crashes might not measure reliability well, e.g., cascading effects of crashes [14] are not covered in our experiment. We collected an extensive amount of data to validate our model; however, we did so in limited experiment time and with injected crashes, simulated by stopping Docker containers. We avoided factors such as other load on the experiment machines; much of the related literature takes a similar approach. To increase internal validity we decided not to run the experiment on a public cloud where, e.g., other load on the experiment machines might have had a significant impact on the results. As a consequence, there is the threat that generalization to a public cloud setting might be limited. As our private cloud setting uses very similar hardware and software stacks as many public cloud offerings, we believe this threat to be small. As the statistical method to compare our model's predictions to the empirical data, we used the MAPE metric as it is widely used and offers good interpretability in our research context. To mitigate the threat that this statistical method might have issues we double-checked three other error measures, which led to similar results.

Conclusions. We investigated the impact of architectural design decisions on system reliability. Regarding **RQ1**, our study concludes that more decentralized routing results in losing a higher number of requests in comparison to more centralized approaches. Regarding **RQ2**, we derived an analytical model for predicting request loss in the studied architectures and empirically validated this model using 36 representative experimental cases. Our results indicate that with a higher number of experimental runs the prediction error is constantly reduced, converging at a prediction error of 8.1%.

References

1. Amiri, A., Krieger, C., Zdun, U., Leymann., F.: Dynamic data routing decisions for compliant data handling in service- and cloud-based architectures: a performance analysis. In: IEEE International Conference on Services Computing (2019)
2. Basiri, A., et al.: Chaos engineering. IEEE Softw. **33**(3), 35–41 (2016)
3. Chappell, D.A.: Enterprise Service Bus. O'Reilly, Sebastopol (2004)
4. Cheung, R.C.: A user-oriented software reliability model. IEEE Trans. Softw. Eng. **2**, 118–125 (1980)
5. Dean, D.J., Nguyen, H., Wang, P., Gu, X.: Perfcompass: toward runtime performance anomaly fault localization for infrastructure-as-a-service clouds. In: 6th USENIX Workshop on Hot Topics in Cloud Computing (HotCloud 14) (2014)
6. Envoy. Service mesh (2019). https://www.learnenvoy.io/articles/service-mesh.html
7. Grassi, V., Patella, S.: Reliability prediction for service-oriented computing environments. IEEE Internet Comput. **10**(3), 43–49 (2006)
8. Hohpe, G., Woolf, B.: Enterprise Integration Patterns. Addison-Wesley, Boston (2003)
9. Homer, A., Sharp, J., Brader, L., Narumoto, M., Swanson, T.: Cloud Design Patterns. Microsoft Press, Redmond (2014)
10. Jamshidi, P., Pahl, C., Mendonça, N.C., Lewis, J., Tilkov, S.: Microservices: the journey so far and challenges ahead. IEEE Softw. **35**(3), 24–35 (2018)

11. Menascé, D.A., Almeida, V.A.: Capacity Planning for Web Services: Metrics, Models, and Methods. Prentice Hall PTR (2001)
12. Microsoft. Sidecar pattern (2010). https://docs.microsoft.com/en-us/azure/architecture/patterns/sidecar
13. Natella, R., Cotroneo, D., Madeira, H.S.: Assessing dependability with software fault injection: a survey. ACM Comput. Surv. (CSUR) **48**(3), 44 (2016)
14. Nygard, M.: Release It!: Design and Deploy Production-Ready Software. Pragmatic Bookshelf (2007)
15. Richardson, C.: Microservice architecture patterns and best practices (2019). http://microservices.io/index.html
16. Sukwong, O., Sangpetch, A., Kim, H.S.: Sageshift: managing slas for highly consolidated cloud. In: 2012 Proceedings IEEE INFOCOM, pp. 208–216 (2012)
17. Trivedi, K.S., Bobbio, A.: Reliability and Availability Engineering: Modeling, Analysis, and Applications. Oxford University Press, Oxford (2017)
18. van Hoorn, A., Aleti, A., Düllmann, T.F., Pitakrat, T.: Orcas: efficient resilience benchmarking of microservice architectures. In: IEEE International Symposium on Software Reliability Engineering Workshops, pp. 146–147. IEEE (2018)
19. Wang, L., Bai, X., Zhou, L., Chen, Y.: A hierarchical reliability model of service-based software system. In: 2009 33rd Annual IEEE International Computer Software and Applications Conference, vol. 1, pp. 199–208, July 2009

Pricing in the Competing Auction-Based Cloud Market: A Multi-agent Deep Deterministic Policy Gradient Approach

Bing Shi[1,2](✉), Lianzhen Huang[1], and Rongjian Shi[1]

[1] Wuhan University of Technology, Wuhan 430070, China
bingshi@whut.edu.cn
[2] Shenzhen Research Institute of Wuhan University of Technology,
Shenzhen 518000, China

Abstract. In the cloud market, there exist multiple cloud providers adopting auction-based mechanisms to offer cloud services to users. These auction-based cloud providers need to compete against each other to maximize their profits by setting cloud resource prices based on their pricing strategies. In this paper, we analyze how an auction-based cloud provider sets the auction price effectively when competing against other cloud providers in the evolutionary market where the amount of participated cloud users is changing. The pricing strategy is affected by many factors such as the auction prices of its opponents, the price set in the previous round, the bidding behavior of cloud users, and so on. Therefore, we model this problem as a Partially Observable Markov Game and adopt a gradient-based Multi-agent deep reinforcement learning algorithm to generate the pricing strategy. Furthermore, we run extensive experiments to evaluate our pricing strategy against the other four benchmark pricing strategies in the auction-based cloud market. The experimental results show that our generated pricing strategy can beat other pricing strategies in terms of long-term profits and the amount of participated users, and it can also learn cloud users' marginal values and users' choices of cloud providers effectively.

Keywords: Auction-based cloud market · Pricing strategy · Markov games · Multi-agent deep reinforcement learning

1 Introduction

Because of economical, scalable, and elastic access to computing resources, the development of cloud computing has achieved significant success in the industry. More and more companies and individuals prefer using computing services over the Internet. This contributes to the vigorous development of the cloud computing market. In the cloud market, there exist different types of cloud resource transaction mechanisms, such as pay as you go, subscription-based transaction. Furthermore, some cloud providers may run auction-based mechanisms to sell

© Springer Nature Switzerland AG 2020
E. Kafeza et al. (Eds.): ICSOC 2020, LNCS 12571, pp. 175–186, 2020.
https://doi.org/10.1007/978-3-030-65310-1_14

resources to users, such as *Amazon*'s Spot Instance. In such a context, cloud providers need to set proper transaction prices for the sale of resources. Moreover, there usually exist multiple cloud providers offering cloud resources, where cloud users can choose to participate in one of the auctions to bid for the resources. In this situation, the resource transaction prices will affect the cloud users' choices of cloud providers and bidding behavior significantly, and in turn, affect the cloud providers' profits. Furthermore, the competition among providers usually lasts for a long time, i.e. the providers compete against each other repeatedly. Therefore, in this paper, we intend to analyze how the cloud provider sets the auction price effectively in order to maximize long-term profits.

In more detail, in the environment with multiple auction-based cloud providers, each cloud user needs to determine which auction mechanism to participate in according to the choice model and then submits the bid to the cloud provider. The auction mechanism then determines the auction price. Users whose bids are not less than the auction prices obtain the resources and pay for it according to the auction prices, not their bids. In this paper, we analyze how to design an appropriate pricing strategy to set the auction price to maximize the cloud provider's profits in the environment with two cloud providers. First, we consider the evolution of the market, where the numbers and the preferences of cloud users are changing. In addition, how cloud users choose the providers and bidding, and how providers set the auction prices are affected by each other, and it is a sequential decision problem. Reinforcement learning is an effective way to solve such problems. Furthermore, this problem involves multiple providers competing against each other. This is a Markov game, which can be solved by Multi-Agent Reinforcement Learning. Specifically, we use a multi-agent deep deterministic policy gradient, named MADDPG to generate the cloud provider's pricing strategy [10]. Finally, we run experiments to evaluate our pricing strategy against four typical pricing strategies. The experimental results show that the pricing strategy generated by our algorithm can not only respond to the opponents' changing prices in time but also learn the marginal values of cloud users and users' choices on providers. Moreover, the pricing strategy generated by our algorithm can beat other strategies in terms of long-term profits.

The structure of this paper is as follows. In Sect. 3, we introduce the basic settings of cloud users and cloud providers. In Sect. 4, we describe how to use the MADDPG algorithm to generate a pricing strategy. We run extensive experiments to evaluate the pricing strategy in different situations in Sect. 5. Finally, we conclude in Sect. 6.

2   Related Work

Since cloud computing involves resource provision and consumption, auction-based mechanisms have been widely used by cloud providers for sale of resources, such as *AmazonEC2's* Spot Instance [8]. In [15], *AmazonEC2* Spot Instance mechanism was investigated from a statistical perspective. The researchers also considered the proportion of idle time for cloud service instances and proposed an elastic Spot Instance method to ensure stable reliability revenues for providers [3]. In [6], a demand-based dynamic pricing model for Spot Instance was proposed by adopting a genetic algorithm. There also exist some works predicting the auction prices of $AmazonEC2$ Spot Instances [2,7]. In [12,14], the authors analyzed how cloud providers using "pay as you go" set prices in the competing environment, but did not take into account the auction-based cloud market and the evolution of cloud users. In [4], the authors proposed a non-cooperative competing model which analyzed the equilibrium price of a one-shot game, but ignored the long-term profits and did not consider the auction-based mechanism as well. Actually, to the best of our knowledge, few works have considered how to set auction prices effectively in the competing environment with multiple auction-based cloud providers.

3 Basic Settings

In this section, we introduce the basic settings of cloud users and cloud providers. We assume that there are two cloud providers P_1 and P_2 in the cloud market, where they compete with each other to maximize their long-term profits. This market is constantly evolving, and we use t to denote the time stage. At the beginning of each stage, each provider publishes its auction price of the last stage. Then each user chooses to be served by a provider based on its choice model of the provider (see Sect. 3.1). However, if the user's expected profit in both providers is negative, it may not enter any providers. After users select the cloud providers, they submit their bids. Now two providers determine the auction prices and obtain the corresponding immediate reward (see Sect. 3.2). The competition enters into the next stage.

3.1 Cloud Users

In this section, we describe the basic settings of cloud users. The amount of cloud users participating in the cloud market varies as the market evolves. Therefore, we model it as a classical logical growth function [11], which is:

$$N(t) = \frac{N_0 N_\infty}{N_0 + (N_\infty - N_0)\,e^{-\delta t}} \tag{1}$$

where $N(t)$ is the number of cloud users at stage t, δ is the temporal evolution rate of the market, and the initial number of cloud users is N_0, the market is saturated when the amount of cloud users entering the market becomes stabilized, then the number of cloud users is N_∞.

Users' Choices of Providers. Cloud users' choices of providers are mainly dependent on their expected utilities in the selected provider. The expected utility of cloud user j choosing to be served by provider i at stage t is:

$$u_{j,i}^t = m_j - p_{i,t} + \eta_{j,i} = v_{j,i}^t + \eta_{j,i} \tag{2}$$

where m_j is the marginal value that user j can receive from per-unit requested resource, $p_{i,t}$ is the auction price set by provider i, and we use $v^t_{j,i} = m_j - p_{i,t}$ to represent the profit that cloud user j can make when choosing provider i at stage t. $\eta_{j,i}$ means that user j has an implicit preference on provider i, which is an independently, identically distributed extreme value, and the density function is $f(\eta_{j,i}) = e^{-\eta_{j,i}} e^{-e^{-\eta_{j,i}}}$.

According to the user's expected utility in Eq. 2 and the density function, user j will choose to be served by provider i ($i' \neq i$) only if its utility is maximized. The probability of cloud user j choosing to be served by provider i at stage t is denoted as $P^t_{j,i}$:

$$P^t_{j,i} = \frac{e^{v^t_{j,i}}}{\sum_{i'} e^{v^t_{j,i'}}} \tag{3}$$

Users' Bidding Model. After each user chooses a provider, it needs to bid for the cloud resource. We adopt a bidding algorithm based on a feedback control system, where cloud users utilize a feedback loop to automatically adjust the submitted bids [1], which is shown in Fig. 1.

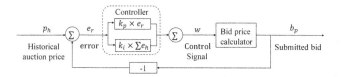

Fig. 1. Cloud users' bidding algorithm

The user's submitted bid for the next stage is b_p:

$$b_p = p_l + \frac{p_u - p_l}{\pi} \times \text{arccot}(w) \tag{4}$$

where p_l and p_u are the lower and upper bound of the cloud service instance respectively, w is a control signal to adjust the user's bid appropriately. The range of $arccot(w)$ is $(0, \pi)$, and thus the user's bid b_p is constrained in (p_l, p_u).

Note that w consists of two parts, which is the current proportional error w_p, and the historical accumulated errors $w_i(t)$:

$$w_p = k_p \times e_r \quad (k_p < 0, p_l - p_u < e_r < p_u - p_l) \tag{5}$$

where k_p is the proportional gain of the control signal. e_r is defined as the difference between the submitted bid at stage t and the auction price of the cloud service instance at stage t, i.e. $e_r = p_h - b_p|_{h=t}$. Therefore e_r is in $(p_l - p_u, p_u - p_l)$.

Since historical errors contain more information to help users to improve their bidding behavior and win bids, we decide to use an integral controller to further study the historical errors, which can be expressed as:

$$w_i(t) = k_i \times \int_0^t e(\tau)d\tau \approx k_i \times \sum_{h=0}^t e_h \quad (k_i < 0, p_l - p_u < e_h < p_u - p_l) \quad (6)$$

where k_i is the integral gain of the control signal, e_h is the historical error at stage h ($0 \leq h \leq t$). Based on Eq. 5 and Eq. 6, we can calculate the control signal w, that is: $w = w_p + w_i \approx k_p \times e_r + k_i \times \sum_{h=0}^t e_h$.

3.2   Cloud Providers

In this section, we introduce the basic settings of cloud providers. Cloud providers incur costs when providing cloud services. Similar to the work in [5], the marginal cost of provider i in a per-unit cloud service at stage t is:

$$c_{i,t} = c_{i,0} \times \left(\sum_{j \in N_{i,t}} d_{j,t} \right)^{-\beta e^{-\rho t}} \quad (7)$$

This equation indicates that the marginal cost of provider i will decrease when the number of cloud users $N_{i,t}$ in demands of cloud services $d_{j,t}$ increase at stage t, where $c_{i,0}$ is the initial cost of cloud provider i, $\beta > 0$ and $\rho > 0$ are two parameters to control the decreased marginal cost when users' demands increase. We then compute the provider's immediate payoff(reward), which is:

$$r_{i,t} = \sum_{j \in N_{i,t}} d_{j,t} \times (p_{i,t} - c_{i,t}) \quad (8)$$

Its long-term profits, which are the discounted cumulative profits over all stages, is calculated as: $R_i = \sum_{t=0}^T \gamma^t r_{i,t}$.

4   MADDPG Algorithm

In this section, we describe how to model the issue as a Partially Observable Markov Game and use MADDPG to solve it to generate a pricing strategy.

4.1   Partially Observable Markov Game

In this paper, two cloud providers repeatedly competing with each other to maximize their profits, which is a sequential-decision problem. Furthermore, since cloud providers and users cannot perceive all information of the world, it is a partially observable Markov game [9].

In more detail, this Markov game consists of a set of states S describing the cloud market, a set of pricing actions A_1, A_2 and a set of the observed states

O_1, O_2 for each provider. We use $s = (p^1_{avg}, p^1_{sd}, p^2_{avg}, p^2_{sd}, b^1_{avg}, b^1_{sd}, b^1_{max}, b^1_{min},$
$b^1_{mid}, b^2_{avg}, b^2_{sd}, b^2_{max}, b^2_{min}, b^2_{mid}, n_{1,t}, n_{2,t}, c_{1,t}, c_{2,t}) \in S$ to denote a state. For
cloud provider P_i, the average and standard deviation of its auction prices
over a period of time are p^i_{avg}, p^i_{sd} respectively. From the cloud users' bids, we
can compute the average, standard deviation, maximum, minimum, and median
value of the bids, which are $b^i_{avg}, b^i_{sd}, b^i_{max}, b^i_{min}, b^i_{mid}$ respectively. We use $n_{i,t}$
to represent the number of cloud users choosing to be served by provider i
at stage t, and use $c_{i,t}$ to denote the marginal cost of provider i at stage t.
Note that in the realistic cloud market, the cloud providers' auction prices
over a period of time are usually accessible to users. However, the number
of cloud users choosing to be served by provider i and users' bids are usu-
ally not public. That is, $p^1_{avg}, p^1_{sd}, p^2_{avg}, p^2_{sd}$ are shared public information of
all providers, but $b^i_{avg}, b^i_{sd}, b^i_{max}, b^i_{min}, b^i_{mid}, n_{i,t}, c_{i,t}$ are private information hidden to the other cloud provider. Therefore, the observation of provider P_i is
$o_i = (p^1_{avg}, p^1_{sd}, p^2_{avg}, p^2_{sd}, b^i_{avg}, b^i_{sd}, b^i_{max}, b^i_{min}, b^i_{mid}, n_{i,t}, c_{i,t}) \in O_i$.

Then we use $\pi_{\theta_i} : O_i \times A_i \to [0, 1]$ to present the pricing strategy of provider i.
After providers take pricing actions, the state transfers to the next state according to the state transfer function $\Delta : S \times A_1 \times A_2 \to S'$, then each provider can
obtain the immediate reward $r_{i,t} : S \times A_i \to \mathbb{R}$, and obtain the corresponding
observation $o_i : S \to O_i$ of the next state. Given the immediate reward made
at stage t, the cloud provider can maximize the long-term profits through an
efficient pricing strategy.

4.2   Multi-Agent Deep Deterministic Policy Gradient

In this section, we introduce how to use MADDPG to generate a pricing strategy
in the competing environment with two cloud providers. MADDPG is a multi-
agent reinforcement learning algorithm based on the Actor-Critic framework
proposed by $OpenAI$, where Actor is a probability-based actuator, while Critic
evaluates every action of Actor to modify the weight of Actor. When the critic
of MADDPG evaluates the actors' actions, it not only considers themselves but
also the rest of the agents [10].

Specifically, the two cloud providers whose strategies $\pi_\theta = \{\pi_1, \pi_2\}$ are
parameterized by $\theta = \{\theta_1, \theta_2\}$. Then the gradient of expected return $J(\theta_i) = E[R_i]$ of cloud provider i is:

$$\nabla_{\theta_i} J(\theta_i) = E_{s \sim p^\mu, a_i \sim \pi_i} [\nabla_{\theta_i} \log \pi_i(a_i|o_i) Q_i^{\pi_\theta}(x, a_1, a_2)] \quad (9)$$

where p^μ is the state distribution, $x = (o_1, o_2)$ is the observed value of all cloud
providers. $Q_i^{\pi_\theta}(x, a_1, a_2)$ is a centralized value function and its input contains not
only some observed information x, but also all providers' actions a_1, a_2. When
Eq. 9 is extended to a deterministic policy, we use μ_{θ_i} w.r.t. parameter θ_i to
represent the provider's strategy. Then its gradient can be written as:

$$\nabla_{\theta_i} J(\mu_{\theta_i}) = E_{s,a \sim D}[\nabla_{\theta_i} \mu_{\theta_i}(a_i|o_i) \nabla_{a_i} Q_i^\mu(x, a_1, a_2)|_{a_i = \mu_{\theta_i}(o_i)}] \quad (10)$$

where D is the experience replay buffer contains tuple $(x, a_1, a_2, r_1, r_2, x')$, in which r_1, r_2 are the immediate rewards, and x' is the two providers' observations in the next stage. The centralized action-value function Q_i^μ is updated as:

$$L(\theta_i) = E_{x,a,r,x'} \left[\left(Q_i^\mu (x, a_1, a_2) - y \right)^2 \right], y = r_i + \gamma Q_i^{\mu'} (x', a_1', a_2') \Big|_{a_j' = \mu_{\theta_j'}'(o_j)} \tag{11}$$

where $\mu' = \{\mu_{\theta_1'}, \mu_{\theta_2'}\}$ is the set of target policies with the delayed parameter θ_i'.

Updating the value function in Eq. 11 requires the pricing strategy of the opponent provider. However, the opponent's pricing strategy is usually private in the realistic environment, and thus hard to be known. Therefore each cloud provider can only estimate the opponent j's pricing strategy $\hat{\pi}_{\varphi_i^j}$ with φ parameter instead. This approximated strategy is learned by maximizing the log probability of provider j's actions with an entropy regularizer, which is:

$$L\left(\varphi_i^j\right) = -E_{o_j,a_j} \left[\log \hat{\pi}_{\varphi_i^j} (a_j | o_j) + \lambda H \left(\hat{\pi}_{\varphi_i^j} \right) \right] \tag{12}$$

where $H\left(\hat{\pi}_{\varphi_i^j}\right)$ is the entropy of the policy distribution. Now y in Eq. 11 can be replaced by the approximated value $\hat{y}$:

$$\hat{y} = r_i + \gamma Q_i^{\mu'} \left(x', \pi_{\varphi_i}' (o_i), \hat{\pi}_{\varphi_i^j}' (o_j) \right), \quad i \neq j \tag{13}$$

where $\hat{\pi}_{\varphi_i^j}' (o_j)$ is the target network of the approximate policy $\hat{\pi}_{\varphi_i^j}$.

To improve the robustness of agents' strategies, sub-strategy will be used to enhance the adaptability of agents. Therefore, in each round of a game, the cloud provider randomly selects a sub-strategy to execute from a set that contains K different sub-strategies. For cloud provider i, the goal is to maximize the ensemble objective, which is:

$$J_e(\mu_{\theta_i}) = E_{k \sim \text{unif}(1,K), s \sim p^\mu, a \sim \mu_{\theta_i^{(k)}}} [R_i(s,a)] \tag{14}$$

where μ_{θ_i} is a set of K different sub-strategies, and $\mu_{\theta_i^{(k)}}$ represents an element in this set. Consequently, the gradient of ensemble objective w.r.t $\theta_i^{(k)}$ is:

$$\nabla_{\theta_i^{(k)}} J_e(\mu_{\theta_i}) = \frac{1}{K} E_{x,a \sim D_i^{(k)}} \left[\nabla_{\theta_i^{(k)}} \mu_{\theta_i^{(k)}} (a_i | o_i) \nabla_{a_i} Q^{\mu_{\theta_i}} (x, a_1, a_2) \Big|_{a_i = \mu_{\theta_i^{(k)}}(o_i)} \right] \tag{15}$$

where $D_i^{(k)}$ is the replay buffer for each sub-strategy $\mu_{\theta_i^{(k)}}$ of agent i.

5 Experiments

5.1 Parameter Settings

In this paper, two cloud providers P_1 and P_2 can set the auction prices in the range of $[10, 100]$. Each round has 200 stages. We set the number of cloud users at initial stage $t = 0$ is $N_0 = 100$, at saturation stage $t = 200$ is $N_\infty = 1000$, the temporal evolution rate of the market is $\delta = 0.07$. The users' marginal values follows a uniform distribution within $[40, 70]$. Then we use two queues $Queue_1, Queue_2$ to store the two providers' historical auction prices, and the length of the queue is $len = 10$. The lower bound price of the cloud service instance equals to the lowest price that the provider can set, i.e. $p_l = 10$, and the upper bound price of the cloud service instance equals to the marginal value that cloud user j can obtain from per-unit requested resource, i.e. $p_u = m_j$. k_p and k_i in the users' bidding model follow a uniform distribution within $(-0.1, 0)$. We set $\beta = 0.01$, $\rho = 0.02$ and $c_{i,0} = 8.0$, and the users' demands for cloud resources follow a uniform distribution of $d_{j,t} \sim U[1, 3]$.

5.2 Training

In this section, we generate a pricing strategy that can maximize the cloud provider's long-term profits in the competing cloud market. The same as the work done in [13], we consider the fictitious self-playing which can learn the optimal pricing strategy from scratch. Therefore, we use MADDPG with fictitious self-playing to train our agents. After training, a pricing strategy based on MADDPG is shown in Fig. 2. From this figure, we find that the prices set by the two cloud providers P_1, P_2 at each stage converge in $[10, 30]$, which is less than the highest auction price range $[40, 70]$ that cloud users can accept. It further indicates that the MADDPG algorithm can learn the marginal values of cloud users, and set the prices a bit lower than the marginal values of most users. By doing this, the cloud provider can maximize its profits while keeping cloud users.

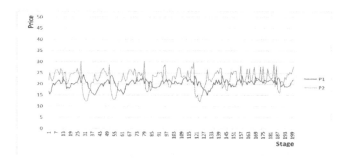

Fig. 2. MADDPG's pricing strategy

5.3 Strategy Evaluation

In this section, we run experiments to evaluate our pricing strategy against four typical pricing strategies, and we evaluate the pricing strategy by using these metrics: auction price set by the pricing strategy, cloud user ratio which is the ratio of the number of cloud users entering in the provider to the total number of users, and cumulative profits which is the long-term profits made by the provider across all stages.

Vs. Random Pricing Strategy. In the market, there exist some fresh competing cloud providers who may explore the market by adopting a random pricing strategy to obtain more information. Therefore, we first evaluate our pricing strategy against the competing provider adopting a random pricing strategy of uniform distribution. The results are shown in Fig. 3, we find that the provider using the MADDPG pricing strategy can attract more cloud users and obtain more cumulative profits than the opponent using a random pricing strategy.

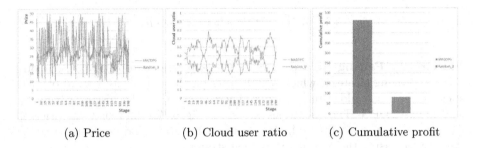

(a) Price   (b) Cloud user ratio   (c) Cumulative profit

Fig. 3. MADDPG vs. Random (uniform distribution)

Vs. Price Reduction Strategy. Some cloud providers may keep reducing the prices to attract cloud users in the cloud market. We consider two kinds of price reduction strategies, named Linear Reduction strategy (RecL) and Exponential Reduction strategy (RecE) where RecL decreases the price linearly while RecE decreases the price rapidly in the initial stages and then becoming smooth when approaching the threshold price. The results are shown in Fig. 4 and Fig. 5. From the experiments, we find that our provider using MADDPG can adjust the price in time to adapt to the changes of the opponent, and thus make the cumulative profits at a higher level.

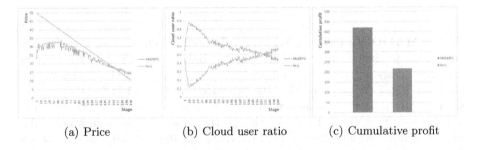

(a) Price   (b) Cloud user ratio   (c) Cumulative profit

Fig. 4. MADDPG vs. Linear Reduction

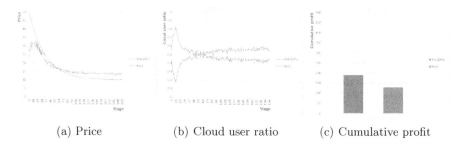

(a) Price   (b) Cloud user ratio   (c) Cumulative profit

Fig. 5. MADDPG vs. Exp reduction

Vs. Greedy Pricing Strategy. Similarly, some cloud providers may adopt a greedy pricing strategy, which only focuses on the immediate reward of each stage, regardless of long-term profits. Therefore, we set the discount factor γ to 0 in MADDPG. The results are shown in Fig. 6. We find that the price of the greedy strategy is slightly higher, so the number of cloud users attracted by the provider using the MADDPG pricing strategy is higher. Again our pricing strategy can beat the greedy pricing strategy in terms of cumulative profits.

(a) Price   (b) Cloud user ratio   (c) Cumulative profit

Fig. 6. MADDPG vs. Greedy

Vs. M-MADDPG Pricing Strategy. To further demonstrate the effectiveness of the pricing strategy generated by MADDPG algorithm, we train a new pricing strategy against itself, and we name it as M-MADDPG. The results are shown in Fig. 7. We can see that the provider using the M-MADDPG pricing strategy has almost the same cumulative profits as that in the MADDPG pricing strategy. This means that even though the opponent can train a particular pricing strategy against the MADDPG pricing strategy, it still cannot beat our pricing strategy.

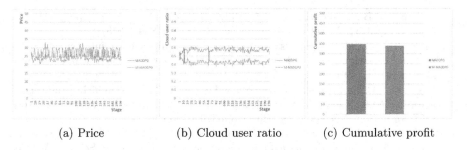

    (a) Price   (b) Cloud user ratio   (c) Cumulative profit

Fig. 7. MADDPG vs. M-MADDPG

6   Conclusion

In this paper, we use the gradient-based multi-agent deep reinforcement learning algorithm to generate a pricing strategy for the competing cloud provider. We also run extensive experiments to evaluate our pricing strategy against the other four typical pricing strategies in terms of long-term profits. Experimental results show that MADDPG based pricing strategy can not only beat the opponent's pricing strategy effectively but also learn the marginal values of cloud users and users' choices of providers. Our work can be used to provide useful insights on designing practical pricing strategies for competing cloud providers.

Acknowledgement. This paper was funded by the Humanity and Social Science Youth Research Foundation of Ministry of Education (Grant No. 19YJC790111), the Philosophy and Social Science Post-Foundation of Ministry of Education (Grant No. 18JHQ060) and Shenzhen Fundamental Research Program (Grant No. JCYJ20190809175613332).

References

1. Åström, K.J., Murray, R.M.: Feedback Systems: An Introduction for Scientists and Engineers. Princeton University Press, Princeton (2010)
2. Cai, Z., Li, X., Ruiz, R., Li, Q.: Price forecasting for spot instances in cloud computing. Future Gener. Comput. Syst. **79**, 38–53 (2018)
3. Dawoud, W., Takouna, I., Meinel, C.: Reliable approach to sell the spare capacity in the cloud. In: Cloud Computing, pp. 229–236 (2012)
4. Feng, Y., Li, B., Li, B.: Price competition in an oligopoly market with multiple IaaS cloud providers. IEEE Trans. Comput. **63**(1), 59–73 (2013)
5. Jung, H., Klein, C.M.: Optimal inventory policies under decreasing cost functions via geometric programming. Eur. J. Oper. Res. **132**(3), 628–642 (2001)
6. Kansal, S., Kumar, H., Kaushal, S., Sangaiah, A.K.: Genetic algorithm-based cost minimization pricing model for on-demand IaaS cloud service. J. Supercomput. **76**, 1–26 (2018)
7. Khandelwal, V., Gupta, C.P., Chaturvedi, A.K.: Perceptive bidding strategy for Amazon EC2 spot instance market. Multiagent Grid Syst. **14**(1), 83–102 (2018)

8. Kumar, D., Baranwal, G., Raza, Z., Vidyarthi, D.P.: A survey on spot pricing in cloud computing. J. Netw. Syst. Manage. **26**(4), 809–856 (2018)

9. Littman, M.L.: Markov games as a framework for multi-agent reinforcement learning. In: Proceedings of the Eleventh International Conference on Machine Learning (ML 1994) (1994)

10. Lowe, R., Wu, Y., Tamar, A., Harb, J., Abbeel, O.P., Mordatch, I.: Multi-agent actor-critic for mixed cooperative-competitive environments. In: Advances in Neural Information Processing Systems, pp. 6379–6390 (2017)

11. Pearl, R., Reed, L.J.: On the rate of growth of the population of the united states since 1790 and its mathematical representation. Proc. Nat. Acad. Sci. U.S.A. **6**(6), 275 (1920)

12. Shi, B., Zhu, H., Wang, J., Sun, B.: Optimize pricing policy in evolutionary market with multiple proactive competing cloud providers. In: Proceedings of the IEEE 29th International Conference on Tools with Artificial Intelligence (ICTAI 2017), pp. 202–209. IEEE (2017)

13. Silver, D., et al.: Mastering the game of go without human knowledge. Nature **550**(7676), 354–359 (2017)

14. Truong-Huu, T., Tham, C.K.: A game-theoretic model for dynamic pricing and competition among cloud providers. In: Proceedings of the 2013 IEEE/ACM 6th International Conference on Utility and Cloud Computing, pp. 235–238. IEEE (2013)

15. Zheng, L., Joe-Wong, C., Tan, C.W., Chiang, M., Wang, X.: How to bid the cloud. ACM SIGCOMM Comput. Commun. Rev. **45**(4), 71–84 (2015)

Dynamic Edge User Allocation with User Specified QoS Preferences

Subrat Prasad Panda, Kaustabha Ray, and Ansuman Banerjee[✉]

Advanced Computing and Microelectronics Unit, Indian Statistical Institute,
Kolkata, India
subratprasad.mail@gmail.com, {kaustabha_r,ansuman}@isical.ac.in

Abstract. Mobile Edge Computing (MEC) policies that bind user service requests to edge servers, seldom take into account user preferences of Quality-of-Service (QoS) and the resulting Quality-of-Experience (QoE). In this paper, we design a novel user-centric optimal allocation policy considering the QoS preferences of users, with an attempt to maximize the overall QoE. Additionally, we propose a real-time mobility aware user-centric heuristic algorithm to solve the allocation problem by accommodating the time varying QoS demands of users. Experimental results on real data sets demonstrate the efficiency of our allocation scheme and a comparison with state-of-art approaches in MEC literature.

Keywords: Edge computing · Server allocation · User migration

1 Introduction

In recent times, Mobile Edge Computing (MEC) [1] has emerged as a new paradigm that allows service providers to deploy services on MEC servers located near base stations. As users move around, their application service invocations are routed to proximate MEC servers to curtail the high latencies of cloud communication networks. A service allocation policy is designed to determine the user-service-server binding, i.e. which service requests from which users are provisioned by which MEC servers in their vicinity, as they move around. In recent years, several allocation policies, static and dynamic, considering different optimization metrics have been proposed in literature [3,4,6–8].

The general philosophy of service allocation policies is to design and optimize a user-mobility aware service-server-user binding that optimizes some quantitative metric (e.g.. latency, energy, throughput) to cater to user application service needs and ensure seamless usage experience. A recent work [6] has proposed a novel view of considering qualitative QoS level offerings by service providers in designing the service bindings. Additionally, the authors have quantitatively correlated QoS values with overall Quality-of-Experience (QoE) of users to demonstrate the existence of thresholds, beyond which, enhancing QoS values no longer enhances a user QoE. This work, however, does not consider a user's QoS preferences when deciding these bindings. Moreover, the binding is static, in other

© Springer Nature Switzerland AG 2020
E. Kafeza et al. (Eds.): ICSOC 2020, LNCS 12571, pp. 187–197, 2020.
https://doi.org/10.1007/978-3-030-65310-1_15

words, once an allocation is decided for a user service invocation to a specific QoS level at an edge server, he is continued to be served at the same level throughout, oblivious to the fact that the user may not be in a position to enjoy services at a higher QoS level always due to battery or other constraints. Also, the policy is not adaptive, in the sense that user movements, joining or leaving of users, and user QoS preferences and preference changes in terms of the required QoS levels, are not accounted for. This motivated us to design a dynamic self-adaptive allocation policy that can address these variations.

Designing an allocation that considers user preferences of QoS levels is challenging due to the dynamics of MEC systems, the stochastic nature of service invocation patterns and the large space of user-service-server binding configurations. In our view, allocation policies in literature are more catered towards the perspective of service providers [5,6], aiming to optimize quantitative metrics, often ignoring users' qualitative preferences of QoS levels when making allocation decisions. QoS levels typically translate to a monotonically increasing footprint on the resource consumption for both the user and the provider, at the server end where the service is provisioned, and at the user end where a communication latency depending on the size of transferred data is incurred. Policies like [6], being user agnostic, may allocate QoS levels to users leading to an added aggravation. In such scenarios, a service provider may also suffer a degradation in throughput since the high QoS levels translate to more resources allocated at the server end which could have been otherwise allocated to other users. In the worst case, an overtly aggressive user-agnostic QoS allocation can lead to new service requests being needlessly denied service.

Our proposal in this paper is a service allocation policy that caters to both user and provider views considering individual QoS preference levels to enhance overall QoE of users in a mobility-aware scenario. The QoS preferences of users can vary over time, for example, a user initially having high battery levels, and preferring to stream services at high QoS levels, may sometime later choose to downgrade his preference depending on the changing battery conditions to alleviate energy utilization spent in data communication. We take into account such user specified adjustments in an attempt to maximize the overall user experience. Additionally, we cater to mobility of users and changing conditions as well. We first formulate the problem of dynamic QoS preference aware edge user allocation and propose an Integer Linear Programming (ILP) formulation for the optimal solution, and a heuristic which produces near optimal QoE allocations. We use the EUA dataset [4–7], a real-world dataset as edge server locations, and the PlanetLab and Seattle Latency dataset [10] to generate latencies representative of MEC environments to validate our approach. Experimental results demonstrate the efficiency of our heuristic which produces near optimal allocations. We compare our results with two state-of-the-art approaches and show that our proposal outperforms both with respect to QoE.

2   A Motivating Example

In this section, we present a motivating example to explain the problem context. Consider the scenario demonstrated in Fig. 1. There are two edge servers E_1 and E_2 and six users u_1, u_2, u_3, u_4, u_5 and u_6. The coverage area of a particular server is marked by a circle, hence any user within the coverage area of a server can use the services hosted at the particular server. For example, u_1 can only access the services from E_1, whereas, u_4 can access the services hosted at both E_1 and E_2. The resource capacity of each server is represented as a resource vector $\langle vCPUs, RAM, storage, bandwidth \rangle$ [6], where $vCPU$ denotes the number of virtual CPUs. For the example scenario, assume the resource capacities of server are denoted by vectors $s_1 = \langle 16, 32, 750, 8 \rangle$ and $s_2 = \langle 16, 16, 500, 4 \rangle$. Edge servers host services at different QoS levels. Provisioning a service at a QoS level consumes a certain amount of server resources. We assume both E_1 and E_2 host a service $\mathcal{P}$ with 3 QoS levels W_1, W_2 and W_3 as in Table 1. Each QoS level has a resource requirement represented by a 4-element resource vector $W = \langle vCPUs, RAM, storage, bandwidth \rangle$ and an associated QoE value. W_3 is the highest QoS level. Each user when invoking $\mathcal{P}$ specifies a desired QoS level, W_1, W_2 or W_3, at which he wishes to be served, and additionally, a lower tolerance threshold QoS level, below which the services are rendered unacceptable to him. The initial QoS preferences of the users are in Table 2. In the scenario demonstrated in Fig. 1, u_3 follows the trajectory as depicted by the curved line while all other users remain stationary. While in its trajectory, at time $t = 0$, demarcated by a black rectangle, u_3 invokes $\mathcal{P}$ with QoS preference as W_3. Simultaneously, u_1, u_2, u_4, and u_5 also invoke $\mathcal{P}$ at $t = 0$, while u_6 does the same at $t = 5$ s. During the course of its trajectory, at $t = 5$ s, u_3 downgrades its QoS preference from W_3 to W_2, at the point indicated by the blue diamond.

Table 1. Available QoS levels

QoS level	Resource requirement	QoE
W_1	$\langle 2, 2, 10, 1 \rangle$	1.5
W_2	$\langle 4, 4, 15, 1.5 \rangle$	4
W_3	$\langle 8, 4, 20, 2 \rangle$	5

Table 2. User QoS details

User	QoS level	QoS Min	Allocation $t=0$ s [6]	Allocation $t=0$ s Our	Allocation $t=5$ s [6]	Allocation $t=5$ s Our
u_1	W_1	Any	E_1, W_2	E_1, W_1	E_1, W_3	E_1, W_1
u_2	Any	Any	E_1, W_2	E_1, W_2	E_1, W_2	E_1, W_3
u_3	W_3	W_2	E_1, W_3	E_1, W_3	E_2, W_3	E_2, W_2
u_4	W_2	Any	E_2, W_3	E_2, W_2	E_1, W_2	E_1, W_2
u_5	W_3	W_2	E_2, W_3	E_2, W_3	E_2, W_3	E_2, W_2
u_6	W_1	Any	Idle	Idle	NA	E_2, W_1

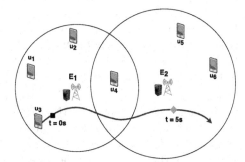

Fig. 1. Representative MEC scenario (Color figure online)

User QoS Preference Agnostic Allocation: A user preference agnostic policy such as [6] does not even take into the account the initial QoS preferences. The allocation is shown in Column 4 of Table 2 as E_k, W_p pairs indicating the edge server

E_k and the QoS level W_p to which the user u_i is bound. Moreover, at $t = 5\,\mathrm{s}$, this policy continues to provision u_3 at W_3 as shown in Column 6, agnostic of the fact that u_3 had requested for a downgrade to W_2. The QoE value experienced by u_3 is 5. In such a scenario, since the bandwidth requirement of W_3 is 2 Mbps, u_3 incurs an additional latency overhead due to increased data transfer. Also, at $t = 5\,\mathrm{s}$, when u_6 invokes the service, E_2 no longer has the needed resources to serve him, considering its serving capacity and the resources already consumed. Given the coverage constraint and the locations shown, u_6 cannot be served by E_1. However, had u_3's QoS level been reduced to W_2 when u_3 changed its preference level, u_6 could be onboarded at E_2.

Our Method at Work: Our user preference aware policy considers the initial preferences, and allocates levels as depicted in Table 2 to the users. Further, at time $t = 5\,\mathrm{s}$, when u_3 indicates its change of preference level, we reduce the QoS level allocated from W_3 to W_2. In such a scenario, for QoS level W_2, the bandwidth requirement is 1.5 Mbps, hence, the additional latency incurred by u_3 earlier is no longer applicable. When we assign W_2 to u_3, the QoE index of u_3 is 4, lower than W_3. Since u_3 requested for a lower QoS level, we consider the corresponding QoE value is good enough. Additionally, since a lower QoS level corresponds to lower resource consumption at the server, we can re-distribute the resources to better serve other users. u_6 can now be onboarded at $t = 5\,\mathrm{s}$.

The example shows the trade-off between resource consumption, latency and QoE in user QoS agnostic versus user QoS preference aware provisioning. The latter is challenging to design considering time-varying user QoS requirements while catering to user mobility. To the best of our knowledge, this is the first work towards mobility-aware dynamic user allocation with user QoS preferences.

3   System Model and ILP Formulation

In this section, we first formalize the system model. We consider a discrete time-slotted model [7]. We denote by $U^t = \{u_1, u_2 \ldots u_n\}$ the set of active users and by $S^t = \{s_1, s_2 \ldots s_m\}$ the set of active edge-servers at time t. Each server s_j has a radius R_j and a capacity vector C_j^t $\langle CPU, RAM, storage, bandwidth\rangle$ at t, denoted as $C_j^t = \langle \left(c_j^1\right)^t, \left(c_j^2\right)^t, \left(c_j^3\right)^t, \left(c_j^4\right)^t\rangle$ in that order. We denote by W_l the demand vector $\langle CPU, RAM, storage, bandwidth\rangle$ of QoS level l, denoted as $\langle w_l^1, w_l^2, w_l^3, w_l^4\rangle$ in that order. A server can only cater to service requests from users within the service radius. For user u_i, the preferred QoS level is denoted as H_i^t, and the threshold L_i^t for the lowest QoS level tolerable. A service allocation policy can choose to serve him at *any* QoS level between the threshold and the preferred level (both inclusive), with an attempt to serve maximum number of users at their preferred levels, thereby, maximizing the overall QoE of all stakeholders, while keeping in view the capacity of each edge server, and the coverage constraint induced by the relative separating distance between the user and the servers. If a user cannot be allocated to any edge-server a suitable QoS level inside the preference range, he has to wait till the required resources are available. We assume a set of q QoS levels. Let E_{il}^t denote the QoE value for u_i at QoS level l, q_i^t the QoS level assigned to u_i at time t, d_{ij}^t the distance between u_i and server s_j, Δ_{ij}^t the latency experienced by u_i allocated to s_j at t. We compute latency Δ_{ij}^t as a function of q_i^t and d_{ij}^t. The latency experienced in any user-server allocation has to honor a maximum limit denoted by δ. We formulate an Integer Linear Program (ILP) for the problem below.

Objective:

$$Maximize: \sum_{t \in T} \sum_{i=1}^{|U^t|} \sum_{j=1}^{|S^t|} \sum_{l=L_i^t}^{H_i^t} x_{ijl}^t \times E_{il}^t \tag{1}$$

where,

$$x_{ijl}^t = \begin{cases} 1, & \text{If user } u_i \text{ is allocated to server } s_j \text{ at QoS level } l \text{ at time } t \\ 0, & \text{Otherwise} \end{cases}$$

Subject to:

1. Coverage Constraint:

$$d_{ij}^t \leq R_j^t \tag{2}$$

2. Capacity Constraint:

$$\sum_{i=1}^{|U^t|} \sum_{l=L_i^t}^{H_i^t} w_l^k \times x_{ijl}^t \leq \left(c_j^k\right)^t : \forall t \in T, \forall j \in \{1, \ldots |S^t|\}, \forall k \in \{1, \ldots 4\} \tag{3}$$

3. Latency Constraint:

$$\sum_{j=1}^{|S^t|} \sum_{l=L_i^t}^{H_i^t} \Delta_{ij}^t \times x_{ijl}^t \leq \delta : \quad \forall t \in T, \ \forall i \in \{1, \ldots |U^t|\} \tag{4}$$

4. User-Server Mapping:

$$\sum_{j=1}^{|S^t|} \sum_{l=L_i^t}^{H_i^t} x_{ijl}^t \leq 1 : \quad \forall t \in T, \ \forall i \in \{1, \ldots |U^t|\} \tag{5}$$

5. Integer Constraint:

$$x_{ijl}^t \in \{0,1\} : \forall t \in T, \forall i \in \{1, .. |U^t|\}, \forall j \in \{1, .. |S^t|\}, \forall l \in \{L_i^t .. H_i^t\} \tag{6}$$

The objective function aims at maximization of the overall QoE of users over the set of time slots t over a period T. The indicator variable x_{ijl}^t at any time instant t, encodes all possible server-user-qos preferences. The objective function implicitly encodes all individual preferences and the threshold in the summation, hence no additional constraints are needed to specify the minimum threshold QoS level as required. At any time instant t, a user u_i can be allocated to s_j if the user is within radius R_j, as expressed by the constraint in Eq. 2. To allocate u_i to s_j at a QoS level l, the resource requirement at s_j is denoted by W_l. The total resources allocated must honor the capacity constraint of each server. Equation 3 ensures that the combined requirements of users allocated to a server remains within the server's total capacity for each dimension CPU, RAM, storage and bandwidth of the resource vector. Equation 4 ensures that users are allocated to servers such that the latency bound is honoured. Equation 5 is used to express that a single service can only be allocated to a single server at a QoS level at any t. Equation 6 specifies that x^t_{ijl} variables are Boolean indicator variables denoting service requests from users, the respective server to which the requests are allocated and required QoS values. As observed in [6], QoS is non-linearly correlated with the QoE for any service, and we represent the QoS-QoE correlation using the logistic function (Eq. (7)) as in [6] with an additional scaling according to the QoS level preference and threshold specified by a user. The QoE E^t_{il} experienced by u_i at time t for level l is expressed as:

$$E^i_l = \frac{E_{max}}{1 + \exp\left\{-\alpha\left(\gamma^t_{il} - \beta^t_i\right)\right\}} \tag{7}$$

The scaling assists to assign lowest QoE value to lowest QoS level and highest QoE value to highest QoS level. E^t_{il} depends on the QoS level W^t_l, his QoS preference H^t_i and the threshold level L^t_i at time t. Here, $\gamma^t_{il} = \frac{\sum_{k=1}^{4} w^k_l}{4}$ is the mean computational demand of QoS level W_l of user u_i at time t; $\beta^t_i = \frac{\gamma^t_{iH^t_i} - \gamma^t_{iL^t_i}}{2}$ is the mid-point of QoE value of user u_i at t. The value E_{max} is the maximum value of QoE and α is the growth factor of the logistics function.

A solution to the ILP gives us for each time slot t, an optimal allocation of user service requests to QoS levels at edge servers, honoring QoS preferences, the latency upper bound and radius constraints. If the ILP solver returns unsatisfiable, we conclude that the user set cannot be allocated to their proximate edge servers, given the constraints. To cater to dynamic mobility and preference changes, we re-evaluate the ILP when any of the following scenarios occur: (a) any user changes the QoS specification; b) users or edge-servers become inactive; c) users move in and out of the service zone of servers; and d) new service requests are placed. However, given the associated computational needs, re-evaluating the ILP frequently turns out to be a non-scalable strategy, as demonstrated in our experimental results presented in Sect. 5. To address this, we design a scalable heuristic to cater to real-world dynamic scenarios, as described in the following.

4   Heuristic Solution

In this section, we present the design of an efficient polynomial time heuristic which generates near-optimal solutions. We use a Red-Black Tree [2] as an indexing data-structure. The algorithm maintains a Red-Black Tree for each edge server and uses a metric defined as i-factor for each user in its service zone as index. This heuristic is used in place of the ILP, and executes whenever any of the events mentioned earlier occur, necessitating a reevaluation of the allocation. However, this being a polynomial time algorithm, is lightweight and can be executed more efficiently than the ILP. Our heuristic has the following steps.

- We first divide the new users into two classes, single-server class (S-class) and multi-server class (M-class). The users within the range of only one edge-server are clustered into S-class and the users withing the range of more than one edge-server are put into the M-class. For example, in Fig. 1, the users u_1, u_2, u_3, u_5 and u_6 are within the range of only one server i.e. E_1 and are hence clustered into S-class. However, u_4 can access both E_1 and E_2, hence is put into the M-class. This categorization is done once for all users at the start, and adjusted at every time slot only if there is a change in user locations, new users join in, or existing users leave.
- The users in both S-class and M-class are allocated an initial QoS level at their minimum threshold specified. Referring to the scenario in Sect. 2, u_1, u_2, u_3 u_4, and u_5 are initially assigned at QoS level W_1, W_1, W_2, W_1 and W_2 respectively. The increment factor (i-factor), discussed later in this section, is computed for all the users in both the S-class and M-class. The i-factor is determined by user's QoS preference and presently assigned QoS level ($plevel$). For determining the allocation, S-class is considered before the M-class since S-class users are bound to a single edge server. Each user is assigned to the edge server according to his i-factor. Users with low i-factor get higher preference to an edge server during the assignment. For M-class users, the allocation policy tries to assign an user to the nearest server with required remaining computation resource, with a motivation to serve him with better latency experience. We examine the users according to their i-factor, compute an initial assignment and update the Red-Black Tree with i-factor as key for each server.
- Our heuristic then attempts to enhance the QoS level of each user (upper bounded by their respective preference levels) and re-evaluates the i-factor after incrementing the QoS level. This process of incrementing continues till all users receive their QoS preference levels or the server exhausts its available resources and we move on to examine the next server in the vicinity of the user from where he can be served.
- For servers which have exhausted their resources, users from M-class may be migrated to the other nearby servers having free resources. Once users have been migrated across nearby servers, the QoS levels have to be re-evaluated. QoS upgrade is re-performed after migration.

The heuristic selects the user with smallest i-factor and increments the QoS level of that user. It then proceeds to update the Red-Black Tree with the re-computed i-factor. Considering our example, at $t = 0$, on enhancement of QoS levels, the users $u_1 \ldots u_5$ are alloted W_1, W_2, W_3, W_2 and W_3 respectively.

Computation of i-factor: The i-factor helps to determine which user causes more alterations to QoS values if the QoS level of a user is increased. Users with lower i-factor values are given higher preferences when the QoS values allocated to them are upgraded. Equation 8 determines the i-factor of a certain user u_i having level preference and threshold of H_i^t and L_i^t respectively with presently assigned QoS level of l at time t. The QoE function E_i^t, E_{max} and α are from Eq. 7 discussed previously. The numerator affects the i-factor by scaling the QoE value according to the present QoS level, i.e., it assigns a higher i-factor as user's reach their preferred QoS levels. The denominator demarcates the difference between H_i^t and L_i^t, the higher the difference, the lower is i-factor.

$$ifactor = \frac{E_{max} \times (E_i^t + l)}{\alpha \times max(H_i^t - L_i^t, 1)} \tag{8}$$

Migrating Users for Improving QoE: Once all the Red-Black trees corresponding to all edge servers have been updated, we find the list of users who can be migrated from the servers which have exhausted their resource capacities and hence, no further QoS upgradation for users are possible. Upon successful migration, our allocation algorithm is re-initiated for possible QoS upgradation.

5   Experiments and Analysis of Results

All experiments were conducted on a machine with Intel Core i5-8250U processor and 8 GB RAM. The ILP model discussed in Sect. 3 was solved using the Python Mixed-Integer-Programming library. The results from our heuristic are compared with the baseline ILP formulated in Sect. 3, the optimal algorithm presented in [6] and the dynamic mobility aware policy in [7].

Experimental Setup: We use the EUA data-set for edge server locations, which includes data of base stations and users within the Melbourne Central Business District area. The coverage area of edge servers are set randomly to values between 200-400 m radius. To simulate different attributes of users over time, we randomly select several users and do the following: a) randomly assign 20% users with 0 m/s for static users, 30% users with random speed between $1 - 2$ m/s for walking users, and the remaining 50% users with speed between $10 - 20$ m/s for users in vehicle; b) randomly assign an initial direction between 0° to 360° which then follows the random way-point mobility model [7]; and c) randomly assign the users' high and low QoS preferences.

We generate latencies from the real world PlanetLab and Seattle latency data-set [10]. Since the PlanetLab and Seattle latency data-set comprises latencies from across the world, which is not fully representative of latencies in an MEC environment, we cluster the data-set into 400 clusters considering devices which are in proximity of each other. A cluster is randomly picked and a representative latency is assigned according to our latency measure derived based on the distance and QoS level, as in [9]. We consider the product of distance and QoS level, which is scaled down according to the number of clusters. A discrete-time slotted model with each slot of 25 s is considered in which the users move and change their QoS preferences dynamically. At the end of each time slot, some user locations are updated, and to 20% of users, we randomly assign new preference levels to simulate dynamic QoS preferences. The number of discrete time slots is kept at 20 for each experiment. To consider various sizes of user population, we vary the number of users from 50 to 250 at intervals of 50 users, while keeping the number of servers to 50 and the server resources at 100% of the cumulative resource requirement of all users at the highest QoS level, distributed uniformly over all servers. Each experiment is averaged over 50 runs. For the QoE model, we set $E_{max} = 5$, $\alpha = 1.5$. We compare the results of our ILP, our heuristic, the static ILP proposed in [6] and MobMig [7], a Mobility-aware dynamic allocation policy. We consider the ILP in [6] by running it in each discrete time step since it is a static formulation. We use MobMig by setting the QoS level as highest possible since MobMig does not support dynamic QoS changes. For comparison, we study the following metrics: a) Average QoE achieved per time slot; b) Average number of users allocated within their QoS preference per time slot; c) Average execution time (CPU time) for evaluation of algorithms; and d) Average latency experienced by users.

Results and Discussion: Figure 2 depicts the average QoE and the average number of users allocated within their QoS preference on the experimental setup with varying users. The results show the effectiveness of the heuristic in being able to generate near optimal solutions comparable with the results from the optimal ILP for both average QoE and average number of users allocated within their QoS preferences. The ILP achieves better allocation of users within their QoS preference having QoE values similar to the ILP in [6]. MobMig [7], being unaware of user QoS preferences allocates users at highest available QoS level when used in a variable QoS scenario. Consequently, the policy leads to a violation in preference levels in a large fraction of users as inferred from Fig. 2b. However, the ILP [6], which seeks to optimize overall QoE, generates near equivalent QoE and number of allocated users as compared to our ILP and heuristic.

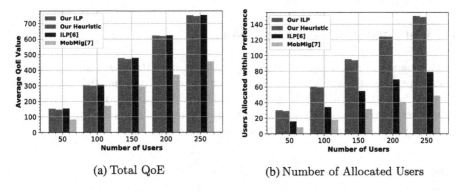

(a) Total QoE   (b) Number of Allocated Users

Fig. 2. Varying users experiment results

The average latency per user is depicted in Fig. 3a. As can be inferred from Fig. 3a, both our optimal and heuristic policies significantly outperform MobMig and the ILP in [6] in terms of average latency incurred by the users. This is because our preference aware policies provide the flexibility to dynamically

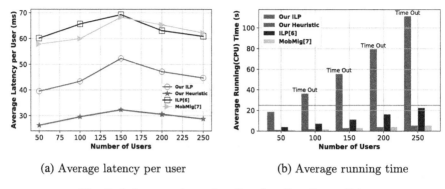

(a) Average latency per user   (b) Average running time

Fig. 3. Latency and running time for allocation policies

adapt QoS values depending on user-qos preference levels and hence conserve resources both at the server end and at the user end. Additionally, at the user-end, adapting to changing QoS levels, prevents higher communication data transfer latencies. As such, our heuristic, which initially assigns the lowest assignable QoS value to users, while progressively upgrading the QoS values depending on resource availability, results in a much lower average latency owing to lower communication overhead. Figure 3b additionally depicts the efficiency of our algorithm in a mobility-driven dynamic scenario where the heuristic takes a fraction of the running time of our ILP. Our heuristic requires lower running times as compared to the ILP in [6] while requiring similar running times to Mob-Mig simultaneously taking QoS-preferences into account. For each algorithm, we consider time-out as 25 s, i.e., the length of each slot. In Fig. 3b, however, we illustrate the time it would have actually taken by the algorithms for the allocation to compare effectiveness.

6   Conclusion and Future Work

In this paper, we have proposed a novel approach to the user-centric dynamic QoS edge user allocation problem. We formulated an optimal ILP and a near optimal heuristic to aid scalability in mobility driven real-world scenarios. As future work, we are working on learning based strategies for modeling user movements, QoS preferences, service invocations and migrations.

References

1. Bonomi, F., Milito, R., Zhu, J., Addepalli, S.: Fog computing and its role in the internet of things. In: MCC, pp. 13–16. ACM (2012)
2. Cormen, T.H., Leiserson, C.E., Rivest, R.L., Stein, C.: Introduction to Algorithms, 3rd edn. The MIT Press, Cambridge (2009)
3. Guo, H., Liu, J., Qin, H.: Collaborative mobile edge computation offloading for IoT over fiber-wireless networks. IEEE Network **32**(1), 66–71 (2018)

4. He, Q., et al.: A game-theoretical approach for user allocation in edge computing environment. IEEE TPDS **31**, 515–529 (2020)
5. Lai, P., et al.: Optimal edge user allocation in edge computing with variable sized vector bin packing. In: Pahl, C., Vukovic, M., Yin, J., Yu, Q. (eds.) ICSOC 2018. LNCS, vol. 11236, pp. 230–245. Springer, Cham (2018). https://doi.org/10.1007/978-3-030-03596-9_15
6. Lai, P., et al.: Edge user allocation with dynamic quality of service. In: Yangui, S., Bouassida Rodriguez, I., Drira, K., Tari, Z. (eds.) ICSOC 2019. LNCS, vol. 11895, pp. 86–101. Springer, Cham (2019). https://doi.org/10.1007/978-3-030-33702-5_8
7. Peng, Q., et al.: Mobility-aware and migration-enabled online edge user allocation in mobile edge computing. In: ICWS, pp. 91–98 (2019)
8. Wang, C., Liang, C., Yu, F.R., Chen, Q., Tang, L.: Computation offloading and resource allocation in wireless cellular networks with mobile edge computing. IEEE TWC **16**(8), 4924–4938 (2017)
9. Wang, S., Guo, Y., Zhang, N., Yang, P., Zhou, A., Shen, X.S.: Delay-aware microservice coordination in mobile edge computing: a reinforcement learning approach. IEEE TMC, pp. 1–1 (2019)
10. Zhu, R., Liu, B., Niu, D., Li, Z., Zhao, H.V.: Network latency estimation for personal devices: a matrix completion approach. IEEE/ACM ToN **25**(2), 724–737 (2016)

Fault-Tolerating Edge Computing with Server Redundancy Based on a Variant of Group Degree Centrality

Wei Du[1,2], Xiran Zhang[1], Qiang He[3(✉)], Wei Liu[1,2], Guangming Cui[3],
Feifei Chen[4], Yuan Ji[1], Chenran Cai[1], and Yanchao Yang[1]

[1] Wuhan University of Technology, Wuhan, China
{whutduwei,zhangxiran,wliu,saltfish,284375,yangyc}@whut.edu.cn
[2] Hubei Key Laboratory of Transportation Internet of Things, Wuhan, China
[3] Swinburne University of Technology, Hawthorn, Australia
{qhe,gcui}@swin.edu.au
[4] Deakin University, Burwood, Australia
feifei.chen@deakin.edu.au

Abstract. In the distributed and dynamic edge computing environment, edge servers are subject to runtime failures. Therefore, edge servers in an area must be fault-tolerated to ensure the reliability of services deployed on those edge servers. Server redundancy is an effective fault tolerance technique and has been widely applied in different distributed computing environments in the past decade. However, conventional fault tolerance techniques are not suitable for edge computing which has unique characteristics, i.e., the constrained coverage areas of individual edge servers (*coverage constraint*) and the partial overlapping between edge servers' coverage areas (*overlapping constraint*). In this paper, we make the first attempt to investigate and tackle the novel edge server redundancy (ESR) problem. We prove that the ESR problem is $\mathcal{NP}$-hard. Then, we introduce a novel optimal approach for identifying a group of edge servers to be redundant. The objective is to maximize the effectiveness of fault tolerance measured by the harmonic mean of the scope and strength of fault tolerance given a redundancy budget. Furthermore, we propose a heuristic approach for finding sub-optimal fault tolerance strategies efficiently in large-scale ESR scenarios. Extensive experiments are conducted on a widely-used real-world dataset to evaluate the proposed approaches against three representative baseline approaches.

Keywords: Edge computing · Fault tolerance · Redundant server identification · Group degree centrality

1 Introduction

Edge computing is a promising distributed computing paradigm that provides computation and storage capacity within end-users' proximity [10]. In such an

© Springer Nature Switzerland AG 2020
E. Kafeza et al. (Eds.): ICSOC 2020, LNCS 12571, pp. 198–214, 2020.
https://doi.org/10.1007/978-3-030-65310-1_16

environment, edge servers, typically facilitated by a micro-data center or a small cluster of servers, usually bind with small base stations to share the computation burdens of mobile and IoT devices and provide high quality-of-service (QoS) for end-users [16]. Therefore, edge servers are the critical components in the edge computing environment. However, edge servers are subject to runtime failures because of various unexpected reasons such as hardware faults, software exceptions, and cyberattacks [3], similar to their counterparts in cloud data centers [22]. In fact, edge servers are more prone to failures and outages than cloud servers due to their geographical dispersion, limited resources and low scalability [1]. In addition, unlike cloud servers that are managed in-house, geographically-distributed edge servers cannot be inspected, repaired or replaced immediately upon failures. Edge server failures will disconnect users from the edge server network if they are not covered by any other edge servers. Therefore, effective and efficient techniques are indispensable for fault-tolerating edge servers to ensure high QoS for end-users served by edge servers. Server redundancy is a promising solution [8]. A redundant server deployed with and isolated from a primary server can take over the workloads when the primary server fails. As the coverage areas of adjacent edge servers usually partially overlap to avoid blank areas, the edge servers sharing overlapping coverage areas also can take over the workloads of the end-users located in the overlapping coverage areas upon each other's failure.

However, it is usually unrealistic for an edge infrastructure provider to make every edge server redundant in a particular area because it can easily incur excessive redundancy costs and operational costs. A cost-effective solution is to identify a group of edge servers to be redundant strategically. In this paper, we refer to those edge servers as *critical edge servers* and the others as *uncritical edge servers*. Given a redundancy budget, i.e., the percentage of critical edge servers, there are two goals to achieve when we attempt to identify the critical edge servers. One is to maximize the *fault tolerance scope*, measured by the total number of uncritical edge servers that share overlapping coverage areas with at least one critical edge server. This way, when an uncritical edge server fails, its workloads can be (partially) taken over (*supported*) by at least one critical edge server, which is fault-tolerated by the redundant edge server. Over an *edge server graph*, where a node represents an edge server and an edge represents whether two edge servers' coverage areas overlap, the scope of fault tolerance achieved by a group of critical edge servers is formally measured by their Group Degree Centrality (GDC) [2], higher the better. Another goal for fault tolerance is to maximize the *fault tolerance strength*, measured by the total number of overlapping areas shared by critical and uncritical edge servers. This way, when an uncritical edge server fails, its end-users can be (partially) taken over by the most critical edge servers on average. Over the edge server graph, the strength of fault tolerance achieved by a group of critical edge servers is formally measured by their Group Degree Intensity (GDI), which will be defined in Sect. 2.1, higher the better. There is usually a conflict between the scope and the strength of a fault tolerance strategy.

Figure 1 illustrates an example area with ten edge servers, i.e., $\{v_1, ..., v_{10}\}$. Each edge server covers a particular geographical area. Their coverage areas partially overlap. The end-users located in an overlapping area can connect to one of the edge servers covering them. In Fig. 1, end-user u_1 can be served by either server v_1 or server v_2. When v_1 or v_2 fails, u_1 is taken over by the other server. This way, v_1 and v_2 are mutually and partially fault-tolerated. A fault tolerance strategy should maximize the number of fault-tolerated edge servers, i.e., the fault tolerance scope. Similarly, u_3 can be served by either v_1 or v_4, Thus, v_1 and v_4 are also mutually fault-tolerated. Servers v_2 and v_4 together increase the possibility that v_1's end-users can still be served when v_1 fails, i.e., the fault tolerance strength.

There might be multiple fault tolerance strategies to optimize the GDC and GDI of a group of critical servers while fulfilling the redundancy budget constraint. In Fig. 1, given a redundancy budget, say 20% of edge servers (i.e., two edge servers can be redundant), two possible fault tolerance strategies are $\{v_1, v_2\}$, which identifies edge servers v_1 and v_2 as critical servers, and $\{v_6, v_7\}$, which identifies edge servers v_6 and v_7 as critical servers. Now let us compare aforementioned two strategies in terms of GDC and GDI. Strategy $\{v_1, v_2\}$ allows servers v_1 and v_2 to support both v_3 and v_4 upon their failures. The GDC of $\{v_1, v_2\}$ is 2 and GDI is 4. On the other hand, strategy $\{v_6, v_7\}$ allows servers v_6 and v_7 to support v_8, v_9 and v_{10} upon their failures. The GDC of $\{v_6, v_7\}$ is 3 and GDI is 3. Obviously, neither $\{v_1, v_2\}$ or $\{v_6, v_7\}$ is superior on both GDC and GDI. Thus, a trade-off is needed for identifying a proper fault tolerance strategy depending on the edge infrastructure provider's preferences.

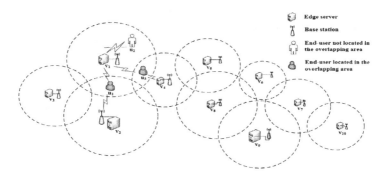

Fig. 1. An example ESR scenario

We refer to the above problem as an *edge server redundancy* (ESR) problem. In this research, we make the first attempt to investigate and tackle this new problem with the aim to maximize their harmonic of GDC and GDI so that both GDI and GDC are taken into account. Solutions to problems remotely similar to the ESR problem have been investigated, e.g., the backup virtual machine placement problem in cloud computing [11, 30] and the critical edge server placement problem [26]. However, due to the unique characteristics of edge computing, including the coverage constraint and overlapping constraint discussed above, traditional server redundancy strategies designed for cloud computing are not applicable for edge computing. Meanwhile, existing studies of edge server placement have not considered the robustness of edge server network. Therefore, a new approach is needed for solving the ESR problem. In this paper, we model the ESR problem as a variant of the group degree centrality problem [2] and propose two approaches for solving it exactly and heuristically, respectively. The major contributions of this paper are as follows:

- The edge servers in an ESR scenario is modelled as an *edge server graph*. Based on this graph, the ESR problem is modelled as a variant of the group degree centrality problem. The concepts of Group Degree Centrality (GDC) and Group Degree Intensity (GDI) are introduced to measure the fault tolerance scope and the fault tolerance strength, respectively. Their harmonic mean is employed to evaluate the overall effectiveness of a fault tolerance strategy.
- We theoretically prove the $\mathcal{NP}$-hardness of the ESR problem.
- An optimal approach is designed for solving the ESR problem optimally based on the Integer Programming technique.
- A heuristic approach is designed for finding sub-optimal solutions to large-scale ESR problems efficiently.
- Extensive experiments are conducted on a widely-used real-world dataset to evaluate the effectiveness and efficiency of the proposed approaches against three baseline approaches.

The remainder of this paper is organized as follows. Section 2 models and formulates the ESR problem. Section 3 introduces the proposed approaches. Section 4 experimentally evaluates the proposed approaches. Section 5 reviews the related work. Section 6 concludes this paper and points out future work.

2 Problem Statement

2.1 Definitions

In this section, we summarize the notations and give four important definitions used in this paper. The key notations are described in Table 1.

In this research, we model the edge servers in an ESR scenario as an edge server graph $G = (V, E)$. A vertex $v_i \in V$ in the graph corresponds to an edge server. Vertices v_i and v_j in G are connected by an edge $(v_i, v_j) \in E$ if their coverage areas partially overlap. *In the remainder of this paper, we will speak inter-changeably of an edge server and its corresponding vertex in graph G.*

The fault-tolerance strategy is defined as follows:

Definition 1 *ESR strategy. Given a set of edge servers $V = \{v_1, ..., v_n\}$, an ESR strategy is a vector $X = \{x_1, ..., x_n\}$, where $x_i (1 \leq i \leq n)$ denotes whether edge server v_i is a critical server to be fault-tolerated, i.e.,*

$$x_i = \begin{cases} 1, & \text{if edge server } v_i \text{ is a critical server} \\ 0, & \text{if edge server } v_i \text{ is an uncritical server} \end{cases} \tag{1}$$

Table 1. Key notations

Notation	Description
$C = \{c_1, c_2, \ldots, c_k\}$	Set of critical edge servers, where $C \subset V,\ |C| = k,\ k = 1, 2, \ldots, m, m \leq n$
E	Set of edges in G representing the corresponding overlapping areas between edge servers
f_i	Number of critical edge servers which support uncritical edge server v_i
$G = (V, E)$	Edge server graph
k	Redundancy budget
$M(C)$	Set of edges connecting uncritical edge servers to critical edge servers, which is a subset of E, i.e. $M(C) \subset E$
$N(C)$	Set of uncritical edge servers connected to critical edge servers, which is a subset of V, i.e. $N(C) \subset V$
$V = \{v_1, \ldots, v_n\}$	Set of vertices (edge servers) in G
$X = \{x_1, \ldots, x_n\}$	An ESR strategy
x_i	Whether edge server v_i is a critical server ($x_i = 1$) or not ($x_i = 0$)
y_i	Whether uncritical edge server v_i is supported by at least one critical server ($y_i = 1$) or not ($y_i = 0$)

Given a group of critical vertices $C \subset V$, the GDC and GDI of C are defined as follows:

Definition 2 *Group Degree Centrality (GDC). The GDC of C, denoted by $gdc(C)$, is the size of set $N(C)$, i.e., $gdc(C) = |N(C)|$, where $N(C)$ is the set of uncritical edge servers that are connected to any critical edge server in C, i.e., $N(C) = \{v_i \in V \setminus C \mid (v_i, v_j) \in E, v_j \in C\}$.*

Definition 3 *Group Degree Intensity (GDI). The GDI of C, denoted by $gdi(C)$, is the size of set $M(C)$, i.e., $gdi(C) = |M(C)|$, where $M(C)$ is the set of edges connecting uncritical edge servers to critical edge servers, i.e., $M(C) = \{(v_i, v_j) \in E \mid v_i \in N(C), v_j \in C\}$.*

Take strategy $X_1 = \{1, 1, 0, 0, 0, 0, 0, 0, 0, 0\}$ for Fig. 1 for example, which identifies edge servers v_1 and v_2 as critical servers. We can obtain that $C = \{v_1, v_2\}$, $N(C) = \{v_3, v_4\}$, $M(C) = \{(v_1, v_3), (v_2, v_3), (v_1, v_4), (v_2, v_4)\}$. There is $gdc(C) = 2$ and $gdi(C) = 4$.

The effectiveness of a fault tolerance strategy is positively correlated with both its GDC and GDI. However, there is a conflict between maximizing GDC and GDI. In general, a high GDC is achieved by distributing fault tolerance while a high GDI requires concentrated fault tolerance. Thus, there is a trade-off between GDC and GDI. This trade-off can be managed domain-specifically, depending on the edge infrastructure provider's preference. In this research, we employ the harmonic mean [6] of GDC and GDI to evaluate the overall effectiveness of a fault tolerance strategy. This is inspired by the widely-used F1-score which is the harmonic mean of precision and recall.

Definition 4 *Harmonic mean (HM). Given a set of critical vertices C, the harmonic mean of its GDC and GDI, denoted by $HM(C)$, is expressed as follows:*

$$HM(C) = \frac{2 \times Ngdc(C) \times Ngdi(C)}{Ngdc(C) + Ngdi(C)} \qquad (2)$$

where $Ngdc(C) = \frac{gdc(C)}{(n-k)}$ is the normalized GDC and $Ngdi(C) = \frac{gdi(C)}{k \times (n-k)}$ is the normalized GDI.

2.2 ESR Model

According to Definition 2, GDC in essence represents the number of uncritical edge servers which share at least one overlapping area with one of critical edge servers. It is also the total number of uncritical edge servers supported by critical edge servers. This is the first optimization goal of the ESR problem, i.e., to maximize $gdc(C)$:

$$maximize \ gdc(C) \qquad (3)$$

According to Definition 3, GDI indicates the number of overlapping coverage areas between uncritical edge servers and critical edge servers. It is also the total number of supports that uncritical edge servers can be obtained from critical edge servers upon runtime failures. This is the second optimization goal, i.e., to maximize $gdi(C)$:

$$maximize \ gdi(C) \qquad (4)$$

Additionally, the total redundancy cost incurred is quantified by the redundancy budget k, i.e.,

$$|C| = k \qquad (5)$$

Finally, as explained in Sect. 2.1, the overall optimization objective of an ESR problem is to maximize the harmonic mean of normalized GDC and GDI, i.e., to maximize $HM(C)$:

$$maximize \ HM(C) \qquad (6)$$

2.3 Problem Hardness

In this section, we demonstrate that the ESR problem is $\mathcal{NP}$-hard by proving the following theorem.

Theorem 1. *The ESR problem is $\mathcal{NP}$-hard.*

Proof. To prove the hardness of the ESR problem, we introduce the maximum k facility location (MKFL) problem. The MKFL problem is a known $\mathcal{NP}$-hard problem [19] and it can be defined as follows. Let $G' = (V', E')$ denote a complete graph, and $p'(i, j) \in \mathbb{N}$ is the profits of function p' between vertex i and j, where $i, j \in V'$. The formulation of MKFL problem is displayed below:

objective:

$$\sum_{v \in V'} \max_{f \in F} p'(v, f) \tag{7}$$

s.t.

$$F \subset V' \text{ with } |F| = k \tag{8}$$

To prove that the ESR problem is $\mathcal{NP}$-hard, we prove that the MKFL problem can be reduced to an instance of the ESR problem. The reduction can be done as follows:

1) add $|C|$ nodes as critical edge servers into the edge server graph $G = (V, E)$ of the ESR problem, i.e., $V \longleftarrow C \bigcup V$;
2) given a set of critical edge servers C, the profit $p(v_i, v_j), v_i \in V, v_j \in C$ equals to $HM(C)/|M(C)|$ iff edge $(v_i, v_j) \in M(C)$ and 0 otherwise, where $|M(C)|$ is the number of edges in $M(C)$; Given an instance MKFL(G', p'), we can construct an instance ESR(G, p) with the reduction above in polynomial time where $|G'| = |G|$ and $p' = p$; For the constraint (8), it is easy to see $C \subset V$ of the ESR problem, and k is a special case of the ESR problem. In terms of the objective of the ESR problem (Eq. (6)), $\sum_{v \in V} \max_{c \in C} p(v, c)$ is the total profits between a set of critical edge servers C and the edge server graph G, which is the same as the objective calculated from Definition 4, and the profit function p equals to p' of MKFL problem. In this case, any solution $\mathcal{Q}$ satisfied objective (7) and constraint (8), also satisfies the objective (6) and constraint (5).

In conclusion, solution $\mathcal{Q}$ satisfies the reduced ESR problem if $\mathcal{Q}$ satisfies the MKFL problem. Thus, the ESR problem is reducible from the MKFL problem and it is $\mathcal{NP}$-hard.

3   Approach Design

3.1   Optimal Approach

To solve the ESR problem exactly, *ESR-IP*, our optimal approach, models it as an Integer Programming (IP) problem that consists of a set of variables $X = \{x_1, ..., x_n\}$ with a domain $D_i = \{0, 1\}, i = 1, ..., n$, listing the possible values for each variable $x_i \in X$, and a set of constraints τ over V. A solution to an IP problem is an assignment of a value to each variable $x_i \in X$ from D_i such that all the constraints τ are fulfilled. To facilitate the calculation of $gdc(C)$ and $gdi(C)$, in the IP model, we define two additional sets of variables y_i $(1 \le i \le n)$ and f_i $(1 \le i \le n)$ as follows:

$$y_i = 1 \; iff \; v_i \in N(C) \tag{9}$$

$$f_i = \begin{cases} \sum_{v_j:(v_i,v_j)\in E} x_j, & x_i = 0 \\ 0, & x_i = 1 \end{cases} \tag{10}$$

where y_i indicates that edge server v_i is an uncritical server connected to a critical server over G and f_i is the number of critical servers supporting uncritical server v_i, Take strategy $X_1 = \{1, 1, 0, 0, 0, 0, 0, 0, 0, 0\}$ for Fig. 1 as an example. We can obtain that $y_3 = 1$, $y_5 = 0$, $f_3 = 2$ and $f_5 = 0$. Please note that $f_i = 0$ when $x_i = 1$ in Eq. (10) ensures that the number of edges between each pair of critical edge servers is not accumulated into GDC and GDI.

Based on $N(C)$ and $M(C)$, we can utilize y_i and f_i to measure the sizes of $N(C)$ and $M(C)$. This way, we can rewrite $gdc(C)$ and $gdi(C)$: $gdc(C) = \sum_{v_i \in V} y_i$, $gdi(C) = \sum_{v_i \in V} f_i$. Now, the IP model of the ESR problem can be formulated as follows:

$$\textbf{objective: } maximize \ \frac{2\sum_{v_i \in V} f_i \sum_{v_i \in V} y_i}{(n-k)(\sum_{v_i \in V} f_i + k \sum_{v_i \in V} y_i)} \tag{11}$$

s.t.

$$y_i \leq \sum_{v_j:(v_i,v_j)\in E} x_j, \forall v_i \in V \tag{12}$$

$$x_i + y_i \leq 1, \forall v_i \in V \tag{13}$$

$$x_i + y_i \geq \frac{1}{\Gamma_i} \sum_{v_j:(v_i,v_j)\in E} x_j, \forall v_i \in V \tag{14}$$

$$\sum_{v_i \in V} x_i = k, \tag{15}$$

$$f_i = (1 - x_i) \sum_{v_j:(v_i,v_j)\in E} x_j, \forall v_i \in V \tag{16}$$

Equation (11) is obtained by applying y_i and f_i to Eq. (6). Constraint (12) ensures that if $y_i = 1$, there is at least one critical server sharing the overlapping coverage area with edge server v_i, i.e., Eq. (9). Constraint (13) ensures that edge server v_i cannot be both a critical server and an uncritical server. Constraint (14) ensures that if $x_i = 0$ and $y_i = 0$, none of the edge servers sharing the overlapping coverage area with server v_i is a critical server. Γ_i is a sufficiently large constant for the tightness of IP relaxation. Here, it is set to k^1. Constraint (15) rewrites constraint (5) and ensures that the number of critical servers is k. Constraint (16) rewrites the piece-wise function f_i as one expression.

The solution to this IP problem is the vector $X = \{x_1, ..., x_n\}$ that achieves (6) while fulfilling (5). Based on X, the edge infrastructure provider can fault-tolerate the identified critical edge servers to maximize the harmonic mean

---

[1] In Constraint (14), there are three possible pairs of values for (x_i, y_i), i.e., $(1, 0), (0, 1)$ and $(0, 0)$. If $(x_i, y_i) = (1, 0)$, $\sum_{v_j:(v_i,v_j)\in E} x_j \leq k - 1$, Γ_i can be set to a value greater than or equals to $k - 1$ to satisfy Constraint (14). If $(x_i, y_i) = (0, 1)$, $\sum_{v_j:(v_i,v_j)\in E} x_j \leq k$, Γ_i can be set to a value greater than or equals to k. If $(x_i, y_i) = (0, 0)$, $\sum_{v_j:(v_i,v_j)\in E} x_j = 0$, Γ_i can be set to any value except 0. In this paper, Γ_i is set to k to fulfill the most tightness of IP relaxation.

of the produced GDI and GDC. For example, given the budget $k = 2$, the optimal solution to the ESR problem presented in Fig. 1 is $C_{k=2} = \{v_4, v_7\}$, i.e., $X_{k=2} = \{0, 0, 0, 1, 0, 0, 1, 0, 0, 0\}$, with $gdi(C_{k=2}) = 7, gdc(C_{k=2}) = 7$ and $HM(C_{k=2}) = 0.58$. Given $k = 4$, there is $C_{k=4} = \{v_1, v_2, v_7, v_8\}$, with $gdi(C_{k=4}) = 11, gdc(C_{k=4}) = 6$ and $HM(C_{k=4}) = 0.63$.

3.2   Heuristic Approach

As proven in Sect. 2.3, the ESR problem is $\mathcal{NP}$-hard. The scales of some real-world ESR scenarios, e.g., city-scale ESR, are very large in the future 5G environment with base station density reaching up to 50 base stations per km^2 [7]. Finding the optimal solutions in such large-scale scenarios may be intractable even in an offline manner. Therefore, we design a heuristic approach named *ESR-H* for finding sub-optimal solutions to large-scale ESR problems effectively and efficiently. Since the harmonic mean is employed to measure the overall effectiveness of a fault tolerance strategy, the proposed heuristic always selects the vertex v from the remaining edge servers that maximizes the harmonic mean of the GDI and GDC produced by all the selected critical servers and v as a group.

The pseudo code of *ESR-H* is presented in Algorithm 1. First, the group of selected critical servers, denoted by C, is initialized as empty (Line 1). Then, the edge server v_i is selected from the set of remaining edge servers V that maximizes the harmonic mean $HM(C \cup \{v_i\})$ of the candidate group of critical servers $C \cup \{v_i\}$ (Line 3). The edge server v_i included into C (Line 4). In the meantime, edge server v_i is removed from V (line 5). This process is repeated until k critical servers have been selected. In the worst-case scenario, the running time of function $HM()$ is $O(n)$. Iterating through all the n edge servers takes $O(n)$ time. Thus, to find a group of k critical servers, the overall computational complexity of *ESR-H* is $O(kn^2)$.

Algorithm 1. Heuristic for edge server redundancy (*ESR-H*)

Input: Edge server graph G, number of critical servers k
Output: A group of critical servers C
 1: Initialization: $C \leftarrow \emptyset$;
 2: **repeat**
 3:    select $v_i \in V$ that maximizes the harmonic mean $HM(C \cup \{v_i\})$ of the candidate group of critical servers $C \cup \{v_i\}$
 4:    $C \leftarrow C \cup \{v_i\}$
 5:    $V \leftarrow V - \{v_i\}$
 6: **until** $|C| = k$
 7: **return** C

---

4   Experimental Evaluation

In this section, we experimentally evaluate the performance of our approaches, i.e., the *ESR-IP* optimization approach and *ESR-H*, against three representative baseline approaches. All the experiments are conducted on a Windows machine equipped with Intel SkyLake6151 (3.0 GHz) and 8 GB RAM. The IP problem discussed in Sect. 3.1 is solved with IBM's CPLEX Optimizer. All the other approaches are implemented with Python 3.6.

4.1   Baseline Approaches

Our approaches are compared with three baseline approaches, namely *Random*, *Greedy-GDC* and *Greedy-GDI*:

- *Random*: This approach randomly picks up a total of k servers as critical edge servers.
- *Greedy-GDC (Greedy-C)*: This approach always picks up the edge server with the greatest GDC as the next critical server until there are k critical edge servers.
- *Greedy-GDI (Greedy-I)*: This approach always picks up the edge server with the greatest GDI as the next critical server until there are k critical edge servers.

4.2   Experimental Setup

Experiment Data. The experiments are conducted on a subset of the widely-used EUA dataset[2] [12,13]. The subset contains the locations of 125 real-world base stations (edge servers) within the Melbourne CBD in Australia.

Experimenting Settings. We conduct two sets of experiments, i.e., Set #1 and Set #2. Set #1 is a set of small-scale experiments, where we run all five approaches. Set #2 is a set of large-scale experiments, where we run only our heuristic approach and three baseline approaches because the optimal approach cannot find a solution within a reasonable amount of time due to the NP-hardness of the ESR problem.

In both Set #1 and Set #2, we vary three setting parameters to simulate different ESR scenarios:

- **Number of edge servers (n).** We select different numbers of edge servers, i.e., $n = 10, 20, \ldots, 100$, to generate different sizes of edge server graphs. Specially, we randomly select the first edge server from the dataset. Then, we select its nearest neighbor edge server. After that, the next edge server to be selected is the nearest neighbor among the neighbors of the first and the second edge servers. This process is iterated until a total of n edge servers are selected.
- **Coverage of edge servers (r).** In order to generate edge server graphs with different densities, the coverage radius of each edge server increases from 0.1 km to 0.28 km. A larger r will allow more edge servers' coverage areas to overlap. Thus, a larger r produces more edges in G.

---

[2] https://github.com/swinedge/eua-dataset.

- **Redundancy budget** (k). The redundancy budget is measured by the percentage of critical edge servers in total edge servers. It changes from 10% to 90%.

The corresponding setting are described in Table 2. Under each setting, we select a different first edge server out of the 125 edge servers. This way, we simulate a total of 125 different ESR scenarios, run the experiment for 125 times and average the results every time the value of a parameter varies.

Performance Metrics. We employ two metrics to evaluate the performance of the approaches: 1) effectiveness: measured by $HM(C)$ (abbr. as HM hereafter), higher the better; 2) efficiency: measured by the computation time taken to find a solution, lower the better.

4.3   Experimental Results

Figures 2, 3 and 4 show the results obtained from the experiment sets #1.1, #1.2 and #1.3 respectively. Overall, *ESR-IP* outperforms the other four approaches with the best average effectiveness (0.719) at the expense of the most average computation time (47.114 s on average) across all the cases in Set #1. *ESR-H* is second to *ESR-IP* with an average effectiveness of 0.702 and outperforms *Greedy-C*, *Greedy-I* and *Random* by 11.76%, 4.53% and 17.97% respectively.

Figure 2 shows that in Set #1.1, as the number of edge servers (n) increases from 10 to 30, the effectiveness of *ESR-IP* decreases from 0.859 to 0.630 while that of *ESR-H* decreases from 0.845 to 0.619. However, in terms of the computation time, *Random*, *Greedy-C*, *Greedy-I* and *ESR-H* outperform *ESR-IP* by 99.99% each on average. The reason for this is that with the increase in n, the

Table 2. Experiment settings

Factor	Number of edge servers (n)	Coverage of each edge server (r)	Redundancy budget (k)
Set #1.1	$10, 11, \ldots, 30$	0.18	30%
Set #1.2	20	$0.10, 0.12, \ldots, 0.28$	30%
Set #1.3	20	0.18	$10\%, 20\%, \ldots, 90\%$
Set #2.1	$40, 50, \ldots, 100$	0.18	30%
Set #2.2	40	$0.10, 0.12, \ldots, 0.28$	30%
Set #2.3	40	0.18	$10\%, 20\%, \ldots, 90\%$

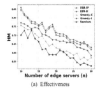 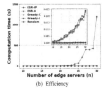 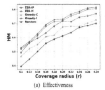 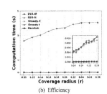

Fig. 2. Results of Set #1.1   **Fig. 3.** Results of Set #1.2

number of uncritical servers that can be supported by critical servers decreases. Thus, the effectiveness of all approaches goes down. At the same time, the scales of edge server graphs become larger. It spends more time to pick up the critical servers. Therefore, the efficiency of all approaches decreases dramatically.

Figure 3 shows the results of Set #1.2, where the coverage radius of each edge server (r) increases from 0.10 to 0.28. As depicted in Fig. 3(a), the effectiveness of *ESR-IP* increases from 0.527 to 0.816 while that of *ESR-H* increases from 0.518 to 0.806. The rationale for this is that the edge server graph is densified with the extension of the edge server's coverage area. More overlapping areas appear and the opportunities for uncritical servers to be supported by critical ones increase. Figure 3(b) shows that the computation time taken by *ESR-IP* increases from 2.556 s to 4.051 s, longer than that of the other four approaches by over 99.8% each on average. These results show that the density of the edge server graph does not impact the efficiency of *ESR-IP* significantly. This conclusion applies to the other four approaches as well.

Figure 4 shows the results of Set #1.3. As depicted in Fig. 4(a), the effectiveness of all approaches fluctuate slightly at first. When the redundancy budget (k) exceeds a certain number, 60% for both *ESR-IP* and *ESR-H*, 70% for *Greedy-C* and 80% for *Greedy-I*, the effectiveness of all approaches except *Random* start to increase steadily. This is due to more critical edge servers caused by the increase in k. Then, more uncritical servers can obtain support from critical servers. We notice that in Fig. 4(b), when k rises, the computation time taken by *ESR-IP* first increases and then decreases. The reason is that the objective function of the IP model, i.e., Eq. (11), is symmetric at the k of 50%.

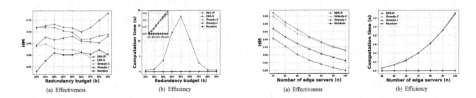

Fig. 4. Results of Set #1.1   **Fig. 5.** Results of Set #1.2

Figures 5, 6 and 7 show the results obtained from the large-scale sets #2.1, #2.2 and #2.3, respectively. Overall, *ESR-H* outperforms *Random*, *Greedy-C* and *Greedy-I* in terms of effectiveness by 84.17%, 11.09% and 11.32% on average, respectively. Comparing with *Random*, the high effectiveness of *ESR-H* comes at the price of higher computation time. In terms of *Greedy-I* and *Greedy-C*, *ESR-H*'s computation time is between that of *Greedy-I* and that of *Greedy-C*. Let us analyze the results on large-scale scenarios in detail to show *ESR-H*'s superiority.

As illustrated in Fig. 5(a), the effectiveness of *ESR-H* is greater than that of *Greedy-C* first. With the increase in n, the gaps between these two approaches' effectiveness are narrowed gradually and almost the same (0.329 versus 0.327) when n achieves 100. The reason is that larger n yet a certain r and k leads to less supports for uncritical servers. Therefore, both GDC and GDI will decrease, but GDI will drop faster than GDC. Then, GDI's impact on the effectiveness will be weakened. When GDI's impact is too small to affect the HM, *ESR-H* is almost equivalent to *Greedy-C*. Thus, the effectiveness of these two approaches are similar to each other. This conclusion is also reinforced by the effectiveness of *Greedy-I* depicted in Fig. 5(a). Furthermore, the similar conclusion can be found in Fig. 5(b). The efficiency of *ESR-H* and *Greedy-C* merge to close values (1.313 versus 1.284). Additionally, *Greedy-I*'s efficiency trends to be closer to that of *ESR-H* and *Greedy-C*. However, its effectiveness is always the lowest one among four approaches, even 31.96% lower than that of *Random* on average. Moreover, the value of *Greedy-I*'s effectiveness decreases continuously to 65.88% lower than that of *ESR-H* when n is 100. As to *Random*, although the efficiency is lowest, the effectiveness is always lower than that of *ESR-H* and *Greedy-C*. Therefore, *ESR-H* and *Greedy-C* are dominant in this experiment.

Figure 6 and Fig. 7 depict similar trends on both effectiveness and efficiency of four approaches. As can be seen in Fig. 6(a) and Fig. 7(a), the effectiveness of *ESR-H* and *Greedy-I* are very close on average (0.549 s versus 0.541 s in Fig. 6(a) and 0.557 s versus 0.545 s in Fig. 7(a)). On the other hand, the effectiveness of *Greedy-C* and *Random* are always lower than that of *ESR-H* and *Greedy-I* (37.20% at the worst case). In Fig. 6(a), the larger r of each edge server raises the number of overlapping areas between adjacent servers. In Fig. 7(a), the number of critical edge servers will be ascended when k rises. In both aforementioned cases, each uncritical server will obtain more supports from different critical servers. As a result, GDI will increase more rapidly than GDC does. GDI will have a greater impact on the value of HM. Then, *ESR-H* is similar to *Greedy-I*. In addition, an interesting result is observed in Fig. 7(a). We can found that *Greedy-C*'s effectiveness descends gradually and lower than that of *Random* at last. This result validates our analysis of the trends of the effectiveness of *ESR-H* and *Greedy-I*. In terms of efficiency, as shown in Fig. 6(b) and Fig. 7(b), *ESR-H*'s computation time is slightly better than that of *Greedy-I* on average (0.0633 s versus 0.0657 s in Fig. 6(b) and 0.152 s versus 0.160 s in Fig. 7(b)). Therefore, *ESR-H* is dominant in these two experiments.

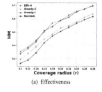
(a) Effectiveness

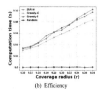
(b) Efficiency

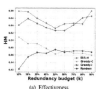
(a) Effectiveness

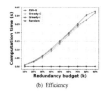
(b) Efficiency

Fig. 6. Results of Set #1.1   **Fig. 7.** Results of Set #1.2

According to all experimental results obtained from sets #2.1, #2.2 and #2.3, *ESR-H* is overall better than three baseline approaches in large-scale scenarios considered in this paper. Moreover, the results also justify that the trade-off between GDC and GDI can be managed, as we have mentioned in Sect. 2.1.

5 Related Work

Edge computing is a new and promising distributed computing paradigm. It offers many opportunities and raises a variety of problems, e.g., edge user allocation [9,12], edge data caching [23–25], edge application placement [14], edge server placement [4,5], etc. However, it has been commonly assumed that the edge computing environment is always reliable. This assumption is in fact not realistic due to the high geographic distribution of edge servers and the lack of centralized reliability management. Thus, it is necessary and critical to investigate the reliability issue in the edge computing environment.

Redundancy is an effective technique for implementing fault tolerance in various distributed environments, such as distributed database systems [18], distributed storage systems [15], wireless sensor networks [27], web environment [20], cloud computing [11,17,29,30] and edge computing [1,3], to guarantee high QoS for end-users [21,28].

In the past decade, redundancy in cloud computing has been extensively investigated. The authors of [29] improve the reliability of cloud applications by tolerating faults of a small part of the most significant components. In [17], Matt et al. utilize monitored data access patterns and take user-defined Quality of Service requirements into account to optimize the placement of data on cloud-based storage services in a redundant, cost- and latency-efficient way. Different from building fault-tolerant cloud applications or utilizing data replication techniques in the aforementioned studies, we employ server redundancy to enhance the reliability of the edge computing environment. Zhou et al. [30] design three algorithms to minimize network resource consumption in the service recovery stage. The authors of [11] propose a redundancy-aware virtual machine (VM) scheduler to optimize the placement and activation of standby VMs while assuring applications' resource entitlements. Obviously, backup VM placement is a popular and effective technique to improve the reliability of cloud-based services. However, existing approaches designed for the conventional cloud computing environment are not suitable for fault-tolerating edge servers because of the unique characteristics of edge computing, i.e., coverage constraint and overlapping constraint. While normal VMs deployed in the cloud computing environment are available to all end-users, redundant edge servers are only accessible to end-users located in the coverage areas of those edge servers. Therefore, the effective strategies proposed in the cloud computing environment cannot be used directly in the edge computing environment.

Recently, researchers are starting to implement redundancy in edge computing. Aral et al. [1] exploit the failure dependencies between edge servers and infer the joint failure probability of a given service deployment. They propose two replica scheduling algorithms to optimize the failure probability and the cost of redundancy, respectively. While their approaches replicate edge services, our approaches deploy redundant edge servers over the edge server network to accommodate server failures. In [3], Chantre et al. address the optimal placement of edge devices for reliable broadcasting services in 5G network functions virtualization-based small cells. However, their optimization objectives are completely different from ours, which are to minimize the costs of service provisioning, service processing time, and loss probability.

Service placement or service redundancy rely on a fault-tolerated edge server network. To the best of our knowledge, our work is the first to tackle the ESR problem in the edge computing environment. The proposed optimal approach achieves high effectiveness and the proposed heuristic approach offers high efficiency for finding sub-optimal solutions to large-scale ESR problems.

6   Conclusion

In the distributed edge computing environment, redundancy-based fault tolerance is challenged with new constraints. To tackle this problem, we modelled the edge servers in an edge server redundancy (ESR) scenario as an edge server graph and formulated the ESR problem as a variant of the group degree centrality problem, an NP-hard problem. We designed an optimal approach that solves the ESR problem with the Integer Programming technique. It find the optimal fault tolerance strategy that trade off between two optimization objectives, i.e., to maximize the fault tolerance scope and to maximize the fault tolerance strength. We also developed a heuristic approach for finding sub-optimal solutions to large-scale ESR problems efficiently. We conducted extensive experiments in different ESR scenarios simulated on a widely-used real-world dataset. The experimental results show that our approaches significantly outperform the baseline approaches.

This research has established a basic foundation for the ESR problem. In our future work, we will take into account the impact of the estimated number of end-users located in overlapping coverage areas, as well as the impacts of the dependency among failed servers and failure probability of each server on fault tolerance strategies. In addition, edge servers' capacities will be considered.

Acknowledgments. This research was partially supported by the Ministry of Education Project of Humanities and Social Sciences (No. 16YJCZH014), Australian Research Council Discovery Projects (DP18010021 and DP200102491) and the Open Fund of Hubei Key Laboratory of Transportation Internet of Things (Wuhan University of Technology) (No. 2018IOT005).

References

1. Aral, A., Brandic, I.: Dependency mining for service resilience at the edge. In: 2018 IEEE/ACM Symposium on Edge Computing (SEC), pp. 228–242 (2018)
2. Borgatti, S.P.: Identifying sets of key players in a social network. Comput. Math. Organ. Theory **12**(1), 21–34 (2006). https://doi.org/10.1007/s10588-006-7084-x

3. Chantre, H.D., Fonseca, N.L.S.D.: Multi-objective optimization for edge device placement and reliable broadcasting in 5G NFV-based small cell networks. IEEE J. Sel. Areas Commun. **36**(10), 2304–2317 (2018)
4. Cui, G., He, Q., Chen, F., Jin, H., Yang, Y.: Trading off between user coverage and network robustness for edge server placement. IEEE Trans. Cloud Comput. (2020). https://doi.org/10.1109/TCC.2020.3008440
5. Cui, G., He, Q., Xia, X., Chen, F., Jin, H., Yang, Y.: Robustness-oriented k edge server placement. In: IEEE/ACM 20th International Symposium on Cluster, Cloud and Grid (CCGrid), pp. 81–90 (2020)
6. Dodge, Y.: Harmonic Mean, pp. 239–241. Springer, New York (2008)
7. Ge, X., Tu, S., Mao, G., Wang, C.X., Han, T.: 5G ultra-dense cellular networks. IEEE Wirel. Commun. **23**(1), 72–79 (2016)
8. Guo, Z., Yang, Y.: Exploring server redundancy in nonblocking multicast data center networks. IEEE Trans. Comput. **64**(7), 1912–1926 (2015)
9. He, Q., Cui, G., Zhang, X., Chen, F., Deng, S., Jin, H., Li, Y., Yang, Y.: A game-theoretical approach for user allocation in edge computing environment. IEEE Trans. Parallel Distrib. Syst. **31**(3), 515–529 (2020)
10. Hu, Y.C., Patel, M., Sabella, D., Sprecher, N., Young, V.: Mobile edge computing-a key technology towards 5G. ETSI White Paper **11**(11), 1–16 (2015)
11. Jung, G., Rahimzadeh, P., Liu, Z., Ha, S., Joshi, K., Hiltunen, M.: Virtual redundancy for active-standby cloud applications. In: IEEE 37th Conference on Computer Communications (INFOCOM), pp. 1916–1924 (2018)
12. Lai, P., et al.: Optimal edge user allocation in edge computing with variable sized vector bin packing. In: 16th International Conference on Service-Oriented Computing (ICSOC), pp. 230–245 (2018)
13. Lai, P., et al.: Edge user allocation with dynamic quality of service. In: 17th International Conference on Service-Oriented Computing (ICSOC), pp. 86–101 (2019)
14. Li, B., et al.: Read: robustness-oriented edge application deployment in edge computing environment. IEEE Trans. Serv. Comput. (2020). https://doi.org/10.1109/TSC.2020.3015316
15. Li, S., Qiang, C., Wan, S., Lu, Q., Xie, C.: HRSPC: a hybrid redundancy scheme via exploring computational locality to support fast recovery and high reliability in distributed storage systems. J. Netw. Comput. Appl. **66**(5), 52–63 (2016)
16. Mach, P., Becvar, Z.: Mobile edge computing: a survey on architecture and computation offloading. IEEE Commun. Surv. Tutorials **19**(3), 1628–1656 (2017)
17. Matt, J., Waibel, P., Schulte, S.: Cost- and latency-efficient redundant data storage in the cloud. In: IEEE 10th Conference on Service-oriented Computing and Applications (SOCA), pp. 164–172 (2017)
18. Muro, S., Ibaraki, T., Miyajima, H., Hasegawa, T.: Evaluation of the file redundancy in distributed database systems. IEEE Trans. Softw. Eng. **11**(2), 199–205 (1985)
19. Owen, S.H., Daskin, M.S.: Strategic facility location: a review. Eur. J. Oper. Res. **111**(3), 423–447 (1998)
20. Salas, J., Perez-Sorrosal, F., Patiño-Martinez, M., Jimenez-Peris, R.: WS-replication: A framework for highly available web services. In: 15th International Conference on World Wide Web (WWW), pp. 357–366 (2006)
21. Sun, X., Wang, S., Xia, Y., Zheng, W.: Predictive-trend-aware composition of web services with time-varying quality-of-service. IEEE Access **8**, 1910–1921 (2020)
22. Wang, L., Trivedi, K.S.: Architecture-based reliability-sensitive criticality measure for fault-tolerance cloud applications. IEEE Trans. Parallel Distrib. Syst. **30**(11), 2408–2421 (2019)

23. Xia, Xiaoyu., et al.: Graph-based optimal data caching in edge computing. In: Yangui, Sami, Bouassida Rodriguez, Ismael, Drira, Khalil, Tari, Zahir (eds.) ICSOC 2019. LNCS, vol. 11895, pp. 477–493. Springer, Cham (2019). https://doi.org/10.1007/978-3-030-33702-5_37

24. Xia, X., Chen, F., He, Q., Grundy, J., Abdelrazek, M., Jin, H.: Online collaborative data caching in edge computing. IEEE Trans. Parallel Distrib. Syst. (2020). https://doi.org/10.1109/TPDS.2020.3016344

25. Xia, X., Chen, F., He, Q., Grundy, J., Abdelrazek, M., Jin, H.: Cost-effective app data distribution in edge computing. IEEE Trans. Parallel Distrib. Syst. $32(1)$, 31–44 (2021)

26. Xu, X., et al.: Load-aware edge server placement for mobile edge computing in 5G networks. In: 17th International Conference on Service-Oriented Computing (ICSOC), pp. 494–507 (2019)

27. Zebbane, B., Chenait, M., Badache, N.: A distributed lightweight redundancy aware topology control protocol for wireless sensor networks. Wireless Netw. $23(6)$, 1–14 (2016)

28. Zhang, Y., et al.: Covering-based web service quality prediction via neighborhood-aware matrix factorization. IEEE Trans. Serv. Comput. (2019). https://doi.org/10.1109/TSC.2019.2891517

29. Zheng, Z., Zhou, T.C., Lyu, M.R., King, I.: Component ranking for fault-tolerant cloud applications. IEEE Trans. Serv. Comput. $5(4)$, 540–550 (2012)

30. Zhou, A., et al.: Cloud service reliability enhancement via virtual machine placement optimization. IEEE Trans. Serv. Comput. $10(6)$, 902–913 (2017)

TD-EUA: Task-Decomposable Edge User Allocation with QoE Optimization

Guobing Zou[1,2], Ya Liu[1], Zhen Qin[1(✉)], Jin Chen[1], Zhiwei Xu[1],
Yanglan Gan[3], Bofeng Zhang[1], and Qiang He[4(✉)]

[1] School of Computer Engineering and Science, Shanghai University, Shanghai, China
{gbzou,ambersoul,zhenqin,cj1125,zhiweixu,bfzhang}@shu.edu.cn
[2] Shanghai Key Laboratory of Computer Software Testing and Evaluating,
Shanghai, China
[3] School of Computer Science and Technology, Donghua University, Shanghai, China
ylgan@dhu.edu.cn
[4] Department of Computer Science and Software Engineering,
Swinburne University of Technology, Melbourne, Australia
qhe@swin.edu.au

Abstract. The edge user allocation (EUA) problem has attracted a lot of attention recently. EUA aims at allocating edge users to nearby edge servers strategically to ensure low-latency network connection. Existing approaches assume that a users' request can only be served by an individual edge server or cannot be served at all. They neglect the fact that a user's request may be decomposable and partitioned into multiple tasks to be performed by different edge servers. To tackle this new task-decomposable edge user allocation (TD-EUA) problem, we model it as an optimization problem. Two novel approaches named TD-EUA-O and TD-EUA-H are proposed, one for finding the optimal solution based on Integer Linear Programming that maximizes users' overall Quality of Experience (QoE), and the other for efficiently finding a sub-optimal solution in large-scale EUA scenarios. Extensive experiments based on a widely-used real-world dataset are conducted to evaluate the effectiveness and efficiency of our approaches. The results demonstrate that our approaches significantly outperform the baseline and the state-of-the-art approach.

Keywords: Edge computing · Edge user allocation · Task decomposition · Quality of Experience · QoE optimization

1 Introduction

The rapidly increasing popularity of mobile and Internet-of-Things (IoT) devices, including mobile phones, wearables, sensors, etc., has promoted the growth of versatile computational-intensive applications, such as face recognition, machine vision, intelligent furniture [6]. Due to the limited computing capabilities and battery power of mobile and IoT devices, their computing tasks are often

© Springer Nature Switzerland AG 2020
E. Kafeza et al. (Eds.): ICSOC 2020, LNCS 12571, pp. 215–231, 2020.
https://doi.org/10.1007/978-3-030-65310-1_17

offloaded to app vendors' servers in the cloud. Nevertheless, with the exponential growth in the number of mobile and IoT devices, it is becoming difficult for cloud computing to handle the huge workload and network congestion. This makes it difficult to provide a low-latency and reliable connection to end-users, especially those that desire real-time responses from applications. For example, delays caused by the traditional centralized computing paradigm may cause operation failures on autopilot and endanger passengers' lives.

To tackle this issue, edge computing, has been proposed as a new distributed computing paradigm [1,15]. In the edge environment, each base station is equipped with a certain amount of computing resources, allowing computing power to be provided to mobile users at the Internet access level. Compared to cloud computing, edge computing places storage and computing resources (such as CPU, memory, bandwidth, etc.,) closer to end-users. An edge server usually cover a specific geographical area [10]. Typically, edge servers are geographically distributed to offer diverse services for different areas. To avoid the existence of an area that is not covered by any edge server, there are overlapping areas between adjacent edges. A user located in the overlapping area can connect to one of the edge servers covering them (*proximity constraint*) that has sufficient computing resources (*resource constraint*) such as CPU, storage, bandwidth, or memory [8,10,11].

While offering new opportunities, edge computing also raises many new challenges, such as the problem of edge user allocation (EUA). As an intermediate supply station, an edge server has limited computing resources. Hence, an app vendor's users in an area must be allocated to edge servers properly to utilize the computing resources hired by the app vendor on the edge servers. Existing research treat each user as a resource request, and each user can only be assigned to one edge server to achieve certain specific optimization objectives, e.g., to minimize the number of edge servers needed [8,10], to maximize the overall user satisfaction measured by their Quality of Experience (QoE) [11] and to increase the ratio of user allocation [14]. However, they ignore the real-world application scenarios where user needs may be decomposable and a user's needs may be satisfied collectively by multiple collaborative edge servers. In a real-world application, a user's request may be composed by multiple tasks, which may need to be performed different edge severs with different resources [20]. Consider a typical game streaming service for example. Players talk to their teammates a lot while playing a game, generating different types of tasks to be performed by edge servers.

The need to handle users' decomposable requests significantly complicates the EUA problem. The fundamental limitation of current EUA approaches assume that a user's needs for computing resources are either fulfilled by an individual edge server nearby, or cannot be fulfilled at all. In this study, we focus on more realistic EUA scenarios where a user's needs may be satisfied by several collaborative edge servers nearby by decomposing its request to a set of tasks to be performed by individual edge servers.

We refer to this problem as a task-decomposable edge user allocation (TD-EUA) problem. To tackle this problem, we model it as an optimization problem and propose two novel approaches, one for finding the optimal solution that maximizes users' overall QoE, and the other for efficiently finding a sub-optimal solution to large-scale TD-EUA problems. To the best of our knowledge, it is the first attempt to tackle the EUA problem where users' requests are decomposable. Our main contributions are as follows:

- We formally define and model the TD-EUA problem, and prove its NP-hardness.
- We propose an optimal approach based on integer linear programming (ILP) for solving the TD-EUA problem that aims to maximize users' overall QoE.
- We propose a heuristic approach for finding a sub-optimal solution to large-scale TD-EUA problems.
- Extensive experiments based on a widely-used real-world dataset are carried out to demonstrate the effectiveness and efficiency of our approaches against a baseline approach and a state-of-the-art approach.

The remainder of the paper is organized as follows. Section 2 provides a motivating example for our research. Section 3 defines and formulates the TD-EUA problem. Section 4 models TD-EUA problem as an optimization problem and presents our approaches in detail. Section 5 shows the experimental evaluation. Section 6 reviews the related work. Finally, we conclude the paper and point out future work in Sect. 7.

2   Motivating Example

A typical example of a task-decomposable EUA application scenario is shown in Fig. 1. In the edge computing environment, there are nine users, $u_1, \cdots, u_9$, four edge server $s_1, \cdots, s_4$, and ten tasks $t_1, t_2, \cdots, t_{10}$, where each task can be performed by a corresponding service deployed on an edge server. Each edge server covers a specific geographical area and has a specific amount of different types of resources available to serve users within its coverage. Edge servers' resource capacities and tasks' resource demand are denoted as a vector $\langle CPU, RAM, storage, bandwidth \rangle$. Each user has a list of tasks and each task may require different amounts of computing resources.

For example, user u_2 has a task list $\{t_2, t_4, t_7, t_8\}$. If the resources available on edge servers s_1, s_2 or s_3 are not limited, user u_2 can be served by any of the three edge servers. Otherwise, the need of u_2 can be partitioned. For example, its tasks t_2, t_4, t_7, t_8 can be served by multiple edge servers. Assume that user u_1 has all the resources it needs from edge server s_2, users u_3 and u_6 are assigned to server s_3, and the workload generated by each task is $\langle 1, 1, 1, 1 \rangle$. As a result, the remaining resources on edge server s_2 or s_3 cannot fulfil the demand of user u_2. Existing EUA approaches cannot handle such case and will allocate user u_2 to the cloud for task processing. However, if the user's requirements can be partitioned, this issue can be addressed. Note that user u_2 is in the overlapping

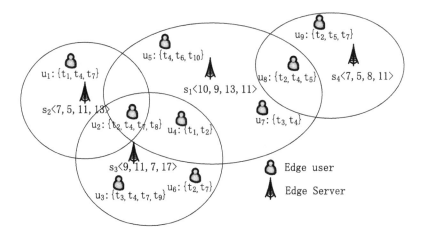

Fig. 1. An example task-decomposable EUA problem.

area of edge servers s_1, s_2, s_3. Tasks t_2 and t_4 can be offloaded to edge server s_2 and task t_7 can be performed by edge server s_3. Then, task t_8 can be performed by edge server s_1. This way, the total workload of the tasks allocated to edge server s_2 is $\langle 5, 5, 5, 5 \rangle$, which not exceed the its remaining capacity ($\langle 7, 5, 11, 13 \rangle$). In the meantime, server s_3 has abundant resources for the tasks assigned to it. What's more, users u_4, u_5, u_7 can be allocated to server s_1 and user u_9 can be allocated to server s_4. Then, user u_8 can allocate its task t_2 to server s_1, tasks t_4 and t_5 to server s_4. While fulfiling the proximity and capacity constraint, this solution allocates all the users' tasks to edge servers, none to the cloud.

There may be other solutions that can also allocate all the users' tasks to edge servers. Finding the optimal one that maximizes users' overall QoE is not trivial, especially in large-scale scenarios. Thus, there is a need for an effective and efficient approach for finding TD-EUA solutions.

3   Problem Formulation

This section defines the TD-EUA problem. The notations and descriptions used in this paper are summarized in Table 1. With the consideration of task decomposition in EUA problem, we give a set of definitions.

Given a finite set of m edge servers $S = \{s_1, s_2, \ldots, s_m\}$, and n edge users $U = \{u_1, u_2, \ldots, u_n\}$ in a particular area, each user has a task list for a request, defined as follows.

Definition 1. *(User Task Decomposition) Given an edge user u, u's request r is composed of a set of tasks, $T(u_i) = \{t_1, t_2, \ldots\}$, where each task t_k can be performed by an edge server.*

From the app vendor's perspective, a TD-EUA solution should allocate as many user requests as possible to edge servers, so that the users' overall QoE is maximized. A user u_i can only offload one or multiple tasks to an edge server s_j under the condition that it is located within s_j's coverage area $cov(s_j)$.

Definition 2. *(Distance-Aware User Coverage) Given an edge user u_i and a set of edge servers $S = \{s_1, s_2, ..., s_n\}$, only the edge servers that cover user u_i may serve u_i, denoted as $S(u_i)$. The edge servers in $S(u_i)$ fulfil the proximity constraint with respect to user u_i:*

$$d_{ij} \leq cov(s_j), \forall i \in 1, 2, \ldots, n; \forall j \in 1, 2, \ldots, m \tag{1}$$

Table 1. Notations

Notation	Description
$D = \{CPU, RAM, storage, bandwidth\}$	A set of computing resource types
$S = \{s_1, s_2, \ldots, s_m\}$	A set of edge servers
$U = \{u_1, u_2, \ldots, u_n\}$	A set of edge users
$T = \{t_1, t_2, \ldots, t_q\}$	A set of tasks decomposed from users' service requests
$c_j = \langle c_j^1, c_j^2, \ldots, c_j^d \rangle$	Computing capacity of edge server s_j
$w_k = \langle w_k^1, w_k^2, \ldots, w_k^d \rangle$	Computing resources demanded for the task t_k
$W_i = \langle W_i^1, W_i^2, \ldots, W_i^d \rangle$	Computing resource that the user u_i gets from the edge server
$T(u_i)$	A set of tasks which user u_i needs in a service request, $T(u_i) \subseteq T$
$T(s_j)$	A set of tasks allocated to server s_j
$U(s_j)$	A set of users that edge server s_j covers, $U(s_j) \subseteq U$
$S(u_i)$	A set of user u_i's candidate servers - edge servers that cover user u_i, $S(u_i) \subseteq S$
$cov(s_j)$	Coverage radius of edge server s_j
d_{ij}	Geographical distance between user u_i and server s_j

Take Fig. 1 as an example. User u_4 can be served by servers s_1 or s_3. Server s_3 can serve users u_2, u_3, u_4, and u_6 as long as it has adequate resources.

The total workload generated by all the tasks allocated to an edge server must not exceed its current capacity. Otherwise, the server will be overloaded.

Definition 3. *(Server Capacity Constraint) Given an edge server s_j and its covered users $U_c = \{u_c^1, u_c^2, ...\}$, where each user in U_c has a set of tasks. We denote $T(s_j) = \{t_{s_j}^1, t_{s_j}^2, ...\}$ as the tasks allocated to server s_j, the total resource demand of which must not exceed its current computing capacity:*

$$\sum_{t_{s_j}^k \in T(s_j)} w_k \leq c_j, \forall s_j \in S \tag{2}$$

Take Fig. 1 for an instance, as the workload generated by each task is $\langle 1, 1, 1, 1 \rangle$, the aggregate workload incurred by users u_3 and u_6 is $\langle 6, 6, 6, 6 \rangle$. It does not exceed the current capacity of server s_3 $\langle 9, 11, 7, 17 \rangle$. Therefore, it is a valid allocation. However, if we allocate users u_1 and u_2's tasks t_2, t_4, t_7 to server s_2, it will be overloaded since the aggregate task workload is $\langle 6, 6, 6, 6 \rangle$, exceeding server s_2's current computing capacity $\langle 7, 5, 11, 13 \rangle$.

Through allocating users' tasks to edge servers, an QoE value can be calculated for each user. In this study, we measure a user's QoE in the same way as [11], which depends on the Quality of the Service (QoS) delivered to the user. As stated in [7,9], QoS is non-linearly correlated with QoE. Generally, it starts to increase slowly at first, then speeds up, and finally converges. Many studies model the correlation between QoE and QoS with the sigmoid function [11]. In [11], the authors use a logistic function, a generalized version of the sigmoid function, to model the QoE-QoS correlation, which is represented as follows:

$$E_i^0 = \frac{L}{1 + e^{-\alpha(x_i - \beta)}} \tag{3}$$

where L is the maximum value of QoE, β is a domain-specific parameter that controls the QoE growth should be, or the mid-point of the QoE function, α, another domain-specific parameter, controls the growth rate of the QoE level, i.e., how steep the change from the minimum to maximum QoE level is, E_i^0 represents the QoE level given user u_i's QoS level W_i, and $x_i = \frac{\sum_{l \in D} W_i^l}{|D|}$. There is $E_i^0 = 0$ if user u_i is not allocated to any edge servers.

Now, we measure the QoE of a user in a TD-EUA scenario, where the its tasks may be allocated to multiple edge servers:

$$E_i = \frac{\sum_{l \in D} W_i^l}{\sum_{l \in D} \sum_{t_k \in T(u_i)} w_k^l} E_i^0 \tag{4}$$

Next, we formally define the TD-EUA problem:

Definition 4. *(TD-EUA) The TD-EUA problem can be represented by a four tuple $TD - EUA = < U, S, T, W >$, where*

(1) $U = \{u_1, u_2, ..., u_n\}$ is a set of edge users and each user has a request;

(2) $S = \{s_1, s_2, ..., s_m\}$ is a set of edge servers, each server has a coverage radius;

(3) $T = \{t_1, t_2, ..., t_q\}$ is a set of tasks decomposed from a user's request;

(4) $W = \{w_1, w_2, ..., w_q\}$ is a set of resource demands from a task in T.

The solution to a TD-EUA problem is a user-task-server assignment, where the each user's tasks are fully or partially allocated to their nearby edge servers. Based on the assignment, a QoE value can be calculated for each user based on its QoS level. From the app vendor's perspective, its objective is to maximize the users' overall QoE.

4   Approaches

To solve a TD-EUA problem, we first model it as an integer linear programming (ILP) problem to find its optimal solution. To solve large-scale TD-EUA problems efficiently, we propose a heuristic approach named TD-EUA-H that finds a sub-optimal TD-EUA solution.

4.1   Optimal Approach

The optimization objective of TD-EUA is to maximize the users' overall QoE, while satisfying the capacity constraint and proximity constraint. In this section, we present TD-EUA-O, our approach for finding the optimal solution to a TD-EUA problem. It models the TD-EUA problem as an ILP problem as follows:

$$\text{objective function: max} \sum_{i=1}^{n} E_i \tag{5}$$

s.t.:

$$x_{i,j,k} = 0 \qquad \forall i, j \in \{i, j | d_{ij} > cov(s_j)\}, \forall k \in \{1, 2, \ldots, |T(u_i)|\} \tag{6}$$

$$\sum_{i=1}^{n} \sum_{k=1}^{q} w_k x_{i,j,k} \leq c_j \qquad \forall j \in \{1, \ldots, m\} \tag{7}$$

$$\sum_{j=1}^{m} x_{i,j,k} \leq 1 \qquad \forall i \in \{1, \ldots, n\}, \forall k \in \{1, \ldots, q\} \tag{8}$$

where $x_{i,j,k}$ is a binary variable indicating that,

$$x_{i,j,k} = \begin{cases} 1, & \text{if user } u_i\text{'s task } t_k \text{ is allocated to server } s_j \\ 0, & \text{otherwise.} \end{cases}$$

The objective (5) maximizes the users' overall QoE. In (5), QoE level E_i depends on the ratio of the resources W_i the user u_i obtains over the total resources requested by u_i. Constraint (6) enforces the proximity constraint.

A user may be located within the overlapping coverage area of multiple edge servers. Constraint (7) makes sure that the aggregate resource demands of all tasks allocated to an edge server must not exceed that server's current computing capacity. Constraint (8) ensures that each task can be allocated to at most one edge server.

The above ILP problem can be solved by an ILP problem solver, e.g., CPLEX or Gurobi. The outcome is the optimal solution to the TD-EUA problem.

4.2   Problem Hardness

Based on the optimization model, we now prove that the TD-EUA problem is $\mathcal{NP}$-hard.

Theorem 1. *Knapsack $\leq_p$ TD-EUA. Therefore, TD-EUA problem is NP-hard.*

Proof. We prove that the TD-EUA problem is $\mathcal{NP}$-hard by reducing the $\mathcal{NP}$-hard Knapsack problem to a specialization of the TD-EUA problem.

Definition 5. *(Knapsack Problem) Given n items and their corresponding weights and values, the aim of a Knapsack problem is to select a group of items so that the total price of the items is the highest within the total weight limit. It can be formally defined as follows:*

$$objective\ function: \max \sum_{i=1}^{n} v_i x_i \tag{9}$$

s.t.:

$$\sum_{i=1}^{n} w_i x_i \leq W \tag{10}$$

$$x_i \in \{0, 1\} \tag{11}$$

where W is the total weight limit and x_i indicates whether the i-th item is selected.

Based on the definition of the Knapsack problem, we now prove that it can be reduced to a special instance of the TD-EUA problem. For ease of exposition, we make the following assumptions: 1) For each task t_k, its requirements for different types of computing resources are the same, i.e., $w_k^1 = w_k^2 = \ldots = w_k^d$; 2) For any edge server s_j, its computing capacities in different dimensions are equal, i.e., $c_j^1 = c_j^2 = \ldots = c_j^d$; 3) The coverage of each edge server is infinite, i.e., a task can be allocated any of the edge server in the area.

Based on the above assumptions, we can obtain a simplified special case of the TD-EUA problem. For the simplified special case, constraints (6)(8) can be combined and projected to (11), because any task can be allocated to any edge server. Moreover, constraint (7) can be projected to objective function (10), since the computing capacities of all the edge servers can be aggregated as an overall resource limit. Clearly, there is a solution to the TD-EUA problem if and only if there is a solution to the corresponding Knapsack problem. Thus, TD-EUA problem is $\mathcal{NP}$-hard.

4.3 Heuristic Approach

Due to the NP-hardness of TD-EUA problem, finding its optimal solution is intractable in large-scale scenarios. This is demonstrated in our experimental results presented in Sect. 5. Thus, we propose a heuristic approach named TD-EUA-H for finding a sub-optimal solution to a TD-EUA problem efficiently. Algorithm 1 presents its pseudo code.

TD-EUA-H goes through three main steps: 1) it employs the skyline algorithm to partition the tasks decomposed from users' requests into two categories, including a group of tasks T_1 requiring more computing resources than any task in the other group T_2; 2) it sorts the tasks within each group according to their required computing resources from high to low; 3) when orderly assigning each task in T_1 to an edge server, for each candidate edge server, it calculates the ratio of the remaining computing resources on that edge server over the number of unallocated tasks covered. Then, it finds the edge server s_j with the highest ratio (Line 15), then allocates the task to that edge server (Lines 13–17). In the same way, it orderly allocates each task t_k in T_2 to an edge server.

The time complexity of TD-EUA-H consists of: 1) using the skyline algorithm to partition q tasks takes $\mathcal{O}(q^2)$ time; 2) labeling and sorting the tasks for each user which depends on the total number of tasks takes $\mathcal{O}(n * q)$ time, where n and q are the number of edge users and tasks, respectively; 3)calculating and

---

Algorithm 1. TD-EUA-H

Input: edge servers S; edge users U; tasks T.
Output: task-server allocation $f : T \rightarrow S$.
 1: $T \overset{skyline}{\longrightarrow} Good(T), Bad(T)$;
 2: **for** each $u_i \in U$ **do**
 3:     **for** each $t_k \in T(u_i)$ **do**
 4:         **if** $t_k \in Good(T)$ **then**
 5:             $T_1 \leftarrow (t_k, u_i)$
 6:         **else**
 7:             $T_2 \leftarrow (t_k, u_i)$
 8:         **end if**
 9:     **end for**
10: **end for**
11: $sort(T_1)_{key} = w_k,\ sort(T_2)_{key} = w_k$
12: **for** each (t_k, u_i) in T_1 **do**
13:     $S(u_i) \leftarrow \{s_j \in S | u_i \in cov(s_j)\}$;
14:     **if** $S(u_i) \neq \phi$ **then**
15:         $j = \text{argmax } c_j/\text{unallocated} \left(|\sum_{u_i \in U(s_j)} \sum_{t_k \in T(u_i)} t_k| \right)$
16:     **end if**
17:     $f \leftarrow f \cup \{t_k, s_j\}$
18: **end for**
19: Perform task-server allocation for T_2

---

ranking m candidate edge servers for each task takes $\mathcal{O}(m \log m)$, and $\mathcal{O}(n * q * m \log m)$ time for all the tasks. Thus, the overall time complexity of TD-EUA-H is $\mathcal{O}(q^2) + \mathcal{O}(n * q) + \mathcal{O}(n * q * m \log m)$. Its complexity indicates that it is an efficient heuristic algorithm with polynomial time for task-decomposable edge user allocation. Thus, it can handle large-scale TD-EUA scenarios.

5   Experiments

5.1   Experimental Setup and Dataset

We conduct a series of experiments to evaluate the effectiveness and efficiency of our approaches. All the experiments are conducted on a machine equipped with an Intel(R) Xeon(R) Gold 6130 CPU@2 and 192 GB RAM. The ILP model in Sect. 4.1 is solved with Gurobi.

The experiments are conducted on the public and widely-used EUA dataset[1]. It contains the locations of the 125 edge servers (base stations) in the Melbourne central business district area in Australia. Following the Gaussian distribution $N(u, \sigma)$, users are distributed in different ways in this area to simulate six different real-world TD-EUA scenarios with different user distributions, as illustrated in Fig. 2, where each black point represents an edge server and each orange point represents a user. Accordingly, six datasets are synthesized with data extracted from the EUA dataset, each corresponding to a specific type of the six user distribution in Fig. 2.

5.2   Competing Methods and Evaluation Metrics

To evaluate the performance of TD-EUA-O and TD-EUA-H, we compare them with two other approaches, including a random baseline and a state-of-the-art approach for solving the EUA problem.

- Random: each task is allocated to a random edge server that has sufficient computing resources to accommodate the task, as long as the user of the task is located within the edge server's coverage area.
- VSVBP [10,11]: it models the EUA problem as a variable sized vector bin packing (VSVBP) problem and aims at maximizing the number of allocated users, while minimizing the number of edge servers needs to be used. This approach treats each user request as a whole, i.e., one user can either be allocated to only one edge server, or cannot be allocated to any edge server at all.

Three widely-used performance metrics are employed in the experiments.

- QoE: it is measured by users' overall QoE, the higher the better.
- Allocation Rate: it is measured by the percentage of users allocated to edge servers of all, the higher the better.
- CPU Time: it is measured by the computation time consumed to find a solution, the lower the better.

---

[1] https://sites.google.com/site/heqiang/eua-repository.
https://github.com/swinedge/eua-dataset.

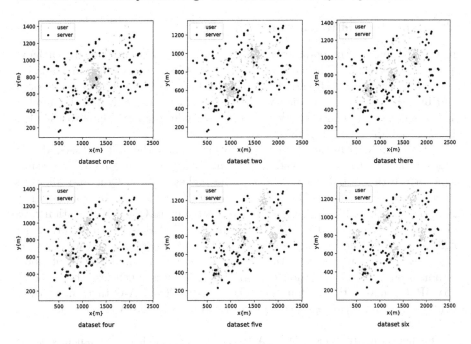

Fig. 2. EUA experimental datasets with different user distributions.

Table 2. Experimental results on different datasets

Methods	Dataset one			Dataset two			Dataset three		
	QoE	AR	CPU Time	QoE	AR	CPU Time	QoE	AR	CPU Time
VSVBP	4,479	0.56	22.512	5,319	0.66	24.312	5,189	0.65	23.145
Random	5,105	0.63	0.014	6,377	0.79	0.016	6,102	0.76	0.015
TD-EUA-H	6,002	0.66	0.034	7,121	0.82	0.046	6,971	0.80	0.041
TD-EUA-O	6,357	0.72	2.591	7,416	0.87	3.241	7,261	0.85	2.756

Methods	Dataset four			Dataset five			Dataset six		
	QoE	AR	CPU Time	QoE	AR	CPU Time	QoE	AR	CPU Time
VSVBP	5,606	0.70	26.235	5,725	0.71	29.324	5,609	0.56	28.165
Random	6,964	0.87	0.018	7,385	0.92	0.018	6,952	0.86	0.018
TD-EUA-H	7,500	0.90	0.045	7,665	0.94	0.048	7,507	0.90	0.047
TD-EUA-O	7,622	0.93	3.212	7,737	0.95	2.234	7,658	0.93	2.946

5.3   Experimental Results and Analysis

In the experiments, the parameters for existing approaches are tuned to achieve optimal performance. The coverage radius of edge servers obeys a Gaussian distribution with $u = 150$ and the number of tasks per user follows a Gaussian distribution with $u = 3$. Further, we set the number of users to 400, the number of edge servers to 125 and the edge server's available computing capacities follow the Gaussian distribution $N(35, 1)$.

Table 2 summarizes the experimental results, where the best and second-best values in each column are marked in dark and light grey, respectively. The results demonstrate that TD-EUA-O achieves the highest overall QoE and allocates the most users. Specifically, TD-EUA-O outperforms VSVBP, Random and TD-EUA-H by 41.92%, 24.52% and 5.91%, respectively, in QoE. In allocation rate, TD-EUA-O is superior to VSVBP, Random and TD-EUA-H with an advantage of 28.57%, 14.28% and 9.09%, respectively. The main reason of the advantage of TD-EUA-O lies in its consideration of task decomposition and pursuit of global optimization. The computation time of TD-EUA-O is much less than that of VSVBP. Compared to Random and TD-EUA-H, TD-EUA-O takes more time, which is expected because of the NP-hardness of the TD-EUA problem as proved in Sect. 4.2.

Our heuristic approach TD-EUA-H also achieves high performance, with an advantage of 34.00% and 17.57% over VSVBP and Random in QoE, and 17.85% and 4.76% in allocation rate. Surprisingly, we can see that the performance of the Random approach is higher than VSVBP, in terms of both QoE and allocation rate. This is because VSVBP either allocates a user request to an edge server as a whole or does not allocate at all, whereas Random can partition a user request into a set of tasks to be allocated. Overall, the results indicate that decomposing users' requests into tasks can significantly improve the allocation rate and users' overall QoE.

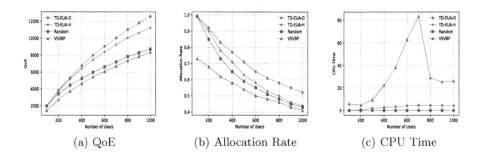

(a) QoE   (b) Allocation Rate   (c) CPU Time

Fig. 3. Performance comparisons on the variations of edge users.

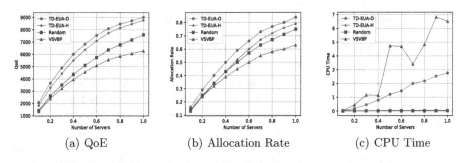

Fig. 4. Performance comparisons on the variations of edge servers.

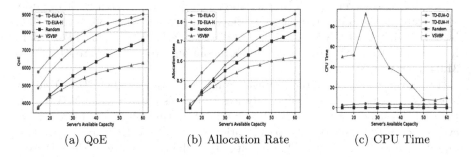

Fig. 5. Performance comparisons on the variations of server's available capacity.

5.4 Performance Impacts of Parameters

To evaluate the performance of our approaches in various TD-EUA scenarios, we vary the following three parameters in the experiments. Each experiment is repeated 100 times to obtain 100 different user distributions so that the impacts of extreme cases, such as overly sparse or dense distributions, are neutralized.

- **Number of edge users (n):** We random distribute 100, 200, ..., 1,000 edge users in the Melbourne CBD.
- **Number of edge servers (m):** A certain percentage of the all of the edge servers (10%, 20%, ..., 100%) in the Melbourne CBD are included in the experiments.
- **Server's available resources (c):** Edge servers' overall capacity is generated following a Gaussian distribution with $\sigma = 1$. The average capacity of each edge server ranges from $u = 15, 20, \ldots$, to 60 in each dimension, e.g., CPU, RAM, storage and bandwidth.

Three sets of experiments #1, #2 and #3 are conducted. In each experiment set, we vary one parameter and fix the other two. The results are shown in Figs. 3, 4, and 5.

Figure 3 compares the performance in experiment set #1, where the number of edge users (n) varies from 100 to 1,000 in steps of 100. Figure 3(a) shows that as n increases, users' overall QoE achieved by different approaches increase. TD-EUA-O achieves the most improvement from 1,989 to 12,559 by 10,570, outperforming TD-EUA-H's 9,244, Random's 6,737, and VSVBP's 6,905. At the beginning, the overall QoE of the four approaches are not that different, because edge servers can provide sufficient computing resources to serve a small number of user requests. As n increases, edge servers' overall computing capacity becomes inadequate, making it hard to achieve high QoE and allocation rate.

The impact of n on allocation rate is shown in Fig. 3(b). Obviously, TD-EUA-O outperforms other approaches again. More specifically, compared with Random and TD-EUA-H, the allocation rate of TD-EUA-O declines more slowly. VSVBP achieves the lowest allocation rate, because it also needs to minimize the number of edge servers hired. Furthermore, as n gradually increases, it is harder to allocate all the users, lowering the allocation rates, from 99.86 % to 52.33 % by 47.33% for TD-EUA-O, from 99.88% to 44.27% by 55.61% for TD-EUA-H, from 99.40% to 43.48% by 55.92% for Random and from 73.01% to 41.96% by 31.04% for VSVBP.

As shown in Fig. 3(c), the average computation time of TD-EUA-O fluctuates slightly and it takes significantly less time consumption than VSVBP. As the problem scales up in n, VSVBP's computation time increases quickly. However, when n exceeds 700, the computation time of VSVBP starts to decrease quickly before it converges. The reason is that the complexity of the TD-EUA problem increases as n increases, producing more possible solutions for VSVBP to inspect. Considering the multi-objective optimization of VSVBP, its solution is not unique, in which it needs to compromise among multiple optimization objectives. Nevertheless, after the turning point, the edge servers cannot accommodate the excessive user requests. Most users are directly allocated to the cloud without further decisions. The computation time of TD-EUA-H is similar to that of Random, slightly less than TD-EUA-O. Thus, TD-EUA-H can accommodate TD-EUA scenarios with large numbers of users.

Figure 4 shows the performance in experiment set #2, where the percentage of the number of edge servers (m) varies from 0.1 to 1.0. As demonstrated, the overall QoE follows a similar trend as in experiment set #1, where TD-EUA-O and TD-EUA-H achieve much higher QoE than Random and VSVBP. As m increases from 10% to 40%, Random achieves performance similar to VSVBP in the resource-scarce situations. Figure 4(b) shows that as m increases, TD-EUA-O and TD-EUA-H continue to achieve high allocation rates. It is worth noting that when m reaches a specific level, the allocation rate achieved by Random is close to that of the TD-EUA-H because the overall computing resources is sufficient to accommodate all the user requests. Figure 4(c) presents the rising trend of the computation time of TD-EUA-O as m keeps increasing. VSVBP takes much more time to find a solution than the other approaches. Its computation time fluctuates. The reason is that VSVBP needs to frequently reselect edge servers to achieve the optimization goal. As for TD-EUA-H and Random, the computation time is always at a low level, similar experiment set #1.

Figure 5 shows the performance comparison in experiment set #3. As the server's available capacity (c) varies from 15 to 60, the overall QoE and allocation rates follow a similar trend as in experiment set #2. In Fig. 5(a), TD-EUA-O and TD-EUA-H outperform the Random and VSVBP in terms of the overall QoE. Especially, With the increase in c, the overall QoE achieved by VSVBP grows slowly, from 3,799 to 6,265 by 2,466, compared with the growth of TD-EUA-O's 3,259 from 5,765 to 9,015, Random's 3,822 from 3,714 to 7,536, and TD-EUA-H's 3,907 from 4,844 to 8,751. Figure 5(b) shows the same trend as Fig. 4(b) on allocation rate as experiment set #2. In Fig. 5(c), compared to other approaches, VSVBP takes the most time to find a solution.

The experimental results show that by considering the task decomposition of service's request, TD-EUA-O and TD-EUA-H outperform the random baseline and the state-of-the-art approach in both QoE and allocation rate with relatively low computation time. In general, TD-EUA-O is the best approach for finding solutions in small-scale instances. In large-scale scenarios, TD-EUA-H is the best option for its second-highest effectiveness of all and its high efficiency.

6 Related Work

With the advances in mobile devices and the Internet of Things, cloud centers may easily be overwhelmed by excessive workloads, causing network latency and congestion. Cisco coined the fog computing, or edge computing, paradigm in 2012 to overcome the major drawback of access latency in cloud computing [1]. Edge computing is an open paradigm that integrates network, computing, storage, and application core capabilities close to end-users to provide low-latency services. Applications deployed and running on the edge can provide fast responses to users' request, meeting their needs for low latency. Service providers can deploy resources on edge servers that are closer to end-users in the edge computing environment. However, an edge server only has a limited computing capacity, making it difficult or sometimes impossible to serve all of the users within its coverage area. Offering many new opportunities, edge computing has also raised a variety of new problems, e.g., edge user allocation (EUA) problem [5,8,10–12,14], edge service placement [2,13,19], edge data management [16–18], edge server placement [3,4], etc.

Recently, the EUA problem as one of the new challenges in the edge computing environment has attracted a lot of attention. Lai et al. [10] made the first attempt to tackle the EUA problem. They modeled the EUA problem as a variable sized vector bin packing problem, and developed an optimal approach for solving the EUA problem with the aim to maximize the number of users allocated and minimize the number of edge servers needed. Then, they further applied user satisfaction as the criterion to measure whether the user allocation is cost-effective, considering that users' resource demands may be differentiated [11]. He et al. [8] proposed a game-theoretic approach for solving the EUA game in a distributed manner. They seek to find the Nash equilibrium of the game as the EUA solution. Peng et al. [14] tackled the EUA problem in an online manner with mobility consideration.

However, existing studies simply assume that a user's demands of computing resources can either be fully fulfilled by a single edge server or cannot be fulfilled at all. In many real-world scenarios, an edge user's request can actually be partitioned into multiple tasks that can be performed by different edge servers. In this paper, we studied the EUA problem with task decomposition and proposed two approaches, TD-EUA-O for finding optimal solutions and TD-EUA-H for finding sub-optimal solutions.

7 Conclusion and Future Work

In this paper, we studied the TD-EUA problem. Instead of serving an user's request as a whole, we consider task decomposition and partition a user's request into individual tasks, which can be performed by different edge servers. To solve the TD-EUA problem, we modeled it as an optimization problem with multiple constraints, and proposed two novel approaches to find TD-EUA solutions that maximize users' overall QoE. The results of experiments conducted on a widely-used real-world dataset demonstrated that our approaches significantly outperform the baseline approach and the state-of-the-art approach. In the future, we will consider the mobility of users and tasks.

Acknowledgments. This work was partially supported by Shanghai Natural Science Foundation (No. 18ZR1414400), National Key Research and Development Program of China (No. 2017YFC0907505), National Natural Science Foundation of China (No. 61772128) and Australian Research Council Discovery Projects (DP18010021 and DP200102491).

References

1. Bonomi, F., Milito, R., Zhu, J., Addepalli, S.: Fog computing and its role in the internet of things. In: International Conference on Mobile Cloud Computing (MCC), pp. 13–16 (2012)
2. Chen, Y., Deng, S., Ma, H., Yin, J.: Deploying data-intensive applications with multiple services components on edge. Mob. Netw. Appl. **25**(2), 426–441 (2020). https://doi.org/10.1007/s11036-019-01245-3
3. Cui, G., He, Q., Chen, F., Jin, H., Yang, Y.: Trading off between user coverage and network robustness for edge server placement. IEEE Trans. Cloud Comput. (2020). https://doi.org/10.1109/TCC.2020.3008440
4. Cui, G., He, Q., Xia, X., Chen, F., Jin, H., Yang, Y.: Robustness-oriented k edge server placement. In: 20th IEEE/ACM International Symposium on Cluster, Cloud and Grid Computing. IEEE (2020). https://doi.org/10.1109/CCGrid49817.2020.00-8
5. Cui, G., et al.: Interference-aware SaaS user allocation game for edge computing. IEEE Trans. Cloud Comput. (2020). https://doi.org/10.1109/TCC.2020.3008440
6. Deng, S., Zhao, H., Fang, W., Yin, J., Dustdar, S., Zomaya, A.Y.: Edge intelligence: the confluence of edge computing and artificial intelligence. CoRR arxiv.org/abs/1909.00560 (2020)

7. Fiedler, M., Hossfeld, T., Tran-Gia, P.: A generic quantitative relationship between quality of experience and quality of service. IEEE Network **24**(2), 36–41 (2010)
8. He, Q., et al.: A game-theoretical approach for user allocation in edge computing environment. IEEE Trans. Parallel Distrib. Syst. **31**(3), 515–529 (2020)
9. Hemmati, M., McCormick, B., Shirmohammadi, S.: QoE-aware bandwidth allocation for video traffic using sigmoidal programming. IEEE MultiMedia **24**(4), 80–90 (2017)
10. Lai, P., et al.: Optimal edge user allocation in edge computing with variable sized vector bin packing. In: Pahl, C., Vukovic, M., Yin, J., Yu, Q. (eds.) ICSOC 2018. LNCS, vol. 11236, pp. 230–245. Springer, Cham (2018). https://doi.org/10.1007/978-3-030-03596-9_15
11. Lai, P., et al.: Edge user allocation with dynamic quality of service. In: Yangui, S., Bouassida Rodriguez, I., Drira, K., Tari, Z. (eds.) ICSOC 2019. LNCS, vol. 11895, pp. 86–101. Springer, Cham (2019). https://doi.org/10.1007/978-3-030-33702-5_8
12. Lai, P., et al.: Cost-effective app user allocation in an edge computing environment. IEEE Trans. Cloud Comput. (2020). https://doi.org/10.1109/TCC.2020.3001570
13. Li, B., et al.: READ: robustness-oriented edge application deployment in edge computing environment. IEEE Trans. Serv. Comput. (2020). https://doi.org/10.1109/TSC.2020.3015316
14. Peng, Q., et al.: Mobility-aware and migration-enabled online edge user allocation in mobile edge computing. In: IEEE International Conference on Web Services (ICWS), pp. 91–98. IEEE (2019)
15. Shi, W., Cao, J., Zhang, Q., Li, Y., Xu, L.: Edge computing: vision and challenges. IEEE Internet Things J. **3**(5), 637–646 (2016)
16. Xia, X., et al.: Graph-based optimal data caching in edge computing. In: Yangui, S., Bouassida Rodriguez, I., Drira, K., Tari, Z. (eds.) ICSOC 2019. LNCS, vol. 11895, pp. 477–493. Springer, Cham (2019). https://doi.org/10.1007/978-3-030-33702-5_37
17. Xia, X., Chen, F., He, Q., Grundy, J., Abdelrazek, M., Jin, H.: Online collaborative data caching in edge computing. IEEE Trans. Parallel Distrib. Syst. (2020). https://doi.org/10.1109/TPDS.2020.3016344
18. Xia, X., Chen, F., He, Q., Grundy, J., Abdelrazek, M., Jin, H.: Cost-effective app data distribution in edge computing. IEEE Trans. Parallel Distrib. Syst. **32**(1), 31–44 (2021)
19. Xiang, Z., Deng, S., Taheri, J., Zomaya, A.: Dynamical service deployment and replacement in resource-constrained edges. Mob. Netw. Appl. **25**(2), 674–689 (2020). https://doi.org/10.1007/s11036-019-01449-7
20. Zhao, H., Deng, S., Zhang, C., Du, W., He, Q., Yin, J.: A mobility-aware cross-edge computation offloading framework for partitionable applications. In: 2019 IEEE International Conference on Web Services (ICWS), pp. 193–200. IEEE (2019)

A Decentralized Reactive Approach to Online Task Offloading in Mobile Edge Computing Environments

Qinglan Peng[1], Yunni Xia[1(✉)], Yan Wang[2], Chunrong Wu[1], Xin Luo[3(✉)], and Jia Lee[1]

[1] Software Theory and Technology Chongqing Key Lab, Chongqing University, Chongqing, China
xiayunni@hotmail.com
[2] Department of Computing, Macquarie University, Sydney, NSW 2109, Australia
[3] Chongqing Institute of Green and Intelligent Technology, Chinese Academy of Sciences, Chongqing, China
luoxin21@cigit.ac.cn

Abstract. In mobile edge computing (MEC) environments, the task offloading towards nearby edge servers usually occurs when local resources are inadequate for computation-intensive applications. While the MEC servers benefit from the close proximity to the end-users to provide services at reduced latency and lower energy costs, they suffer from limitations in computational and radio resources, which calls for smart, timely, and efficient offloading methods and strategies. In this paper, we consider an arbitrary request arrival pattern and formulate the MEC-oriented task offloading problem as an online multi-dimensional integer linear programming. We propose a decentralized reactive approach by adopting a dynamic-learning mechanism to yield online offloading decisions upon request arrivals. Experiments based on real-world MEC environment datasets show that our method outperforms state-of-the-art ones in terms of offloading responsiveness and efficiency.

Keywords: Mobile edge computing · Task offloading · Reactive scheduling · Decentralized scheduling

1 Introduction

Due to restricted battery power, storage, and computational capacity, mobile devices face challenges in executing delay-sensitive and resource-hungry mobile applications such as augmented reality and online gaming [6]. As a newly emerging computing paradigm, edge computing shows great capability in supporting and boosting such computation-intensive mobile applications. In the mobile edge computing (MEC) environments, the mobile edge is enhanced with computation resources and storage capabilities, possibly by the dense deployment of computational servers or by strengthening the already-deployed edge entities such as small-cell base stations. Consequently, mobile devices are able to offload their

© Springer Nature Switzerland AG 2020
E. Kafeza et al. (Eds.): ICSOC 2020, LNCS 12571, pp. 232–247, 2020.
https://doi.org/10.1007/978-3-030-65310-1_18

computationally intensive tasks to the edge servers to alleviate the insufficiency of local computing power and capacity [4].

In practice, MEC-oriented offloading requests can be dynamically submitted in real-time by end-users and specified with timing constraints. They require both logical and temporal correctness of computations. Due to the dynamic nature in MEC environments and the heterogeneity of both real-time tasks and edge servers, traditional centralized offloading strategies, where an offloading decision for a batch of requests is made at the centralized scheduler and performed simultaneously, can lead to bad user-perceived Quality-of-Service (QoS) and long waiting time of end-users. Intuitively, such long waiting time and low system responsiveness are usually caused by the fact that asynchronous requests have to gather at the scheduler first before the synchronous offloading decisions for a batch of such requests are made and carried out.

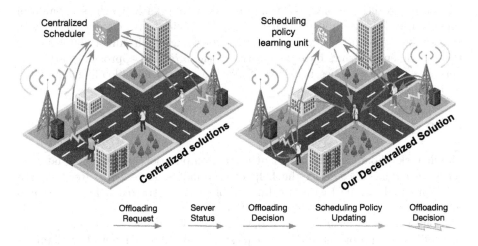

Fig. 1. System architecture comparison between ours and traditional ones.

In this paper, instead of considering centralized and batch-processing-based offloading decision-making, we propose a decentralized reactive approach to yield online offloading decisions upon request arrivals. Figure 1 shows the differences between ours and the traditional ones. It can be seen in the traditional solution that a centralized scheduler requires a global view of system status and all offloading requests are forwarded to it before offloading decisions are made and performed. Consequently, in addition to low system responsiveness, the centralized scheduling pattern can be susceptible to single-point-of-failures (SPOFs) [16] that affect all server nodes when the central one crashes and cause high communication overhead among the central scheduler and edge servers. There are also some studies, e.g., [10,17,23], that proposed distributed solutions by utilizing the parallelism feature of game-theory or alternating direction method of multipliers (ADMM). However, they still need a centralized coordinator to exchange sub-decisions to reach the final decision. In contrast, our approach is completely decentralized, where the online offloading decisions are locally made by and applied to individual mobile users themselves instead of a centralized scheduler. Moreover, in our work, a significant difference exists from the traditional system architectures, namely, our proposed architecture is empowered by a learning unit which is responsible of continuously learning scheduling policies and pushing them to end-users, the dynamicity (e.g., the fluctuation of offloading request arrival rates and uneven geographical distribution of requests) of MEC environments is thus captured and tackled.

The main contributions of this work are as follows: 1) we propose a completely decentralized architecture for MEC-oriented online task offloading problem by devolving the offloading decision-making power from a centralized scheduler to end-users themselves; 2) instead of assuming the request arrival rates are pre-given or follow certain distributions, we consider an arbitrary request arrival pattern, which is more in line with the practical application scenarios; 3) we present an efficient reactive dynamic-learning-based [1] approach which is capable of continuously learning and updating scheduling policies. We conduct a series of case studies based on two well-known real-world edge environment datasets and the experimental results have demonstrated the proposed approach clearly outperforms traditional ones in terms of average end-to-end offloading delay and decision-making time.

2   Related Work

Mobile task offloading aims at executing the computation-intensive and latency-sensitive mobile tasks with the help of external resources [16]. Recently the MEC-oriented mobile task offloading problem has attracted a lot of research interests and extensive efforts are devoted to it.

Some studies focus on the static optimization of multiple-server multiple-user task offloading problems during a request arrival batch window. For example, Chen et al. [4] formulate the task offloading problem at a certain time point as a mixed-integer-programming (MIP) problem, then they decompose and convert it into two convex optimization ones and develop a Lagrange-multiplier-based algorithm to solve them. Alameddine et al. [2] take the offloading request admission rate as the target and propose a Logic-Based-Benders-Decomposition-based method to reduce the searching space of the MIP problem. Yang et al. [23] consider both energy consumption and latency as offloading targets, they formulate the offloading problem as a potential game and present a distributed game-theoretical approach to solving it. Dai et al. [5] propose a two-tier computation offloading framework to cope with the heterogeneous networks and multiple mutually dependent mobile tasks, then the semi-definite-program and linear-convex-program are employed to yield user association plan and offloading decisions, respectively. Yang et al. [22] formulate the offloading decision problem as a classification one and propose a feedforward neural network model to optimize the offloading decisions.

There are also some studies considering the long-term offloading QoS as target and present the corresponding online solutions. For example, Liu et al. [14] and Du et al. [7] assume the task arrivals are i.i.d. over time and their average arrival rates are pre-given. Chen *et al.* [3] and Xu *et al.* [21] consider that task arrivals follow a Poisson process and they both use random arrival rates to capture the temporal variation of task arrival pattern at different time. While Zhao *et al.* [24] assume the offloading demands of mobile users follow a binomial distribution with a pre-given probability. Based on these assumptions, they all build a local-edge two-tier queue model and utilize a Lyapunov optimization technique to maintain the stability of the system to achieve an online optimization. Huang *et al.* [11] present a deep-reinforcement-learning-based method to get online offloading decisions. However, their approach is a centralized one and they only consider one edge server in their system model.

A careful investigation into the aforementioned studies shows that they are still limited in three ways: 1) most of the existing studies base themselves upon centralized architecture that needs a central scheduler to yield offloading solutions, which may suffer from SPOFs and low system responsiveness; 2) the batch-processing scheduling mode of some static studies, e.g., [4,10], may result in additional waiting time, which may lead to bad user-perceived QoS and long waiting time; 3) some online studies, e.g., [3,14,24], are based on the assumptions that the offloading request arrival rates are pre-given or follow certain distributions. However, these assumptions are unrealistic in real-world application scenarios where offloading requests could arrive at an arbitrary time and their arrival rates fluctuate over time. Therefore, a decentralized reactive approach that adapts to a more general application scenario is in high demand.

3 Preliminary

In this section, we present our system model and give the problem formulation of online task offloading in MEC environments. Table 1 lists the notations used in our system model.

Table 1. List of notations

Notation	Description	Notation	Description
a_j	Arrival time of task t_j.	q_i	Maximum size of the task queue of edge server e_i.
b_i	Maximum total size of tasks that server e_i can handle in period P.	q_{ji}	Instantaneous task queue size of server e_i when task t_j arrivals.
c_i, c_j	Computing capability of edge server e_i, requester of task t_j.	r_i	Radius of edge server e_i' signal coverage.
d_{ji}	Distance between server e_i and user who invokes task t_j.	r_{ji}	Uplink data rate between edge server e_i and the requester of task t_j.
e_i	The i-th edge server in E.	$\mathbb{R}_{ji}$	Response time of offloading t_j to e_i.
E	The set of edge servers.	s_j	Data content size of t_j.
f_{ji}	Transmission delay of uploading the data of task t_j to server e_i.	t_j	The j-th task in T.
h_{ji}	Execution time of task t_j on the e_i.	T	The set of offloading requests.
l_i, l_j	Real-time geographic location of server e_i, requester of task t_j.	u_i	Utility value of server e_i that has been learned.
m	The count of edge servers in E.	v_j	Earliest start time of task t_j on server e_i.
n	The count of Offloading requests in T.	x_{ji}	An indicator to identify whether task t_j is scheduled to server e_i.
o_j	The count operations in task t_j.	ϵ	Decision repository length factor

3.1 System Model

As shown in Fig. 1, in the MEC environments, base stations are equipped with a certain amount of computing resources (i.e., edge servers) to fulfill users' offloading demands. Suppose that there are m edge servers in total in the MEC environments, and we use a set $E = \{e_1, e_2, ..., e_m\}$ to represent them. Each edge server can be described by a 4-tuple (l_i, r_i, c_i, q_i), where l_i is the geographic location of server e_i, r_i its radius of signal coverage, c_i its computing capability (e.g., CPU cycles per second [2,14]), and q_i its task queue length.

Mobile users in MEC environments who act in this region are allowed to offload their computational tasks to nearby available edge servers, and we use a set $T = \{t_1, t_2, ..., t_n\}$ to represent the set of n tasks offloaded by users in a period P. Each task can be described by a 5-tuple $(a_j, l_j, o_j, s_j, c_j)$, where a_j is the arrival time of task t_j, l_j the location of the user who offloaded t_j, o_j the computation amount (i.e., the CPU cycles needed to complete the task) of t_j, s_j the size of data contents of t_j, and c_j the computing capability of the requester of t_j itself.

In this paper, we consider that mobile users' computational tasks can be executed by both signal reachable edge servers [10,12,13] and local mobile devices [2,5,23]. We use d_{ji} to identify the distance between server e_i and the requester of task t_j. Like various well-known data processing and AI service engines (e.g., Apache Spark[1], Flink[2], and Tensorflow Serving [8]) do, edge servers in our model have multiple computing units and

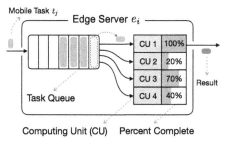

Fig. 2. Offloading request processing flow at edge server.

handle incoming tasks on a First-Come-First-Service (FCFS) basis as shown in Fig. 2. Therefore, given the status of server e_i at time a_j, the end-to-end delay of offloading task t_j to server e_i can be estimated as:

$$
\mathbb{R}_{ji} = \begin{cases} f_{ji} + (v_j - a_j) + h_{ji}, & d_{ji} \leq r_i, \quad i = 1, 2, ..., m \\ h_{ji}, & i = 0 \end{cases}
\tag{1}
$$

where f_{ji} is the data transmission delay, h_{ji} is the task execution delay, v_j is the earliest start time of t_j on e_i, and thus $(v_j - a_j)$ is the waiting time of t_j at e_i's task queue. If there are no available edge servers around the requester of t_j, the offloading request t_j is declined and it will be executed by users' local devices, we use $i = 0$ to represent this situation. It can be seen that the end-to-end delay of offloading a mobile task to an edge server (i.e., $i \neq 0$) consists of three parts:

---

[1] https://spark.apache.org/docs/latest/job-scheduling.html.
[2] https://ci.apache.org/projects/flink/flink-docs-stable/internals/job_scheduling.html.

task uploading delay f_{ji}, waiting time $(v_j - a_j)$, and the execution delay h_{ji}. The task execution delay h_{ji} can be estimated as [2,4,22]:

$$
h_{ji} = \begin{cases} o_j/c_i, & d_{ji} \leq r_i, \quad i = 1, 2, ..., m \\ \\ o_j/c_j, & i = 0 \end{cases} \tag{2}
$$

And the data transmission delay f_{ji} can be estimated as $f_{ji} = s_j/r_{ji}$, where r_{ji} is the user's uplink data rate and it can be calculated as [4]:

$$
r_{ji} = \beta \log_2 \left(1 + \frac{p_j g_{ji}}{\delta^2}\right), \tag{3}
$$

where β is the channel bandwidth, p_j the transmission power of the requester of task t_j, g_{ji} the channel gain between the server e_i and the requester of t_j, and δ^2 the background noise power.

3.2 Problem Formulation

Based on the above system model, we have great interest to know: for a given region where m edge servers are deployed with heterogeneous resource configurations and n offloading requests asynchronously raised in a period P, how to appropriately respond and take offloading actions with optimized offloading efficiency in terms of end-to-end offloading delay. The problem can be formulated as follows:

$$
Min: \quad \frac{1}{n}\left(\sum_{j=1}^{n}\sum_{i=0}^{m} \mathbb{R}_{ji}x_{ji}\right) \tag{4a}
$$

$$
s.t: \quad d_{ji} \leq r_i, \qquad\qquad\qquad \forall x_{ji} \neq 0 \tag{4b}
$$

$$
s_j + q_{ji} \leq q_i, \qquad \forall j = 1, 2, ..., n, \quad \forall i = 1, 2, ..., m \tag{4c}
$$

$$
\sum_{j=1}^{n} o_j x_{ji} \leq b_i, \qquad\qquad\qquad \forall i = 0, 1, ..., m
$$

$$
\sum_{i=1}^{m} 0 \leq x_{ji} \leq 1, \qquad\qquad\qquad \forall j = 1, 2, ..., n
$$

where $x_{ji} \in \{0, 1\}$ is the offloading decision that indicates whether task t_j is going to be scheduled to server e_i (e_0 represents local device), which is made in real-time upon t_j arrivals. b_i is the maximum computation amount that e_i can process within the period P, which can be estimated as $c_i \times P$, and q_{ji} the instantaneous task queue size of e_i when t_j arrives.

As shown in (4a), the objective is to minimize the average end-to-end delays of offloaded tasks arriving in a period P. (4b) and (4c) are the constraints of offloading distance and task queue capacity. (4d) indicates that an edge server is feasible to an offloading requester only if it has enough computation amount.

Note that in this paper, we consider users' offloading requests could arrive at an arbitrary time and we aim at yielding online offloading decision in a reactive manner upon request arrivals. The specifications of individual offloading requests are unknown before being raised and thus the problem can be formulated as an Online-Multidimensional-Integer-Linear-Programming with no optimal online solutions [1,9].

4 Proposed Dynamic-Learning-Based Approach

For the problem formulated above, in this section, we adopt a dynamic-learning mechanism [1] and propose a decentralized reactive approach, shorts for DRA, to yield reactive and online offloading decisions. Figure 3 shows the process of the proposed approach.

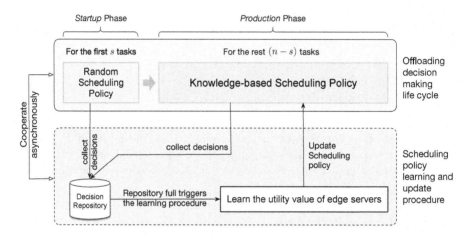

Fig. 3. The process of proposed DRA approach.

It can be seen that at the *startup* phase, a random scheduling policy is performed for the first s requests to collect training data to start the dynamic-learning procedure. The initial length of the decision repository is set to s and a dynamic-learning procedure is triggered to learn the scheduling policies when the repository is full. After that, our approach moves forward into the *production* phase, where the offloading decisions are made by the learned knowledge-based scheduling policies. Note that, due to the high dynamicity of the MEC environments, scheduling policies in this phase are evolvable and our learning procedure keeps updating and pushing them to end-users.

The knowledge-based scheduling policies are learned by reviewing the effect of past decisions. We use σ_j to denote the reward (i.e, end-to-end delay) of the j-th decision, and $y_j \in \{0,1\}$ to determine the correctness of the j-th decision from the reviewing perspective. The above determination problem can be formulated to a linear programming (LP) as shown in (5).

Primal-LP	**Dual-LP**

$$Min: \ \frac{1}{n}\left(\sum_{j=1}^{s}\sigma_j y_j\right)$$

$$Max: \ \sum_{i=1}^{m}(1-\epsilon)\frac{s}{n}b_i u_i + \sum_{j=1}^{s} z_j$$

$$s.t: \ \sum_{j=1}^{s} o_j y_j \leq (1-\epsilon)\frac{s}{n}b_i, \qquad \forall i$$

$$s.t: \ \sum_{i=1}^{m} o_j u_i + z_j \geq \sigma_j, \qquad \forall j$$

$$0 \leq y_j \leq 1, \qquad \forall j$$

$$u_i, z_j \geq 0, \qquad \forall i, j$$

$$i = 1, 2, ..., m, \quad j = 1, 2, ..., n$$

$$i = 1, 2, ..., m, \quad j = 1, 2, ..., n$$

We also present its dual problem in (6), let $(\hat{\mathbf{u}}, \hat{\mathbf{z}})$ be its optimal solution, where vector $\hat{\mathbf{u}}$ indicates the utility value for all edge servers and it can be used to evaluate the gains of offloading decisions. We use a function $G(\hat{\mathbf{u}}, t_j)$ to represent the knowledge-based scheduling policy in the *production* phase:

$$G(\hat{\mathbf{u}}, t_j) = \begin{cases} 0, & \text{if } (\mathbb{R}_{ji} - \sum_{i=1}^{m} u_i o_j) \leq 0 \\ \underset{i}{\operatorname{argmin}}(\mathbb{R}_{ji} - \sum_{i=1}^{m} u_i o_j), & \text{otherwise} \end{cases} \tag{5}$$

where $i = 1, 2, ..., m$ and $d_{ji} \leq r_i$.

Algorithm 1 shows the specific steps of the proposed approach. It can be seen that DRA starts with initializing the decision repository R with $\varnothing$ and setting its length to $s = n\epsilon$ (as shown in lines 1–2), where $\epsilon \in (0, 1)$. Then, it performs a random scheduling policy to schedule the first s tasks and collects the corresponding decisions to R (as shown in lines 3–12). If the length of R equals s, it begins to learn the utility value of each edge server by solving the dual problem defined in (6). After that, for the rest incoming tasks, a knowledge-based scheduling policy is performed to reactively yield online offloading decisions (as shown in lines 13–25). Note that, once the decision repository is full, the learning procedure is triggered and the length of the repository is doubled to collect more decisions to realize dynamic learning (as shown in lines 15–17).

For the *startup* phase of our approach, the time complexity of getting nearby edge servers and filtering out unavailable ones (i.e., edge servers without enough computing power or full task queues) is $O(m)$, the time complexity of making a random offloading decision is $O(1)$. Thus, the total time complexity of making an offloading decision in the startup phase is $O(m)$. For the *production* phase, the time complexity of getting nearby available servers is also $O(m)$, but the time complexity of making an offloading decision by a knowledge-based scheduling policy, i.e., $G(\hat{\mathbf{u}}, t_j)$, is $O(m \log m)$. Thus, the total time complexity of making an offloaded decision in the production phase is $O(m \log m)$.

Competitive ratio analysis is a useful way to evaluate the optimality of online algorithms. An online algorithm is c-competitive if its expected performance could reach at least c factor of the optimal solution of the problem form the offline perspective. As proved by Agrawal et al. [1], the proposed DRA achieves a $1 - O(\sqrt{m \log n/B})$ competitiveness, where $B = min(b_i)$.

Algorithm 1: DRA

Input: Edge server count m; Offloading request count n; Edge server set E;
Task set T; decision repository length base factor ϵ

1 Initialize offloading decision repository $R \leftarrow \varnothing$

2 Set the length of repository $s \leftarrow n\epsilon$

3 **foreach** t_j in the first s tasks of T **do**

4 | Initialize offloading decision $\boldsymbol{x_j} \leftarrow [0, 0, ..., 0]$

5 | $E' \leftarrow$ Get all available edge servers around the invoker of t_j from E

6 | **if** $E' = \varnothing$ **then**

7 | ⌊ $x_{j0} \leftarrow 1$

8 | **else**

9 | | $i \leftarrow$ Randomly select an edge server e_i in S and record i

10 | ⌊ $x_{ji} \leftarrow 1$

11 | Schedule task t_j according to offloading decision $\boldsymbol{x_j}$

12   ⌊ Add $\boldsymbol{x_j}$ to decision repository R

13 **foreach** t_j in the rest tasks of T **do**

14 | Initialize decision $\boldsymbol{x_j} \leftarrow [0, 0, ..., 0]$

15 | **if** $length(R) = s$ **then**

16 | | $(\hat{\mathbf{u}}, \hat{\mathbf{y}}) \leftarrow$ Solve the dual problem defined in (6)

17 | ⌊ $s \leftarrow s \times 2$

18 | $E' \leftarrow$ Get all available edge servers around the invoker of t_j from E

19 | **if** $E' = \varnothing$ **then**

20 | ⌊ $x_{j0} \leftarrow 1$

21 | **else**

22 | | $i \leftarrow G(\hat{\mathbf{u}}, t_j)$

23 | ⌊ $x_{ji} \leftarrow 1$

24 | Schedule task t_j according to offloading decision $\boldsymbol{x_j}$

25   ⌊ Add $\boldsymbol{x_j}$ to decision repository R

---

5   Experiments and Analysis

In this section, we conduct a series of case studies based on two real-world edge environment datasets to evaluate the performance of our proposed approach in terms of offloading responsiveness and efficiency.

5.1   Experiment Settings

EUA [12] and Telecom [18–20] are two well-known edge environment datasets, where EUA dataset[3] includes the geographic positions of edge servers and users in a CBD area in Melbourne, Australia, and Telecom dataset[4] contains the geographic positions of edge servers and the arrival time of edge users in the

---

[3] https://github.com/swinedge/eua-dataset.
[4] http://www.sguangwang.com/TelecomDataset.html.

Table 2. The details of two test cases in our experiment

Settings	Case	
	EUA [12]	Telecom [20]
Location	CBD area, Melbourne, AU	Central Urban area, Shanghai, CN
Upper-left coordinate	(−37.813134, 144.951300)	(31.233580, 121.423307)
Lower-right coordinate	(−37.815240, 144.974820)	(31.196371, 121.494572)
Area	$2.04\,km^2$	$32.67\,km^2$
Base station count	125	190
Edge user count	4000 ∼ 8000	10000 ∼ 20000
Experimental duration	2 h (7200 s)	2 h (7200 s)

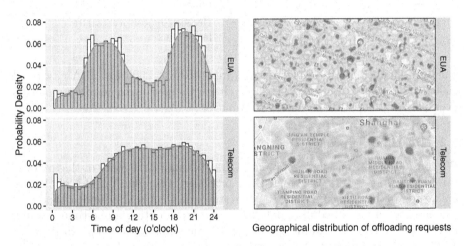

Fig. 4. Geographic distribution and arrival time probability density of offloading requests during a day.

urban area of Shanghai, China. In our experiments, we consider the whole region of the EUA dataset and the central region of the Telecom dataset as test cases, and Table 2 shows the details of them. As for the request arrival time data of the EUA case and user position data of the Telecom case, we use Uber request arrival time and Shanghai's taxi trajectories to make a supplement as illustrated in Fig. 4. It can be seen that users' offloading requests are distributed unevenly in different geographical areas and the arrival rates fluctuate over time. We choose the requests which arrive from 8 AM to 10 AM (i.e., P equals to 2 h) to conduct our case studies.

In this paper, we consider both heterogeneous edge servers configurations and offloading requests. Table 3 shows the configurations of edge servers, users' mobile devices, and offloading requests in our experiments [4,5]. We scale the computing capability of edge servers from 75% to 125% to evaluate the performance of our approach and baselines under different edge resources. We also

Table 3. Experiment configuration

Parameters	Value	Parameters	Value
Computing capabilities of edge servers	$2.2 \sim 3.8$ GHz	Computing units count of edge servers	$4 \sim 12$
RAM size of edge servers	16 GB $\sim$ 2 TB	Computing capabilities of mobile devices (equivalent)	$0.8 \sim 1.2$ GHz
Computation amount of offloading requests	$50 \sim 100$ cycles/bit	Data amount of offloading requests	$5 \sim 100$ MB
Communication channel gain	$127 + 30 \times \log d$	Transmission power	0.5 W
Bandwidth of mobile devices	20 MHz	Background noise power	2×10^{-13} W
Radius of edge servers' signal coverage	$300 \sim 600$ m	Decision repository length factor ϵ	0.01

scale the number of offloading requests from 4000 to 8000 for EUA cases and 10000 to 20000 for Telecom cases to evaluate the performance of ours and its peers under different offloading request loads.

5.2 Baseline Approaches

We consider a conventional approach (OLA [9]) and three state-of-the-art ones (MobMig [15], GD [13], and SO [12]) as baselines, where OLA and MobMig are online approaches while GD and SO are static ones. OLA is an online method that is able to learn the scheduling policy like ours by adopting a one-time-learning mechanism, but its scheduling policy is non-renewable once determined; Mob-Mig is also an online best-fit-decreasing-based method that always schedules the offloaded mobile tasks to their nearby available edge servers with the shortest expected end-to-end delay; while GD is a static method that employs a greedy heuristic to schedule the offloaded mobile tasks to their nearby available edge servers with the highest remaining computation capability; and SO is a static method that employs IBM CPLEX Optimizer to solve the integer linear programming (ILP) problem of multiple-user multiple-server allocation in a batch-processing way.

Our approach and baselines are all implemented by Matlab R2020b, and the LP and ILP problems in our approach and its peers are solved by the Matlab built-in *linprog* and *intlinprog* functions. The experiments are conducted on a personal computer with macOS Catalina, 3.6 GHz Quad-Core Intel Core i3 processor, 8 GB memory, and 256 GB storage.

5.3 Responsiveness Evaluation

Results: Figure 5 compares the average end-to-end delays of our approach and baselines under different edge resources and request loads. It can be seen that

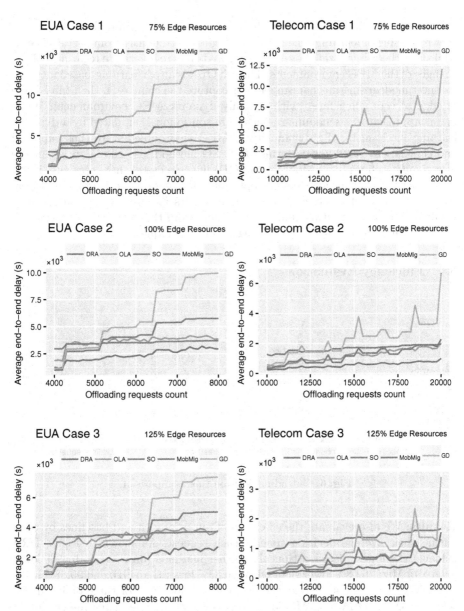

Fig. 5. Average end-to-end delay comparison.

our proposed DRA approach gets the lowest average end-to-end delay in the most of the cases of two datasets. More specifically, the proposed DRA can achieve a 35.72%, 32.89%, 42.26%, and 59.79% lower end-to-end delay on average compared with OLA, SO, MobMig, and GD respectively in EUA cases, and it can also achieve a 50.43%, 64.41%, 51.12%, 74.86% lower end-to-end delay on average than them in Telecom cases.

Analysis: DRA beats MobMig and GD because it is a learning-based approach that is capable of learning scheduling strategies continuously from past decisions, while the scheduling strategies of MobMig and GD are invariable regardless of the changes of the MEC environments. Though OLA is also a learning-based method, its one-time-learning mechanism can not capture the changes in the utility value of edge servers when faced with a highly dynamic MEC environments. While in our approach, the scheduling policies are continuously updated by a dynamic learning mechanism, the dynamicity of MEC environments are thus captured and that is why DRA outperforms OLA. SO method also shows an advantage over some baselines (e.g., MobMig and GD) in some cases, that is because it is a static method that always gets the optimal offloading decisions from the global view at the end of a batch window. However, its batch-processing mode may result in additional waiting time and it suffers from the decision time explosion problem when faced with an increasing number of requests.

5.4 Efficiency Evaluation

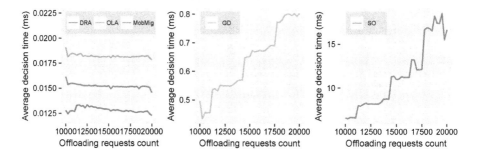

Fig. 6. Offloading decision time comparison.

Results: We also evaluate the efficiency of our approach and baselines by comparing their average decision time of each request. As shown in Fig. 6, DRA achieves the lowest decision time than other methods (on average, 9.59% lower than MobMig; 26.98% lower than OLA; 96.83% lower than GD; and 99.88% lower than SO). It can be seen that the average decision time of three online methods (i.e., DRA, OLA, and MobMig) keeps steady with the increasing of request count, while that figures for GD and SO methods show a rapidly increasing trend. Besides, the average decision time of all online methods is around 0.015 ms, while that figures for GD and SO methods are around 0.7 ms and 15 ms, which are two and three orders of magnitude higher than online ones, respectively.

Analysis: The time complexity of making an offloading decision of DRA, OLA, and MobMig methods are all $O(m \log m)$, where m is the number of edge servers, thus they are not sensitive to the increasing request count. The reason why the DRA method achieves a lower decision-making time than other online methods lies in that its a decentralized approach where offloading decisions are made by end-users themselves locally instead of a centralized scheduler, the request forwarding delays are thus avoided and offloading decision time is shortened. The time complexity of GD is $O(n'm\log m)$, where n' is the number of requests that arrive in the same batch window, thus its decision time shows a growth trend with the increasing of request count. Similarly, the SO method also shows such a trend, but its global optimization strategy consumes more time.

6 Conclusion and Further Work

This paper targets at the online mobile task offloading in MEC environments. We consider the arbitrary arrival pattern of offloading requests and formulate the online MEC-oriented task offloading problem as a multi-dimension online integer linear programming problem. We employ a dynamic-learning mechanism and propose a decentralized reactive approach to solve it, the proposed approach is capable of continuously learning and updating scheduling policy to cope with the highly dynamic MEC environments. Case studies based on two real-world edge datasets have verified the effectiveness and efficiency of the proposed approach.

In our further studies, the following concerns will be addressed: 1) some time-series prediction and trajectories prediction methods could be utilized to predict the future request arrival rates and the request densities in different areas, which can be used to perform a load-balance and task-migration in advance to serve more users; 2) we only consider CPU tasks in this paper, GPU and CPU-GPU hybrid task offloading problem will be investigated in our future works; 3) more QoS metrics such as offloading monetary cost, reliability, and energy consumption of mobile devices will be considered, evaluated, and added to our system model.

Acknowledgements. This work is supported in part by the Graduate Scientific Research and Innovation Foundation of Chongqing, China (Grant No. CYB20062 and CYS20066), and the Fundamental Research Funds for the Central Universities (China) under Project 2019CDXYJSJ0022. The author gratefully acknowledges the support of K.C.Wong Education Foundation, Hong Kong.

References

1. Agrawal, S., Wang, Z., Ye, Y.: A dynamic near-optimal algorithm for online linear programming. Oper. Res. **62**(4), 876–890 (2014)
2. Alameddine, H.A., Sharafeddine, S., Sebbah, S., Ayoubi, S.: Dynamic task offloading and scheduling for low-latency IoT services in multi-access edge computing. IEEE J. Sele. Areas Commun. **37**(3), 668–682 (2019)
3. Chen, L., Zhou, S., Xu, J.: Computation peer offloading for energy-constrained mobile edge computing in small-cell networks. IEEE/ACM Trans. Netw. **26**(4), 1619–1632 (2018)
4. Chen, M., Hao, Y.: Task offloading for mobile edge computing in software defined ultra-dense network. IEEE J. Sel. Areas Commun. **36**(3), 587–597 (2018)

5. Dai, Y., Xu, D., Maharjan, S., Zhang, Y.: Joint computation offloading and user association in multi-task mobile edge computing. IEEE Trans. Veh. Technol. **67**(12), 12313–12325 (2018)

6. Deng, S., Wu, H., Yin, J.: Mobile service provisioning. Mobile Service Computing. ATSTC, vol. 58, pp. 279–329. Springer, Singapore (2020). https://doi.org/10.1007/978-981-15-5921-1_8

7. Du, W., et al.: Service capacity enhanced task offloading and resource allocation in multi-server edge computing environment. In: 2019 IEEE International Conference on Web Services (ICWS), pp. 83–90 (2019)

8. Fang, Z., Lin, J.H., Srivastava, M.B.: Multi-tenant mobile offloading systems for real-time computer vision applications. In: Proceedings of the 20th International Conference on Distributed Computing and Networking, pp. 21–30 (2019)

9. Feldman, J., Henzinger, M., Korula, N., Mirrokni, V.S., Stein, C.: Online stochastic packing applied to display ad allocation. In: de Berg, M., Meyer, U. (eds.) ESA 2010, Part I. LNCS, vol. 6346, pp. 182–194. Springer, Heidelberg (2010). https://doi.org/10.1007/978-3-642-15775-2_16

10. He, Q., et al.: A game-theoretical approach for user allocation in edge computing environment. IEEE Trans. Parallel Distrib. Syst. **31**(3), 515–529 (2019)

11. Huang, L., Bi, S., Zhang, Y.J.: Deep reinforcement learning for online computation offloading in wireless powered mobile-edge computing networks. IEEE Trans. Mob. Comput. **19**(11), 2581–2593 (2020)

12. Lai, P., et al.: Optimal edge user allocation in edge computing with variable sized vector bin packing. In: Pahl, C., Vukovic, M., Yin, J., Yu, Q. (eds.) ICSOC 2018. LNCS, vol. 11236, pp. 230–245. Springer, Cham (2018). https://doi.org/10.1007/978-3-030-03596-9_15

13. Lai, P., et al.: Edge user allocation with dynamic quality of service. In: Yangui, S., Bouassida Rodriguez, I., Drira, K., Tari, Z. (eds.) ICSOC 2019. LNCS, vol. 11895, pp. 86–101. Springer, Cham (2019). https://doi.org/10.1007/978-3-030-33702-5_8

14. Liu, C.F., Bennis, M., Debbah, M., Poor, H.V.: Dynamic task offloading and resource allocation for ultra-reliable low-latency edge computing. IEEE Trans. Commun. **67**(6), 4132–4150 (2019)

15. Peng, Q., et al.: Mobility-aware and migration-enabled online edge user allocation in mobile edge computing. In: 2019 IEEE International Conference on Web Services (ICWS), pp. 91–98. IEEE (2019)

16. Rafique, W., Qi, L., Yaqoob, I., Imran, M., u. Rasool, R., Dou, W.: Complementing IoT services through software defined networking and edge computing: a comprehensive survey. IEEE Commun. Surv. Tutor. **22**(3), 1761–1804 (2020)

17. Sun, M., Xu, X., Tao, X., Zhang, P.: Large-scale user-assisted multi-task online offloading for latency reduction in D2D-enabled heterogeneous networks. IEEE Trans. Netw. Sci. Eng. (2020). https://doi.org/10.1109/TNSE.2020.2979511

18. Wang, S., Guo, Y., Zhang, N., Yang, P., Zhou, A., Shen, X.S.: Delay-aware microservice coordination in mobile edge computing: a reinforcement learning approach. IEEE Trans. Mob. Computi. (2019). https://doi.org/10.1109/TMC.2019.2957804

19. Wang, S., Zhao, Y., Huang, L., Xu, J., Hsu, C.H.: Qos prediction for service recommendations in mobile edge computing. J. Parallel Distrib. Comput. **127**, 134–144 (2019)

20. Wang, S., Zhao, Y., Xu, J., Yuan, J.: Edge server placement in mobile edge computing. J. Parallel Distrib. Comput. **127**, 160–168 (2019)

21. Xu, J., Chen, L., Zhou, P.: Joint service caching and task offloading for mobile edge computing in dense networks. In: IEEE INFOCOM 2018-IEEE Conference on Computer Communications, pp. 207–215. IEEE (2018)
22. Yang, B., Cao, X., Bassey, J., Li, X., Qian, L.: Computation offloading in multi-access edge computing: a multi-task learning approach. IEEE Trans. Mob. Comput. (2020). https://doi.org/10.1109/TMC.2020.2990630
23. Yang, L., Zhang, H., Li, X., Ji, H., Leung, V.C.: A distributed computation offloading strategy in small-cell networks integrated with mobile edge computing. IEEE/ACM Trans. Netw. **26**(6), 2762–2773 (2018)
24. Zhao, H., Deng, S., Zhang, C., Du, W., He, Q., Yin, J.: A mobility-aware cross-edge computation offloading framework for partitionable applications. In: 2019 IEEE International Conference on Web Services (ICWS), pp. 193–200. IEEE (2019)

Mobility-Aware Service Placement for Vehicular Users in Edge-Cloud Environment

Rahul Mudam[1], Saurabh Bhartia[1], Soumi Chattopadhyay[1(✉)], and Arani Bhattacharya[2]

[1] Indian Institute of Information Technology, Guwahati, India
soumi@iiitg.ac.in
[2] Indraprastha Institute of Information Technology, Delhi, India

Abstract. In the era of Internet-of-Things (IoT), both the number of web services and the number of users invoking them are increasing everyday. These web services utilize a cloud server for access to sufficient compute resources for service delivery. A disadvantage of cloud computing is that it is known to have a high latency because of its large distance (both physical distance as well as number of hops) from the end user device. A key technique of enabling low-latency web services, called edge computing, brings the compute resources closer to the end device. Edge computing enables better resource utilization and it reduces latency. However, since there are numerous compute resources or 'edge resources', determining where the services should be placed becomes a new challenge. In this paper, we consider the case of public transport vehicles utilizing edge computing to reduce latency while providing such web services. We first model the dynamic service placement problem considering user mobility. We then propose two algorithms to solve this problem. The first algorithm utilizes an Integer Linear Programming (ILP) to obtain an optimal solution, albeit at the cost of scalability. We then propose a heuristic algorithm to achieve a low latency, while also scaling to large problem instances. We validate the performance of both the techniques through extensive trace-driven simulations.

1 Introduction

With the recent improvement of wireless connectivity, services are generally delivered by software vendors from data centers. This paradigm of delivering services, called cloud computing [17], has made it easier for software vendors to provide new services or upgrade their existing ones. However, cloud computing being inherently centralized, fails to deliver low latency to users [2]. With latency becoming a major factor in satisfying users, multiple works have proposed using a more decentralized architecture, that complements the existing data centers. This decentralized architecture is known as edge computing [17]. In edge computing, data is placed in locations that are physically and logically closer to the user. This could be either mini-data centers associated with the network base

© Springer Nature Switzerland AG 2020
E. Kafeza et al. (Eds.): ICSOC 2020, LNCS 12571, pp. 248–265, 2020.
https://doi.org/10.1007/978-3-030-65310-1_19

stations [18], or compute resources provided by a third party [13]. Edge computing promises to deliver low-latency services, while maintaining the advantages of data centers.

However, utilizing edge computing to deliver services in practice has a number of challenges. For example, it is possible for users to move around in vehicles. Such movement of users makes it challenging to decide the edge device where data and state of services should be placed that are sought by users [24]. While a number of works have studied this problem of service placement, most of them do not consider the mobility of users [2,16]. Works that have looked at the mobility of users either focus on a single user [1,10] or depend on more compute-intensive techniques like path prediction or other forms of learning [3,9,10,14,25]. Many of them also do not consider the memory constraints imposed by edge devices.

In this paper, we study the service placement problem in a dynamic environment considering user mobility, viz., physical mobility of users while accessing said services. We consider the case of users situated in moving vehicles, from which they are accessing a set of services at different points of time. This also includes the possibility of the vehicles themselves accessing services, in particular, in the case of autonomous or semi-autonomous vehicles. The objective therefore is to dynamically place/re-place the services either on the cloud or on an edge device to minimize the overall latency felt by the users. Here, we first model the service placement problem in a dynamic environment. We then propose an optimal (oracle) algorithm to solve this problem using Integer Linear Programming (ILP). Though the optimal algorithm gives a solution, it assumes that information about the entire trajectory of the vehicle is available a priori. We show that it also suffers from scalability issues, i.e. for a large dataset, it is incapable of generating results in real-time.

To circumvent this problem, we utilize the ILP to solve the problem in stages. We utilize the fact that although the entire trajectory of the vehicles is usually not known in advance, users tend to know their next few destinations. This information is usually available from location-based applications such as Google Maps. Using this information, we are able to repeatedly run the ILP to obtain solutions for different time windows. Finally, we also propose a heuristic called First Come First Serve (FCFS) that utilizes information about only one destination to solve the service placement problem.

Our evaluation utilizes traces of publicly available datasets. We show that our technique reduces latency significantly (around 6.76 times better) compared to multiple baseline techniques. We also show that the FCFS heuristic in most cases performs close to the optimal solution given by ILP. Finally, we also show that the execution overhead of our heuristic is negligible compared to the amount of reduction in latency.

We summarize our contributions as follows:

1. We model the dynamic service placement problem considering user mobility and formulate it as a ILP to minimize the overall latency.
2. We propose two techniques of obtaining a realistic solution. The first technique solves the ILP in multiple time windows. The second technique uses a

heuristic algorithm called FCFS using information about the next destination of the vehicle.
3. We perform extensive experiments based on real dataset to compare the optimal and FCFS algorithms with multiple baseline techniques. We show that FCFS provides on average 6.76 times lower latency than the best baseline, while adding an overhead of only order of tens of milliseconds.

2 Problem Formulation

In this section, we design a mathematical model of the dynamic service placement problem (DSPP). We consider our model as *dynamic* since here we assume that the location of the trajectory changes over time. In other words, the relative position between the user and each edge device keeps on changing over time. We begin with describing our system under consideration. We model our system as eight tuples $\mathcal{M} = (\mathcal{C}, \mathcal{E}, \mathcal{N}, \mathcal{R}, \mathcal{T}, \mathcal{H}, \mathcal{S})$:

1. A set of n execution platforms $Ex = \mathcal{C} \cup \mathcal{E}$, where
   (a) $\mathcal{C} = \{\mathcal{C}_1, \mathcal{C}_2, \ldots, \mathcal{C}_k\}$ is a set of cloud servers.
   (b) $\mathcal{E} = \{\mathcal{E}_{k+1}, \mathcal{E}_{k+2}, \ldots, \mathcal{E}_n\}$ is a set of edge devices.
2. A set of network parameters $\mathcal{N}$.
3. A vehicular road route map $\mathcal{R}$.
4. A set of vehicular trajectories $\mathcal{T} = \{\mathcal{T}_1, \mathcal{T}_2, \ldots, \mathcal{T}_m\}$.
5. A set of handheld devices $\mathcal{H} = \{\mathcal{H}_1, \mathcal{H}_2, \ldots, \mathcal{H}_m\}$, where each $\mathcal{H}_i \in \mathcal{H}$ is associated with a unique $\mathcal{T}_i \in \mathcal{T}$.
6. A set of services $\mathcal{S} = \{\mathcal{S}_1, \mathcal{S}_2, \ldots, \mathcal{S}_r\}$.

We now discuss the characterization of each of the components of $\mathcal{M}$ in details.

1. Each execution platform $Ex_i \in Ex$ is characterized by three tuples (U_i, D_i, TC_i), where U_i, D_i and TC_i refer to the uplink speed, downlink speed and the total memory capacity of Ex_i, respectively. We assume each cloud server to have sufficient memory, i.e., $\forall \mathcal{C}_i \in \mathcal{C}$, TC_i is infinite, so that the execution of the web services is not constrained by the memory capacity of a cloud server. This assumption is true for most commercial cloud servers.
2. The set of network parameters $\mathcal{N}$ contains an average propagation delay $PD_{i,j}$ of an execution platform $Ex_i \in Ex$ from a location $\mathcal{L}_j$.
3. The route map $\mathcal{R} = (\mathcal{L}, E)$ is given as a graph, where
   - $\mathcal{L}$ is the set of vertices of the graph. Each vertex $\mathcal{L}_i \in \mathcal{L}$ of $\mathcal{R}$ represents a location.
   - E is the set of links of the graph. Each link $e_{ij} = (\mathcal{L}_i, \mathcal{L}_j) \in E$ indicates the existence of a vehicular road between locations $\mathcal{L}_i$ and $\mathcal{L}_j$.
4. Each trajectory of a vehicle $\mathcal{T}_i$ is modeled as the tuple of the following tuples:
   $\mathcal{T}_i = ((\mathcal{L}_{i1}, TS_{i1}, TS'_{i1}, \hat{S}_{i1}), (\mathcal{L}_{i2}, TS_{i2}, TS'_{i2}, \hat{S}_{i2}), \ldots, (\mathcal{L}_{ix}, TS_{ix}, TS'_{ix}, \hat{S}_{ix}))$,
   where
   (a) The vehicle passes through the locations $\mathcal{L}_{i1}, \mathcal{L}_{i2}, \ldots, \mathcal{L}_{ix}$.
   (b) At timestamp TS_{ij} the vehicle reaches the location $\mathcal{L}_{ij}$ and at timestamp TS'_{ij} the vehicle leaves $\mathcal{L}_{ij}$.

(c) $\hat{S}_{ij}$ is the set of services invoked by $\mathcal{T}_i$ at location $\mathcal{L}_{ij}$.

Since we target services invoked on public transport vehicles, we expect the timestamps and the routes taken to be known in advance.

5. Each handheld device $\mathcal{H}_i \in \mathcal{H}$ is characterized by two tuples (U_i^h, D_i^h), where U_i^h and D_i^h refer to the uplink and downlink speeds, respectively.

6. $\mathcal{S}$ is the set of services invoked by the vehicles. The data requirement of each service varies across the trajectories. Therefore, each service $\mathcal{S}_i \in \mathcal{S}$ of a trajectory $\mathcal{T}_j \in \mathcal{T}$ is defined as 3-tuple: $\mathcal{S}_i = (Ip_{i,j}, Op_{i,j}, PM_{i,j})$, where

   (a) $Ip_{i,j}$ is the average input file size required to be uploaded to an execution platform from the handheld device of the trajectory $\mathcal{T}_j$ to invoke the service $\mathcal{S}_i$.

   (b) $Op_{i,j}$ is the average output file size generated by $\mathcal{S}_i$ and to be downloaded from the respective execution platform to the handheld device of $\mathcal{T}_j$.

   (c) $PM_{i,j}$ is the worst case peak memory required by $\mathcal{S}_i$ to be executed when invoked from $\mathcal{T}_j$.

Our model is generic enough to handle interactive services as well. An interactive service can be divided into multiple blocks, where each block can be represented by a service as defined above. Therefore, an interactive service, in our model, can be treated as multiple atomic services.

We now define the notion of latency for $\mathcal{S}_i$ of $\mathcal{T}_j$. Consider $\mathcal{S}_i$ being invoked from $\mathcal{H}_j$ from TS_x to $TS_{x+k'}$ while traveling through $\mathcal{L}_{l0}, \mathcal{L}_{l1}, \ldots, \mathcal{L}_{lk'}$. Also consider in each TS_k, for $k \in \{x, x+1, \ldots, x+k'\}$, $\mathcal{S}_i$ is executed in $Ex_{pk} \in Ex$. The latency for $\mathcal{S}_i$ of $\mathcal{T}_j$ is computed as:

1. *Initial Upload:* At the initial timestamp TS_x, when $\mathcal{S}_i$ of $\mathcal{T}_j$ starts its execution, the input file (i.e., $IP_{i,j}$) of $\mathcal{S}_i$ of $\mathcal{T}_j$ is uploaded to Ex_{p0} from location $\mathcal{L}_{l0}$.

2. *Final Download:* At the final timestamp $TS_{x+k'+1}$, when $\mathcal{S}_i$ of $\mathcal{T}_j$ finishes its execution, the output file (i.e., $OP_{i,j}$) of $\mathcal{S}_i$ of $\mathcal{T}_j$ is downloaded from $Ex_{pk'}$ to $\mathcal{H}_j$ at $\mathcal{L}_{l(k'+1)}$.

3. *Intermediate Transfer:* In an intermediate timestamp TS_k, for $x < k \le (x+k')$, when $\mathcal{S}_i$ of $\mathcal{T}_j$ continues its execution, the state of $\mathcal{S}_i$ of $\mathcal{T}_j$ may be transferred from $Ex_{p(k-1)}$ to Ex_{pk} through the handheld device $\mathcal{H}_j$ at location $\mathcal{L}_{lk}$. The state size of a service is represented by its peak memory, i.e., $PM_{i,j}$.

The uploading/downloading latency for $\mathcal{S}_i$ of $\mathcal{T}_j$ has two key components: (a) transmission delay and (b) propagation delay. The service uploading/downloading is associated with three different events: (i) data uploading from the sender device, (ii) data propagation from a sender device to the receiver device, (iii) data downloading to the receiver device. While (i) and (iii) together determine the transmission delay, (ii) decides the propagation delay. Mathematically, the latency is defined as:

$$\left(\underbrace{\underbrace{\frac{IP_{i,j}}{U_j^h}}_{\text{uploading}} + \underbrace{PD_{l0,p0}}_{\text{propagation delay}} + \underbrace{\frac{IP_{i,j}}{D_{p0}}}_{\text{downloading}}\right) + \underbrace{\left(\frac{OP_{i,j}}{U_{pk'}} + PD_{pk',l(k'+1)} + \frac{OP_{i,j}}{D_j^h}\right)}_{\text{Final Download}} +$$
$$\underbrace{}_{\text{Initial Upload}}$$

$$\underbrace{\sum_{k=1}^{k'}\left(\underbrace{\left(\frac{PM_{i,j}}{U_{p(k-1)}} + PD_{p(k-1),lk} + \frac{PM_{i,j}}{D_j^h}\right)Ex_{p(k-1)}}_{\text{download from}} + \underbrace{\left(\frac{PM_{i,j}}{U_j^h} + PD_{lk,pk} + \frac{PM_{i,j}}{D_{pk}}\right)Ex_{pk}}_{\text{upload to}}\right)I_{p(k-1),pk}}_{\text{Intermediate Transfer}}$$

$$\tag{1}$$

where, $I_{p(k-1),pk}$ is an indicator variable, indicates if state of $\mathcal{S}_i$ of $\mathcal{T}_j$ is transferred from one execution platform to another in the intermediate timestamps. Formally:

$$I_{p(k-1),pk} = \begin{cases} 1, & \text{if } Ex_{p(k-1)} \neq Ex_{pk} \\ 0, & \text{otherwise} \end{cases} \tag{2}$$

The key objective of this work is to reduce the overall latency across all services of all trajectories. Since the edge compute resources available are usually fixed, this requires us to design an algorithm to decide where to place each of the services. We model this objective as that of reducing the sum of latencies across all the services and all the users.

3   Detailed Methodology

In this section, we present our methodology to solve DSPP. We first propose the optimal solution for DSPP, followed by a heuristic solution based on First Come First Serve (FCFS).

3.1   Optimal Algorithm

Our optimal solution is based on the Integer Linear Programming (ILP) formulation. We first define a set of Boolean variables $\mathcal{B}$ as follows:

$$y_{i,j,k,l,p,u} = \begin{cases} 1, & \text{if } \mathcal{S}_i \text{ of } \mathcal{T}_j \text{ is uploaded to } Ex_p \text{ from } \mathcal{L}_l \text{ at } TS_k \\ 0, & \text{otherwise} \end{cases}$$

$$y_{i,j,k,l,p,d} = \begin{cases} 1, & \text{if } \mathcal{S}_i \text{ of } \mathcal{T}_j \text{ is downloaded from } Ex_p \text{ at } \mathcal{L}_l \text{ at } TS_k \\ 0, & \text{otherwise} \end{cases}$$

$$z_{i,j,k,p} = \begin{cases} 1, & \text{if } \mathcal{S}_i \text{ of } \mathcal{T}_j \text{ is executing in } Ex_p \text{ at } TS_k \\ 0, & \text{otherwise} \end{cases}$$

We now design the objective function and the set of constraints required to formulate the ILP using $\mathcal{B}$. It may be noted that in this formulation, the objective is to minimize the overall latency across all services of all trajectories, which is obtained by choosing the appropriate value of each Boolean variables in $\mathcal{B}$ by the ILP solver. Therefore, the objective function is formulated by summing up the latency of all services of all trajectories. However, the latency expression of $\mathcal{S}_i$ of $\mathcal{T}_j$, which is used in the objective function of ILP, is different from Expression (1). In the definition of the latency of $\mathcal{S}_i$ of $\mathcal{T}_j$, we consider that the execution platform, where $\mathcal{S}_i$ of $\mathcal{T}_j$ to be placed in each timestamp is known to us. However, in the objective function of this formulation, the execution platform is to be decided by the ILP solver itself. Therefore we need to reformulate the latency expression for each service of each trajectory. We now discuss the three cases again, which we discussed earlier to define the latency.

Let the execution time span of $\mathcal{S}_i$ of $\mathcal{T}_j$ from timestamp TS_x to $TS_{x+k'}$ be denoted by $\Gamma_{ij} = \{TS_{x+0}, TS_{x+1}, \ldots, TS_{x+k'}\}$, while $\mathcal{T}_j$ is at location $\mathcal{L}_{lk}$ at $TS_{x+k} \in \Gamma_{ij}$.

- *Initial Upload*: At the initial timestamp (i.e., at TS_x), $\mathcal{S}_i$ of $\mathcal{T}_j$ is uploaded to an execution platform to be decided by the ILP solver, and captured by the following.

$$\lambda_{ij}^1 = \sum_{Ex_p \in Ex} \left(\frac{IP_{i,j}}{U_j^h} + PD_{l0,p} + \frac{IP_{i,j}}{D_p} \right) y_{i,j,x,l0,p,u} \tag{3}$$

We note that in Expression (3), only one Boolean variable corresponding to the execution platform, where $\mathcal{S}_i$ of $\mathcal{T}_j$ is to be uploaded initially, is set to 1 by the ILP solver. We ensure this by adding a constraint, which is discussed later.
- *Intermediate Transfer*: In each intermediate timestamp, $\mathcal{S}_i$ of $\mathcal{T}_j$ has two options: either $\mathcal{S}_i$ of $\mathcal{T}_j$ continues its execution in the same platform executing in the previous timestamp, or it gets downloaded from the previous execution platform and uploaded to some other execution platform. Mathematically,

$$\lambda_{ij}^2 = \sum_{k=1}^{k'} \left(\sum_{Ex_p \in Ex} \left(\frac{PM_{i,j}}{U_p} + PD_{p,lk} + \frac{PM_{i,j}}{D_j^h} \right) y_{i,j,k,lk,p,d} \right.$$
$$\left. + \sum_{\substack{Ex_q \in Ex, \\ Ex_p \neq Ex_q}} \left(\frac{PM_{i,j}}{U_j^h} + PD_{lk,q} + \frac{PM_{i,j}}{D_q} \right) y_{i,j,k,lk,q,u} \right) \tag{4}$$

- *Final Download*: In this case, $\mathcal{S}_i$ of $\mathcal{T}_j$ has to be downloaded from its last execution platform, which is expressed by the following expression.

$$\lambda_{ij}^3 = \sum_{Ex_p \in Ex} \left(\frac{OP_{i,j}}{U_p} + PD_{p,l(k'+1)} + \frac{OP_{i,j}}{D_j^h} \right) y_{i,j,(k'+1),l(k'+1),p,d} \tag{5}$$

We now formulate the objective function of the ILP as follows:

$$\text{Minimize:} \sum_{T_j \in \mathcal{T}} \sum_{S_i \in T_j} \left(\lambda_{ij}^1 + \lambda_{ij}^2 + \lambda_{ij}^3 \right) \tag{6}$$

We now discuss the set of constraints required for this formulation. First, the number of times each S_i of T_j has been uploaded to an execution platform Ex_p has to be equal to the number of times the same has been downloaded from Ex_p.

$$\forall T_j \in \mathcal{T} \text{ and } \forall S_i \in T_j; \forall Ex_p \in Ex \quad \sum_{TS_x \leq TS_k \leq TS_{k'}} y_{i,j,k,lk,p,u} = \sum_{TS_x \leq TS_k \leq TS_{k'+1}} y_{i,j,k,lk,p,d} \tag{7}$$

where, the execution time span of S_i of T_j is from TS_x to $TS_{x+k'}$, while T_j passes through location $\mathcal{L}_{lk}$ at TS_k.

Each S_i of T_j continues its execution on Ex_p at TS_k if S_i of T_j has been uploaded to Ex_p, but not yet downloaded from Ex_p. We have the following constraint to capture this fact:

$$\forall T_j \in \mathcal{T} \text{ and } (\forall S_i \in T_j); \quad \forall TS_k \in \Gamma_{ij}; \quad \forall Ex_p \in Ex$$
$$z_{i,j,k,p} = \sum_{TS_\psi \leq TS_k} y_{i,j,\psi,l\psi,p,u} - \sum_{TS_\psi \leq TS_k} y_{i,j,\psi,l\psi,p,d} \tag{8}$$

where, T_j passes through location $\mathcal{L}_{l\psi}$ at TS_ψ.

The following constraint ensures that each S_i of T_j must execute on exactly one execution platform in each timestamp throughout its time span.

$$\forall T_j \in \mathcal{T} \ \& \ (\forall S_i \in T_j); \forall TS_k \in \Gamma_{ij}; \sum_{Ex_p \in Ex} z_{i,j,k,p} = 1 \tag{9}$$

Our final constraint is related to the memory capacity of each edge device. At each timestamp TS_k, the memory constraint of each edge device has to be satisfied. An edge device cannot accept any service, if it does not have residual memory capacity to satisfy the service's memory requirement.

$$\forall TS_k \in \mathcal{T}; \forall Ex_p \in \mathcal{E}; \quad \sum_{T_j \in \mathcal{T}} \sum_{S_i \in T_j} PM_{i,j} * z_{i,j,k,p} \leq TC_p \tag{10}$$

where TC_p is total capacity of $\mathcal{E}_p$.

Although the ILP provides an optimal solution to DSPP that minimizes total latency, it does not scale for large problem instances. Moreover, we may not always have complete knowledge about all the trajectories in advance. Thus, we propose a window-based optimal strategy to overcome this problem.

3.2   Window-Based Optimal Algorithm

The crux of the window-based optimal strategy is that we do not require to have complete information about all the trajectories in advance. However, if we have prior knowledge of the next few timestamps, say ω number of timestamps, then also we can apply the same optimal algorithm on each sub-part of the trajectories. The main idea of this algorithm is to divide the entire set of timestamps into multiple windows of size ω and solve the problem optimally for each window individually. We note that we need to transfer the previous state of the system (i.e., which service of which trajectory is executing on which execution platform) to its next state to obtain the optimal solution for the next window. Clearly, when ω is the total number of timestamps across all trajectories, the window-based optimal algorithm generates the optimal solution. For a smaller value of ω, although this approach does not produce an optimal solution, this approach increases the scalability as compared to the optimal algorithm, since it handles a smaller set of variables at a time.

In case of large number of timestamps, the window-based optimal algorithm scales better compared to the optimal approach. Therefore, we can use this approach as an online technique. However, for a large number of trajectories, edge devices, or the number of services per timestamp per trajectory in one window, the window-based optimal algorithm does not scale as well in real-time. This can increase the computation overhead of running it online. Therefore, in the next subsection, we propose a scalable heuristic algorithm, which can solve the placement problem dynamically in real-time.

3.3   Heuristic Using FCFS

We now discuss our heuristic algorithm, which solves DSPP by first come first serve (FCFS) scheduling. In FCFS, if a service $\mathcal{S}_i$ of a trajectory $\mathcal{T}_j$ starts its execution earlier on an execution platform Ex_p than another service $\mathcal{S}_{i'}$ of $\mathcal{T}_{j'}$, $\mathcal{S}_i$ of $\mathcal{T}_j$ gets higher priority over $\mathcal{S}_{i'}$ of $\mathcal{T}_{j'}$ on Ex_p. In case of tie, it gets resolved arbitrarily. The FCFS algorithm is an online algorithm as it runs on each timestamp. Therefore, this algorithm does not require the trajectory information in advance.

If a service $\mathcal{S}_i$ of a trajectory $\mathcal{T}_j$ executes at timestamp TS_k, we have three possibilities. Analyzing each of the possibilities, the service placement decision is taken. We now discuss the principle of the FCFS algorithm.

1. $\mathcal{S}_i$ of $\mathcal{T}_j$ is placed to the fastest execution platform accessible from the current location having the residual capacity to accommodate the service for processing at TS_k, if $\mathcal{S}_i$ of $\mathcal{T}_j$ starts its execution at TS_k.
   The fastest execution platform is the one having latency equal to $\min_{Ex_q \in Ex}\left(\frac{IP_{i,j}}{U_j^h} + PD_{lk,q} + \frac{IP_{i,j}}{D_q}\right)$.
2. If $\mathcal{S}_i$ of $\mathcal{T}_j$ starts its execution before TS_k and it is already on the fastest edge device accessible from the current location or on the cloud, no action needs to be taken.
3. If $\mathcal{S}_i$ of $\mathcal{T}_j$ starts its execution before TS_k and it is neither on the fastest edge device accessible from the current location nor on the cloud, $\mathcal{S}_i$ of $\mathcal{T}_j$ may need to be transferred from the current edge device to the fastest execution platform accessible from the current location having capacity to accommodate it. However, this decision is taken based on a look-ahead in the next K timestamps, where K is an input to this algorithm, as discussed below.

Consider the execution time span of $\mathcal{S}_i$ of $\mathcal{T}_j$ is up to $TS_{x+k'}$, while $\mathcal{T}_j$ passes through location $\mathcal{L}_{lk}$ at TS_k. Also consider $\mathcal{S}_i$ of $\mathcal{T}_j$ executed on Ex_q at TS_{k-1}. We first define a transfer latency $Tr(Ex_q, TS_\psi, \mathcal{L}_{l\psi})$ from Ex_q to the fastest execution platform accessible from $\mathcal{L}_{l\psi}$ at TS_ψ as:

$$Tr(\cdot) = \left(\frac{PM_{i,j}}{U_q} + PD_{l\psi,q} + \frac{PM_{i,j}}{D_j^h} \right) + \min_{Ex_p \in Ex} \left(\frac{PM_{i,j}}{U_j^h} + PD_{l\psi,p} + \frac{IP_{i,j}}{D_p} \right) \qquad (11)$$

The execution platform chosen Ex_c for $\mathcal{S}_i$ of $\mathcal{T}_j$ at TS_k is:

$$Ex_c = \begin{cases} Ex_q, & \text{if } Tr(Ex_q, TS_k, \mathcal{L}_{lk}) \geq \min_{TS_\psi} Tr(Ex_q, TS_\psi, \mathcal{L}_{l\psi}) \\ Ex_p, & \text{otherwise} \end{cases} \qquad (12)$$

where, $TS_k \leq TS_\psi \leq \min(TS_{k+K}, TS_{x+k'})$, Ex_p is the fastest platform accessible from $\mathcal{L}_{lk}$ and has residual capacity to accommodate $\mathcal{S}_i$ of $\mathcal{T}_j$. The above equation checks whether the total time required to transfer $\mathcal{S}_i$ of $\mathcal{T}_j$ at TS_k from $\mathcal{E}_q$ to $\mathcal{E}_p$ is less than the time required to transfer it in the later timestamps. If that is the case, $\mathcal{S}_i$ of $\mathcal{T}_j$ is transferred at TS_k. Otherwise, $\mathcal{S}_i$ of $\mathcal{T}_j$ continues its execution on Ex_q.

We make the following observations about FCFS:

1. Since FCFS is an online algorithm, it is executed in each timestamp in each handheld device, which adds an additional overhead in the overall latency. Experimentally, we have shown that the overhead incurred due to the execution of this algorithm is very small.
2. Whenever an edge device accepts any service for execution, it broadcasts its own residual capacity. Therefore, computation of residual capacity of edge devices does not have any impact on the latency computation.
3. The quality of this algorithm depends on the value of K. In general, with an increase in the value of K, the solution quality, i.e., the latency monotonically improves. However, after certain value of K, this improvement stagnates. We also note that with an increase in the value of K, the computation time of the FCFS algorithm increases up to a certain value of K. Unless mentioned otherwise, we consider the value of K as 1. However, in the experimental section, we have shown the trade-off between the computation time and the solution quality in terms of the latency for different values of K.

Time Complexity: The FCFS algorithm iterates over each timestamp, and in one timestamp, the algorithm iterates over each trajectory to find out what all services are executed in that timestamp. It accordingly places the services on an appropriate execution platform to obtain a low latency. Therefore, the complexity of the FCFS algorithm is polynomial in the size of the set of trajectories. More specifically, the worst-case time complexity of the FCFS algorithm is the order of the size of the set of trajectories, i.e., $O(|\mathcal{T}|)$, since each trajectory is defined as the set of services accessed across all timestamps.

4   Experimental Results

In this section, we present our experimental results with analysis. We implemented our proposed framework in Python. All experiments were performed on a system with the following configuration: AMD Ryzen 5 3550H with Radeon Vega Mobile Gfx, 2100 MHz, 4 Cores(s), 8 logical processor(s) @ 2.10 GHz with 8 GB DDR4 RAM. We used Gurobi [5] as the ILP solver. We begin with a discussion of the datasets used for our evaluations.

4.1   Dataset Generation

We conducted our experiments on a real dataset, which we generated for the evaluation and a set of synthetically generated datasets. We now discuss these two datasets in detail.

Real Dataset Generation. We could not find any real benchmark dataset that can be used directly to evaluate the performance of our proposed framework. Therefore, we designed our own dataset by combining multiple datasets to model various dimensions of our problem model. We now demonstrate each component of $\mathcal{M} = (\mathcal{C}, \mathcal{E}, \mathcal{N}, \mathcal{L}, \mathcal{R}, \mathcal{T}, \mathcal{H}, \mathcal{S})$ below.

In our real dataset, we considered only one cloud server. We used the Pantheon[1] dataset to generate the uplink and downlink speeds of the cloud. We assumed one edge device per location and generated the uplink and downlink speeds of each edge device randomly between 3 MBps to 10 MBps. We obtained these values by observing actual transmission speeds using a Wi-Fi dongle connected to a Raspberry Pi. The size of the memory of each edge device was generated randomly between 512 MB to 4 GB considering the configuration of Raspberry Pi. The propagation delay from a location to an edge device was generated randomly following a distribution, which was obtained from our collected ping latency data. We conducted an experiment to collect the ping latency of our institute server from different locations. The propagation delay from a location to the cloud was generated from the distribution obtained from our collected data containing the ping latency of Amazon and Google servers from different locations. The set of locations, route map and the set of vehicular trajectories were constructed from gatech[2] dataset. The gatech dataset contains 10 different user trajectories, where the positions of the vehicles were captured in terms of latitude and longitude pairs. We first extracted the latitude-longitude pairs from the dataset. We then used K-means [8] algorithm with Haversine distance [20] function to discretize the set of locations. The route map was generated from the vehicular trajectories of gatech dataset. To obtain the set of services and their duration of invocations per user, we used Carat[3] dataset. The uplink and downlink speeds of each handheld

---

[1] https://www.pantheon.stanford.edu/summary/?page=1.

[2] https://www.crawdad.org/gatech/vehicular/20060315/.

[3] https://www.cs.helsinki.fi/group/carat/data-sharing/.

device were estimated from a distribution, obtained from the uplink and downlink speeds of a set of cell phones. Finally, we generated the input, output and the worst case memory requirement of each service by random sampling from our collected dataset. We performed an experiment on publicly available service APIs to obtain the input, output and the worst case memory requirement.

Synthetic Dataset Generation. To show the performance scalability of our framework, we extended our experiments on synthetically generated dataset, which we discuss below. For each instance of the dataset, externally, we provided the number of edge devices and clouds, the number of trajectories, the total number of services, the number of timestamps, and the number of services per trajectory per timestamp. For each dataset, we first randomly generated the graph representing the route map. The number of vertices in the graph was equal to the number of edge devices. We used a probability p following the uniform distribution to generate a link between each pair of vertices. We note that a trajectory of our system is nothing but a path of the graph, which was chosen randomly. Finally, for each trajectory tuple, we randomly assigned two timestamps. The first timestamp shows the time to enter into the location, while the second timestamp shows the time to leave the location. The rest of the part of each dataset were generated similarly, as described above.

4.2 Comparative Methods

We compared our methods with three baseline techniques:

1) Proactive method: This method assumes that if a service of a trajectory is uploaded to any execution platform, it continues the execution until the execution platform becomes inaccessible from the current location of the vehicular trajectory. In this approach, a service of a trajectory is uploaded, if required, to the fastest execution platform accessible from the current location of the trajectory having the residual capacity to accommodate the service. The inaccessibility of an execution platform is measured in terms of its propagation delay. A service of a trajectory is transferred from one execution platform to another when the propagation delay of the former execution platform is more than a given threshold value from the current location of the trajectory.

2) Reactive method: In this method, each service of a trajectory changes the execution platform along with the vehicular trajectory across the span of the service. Here, in each location of a trajectory, a service of the trajectory is uploaded to the fastest execution platform accessible from the current location of the trajectory having the residual capacity to accommodate the service.

3) Cloud-based method: In this method, each service of each trajectory is uploaded to the cloud. The service continues its execution in the cloud until it finishes. Finally, the service gets downloaded from the cloud to the handheld device.

Table 1. Comparative study on the real dataset (all in seconds)

Network parameters				
$|\mathcal{T}|$	$|\mathcal{S}|$	$|\mathcal{E}|$	$|TS|$	$\#\mathcal{S}/\mathcal{T},TS$
10	121	10	10	2 to 5
Comparative study with different algorithms				
Subject	Optimal	FCFS	Proactive	Reactive	Cloud
Lat	–	12.52	12.52	17.37	291.11
CT	–	0.01	0.02	0.024	0.02
FCFS with K-look ahead				
K	2	3	5	7	10
Lat	8.61	6.14	6.07	6.07	6.07
CT	0.01	0.01	0.01	0.02	0.02

**note: $\#\mathcal{S}/\mathcal{T},TS$ the number of services per trajectory per timestamp

4.3 Analysis on Real Dataset

In this section we briefly discuss our experimental analysis. We begin with analyzing the results obtained on the real dataset. Table 1 shows the results on the real dataset. From the table we have the following observations:

1. **Performance of FCFS:** The proposed First Come First Serve (FCFS) algorithm (with look-ahead 1) was as good as the proactive technique and better than the reactive and cloud-based techniques in terms of latency.
2. **Performance of Optimal:** The optimal algorithm was unable to produce any result due to the size of the dataset.
3. **Execution time of FCFS:** Our FCFS algorithm was able to generate the results in the order of tens of milliseconds.
4. **Impact of look-aheads on FCFS:** As we increased the number of look-aheads K, the latency monotonically reduced. However, this improvement stagnates beyond $K = 5$. This is because for our available dataset, the entire set of decision parameters can usually be obtained by FCFS when $K \geq 5$. As is evident from Table 1, the execution timespan of any service is bounded by 5 timestamps.

To generalize the overall characteristics of our proposed optimal and FCFS algorithms, we further extended our experiments on synthetically generated datasets.

4.4 Analysis on Synthetically Generated Dataset

In this analysis, we varied different network parameters, i.e., the number of trajectories ($|\mathcal{T}|$), the number of edge devices ($|\mathcal{E}|$), the number of timestamps ($|TS|$), the number of services ($|\mathcal{S}|$), and the number of services per trajectory per timestamp ($\#\mathcal{S}/\mathcal{T}, TS$), to analyze the performance of different algorithms. At a time we varied only one parameter while keeping the rest of the parameters constant.

We first performed an experiment with a smaller dataset. Figures 1(a)–(e) shows the comparative study between different algorithms. We have the following observations:

1. **Performance of Optimal Algorithm:** As evident from Figs.1(a)–(e), the optimal algorithm produced the best results in terms of latency. However, the optimal algorithm was quite expensive in terms of computation time. For a relatively large dataset, the optimal algorithm was, therefore, unable to produce any result.

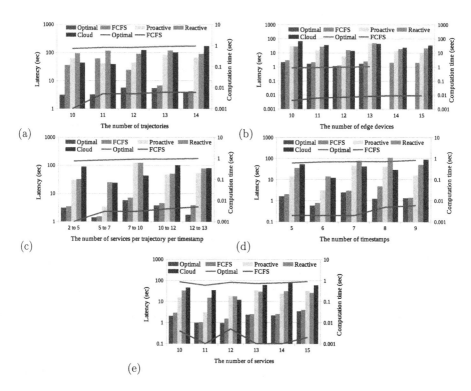

Fig. 1. Comparative study between different methods by varying the number of (a) trajectories ($|\mathcal{S}| = 10$; $|\mathcal{E}| = 5$; $|TS| = 5$; $\#\mathcal{S}/\mathcal{T}, TS = 2-5$); (b) edge devices ($|\mathcal{T}| = 5$; $|\mathcal{S}| = 10$; $|TS| = 5$; $\#\mathcal{S}/\mathcal{T}, TS = 2-5$); (c) services per trajectory per timestamp ($|\mathcal{T}| = 5$; $|\mathcal{S}| = 20$; $|\mathcal{E}| = 5$; $|TS| = 5$); (d) timestamps ($|\mathcal{T}| = 5$; $|\mathcal{S}| = 10$; $|\mathcal{E}| = 5$; $\#\mathcal{S}/\mathcal{T}, TS = 2-5$); (e) services ($|\mathcal{T}| = 5$; $|\mathcal{E}| = 10$; $|TS| = 5$; $\#\mathcal{S}/\mathcal{T}, TS = 2-5$)

2. **Comparison between FCFS and Optimal Algorithms:** On average, the optimal algorithm was 2.43 times better than the FCFS algorithm in terms

of latency, while the FCFS algorithm was 306 times faster than the optimal algorithm. This signifies the purpose of the FCFS algorithm.

3. **Comparison between FCFS and baseline techniques:** In few cases, the FCFS algorithm was worse than the proactive or cloud-based techniques. As apparent from Figs. 1(a)–(e), in only 1 out of 27 cases, the proactive technique and the cloud-based technique had 1.5 times and 1.6 times lower latency than the FCFS, respectively. However, on average, the FCFS algorithm had 6.76 times lower latency than the best algorithm among proactive, reactive, and cloud-based techniques (in each case).

4. **Variation of network parameters:** As observed from Figs. 1(a)–(e), with the increase in the number of trajectories, edge devices, timestamps or services per trajectory per timestamp, the computation time of both the optimal and the FCFS algorithms monotonically increased. However, the number of services did not influence the computation time. While the number of services increases the variation of services to be invoked, it does not increase the total number of services invoked from each trajectory.

As discussed earlier, for a large dataset, the optimal algorithm was not able to produce any result. However, our FCFS algorithm is scalable enough to generate results in a reasonable time limit. Figures 2(a)–(e) show the results on larger

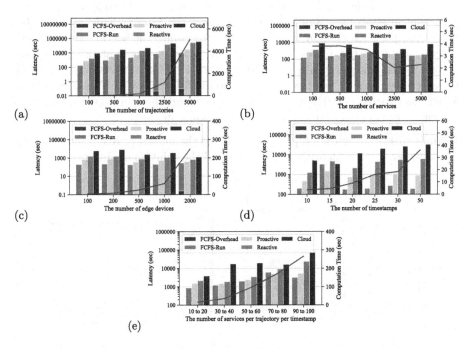

Fig. 2. Comparative analysis on large datasets by varying the number of (a) trajectories; (b) edge devices; (c) services per trajectory per timestamp; (d) timestamps; (e) services; Unless otherwise mentioned, the general configuration of the network parameters for this experiment are: $|\mathcal{T}| = 100$; $|\mathcal{S}| = 100$; $|\mathcal{E}| = 100$; $|TS| = 10$; $\#\mathcal{S}/\mathcal{T}, TS = 5 - 10$ (Color figure online)

datasets. A similar trend was observed from the larger datasets as well. Here, in Figs. 2(a)–(e), we reported the overall time taken by the FCFS algorithm across all trajectories across all timestamps (as shown by the blue line graph in Fig. 2). However, in each case, we also reported the latency overhead (i.e., the computation time of the FCFS algorithm in each trajectory in each timestamp) added due to the computation time of the FCFS algorithm. We note that for the larger dataset, the latency overhead generated due to the computation time of the FCFS algorithm was significant, as shown in Figs. 2(a)–(e). However, the FCFS algorithm was still 2.57 times better than the best technique among proactive, reactive, and cloud-based methods (in each case) in terms of latency. We further note that only in 3 out of 26 cases, the proactive technique was 1.5 times better than the FCFS in terms of latency.

4.5   Impact of Tunable Parameters

We now discuss the impact of two tunable parameters on the trade-off between solution quality and computation time.

Impact of Window Size (ω): We first discuss the impact of window size in case of window-based optimal algorithm. We compared the solution quality (i.e., latency) of the window based optimal algorithm for different window sizes with the optimal algorithm. Figure 3(a) shows the latency and overhead due to the computation time of the algorithm across different window sizes for five different datasets (i.e. Cases 1–5), where each dataset represents a different set of parameter configurations. As evident from Fig. 3(a), on average, with the increase in the size of window, the solution quality improved. This is expected, as with an increase in the window size, in general the window-based optimal algorithm gradually approaches the optimal solution.

Impact of Lookaheads (K): We now discuss the impact of K in the case of the K-look-ahead FCFS algorithm. We compared the solution quality (i.e., latency)

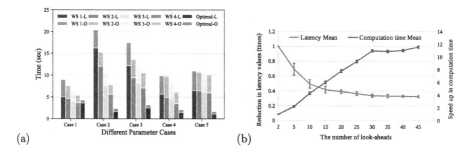

Fig. 3. Trade-off between computation delay and latency for (a) window-based optimal algorithm; (b) FCFS with K-look ahead. For (a), the darker colors (labels ending with a suffix '-L') denote latency, while the lighter colors (labels ending with a suffix '-O') denote overhead.

of the K-look-ahead FCFS algorithm for a specific value of K with the 1-look-ahead FCFS algorithm. Figure 3(b) shows the means and standard deviations of latency improvement and computation time degradation. While the latency improvement was calculated as the ratio between the latency obtained by 1-look-ahead FCFS and K-look-ahead FCFS, the computation time degradation was determined by the ratio between the time taken by K-look-ahead FCFS and 1-look-ahead FCFS. As evident from Fig. 3(b), with the increase in the value of K, the solution quality monotonically improved, and computation time degraded. However, we note that after a certain limit, the solution quality did not improve significantly with an increase in the value of K. The trade-off between the solution quality and the computation time gets captured by the value of K.

In summary, FCFS provides a good balance between the solution quality (i.e., latency value) and computation time. The solution quality can be improved further at the cost of computation time using K-look-ahead FCFS.

5 Related Work

The rise of low-latency applications for the Internet of Things has made it necessary to utilize edge devices, instead of depending only on cloud services [2,7,14]. Multiple studies have appeared in the literature about providing such low-latency services. The first category deals with service placement in an edge-cloud environment, whereas the second category handles service requests for users of vehicles.

Service Placement in Edge-Cloud Environment: The problem of service placement in edge-cloud environment has received attention recently [11,16,19,23]. One of the earliest solutions to the service placement problem was proposed in [16], where the authors first provided an (IoT) model along with the Quality of Service (QoS) requirement of the services and formulates Fog Service Placement Problem (FSPP) based on QoS requirements. In [4,6,15,19,23], the authors model the application placement problems and then propose a solution based on the different changing dynamics of the network and requests. None of these studies focus on user mobility. Our work builds on these ideas to propose an algorithm that considers the mobility of users.

Edge Service for Vehicular Users: The authors in [24] identified the requirement of the mobility problem, highlighted the advantages of mobility and discovered open challenges in this direction. In [1] and [25], the authors considered an application with multiple components to be placed on the set of edge devices across multiple timestamps for a moving user. Finally, [3] utilized a simulation tool to benchmark the performance of various algorithms. In contrast, our objective is to minimize the overall latency while multiple mobile users access different services at various points of time of their journey.

A number of works also consider optimizing service placement for moving user devices [3,9,10,21,22]. Mobmig [12] focused on solving the service placement problem in the context of edge users from moving vehicles by looking at the direction of its movement. However, its primary focus is on load balancing, and not on minimizing overall latency. References [21] and [22] model the problem of service placement as an Markov Decision Process (MDP). Unlike our work, these analytical model do not consider multiple users and multiple services to reduce the complexity of their model. Reference [10] utilized Thompson Sampling to handle the uncertainties inherent in placing services on edge clouds. However, it considers the response time of only a single user at a time, and considers a much simpler service model without considering the diversity of data requirements for different services. Moreover, these studies [9,10] do not consider the dimension of memory requirement and availability, preferring to focus only on optimizing latency. In contrast, our work focuses on optimizing service latency while adhering to the memory constraint imposed by edge devices.

6   Conclusion

In this paper, we study the dynamic service placement problem in a distributed edge-cloud environment with emphasis on user mobility. We first model the problem and propose an optimal solution to this. To improve its scalability, we further propose a heuristic algorithm considering FCFS scheduling. The experimental results on real and synthetic datasets show the effectiveness of our proposal. One limitation of this work is the assumption of having prior knowledge of the service invocation logs. In the future, we will utilize techniques shown by prior studies to predict services invoked to relax this assumption.

Acknowledgment. We would like to acknowledge Dr. Ansuman Banerjee, Indian Statistical Institute and Dr. Nanjangud C Narendra, Ericsson Research Bangalore for their initial discussions on this project.

References

1. Bahreini, T., Grosu, D.: Efficient placement of multi-component applications in edge computing systems. In: ACM/IEEE Symposium on Edge Computing, p. 5. ACM (2017)
2. Bhattacharya, A., De, P.: Computation offloading from mobile devices: can edge devices perform better than the cloud? In: ARMS-CC Workshop, pp. 1–6 (2016)
3. Deng, S., Huang, L., Taheri, J., Yin, J., Zhou, M., Zomaya, A.Y.: Mobility-aware service composition in mobile communities. IEEE TSMC Syst. **47**(3), 555–568 (2017)
4. Farhadi, V., et al.: Service placement and request scheduling for data-intensive applications in edge clouds. In: IEEE INFOCOM, pp. 1279–1287 (2019)
5. Gurobi Optimization, L.: Gurobi optimizer reference manual (2019). http://www.gurobi.com
6. He, T., et al.: It's hard to share: joint service placement and request scheduling in edge clouds with sharable and non-sharable resources. In: IEEE ICDCS, pp. 365–375 (2018)
7. Lin, L., et al.: Computation offloading toward edge computing. Proc. IEEE **107**(8), 1584–1607 (2019)

8. MacQueen, J., et al.: Some methods for classification and analysis of multivariate observations. In: Fifth Berkeley Symposium on Mathematical Statistics and Probability, vol. 1, pp. 281–297 (1967)

9. Ouyang, T., Zhou, Z., Chen, X.: Follow me at the edge: mobility-aware dynamic service placement for mobile edge computing. IEEE J. Sel. Areas Commun. **36**(10), 2333–2345 (2018). https://doi.org/10.1109/JSAC.2018.2869954

10. Ouyang, T., Li, R., Chen, X., Zhou, Z., Tang, X.: Adaptive user-managed service placement for mobile edge computing: an online learning approach. In: IEEE INFOCOM, pp. 1468–1476. IEEE (2019)

11. Pasteris, S., Wang, S., Herbster, M., He, T.: Service placement with provable guarantees in heterogeneous edge computing systems. In: IEEE INFOCOM, pp. 514–522 (2019)

12. Peng, Q., et al.: Mobility-aware and migration-enabled online edge user allocation in mobile edge computing. In: IEEE ICWS, pp. 91–98, July 2019

13. Rausch, T., Avasalcai, C., Dustdar, S.: Portable energy-aware cluster-based edge computers. In: 2018 IEEE/ACM Symposium on Edge Computing (SEC), pp. 260–272, October 2018

14. Rejiba, Z., Masip-Bruin, X., Marín-Tordera, E.: A survey on mobility-induced service migration in the fog, edge, and related computing paradigms. ACM Comput. Surv. **52**(5), 90:1–90:33 (2019)

15. Selimi, M., et al.: Practical service placement approach for microservices architecture. In: IEEE/ACM CCGRID, pp. 401–410 (2017)

16. Skarlat, O., Nardelli, M., Schulte, S., Dustdar, S.: Towards QoS-aware fog service placement. In: IEEE ICFEC, pp. 89–96 (2017)

17. Tong, L., Li, Y., Gao, W.: A hierarchical edge cloud architecture for mobile computing. In: IEEE INFOCOM, pp. 1–9 (2016)

18. Tran, T.X., et al.: Collaborative mobile edge computing in 5g networks: new paradigms, scenarios, and challenges. IEEE Commun. Mag. **55**(4), 54–61 (2017)

19. Urgaonkar, R., Wang, S., He, T., Zafer, M., Chan, K., Leung, K.K.: Dynamic service migration and workload scheduling in edge-clouds. Perform. Eval. **91**, 205–228 (2015)

20. Van Brummelen, G.: Heavenly Mathematics: The Forgotten Art of Spherical-trigonometry. Princeton University Press, Princeton (2012)

21. Wang, S., Guo, Y., Zhang, N., Yang, P., Zhou, A., Shen, X.S.: Delay-aware microservice coordination in mobile edge computing: A reinforcement learning approach. IEEE Trans. Mob. Comput. 1 (2019)

22. Wang, S., Urgaonkar, R., Zafer, M., He, T., Chan, K., Leung, K.K.: Dynamic service migration in mobile edge computing based on Markov decision process. IEEE/ACM Trans. Networking **27**(3), 1272–1288 (2019)

23. Wang, S., Zafer, M., Leung, K.K.: Online placement of multi-component applications in edge computing environments. IEEE Access **5**, 2514–2533 (2017)

24. Waqas, M., Niu, Y., Ahmed, M., Li, Y., Jin, D., Han, Z.: Mobility-aware fog computing in dynamic environments: understandings and implementation. IEEE Access **7**, 38867–38879 (2018)

25. Zhao, H., Deng, S., Zhang, C., Du, W., He, Q., Yin, J.: A mobility-aware cross-edge computation offloading framework for partitionable applications. In: IEEE ICWS, pp. 193–200. IEEE (2019)

Machine Learning for Service Oriented Computing

Feature Model-Guided Online Reinforcement Learning for Self-Adaptive Services

Andreas Metzger[1]($\boxtimes$) (iD), Clément Quinton[2](iD), Zoltán Ádám Mann[1](iD), Luciano Baresi[3](iD), and Klaus Pohl[1](iD)

[1] paluno, University of Duisburg-Essen, Essen, Germany
{andreas.metzger,zoltan.mann,klaus.pohl}@paluno.uni-due.de
[2] University of Lille, Inria, CRIStAL UMR CNRS, 9189 Lille, France
clement.quinton@univ-lille.fr
[3] Politecnico di Milano, Milan, Italy
luciano.baresi@polimi.it

Abstract. A self-adaptive service can maintain its QoS requirements in the presence of dynamic environment changes. To develop a self-adaptive service, service engineers have to create self-adaptation logic encoding when the service should execute which adaptation actions. However, developing self-adaptation logic may be difficult due to design time uncertainty; e.g., anticipating all potential environment changes at design time is in most cases infeasible. Online reinforcement learning addresses design time uncertainty by learning suitable adaptation actions through interactions with the environment at runtime. To learn more about its environment, reinforcement learning has to select actions that were not selected before, which is known as exploration. How exploration happens has an impact on the performance of the learning process. We focus on two problems related to how a service's adaptation actions are explored: (1) Existing solutions randomly explore adaptation actions and thus may exhibit slow learning if there are many possible adaptation actions to choose from. (2) Existing solutions are unaware of service evolution, and thus may explore new adaptation actions introduced during such evolution rather late. We propose novel exploration strategies that use feature models (from software product line engineering) to guide exploration in the presence of many adaptation actions and in the presence of service evolution. Experimental results for a self-adaptive cloud management service indicate an average speed-up of the learning process of 58.8% in the presence of many adaptation actions, and of 61.3% in the presence of service evolution. The improved learning performance in turn led to an average QoS improvement of 7.8% and 23.7% respectively.

Keywords: Adaptation · Reinforcement learning · Feature model · Cloud service

© Springer Nature Switzerland AG 2020
E. Kafeza et al. (Eds.): ICSOC 2020, LNCS 12571, pp. 269–286, 2020.
https://doi.org/10.1007/978-3-030-65310-1_20

1   Introduction

A *self-adaptive* service is capable of modifying its own structure and behavior at runtime based on its perception of the environment, of itself and of its requirements [9,20,28]. As an example, take a self-adaptive web service. Faced with a sudden increase in workload, the web service may reconfigure itself by deactivating optional system features. An online store, for instance, may deactivate its resource-intensive recommender engine in the presence of a high workload. By adapting itself at runtime, the web service is able to maintain its QoS requirements (here: performance) under changing workloads.

To develop a self-adaptive service, service engineers have to develop *self-adaptation logic* that encodes when and how the service should adapt itself. Among other concerns, this requires anticipating the potential environment states the service may encounter at runtime to define when the service should adapt itself. However, anticipating all potential environment states at design time is in most cases infeasible due to *design time uncertainty* [8,10]. In addition, due to simplified design assumptions, the precise effect of an adaptation action may not be known and thus accurately determining how the service should adapt itself is difficult [10]. As an example, while service engineers may know in principle that activating more features will have a negative impact on performance, exactly determining the performance impact is more challenging [30].

Online reinforcement learning (RL) is an emerging approach to address design time uncertainty of self-adaptive services by employing RL at runtime (see existing solutions discussed in Sect. 6). In general, RL aims to learn suitable actions via an agent's interactions with its environment [31]. The agent receives a reward for executing an action. The reward expresses how suitable that action was. The goal of RL is to optimize cumulative rewards.

1.1   Problem Statement

RL faces the exploration-exploitation dilemma [31]. To optimize cumulative rewards, actions should be selected that have shown to be suitable, which is known as *exploitation*. However, to discover such actions in the first place, actions that were not selected before should be selected, which is known as *exploration*. How exploration happens has an impact on the performance of the learning process [4,13,31]. We focus on two problems related to how a service's set of possible adaptation actions, *i.e.*, its *adaptation space*, is explored.

Random Exploration of Adaptation Space. Existing online RL solutions for self-adaptive services propose randomly selecting adaptation actions for exploration (see Sect. 6). The effectiveness of exploration therefore directly depends on the size of the adaptation space, because each adaptation action has an equal chance of being selected. Some RL algorithms can cope with a large space of actions, but require that the space of actions is continuous in order to generalize over unseen actions [23]. Self-adaptive services may have large, discrete adaptation spaces; *e.g.*, if their adaptation actions entail changes of service compositions

[22] or reconfigurations of service features [19]. A simple example is a service composition consisting of eight abstract services that may allow dynamically binding 2 concrete services each. Assuming no temporal or logical constraints on adaptation, this constitutes $2^8 = 256$ possible adaptation actions. In the presence of such large, discrete adaptation space, random exploration thus may lead to slow learning at runtime [4,13,31].

Evolution-Unaware Exploration of Adaptation Space. Existing online RL solutions are unaware of service evolution [16,29]. They do not consider that a self-adaptive service – like any service – may undergo evolution [25]. In contrast to self-adaptation, which refers to the automatic modification of the service by itself, evolution refers to the modification of the service by humans [20]. During evolution, service engineers may modify the service to correct bugs, remove no longer used features, or introduce new features. Service evolution means that the adaptation space may change, *e.g.*, existing adaptation actions may be removed or new adaptation actions may be added. Some RL algorithms can cope with environments that change over time, so called non-stationary environments [23,31]. However, a change of the adaptation space cannot be determined by observing the environment, as the adaptation space is an intrinsic property of the RL agent. As a result, existing solutions may explore new adaptation actions only with low probability (as all adaptation actions have an equal chance of being selected). It may thus take quite long until the new adaptation actions have been explored.

1.2   Contributions

We introduce exploration strategies for online RL that address (1) a service's potentially large adaptation space, and (2) changes of its adaptation space due to evolution. Our exploration strategies use *feature models* [21] to give structure to the service's adaptation space and thereby leverage additional information to guide exploration. A feature model is a tree or a directed acyclic graph of features, organized hierarchically. An adaptation action is represented by a valid feature combination specifying the target run-time configuration of the service.

Our strategies traverse the feature model to select the next adaptation action to be explored. By leveraging the structure of the feature model, our strategies guide the exploration process. In addition, our strategies detect added and removed adaptation actions by analyzing the change of the feature model due to evolution. Adaptation actions removed as a result of evolution are no longer explored, while added adaptation actions are explored first.

We implement our strategies as part of the Q-Learning RL algorithm [31] widely used in the related work (see Sect. 6). We experimentally assess our strategies using an actual cloud resource management service and compare the learning performance with that of the widely used ϵ-greedy random exploration strategy.

In what follows, Sect. 2 explains fundamentals and a running example. Sect. 3 describes our exploration strategies and how they are integrated with RL algorithms. Sect. 4 presents the design and results of our experiments. Sect. 5 provides a critical discussion. Sect. 6 analyzes related work.

2 Fundamentals

Feature Models and Self-adaptation. A *feature model* is a tree of features organized hierarchically [21]. A feature can be decomposed into mandatory, optional or alternative sub-features. A mandatory sub-feature has to be activated if its parent feature is activated. While an optional sub-feature may or may not be activated, at least one of the alternative sub-features has to be activated if their parent feature is activated. Additional constraints, such as "excludes" or "requires", express inter-feature dependencies. Thereby, a feature model describes the possible and allowed feature combinations.

Feature models are traditionally used in software product line engineering to define the set of system variants at design time [21]. Dynamic software product lines extend the use of feature models to describe possible run-time configurations of a system [14]. A feature model thereby can be used to define a self-adaptive system's adaptation space, where each adaptation action is expressed in terms of a possible runtime configuration, *i.e.*, feature combination [12].

Figure 1 shows the feature model of a self-adaptive web service as an example. The DataLogging feature is mandatory (which means it is always active), while the ContentDiscovery feature is optional. The DataLogging feature has three alternative sub-features, *i.e.*, at least one data logging sub-feature must be active: Min, Medium or Max. The ContentDiscovery feature has two optional sub-features Search and Recommendation. The constraint Recommendation ⇒ Max ∨ Medium specifies that a sufficient level of data logging is required to collect enough information about the web service's users and transactions to make good recommendations.

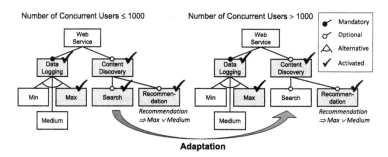

Fig. 1. Feature model and adaptation of example web service

Let us consider the above web service should adapt to changing number of concurrent users to keep its response time below 500 ms. A service developer may express an adaptation rule for the web service such that it turns off some of the features in the presence of more users, thereby reducing the resource needs of the service. The right-hand side of Fig. 1 shows a concrete example for such an adaptation. If the service faces an environment state of more than 1000 concurrent users, the service self-adapts by deactivating the Search feature.

Reinforcement Learning (RL). RL aims to learn suitable actions via an agent's interactions with its environment [31]. At a given time step t, the agent selects an action a (from its adaptation space) to be executed in environment state s (see Fig. 2). As a result, the environment transitions to s' at time step $t + 1$ and the agent receives a reward r for executing the action. The reward r together with the information about the next state s' are used to update the knowledge of the agent. The goal of RL is to optimize cumulative rewards. As mentioned in Sect. 1, a trade-off between *exploitation* (using current knowledge) and *exploitation* (gathering new knowledge) must be made. For a self-adaptive service, "agent" refers to the self-adaptation logic of the service and "action" refers to an adaptation action [24].

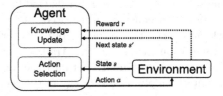

Fig. 2. RL concept

3 Feature-Model-Guided Exploration

As motivated in Sect. 1, our exploration strategies use feature models (FM) to guide the exploration process. We first explain how our *FM-guided exploration strategies* can be integrated into an existing RL algorithm and then introduce the realization of these strategies.

3.1 Integration into Reinforcement Learning

Algorithm 1 shows how our FM-guided strategies can be integrated into RL by using the well-known Q-Learning algorithm as basis. We chose Q-Learning because it is the most widely used algorithm in the related work (see Sect. 6).

Algorithm 1. Q-Learning with FM-guided Exploration

1: **function** FMQ-LEARNING(FeatureModel $\mathcal{M}$; Double α, γ, ϵ, δ)
2:     Initialize $Q(s, a)$ for all $s \in S$ (state space) and $a \in A$ (adaptation space);
3:     Determine current state s;
4:     **repeat**
5:         Set<Feature> a = GETNEXTACTION($\mathcal{M}$, s); // **Action Selection**
6:         Adapt service to configuration a; Observe reward r; Observe new state s';
7:         $Q(s, a) \leftarrow Q(s, a) + \alpha[r + \gamma\max_{a' \in A}Q(s', a') - Q(s, a)]$; // **Knowledge Update**
8:         $s \leftarrow s'$;
9:     **until** last time step
10: **end function**
11:
12: **function** GETNEXTACTION(FeatureModel $\mathcal{M}$, State s)
13:     Set<Feature> $a \leftarrow \text{argmax}_a Q(s, a)$; // Exploit existing knowledge
14:     INITFMEXPLORATION($\mathcal{M}$, a); // initialize the FM-guided strategies, see Algorithm 2
15:     **if** random() $< \epsilon$ **then** // Explore new actions
16:         **if** random() $< \delta$ **then return** $getRandomConfiguration(\mathcal{M})$;
17:         **else**
18:             **return** $getNextConfiguration()$; // see Algorithm 2
19:         **end if**
20:     **end if**
21:     **return** a;
22: **end function**

Q-Learning employs a value function for representing the learned knowledge. The value function $Q(s, a)$ gives the expected cumulative reward when performing a particular action a in a given state s [31]. Q-Learning offers two hyperparameters: the learning rate α, which defines to what extent newly acquired knowledge overwrites old knowledge, and the discount factor γ, which defines the relevance of future rewards (see knowledge update in line 7).

Our strategies are integrated into RL within the GETNEXTACTION function, which selects the next adaptation action while trading off exploration and exploitation. To make this trade-off we use the ϵ-greedy strategy as a baseline, as it is a standard action selection strategy in reinforcement learning and the most widely used strategy in the related work (see Sect. 6). With probability $1 - \epsilon$, ϵ-greedy exploits existing knowledge by selecting the action a that has the highest Q value and thus highest expected reward (line 13). With probability ϵ, ϵ-greedy randomly explores a new action. In contrast to this random exploration, we use our FM-guided exploration strategies by calling the GETNEXTCONFIGU- RATION function (line 18). The different realizations of GETNEXTCONFIGURATION are explained below. To prevent FM-guided exploration from prematurely converging to a local minimum, we follow the literature and use a small amount of randomness [26], i.e., we perform random exploration with probability $\delta \cdot \epsilon$.

3.2   Leveraging the Feature Model Structure for Exploration

Incremental Exploration Strategy. This strategy takes advantage of the semantics typically encoded in the structure of feature models. Non-leaf features in a feature model are usually abstract features used to better structure variability [36]. These abstract features often do not have an impact at implementation level, but delegate their realization to their sub-features. Sub-features thus may offer different realizations of their abstract parent feature. The sub-features of a common parent feature, i.e., sibling features, can thus be considered semantically connected. In the example from Sect. 2, the ContentDiscovery feature has two sub-features Search and Recommendation offering different concrete ways how a user may discover online content. The idea behind the Incremental strategy is to exploit the information about these potentially semantically connected sibling features and explore them first before exploring other features. Note that this entails a random selection of the order of sub-features. Table 1 shows an excerpt of a typical exploration sequence of the Incremental strategy with the step-wise exploration of sibling features highlighted in gray.

Table 1. Example exploration via Incremental strategy (excerpt)

	Logging	Min	Medium	Max	Content Disc.	Search	Recommend.
1	✓			✓	✓		✓
2	✓		✓		✓		✓
3	✓		✓		✓	✓	✓
4	✓			✓	✓	✓	✓
5	✓		✓		✓	✓	
6	✓	✓			✓	✓	
7	...	...	...	...	...	...	...

The Incremental strategy is realized by Algorithm 2, which starts by randomly selecting an arbitrary leaf feature f (*i.e.*, a feature with no sub-features) among all leaf features that are part of the current configuration (lines 5– 6). Then, the set of configurations C_f containing feature f is computed, while the sibling features of feature f are gathered into a dedicated *siblings* set (line 7).

Algorithm 2. Incremental Strategy

```
1: Set<Feature> leaves, configuration, siblings;
2: Set<Set<Feature>> Cf; Feature f;
3:
4: function INITFMEXPLORATION(FeatureModel M, Set<Feature> currentConfiguration)
5:     leaves ← getLeaves(currentConfiguration);
6:     f ← randomSelect(leaves);
7:     Cf ← getConfigurationsWithFeature(f); siblings ← siblings(f);
8: end function
9:
10: function GETNEXTCONFIGURATION()
11:     if Cf ≠ ∅ then
12:         configuration ← randomSelect(Cf); Cf ← Cf \ {configuration};
13:         return configuration;
14:     else
15:         if siblings ≠ ∅ then
16:             f ← randomSelect(siblings);
17:             siblings ← siblings \ {f}; Cf ← getConfigurationsWithFeature(f);
18:         else
19:             if parent(f) ≠ ∅ then
20:                 f ← parent(f); siblings ← siblings(f);
21:                 Cf ← getConfigurationsWithFeature(f);
22:             else // Root feature reached
23:                 return ∅;
24:             end if
25:         end if
26:         return GETNEXTCONFIGURATION();
27:     end if
28: end function
```

While C_f is non-empty, the strategy explores one randomly selected configuration from C_f and removes the selected configuration from C_f (lines 11–13). If C_f is empty, then a new set of configurations containing a sibling feature of f is randomly explored, provided such sibling feature exists (lines 15–17). If no configuration containing f or a sibling feature of f is found, then the strategy moves on to the parent feature of f, which is repeated until a configuration is found (line 13) or the root feature is reached (line 22).

Feature Degree Exploration Strategy. Even though the Incremental strategy makes use of the structure of the feature model, it still randomly determines the order in which leaf and sibling features are explored. To better guide the decision about which of these features to explore, we make use of the concept of feature degree. We define the feature degree for a given feature f as the number of configurations that contain f. The intuition here is that there may be a higher probability of finding a suitable configuration when considering features with high feature degrees, as they are present in more configurations.

In our example, the feature degree of Search is 5, while of Recommendation it is only 4 (due to the constraint requiring at least the Medium logging level).

The Feature Degree strategy thus first explores all configurations involving the Search feature before exploring other configurations. Table 2 shows an excerpt of a typical exploration sequence of the Feature Degree strategy (the exploration of the sibling feature with highest feature degree highlighted in gray).

Table 2. Example exploration via Feature Degree strategy (excerpt)

	Logging	Min	Medium	Max	Content Disc.	Search	Recommend.
1	✓			✓	✓		✓
2	✓		✓		✓	✓	✓
3	✓			✓	✓	✓	✓
4	✓		✓		✓	✓	
5	✓	✓			✓	✓	
6	...	...	...	...	...	...	...

The Feature Degree strategy is realized by modifying Algorithm 2 to make use of the feature degree as shown in Algorithm 3. On the one hand, the feature degree is used to determine which leaf feature to start exploring from. Instead of randomly selecting a leaf feature as done in Algorithm 2 (line 6), the Feature Degree strategy selects a leaf feature with the highest feature degree. On the other hand, instead of randomly choosing sibling features as done in Algorithm 2 (line 16), the Feature Degree strategy explores the sibling in descending order of their feature degrees. To realize the *featureDeg* function, existing feature model analysis tools, such as [35], can be used to efficiently compute the number of possible configurations containing f.

Algorithm 3. Feature Degree Strategy

```
5:      leaves ← getLeaves(currentConfiguration);
6:      f ← argmax_{f∈leaves}(featureDeg(f));
        [...]
16:         if siblings ≠ ∅ then
17:             f ← argmax_{f∈siblings}(featureDeg(f));
```

3.3   Leveraging Feature Model Differences for Exploration

To capture changes in the service's adaptation space due to evolution, we propose analyzing the differences in feature models before ($\mathcal{M}$) and after ($\mathcal{M}'$) an evolution step. Following the product line literature, we consider two main types of changes of feature models [34]:

Added configurations (feature model generalization). New configurations may be added to the adaptation space by (*i*) introducing new features to $\mathcal{M}'$, or (*ii*) removing or relaxing existing constraints (*e.g.*, by changing a sub-feature from mandatory to optional, or by removing "requires" or "excludes" constraints). In the example from Sect. 2, a new sub-feature Optimized might be added to the DataLogging feature, providing a more resource efficient logging implementation. Thereby, new configurations are added to the adaptation space, such as

{DataLogging, Optimized, ContentDiscovery, Search}. As another example, the Recommendation implementation may have been improved and it now can work with the Min logging feature. This removes the constraint shown in Fig. 1, and adds new configurations such as {DataLogging, Min, ContentDiscovery, Recommendation}.

Removed configurations (feature model specialization). Symmetrical to above, configurations may be removed from the adaptation space by (i) removing features from $\mathcal{M}$, or (ii) by adding or tightening constraints in $\mathcal{M}'$.

To determine these changes of feature models, we compute a set-theoretic difference between valid configurations expressed by feature model $\mathcal{M}$ and feature model $\mathcal{M}'$. Detailed descriptions of feature model differencing as well as efficient tool support can be found in [1,5]. The feature model differences provide us with adaptation actions added to the adaptation space ($\mathcal{M}' \setminus \mathcal{M}$), as well as adaptation actions removed from the adaptation space ($\mathcal{M} \setminus \mathcal{M}'$).

Our evolution-aware strategies thus first explore the configurations that were added to the adaptation space, and then explore the remaining configurations if needed. The rationale is that added configurations might offer new opportunities for finding suitable adaptation actions and thus should be explored first. Configurations that were removed are no longer executed and thus the learning knowledge can be pruned accordingly. In the Q-Learning realization (Sect. 3.1), we remove all tuples (s, a) from Q, where a represents a removed configuration.

Such evolution-aware exploration can also be introduced to ϵ-greedy. Instead of randomly exploring the whole new adaptation space, exploration is limited to first randomly exploring the set of new configurations.

4   Experiments

We experimentally assess our FM-guided exploration strategies and compare them with ϵ-greedy as the strategy used in the related work (see Sect. 6).

Research Questions. We aim to answer the following research questions:

RQ1: How does learning performance using FM-guided exploration compare to using ϵ-greedy and how does it impact on QoS?

RQ2: How does learning performance using evolution-aware exploration strategies compare to evolution-unaware exploration and how does it impact on QoS?

Experiment Setup. We use a self-adaptive cloud resource management service, CloudRM[1], as subject system [17]. CloudRM controls the allocation of computational tasks to virtual machines (VMs) and the allocation of virtual machines to physical machines in a cloud data center. CloudRM can be adapted by reconfiguring it to use different allocation algorithms, and the algorithms can be adapted by using different sets of parameters. We implemented a separate adaption logic for CloudRM by using the extended Q-Learning algorithm as introduced in Sect. 3.1. In total, CloudRM provides 344 possible adaptation

---

[1] https://sourceforge.net/p/vm-alloc/task_vm_pm.

actions. These are structured in a feature model that is four levels deep and includes 65 different features. The feature model together with the code of our algorithms and the data of our experiments are available online[2].

Our experiments are based on a real-world workload trace with 10,000 tasks, in total spanning over a time frame of 29 days [18]. The CloudRM algorithms decide on the placement of new tasks whenever they are entered into the system (as driven by the workload trace). To allow sufficient time in the experiment to observe the impact of an adaptation, CloudRM is allowed to run one hour before the next adaptation action is executed. For RQ2, the same workload was replayed after each evolution step to ensure consistency among the results.

We define the reward function for online RL as $r = -(\rho \cdot e + (1 - \rho) \cdot m)$, with e being the energy consumption and m being the number of VM manipulations (*i.e.*, migrations and launches), each normalized to be on the same scale. We use $\rho = 0.8$, meaning we give priority to reducing energy consumption, while still maintaining a low number of VM manipulations. If several adaptation actions show similar energy consumption, the one that achieves this with less VM manipulations receives a higher reward.

To determine suitable hyper-parameter values (see Sect. 3.1), we performed hyper-parameter tuning (via grid search). We used the best performing learning rate $\alpha = 0.85$ and discount factor $\gamma = 0.2$ for ϵ-greedy and used this also for our FM-guided strategies. To facilitate convergence of the learning process, we used an ϵ decay approach. This is a typical approach in RL, meaning that ϵ starts at 1 and diminishes with a predefined rate after each time step. We used an ϵ decay rate of 0.97 (*i.e.*, $\epsilon < 1\%$ after time step 150), as this led to fastest convergence with highest asymptotic rewards for ϵ-greedy. For the FM-guided strategies we used a δ decay rate of 0.9 (*i.e.*, $\delta < 1\%$ after time step 45). Due to the stochastic nature of the learning strategies (both ϵ-greedy and to a lesser degree our strategies involve random decisions), we repeated the experiment 100 times and averaged results.

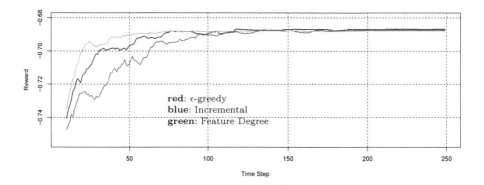

Fig. 3. Learning curves (RQ1)

---

[2] https://git.uni-due.de/online-reinforcement-learning/icsoc-2020-artefacts.

Results for RQ1. Figure 3 visualizes the learning process for the different exploration strategies by showing how rewards develop over time. As visible, the FM-guided exploration strategies (Incremental and Feature Degree) more quickly reach maximum rewards than ϵ-greedy (our baseline).

Table 3 characterizes the learning process of the different strategies by using the metrics presented in [32]: *Asymptotic performance* (maximum reward at end of learning process, here: average rewards of time steps 200–250), *total reward* (area between reward curve and asymptotic reward), *time to threshold* (time step when $x\%$ of asymptotic reward is reached for first time, here: $x = 90$), *jumpstart* (rewards at beginning of learning process, here: at time step 10). In addition, the table shows how the learning performance of the different strategies impact on the QoS characteristics of CloudRM.

Results indicate that our FM-guided exploration strategies lead to a consistent improvement of the learning process. In addition, the Feature Degree strategy performs better than the Incremental strategy, suggesting that considering additional information about the service's features has an effect. Our FM-guided strategies perform better when compared with ϵ-greedy wrt. total reward (58.8% on average), time to threshold (48.6% on average), and jumpstart (1.3% on average), while performing comparably wrt. asymptotic performance. Considering the impact on QoS, FM-guided learning consistently leads to less VM manipulations and sightly lower energy consumption. While savings in energy are rather small (less than 1%), FM-guided learning reduces the number of virtual machine manipulations by 7.8% on average. This is caused by the different placement algorithms having a rather small difference wrt. energy optimization, but having a much larger difference wrt. optimizing the number of virtual machine manipulations.

Table 3. Comparison of exploration strategies (RQ1)

	Learning performance				QoS impact	
	Asymptotic performance	Time to threshold	Jumpstart	Total reward	Energy (kWh)	Number VM manipulations
ϵ-greedy	−0.6873	74	−0.7474	−2.0110	2511	761
Incremental	−0.6868	47	−0.7407	−0.9946	2507	713
Improvement	*0.1%*	*36.5%*	*0.9%*	*50.5%*	*0.1%*	*6.2%*
Feature Degree	−0.6878	29	−0.7351	−0.6644	2508	690
Improvement	*−0.1%*	*60.8%*	*1.7%*	*67.0%*	*0.1%*	*9.3%*
Avg. improvement	*0.0%*	*48.6%*	*1.3%*	*58.8%*	*0.1%*	*7.8%*

Results for RQ2. We compare three evolution-aware strategies (evolution-aware ϵ-greedy, evolution-aware Incremental, and evolution-aware Feature Degree) with their respective evolution-unaware counterparts (*i.e.*, the strategies used for RQ1). It should be noted that even though we provide the evolution-unaware strategies with the information about the changed adaptation space (so they can fully explore it), we have not modified them such as to differentiate between old and new adaptation actions.

We use a 3-step evolution scenario incrementally adding features and thus adaptation actions to CloudRM. Initially, CloudRM offers the Simple placement feature (creating a dedicated virtual machine for each task) and Multiple placement features (allowing a given number of tasks to be deployed on a virtual machine), offering 26 adaptation actions. In evolution step #1, the Maxsize placement feature is added, which creates virtual machines of a fixed capacity and selects virtual machines using the First-Fit (FF) heuristic, adding 30 adaptation actions. In evolution step #2, the Maxsize placement feature is enhanced by allowing different VM capacities and adding two new virtual machine selection heuristics: Best-Fit (BF) and Worst-Fit (WF), adding 72 adaptation actions. In evolution step#3, the Consolidation_Friendly placement feature is added, which selects a physical machine that can accommodate the given task, and then selects a virtual machine hosted on the physical machine, adding 216 adaptation actions.

Like for RQ1, Fig. 4 visualizes the learning process for the different exploration strategies. After each evolution step, we observe the learning process for 250 time steps, before moving to the next step of the evolution scenario.

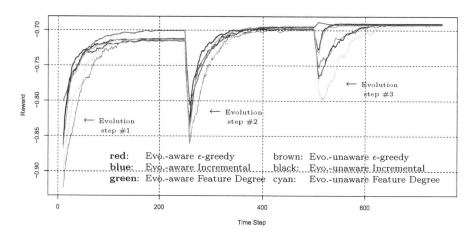

Fig. 4. Learning curves across evolution steps (RQ2)

Table 4 shows the results of learning performance and QoS impact across all three evolution steps. We computed the metrics separately for each of the evolution steps and report their averages.

The evolution-aware strategies consistently perform better than their evolution-unaware counterparts wrt. total reward (61.3% on average), time to threshold (51.0% on average), jumpstart (5.1% on average), and asymptotic performance (0.4% on average). With respect to the impact on QoS, the evolution-aware strategies reduce the number of virtual machine manipulations by 23.7% on average, while keeping energy consumption around the same as the non-evolution-aware strategies. As can be seen, the evolution-unaware FM-guided strategies (from RQ1) may perform much worse than any of the evolution-aware

Table 4. Comparison of exploration strategies across evolution steps (RQ2)

	Learning performance				QoS impact	
	Asymptotic performance	Time to threshold	Jumpstart	Total reward	Energy (kWh)	Number VM manipulations
ε-greedy						
Evo.-aware	−0.6964	35.33	−0.7645	−1.2623	2616	1028
Evo.-unaware	−0.7012	75.00	−0.8437	−4.8926	2615	1482
Improvement	*0.7%*	*52.9%*	*9.4%*	*74.2%*	*−0.1%*	*30.6%*
Incremental						
Evo.-aware	−0.6997	32.33	−0.8027	−1.5256	2611	1054
Evo.-unaware	−0.7013	59.33	−0.8161	−3.0479	2618	1316
Improvement	*0.2%*	*45.5%*	*1.6%*	*49.9%*	*0.3%*	*19.9%*
Feature Degree						
Evo.-aware	−0.6996	39.00	−0.8098	−2.1185	2614	1033
Evo.-unaware	−0.7013	85.67	−0.8455	−5.2652	2616	1301
Improvement	*0.3%*	*54.5%*	*4.2%*	*59.8%*	*0.1%*	*20.5%*
Avg. Improvement	*0.4%*	*51.0%*	*5.1%*	*61.3%*	*0.1%*	*23.7%*

ones. This is because they again explore old adaptation actions, many of which were not suitable. Finally, it can be observed that evolution-aware ϵ-greedy may even outperform the other evolution-aware strategies. This suggests that, during evolution, considering the changes of the adaptation space has a much larger effect than considering the structure of the adaptation space.

5 Discussion

Validity Risks. We used an actual cloud resource management service and a real-world workload trace to measure learning performance and the impact of the different exploration strategies on QoS characteristics. Still results are only for a single system, which limits generalizability.

We purposefully chose ϵ-greedy as a baseline, because it was the exploration strategy used in existing online RL approaches for self-adaptive services (see Setc. 6). Alternative exploration strategies were proposed in the field of machine learning. Examples include Boltzmann exploration, where actions with a higher expected reward (e.g., Q value) have a higher chance of being explored, or UCB action selection, where actions are favored that have been less frequently explored [31]. Another alternative is to use policy-based RL, which in contrast to value-based RL such as Q-Learning, directly represents the policy as a neural network, and thus intrinsically exhibits stochastic action selection behavior [24]. A comparison among those alternatives is beyond the scope of the current paper, because a fair comparison would require the careful variation and analysis of a range of many additional hyper-parameters.

We focused on evolution steps that increase the size of the adaptation space to assess to what extent our strategies are able to capture adaptation spaces of increasingly larger size. Our experiments may be complemented by analyzing how the different strategies compare to each other when the size of the adaptation space is reduced. Even though in an adaptation space of reduced size, fewer configurations have to be explored – thus leading in principle to faster learning – there still may be differences in the way these fewer configurations are explored.

Limitations and Assumptions. We assume that feature models are complete with respect to the coverage of the adaptation space and that during an evolution step they are always consistent and up to date. A further possible change during service evolution can be the modification of a feature's implementation, which is currently not visible in the feature models. Encoding such kind of modification thus could further improve our online learning strategies.

One aspect that impacts FM-guided exploration is the depth of the feature models. On the one hand, if the feature model has only few levels, the FM-guided exploration strategies behave very similar to random exploration, because such models do not provide enough structure. On the other hand, based on initial experiments with the RL approach in [24], providing an RL agent with too structured knowledge might in fact hinder learning an optimal policy. How to define feature models at the right level of detail thus deserves further investigation.

In the realization of the exploration strategies (both ϵ-greedy and FM-guided), we assumed we can always switch from a configuration to any other possible configuration. We were not concerned with the technicalities of how to reconfigure the running service (which, for example, is addressed in [7]). We also did consider constraints concerning the order of adaptations. In practice, only certain paths may be permissible to reach a configuration from the current one. To consider such paths, online RL may be enhanced by building on work such as [27].

6   Related Work

The following authors applied online RL to self-adaptive services and considered different approaches to improve the performance of the learning process. Yet, they did not consider large adaptation spaces nor service evolution. Tesauro *et al.* use Q-Learning for autonomic resource allocation in data centers [33]. Xu *et al.* employ Q-Learning (with ϵ-greedy) for the automatic configuration of cloud virtual machines and applications [39]. Both suggest offline learning to increase the jumpstart at runtime. Barrett *et al.* propose using Q-Learning with ϵ-greedy for autonomic cloud resource allocation [3]. They propose parallel learning to speed up the learning process. Caporuscio *et al.* propose using two-layer hierarchical RL for multi-agent service assembly [6]. They observe that by sharing monitoring information, learning happens faster than when learning in isolation. Arabnejad *et al.* apply fuzzy RL with ϵ-greedy to learn fuzzy adaptation rules [2]. They also demonstrate that transfer learning may speed up learning [15]. Wang *et al.* use Q-Learning (using ϵ-greedy) together with function approximation. They use neural networks to generalize over unseen environment states and thereby facilitate learning in the presence of many environment states, *i.e.*, they address large state spaces but not large action spaces [38]. Moustafa and Zhang propose multi-agent Q-Learning with ϵ-greedy for adaptive service compositions [22].

To speed up learning, they use collaborative learning, where multiple systems simultaneously explore the set of concrete services to be composed. Zhao *et al.* propose using RL (using ϵ-greedy) combined with case-based reasoning to generate and update adaptation rules for web applications [40]. Their approach may take as long to converge as learning from scratch, but it may offer a higher jumpstart.

Bu *et al.* explicitly consider large adaptation spaces [4]. They employ Q-Learning (using ϵ-greedy) for self-configuring cloud virtual machines and applications. They reduce the size of the adaptation space by splitting it into coarse-grained sub-sets for each of which they find a representative adaptation action using the simplex method. Their experiments indicate that their approach indeed can speed up learning. Yet, they do not consider service evolution.

Dutreilh *et al.* explicitly consider service evolution [11]. They employ Q-Learning for autonomic cloud resource management and speed up learning by providing a good initial estimate for the Q-function, as well as by using statistical estimates about the environment behavior. They indicate that system evolution may imply a change of system performance and sketc.h an idea on how to detect such drifts in system performance. Yet, they do not consider that evolution may also introduce or remove adaptation actions. As explained in Sect.1, such a change in the adaptation space cannot be determined by observing the environment, as the adaptation space is an intrinsic property of the RL agent.

In our previous work, we used online RL for a self-adaptive cloud service [24]. We addressed the problem of large environment spaces (similar to Wang *et al.*) but did neither consider large action spaces nor service evolution. In earlier work, we sketc.hed the principal dependencies between learning and evolution, but did not provide concrete technical solutions [29].

A different line of work uses supervised machine learning to reduce the size of the adaptation space. As an example, Van Der Donckt *et al.* use deep learning to determine a representative and much smaller subset of the adaptation space [37]. Supervised learning requires sufficient labeled training data representative of the service's environment, which may be challenging due to design time uncertainty.

7 Conclusion

We introduced feature-model-guided exploration strategies for online reinforcement learning that address potentially large adaptation spaces and the change of the adaptation space due to service evolution. Experimental results for an adaptive cloud management service indicate a speed up of the learning process and an improvement of QoS characteristics.

As part of our future work, we will perform additional experiments, considering further types of services and the comparison with alternative exploration strategies. We also aim to integrate our strategies with more advanced reinforcement learning algorithms, such as policy-based reinforcement learning. In addition, we aim to address the current limitations of our strategies and will, for instance, also consider feature modifications during evolution.

Acknowledgments. We cordially thank Amir Molzam Sharifloo for constructive discussions during the conception of initial ideas, as well as Alexander Palm for his comments on earlier drafts. Our research received funding from the EU's Horizon 2020 R&I programme under grants 780351 (ENACT) and 871525 (FogProtect).

References

1. Acher, M., Heymans, P., Collet, P., Quinton, C., Lahire, P., Merle, P.: Feature model differences. In: Proceedings of the 24th International Conference on Advanced Information Systems Engineering, CAiSE 2012, pp. 629–645 (2012)
2. Arabnejad, H., Pahl, C., Jamshidi, P., Estrada, G.: A comparison of reinforcement learning techniques for fuzzy cloud auto-scaling. In: 17th Intl Symposium on Cluster, Cloud and Grid Computing, CCGRID 2017, pp. 64–73 (2017)
3. Barrett, E., Howley, E., Duggan, J.: Applying reinforcement learning towards automating resource allocation and application scalability in the cloud. Concurr. Comput. Pract. Exp. **25**(12), 1656–1674 (2013)
4. Bu, X., Rao, J., Xu, C.: Coordinated self-configuration of virtual machines and appliances using a model-free learning approach. IEEE Trans. Parallel Distrib. Syst. **24**(4), 681–690 (2013)
5. Bürdek, J., Kehrer, T., Lochau, M., Reuling, D., Kelter, U., Schürr, A.: Reasoning about product-line evolution using complex feature model differences. Autom. Softw. Eng. **23**(4), 687–733 (2015). https://doi.org/10.1007/s10515-015-0185-3
6. Caporuscio, M., D'Angelo, M., Grassi, V., Mirandola, R.: Reinforcement learning techniques for decentralized self-adaptive service assembly. In: Aiello, M., Johnsen, E.B., Dustdar, S., Georgievski, I. (eds.) ESOCC 2016. LNCS, vol. 9846, pp. 53–68. Springer, Cham (2016). https://doi.org/10.1007/978-3-319-44482-6_4
7. Chen, B., Peng, X., Yu, Y., Nuseibeh, B., Zhao, W.: Self-adaptation through incremental generative model transformations at runtime. In: 36th International Conference on Software Engineering, ICSE 2014, pp. 676–687 (2014)
8. Chen, T., Bahsoon, R.: Self-adaptive and online QoS modeling for cloud-based software services. IEEE Trans. Software Eng. **43**(5), 453–475 (2017)
9. de Lemos, R., et al.: Software engineering for self-adaptive systems: a second research roadmap. In: de Lemos, R., Giese, H., Müller, H.A., Shaw, M. (eds.) Software Engineering for Self-Adaptive Systems II. LNCS, vol. 7475, pp. 1–32. Springer, Heidelberg (2013). https://doi.org/10.1007/978-3-642-35813-5_1
10. D'Ippolito, N., Braberman, V.A., Kramer, J., Magee, J., Sykes, D., Uchitel, S.: Hope for the best, prepare for the worst: multi-tier control for adaptive systems. In: 36th International Conference on Software Engineering, ICSE 2014, pp. 688–699 (2014)
11. Dutreilh, X., Kirgizov, S., Melekhova, O., Malenfant, J., Rivierre, N., Truck, I.: Using reinforcement learning for autonomic resource allocation in clouds: towards a fully automated workflow. In: 7th International Conference on Autonomic and Autonomous Systems, ICAS 2011, pp. 67–74 (2011)
12. Esfahani, N., Elkhodary, A., Malek, S.: A learning-based framework for engineering feature-oriented self-adaptive software systems. IEEE Trans. Softw. Eng. **39**(11), 1467–1493 (2013)
13. Filho, R.V.R., Porter, B.: Defining emergent software using continuous self-assembly, perception, and learning. TAAS **12**(3), 16:1–16:25 (2017)
14. Hinchey, M., Park, S., Schmid, K.: Building dynamic software product lines. IEEE Comput. **45**(10), 22–26 (2012)

15. Jamshidi, P., Velez, M., Kästner, C., Siegmund, N., Kawthekar, P.: Transfer learning for improving model predictions in highly configurable software. In: 12th International Symposium on Software Engineering for Adaptive and Self-Managing Systems, SEAMS 2017, pp. 31–41 (2017)
16. Kinneer, C., Coker, Z., Wang, J., Garlan, D., Le Goues, C.: Managing uncertainty in self-adaptive systems with plan reuse and stochastic search. In: 13th International Symposium on Software Engineering for Adaptive and Self-Managing Systems, SEAMS 2018, pp. 40–50 (2018)
17. Mann, Z.Á.: Interplay of virtual machine selection and virtual machine placement. In: Aiello, M., Johnsen, E.B., Dustdar, S., Georgievski, I. (eds.) ESOCC 2016. LNCS, vol. 9846, pp. 137–151. Springer, Cham (2016). https://doi.org/10.1007/978-3-319-44482-6_9
18. Mann, Z.Á.: Resource optimization across the cloud stack. IEEE Trans. Parallel Distrib. Syst. **29**(1), 169–182 (2018)
19. Metzger, A., Bayer, A., Doyle, D., Molzam Sharifloo, A., Pohl, K., Wessling, F.: Coordinated run-time adaptation of variability-intensive systems: An application in cloud computing. In: 1st International Workshop on Variability and Complexity in Software Design, VACE 2016 (2016)
20. Metzger, A., Di Nitto, E.: Addressing highly dynamic changes in service-oriented systems: Towards agile evolution and adaptation. In: Agile and Lean Service-Oriented Development: Foundations, Theory and Practice, pp. 33–46 (2012)
21. Metzger, A., Pohl, K.: Software product line engineering and variability management: achievements and challenges. In: Future of Software Engineering, FOSE 2014, pp. 70–84 (2014)
22. Moustafa, A., Zhang, M.: Learning efficient compositions for QoS-aware service provisioning. In: IEEE International Conference on Web Services, ICWS 2014, pp. 185–192 (2014)
23. Nachum, O., Norouzi, M., Xu, K., Schuurmans, D.: Bridging the gap between value and policy based reinforcement learning. In: Advances in Neural Information Processing Systems 12 (NIPS 2017), pp. 2772–2782 (2017)
24. Palm, A., Metzger, A., Pohl, K.: Online reinforcement learning for self-adaptive information systems. In: Yu, E., Dustdar, S. (eds.) International Conference on Advanced Information Systems Engineering, CAiSE 2020 (2020)
25. Papazoglou, M.P.: The challenges of service evolution. In: 20th International Conference on Advanced Information Systems Engineering, CAiSE 2008, pp. 1–15 (2008)
26. Plappert, M., et al.: Parameter space noise for exploration. In: 6th International Conference on Learning Representations, ICLR 2018, OpenReview.net (2018)
27. Ramirez, A.J., Cheng, B.H.C., McKinley, P.K., Beckmann, B.E.: Automatically generating adaptive logic to balance non-functional tradeoffs during reconfiguration. In: 7th International Conference on Autonomic Computing, ICAC 2010, pp. 225–234 (2010)
28. Salehie, M., Tahvildari, L.: Self-adaptive software: landscape and research challenges. TAAS **4**(2), 1–42 (2009)
29. Sharifloo, A.M., Metzger, A., Quinton, C., Baresi, L., Pohl, K.: Learning and evolution in dynamic software product lines. In: 11th International Symposium on Software Engineering for Adaptive and Self-Managing Systems, SEAMS 2016, pp. 158–164 (2016)

30. Siegmund, N., Grebhahn, A., Apel, S., Kästner, C.: Performance-influence Models for Highly Configurable Systems. In: Proceedings of the 2015 10th Joint Meeting on Foundations of Software Engineering, ESEC/FSE 2015, pp. 284–294. ACM, New York (2015)
31. Sutton, R.S., Barto, A.G.: Reinforcement Learning: An Introduction, 2nd edn. MIT Press, Cambridge (2018)
32. Taylor, M.E., Stone, P.: Transfer learning for reinforcement learning domains: a survey. J. Mach. Learn. Res. **10**, 1633–1685 (2009)
33. Tesauro, G., Jong, N.K., Das, R., Bennani, M.N.: On the use of hybrid reinforcement learning for autonomic resource allocation. Cluster Comput. **10**(3), 287–299 (2007)
34. Thüm, T., Batory, D., Kastner, C.: Reasoning about edits to feature models. In: 31st International Conference on Software Engineering, ICSE 2009, pp. 254–264 (2009)
35. Thüm, T., Kästner, C., Benduhn, F., Meinicke, J., Saake, G., Leich, T.: FeatureIDE: an extensible framework for feature-oriented software development. Sci. Comput. Program. **79**, 70–85 (2014)
36. Thüm, T., Kästner, C., Erdweg, S., Siegmund, N.: Abstract features in feature modeling. In: 15th International Conference on Software Product Lines, SPLC 2011, pp. 191–200 (2011)
37. Van Der Donckt, J., Weyns, D., Quin, F., Van Der Donckt, J., Michiels, S.: Applying deep learning to reduce large adaptation spaces of self-adaptive systems with multiple types of goals. In: 15th International Symposium on Software Engineering for Adaptive and Self-Managing Systems, SEAMS 2020. ACM (2020)
38. Wang, H., Gu, M., Yu, Q., Fei, H., Li, J., Tao, Y.: Large-scale and adaptive service composition using deep reinforcement learning. In: 15th Intl Conference on Service-Oriented Computing (ICSOC 2017), pp. 383–391 (2017)
39. Xu, C., Rao, J., Bu, X.: URL: A unified reinforcement learning approach for autonomic cloud management. J. Parallel Distrib. Comput. **72**(2), 95–105 (2012)
40. Zhao, T., Zhang, W., Zhao, H., Jin, Z.: A reinforcement learning-based framework for the generation and evolution of adaptation rules. In: International Conference on Autonomic Computing, ICAC 2017, pp. 103–112 (2017)

FAST: A Fairness Assured Service Recommendation Strategy Considering Service Capacity Constraint

Yao Wu[1], Jian Cao[1(✉)], and Guandong Xu[2]

[1] Shanghai Jiao Tong University, Shanghai, China
{wuyaoericyy,cao-jian}@sjtu.edu.cn
[2] University of Technology Sydney, Sydney, NSW, Australia
Guandong.Xu@uts.edu.au

Abstract. An excessive number of customers often leads to a degradation in service quality. However, the capacity constraints of services are ignored by recommender systems, which may lead to unsatisfactory recommendation. This problem can be solved by limiting the number of users who receive the recommendation for a service, but this may be viewed as unfair. In this paper, we propose a novel metric *Top-N Fairness* to measure the *individual fairness* of multi-round recommendations of services with capacity constraints. By considering the fact that users are often only affected by top-ranked items in a recommendation, *Top-N Fairness* only considers a sub-list consisting of top N services. Based on the metric, we design *FAST*, a *F*airness *A*ssured service recommendation *ST*rategy. *FAST* adjusts the original recommendation list to provide users with recommendation results that guarantee the long-term fairness of multi-round recommendations. We prove the convergence property of the variance of *Top-N Fairness* of *FAST* theoretically. *FAST* is tested on the Yelp dataset and synthetic datasets. The experimental results show that *FAST* achieves better recommendation fairness while still maintaining high recommendation quality.

Keywords: Fairness · Service recommendation · Capacity constraints

1 Introduction

In service recommendation, a user's degree of satisfaction with an item is affected by many factors. *Capacity constraints*, which affect many service recommendation scenarios like dining, accommodation, fitness, haircuts, massages, medical services and so on, is a special factor that decides how many customers can receive a service with an assured level of quality. For example, a restaurant often has a capacity constraint on the number of customers who can be served during their dining hours. If too many customers arrive at a restaurant, their dining experience will be unpleasant or in the worst case, some customers will be very disappointed. However, recommender systems make recommendations

© Springer Nature Switzerland AG 2020
E. Kafeza et al. (Eds.): ICSOC 2020, LNCS 12571, pp. 287–303, 2020.
https://doi.org/10.1007/978-3-030-65310-1_21

to customers which only align with their preferences, and this may lead to dissatisfaction.

The solution of previous studies about recommendation with capacity constraint was to recommend the service to a limited number of users, or to penalize the service's relevant score when the recommended users exceeded the service's capacity [9], making it less likely to be recommended. But such an approach brings a new problem, namely it is unfair to those users who may also like this restaurant according to their preference information.

Fairness is already a concern in recommendation algorithm design [22]. At present, the research on recommendation fairness mainly considers *group fairness* [25], trying to eliminate the influence of specific group attributes on the recommendation results, or removing the difference in recommendation results between groups caused by data bias, such as ensuring that gender or nationality does not affect the recommended results. Unlike these studies, the fairness we consider here is *individual fairness* [24], which ensures the same quality of recommendation for different users when capacity constraints are considered. To the best of our knowledge, we are the first to formalize the fairness ensured recommendation problem for services with capacity constraints. The contributions of this paper are as follows:

- We propose a metric *Top-N Fairness* to measure the fairness of recommendation under capacity constraint.
- We design a strategy named *FAST* (*F*airness *A*ssured service recommendation *ST*rategy) to ensure the long-term fairness of multi-round recommendations. We also prove the convergence property of the variance of *Top-N Fairness* of *FAST* theoretically.
- Experiment results on a real-world dataset and synthetic datasets show *FAST* can achieve higher fairness compared with baseline methods while still preserving high recommendation quality.

The rest of the paper is organized as follows. Section 2 discusses the related work. Section 3 formalizes the fairness assured multi-round recommendation problem for services with capacity constraints. Section 4 presents the fairness assured service recommendation strategy. The experiment results are illustrated in Sect. 5. We conclude the paper in Sect. 6.

2   Related Work

Many researchers have begun to focus on metrics other than recommendation accuracy to measure the performance of recommender systems [10,19], and fairness is one of the important metrics.

Currently, the research on fairness in recommender system can be roughly divided into two categories: *group fairness* and *individual fairness*. Ensuring *group fairness* requires that the attributes of a specific group will not affect the recommendation results so the disadvantaged group can be given the same opportunities as the superior group [3,4,23,25,26]. Geyik et al. [11] proposed a re-ranking algorithm that reorders the results based on the recommended scores so that the distribution of the results meets the proportion of specific parameters; and Bose et al. [6] tried to remove information about protected sensitive attributes in graph embedding by learning a series of adversarial filters. These approaches designed to ensure *group fairness* usually can only guarantee fair treatment in terms of one or a few attributes. However, when fairness in terms of some attributes is guaranteed, the unfairness related to other attributes may not be avoidable.

Our approach focuses on the *individual fairness* level, which has been considered by very few researchers. This metric puts emphasis on the view that similar users should be treated similarly [5,11]. Rastegarpanah et al. [21] improved fairness by generating antidote data. The *individual fairness* to be maintained by the recommender system in their work was inspired by [24], and is defined as the equality of users' prediction accuracies. Our definition of *individual fairness* is similar to theirs, but our interpretation of equal quality is different, which is the extent to which the final recommendation results considering fairness match the initial recommendation results considering a user's preference should be equal between users.

Some research classifies approaches considering fairness from other perspectives. [7] divided fairness-related criteria into consumers (C-fairness), providers (P-fairness) [17,20], and both (CP-fairness) [18] according to the stakeholders that systems consider; [24] classified approaches from the perspective of the time that the mechanism works in the system, and divided the fairness mechanism into pre-processing [8,14], in-processing [2,6] and post-processing [15,16] approaches. Our study considers consumer fairness and proposes a post-processing approach that further processes the existing recommendation results to obtain results that ensure individual fairness.

3   Fairness Assured Multi-round Recommendation Problem for Services with Capacity Constraints

We suppose that there is a conventional recommendation algorithm in the system, which provides a predicted rating matrix R and the original recommendation lists L for all users based on R. If we push L directly to users, there is a high possibility that it will break the capacity constraints C of services. To solve this problem, we design a strategy to adjust L and generate new recommendation lists L^T which can make recommendations as fair as possible without breaking capacity constraints while still preserving recommendation quality.

3.1   Notations

We use the following notations:

- $S = \{s_1, s_2, ..., s_m\}$ is a set of recommended services.
- $C = \{c_1, c_2, ..., c_m\}$ is a set of services' capacity constraints.

- $U = \{u_1, u_2, ..., u_n\}$ is a set of users.
- $R = [r_{1,1}, r_{1,2}, ..., r_{n,m}]$ is a relevant rating matrix produced by the original recommendation algorithm of the system.
- $L = \{l_1, l_2, ..., l_n\}$ is a set of original recommendation lists based on R.
- $L^T = \{l_1^T, l_2^T, ..., l_n^T\}$ is a set of recommendation lists finally outputted to users in the Tth round recommendation.
- δ_i^T is a variable to indicate whether user u_i uses the recommender system in the Tth recommendation or not, where $\delta_i^T = 1$ denotes yes and $\delta_i^T = 0$ denotes no.

3.2 Capacity Constraints

We suppose each recommended service s_j has a capacity constraint c_j. When there are multiple customer channels for a service, we only consider customers from the recommender system under discussion, as do the capacity constraints. In order to simplify the representation, unless otherwise specified, the capacity constraint of a service in our paper refers to the limited number of users to whom the recommendation system can recommend this service. This data can be obtained by dividing the allowed service capacity for the recommender system by the conversion rate of recommendation, which is the attendance ratio of users who are recommended a service.

3.3 Recommendations on Top-N Services

In practice, the recommendation results are shown in a limited space, such as web pages or APPs. Although longer lists can be shown to customers by pagination, research on user behaviors shows that most users only look at a few results before deciding, and they are more likely to notice highly ranked results [12]. According to some reports, even an item at position 5 is largely ignored [13]. Therefore, we choose to ignore the influence of services in lower positions. To be more specific, we only consider the influence of a service's capacity constraint or a user's fairness when this service appears in the user's original top-N service recommendation list.

We denote the sub-list of the top N services of user u_i's original recommendation list as $l(N)_i$. At the same time, for each recommended service s_j, users whose $l(N)_i$ include s_j are denoted as a user set U_j, and the number of users in U_j is often greater than the capacity constraint of s_j.

3.4 Measuring the Fairness of Recommendations

Based on intuition, we divide the fairness status of a recommender system into three levels, and the fairness metric we design should be able to express these three levels of fairness:

1. *Perfect Fair Status*: At this level, every service in a user's recommendation list is fairly recommended. Each user reaches an absolutely fair status on

every service in his recommendation list and also an absolutely fair status of the whole top-N service recommendation list.

2. *Individual Level Fair Status*: Each service is not necessarily allocated fairly, but each user can reach a fair status according to the top-N service recommendation list. In this case, a user may lose the chance of being allocated some services in his recommendation list, but he has more chance than the others on other services, and the summation of the fairness degree on the top-N service recommendation list offsets these deviations against each other, thereby achieving a fair status at an individual level.

3. *Relatively Fair Status*: The system cannot ensure that every user reaches an absolutely fair status, but the degree of unfairness among the users is the same, thus achieving a relatively fair status at an individual level.

Obviously, for a single round recommendation, it is unlikely to ensure fairness for all users due to capacity constraints. Instead, we measure the long-term fairness in the multi-round recommendation process in which users' fairness can accumulate over recommendations. We define two kinds of appearance probabilities of service to measure the chance of a service being allocated to users.

Definition 1 (Overall Appearance Probability). *The probability of a service s_j appearing in the recommendation lists of all users in U_j up to T^{th} round recommendation is:*

$$p_j^T = \frac{\sum_{u_i \in U_j} \sum_{t=0}^{T} \delta_i^t \cdot In\_tn(s_j, l_i^t, N)}{\sum_{u_i \in U_j} \sum_{t=0}^{T} \delta_i^t} \tag{1}$$

$$In\_tn(s_j, list, N) = \begin{cases} 0 \text{ if } s_j \text{ is not in the top } N \text{ sub-list of } list \\ 1 \text{ if } s_j \text{ is in the top } N \text{ sub-list of } list \end{cases} \tag{2}$$

Definition 2 (Actual Appearance Probability). *The probability of a service s_j appearing in the recommendation lists of user u_i up to T^{th} round recommendation is:*

$$p_{i,j}^T = \frac{\sum_{t=0}^{T} \delta_i^t \cdot In\_tn(s_j, l_i^t, N)}{\sum_{t=0}^{T} \delta_i^t} \tag{3}$$

If u_i receives a fair recommendation on s_j, the *Actual Appearance Probability* of s_j to u_i should be equal to the *Overall Appearance Probability* of s_j. Thus, the difference between the above two appearance probability values represents the fairness degree of user u_i on service s_j. Furthermore, we divide the difference by *Overall Appearance Probability* to smooth the difference in capacity conflicts between different services and obtain the following definition:

Definition 3 (Service Fairness Degree). *Fairness degree of user u_i on service s_j up to T^{th} round recommendation:*

$$F_{i,j}^T = \frac{p_{i,j}^T - p_j^T}{p_j^T} \tag{4}$$

If $F_{i,j}^T$ is greater than zero, it means u_i is allocated to service s_j more frequently than the others in U_j; If $F_{i,j}^T$ is less than zero, service s_j appears in his
recommendation lists with fewer opportunities than the others; If $F_{i,j}^T$ is equal
to zero, it means u_i receives a fair recommendation for s_j. At the same time,
we can add the service fairness degrees of all the services in user's $l(N)_i$ list and
obtain the overall fairness degree at an individual level. We call it the fairness
degree of Top-N recommendation(or *Top-N Fairness* for short):

Definition 4 (Top-N Fairness). *Overall fairness degree of user u_i up to T^{th}
round recommendation:*

$$F_i^T = \sum_{s_j \in l(N)_i} F_{i,j}^T \tag{5}$$

With the measurement of fairness, we can represent three levels of fairness
in a formalized way:

1. *Perfect Fair Status:* $\forall u_i \in U$ and $\forall s_j \in l(N)_i$, $F_{i,j}^T = 0$.
2. *Individual Level Fair Status:* $\forall u_i \in U, F_i^T = 0$.
3. *Relatively Fair Status:* $\forall u_i, u_j \in U, F_i^T = F_j^T$.

These three fairness statuses share the same feature, the variance of *Top-N
fairness* among users is equal to zero. Therefore, we use the **variance among
users' Top-N Fairness** $D(F_i^T)$ as a measure of the fairness of recommender
systems, where the smaller the variance, the fairer the recommender system.

3.5   Quality of Recommendations

When the original recommendation lists L are adjusted to generate new recommendation lists L^T, those services whose capacity is constrained are removed
from the list, hence the recommendation list cannot fully meet the users' preferences, and the quality of the recommendation list decreases.

Following the idea in Sect. 3.3, we only consider the quality of $l(N)_i$. In the
new list l_i^T, quality declines when a service is removed, and we use the predicted
rating score of the service as a measure of the degree of decline. Therefore, the
quality of a new recommendation list l_i^T will be the sum of the rating scores of
all the services belonging to $l(N)_i$ and l_i^T at the same time. Taking into account
that users may have different rating habits, i.e., some users like to give positive
reviews while others prefer bad reviews, we use the highest rating of $l(N)_i$ as the
denominator to normalize the quality score. Moreover, the positions of services
in the recommendation lists also reflect their importance to a user. The quality
measurement can be extended by giving each service a logarithmic discount
based on its position in $l(N)_i$. The quality of the recommendation lists of the
entire system can be obtained by adding the recommendation list quality of each
user.

Definition 5 (Quality of Recommendation List). *Quality of outputted recommendation list l_i^T of user u_i on T^{th} round recommendation:*

$$q_i^T = \frac{\sum_{s_j \in l(N)_i \cap l(N)_i^t} \frac{r_{i,j}}{\log_2(p_{i,j}^T + 1)}}{r_{i,l(N)_i[0]}} \tag{6}$$

where $l(N)_i[0]$ represents the subscript index of the service appearing at the top position of $l(N)_i$, and $p_{i,j}^T$ is the position of service s_j in $l(N)_i$.

Our problem is to generate L^t based on a strategy so that the capacity constraint will not be violated while the fairness of the recommendation quality of each user can be assured along with an increase in recommendation times.

4 A Fairness Assured Service Recommendation Strategy

When only fairness is considered, the problem can be reduced to a Knapsack problem which has been proven to be a non-deterministic polynomial complete problem. We analogize the capacity constraint of services as the capacity of the knapsack, the users' recommendation lists as the items put in the knapsack, and fairness as the objective. When further taking the quality of recommendation lists into consideration, the problem becomes more complicated. So we choose heuristic strategies to solve the problem.

In practical applications, service recommendations can be divided into two scenarios. The first is service recommendation for a fixed user set where the list of users receiving recommendations remains basically unchanged for a period of time, like an active advertising push, recommendations for members, high-end service recommendations, etc. This ensures the recommendation process in a stable environment, and the fairness of users is fully accumulated. The second is for a dynamic user set in which not all users receive recommendations each round or new users join, like recommendations for dining, movies to watch, medical services, etc. By considering the above situations, we design two versions of *FAST*, *F-FAST* for a fixed user set and *D-FAST* for a dynamic user set.

4.1 Fairness Assured Service Recommendation Strategy for a Fixed User Set - *F-FAST*

In order for users to reach a fair state as soon as possible, users with lower *Top-N Fairness* should get more opportunities than users with higher *Top-N Fairness*. Under the premise of limited service capacity, we preferentially meet the needs of recommendation list for users with lower *Top-N Fairness*. To maintain a high level of recommendation list quality, when adjusting the original recommendation list L, we choose not to change the order of services in the list, and only delete from the list several services with insufficient capacity, and keep higher ranked services. Based on the above ideas, we design a heuristic algorithm based on greedy ideas.

The algorithm works as follows. Users are sorted according to their *Top-N Fairness* from the lowest to the highest. The user with the lowest *Top-N Fairness* will be recommended first. For a user u_i, a service with the highest rating score in $l(N)_i$ will be recommended as long as its capacity is still sufficient. If a service reaches its capacity constraint, the next best service in $l(N)_i$ will be recommended. After a service is recommended, the user's *Top-N Fairness* and the capacity of the recommended service are updated. Then all users' *Top-N Fairness* are sorted from the lowest to the highest again, and the next service is recommended in turn. This process ends when an attempt has been made to recommend every service in all users' $l(N)_i$ (regardless of whether they are actually recommended to the user or not) or the capacities of all services have been exhausted. Finally, the algorithm fills the remaining empty positions in each user's recommendation list with services whose positions are larger than N in his original list l_i in sequence. The pseudo-code of *F-FAST* is shown in Algorithm 1.

Algorithm 1. Fairness Assured Service Recommendation Algorithm for A Fixed User Set

---

Input: N: Parameter Top-N;
    $l_1, l_2,..., l_n$: Original recommendation list of n users;
    $l(N)_1, l(N)_2,..., l(N)_n$: Original top-$N$ recommendation list of n users;
    R: Rating matrix;
    $c_1, c_2,..., c_m$: Capacity constraints of m services;
    $U_1, U_2,..., U_m$: U_j list of m services;
    $F_1^{T-1}, F_2^{T-1},..., F_n^{T-1}$: *Top-N Fairness* of n users up to last recommendation.
Output: $l_1^T, l_2^T,..., l_n^T$: Recommendation list for n users in T^{th} round;
1: **for** $time = 0 \rightarrow n \times N - 1$ **do**
2:    Sort users according to F_i^{T-1} from lowest to highest
3:    $rec\_user \leftarrow$ user with the lowest F_i^{T-1}
4:    **for** s_j in $l(N)_{rec\_user}$ **do**
5:        **if** $c_j > 0$ **then**
6:            insert s_j into $l_{rec\_user}^T$;
7:            $c_j = c_j - 1$;
8:            Update $F_{rec\_user}^{T-1}$;
9:            break;
10:        **end if**
11:    **end for**
12: **end for**
13: Fill l_i^T whose positions are larger than N in l_i in sequence;
14: **return** $l_1^T, l_2^T,..., l_n^T$;

F-FAST also has three properties, and for the relevant proofs of **THEOREM 1,2** refer to Appendix A.

Theorem 1. *The sum of Top-N Fairness of all the users in each round is equal to zero,* $\sum_{u_i \in U} F_i^T = 0$.

Theorem 2. *Variance among Top-N fairness of all users $D(F_i^T)$ converges to 0 with the recommended round T.*

Theorem 3. *The system can reach the Individual Level Fair Status,* $\forall u_i \in U, F_i^T = 0$.

Theorem 1 indicates that the sum of *Top-N Fairness* is stable, and Theorem 2 indicates *F-FAST* can ensure long-term fairness for multi-round recommendations. By combining Theorem 1 and Theorem 2, we can conclude that F_i^T of each user in the system will eventually converge to 0, so that the system can reach the *Individual Level Fair Status* which is Theorem 3.

4.2 Fairness Assured Service Recommendation Strategy for a Dynamic User Set - *D-FAST*

D-FAST is applied to the situation where the user set receiving recommendations changes from time to time. In this situation, we cannot guarantee the validity of Theorem 1. The average fairness of users receiving recommendations is different in each round, which leads to changes in the baseline of *Top-N Fairness*.

Therefore, before generating the recommendation lists, the user's *Top-N Fairness* needs to be calculated again to make up for the baseline change. The strategy works as follows: the average *Top-N Fairness* of users is recorded after each round, and at the beginning of a new round, the user's *Top-N Fairness* is updated by adding the difference between the average *Top-N Fairness* in his last round and the average *Top-N Fairness* in this round. In addition, for a new user, his *Top-N Fairness* and the average *Top-N Fairness* of the last round will both be set to zero. The remaining operations are the same as Algorithm 1.

4.3 Time Complexity

The time complexity of *F-FAST* is analyzed as follows. When recommending a service, *F-FAST* first sorts users according to their *Top-N Fairness*. The complexity of sorting n users will be $O(nlog(n))$ when using the Quick Sort Algorithm or the Merge Sort Algorithm. Then *F-FAST* recommends a service to the user with the lowest *Top-N Fairness*. These are operations with a single instruction, so the complexity of recommending an item is $O(nlog(n)+1)$. In a round of recommendations, we need to recommend a maximum of $n \times N$ services, where N is a small constant. So, in a round of recommendations, the worst case time complexity of *F-FAST* is $O(n^2log(n))$.

There is only one additional step for *D-FAST* which is at the beginning of each round, that is, to update the *Top-N Fairness* of all users, and its time complexity is also $O(n^2log(n))$.

5 Experiments

Datasets and Metrics. We conduct experiments on a real-world dataset and a synthetic datasets. Our code and datasets are released on Zenodo[1].

Yelp Dataset. The data is provided by the Yelp Dataset Challenge [1]. We select two cities with the largest number of businesses, i.e., Phoenix and Toronto. After

---

[1] https://zenodo.org/record/3661863#.XkJGb2gzZPY.

filtering out users less than 10 reviews and businesses less than 30 reviews, we obtain the dataset for Phoenix, which contains 11,252 users, 3774 businesses and 194,188 reviews. The Toronto dataset contains 8867 users, 3,505 businesses, and 1,190,64 reviews.

Synthetic Datasets. We generate synthetic datasets to test the performance of the algorithms under different parameter settings. For this purpose, we generate 4 synthetic datasets with different situations of capacity conflicts when N is set to 5:

- *Very Popular Services*: the number of users in U_j is more than 2 times its capacity.
- *Popular Services*: the number of users in U_j is 1–2 times its capacity.
- *Ordinary Services*: the number of users in U_j is 0.9–1.0 times its capacity.
- *Unpopular Services*: the number of users in U_j is 0.9 times its capacity.

The capacity of each service is a random number from 50 to 100. Each dataset contains 800 users and 50 services.

Metrics. We measure the total quality of the recommendations of each user and the variance of the *Top-N Fairness* of all users at the same time.

5.1   Compared Approaches

This is the first time that the fairness assured multi-round recommendation problem for services with capacity constraints is defined and there is no existing algorithm for this problem. Thus, we compare our approach against the following three baseline methods.

Integer Linear Programming. We use Integer Linear Programming (ILP) to maximize the quality of recommendations. We take the capacity constraints as the limitations and the quality of recommendations as the target.

Greedy Algorithm to Maximize Quality of Recommendation. The size of the problem that can be solved by ILP is limited, so when processing the Yelp dataset, we replace the ILP method with a greedy heuristic algorithm. The idea of the algorithm is to recommend services that ensure the best quality of recommendation each time as long as the capacity constraint of a service is not violated.

Random Strategy. For a service s_j, we randomly select a number of users which equals s_j's capacity constraint from its U_j list in each round. Obviously, this strategy can also ensure the *Top-N Fairness* in the long run.

5.2   Results on Yelp Dataset

We perform 50 rounds of recommendations on a fixed user set on the Yelp dataset. Since recommendations are pushed to a fixed user set, *F-FAST* is executed to generate the recommendations. In this experiment, we set N to 5, and Fig. 1 shows the results.

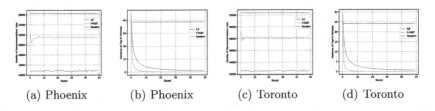

| (a) Phoenix | (b) Phoenix | (c) Toronto | (d) Toronto |

Fig. 1. Quality of recommendation and variance of *Top-N Fairness* on Yelp dataset

From the figure, we can draw two conclusions. First, *F-FAST* makes the system reach a relatively balanced state (variance of *Top-N Fairness* approaches zero) faster, and the degree of fairness is also the highest. Although the random strategy can also achieve a relatively fair situation, compared to *F-FAST*, the speed at which it arrives at a stable status of fairness is much slower. Second, regarding recommendation quality, *F-FAST* has a small loss while the random strategy leads to significant losses. *F-FAST* loses 7% of recommendation quality compared with the ILP method but it is nearly 20% higher than the random strategy.

5.3 Results on Synthetic Datasets

Comparisons Between Different Levels of Capacity Constraints. We conduct 100 rounds of recommendations on a fixed user set on four synthetic datasets. In four groups of experiments, N is uniformly set to 5, and results are shown in Fig. 2. It can be seen from Figs. 2a, b, c and d that as capacity conflict being more intense, the quality of recommendations tends to decrease. The reason for this is when capacity conflict becomes more intense, users have less chances of being assigned one of the top-N services in his original list, which in turn leads to a decrease in quality. Figures 2e, f, g and h show that as the capacity conflicts become more intense, the total fairness of ILP and the random strategy basically show a downward trend, while the *F-FAST* is not affected by the intensity of capacity conflicts. At the same time, *F-FAST* arrives at a stable status of fairness faster than the random strategy in all scenarios.

Comparisons Between Different N. Figure 3 shows the performance of algorithms under different N. This experiment is performed on **Synthetic Dataset 2** under the premise of users being fixed, and a total of 100 rounds of recommendations are carried out for each experiment.

As can be seen from the figures, as N rises, the overall recommendation quality improves, but the rate of growth continues to decrease. It is worth noting that when N is greater than 10, the quality of ILP and *F-FAST* virtually does not increase and the quality of the random strategy even starts to decline. The reason for this is the impacts of the services in the lower positions in the original recommendation list is smaller. It can be noted that as N rises, the variance of *Top-N Fairness* rises instead. This shows that for *F-FAST*, a longer top-N

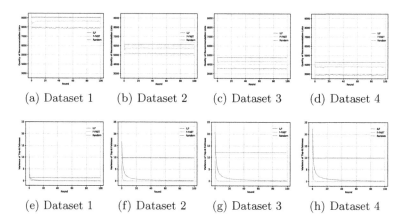

Fig. 2. Recommendation quality and variance of *Top-N Fairness* under different levels of capacity constraints

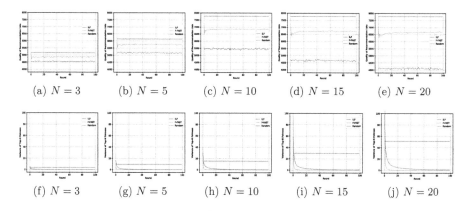

Fig. 3. Recommendation quality and variance of *Top-N Fairness* under different N

recommendation list will be of benefit to recommendation quality but will impair fairness.

Comparisons Between Different Degrees of User Dynamics. We simulate the performance of the algorithms under different user dynamics by changing the proportion of recommended users in each round. Figures 4 shows the results of the experiment on **Synthetic Dataset 2**.

It can be seen that both *F-FAST* and *D-FAST* perform very well on the dynamic user set with little loss of recommendation quality, and the variance of *Top-N Fairness* is still close to zero. It is worth noting that *D-FAST* can achieve lower fairness variance and higher recommendation quality than *F-FAST*, which validates the measure of updating the *Top-N Fairness* of each user according to their actual situations in *D-FAST* which indeed improves the performance.

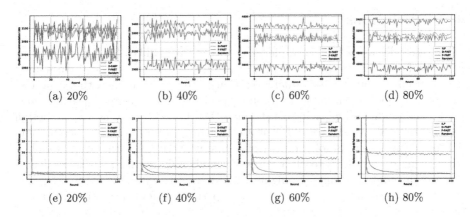

| (a) 20% | (b) 40% | (c) 60% | (d) 80% |

| (e) 20% | (f) 40% | (g) 60% | (h) 80% |

Fig. 4. Recommendation quality and variance of *Top-N Fairness* under different degrees of user dynamics

Fairness of New Users. We compare how quickly the approaches can ensure a new user reaches a relatively fair state. We add a new user to a stable recommendation environment on **Synthetic Dataset 2** after 100 rounds of recommendations. We apply these four methods to the new recommendation environment after adding a new user, and compare the performance of the four methods on the *Top-N Fairness* of the new user. The results are shown in Fig. 5. Since the user set remains the same after adding new users, the process and results of *F-FAST* and *D-FAST* are the same, so we only show the results of *D-FAST*.

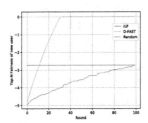

Fig. 5. Trend of *Top-N Fairness* for a new user

As can be seen, *D-FAST* ensures the new user reaches a relatively fair state (*Top-N Fairness* being close to 0) in about 30 rounds of recommendation and this status is maintained. In contrast, although the random strategy can also ensure the *Top-N Fairness* of a new user continues to approach 0, it is much slower. The ILP method cannot improve the fairness of new users.

6   Conclusions

This paper discusses the contradiction between the quality of recommendations and the fairness of users under the constraints of service capacity. We mainly consider fairness at the individual level, that is, to provide users with recommendations of equal quality, and propose a novel fairness measure *Top-N Fairness* under the premise of capacity constraints. Based on this new metric, we design two heuristic algorithms for different user situations to resolve the contradiction. Through theoretical proofs and experiments, we verify that the proposed algorithms can ensure users reach a fair state while only sacrificing a small degree of recommendation quality. Going ahead, We want to extend individual fairness to group fairness and carry out relevant experimental and theoretical research.

Acknowledgement. This work is partially supported by National Key Research and Development Plan (No. 2018YFB1003800).

A   Properties of *F-FAST*

THEOREM 1. *The sum of Top-N Fairness of all the users in each round is equal to zero,* $\sum_{u_i \in U} F_i^T = 0$.

PROOF. According to Eq. (4), the sum of *Top-N Fairness* can be formulated as:

$$\sum_{u_i \in U} F_i^T = \sum_{u_i \in U} \sum_{s_j \in l(N)_i} \frac{p_{i,j}^T - p_j^T}{p_j^T} = \sum_{s_j \in S} \sum_{u_i \in U_j} \frac{p_{i,j}^t - p_j^T}{p_j^T} \tag{7}$$

Since all users will receive recommendations in every round, δ_i^t will all be equal to 1, and according to Eq. (1) and Eq. (3), p_j^T and $p_{i,j}^t$ can be re-expressed as:

$$p_j^T = \frac{\sum_{u_i \in U_j} \sum_{t=0}^{T} In\_tn(s_j, l_i^t, N)}{\sum_{u_i \in U_j} T}, p_{i,j}^T = \frac{\sum_{t=0}^{T} In\_tn(s_j, l_i^t, N)}{T} \tag{8}$$

Then the sum of *Top-N Fairness* will be:

$$\sum_{u_i \in U} F_i^T = \sum_{s_j \in S} \sum_{u_i \in U_j} \frac{\frac{\sum_{t=0}^{T} In\_tn(s_j, l_i^t, N)}{T}}{\frac{\sum_{u_i \in U_j} \sum_{t=0}^{T} In\_tn(s_j, l_i^t, N)}{\sum_{u_i \in U_j} T}} - \sum_{s_j \in S} \sum_{u_i \in U_j} 1 \tag{9}$$

After reducing Eq. (9), we can get:

$$\sum_{u_i \in U} F_i^T = \sum_{s_j \in S} \left(\frac{\sum_{u_i \in U_j} T}{T} - \sum_{u_i \in U_j} 1 \right) = 0 \tag{10}$$

THEOREM 2. *Variance among Top-N fairness of all users* $D(F_i^T)$ *converges to 0 with the recommended round T.*

PROOF. According to **THEOREM 1**, we can get the mean of *Top-N Fairness* of all users equals to zero, and the variance can be formulated as:

$$D(F_i^T) = \frac{\sum_{u_i \in U} \left(F_i^T\right)^2}{n} \tag{11}$$

According to Eq. (4), we know that:

$$\sum_{u_i \in U} \left(F_i^T\right)^2 = \sum_{u_i \in U} \left(\sum_{s_j \in l(N)_i} \frac{p_{i,j}^T - p_j^T}{p_j^T}\right)^2 \tag{12}$$

Since every user receives a recommendation in each round, p_j^T of each service should be a constant. We discuss this issue in the following two cases.

For services without capacity conflicts: $c_j \geqslant len(U_j)$. Each service s_j can be assigned to every user in its U_j in each round. So p_j^T and $p_{i,j}^T$ will always be 1. So the addends in summation formula of *Top-N Fairness* are always equal to 0 and can be ignored in this discussion.

For services with capacity conflicts: $c_j < len(U_j)$. Each service s_j will always be assigned to c_j users, so p_j^T will be a constant less than 1, and we call it $Const_j$:

$$p_j^T = c_j/len(U_i) = Const_j < 1 \tag{13}$$

Then, Eq. (12) will be:

$$\sum_{u_i \in U} \left(F_i^T\right)^2 = \sum_{u_i \in U} \left[\sum_{s_j \in l(N)_i} \left(\frac{p_{i,j}^T}{Const_j} - 1\right)\right]^2 \tag{14}$$

The only variable in Eq. (14) is $p_{i,j}^t$, and according to Eq. (8), we can get:

$$p_{i,j}^{T+1} = \frac{\sum_{t=0}^{T} In\_tn(s_j, l_i^t, N)}{T+1} + \frac{In\_tn(s_j, l_i^{T+1}, N)}{T+1} \tag{15}$$

According to **THEOREM 1**, we can divide users into two groups, users with low *Top-N Fairness*($F_i^T < 0$) and users with high *Top-N Fairness*($F_i^T \geqslant 0$).

For users with low *Top-N Fairness*, addends with $p_{i,j}^T < Const_j$ occupy the main influence factor in the summation formula of *Top-N Fairness* in this situation. As designed in our strategy, users with low *Top-N Fairness* will always be allotted first, that:

$$1 > Const_j > P_{i,j}^{T+1} = \frac{\sum_{t=0}^{T} In\_tn(s_j, l_i^t, N) + 1}{T+1} > \frac{\sum_{t=0}^{T} In\_tn(s_j, l_i^t, N)}{T} = P_{i,j}^T \tag{16}$$

According to Eq. (14), we know that

$$\left|F_i^{T+1}\right| < \left|F_i^T\right|, (F_i^{T+1})^2 < (F_i^T)^2 \tag{17}$$

For users with high *Top-N Fairness*, addends with $P_{i,j}^T \geqslant Const_j$ occupy the main influence factor in the summation formula of *Top-N Fairness* in this situation. Also, according to our recommendation strategy, these users will always be assigned last and will most likely not be assigned under the condition that service capacity is limited, so that:

$$Const_j \leqslant p_{i,j}^{T+1} = \frac{\sum_{t=0}^{T} In\_tn(s_j, l_i^t, N)}{T+1} < \frac{\sum_{t=0}^{T} In\_tn(s_j, l_i^t, N)}{T} = P_{i,j}^T \tag{18}$$

According to Eq. (14), we can also get:

$$\left| F_i^{T+1} \right| < \left| F_i^T \right|, (F_i^{T+1})^2 < (F_i^T)^2 \tag{19}$$

In both cases, $(F_i^T)^2$ becomes smaller as the round of recommendation increases. When a user's F_i^T is not equal to the average F_i^T of users, *F-FAST* will continue to work until F_i^T of all users is equal, and we can get that $D(F_i^T)$ will converge to 0, thus **THEOREM 2** is true.

References

1. Yelp dataset challenges. https://www.yelp.com/dataset/challenge/. Accessed 18 Dec 2019
2. Agarwal, A., Beygelzimer, A., Dudík, M., Langford, J., Wallach, H.: A reductions approach to fair classification. arXiv preprint arXiv:1803.02453 (2018)
3. Asudeh, A., Jagadish, H., Stoyanovich, J., Das, G.: Designing fair ranking schemes. In: Proceedings of the 2019 International Conference on Management of Data, pp. 1259–1276. ACM (2019)
4. Beutel, A., et al.: Fairness in recommendation ranking through pairwise comparisons. arXiv preprint arXiv:1903.00780 (2019)
5. Biega, A.J., Gummadi, K.P., Weikum, G.: Equity of attention: amortizing individual fairness in rankings. In: The 41st International ACM SIGIR Conference on Research & Development in Information Retrieval, pp. 405–414. ACM (2018)
6. Bose, A.J., Hamilton, W.: Compositional fairness constraints for graph embeddings. arXiv preprint arXiv:1905.10674 (2019)
7. Burke, R.: Multisided fairness for recommendation. arXiv preprint arXiv:1707.00093 (2017)
8. Calmon, F., Wei, D., Vinzamuri, B., Ramamurthy, K.N., Varshney, K.R.: Optimized pre-processing for discrimination prevention. In: Advances in Neural Information Processing Systems, pp. 3992–4001 (2017)
9. Christakopoulou, K., Kawale, J., Banerjee, A.: Recommendation with capacity constraints. In: Proceedings of the 2017 ACM on Conference on Information and Knowledge Management, pp. 1439–1448 (2017)
10. Ge, M., Delgado-Battenfeld, C., Jannach, D.: Beyond accuracy: evaluating recommender systems by coverage and serendipity. In: Proceedings of the fourth ACM Conference on Recommender Systems, pp. 257–260. ACM (2010)
11. Geyik, S.C., Ambler, S., Kenthapadi, K.: Fairness-aware ranking in search & recommendation systems with application to linkedin talent search. arXiv preprint arXiv:1905.01989 (2019)

12. Joachims, T., Granka, L., Pan, B., Hembrooke, H., Radlinski, F., Gay, G.: Evaluating the accuracy of implicit feedback from clicks and query reformulations in web search. ACM Trans. Inf. Syst. (TOIS) **25**(2), 7 (2007)

13. Joachims, T., Radlinski, F.: Search engines that learn from implicit feedback. Computer **40**(8), 34–40 (2007)

14. Kamiran, F., Calders, T.: Data preprocessing techniques for classification without discrimination. Knowl. Inf. Syst. **33**(1), 1–33 (2012)

15. Karako, C., Manggala, P.: Using image fairness representations in diversity-based re-ranking for recommendations. In: Adjunct Publication of the 26th Conference on User Modeling, Adaptation and Personalization, pp. 23–28. ACM (2018)

16. Liu, W., Burke, R.: Personalizing fairness-aware re-ranking. arXiv preprint arXiv:1809.02921 (2018)

17. Mehrotra, R., McInerney, J., Bouchard, H., Lalmas, M., Diaz, F.: Towards a fair marketplace: counterfactual evaluation of the trade-off between relevance, fairness & satisfaction in recommendation systems. In: Proceedings of the 27th ACM International Conference on Information and Knowledge Management, pp. 2243–2251 (2018)

18. Patro, G.K., Chakraborty, A., Ganguly, N., Gummadi, K.P.: Incremental fairness in two-sided market platforms: on smoothly updating recommendations. In: AAAI, February 2020

19. Pu, P., Chen, L., Hu, R.: A user-centric evaluation framework for recommender systems. In: Proceedings of the Fifth ACM Conference on Recommender Systems, pp. 157–164. ACM (2011)

20. Qian, S., Cao, J., Mouël, F.L., Sahel, I., Li, M.: SCRAM: a sharing considered route assignment mechanism for fair taxi route recommendations. In: Proceedings of the 21th ACM SIGKDD International Conference on Knowledge Discovery and Data Mining, pp. 955–964 (2015)

21. Rastegarpanah, B., Gummadi, K.P., Crovella, M.: Fighting fire with fire: using antidote data to improve polarization and fairness of recommender systems. In: Proceedings of the Twelfth ACM International Conference on Web Search and Data Mining, pp. 231–239. ACM (2019)

22. Stratigi, M., Kondylakis, H., Stefanidis, K.: Fairness in group recommendations in the health domain. In: 2017 IEEE 33rd International Conference on Data Engineering (ICDE), pp. 1481–1488. IEEE (2017)

23. Yao, S., Huang, B.: Beyond parity: fairness objectives for collaborative filtering. In: Advances in Neural Information Processing Systems, pp. 2921–2930 (2017)

24. Zafar, M.B., Valera, I., Gomez Rodriguez, M., Gummadi, K.P.: Fairness beyond disparate treatment & disparate impact: learning classification without disparate mistreatment. In: Proceedings of the 26th International Conference on World Wide Web, pp. 1171–1180. International World Wide Web Conferences Steering Committee (2017)

25. Zehlike, M., Bonchi, F., Castillo, C., Hajian, S., Megahed, M., Baeza-Yates, R.: FA* IR: a fair top-k ranking algorithm. In: Proceedings of the 2017 ACM on Conference on Information and Knowledge Management, pp. 1569–1578. ACM (2017)

26. Zhu, Q., Zhou, A., Sun, Q., Wang, S., Yang, F.: FMSR: a fairness-aware mobile service recommendation method. In: 2018 IEEE International Conference on Web Services (ICWS), pp. 171–178. IEEE (2018)

Real-Time Automatic Configuration Tuning for Smart Manufacturing with Federated Deep Learning

Yilei Zhang[1,2]([⊠]), Xinyuan Li[1], and Peiyun Zhang[1]

[1] Anhui Normal University, Wuhu, China
stonezyl@gmail.com, {zx95,zpyanu}@mail.ahnu.edu.cn
[2] The Chinese University of Hong Kong, Hong Kong, China

Abstract. Manufacturing systems contain a large number of parameters, and a proper configuration of parameters is very important to ensure the stability of product quality. Traditional configuration methods rely heavily on manual tuning, which is labor-intensive, time-consuming, and poor performance. In this paper, we propose to build deep learning models on the vast amount of industrial data collected by IIoT devices for automatic configuration tuning. In order to address key challenges such as high data redundancy, limited device capacity, latency-sensitivity, and system heterogeneity, we propose a two-level federated deep learning framework. We first extract representative features from redundant data, and reduce network traffic and latency through joint training on plants and the cloud. Timely configuration tuning is made through local models of plants, and the tuning accuracy is improved through the global model in the cloud. We have deployed and evaluated the performance of the proposed model in real-world smart manufacturing systems, and the experimental results confirm its effectiveness.

Keywords: Configuration tuning · Smart manufacturing · Industrial Internet of Things · Deep learning · Federated learning

1 Introduction

With the recent advancements in Internet of Things (IoT) technology, the manufacturing industry is evolving from conventional automated manufacturing to smart manufacturing. Under this new paradigm, Industrial Internet of Things (IIoT) becomes an critical technology which connects a massive number of manufacturing IoT devices (e.g., sensors, actuators, controller, robots, machines, etc.) in production lines and manufacturing processes with computing platforms (e.g., edge nodes, cloud servers, etc.) through communication links [21]. The continuously monitoring, measurement and sensing of IoT devices produces unprecedented volume of industrial data, which has the following characteristics: high volume, high heterogeneity, high redundancy, high velocity, and high value. The

© Springer Nature Switzerland AG 2020
E. Kafeza et al. (Eds.): ICSOC 2020, LNCS 12571, pp. 304–318, 2020.
https://doi.org/10.1007/978-3-030-65310-1_22

analytics of IIoT data can potentially enhance decision efficiency, improve product quality, and increase productivity.

Manufacturing configuration refers to adjusting a large number of parameters in the production line to achieve the desired performance of the smart manufacturing systems. Optimizing configuration is particularly important to ensure product quality [6,18]. Generally, there are a large number of configuration options that control the behavior of various aspects of the manufacturing system. For example, the target manufacturing system studied in this paper is one of the largest cigarette production systems in the world, with tens of thousands of adjustable production line parameters. Under this complexity, tuning a larger number of configuration parameters requires in-depth understanding of the target manufacturing system, professional domain knowledge and extensive experience. The traditional manufacturing configuration mainly relies on manual tuning, which has become a labor-intensive, time-consuming and error-prone task due to the complex and high-dimensional configuration space, the instability of raw material quality, and the time constraint for configuration tuning. It is still an arduous task to make real-time automatic configuration adjustment to ensure the stability of product quality.

Big data analytics on a large amount of valuable IIoT data provides a viable way to realize the intelligent model of automated manufacturing process control. In recent years, deep learning techniques has been widely used in the IoT for big data-driven modeling [14] and analysis [8,12] of the underlying interactions between parameters. However, due to the extremely complex and highly dynamic nature of smart manufacturing systems, general deep learning models are not suitable to be directly applied in IIoT. Specifically, there are four main challenges in automatic configuration and tuning of smart manufacturing systems:

- **Data redundancy:** Different from traditional IoT data generated mainly by personal devices, the raw data in IIoT is generated at extremely high rates from various manufacturing devices. The large amount of original time series data has excessively spatial and temporal redundancy information, which will seriously affect the effectiveness and efficiency of the deep learning model. Managing and extracting valuable features from the massive redundant data is crucial for effective real-time data analysis.
- **Device capability:** Conventional deep learning approaches require considerable number of samples and multiple rounds of training to achieve promising results. In order to analyze the huge amounts of data with high dimension and high dynamic natures, deep learning models put forward extremely high demands on the computation power and storage capacity of the devices. However, due to the capability and energy limitations of IIoT devices, the conventional deep learning models might be too complicated to be executed on the IIoT devices.
- **Time sensitivity:** Due to the high-speed transmission and processing of raw materials on the assembly line, even misconfiguration in a short period of time may cause thousands of defective products to be produced. Real-time configuration tuning make the task of IIoT data analysis latency-sensitive. It is

infeasible to train and deploy a deep learning model on a remote cloud server with powerful computing capacity, because transmitting a large amount of data to a remote cloud server will cause severe delays. Network Congestion caused by massive data transmission will further increase the latency. In addition, deep learning models require a long time for multiple rounds of training, which makes the results of data analysis can not be transmitted in a timely manner.

- **System Heterogeneity:** In order to facilitate automatic configuration, diverse data from different settings are needed to train deep learning models. For example, different batches of raw materials have different characteristics, and specific configuration is required even in the same manufacturing system. Raw materials with similar characteristics from the same supplier need different configurations in different manufacturing systems. However, smart manufacturing systems are heterogeneous even in the same industrial sector. How to use data from different manufacturing systems in the same industrial sector to improve model effectiveness is a very challenging task.

To address these challenges, we propose a federated deep learning model, named REACT, for **RE**al-time **A**utomatic **C**onfiguration **T**uning of smart manufacturing systems. Specifically, the deep learning model is jointly trained on the edge servers and cloud servers by leveraging edge computing and federated learning techniques. In order to mitigate data redundancy and reduce network traffic, we extract several features from the original time series data generated by IIoT devices. Deep learning process is offloaded from cloud to edge on small local datasets so that network congestion can be mitigated and response latency can be reduced. The parameters of local models are sent to the remote cloud server and aggregated to generate a more powerful federated model, which is then sent back to each edge server for precise and timely local configuration tuning. In order to facilitate the federated deep learning among heterogeneous smart manufacturing systems in the same industrial sector, we design a two-level learning framework for configuration tuning at different granularities.

To evaluate the effectiveness of our model, we collected a large-scale real-world manufacturing dataset from one of the largest cigarette manufacturing group in the world. The dataset includes raw material product data, product quality data, equipment and process configuration parameters, and workshop environment data in the cigarette production process. Given the raw material product data, product quality data, and workshop environment data, we evaluate the accuracy of configuration tuning by comparing the proposed configuration of our model with the actual configuration. Our experimental results shows that REACT significantly outperforms the baseline methods. We have also deployed our model in real-world manufacturing process, and comparing the quality of the product with other baseline methods. The evaluation results indicate that REACT can significantly improve the quality stability of products produced in a complex and highly dynamic production environment.

In summary, the main contributions of this paper are as follows:

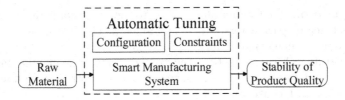

Fig. 1. Configuration tuning problem.

- To the best of our knowledge, we are among the first to identify and formally define the **tuning problem** of real-time automatic configuration in the smart manufacturing process for the stability of product quality.
- We propose a novel **two-level federated deep learning framework** that enables collaborative modeling among heterogeneous manufacturing systems for timely configuration tuning.
- We have deployed and conducted extensive experiments to validate the effectiveness of REACT in **real-world smart manufacturing systems**.

The rest of this paper is organized as follows. Section 2 introduces and formally describes the configuration tuning problem in smart manufacturing. Section 3 presents the details of our proposed model. Section 4 describes our experimental setup and the quantitative evaluation results. Related work and final remarks are discussed in Sect. 5 and Sect. 6, respectively.

2   Problem Statement

In this paper, we study the problem of configuration tuning of smart manufacturing systems. As shown in Fig. 1, the goal of the tuning problem is to find the optimal configuration to maximize system output under a given production condition. Specifically, there are five major factors in the problem:

- **Smart Manufacturing System** (S): The target system is a smart manufacturing system consisting of many production lines and processes that are used to produce a specific product. It usually provides a large number of configurable parameters.
- **Raw Material** (I): The input to a manufacturing system is usually the raw material with many quality parameters that are used to describe its characteristics and state, including category type, numerical type, etc. These parameters can be given or measured during the production process.
- **Stability of Product Quality** (O): The output of a manufacturing system is the performance. The stability of product quality is usually a more important indicator for measuring the performance of a manufacturing system than product quality, productivity and other indicators. The stability of product quality is generally measured by statistical characteristics such as variance of product quality.

- **Configuration** (C): Configuration refers to the setting of various parameters such as machine parameters, process parameters, etc. It can be set up before production or tuned timely during production.
- **Constraints** (CS): In practice, the configuration of a manufacturing system is subject to many constraints, such as time constraints, equipment constraints, network constraints, etc.

The configuration tuning problem can be formally defined as follows:

$$\max_{C} O(S, I, C), \quad s.t. \ CS \tag{1}$$

Without losing generality, in this paper we study the problem of configuration tuning using cigarette manufacturing systems as an example. Figure 2 illustrates a typical cigarette manufacturing architecture. Multiple plants belonging to one or more companies are usually distributed in different geographical locations. Each plant has one or multiple production lines. A production line consists of many processes. Due to differences in equipment and brands, the process sequence is not exactly the same for different production lines. There are many common processes between production lines. The input to a production line is the raw material, which has different characteristics for each batch. Specific manufacturing parameters for each batch of raw material are required according to the quality requirements of the final product.

3   REACT: Real-Time Automatic Configuration Tuning

In this section, we present the design of REACT. We first introduce the architecture of the two-level federated deep learning in Sect. 3.1. We extract time series features from the IIoT raw data to reduce redundancy in Sect. 3.2. The detailed line level and process level federated configuration tuning models are described in Sect. 3.3 and Sect. 3.4, respectively.

3.1   Two-Level Federated Deep Learning Framework

Figure 2 illustrates the framework of federated configuration tuning model. Each production line has a capacity limited server (e.g., edge server) on which real-time data streams from the line are processed. Line servers in the same plant are all connected to one plant server, and process level federal learning takes place first within the plant. Different plant servers are linked to a parameter server in the cloud, where line level and process level model parameters learned within the plant are aggregated to produce a better global model. Optimized global model parameters are then sent to each plant server for configuration tuning. Process level model parameters are further sent to the line server to update the local model on each line server. To avoid the impact of unreliable model parameters uploaded by plants with malicious behavior on the global model, we assign a reputation value to each plant that represents the credibility of the data from this plant. The global model is also aggregated with reputation values as weights.

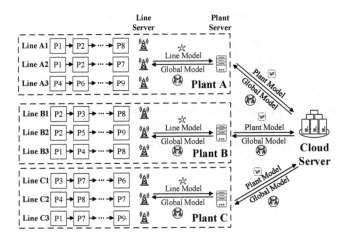

Fig. 2. Framework of federated configuration tuning.

3.2 Feature Extraction

IIoT data is generated at extremely high rates with overly redundant information. It is typically expressed as a time series with temporal dependencies between data points. In order to reduce data redundancy and incorporate the contextual relevance of configuration parameters into the model, we extracted features related to time series to retain contextual information and temporal information [20]. These features can be categorized into two groups: statistical features and temporal features.

In order to facilitate the feature extraction process in the following algorithms, we define w as the size of the sliding window. w can be calculated from the most dominant frequency p of the time series, which can be estimated by the Discrete Fourier Transform (DFT).

Statistical Features. Statistical features describe the basic characteristics of a time series. They can describe the characteristics specific to different parameters, and are used to represent the status of the machines, products, or workshop environments. For example, if the average temperature in a time window is higher during baking, it may indicate that the moisture content of the product is lower. The statistical features we extracted are listed in Table 1. They are calculated every other window of size w. The short-term characteristics of the time series represented by these statistical features are mean, median, quartile deviation, standard variance, autocorrelation, etc.

Temporal Features. Temporal features describe the changes of a time series over time. They can be used to detect the changes in the status of raw materials, machines, workshop environments, etc. We extract temporal features by comparing the data in two consecutive windows. We also calculated the difference d_w

Table 1. Statistical features

Feature	Description
Mean	Mean
Median	Median
Standard variance	Standard variance
Quartile deviation	The absolute measure of dispersion
ACF1	First order of autocorrelation
ACFremainder	Autocorrelation of remainder
Trend	Strength of trend
Linearity	Strength of linearity computed on trend of STL decomposition
Curvature	Strength of curvature computed on trend of STL decomposition
Entropy	Spectral entropy
ARCHtest.p	P value of Lagrange Multiplier (LM) test for ARCH model
GARCHtest.p	P value of Lagrange Multiplier (LM) test for GARCH model

between two windows with a distance of $2p$, $4p$, and $8p$. The temporal features we extracted are listed in Table 2.

Table 2. Temporal features

Feature	Description
MaxLevelShift	Max trimmed mean between two consecutive windows
MaxVarShift	Max variance shift between two consecutive windows
MaxKLShift	Max shift in Kullback-Leibler divergence between two consecutive windows
Lumpiness	Changing variance in remainder
d_{2p}	The differences between two windows with a distance of $2p$
d_{4p}	The differences between two windows with a distance of $4p$
d_{8p}	The differences between two windows with a distance of $8p$

3.3 Federated Configuration Tuning in Line Level

Since the smart manufacturing systems of different plants are diverse, their parameters are not exactly the same. It is not feasible to conduct federated learning directly for configuration tuning on all parameters. To facilitate the collaborative modeling among plants, we divide the parameters into two levels: line level and process level. Line level parameters (e.g., quality parameters for intermediate products) are commonly shared among plants in the same industrial sector. The federated configuration tuning learning consists of three steps:

1. The cloud parameter server delivers the global model to all plants, and each production line server (i.e. the edge server corresponding to a production line) get a local copy of the global model.

2. Each line trains the model on local data and uploads the model updates rather than local data to the cloud parameter server.
3. The cloud parameter server aggregates the updates from all lines to get an updated global model, and then sends the updated global model to all plants.

Let $\mathcal{D}_i$ be the local data on the i-th line, $\mathcal{D} = \cup_i \mathcal{D}_i$ represent the data on all L lines. $\mathcal{D}_i = \{\mathbf{x}_j, \mathbf{y}_j\}_{j=1}^{|\mathcal{D}_i|}$, where $\mathbf{x}_j$ is the features (e.g., time series features, categorical features, etc.) of the j-th sample (i.e., time series data of several parameters in the j-th time window), and $\mathbf{y}_j$ is the corresponding label (i.e., line level parameters in the specific time window). $|\mathcal{D}_i|$ represents the number of data samples of $\mathcal{D}_i$. $\mathbf{w}_i$ is the parameters of a deep learning model for configuration tuning in the i-th line. $f(\mathbf{x}_j, \mathbf{y}_j, \mathbf{w}_i)$ is the loss function of the j-th data sample, which reflects the prediction error of the model for the j-th data sample. Examples of the loss function are mean square error, cross-entropy, etc. For simplicity, we denote $f(\mathbf{x}_j, \mathbf{y}_j, \mathbf{w}_i)$ by $f_j(\mathbf{w}_i)$ to hereafter. The training process in a line is to learn an optimal $\mathbf{w}_i$ with the local data to minimize the loss function. The loss function of the i-th line is defined as:

$$F_i(\mathbf{w}_i) = \frac{1}{|\mathcal{D}_i|} \sum_j f_j(\mathbf{w}_i). \tag{2}$$

In a deep learning model, $\mathbf{w}_i$ can be leaned through an iterative process of gradient descent. Denote η as the learning rate, and in the k-th iteration, the model parameters are updated as:

$$\mathbf{w}_i^k = \mathbf{w}_i^{k-1} - \eta \nabla F_i(\mathbf{w}_i^{k-1}). \tag{3}$$

Accordingly, the loss function of the global model in the cloud parameter server can be calculated as a weighted average of the local loss functions, as follows:

$$F(\mathbf{w}) = \frac{\sum_i |\mathcal{D}_i| F_i(\mathbf{w}_i)}{|\mathcal{D}|} \tag{4}$$

FAVG algorithm [11] is widely used to aggregate the local gradient descents from lines to form a global gradient descent. The aggregation is performed after every κ iterations of gradient decent on each line. Within a certain time constraints (e.g., latency restriction, energy restriction, etc.), this learning process can be repeated several rounds for a higher accuracy rate. For the k-th iteration, the model parameters on the i-th line is updated as follows:

$$\mathbf{w}_i^k = \begin{cases} \mathbf{w}_i^{k-1} - \eta \nabla F_i(\mathbf{w}_i^{k-1}) & k \bmod \kappa \neq 0, \\[2em] \dfrac{\sum_i |\mathcal{D}_i|(\mathbf{w}_i^{k-1} - \eta \nabla F_i(\mathbf{w}_i^{k-1}))}{|\mathcal{D}|} & k \bmod \kappa = 0. \end{cases} \tag{5}$$

The GRU model [3] is an effective approach for time series prediction. In general, the GRU models aims at generating a output sequence $\mathbf{y} = (\mathbf{y}_1, \mathbf{y}_2, ...)$

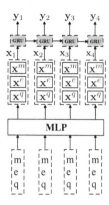

Fig. 3. Structure of the GRU model in line level.

given the input sequence $\mathbf{x} = (\mathbf{x}_1, \mathbf{x}_2, ...)$. In this paper, we extends the GRU model for solving the configuration tuning problem.

Figure 3 illustrates the over architecture of the GRU model. The input $\mathbf{x}_j$ consists of three types of features: material quality features, shop environment features, and desired product quality features. We denote the features of material quality, shop environment, and product quality as $\mathbf{x}_j^m$, $\mathbf{x}_j^e$, and $\mathbf{x}_j^q$, respectively. To incorporate these features into GRU, we first represent the categorical feature values into feature embedding via multilayer perceptions (MLPs), i.e., fully connected layers. The embedding of material quality categorical features m is defined as:

$$\mathbf{x}_j^{mc} = tanh(\mathbf{W}^M Emb(m)), \forall m = 1, 2, .., N_m, \tag{6}$$

where $\mathbf{W}^M$ is the trainable weight matrix in the MLP, and $\mathbf{x}_j^{mc}$ are the embedding vectors of all categorical material quality features. $Emb(m) \in \mathbb{R}^{N_M}$ is the vector representation of m, and $Emb(\cdot)$ indicates one general embedding layer to obtain the latent representation of m. $\mathbf{x}_j^m$ is then represented by:

$$\mathbf{x}_j^m = [\mathbf{x}_j^{mt}; \mathbf{x}_j^{mc}], \tag{7}$$

where $\mathbf{x}_j^{mt}$ is the time series feature vector, and $[;]$ is the concatenation of two vectors.

Similarly, we can obtain the categorical feature vectors of shop environment and product quality by:

$$\mathbf{x}_j^{ec} = tanh(\mathbf{W}^E Emb(e)), \forall e = 1, 2, .., N_e, \tag{8}$$

$$\mathbf{x}_j^{qc} = tanh(\mathbf{W}^Q Emb(q)), \forall q = 1, 2, .., N_q, \tag{9}$$

and represent $\mathbf{x}_j^e$, $\mathbf{x}_j^q$ by:

$$\mathbf{x}_j^e = [\mathbf{x}_j^{et}; \mathbf{x}_j^{ec}]. \tag{10}$$

$$\mathbf{x}_j^q = [\mathbf{x}_j^{qt}; \mathbf{x}_j^{qc}]. \tag{11}$$

We then concatenate $\mathbf{x}_j^m$, $\mathbf{x}_j^e$, and $\mathbf{x}_j^q$ to obtain the input vector $\mathbf{x}_j$ by:

$$\mathbf{x}_j = [\mathbf{x}_j^m; \mathbf{x}_j^e; \mathbf{x}_j^q]. \tag{12}$$

3.4 Federated Configuration Tuning in Process Level

A production line consists of multiple processes. Due to the heterogeneous of smart manufacturing systems in different plants, production lines have different process sequences. Even process sequences for multiple production lines in the same plant are not identical. Therefore, we conduct independent federated configure tuning for each process. Directly applying federated learning between lines and cloud server for a large number of processes will introduce high communication cost and lead to high latency. Therefore, the federated learning is conducted in a hierarchical manner. We first conduct federated learning with data from the same process on different production lines within a plant. The local models from different plants are then further aggregated in the cloud parameter server. It is worth noting that if a process is exclusive to a particular production line, then the configuration of that process cannot be learned through federated learning, which is obviously acceptable.

Specifically, we consider P plants indexed by p, with disjoint Line sets $\{\mathcal{L}^p\}_p$, and $\mathcal{D}_i^p$ denotes the local data within the i-th line in the p-th plant. $\mathcal{D}^p = \cup_i \mathcal{D}_i^p$ denotes the aggregated dataset in plant p. After every κ_1 iterations of local learning in each line, the plant parameter server aggregates models from local lines. Then after every κ_2/κ_1 aggregations on each plant, the cloud parameter server aggregates all the models of plants. For the k-th iteration, the local model parameters on the i-th line of plant p is updated as follows:

$$\mathbf{w}_i^k = \begin{cases} \mathbf{w}_i^{k-1} - \eta \nabla F_i(\mathbf{w}_i^{k-1}) & k \bmod \kappa_1 \neq 0 \\ & k \bmod \kappa_2 \neq 0, \\[2mm] \dfrac{\sum\limits_{i \in \mathcal{L}^p} |\mathcal{D}_i^p|(\mathbf{w}_i^{k-1} - \eta \nabla F_i(\mathbf{w}_i^{k-1}))}{|\mathcal{D}^p|} & k \bmod \kappa_1 = 0, \\[4mm] \dfrac{\sum_i |\mathcal{D}_i|(\mathbf{w}_i^{k-1} - \eta \nabla F_i(\mathbf{w}_i^{k-1}))}{|\mathcal{D}|} & k \bmod \kappa_2 = 0. \end{cases} \tag{13}$$

Similarly, we extends the basic GRU model to solve the configuration tuning problem in process level. The input $\mathbf{x}_j$ consists of three types of features: incoming material quality features, machine inner environment features, and outgoing material quality features. We denote the features of incoming material quality, machine inner environment, and outgoing material quality as $\mathbf{x}_j^{m_i}$, $\mathbf{x}_j^{e_m}$, and $\mathbf{x}_j^{m_o}$, respectively. The output $\mathbf{y}_j$ represents the process level configuration parameters (e.g., machine parameters). After concatenating the categorical feature vector and the time series feature vector, we obtain the input vector $\mathbf{x}_j$ by:

$$\mathbf{x}_j = [\mathbf{x}_j^{m_i}; \mathbf{x}_j^{e_m}; \mathbf{x}_j^{m_o}]. \tag{14}$$

Table 3. Descriptions of manufacturing dataset

Attribute	Value
#Plants	7
#Cities	5
#Manufacturing Systems	3
#Brands	2
#Lines	12
#Distinct Processes	26
#Distinct Configurable Parameters	105
#Distinct Features.	536

4   Experiments

We have deployed REACT model in cigarette manufacturing systems and collected a real-world dataset. In this section, we conduct experiments to evaluate the effectiveness of REACT on the dataset. We also evaluated the performance of real manufacturing systems where REACT was deployed.

4.1   Experimental Settings

We collected a dataset from one of the largest cigarette manufacturers in the world. This dataset is collected during the production process from leaf to cigarette, with a total of 7 cigarette plants of the manufacturer located in 5 different cities. There are 3 different manufacturing systems that involve 2 brands of cigarettes. There are 12 lines in total with 26 distinct processes. The distinct configuration parameters and distinct features are 105 and 536, respectively. Note that on a particular line, the configuration parameters is a subset of the total parameters. The descriptions of the dataset are summarized in Table 3.

4.2   Metrics

We assess the accuracy of REACT in comparison with other approaches by MAE (Mean Absolute Error):

$$MAE = \frac{1}{|\mathcal{D}_t|} \sum_{j \in \mathcal{D}_t} ||\mathbf{y}_j - \hat{\mathbf{y}}_j||, \tag{15}$$

where $\mathbf{y}_j$ is the real configuration vector of the j-th sample, $\hat{\mathbf{y}}_j$ is the REACT generated configuration vector. $\mathcal{D}_t$ is the set of testing samples. Note that all the parameters are normalized before training. Given the features $\mathbf{x}$, MAE assesses how accurate the model is in generating the configurations compared to the real configurations. In other words, the MAE evaluates how well the model captures the relationship between incoming materials, configurations, and outgoing products.

4.3   Accuracy

To evaluate the performance of REACT, we compare it with general deep learning models:

- GRU [3]: This is the extended version of basic GRU model as introduced in Sect. 3.3. It is trained only on the local data of a line.
- REACT: Federated configuration tuning model proposed in this paper.

We used the data from the first $d\%$ of the time windows to train the model, and test the model with data from the remaining time windows. We vary d from 10 to 30 with a step of 5. We randomly set two plants (i.e., 28% of the plants) as untrustworthy , and add random noise to the corresponding data. The comparison is carried out 10 times. Figure 4 shows the average accuracy of the compared models. The results show that federated learning framework leveraging more useful information from larger volume of data significantly improve the accuracy results.

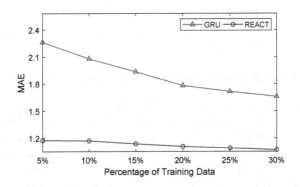

Fig. 4. Accuracy results.

4.4   Case Study

To evaluate the effectiveness of REACT, we deploy REACT into real-world manufacturing systems and compared the performance of these systems with and without running the REACT model. We also deploy the general deep learning model (i.e., extended version of basic GRU) into the manufacturing systems. The performance of a manufacturing system is evaluated in terms of product yield rate.

The performance results are shown in Fig. 5. We observe that compared with the manual configuration, which is not conducted in a timely manner, real-time automatic configuration tuning achieves significant improvements. GRU achieves an average of 3.3% improvement over manual method. REACT achieves an average of 7.8% improvement over manual method. REACT outperforms GRU on all

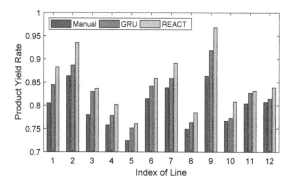

Fig. 5. Product yield rate.

production lines, meaning that Federated Learning can use data from different manufacturing systems in multiple plants to gain a deeper understanding of the production process.

5   Related Work

5.1   Smart Manufacturing and Configuration

IIoT plays a important role of connecting the physical environment of manufacturing to the computing platforms and decision-making models in the smart manufacturing paradigm [4]. The big data analytics on tremendous volume of real-time data generated by IIoT devices provides a feasible way to realized intelligent models of automated manufacturing decision making. Bui et al. [2] proposed dynamic decision making approach for vehicles in IoT. Wang et al. [15] IIoT data analytics for flexible manufacturing.

Optimal Configuration have widely studied in manufacturing systems to improve productivity [6,7,18]. Most of the configuration selection methods [18] rely on simulation to emulate the operations in digital twin [13], which is a digital copy of real systems. Due to the large volume of IIoT data and tight time constraint, these methods can not provide optimal configuration parameters in time. Different from existing studies, we focus on automating configuration tuning in a timely manner for smart manufacturing.

5.2   Deep Learning

The key to IIoT intelligence is data analysis. In recent years, deep learning techniques are widely used in smart manufacturing [14] for solving detection [12], prediction [8], and other problems. While a deep learning model can capture the underlying correlations between variables, the massive training data, time, and high capacity devices it requires makes it difficult to use directly in manufacturing. In contrast to previous studies that have focused on improving model accuracy, our goal is to facilitate deep learning models in complex, resource-limited smart manufacturing environments through a federated modeling framework.

5.3 Federated Learning

Federated learning techniques have been used by major service providers [1] for train models over remote devices. In federated learning, a star network, where a central server is connected to a network of devices, is the main communication topology [16]. The decentralized training has been demonstrated to be effective when operating on networks with low bandwidth or high latency [5]. Federated learning techniques have been widely used for communication efficiency [9], privacy [10,19] and security [17] issues in IIoT. Different from these studies, we focus on collaborative modeling among heterogeneous systems, and propose a novel two-level federated learning framework.

6 Conclusion

In smart manufacturing systems, real-time configuration tuning is critical to ensure the stability of product quality. In this paper, we propose a novel two-level federated deep learning approach to enable collaborative modeling among heterogeneous manufacturing systems on the massive IIoT data. The model is trained in a plant-cloud collaboration manner, and can make accurate configuration tuning in time. We have deployed the proposed model in real-world smart manufacturing systems, and conducted extensive experiments to evaluate the effectiveness of the model. The experimental results show that our model can significantly improve the stability of product quality compared to the conventional methods.

Acknowledgment. The work described in this paper was supported by the National Natural Science Foundation of China (61802003, 61872006), and the Anhui Innovation Program for Overseas Students.

References

1. Bonawitz, K., et al.: Towards federated learning at scale: system design. arXiv preprint arXiv:1902.01046 (2019)
2. Bui, K.N., Jung, J.J.: ACO-based dynamic decision making for connected vehicles in IoT system. IEEE Trans. Ind. Inf. **15**(10), 5648–5655 (2019)
3. Cho, K., et al.: Learning phrase representations using RNN encoder-decoder for statistical machine translation. In: Proceedings of the 2014 Conference on Empirical Methods in Natural Language Processing (EMNLP), pp. 1724–1734 (2014)
4. Dai, H.N., Wang, H., Xu, G., Wan, J., Imran, M.: Big data analytics for manufacturing internet of things: opportunities, challenges and enabling technologies. Enterp. Inf. Syst. 1–25 (2019)

5. He, L., Bian, A., Jaggi, M.: COLA: decentralized linear learning. In: Advances in Neural Information Processing Systems, pp. 4536–4546 (2018)
6. Koren, Y., Gu, X., Guo, W.: Choosing the system configuration for high-volume manufacturing. Int. J. Prod. Res. **56**, 476–490 (2018)
7. La Feperdomo, I., Beruvides, G., Quiza, R., Haber, R.E., Rivas, M.: Automatic selection of optimal parameters based on simple soft-computing methods: a case study of micromilling processes. IEEE Trans. Ind. Inf. **15**(2), 800–811 (2019)
8. Lin, Y., Zhang, Y., Lin, I., Chang, C.: Predicting logistics delivery demand with deep neural networks. In: International Conference Industrial Technology and Management (2018)
9. Liu, L., Zhang, J., Song, S.H., Letaief, K.B.: Client-edge-cloud hierarchical federated learning. arXiv: Networking and Internet Architecture (2019)
10. Lu, Y., Huang, X., Dai, Y., Maharjan, S., Zhang, Y.: Blockchain and federated learning for privacy-preserved data sharing in industrial IoT. IEEE Trans. Ind. Info. **16**(6), 4177–4186 (2020)
11. McMahan, B., Moore, E., Ramage, D., Hampson, S., y Arcas, B.A.: Communication-efficient learning of deep networks from decentralized data. In: Artificial Intelligence and Statistics, pp. 1273–1282 (2017)
12. Ren, R., Hung, T., Tan, K.C.: A generic deep-learning-based approach for automated surface inspection. IEEE Trans. Syst. Man Cybern. **48**(3), 929–940 (2018)
13. Tao, F., Cheng, J., Qi, Q., Zhang, M., Zhang, H., Sui, F.: Digital twin-driven product design, manufacturing and service with big data. Int. J. Adv. Manufact. Technol. **94**(9), 3563–3576 (2018)
14. Wang, J., Ma, Y., Zhang, L., Gao, R.X., Wu, D.: Deep learning for smart manufacturing: methods and applications. J. Manufact. Syst. **48**, 144–156 (2018)
15. Wang, J., Sun, Y., Zhang, W., Thomas, I., Duan, S., Shi, Y.: Large-scale online multitask learning and decision making for flexible manufacturing. IEEE Trans. Ind. Inf. **12**(6), 2139–2147 (2016)
16. Yang, Q., Liu, Y., Chen, T., Tong, Y.: Federated machine learning: concept and applications. ACM Trans. Intell. Syst. Tech. (TIST) **10**(2), 1–19 (2019)
17. Yin, B., Yin, H., Wu, Y., Jiang, Z.: FDC: a secure federated deep learning mechanism for data collaborations in the internet of things. IEEE Internet Things J. 1 (2020)
18. Zhang, G., Spaak, A., Martinez, C., Lasko, D.T., Zhang, B., Fuhlbrigge, T.A.: Robotic additive manufacturing process simulation - towards design and analysis with building parameter in consideration. In: International Conference on Automation Science and Engineering, pp. 609–613 (2016)
19. Zhang, X., Chen, X., Liu, J.K., Xiang, Y.: DeepPAR and DeepDPA: privacy preserving and asynchronous deep learning for industrial IoT. IEEE Trans. Ind. Inf. **16**(3), 2081–2090 (2020)
20. Zhang, X., et al.: Cross-dataset time series anomaly detection for cloud systems. In: USENIX Annual Technical Conference, pp. 1063–1076 (2019)
21. Zheng, P., et al.: Smart manufacturing systems for industry 4.0: conceptual framework, scenarios, and future perspectives. Front. Mech. Eng. **13**(2), 137–150 (2018)

A Trust and Energy-Aware Double Deep Reinforcement Learning Scheduling Strategy for Federated Learning on IoT Devices

Gaith Rjoub[1], Omar Abdel Wahab[2(⊠)], Jamal Bentahar[1], and Ahmed Bataineh[1]

[1] Concordia University, Montreal, QC, Canada
{g_rjoub,bentahar,ah_batai}@encs.concordia.ca
[2] Université du Québec en Outaouais, Gatineau, QC, Canada
omar.abdulwahab@uqo.ca

Abstract. Federated learning is a revolutionary machine learning approach whose main idea is to train the machine learning model in a distributed fashion over a large number of edge/end devices without having to share the raw data. We consider in this work a federated learning scenario wherein the local training is carried out on IoT devices and the global aggregation is done at the level of an edge server. One essential challenge in this emerging approach is scheduling, i.e., how to select the IoT devices to participate in the distributed training process. The existing approaches suggest to base the scheduling decision on the resource characteristics of the devices to guarantee that the selected devices would have enough resources to carry out the training. In this work, we argue that trust should be an integral part of the decision-making process and therefore design a trust establishment mechanism between the edge server and IoT devices. The trust mechanism aims to detect those IoT devices that over-utilize or under-utilize their resources during the local training. Thereafter, we design a Double Deep Q Learning (DDQN)-based scheduling algorithm that takes into account the trust scores and energy levels of the IoT devices to make appropriate scheduling decisions. Experiments conducted using a real-world dataset (https://www.cs.toronto.edu/~kriz/cifar.html) show that our DDQN solution always achieves better performance compared to the DQN and random scheduling algorithms.

Keywords: Federated learning · Edge computing · Internet of Things (IoT) · Double Deep Q-Learning (DDQN) · Trust · IoT Selection

1 Introduction

With the increasing reliance on Internet of Things (IoT) applications and social media platforms, the volume of data that need to be stored and processed is

© Springer Nature Switzerland AG 2020
E. Kafeza et al. (Eds.): ICSOC 2020, LNCS 12571, pp. 319–333, 2020.
https://doi.org/10.1007/978-3-030-65310-1_23

becoming enormous. Cloud computing has long been a great solution to deal with this challenge, owing to the wide array of benefits it has proved to offer for data providers [3,6,19,21,22]. These benefits include multi-tenancy, elasticity, virtualization and reduced storage and processing costs. Consequently, instead of acquiring and continuously maintaining expensive hardware equipment to store and analyze big data, companies can now migrate these duties to the cloud to be done in a more efficacious and cost-efficient manner. The increasing data privacy and network communication concerns play against the adoption of a centralized cloud-based data storage and analytics approach. First, data owners often feel reluctant to share their data with the cloud platform [2]. This is because these owners will no longer have any control on their own data and hence are not sure which other (possible unauthorized) parties will have access to their sensitive data. Moreover, the cloud data centers are mostly located in geographical areas that are quite far from the IoT devices. This entails high communication cost and delay to transmit data to the cloud for processing and receive back the insights from the cloud for decision-making. These factors have pushed the research community to design distributed data analytics approaches that are executed either by the end devices or at the edge of the network [7,26].

1.1 Problem Statement

Inspired by this idea, the concept of *Federated Learning (FL)* has recently been proposed to allow end devices to collaboratively train a single machine learning model without having to share their raw data. FL consists of two main phases, i.e., local training and global computation. In the local training phase, a parameter server (e.g., edge node) initializes the machine learning model and then shares initial parameters with the end devices. These devices then use the shared parameters to train the model on their own data. Finally, they share the updated parameters obtained through training the model on their data with the parameter server. In the global computation phase, the parameter server aggregates all the received updates to reconstruct a global machine learning model. This process repeats until a certain accuracy level is attained.

One substantial challenge in federated learning is how to select the end devices that will participate in the collaborative training. Several approaches have been proposed to tackle this challenge [15,24,25]. Most existing approaches rely on the devices' resource characteristics when taking their decisions. Despite the importance of the resource factor, we argue in this work that the reliability of the devices cannot be overlooked. In fact, the presence of unreliable devices in the federated training might lead to performance degradation and even security hazards. Unreliable devices might, for example, use bogus data to do their local training. To address this problem, we propose in this paper a scheduling solution for federated learning that takes into account both the resources availability (in terms of energy level) and trustworthiness of the IoT devices. The considered scenario consists of an edge server which plays the role of the parameter server that is responsible for the global computation phase and IoT devices that are responsible for the local training phase. A fundamental challenge in federated learning is the uncertainty that the edge server faces regarding the resource and trust levels of the IoT devices. We address this challenge by proposing a Double Deep Q-Network (DDQN) reinforcement learning-based algorithm. Compared to the traditional reinforcement learning approaches, DDQN has the advantage of reducing the overestimation of Q values and thus helps us achieve a faster training and have a more stable learning. Moreover, as argued in [11,13,23], DDQN reveals better performance compared to classic optimization methods such as Monte-Carlo search, swarm intelligence, genetic algorithms and Bayesian methods.

1.2   Contributions

The main contributions of the paper can be summarized as follows:

- We propose a trust establishment technique for the IoT devices. The algorithm monitors the CPU and memory consumption of the IoT devices and employs a modified Z-score statistical method to identify the IoT devices that exhibit any abnormal behavior in terms of over-consumption or under-consumption. This is of prime importance to detect those devices that do not dedicate enough resources to serve the federated learning tasks as well as those that carry out additional computations to achieve some malicious objectives. The modified Z-score is more robust than the standard Z-score technique since it relies on the median (instead of the mean) for calculating the Z-score. It is thus less influenced by the outliers. Moreover, compared to classification techniques such as Support Vector Machine (SVM) and decision tree, the modified Z-score technique needs less training time and can hence be executed with less overhead.
- We propose a DDQN algorithm which enables the edge servers to find the optimal scheduling decisions in terms of energy efficiency and the trustworthiness. In particular, we first formulate a stochastic optimization problem that seeks to derive to set of IoT devices that, by sending the federated learning tasks to them, the edge server can maximize the trust and at the same time minimize the energy cost. Then, a DDQN algorithm is designed to solve the optimization problem while modeling the uncertainty that the server faces regarding the resource and trust levels of the IoT devices.
- We study the proposed solution experimentally in an image recognition scenario using a Convolutional Neural Network (CNN). The experimental results reveal that our solution shows a better performance compared to the DQN and random scheduling algorithms.

1.3   Organization

The rest of the paper is organized as follows. In Sect. 2, we conduct a literature review on the existing task scheduling approaches in cloud and edge computing settings, and in the context of federated learning. We also survey the main deep and reinforcement learning-based resource management approaches. In Sect. 3, we describe the details of the proposed task scheduling approaches. In Sect. 4, we explain the experimental environment, evaluate the performance of our scheduling solution, and present empirical analysis of our results compared to other two existing scheduling approaches. In Sect. 5, we conclude the paper.

2 Related Work

In this section, we survey the main task scheduling approaches in federated learning as well as in edge computing environments.

2.1 Task Scheduling with Federated Learning

In [4], the authors study the problem of training FL algorithms over a realistic wireless network. To do so, the authors formulate an optimization problem that jointly considers user selection and resource allocation to minimize the value of the loss function. To solve this problem, a closed-form expression of the expected convergence rate of the FL algorithm that considers the wireless factors is derived. In [1], the authors adopt a DQN algorithm that allows the server to learn and find optimal decisions without any a priori knowledge of the network dynamics. The authors employ Mobile Crowd-Machine Learning (MCML) to address data privacy issues of traditional machine learning. In [8], the authors propose a segment-level decentralized federated learning to improve the efficiency of network capacity utilization among client nodes. In particular, the authors propose a segmented gossip approach, which not only makes full utilization of node-to-node bandwidth, but also achieves good training convergence. In [16], the authors present *FedCS*, a protocol that aims to improve the efficiency of FL in a mobile edge computing environment with heterogeneous clients. FedCS proposes to solve a client selection problem with resource constraints, which allows the server to aggregate as many client updates as possible and to accelerate the training convergence rate. In [15], the authors present DQN algorithm for resource allocation in a mobility-aware federated learning network. The authors propose to employ the DQN to enable the model owner to find the optimal decisions in terms of energy and channels without any a priori knowledge about the network. The authors formulate the energy and channel selection decision of the model owner as a stochastic optimization problem. The optimization problem aims to maximize the number of successful transmissions of the model owner while minimizing the energy and channel costs.

2.2 Task Scheduling in Cloud and Edge Computing

In [18], the authors propose a trust-aware scheduling solution called *BigTrustScheduling* that is particularly useful for big data tasks. The solution consists of three stages: VMs' trust level computation to derive a trust value for each VM based on its underlying performance, task priority level determination based on resource requirements and prices, and trust-aware scheduling that minimizes the makespan and cost of task execution. In [12], the authors propose a smart manufacturing factory framework based on edge computing and investigates the Job Shop Scheduling (JSP) under such a setting. Moreover, the authors adjust the DQN with an edge computing framework to solve the JSP. In [5], the authors consider the characteristics of autonomous-driving tasks to select more suitable mobile edge computing (MEC) servers for task migration. To improve the earliest deadline first algorithm through the replacement and recombination of tasks, the authors propose a Best Fit Replacement Scheduling (BFRS) technique that enables more tasks to be executed at every stage, while considering the time constraints of tasks, the urgency difference among them and their vulnerability to environmental impacts. In [9], the authors aim to reach an optimal revenue for edge service providers in the contexts of dynamic task scheduling and resource management in MEC environment. Moreover, the authors prove to achieve a favorable property called total unimodularity. This property further helps in designing an equivalent linear programming problem which can be efficiently and elegantly solved with polynomial computational complexity.

Overall, the existing scheduling approaches in federated learning, cloud and edge computing focus on the resource characteristics of the participant devices, but overlook the reliability of these devices. In this work, we consider both the resource and trust components to guarantee high-quality and reliable performance of the federated training. Moreover, different from the scheduling approaches that employ traditional deep Q learning approaches, we formulate in this paper the scheduling problem as a double deep Q learning model. This is important to consider the uncertainty that the server faces about the trust and resource characteristics of the IoT devices, while avoiding the problem of overoptimism when choosing the scheduling actions.

3   Trust-Aware IoT Scheduling for Federated Learning

3.1   Trust Establishment Mechanism

In Algorithm 1, we propose a statistical trust establishment method for IoT devices based on monitoring the CPU and RAM consumption of the devices to identify the ones that exhibit some abnormal resource consumption behavior, and the devices whose consumption goes down the normal minimal habitual consumption (e.g., failed IoTs). This is important to detect those devices that do not dedicate enough resources to serve the FL tasks as well as those that exhibit some overly high consumption which could be an indication of some malicious behavior. For example, some malicious devices might optimize for a malicious objective that aims to generate targeted misclassification. Such devices are expected to spend more resources than the regular devices that only try to optimize for the underlying federated task. Note that, every edge server monitors IoT devices that are located within its range. Thus, Algorithm 1 is executed by each edge server. The proposed method capitalizes on the modified Z-score statistical technique. Modified Z-score is a standardized score that measures outlier strength, i.e., how much a particular score differs from the typical score by checking the dependability of a particular score on a certain typical score.

This method shows a greater robustness to outliers compared to some other statistical techniques (e.g., traditional Z-Score, Tukey method, etc.) since it capitalizes on the median $\bar{x}$ instead of the mean μ. In our algorithm, this method approximates the difference of a certain score from the median using the median absolute deviation $MAD_j^z(t)$ of a metric z (e.g., CPU, RAM) consumed by a device j during a time window $[t - \delta, t]$ (Algorithm 1 line 6).

Algorithm 1. IoT Trust

Inputs:

1: j: an IoT being monitored by the edge computing server
2: $M = \{CPU, \ memory\}$: the set of IoT's metrics to be analyzed by the edge server
3: δ: size of time window after which the algorithm is to be repeated
   Variables:
4: $M_j^z(t)$: a table recording $x_j^z(i)$ ($i = t - \delta, t - \delta + 1, \ldots, t$), the amounts of $z \in M$ consumed by j during the time interval $[t - \delta, t]$
5: $\bar{x}_j^z(t)$: the median of $M_j^z(t)$ (median consumption of $z \in M$ by j during the time interval $[t-\delta, t]$)
6: $MAD_j^z(t)$: the median absolute deviation of $M_j^z(t)$, i.e., $MAD_j^z(t) = median \left\{ \left| x_j^z(i) - \bar{x}_j^z(t) \right| \right\}$ for all $t - \delta \leq i \leq t$
7: $\alpha_j^z(i, t)$: the modified Z-score of $x_j^z(i) \in M_j^z(t)$
8: $AbnormalMetrics_j^z$: sum of unusual consumption of $z \in M$ by j
9: $CountAbnormalMetrics_j^z$: a counter enumerating the occurrence of unusual consumption of $z \in M$ by j
10: $AvgAbnormalMetrics_j^z$: j's average unusual consumption of $z \in M$
11: $PropAbnormalMetrics_j^z$: j's unusual consumption of $z \in M$ proportionally to the upper and lower consumption limits of this z
12: $AbnormalMetrics_j$: the number of abnormal usages of all the metrics by j.
   Output:
13: Γ_j: trust value of j

14: **Initialize** $AbnormalMetrics_j$ to 0
15: **for each** metric $z \in M$ **do**
16:     **Initialize** $AbnormalMetrics_j^z$ **and** $CountAbnormalMetrics_j^z$ **to** 0
17:     **Initialize** $AvgAbnormalMetrics_j^z$ **and** $PropAbnormalMetrics_j^z$ **to** 0
18:     Compute the median $\bar{x}_j^z(t)$ of $M_j^z(t)$
19:     Compute the $MAD_j^z(t)$ of $M_j^z(t)$
20:     Compute $\alpha_j^z(i, t) = \dfrac{\varrho(x_j^z(i) - \bar{x}_j^z(t))}{MAD_j^z(t)}$
21:     **for each** data point $x_j^z(i) \in M_j^z(t)$ **do**
22:         **if** $\alpha_j^z(i, t) \geq \varphi$ **then**
23:             $AbnormalMetrics_j^z = AbnormalMetrics_j^z + x_j^z(i)$
24:             $CountAbnormalMetrics_j^z = CountAbnormalMetrics_j^z + 1$
25:         **end if**
26:     **end for**
27:     **if** $CountAbnormalMetrics_j^z > 0$ **then**
28:         $AvgAbnormalMetrics_j^z = AbnormalMetrics_j^z / CountAbnormalMetrics_j^z$
29:         $PropAbnormalMetrics_j^z = \dfrac{\varphi}{AvgAbnormalMetrics_j^z}$
30:         $AbnormalMetrics_j = AbnormalMetrics_j + 1$
31:     **end if**
32: **end for**
33:     **if** $AbnormalMetrics_j = 0$ **then**
34:         $\Gamma_j = 1$
35:     **else**
36:         $\Gamma_j = \dfrac{\sum_{z \in M} PropAbnormalMetrics_j^z}{AbnormalMetrics_j}$
37:     **end if**
38: **return** Γ_j

More specifically, the modified Z-score $\alpha_j^z(i,t)$ is calculated through dividing the difference between the consumption $x_j^z(i)$ of the device j in terms of the resource metric z at time moment $i \in [t - \delta, t]$ and the median consumption of that device in terms of that metric within the time interval $[t - \delta, t]$ by the median absolute deviation of the metric z (Algorithm 1 line 20). The constant $\varrho = 0.6745$ is needed because $\mathbb{E}(MAD_j^z(t)) = 0.6745\sigma$ for a large number n of samples. Observations will be labeled outliers when $\alpha_j^z(i,t) \geq \varphi$, where $\varphi = 3.5$ as argued in [10]. This limit quantifies the patterns of maximal and minimal habitual utilization of each IoT device within a certain time interval. Thus, any future consumption that exceeds or falls under this limit is deemed to be unusual. The Algorithm then checks for any future consumption of the IoT to determine whether there exists any consumption that exceeds or falls under the computed abnormal limit (Algorithm 1 - lines 22–23). If such a case is encountered, this observation is added to a table that registers each IoT's unusual consumption (if any) (Algorithm 1 - line 24). The average unusual consumption for each metric is then computed (Algorithm 1 - line 28). The Algorithm then computes the trust value of each IoT by dividing the sum of the proportional abnormal consumption over all the metrics by the number of metrics that the device has overused/underused (if any) (Algorithm 1 - line 36). If no metric has been overused/underused, the initial trust in the IoT's trustworthiness would be set to 1 (Algorithm 1 - line 34), which represents a full trust in that device.

3.2 DDQN Scheduling Policy

Reinforcement learning [14,17] is an active research and application area of machine learning that has been applied to solve uncertainty-driven problems wherein exact models are often infeasible. It aims at guiding a certain agent on how to react to the changes that take place in the environment. The agent performs the appropriate actions that maximize its cumulative reward according to the current state of the environment. In this work, we propose a trust and energy-aware dynamic Double Deep Q Network (DDQN) scheduling method. The proposed method consists of a multi-layered neural network that, for a given state outputs a vector of actions given a set of parameters of the network. The problem is formulated as a global Markov Decision Process (MDP) where the system global states and global actions are formulated as the combination of IoT devices local states and actions. It is defined by the tuple $\langle S, A, T, R, \gamma \rangle$, where:

- S: the set of global states of the system.
- A: the set of joint actions of all the IoT devices.
- T: the transition probability function defined as: $T(s, a, s') = Pr(s'|s, a)$, where $s, s' \in S$ and $a \in A$.
- $R : S \times A \times S \mapsto \mathbb{R}$: the reward function of the model.
- γ: a discount factor that decreases the impact of the past reward.

Let S_j be the set of local states of the IoT device j and J the set of all the devices. The global state space S is obtained through the Cartesian product of

IoT devices local states: $S = \prod_{j \in J} S_j$. Each local state $s_j \in S_j$ is as follows:

$$s_j = (\Gamma_j, \chi_j); \qquad \Gamma_j \in [0,1], \chi_j \in \{0,1,\ldots,\chi^{max}\} \tag{1}$$

where Γ_j is the trust value of the IoT device j computed in Algorithm 1 and χ_j is the energy state of j. Trust and energy state are dynamic, so they could change from state to state. The global action space of the parameter edge server is the joint action space of each device: $A = \prod_{j \in J} A_j$ where A_j is the set of local actions of j. A local action $a_j \in A_j$ is as follows:

$$a_j = (\sigma_j, l_j^\chi, \xi_j); \qquad \sigma_j \in \{0,1\}, l_j^\chi \in \{0,1,\ldots,\chi^{max}\}, \xi_j \in \mathbb{R} \tag{2}$$

where $\sigma_j = 1$ means the parameter server assigns a training task to the IoT device j; $\sigma_j = 0$ otherwise, l_j^χ refers to the amount of energy needed by the IoT device j to download, train and upload the model, and ξ_j is the cost of transmitting the model from the parameter server to the device j and running the model. For an action to be feasible from a global state s to s', the following condition should hold:

$$l_j^\chi(s') \leq \chi_j(s) \quad \forall j \in J \tag{3}$$

where $l_j^\chi(s')$ refers to l_j^χ in the action leading to s' and $\chi_j(s)$ is χ_j in s. Finally, to define the reward function R, the objective of maximizing the selection of trusted IoT devices having enough energy to receive and perform the training task is considered. The cost ξ_j is also considered proportional to the maximum cost ξ^{max}. The reward ψ_j for the device j is a function of state $s \in S$ and action $a \in A$ as follows:

$$\psi_j(s,a) = \begin{cases} \Gamma_j \cdot \chi_j - \frac{\xi_j}{\xi^{max}}, & \text{if } l_j^\chi \leq \chi_j. \\ -\frac{\xi_j}{\xi^{max}}, & \text{otherwise.} \end{cases} \tag{4}$$

Thus, along with the trust scores of the IoT devices, the edge server accounts for the available energy level of the devices to make sure that these devices have enough battery capacity to download, train and upload the model.

The global reward of the parameter server is as follows:

$$R(s,a) = \sum_{j \in J} \psi_j(s,a) \tag{5}$$

The parameter edge server determines the optimal policy $\pi^* : S \rightarrow A$ that indicates the actions to be taken at each state to maximize the cumulative reward. The essential goal of the Q-learning (QL) algorithm used to find π^* is to update the Q-value of a state-action pair, $Q(s,a)$, which encodes the expected future discounted reward for taking action a in state s. The optimal action-value function $Q^*(s,a)$ is $Q^*(s,a) = \max_\pi Q_\pi(s,a)$. This optimal value function can be nested within the Bellman optimality equation as follows:

$$Q^*(s,a) = R(s,a) + \gamma \sum_{s' \in S} Pr(s'|s,a) . \max_{a' \in A} Q^*(s',a') \tag{6}$$

Depending on the Q-table that results from updating the $Q(s, a)$ values, the parameter server determines the optimal action from any state to maximize the cumulative reward. The QL algorithm is practical for networks with small state and action spaces only, but when the number of network participants increases (which is the case of IoT networks that consist of a large number of devices), the problem of assigning training tasks to the IoT devices becomes high dimensional. The Deep QL (DQL) algorithm (a combination of QL and deep neural network DNN) comes into play to solve the high dimensionality problem. The input of the DNN is one of states of the online network, and the outputs are the Q-values $Q(s, a; \theta)$ of all the possible actions, with θ being the weight matrix of the DNN. The DNN needs to be trained by using experiences $(s, a, R(s, a), s')$ to obtain the approximate values $Q^*(s, a)$. We use the Mean Square Error (MSE) to define the loss function and DNN uses the Bellman equation to minimize this loss function as follows:

$$L(\theta_i) = E[(R(s, a) + \gamma \arg \max_{a' \in A} Q(s', a'; \theta'_i) - Q(s, a; \theta_i))^2] \qquad (7)$$

where θ_i represents the parameters of the online network at the ith iteration, θ'_i represents the parameters of the target network at the ith iteration, and $E[.]$ denotes the expected value. Note that the action a is selected based on the ϵ-greedy policy. By using the max operator (which uses the same Q-values to select and to evaluate an action in standard QL and DQN), we observe that it is more likely that this operator selects overestimated values, resulting in overoptimistic estimates. To prevent such a problem, we should decouple the action selection from the evaluation by employing the Double Deep Q-network (DDQN) [20]. The main feature of DDQN is the use of two separate DNNs, i.e., an online network with weight set θ and a target network with weight set θ''. The DDQN employs two valuation functions for two autonomous DNNs learned through randomly assigning experiences to update one of the two value functions, resulting in two sets of weights θ for the first DNN and θ'' for the second DNN. At each iteration, the weights of the online network are updated, while those of the target network are kept constant to determine the greedy policy. The target function of the DDQN error is defined by:

$$T_{DDQN}(s, a, s') = R(s, a) + \gamma Q(s', \arg \max_{a' \in A} Q(s', a'; \theta); \theta'') \qquad (8)$$

To compute the optimal value $Q(s', a'; \theta)$, the weight θ of the online network uses the next state s' to select an action, while the target network θ'' uses the next state s' to evaluate the action. Then, a stochastic gradient descent step is performed to update the weights of the online networks θ based on the loss

3.3 DDQN-Based Federated Learning Model

In this section, we describe how the FL process can be executed after integrating our trust establishment and scheduling mechanisms. A DNN model is distributed over the IoT devices to be collaboratively trained following the

FL framework. Let D_j be a local dataset collected by the IoT device j, $D_j = \{(x_{1_j}, y_{1_j}), \ldots, (x_{n_j}, y_{n_j})\}$, where x_{i_j} is the ith training sample and y_{i_j} represents the corresponding ground-truth label. In this work, we take a general Convolutional Neural Network (CNN) model for analysis. The edge server receives the local gradient vectors from the trusted IoT devices and then aggregates (averages) them to obtain the global gradient using Eq. (9):

$$g[\nu] = \frac{1}{\sum_{j \in J} |\vartheta_j|} \sum_{j \in J} |\vartheta_j| g_j[\nu] \tag{9}$$

where ϑ_j is a subset of local data collected from the IoT device j for a training period ν, with $\vartheta_j \subseteq D_j$, and $g_j[\nu]$ being the local gradient which is computed as per Eq. (10).

$$g_j[\nu] = \nabla_{w_j} L_j(w_j, \vartheta_j) \tag{10}$$

where w_j is the local parameter set of the CNN model, L_j is the local loss function on the IoT device j to measure the training error and $\nabla_{w_j} L_j(.)$ is the gradient of the loss function L_j with respect to w_j.

Algorithm 2. DDQN-based Federated Learning Algorithm for IoT Selection

---

1: Initialize the global parameter set of the CNN model
2: **for** each round $\tau = 1, 2, \ldots$ **do**
3:       Use Algorithm 1 to compute the trust scores of all the IoT devices
4:       Use DDQN to select a subset $\mathcal{E} \subseteq J$ of IoT devices to participate in the training
5:       Send W_τ to each selected IoT
6:       **for** each IoT device $j \in \mathcal{E}$ **do**   % $\mathcal{E} = \{1, 2, \ldots, E\}$
7:             Execute **IoTLocalUpdate**(W_τ)   % See Algorithm 3
8:       **end for**
9:             $W_\tau = \frac{1}{n} \sum_{j=1}^{E} n_j w_j$
10: **end for**

In Algorithms 2 and 3, we describe the federated learning process after embedding our proposed trust establishment mechanism and DDQN scheduling policy to improve the selection of IoT devices. In Algorithm 2, n_j is the data size available on IoT j, n is the size of the whole data across all devices, E is the total number of selected devices, τ is the training communication round index and W_τ is the global parameter set at round τ.

Algorithm 3. IoT Local Training

1: **IoTLocalUpdate**(W_τ)
2:       $w_j = W_\tau$
3:       **for** each local iteration $t = 1$ to T **do**
4:               $w_j = w_j - \eta \nabla_{w_j} L_j(w_j, \vartheta_j)$ % η is the learning rate
5:       **end for**
6:       return w_j to the edge server

Each IoT device runs the stochastic gradient descent (SGD) algorithm based on the received global gradient. The local loss function on each device j is defined as per Eq. (11):

$$L_j\left(w_j\right) = \frac{1}{N_j} \sum_{(x,y) \in D_j} \ell\left(w_j, x, y\right) \tag{11}$$

where $\ell\left(w_j, x, y\right)$ is the sample-wise loss function that quantifies the prediction error between the learning output (via input x and parameter w_j) and the ground-truth label y, and N_j is the number of data samples of the device j. Each device seeks to minimize the local loss function defined in Eq. (11) to minimize the training error. On a global level, the main target of the training task at the edge server is to optimize the parameters towards minimizing the global loss function $L(W)$ via the SGD algorithm expressed as follows:

$$L(W) = \frac{1}{\sum_{j=1}^{E} N_j} \sum_{j=1}^{E} N_j L_j(w_j) \tag{12}$$

4 Implementation and Experiments

4.1 Experimental Setup

To carry out our experiments, we use TensorFlow Federated (TFF), which is an open-source framework for machine learning on decentralized data. TFF supports a variety of distributed learning scenarios executed on a large number of heterogeneous devices having diverse capabilities. We train a CNN model on the CIFAR-10 dataset[1] to evaluate the performance and efficiency of our solution. The dataset consists of 50,000 training images and 10,000 testing images divided across 10 object classes. The employed CNN model consists of six 3×3 convolution layers as follows: 32, 32, 64, 64, 128, 128. Each layer is activated by a Rectified Linear Unit (ReLU) and batch normalized. Every pair of convolution layers is followed by a 2×2 max pooling layer, followed by three fully-connected layers (where each fully connected layer takes a 2D input of 382 and 192 units) with ReLU activation and another 10 units activated by soft-max. The model is trained on IoT devices using the Stochastic Gradient Descent (SGD) algorithm with a batch size of 128 rows. The training dataset was distributed over a set of 1000 IoT devices (i.e., $|J| = 1000$) of 4 types: type-1 with 1 CPU core and 1.75 GB RAM, type-2 with 2 CPU cores and 3.5 GB RAM, type-3 with 4 CPU cores and 7 GB RAM, and type-4 with 8 CPU cores and 14 GB RAM. At each iteration, the edge server selects the top 50 IoT devices returned by the scheduling algorithm (i.e., $E = 50$).

We evaluate the performance of the proposed DDQN solution with the traditional DQN [15] which has lately been used for client selection in federated learning and with the random scheduling approach, the default approach in federated learning. The proposed DDQN model consists of two Deep Neural

---

[1] https://www.cs.toronto.edu/~kriz/cifar.html.

Networks (DNNs), where each DNN has a size of $32 \times 32 \times 32$. The Adam optimizer is used to adjust the learning rate during the training. The learning rate η is initially set to 0.01 to avoid losing the local minima. In general, the deep Q learning approach prefers the long-term reward; therefore, we set the value of the discount factor γ to 0.9. We use the ϵ-greedy policy with $\epsilon = 0.9$ that balances between the exploration and exploitation. During the training phase, ϵ is linearly reduced to zero to move from exploration to exploitation. Our application is written in Python, version 3, and executed in a 64-bit Windows 7 environment on a machine equipped with an Intel Core i7-6700 CPU 3.40 GHz Processor and 16 GB RAM.

4.2   Experimental Results

In Figs. 1, 2 and 3, we measure the accuracy of the CNN that was trained by IoT devices selected by the DDQN (Fig. 1), DQN (Fig. 2), and random scheduling (Fig. 3) approaches. We ran the experiments over 2000 iterations to study the scalabilty of the different considered solutions. The accuracy obtained by the DDQN approach is higher than that obtained by the DQN and random approaches. In particular, the accuracy levels obtained by the DDQN, DQN, and random approaches are of 87%, 71%, and 35% respectively. Moreover, we notice from the figures that the DDQN approach convergences faster than the DQN and random approaches to a stable accuracy level. The improvements with regard to the random scheduling approach mainly stem from the fact that our solution leverages the trust energy values of the IoT devices when selecting the devices that will participate in the training. Compared to the traditional DQN, our solution improves the accuracy since it relies on a double Q learning model that provides a better estimate of the potential actions due to its second Q-function approximator, which helps avoid *overoptimism*. In DQN, on the other hand, the Q values are noisy; thus when we take the maximum over all the actions, there is a considerable risk of obtaining an overestimated value.

In Fig. 4, we provide experimental comparisons in terms of cumulative reward. We ran the experiments over 10,000 iterations. The reward obtained by the DDQN is much higher than those obtained by the DQN and random approaches. In particular, the rewards obtained by the DDQN, DQN, and random approaches are 175, 115, and 60, respectively. This means the proposed DDQN approach enables the edge server to better learn the scheduling policy that best maximizes the reward.

In the random approach, the edge server randomly selects IoT devices, which increases the risk of selecting unreliable devices or devices that have insufficient energy levels. This endangers the whole collaborative training process and makes the performance unstable. Moving to the traditional DQN approach, its overestimation of the future actions leads to a natural reduction in the overall reward that results from the chosen actions.

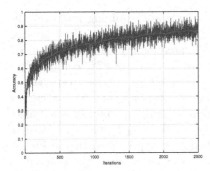

Fig. 1. Performance of the trained CNNs with DDQN scheduling

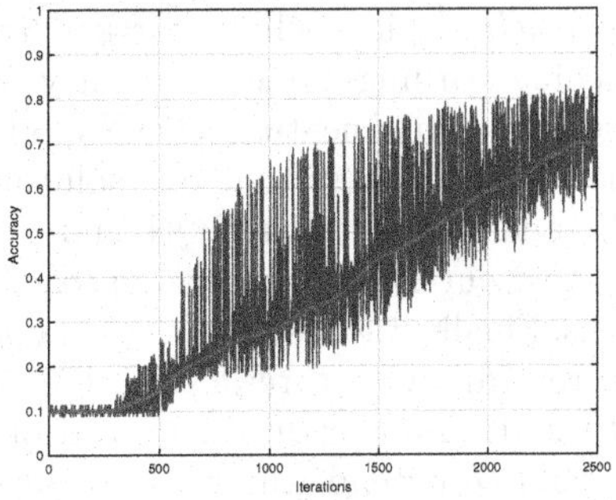

Fig. 2. Performance of the trained CNNs with DQN scheduling

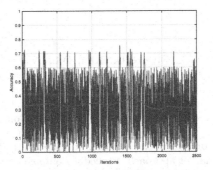

Fig. 3. Performance of the trained CNNs with random scheduling

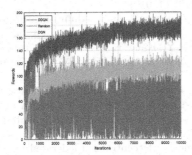

Fig. 4. Reward values in DDQN, DQN, and Random scheduling policies

5   Conclusion

We designed and formulated a trust and energy-aware FL scheduling approach in IoT environments using DDQN. Experiments conducted on the CIFAR-10 real-world dataset reveal that our solution outperforms, in terms of accuracy and cumulative reward, the most commonly used scheduling approaches in FL, i.e., DQN and random scheduling. Our solution accurately selects the appropriate set of IoT devices whose participation in the federated training improves the machine learning model's accuracy. We study the accuracy of the three studied models by implementing a CNN model in a federated fashion on the IoT devices. The results suggest that our solution yields an accuracy of 87% compared to 71% and 35% for the DQN and random scheduling approaches respectively. Besides, our DDQN-based approach convergences faster to a stable accuracy levels. Finally, the results reveal that our proposed scheduling solution maximizes the reward (with a reward of 175) compared to the DQN (with a reward of 115) and random (with a reward of 60) scheduling approaches. In the future, we plan to extend this work by investigating and formulating the scheduling approach using Dueling Double Deep Q Network (DDDQN), which could help better reduce the overhead and time complexity of the scheduling process by avoiding unnecessary computations.

References

1. Anh, T.T., Luong, N.C., Niyato, D., Kim, D.I., Wang, L.C.: Efficient training management for mobile crowd-machine learning: a deep reinforcement learning approach. IEEE Wirel. Commun. Lett. **8**(5), 1345–1348 (2019)
2. Bataineh, A.S., Mizouni, R., Bentahar, J., Barachi, M.E.: Toward monetizing personal data: a two-sided market analysis. Future Gener. Comput. Syst. **111**, 435–459 (2020)
3. Bataineh, A.S., Mizounib, R., El Barachic, M., Bentahara, J.: Monetizing personal data: a two-sided market approach. Procedia Comput. Sci. **83**, 472–479 (2016)
4. Chen, M., Yang, Z., Saad, W., Yin, C., Poor, H.V., Cui, S.: A joint learning and communications framework for federated learning over wireless networks. arXiv preprint arXiv:1909.07972 (2019)
5. Dai, H., Zeng, X., Yu, Z., Wang, T.: A scheduling algorithm for autonomous driving tasks on mobile edge computing servers. Syst. Arch. **94**, 14–23 (2019)
6. Ding, D., Fan, X., Zhao, Y., Kang, K., Yin, Q., Zeng, J.: Q-learning based dynamic task scheduling for energy-efficient cloud computing. Future Gener. Comput. Syst. **108**, 361–371 (2020)
7. Drawel, N., Bentahar, J., Laarej, A., Rjoub, G.: Formalizing group and propagated trust in multi-agent systems. In: Bessiere, C. (ed.) Proceedings of the Twenty-Ninth International Joint Conference on Artificial Intelligence, IJCAI 2020, pp. 60–66 (2020)
8. Hu, C., Jiang, J., Wang, Z.: Decentralized federated learning: a segmented gossip approach. arXiv preprint arXiv:1908.07782 (2019)
9. Huang, J., Li, S., Chen, Y.: Revenue-optimal task scheduling and resource management for IoT batch jobs in mobile edge computing. Peer-to-Peer Netw. Appl., 1–12 (2020)
10. Iglewicz, B., Hoaglin, D.C.: How to Detect and Handle Outliers, vol. 16. ASQ Press (1993)
11. Lei, L., Tan, Y., Zheng, K., Liu, S., Zhang, K., Shen, X.: Deep reinforcement learning for autonomous internet of things: model, applications and challenges. IEEE Commun. Surv. Tutor. **22**(3), 1722–1760 (2020)
12. Lin, C.C., Deng, D.J., Chih, Y.L., Chiu, H.T.: Smart manufacturing scheduling with edge computing using multiclass deep Q network. IEEE Trans. Ind. Inform. **15**(7), 4276–4284 (2019)

13. Luo, S.: Dynamic scheduling for flexible job shop with new job insertions by deep reinforcement learning. Appl. Soft Comput., 106208 (2020)
14. Mao, H., Alizadeh, M., Menache, I., Kandula, S.: Resource management with deep reinforcement learning. In: Proceedings of the 15th ACM Workshop on Hot Topics in Networks, pp. 50–56 (2016)
15. Nguyen, H.T., Luong, N.C., Zhao, J., Yuen, C., Niyato, D.: Resource allocation in mobility-aware federated learning networks: a deep reinforcement learning approach. arXiv preprint arXiv:1910.09172 (2019)
16. Nishio, T., Yonetani, R.: Client selection for federated learning with heterogeneous resources in mobile edge. In: IEEE International Conference on Communications (ICC), pp. 1–7 (2019)
17. Rjoub, G., Bentahar, J., Abdel Wahab, O., Saleh Bataineh, A.: Deep and reinforcement learning for automated task scheduling in large-scale cloud computing systems. Concurr. Comput. Pract. Exp. (2020)
18. Rjoub, G., Bentahar, J., Wahab, O.A.: BigTrustScheduling: trust-aware big data task scheduling approach in cloud computing environments. Future Gener. Comput. Syst. **110**, 1079–1097 (2020)
19. Rjoub, G., Bentahar, J., Wahab, O.A., Bataineh, A.: Deep smart scheduling: a deep learning approach for automated big data scheduling over the cloud. In: 7th International Conference on Future Internet of Things and Cloud (FiCloud), pp. 189–196 (2019)
20. Van Hasselt, H., Guez, A., Silver, D.: Deep reinforcement learning with double Q-learning. In: Thirtieth AAAI Conference on Artificial Intelligence (2016)
21. Wahab, O.A., Bentahar, J., Otrok, H., Mourad, A.: Resource-aware detection and defense system against multi-type attacks in the cloud: repeated Bayesian stackelberg game. IEEE Trans. Dependable Secur. Comput. (2019)
22. Wahab, O.A., Cohen, R., Bentahar, J., Otrok, H., Mourad, A., Rjoub, G.: An endorsement-based trust bootstrapping approach for newcomer cloud services. Inf. Sci. **527**, 159–175 (2020)
23. Wang, X., Han, Y., Wang, C., Zhao, Q., Chen, X., Chen, M.: In-edge AI: intelligentizing mobile edge computing, caching and communication by federated learning. IEEE Netw. **33**(5), 156–165 (2019)
24. Yang, H.H., Liu, Z., Quek, T.Q.S., Poor, H.V.: Scheduling policies for federated learning in wireless networks. IEEE Trans. Commun. **68**(1), 317–333 (2020)
25. Zhou, Z., Yang, S., Pu, L., Yu, S.: CEFL: online admission control, data scheduling, and accuracy tuning for cost-efficient federated learning across edge nodes. IEEE Internet Things J. **7**(10), 9341–9356 (2020)
26. Zhu, G., Liu, D., Du, Y., You, C., Zhang, J., Huang, K.: Toward an intelligent edge: wireless communication meets machine learning. IEEE Commun. Mag. **58**(1), 19–25 (2020)

Smart Data and Smart Services

A Spectrum of Entropy-Based Precision and Recall Measurements Between Partially Matching Designed and Observed Processes

Anna Kalenkova(✉)[iD] and Artem Polyvyanyy[iD]

School of Computing and Information Systems, The University of Melbourne,
Parkville, VIC 3010, Australia
{anna.kalenkova,artem.polyvyanyy}@unimelb.edu.au

Abstract. Modern software systems are often built using service-oriented principles. Atomic components, be that web- or microservices, allow constructing flexible and loosely coupled systems. In such systems, services are building blocks orchestrated by business processes the system supports. Due to the complexity and heterogeneity of industrial software systems, implemented processes may deviate from those initially designed. In this paper, we propose a *spectrum* of conformance measurements. The spectrum results from a generalization of the recently introduced entropy-based approaches for measuring *precision* and *recall* between *observed* process executions and *designed* process models. The new generalized measures of precision and recall inherit the desired for this class of measures properties and provide analysts with flexible control over the sensitivity for identifying commonalities and discrepancies in the compared processes and performance of the techniques. The reported evaluation based on our implementation of the measures over real-world event logs and automatically discovered models confirms the feasibility of using the approach in industrial settings.

1 Introduction

In a service-oriented architecture (SOA), business processes can be implemented as compositions of loosely coupled services that interact to achieve concrete business goals [10]. The historical data on executions of such processes are often recorded in event logs. These logs can be subsequently analyzed to discover, check, and improve service compositions [1] using process mining techniques. Process mining combines studies of inferences from data in data mining and machine learning with process modeling and analysis to tackle the problems of discovering, monitoring, and improving real-world processes [2]. One of the core problems in process mining is *conformance checking* [5], which studies relationships between processes recorded in an event log and described by a process model to characterize and/or measure commonalities and discrepancies between the *observed* real-world and *designed* processes. Two core measures in

E. Kafeza et al. (Eds.): ICSOC 2020, LNCS 12571, pp. 337–354, 2020.
https://doi.org/10.1007/978-3-030-65310-1_24

conformance checking are *precision* and *recall*. A precise process model should not allow for behavior unrelated to what was seen in the event log, while a model with good recall should allow for the behavior seen in the event log.

In our previous work, we devised two approaches for measuring recall and precision between process models and event logs [19, 21] founded on the notion of topological entropy [6] of the behaviors, i.e., collections of traces, that they describe. The measures presented in [21] have been recently recognized in [23] as the *only* recall and precision measures, among the evaluated state-of-the-art measures, that satisfy all the desired properties. For example, they are deterministic, depend only on the underlying behaviors and not on their representations, and are monotone, i.e., the more common behavior the model and log have, the greater the recall and precision values are. These measures can be computed for behaviors that describe arbitrary, including infinite, collections of traces. However, they rely on the exact matching of traces, i.e., two different traces are always treated as totally dissimilar, even if they differ only in a single task. In [19], we extended the measures to account for partially matching traces. Instead of measuring the original collections of traces, the new measures quantify and compare the "diluted" behaviors, where the diluted version of a behavior consists of all the traces obtained from original traces by skipping an arbitrary number of tasks; note that once a task is skipped the order of the remaining tasks in the resulting trace does not change. These new measures inherit the properties of the original measures and enjoy some further properties specific to the partial matching of traces. For example, the more common subtraces the model and log describe, the greater the recall and precision values are.

The two approaches for measuring recall and precision presented in [19, 21] address two *extremes*, i.e., no support for partial matching of traces and ability to detect and quantify any partial similarity between traces. Such extreme approaches are doomed for limitations. The former approach may overlook the commonalities in traces, while the latter may miss the discrepancies. This calls for a *compromise* approach.

In this paper, we present a novel technique for measuring precision and recall between two (not necessarily finite) collections of partially matching traces that can be configured as to when two different traces should be considered similar. The configuration consists of two non-negative integers that specify the maximum numbers of tasks that can be skipped in traces in each of the two compared collections to arrive at the same trace and, consequently, accept the compared traces as similar. For example, traces $\langle a, b, c \rangle$ and $\langle b, d, c, e \rangle$ are *dissimilar* if one is allowed to skip only one task in each trace. However, they can be accepted as *similar* if one is allowed to skip two tasks in the latter trace. Indeed, one arrives at the trace $\langle b, c \rangle$ by skipping task a in the former trace and tasks d and e in the latter trace. Hence, two traces are said to be similar if they have a common subtrace that can be constructed by skipping up to the configured number of tasks in each trace. Such common subtrace captures the common behavior of the compared traces. The technique then proceeds by measuring the amount of all common subtraces in both collections as per the supplied configuration.

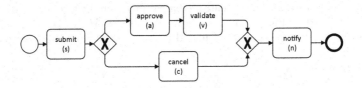

Fig. 1. A BPMN model of a loan application process.

The new technique results in a *discrete spectrum* of recall and precision measurements induced by all the configurations in the Cartesian square of the natural numbers ($\mathbb{N}_0 \times \mathbb{N}_0$). In this spectrum, the (k, m) configuration suggests that up to k and m skips are allowed in the traces of log and model, respectively. The recall and precision measures for the $(0, 0)$ configuration correspond to the exact matching measures from [21]. Using a formal proof, we show that measures for the (k, m) configurations approach the partial matching measures from [19] when $k, m \to \infty$, allowing for a gradual adjustment of the analysis between the two extremes.

Process analysts can rely on our new technique to (in a flexible way) adjust the "sensitivity" of the measured recall and precision values to mismatches in the compared behaviors. Such an adjustment may, for instance, be guided by domain knowledge. An analyst may know that logs are recorded with noise, e.g., a sequence of initialization tasks at the start of each trace, and, thus, adjust the allowed skips in log traces accordingly. In addition, the new measures demonstrate good runtime characteristics for the practically relevant range of configurations. The most computationally demanding step of the partially matching approach from [19] is the construction of a deterministic version of the automaton that encodes the completely diluted version of the original behavior. This step has exponential worst-case time complexity and, unfortunately, close-to-worst cases manifest often for industrial datasets [19]. However, as confirmed through our evaluations, for configurations (x, y), where $x, y \leq 10$, the worst-case complexity manifests only for sub-problems of small sizes, or not at all.

Section 2 motivates the problem addressed in this paper and demonstrates our approach for solving the problem by means of an intuitive example. Next, Sect. 3 introduces the basic notions used in the discussions of the subsequent sections. Then, Section 4 presents our approach and discusses several its properties. Sect. 5 presents the results of our evaluations of the new measures. Sect. 6 positions our work among the state-of-the-art results in conformance checking. Sect. 7 concludes the paper.

2 Motivating Example

Consider the example loan application process in Fig. 1. First, the client submits an application. Then, the submitted application is reviewed by a bank analyst and either approved or canceled. If the application is approved, it is then validated. In both cases, the client is eventually notified. The BPMN model in Fig. 1

Table 1. The spectrum of the entropy-based precision and recall measurements between the model in Fig. 1 that describes set of traces $M = \{\langle s, a, v, n \rangle, \langle s, c, n \rangle\}$ and event log $L = \{\langle s, a, n \rangle\}$ calculated for different numbers of skipped tasks in traces of M and L.

	$L^{(0)}$	$L^{(1)}$	$L^{(2)}$	$L^{(3)}$		$L^{(0)}$	$L^{(1)}$	$L^{(2)}$	$L^{(3)}$
$M^{(0)}$	0.000	0.000	0.000	0.000	$M^{(0)}$	0.000	0.000	0.000	0.000
$M^{(1)}$	1.000	0.793	0.568	0.464	$M^{(1)}$	0.549	0.670	0.670	0.670
$M^{(2)}$	1.000	1.000	0.908	0.741	$M^{(2)}$	0.382	0.589	0.745	0.745
$M^{(3)}$	1.000	1.000	1.000	1.000	$M^{(3)}$	0.299	0.459	0.642	0.785

(a) Recall   (b) Precision

describes the expected process behavior. This behavior can be described by the set of traces $M = \{\langle s, a, v, n \rangle, \langle s, c, n \rangle\}$, which contains the two traces that the model supports.[1]

Suppose that the corresponding event log L contains only one trace $t = \langle s, a, n \rangle$. Then, the model and log have no common traces, i.e., $M \cap L = \emptyset$. Consequently, precision and recall measures founded on the exact matching of traces, e.g., the entropy-based approach presented in [21], are equal to zero, suggesting no similarity between the behaviors of the model and log. Despite different, the traces in M and L show some similarity. For example, it holds that t and traces in M contain subtrace $\langle s, n \rangle$.

The partial matching approach from [19] addresses the above issue by comparing collections of diluted traces. For example, the diluted versions of L and M are $\{\langle s, a, n \rangle, \langle s, a \rangle, \langle s, n \rangle, \langle a, n \rangle, \langle s \rangle, \langle a \rangle, \langle n \rangle, \langle \rangle\}$ and $\{\langle s, a, v, n \rangle, \langle a, v, n \rangle, \langle s, v, n \rangle, \langle s, a, n \rangle, \langle s, a, v \rangle, \langle s, c, n \rangle, \langle v, n \rangle, \langle a, n \rangle, \langle a, v \rangle, \langle s, n \rangle, \langle s, v \rangle, \langle s, a \rangle, \langle s, c \rangle, \langle c, n \rangle, \langle s \rangle, \langle a \rangle, \langle v \rangle, \langle n \rangle, \langle c \rangle, \langle \rangle\}$, where $\langle \rangle$ is the empty trace. We denote the former set and the latter set as L^∞ and M^∞, respectively. The diluted traces can be used to identify commonalities and discrepancies between the original traces. For example, it holds that $\langle s, n \rangle \in L^\infty \cap M^\infty$ and $\langle s, c, n \rangle \in M^\infty \setminus L^\infty$. The partial matching precision and recall measures between a model and log quantify the commonalities and discrepancies in their diluted traces. Since $L^\infty \subset M^\infty$, such diluted recall is equal to 1.0, suggesting that the model allows for the behavior seen in the log perfectly. As $M^\infty \not\subset L^\infty$, such diluted precision is not perfect. The particular precision value obtained using the technique from [19] is 0.785; note that the absolute value is of less interest here as these are the relations between the measurements that allow comparing different behaviors.[2]

The above examples highlight the limitations of the two extreme approaches mentioned in the Introduction. The approach founded on the exact matching

---

[1] We use short task names to specify traces, while the corresponding full names are in Fig. 1.

[2] In general, precision and recall measure of one suggest perfect conformance, while the values of zero suggest no behavioral similarities between the compared model and log.

of traces overlooks the existing partial commonalities in traces, while the approach that relies on the arbitrary skips of tasks in traces misses to identify the discrepancies, cf. recall of 1.0.

Consider two sets $L^{(1)}$ and $M^{(1)}$ with all the traces constructed from the traces in L and M, respectively, by skipping at most one task in a trace from the original set, i.e., $L^{(1)} = \{\langle s, a, n \rangle, \langle a, n \rangle, \langle s, n \rangle, \langle s, a \rangle\}$ and $M^{(1)} = \{\langle s, a, v, n \rangle, \langle a, v, n \rangle, \langle s, v, n \rangle, \langle s, a, n \rangle, \langle s, a, v \rangle, \langle s, c, n \rangle, \langle c, n \rangle, \langle s, n \rangle, \langle s, c \rangle\}$. It holds that $L^{(1)} \cap M^{(1)} = \{\langle s, a, n \rangle, \langle s, n \rangle\}$, $L^{(1)} \setminus M^{(1)} \neq \emptyset$, and $M^{(1)} \setminus L^{(1)} \neq \emptyset$. Hence, sets $L^{(1)}$ and $M^{(1)}$ contain information about commonalities and discrepancies of log and model. The entropy-based recall and precision computed based on the traces in $L^{(1)}$ and $M^{(1)}$ are equal to 0.793 and 0.670, respectively, and, thus, confirm that the behaviors are neither completely different, nor are in the subsumption relation. Again, the absolute values of precision and recall are irrelevant, as they indeed satisfy the monotonicity properties discussed later. Importantly, these measure neither suggest perfect match nor the complete dissimilarity of the compared behaviors.

Tables 1a and b demonstrate the spectrum of precision and recall values calculated for the traces in L and M. Given a set of traces X, by $X^{(k)}$, $k \in \mathbb{N}_0$, we denote the set of all traces obtained from the traces in X by skipping up to k arbitrary tasks in the original traces. Thus, it holds that $M^{(0)} = M$ and $L^{(0)} = L$. For this example, it also holds that $M^{(m)} = M^\infty$ and $L^{(m)} = M^\infty$, where $m \geq 3$.

Note that the recall values do not decrease when more skips are allowed in the model traces, i.e., $recall^{(k,m)}(M, L) \leq recall^{(k+1,m)}(M, L)$, $k, m \in \mathbb{N}_0$; here, k and m refer to the numbers of allowed skips in M and L, respectively, used to compute the conformance values (refer to Sect. 4 for details). Indeed, by extending the behavior of the model more, we can use it to cover more of the traces in the log. On the other hand, precision values do not decrease when more skips are allowed in the log traces, i.e., $prec^{(k,m)}(M, L) \leq prec^{(k,m+1)}(M, L)$, $k, m \in \mathbb{N}_0$, as by extending the behavior of the log we can use it to cover more behavior of the model. These properties of precision and recall measures are formally proved in Sect. 4.3.

3   Basic Notions

This section introduces basic notions and definitions used in the remainder of the paper.

3.1   Sequences, Languages, and Event Logs

Let X be a set of elements. The *power set* of X, denoted as $\mathcal{P}(X)$, is the set of all subsets of X. By $\langle x_1, x_2, \ldots, x_k \rangle$, where $x_1, x_2, \ldots, x_k \in X$, $k \in \mathbb{N}$, we denote a *sequence* of elements from X of length k. The *empty sequence* of zero length is represented by $\langle \rangle$. By X^*, we denote the set of all finite sequences over X. A *concatenation* of two sequences $\langle x_1, x_2, \ldots, x_k \rangle$ and $\langle y_1, y_2, \ldots, y_l \rangle$ is denoted by $\langle x_1, x_2, \ldots, x_k \rangle \cdot \langle y_1, y_2, \ldots, y_l \rangle$ and is the sequence $\langle x_1, x_2, \ldots, x_k, y_1, y_2, \ldots, y_l \rangle$.

Given a sequence x and a set K, by $x|_K$, we denote a sequence obtained from x by removing all elements of x that are not members of K without changing the order of the remaining elements, e.g., it holds that $\langle a, c, b, a, d, c \rangle|_{\{c,d\}} = \langle c, d, c \rangle$.

An *alphabet* is any nonempty finite set. The elements of an alphabet are its *labels*. A *language* L over an alphabet Σ is a (not necessarily finite) set of sequences, or *words*, of labels from Σ, i.e., $L \subseteq \Sigma^*$. By $C_n(L)$, we denote the set of all words in L of length n. By Ξ, we denote a universe of all possible *observable* labels, while τ, $\tau \notin \Xi$, denotes a special *silent* label. Let L_1 and L_2 be two languages. Then, their concatenation is the language $L = \{l_1 \cdot l_2 \mid l_1 \in L_1, l_2 \in L_2\}$, denoted by $L_1 \circ L_2$. Given a language L, L^* is the language defined by $\bigcup_{n=0}^{\infty} L^n$, where $L^0 = \{\langle \rangle\}$, $L^n = L^{n-1} \circ L$.

Let E be a finite nonempty set of *tasks*, or *events*. A finite language $L \subset E^*$ is an *event log* and its words are called *traces* [2].

3.2   Finite Automata

A *nondeterministic finite automaton* (NFA) is a 5-tuple $(Q, \Lambda, \delta, q_0, A)$, where Q is a finite nonempty set of *states*, $\Lambda \subseteq \Xi$ is a set of *labels*, $\delta : Q \times (\Lambda \cup \{\tau\}) \to \mathcal{P}(Q)$ is the *transition function*, $q_0 \in Q$ is the *start state*, and $A \subseteq Q$ is the *set of accept states*.

An NFA induces a collection of computations. A *computation* of an NFA $B = (Q, \Lambda, \delta, q_0, A)$ is either the empty word or a word $\sigma = \langle a_1, \ldots, a_n \rangle$, $n \in \mathbb{N}$, where $a_i \in \Lambda \cup \{\tau\}$, $i \in [1 .. n]$, and exists a sequence of states $\langle q_0, q_1, \ldots, q_n \rangle$, such that for every $k \in [1 .. n]$ it holds that $q_k \in \delta(q_{k-1}, a_k)$. We say that σ *leads from* q_0 to q_n. By convention, the empty word leads to the start state. NFA B *accepts* a word $w \in \Lambda^*$ iff exists a computation $\sigma \in (\Lambda \cup \{\tau\})^*$ that leads to one of its accept states and it holds that $w = \sigma|_\Lambda$. The *language* of B is denoted by $lang(B)$ and is the set of all words B accepts. We also say that B *recognizes* $lang(B)$.

A *deterministic finite automaton* (DFA) is an NFA $(Q, \Lambda, \delta, q_0, A)$, where for every $q \in Q$ it holds that $\delta(q, \tau) = \emptyset$, and for every $q \in Q$ and every $a \in \Lambda$, $|\delta(q, a)| \leq 1$. For a language L recognized by an NFA, exists a DFA that recognizes L [12].

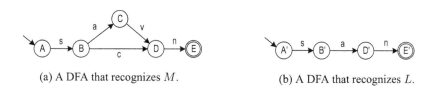

(a) A DFA that recognizes M.   (b) A DFA that recognizes L.

Fig. 2. Two DFAs that recognize languages M and L.

Figures 2a and b present DFAs that recognize, respectively, languages M and L discussed in Sect. 2. States are shown as circles, start states are marked with incoming arrows, transitions are encoded as arcs, and accept states are shown with double border.

A DFA $(Q, \Lambda, \delta, q_0, A)$ is *ergodic* if its underlying graph is strongly irreducible, i.e., for all $(q, p) \in Q \times Q$, $q \neq p$, there is a sequence of states $\langle q_1, \ldots, q_n \rangle \in Q^*$, $n \in \mathbb{N}$, such that $q_1 = q$, $q_n = p$, and for every $k \in [1 .. n - 1]$ there exists $\lambda \in \Lambda$ such that $q_{k+1} \in \delta(q_k, \lambda)$. A language L is *regular* iff there exists a DFA that recognizes L. A regular language L is *irreducible* iff it is a language of an ergodic DFA [6].

3.3 Topological Entropy

Let Σ be an alphabet and let $L \subseteq \Sigma^*$ be an irreducible language over Σ. The *topological entropy* of L, which estimates the cardinality of L by measuring the ratio of the number of distinct words in L to the length of these words, is given below [6]:

$$ent(L) = \limsup_{n \to \infty} \frac{\log |C_n(L)|}{n}. \tag{1}$$

The languages recognized by automata and event logs are *regular*; note that an event log can be encoded as a DFA, cf. Fig. 2b. But, not all such languages are *irreducible*. Given a regular language L, in [21], the authors proposed to compute the *short-circuit* topological entropy of L, denoted by $ent\bullet(L)$, as the topological entropy of the irreducible language $(L \circ \{\langle \chi \rangle\})^* \circ L$, $\chi \notin \Sigma$, i.e., $ent\bullet(L) = ent((L \circ \{\langle \chi \rangle\})^* \circ L)$. Note that one can always construct a DFA that recognizes $(L \circ \{\langle \chi \rangle\})^* \circ L$ from a DFA B that recognizes L by adding fresh transitions in B that are labeled with χ and connect the accept states of B with its start state. For example, the short-circuit topological entropy of the language recognized by the automaton in Fig. 2a is equal to the topological entropy of the language recognized by the automaton in Fig. 3.[3]

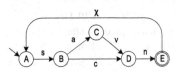

Fig. 3. A DFA that recognizes language $(M \circ \{\langle \chi \rangle\})^* \circ M$.

Finally, this result follows immediately from the definition of the short-circuit topological entropy and Lemma 4.7 in [21]:

Corollary 3.1 (Topological entropy). *Let L_1 and L_2 be two regular languages.*

1. *If $L_1 = L_2$, then $ent\bullet(L_1) = ent\bullet(L_2)$;*
2. *If $L_1 \subset L_2$, then $ent\bullet(L_1) < ent\bullet(L_2)$.*

4 Comparing Designed and Observed Processes

This section describes existing entropy-based conformance checking techniques and proposes a new approach that can control the number of skipped tasks.

---

[3] The topological entropy of an ergodic DFA is given by the logarithm of the Perron-Frobenius eigenvalue of its adjacency matrix [6].

4.1   Existing Entropy-Based Conformance Checking Techniques

Conformance checking techniques [5] measure the discrepancies and commonalities between the behaviors described in process models and event logs. *Precision* estimates the share of the common model and log behavior with respect to the overall model behavior, while *recall* assesses the share of the log behavior captured by the model.

The *exact matching* conformance checking approach for measuring precision and recall proposed in [21] relates two regular languages of a process model (M) and event log (L) with their intersection; note that the intersection of M and L is also a regular language [12]. The measurements of the behaviors encoded in these languages are carried out using the short-circuit topological entropy. The entropy-based precision (*prec*) and recall (*recall*) values between the model and log are then defined as shown below [21]:

$$prec(M, L) = \frac{ent\bullet(M \cap L)}{ent\bullet(M)}, \qquad recall(M, L) = \frac{ent\bullet(M \cap L)}{ent\bullet(L)}.$$

As follows from Corollary 3.1, for any two regular languages M and L, it holds that $prec(M, L)$ and $recall(M, L)$ values belong to the interval $[0, 1]$. In contrast to other conformance checking techniques, this approach is *trace monotone* [23], i.e., the higher the share of the model traces that are presented in the log, the higher the precision value, and similarly, the higher the share of the log traces that are captured by the model, the higher the recall value. As shown in Sect. 2, this approach can be too restrictive and in case $M \cap L = \emptyset$, $prec(M, L) = recall(M, L) = 0$.

The *partial matching* precision and recall measures described in [19] compare regular languages that allow for arbitrary skips within the model and log behaviors. First, for regular languages M and L that encode the model behavior and the log behavior, respectively, M^∞ and L^∞ are constructed. NFAs that recognize languages M^∞ and L^∞ for the example behaviors discussed in Sect. 2 are shown in Fig. 4. Then, these NFAs are converted to equivalent DFAs [12] and, finally, the precision and recall values for these "diluted" languages are calculated:

$$prec^{(\infty,\infty)}(M, L) = \frac{ent\bullet(M^\infty \cap L^\infty)}{ent\bullet(M^\infty)}, \qquad recall^{(\infty,\infty)}(M, L) = \frac{ent\bullet(M^\infty \cap L^\infty)}{ent\bullet(L^\infty)}.$$

Such conformance checking technique assesses the share of the common log and model behavior, including all the shared subtraces. In contrast to the original exact matching approach, the partial matching technique is not restrictive. Moreover, it "dilutes" the initial languages by adding extra behavior that, in some cases, results in too many matches, which hampers analysis. Recall that for the languages discussed in Sect. 2, it holds that $recall^{(\infty,\infty)}(M, L) = 1.0$, as $L^\infty \subset M^\infty$, while $recall(M, L) = 0.0$, because M and L do not have common traces, i.e., $M \cap L = \emptyset$.

(a) An NFA that recognizes language M^∞.   (b) An NFA that recognizes language L^∞.

Fig. 4. Two NFAs that recognize languages M^∞ and L^∞ discussed in Sect. 2.

4.2 k-Skips Conformance Checking

The primary task of the proposed technique is to assess the log and the model similarities assuming that some predefined numbers of steps can be skipped. Suppose the event log contains traces with additional steps not presented within the original model. In that case, this approach can still consider these traces, because a limited number of skips within the log is allowed. Similarly, the behavior of the model with a controlled number of skips can match some of the event log traces that skip the model's tasks.

Let M and L be two regular languages capturing the behavior of a process model and event log, respectively. Suppose that $M^{(l)}$ and $L^{(k)}$, where $l, k \in \mathbb{N}_0$, are languages obtained from M and L by allowing up to l and k skips in the original traces of M and L. Then, we define the precision and recall measures for these allowed skips as follows:

$$prec^{(l,k)}(M, L) = \frac{ent\bullet(M^{(l)} \cap L^{(k)})}{ent\bullet(M^{(l)})}, \quad recall^{(l,k)}(M, L) = \frac{ent\bullet(M^{(l)} \cap L^{(k)})}{ent\bullet(L^{(k)})}.$$

Again, according to Corollary 3.1, these precision and recall values belong to the interval $[0, 1]$. While the entropy calculation techniques [6,21] and the set operations over regular languages [12] are well-defined, we still need to build $M^{(l)}$ and $L^{(k)}$ languages. Without loss of generality, we consider language $L^{(k)}$ and define it constructively using Algorithm 1 by building a DFA that recognizes $L^{(k)}$.

Firstly, this algorithm constructs an NFA B_{NFA} that recognizes language $L^{(k)}$. To that end, $k + 1$ copies of the DFA that recognizes L and referred to as *layers* are added to the NFA (Lines 1 and 5). The start state of B_{NFA} is the start state of the first layer (Layer 0). The transition function δ is considered as a relation (a set of pairs) in this algorithm. As suggested in Line 10, for each transition (q^{i-1}, a) of Layer $i - 1$, a transition (q^{i-1}, τ) leading to the only state in the set $\delta(q^i, a)$, where q^{i-1} and q^i are copies of the same state at Layers $i - 1$ and i, respectively, is added.

The NFA constructed by Algorithm 1 for the language $M^{(2)}$, where M is the language discussed in Sect. 2, is presented in Fig. 5a. This automaton contains three layers connected by additional transitions labeled by τ. The layers of B_{NFA} correspond to the number of skips made. For instance, visiting a state at Layer 1 means that one skip has been made in the computation and, hence, it is still possible to make one more skip by visiting a state at Layer 2.

Once the NFA has been constructed, it is converted to an equivalent DFA using the approach from [12] (Line 14). Figure 5b shows the minimal DFA constructed from the NFA in Fig. 5a. The states of this DFA correspond to sets of the NFA states, i.e., $S_0 = \{A, B', C'', D''\}$, $S_1 = \{D, D', E', E''\}$, $S_2 = \{E, E', E''\}$, $S_3 = \{C', D''\}$, $S_4 = \{D''\}$, $S_5 = \{B, C', D', D'', E''\}$, and $S_6 = \{C, D', E''\}$. NFA states A', A'', and B'' (highlighted in gray in Fig. 5a) are *dead*, because they cannot be reached from the start state A and, thus, are not represented in the resulting DFA.

Algorithm 1: Construct a DFA that recognizes language $L^{(k)}$

Input: A DFA $B^0 = (Q^0, \Lambda, \delta^0, q_0^0, A^0)$ that recognizes language L and $k \in \mathbb{N}$.
Output: A DFA B_{DFA} that recognizes language $L^{(k)}$.

1 $Q \leftarrow Q^0$; $\delta \leftarrow \delta^0$; $q_0 \leftarrow q_0^0$; $A \leftarrow A^0$;
2 $B_{NFA} \leftarrow (Q, \Lambda, \delta, q_0, A)$;   /* Initialize an NFA B_{NFA} */
3 **for** $i \leftarrow 1$ **to** k **do**
4 $\quad$ $Q^i \leftarrow Q^0$; $\delta^i \leftarrow \delta^0$; $A^i \leftarrow A^0$;   /* Clone states and transitions */
5 $\quad$ $Q \leftarrow Q \cup Q^i$; $\delta \leftarrow \delta \cup \delta^i$; $A \leftarrow A \cup A^i$;   /* Add next layer */
6 $\quad$ /* Connect layers   */
7 $\quad$ **foreach** $q^{i-1} \in Q^{i-1}$, $a \in \Lambda$ **do**
8 $\quad\quad$ **if** $\delta(q^{i-1}, a) \neq \emptyset$ **then**
9 $\quad\quad\quad$ /* q^{i-1}, q^i are copies of the same state from Q^0 */
10 $\quad\quad\quad$ $\delta \leftarrow \delta \cup \{((q^{i-1}, \tau), \delta(q^i, a))\}$;
11 $\quad\quad$ **end**
12 $\quad$ **end**
13 **end**
14 $B_{DFA} \leftarrow Determinize(B_{NFA})$;
15 **return** B_{DFA};

4.3 Formal Properties

According to Algorithm 1, for any regular language L, it holds that $L^{(0)} = L$, and for any $k \geq 1$, by construction, it holds that $L^{(k-1)} \subseteq L^{(k)}$. From the monotonicity of $ent\bullet$ measure, refer to Corollary 3.1, it holds that $ent\bullet(L^{(k-1)}) \leq ent\bullet(L^{(k)})$, for any $k \geq 1$. This leads to the following two propositions.

Proposition 4.1. *Let M and L be two regular languages.*
Then, it holds that $prec^{(l,k)}(M, L) \leq prec^{(l,k+1)}(M, L)$, where $l, k \in \mathbb{N}_0$.

Proof. By definition, it holds that $prec^{(l,k)}(M, L) = {}^{ent\bullet(M^{(l)} \cap L^{(k)})}\!/\!_{ent\bullet(M^{(l)})}$ and $prec^{(l,k+1)}(M, L) = {}^{ent\bullet(M^{(l)} \cap L^{(k+1)})}\!/\!_{ent\bullet(M^{(l)})}$. Since it holds that $(M^{(l)} \cap L^{(k)}) \subseteq (M^{(l)} \cap L^{(k+1)})$, then ${}^{ent\bullet(M^{(l)} \cap L^{(k)})}\!/\!_{ent\bullet(M^{(l)})} \leq {}^{ent\bullet(M^{(l)} \cap L^{(k+1)})}\!/\!_{ent\bullet(M^{(l)})}$. □

Proposition 4.2. *Let M and L be two regular languages.*
Then, it holds that $recall^{(l,k)}(M, L) \leq recall^{(l+1,k)}(M, L)$, where $l, k \in \mathbb{N}_0$

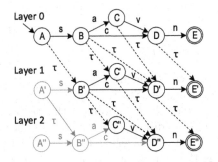

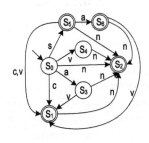

(a) An NFA that recognizes language $M^{(2)}$.   (b) A DFA that recognizes language $M^{(2)}$.

Fig. 5. Two automata that recognize languages $M^{(2)}$ and $L^{(2)}$.

The proof of Proposition 4.2 is similar to that one of Proposition 4.1.

Propositions 4.1 and 4.2 confirm the monotonicity of the k-skips measures. The next result states that the k-skips measures tend to the partial measure extreme as k approaches the infinity.

Theorem 4.1. *Let L be a regular language over Σ.*
Then, it holds that $\lim_{k \to \infty} ent\bullet(L^{(k)}) = ent\bullet(L^\infty)$.

Proof. By definition, limit superior of $\{\log |C_n((L^\infty \circ \{\langle \chi \rangle\})^* \circ L^\infty)|/n\}$, $\chi \notin \Sigma$, when n tends to ∞, is equal to $ent\bullet(L^\infty)$. Let $x_n = \log |C_n((L^\infty \circ \{\langle \chi \rangle\})^* \circ L^\infty)|/n$. Suppose that $\{x_{n_l}\}_{l=1}^\infty$, where $n_1 < n_2 < \dots$, is a subsequence, such that $x_{n_l} \to ent\bullet(L^\infty)$, as $l \to \infty$. By the definition of limit, $\forall \varepsilon > 0 \exists N(\varepsilon) \forall l \geq N$, where N is a number that depends on ε, it holds that $|x_{n_l} - ent\bullet(L^\infty)| < \varepsilon$. Consider a large enough $K(l)$ such that $\forall k > K$, $|C_{n_l}((L^{(k)} \circ \{\langle \chi \rangle\})^* \circ L^{(k)})| = |C_{n_l}((L^\infty \circ \{\langle \chi \rangle\})^* \circ L^\infty)|$. Let y_n^k be a sequence $\log |C_n((L^{(k)} \circ \{\langle \chi \rangle\})^* \circ L^{(k)})|/n$. Then, $\forall \varepsilon > 0 \exists N(\varepsilon) \forall l \geq N$ holds that $\exists K(l)$, such that $\forall k > K : |y_{n_l}^k - ent\bullet(L^\infty)| < \varepsilon$. Since $y_{n_l}^k \to ent\bullet(L^{(k)})$, as $l \to \infty$, it holds that $\forall \varepsilon > 0 \exists K(\varepsilon)$, such that $\forall k > K : |ent\bullet(L^{(k)}) - ent\bullet(L^\infty)| < \varepsilon$. Therefore, $\lim_{k \to \infty} ent\bullet(L^{(k)}) = ent\bullet(L^\infty)$. $\square$

Similarly to Theorem 4.1, the following theorem can be formulated and proved.

Theorem 4.2. *Let M and L be two regular languages over Σ. Then, it holds that* $\lim_{k \to \infty} ent\bullet(M^{(k)} \cap L) = ent\bullet(M^\infty \cap L)$ *and* $\lim_{k \to \infty} ent\bullet(M^{(k)} \cap L^{(k)}) = ent\bullet(M^\infty \cap L^\infty)$.

The next corollary follows immediately from Theorems 4.1 and 4.2.

Corollary 4.1. *Let M and L be two regular languages over Σ. Then, it holds that:*

- $\lim\limits_{k,l\to\infty} prec^{(l,k)}(M,L) = prec^{(\infty,\infty)}(M,L),\ \lim\limits_{k,l\to\infty} recall^{(l,k)}(M,L) = recall^{(\infty,\infty)}(M,L);$
- $\lim\limits_{l\to\infty} prec^{(l,k)}(M,L) = prec^{(\infty,k)}(M,L),\ \lim\limits_{l\to\infty} recall^{(l,k)}(M,L) = recall^{(\infty,k)}(M,L);$ and
- $\lim\limits_{k\to\infty} prec^{(l,k)}(M,L) = prec^{(l,\infty)}(M,L),\ \lim\limits_{k\to\infty} recall^{(l,k)}(M,L) = recall^{(l,\infty)}(M,L).$

In practice, the results of Corollary 4.1 allow balancing smoothly between the two extremes of the exact and partial measures. Starting with the exact measurements when $k = 0$ and $l = 0$, we can gradually approach the partial measurements by increasing parameters k and l. As discussed in [12], the number of states can grow exponentially when an NFA is converted to a DFA that recognizes the same language. The following theorem defines a condition under which the number of states is polynomially bounded.

Theorem 4.3. *Let $B = (Q, \Lambda, \delta, q_0, A)$ be a DFA and let $k \in \mathbb{N}$ such that $lang(B) = L$ and for any symbol $a \in \Lambda$, any state $q \in Q$, and any two (possibly empty) sequences of transitions of length less than or equal to k, one leading from q to $q' \in Q$ and the other leading from q to $q'' \in Q$ and enabling a in q' and q'', i.e., $\delta(q', a) \neq \emptyset$ and $\delta(q'', a) \neq \emptyset$, it holds that $q' = q''$. Then, there exists a DFA $B^k = (Q^k, \Lambda, \delta^k, q_0^k, A^k)$ such that $lang(B^k) = L^{(k)}$ and $|Q^k| \leq (k+1) \cdot |Q|$.*

Proof. Consider NFA B_{NFA} constructed from B at lines 1–13 of Algorithm 1. Let $closure(q)$ denote the set of all states that can be reached from a state q of B_{NFA} via τ-transitions, including q. By induction, we prove that each state of the resulting DFA B^k obtained by determinization [12] of B_{NFA} is a *closure* of one state from B_{NFA}. Basis of induction: According to the determinization algorithm [12], $q_0^k = closure(q_0)$, and hence, we say q_0^k corresponds to q_0. Step of induction: Let $q^k \in Q^k$ be a *closure* of a state $\hat{q}_1$, i.e., $q^k = \{\hat{q}_1, \hat{q}_2, \hat{q}_3, \ldots, \hat{q}_m\}$, where $\hat{q}_1, \hat{q}_2, \hat{q}_3, \ldots, \hat{q}_m$ are some states of B_{NFA}. By construction (see Algorithm 1), states $\hat{q}_1, \hat{q}_2, \hat{q}_3, \ldots, \hat{q}_m$ may belong to different layers of the NFA and for each state $\hat{q}_i$, $i \in [1 .. m]$, there exists a (possibly empty) sequence of τ-transitions with a maximum length of k leading from $\hat{q}_1$ to $\hat{q}_i$. Again, by construction, states $\hat{q}_1, \hat{q}_2, \hat{q}_3, \ldots, \hat{q}_m$ correspond to some states $q_1, q_2, q_3, \ldots, q_l$, $l \leq m$, of B and each sequence of τ-transitions with a maximum length of k in the NFA corresponds to some sequence of transitions with a maximum length of k in B. Suppose that for some $\hat{q}_j$, $j \in [1 .. m]$, exists $b \in \Lambda$ such that $\delta(\hat{q}_j, b) \neq \emptyset$; transition $\delta(\hat{q}_j, b)$ corresponds to a DFA transition and can contain not more than one NFA state. Let $\delta(\hat{q}_j, b) = \{\hat{q}_*\}$, where $\hat{q}_*$ is a state of the NFA. Then, for any $\hat{q}_p$, $p \in [1 .. m]$, $p \neq j$, it holds that $\delta(\hat{q}, b) = \emptyset$; otherwise, there is more than one transition labeled by b within corresponding sequences of states belonging to $\{q_1, q_2, q_3, \ldots, q_l\}$ in DFA B, and since the length of these sequences is less or equal to k, we obtain a contradiction to the conditions of the theorem. Hence, according to the determinization algorithm in [12], $\delta^k(q^k, b) = closure(\hat{q}_*)$, i.e., the next state of B^k is a *closure* of a state from B_{NFA}. Thus, each state of B^k corresponds to a *closure* of some state of B_{NFA}. Since B_{NFA} has at most $(k+1) \cdot |Q|$ states, it holds that $|Q^k| \leq (k+1) \cdot |Q|$.   □

This theorem proves that if the original DFA that recognizes language L does not contain occurrences of the same symbol within k-length sequences of transitions, the size of the DFA recognizing language $L^{(k)}$ is bounded linearly by the size of the NFA constructed by Algorithm 1. Real-life logs and models can contain task repetitions and this, as shown in [12], can potentially lead to the state space explosion in DFAs modeling event log languages with skips. However, as shown in the next section, such cases manifest rarely in practice and pose practical limitations only for large values of k.

5 Evaluation

This section presents results of applying our approach to computing the spectrum of entropy-based precision and recall measurements on the real-world event data. All the experiments were carried out using Intel Xeon Gold 6154 CPU @3.00 GHz with 128 GB RAM and can be reproduced with our publicly available tool [18].

To perform the experiments, we used logs of real-world IT-systems made publicly available by the IEEE Task Force on Process Mining.[4] Prior to the analysis, we filtered out infrequent events that appear in less than 80% of traces using the "filter log using simple heuristics" Process Mining (ProM) plug-in [9]. Hence, we used the same logs as in [19]. Table 2 summarizes characteristics of the filtered logs by showing the total number of unique traces (# Traces), size of the alphabet (# Ev. Classes), and the total number of event occurrences (# Events). Next, we applied the *Inductive* miner [13] to automatically construct Petri nets from the logs. For each Petri net, its reachability graph, represented as a DFA, was constructed. The event logs were also encoded as DFAs. Finally, these DFAs and Algorithm 1 were used to compute the precision and recall values presented in Sect. 4.2 for different parameters.

Table 3 presents the numbers of states in DFAs that encode the behaviors of process models ($M^{(k)}$), event logs ($L^{(k)}$), and their intersections ($M^{(k)} \cap L^{(k)}$) for different values of k, $k \in \{0, 1, 2, 5, 10, 20, \infty\}$, and the times (in milliseconds) taken to construct the DFAs; we used the technique from [19] to construct DFAs with arbitrary skips ($k = \infty$). If no DFA was constructed (using 128 GB of memory), the corresponding values are

Table 2. Characteristics of event logs.

No.	Event log	# Traces	# Ev. Classes	# Events
1	BPIC'12	2,320	18	164,144
2	BPIC'13 closed	111	3	5,179
3	BPIC'13 open	45	3	1,403
4	BPIC'13 incid.	832	4	44,607
5	WABO 1	709	64	25,823
6	WABO 2	449	85	20,420
7	WABO 3	756	56	28,482
8	WABO 4	580	61	21,848
9	WABO 5	704	68	29,513

not provided. The results show that the numbers of states and the times start to grow as k increases (up to k of 5 for event logs 2 and 3, and $k \in \{10, 20\}$ for the other logs), and then drop. The non-linear growth of states with increasing k (see, for example, event log 4 and the corresponding log DFAs for $k = 5$ and $k = 10$) can be explained by the fact that for large k, events are more likely to be repeated in k-length subsequences and, thus, Theorem 4.3 does not apply.

---

[4] https://data.4tu.nl/repository/collection:event_logs_real.

The decreases in the numbers of states relate to the cases when allowing too much behavior leads to DFAs with less number of states; indeed, the fully permissive *flower* model that recognizes all possible traces over a given alphabet contains only one state [2]. Note that all the results for parameters $k \leq 10$ were computed and are suitable for practical applications. Indeed, the precision and recall values computed for up to ten skips are sufficient for many practical scenarios. Note also that all the (not shown in the table) eigenvalues of the corresponding adjacency matrices were computed fast, always under two minutes and often within couple of seconds.

Table 4 presents (parts of) the corresponding spectrums of the precision and recall values. Using such spectrums, one can smoothly balance between the two extremes of the exact matching ($k = 0$) and the partial matching ($k = \infty$). Note that the values also confirm the result of Theorem 4.2, which states that $prec^{(k,k)}$ and $recall^{(k,k)}$ approach $prec^{(\infty,\infty)}$ and $recall^{(\infty,\infty)}$ when k approaches infinity.

6   Related Work

Over the past decade, a plethora of conformance checking methods [5] have been developed and proven to be effective in analyzing real-world process data. These methods vary in types of process models and event logs being analyzed, as well as in types of results being produced. Conformance checking techniques can produce a single number assessing the behavioral similarities of process models and event logs (*quantitative* conformance checking) or can provide rich diagnostic information highlighting deviations in model and log behaviors (*qualitative* conformance checking). In this paper, we develop and investigate a novel quantitative conformance checking technique.

Existing quantitative conformance checking techniques include such methods as *Projected conformance checking* [14], *k-order Markovian abstractions* [4], *Escaping edges* [17], *Set difference* [11], *Negative events* [7], *Anti-alignments* [8], and *Entropy-based exact* [21] and *partial matching* [19]. Several quantitative stochastic conformance checking approaches have been recently proposed [15, 16, 20]; these account for the relative likelihoods of traces described in models and recorded in logs. Finally, methods that combine quantitative and qualitative conformance checking techniques visualize the conformance diagnostics over the process model and are based on *alignment, token replay,* or *footprint* matrices, refer to [3, 22], and [2], respectively.

In [23], the authors propose various properties that precision and recall measures need to fulfill. Among precision and recall measures [2, 3, 7, 8, 11, 14, 17, 21, 22, 24] being analyzed in [23], only the entropy-based exact matching [21] fulfills all the formal properties. The entropy-based exact and partial matching techniques were also compared to other conformance checking techniques [3, 4, 7, 8, 11, 14, 17] during a qualitative analysis provided in [19]. As demonstrated in [19], the entropy-based methods [19, 21] prove their applicability to accurately rank models by their precision values in accordance with the share of behavior not present in the analyzed event log. Although the existing

Table 3. Numbers of states in DFAs and construction times (in milliseconds).

Event log	DFA	# States/time (in milliseconds)						
		$k=0$	$k=1$	$k=2$	$k=5$	$k=10$	$k=20$	$k=\infty$
1	$L^{(k)}$	9,102/2,129	18,283/24,208	31,936/48,462	98,523/125,806	367,203/330,671	1,360,759/1,636,200	90,557/95,370
	$M^{(k)} \cap L^{(k)}$	9,102/15	18,283/31	31,936/51	98,523/230	367,203/949	1,360,759/4,477	90,557/215
	$M^{(k)}$	4/4	4/8	3/12	3/4	3/7	3/20	3/4
2	$L^{(k)}$	156/15	381/47	696/74	1,185/172	1,213/399	216/1,000	216/44
	$M^{(k)} \cap L^{(k)}$	16/27	83/31	230/39	936/63	1,274/82	216/4	216/0
	$M^{(k)}$	3/4	7/4	9/8	15/8	25/8	45/15	1/8
3	$L^{(k)}$	33/4	51/7	62/12	69/19	17/35	17/63	17/7
	$M^{(k)} \cap L^{(k)}$	33/0	51/0	62/0	69/4	17/4	17/0	17/0
	$M^{(k)}$	3/7	5/4	7/8	13/8	23/8	43/15	1/8
4	$L^{(k)}$	2,032/121	7,451/1,324	23,733/2,906	417,814/37,495	11,331,602/1,599,223	—	24,336/1,379,026
	$M^{(k)} \cap L^{(k)}$	6/137	3,736/324	19,332/1,199	440,216/33,502	11,635,787/1,632,042		24,336/39
	$M^{(k)}$	5/8	9/4	13/4	25/11	45/12		1/8
5	$L^{(k)}$	10,784/2,277	25,259/33,135	48,686/64,729	254,067/202,598	2,020,868/1,230,863	—	—
	$M^{(k)} \cap L^{(k)}$	10,784/19	25,259/51	48,686/125	254,067/1,344	2,020,868/18,595		
	$M^{(k)}$	13/59	24/82	32/71	56/102	96/118		
6	$L^{(k)}$	12,316/2,110	26,892/44,344	46,613/81,855	182,837/217,852	1,308,926/1,188,256	—	
	$M^{(k)} \cap L^{(k)}$	6,482/1,277	23,576/8,098	47,467/27,151	218,291/174,728	1,308,926/11,282		
	$M^{(k)}$	15/50	27/63	37/54	73/63	133/148		
7	$L^{(k)}$	9,590/4,044	23,647/31,585	47,422/56,458	275,803/210,160	2,040,917/1,931,814	—	1,665,113/1,370,908
	$M^{(k)} \cap L^{(k)}$	8,140/797	23,747/12,993	48,265/37,546	275,969/263,653	2,040,917/21,566		1,665,113/18,392
	$M^{(k)}$	29/82	55/78	76/97	145/270	265/2,181		5/97
8	$L^{(k)}$	9,187/2,824	21,579/24,970	41,584/48,922	233,666/197,214	2,243,180/1,454,254	—	
	$M^{(k)} \cap L^{(k)}$	7,981/1,207	21,215/8,524	43,074/28,967	236,664/233,901	2,243,180/24,525		
	$M^{(k)}$	57/164	116/211	176/312	356/1,800	656/22,498		
9	$L^{(k)}$	12,891/8,165	30,325/61,564	58,596/106,293	326,177/359,597	2,994,538/2,666,084	—	
	$M^{(k)} \cap L^{(k)}$	12,891/27	30,325/23,771	58,621/108,520	326,177/1,726	2,994,538/27,819		
	$M^{(k)}$	13/50	23/62	28/54	49/67	89/101		

Table 4. Precision and recall values.

Event log	$prec^{(k,k)}/recall^{(k,k)}$						
	$k = 0$	$k = 1$	$k = 2$	$k = 5$	$k = 10$	$k = 20$	$k = \infty$
1	0.147/1.000	0.194/1.000	0.241/1.000	0.386/1.000	0.547/1.000	0.650/1.000	0.709/1.000
2	0.918/0.797	0.981/0.856	0.990/0.918	0.959/0.997	0.946/1.000	0.961/1.000	0.960/1.000
3	0.903/1.000	0.950/1.000	0.955/1.000	0.974/1.000	0.980/1.000	0.980/1.000	0.980/1.000
4	0.575/0.824	0.679/0.952	0.763/0.988	0.936/1.000	0.973/1.000	–	0.995/1.000
5	0.025/1.000	0.034/1.000	0.046/1.000	0.087/1.000	0.145/1.000	–	–
6	0.016/0.991	0.023/0.979	0.031/0.877	0.072/0.830	0.791/1.000	–	–
7	0.030/1.000	0.043/1.000	0.057/1.000	0.095/1.000	0.137/1.000	–	0.393/1.000
8	0.027/1.000	0.037/1.000	0.048/1.000	0.090/1.000	0.135/1.000	–	–
9	0.020/1.000	0.025/0.861	0.032/0.386	0.083/1.000	0.859/1.000	–	–

entropy-based measures have advantages over other conformance checking techniques, they present two different extreme measures. The exact entropy-based matching technique is too restrictive, while the partial entropy-based technique substantially extends the log and the model behaviors prior to the comparison. This paper presents an approach that gradually balances between these two different measures.

7 Conclusion and Future Work

This paper proposes a spectrum of conformance measurements for finding deviations between designed and observed processes. The new conformance values inherit properties of the recently proposed entropy-based techniques and provide flexible control over the sensitivity for identifying differences in the compared processes. We prove that with the new conformance measures, one can smoothly balance between the two existing extreme entropy-based techniques. Additionally, we analyzed the new methods' performance characteristics and showed their scalability for analyzing real-world event data. In future work, we plan to extend the techniques by providing qualitative information on differences between designed and observed processes, including the identification and visualization of deviations.

Acknowledgments. This work was in part supported by the Australian Research Council project DP180102839.

References

1. van der Aalst, W.: Service mining: using process mining to discover, check, and improve service behavior. IEEE Trans. Serv. Comput. **6**(4), 525–535 (2013)
2. van der Aalst, W.: Process Mining: Data Science in Action. Springer, Heidelberg (2016). https://doi.org/10.1007/978-3-662-49851-4
3. Adriansyah, A., Munoz-Gama, J., Carmona, J., van Dongen, B., van der Aalst, W.: Measuring precision of modeled behavior. Inf. Syst. e-Bus. Manag. **13**(1), 37–67 (2015)

4. Augusto, A., Armas-Cervantes, A., Conforti, R., Dumas, M., La Rosa, M., Reissner, D.: Abstract-and-compare: a family of scalable precision measures for automated process discovery. In: Weske, M., Montali, M., Weber, I., vom Brocke, J. (eds.) BPM 2018. LNCS, vol. 11080, pp. 158–175. Springer, Cham (2018). https://doi.org/10.1007/978-3-319-98648-7_10

5. Carmona, J., van Dongen, B., Solti, A., Weidlich, M.: Conformance Checking—Relating Processes and Models. Springer, Cham (2018). https://doi.org/10.1007/978-3-319-99414-7

6. Ceccherini-Silberstein, T., Machì, A., Scarabotti, F.: On the entropy of regular languages. Theor. Comput. Sci. **307**, 93–102 (2003)

7. De Weerdt, J., De Backer, M., Vanthienen, J., Baesens, B.: A robust F-measure for evaluating discovered process models. In: CIDM, pp. 148–155. IEEE (2011)

8. van Dongen, B.F., Carmona, J., Chatain, T.: A unified approach for measuring precision and generalization based on anti-alignments. In: La Rosa, M., Loos, P., Pastor, O. (eds.) BPM 2016. LNCS, vol. 9850, pp. 39–56. Springer, Cham (2016). https://doi.org/10.1007/978-3-319-45348-4_3

9. van Dongen, B.F., de Medeiros, A.K.A., Verbeek, H.M.W., Weijters, A.J.M.M., van der Aalst, W.M.P.: The ProM framework: a new era in process mining tool support. In: Ciardo, G., Darondeau, P. (eds.) ICATPN 2005. LNCS, vol. 3536, pp. 444–454. Springer, Heidelberg (2005). https://doi.org/10.1007/11494744_25

10. Erl, T.: Service-Oriented Architecture: Concepts, Technology, and Design. Prentice Hall PTR, Upper Saddle River (2005)

11. Greco, G., Guzzo, A., Pontieri, L., Sacca, D.: Discovering expressive process models by clustering log traces. IEEE Trans. Knowl. Data Eng. **18**(8), 1010–1027 (2006)

12. Hopcroft, J., Motwani, R., Ullman, J.: Introduction to Automata Theory, Languages, and Computation, 3rd edn. Pearson International Edition, Addison-Wesley (2007)

13. Leemans, S.J.J., Fahland, D., van der Aalst, W.M.P.: Discovering block-structured process models from incomplete event logs. In: Ciardo, G., Kindler, E. (eds.) PETRI NETS 2014. LNCS, vol. 8489, pp. 91–110. Springer, Cham (2014). https://doi.org/10.1007/978-3-319-07734-5_6

14. Leemans, S.J.J., Fahland, D., van der Aalst, W.M.P.: Scalable process discovery and conformance checking. Softw. Syst. Model. **17**(2), 599–631 (2016). https://doi.org/10.1007/s10270-016-0545-x

15. Leemans, S.J.J., Polyvyanyy, A.: Stochastic-aware conformance checking: an entropy-based approach. In: Dustdar, S., Yu, E., Salinesi, C., Rieu, D., Pant, V. (eds.) CAiSE 2020. LNCS, vol. 12127, pp. 217–233. Springer, Cham (2020). https://doi.org/10.1007/978-3-030-49435-3_14

16. Leemans, S.J.J., Syring, A.F., van der Aalst, W.M.P.: Earth movers' stochastic conformance checking. In: Hildebrandt, T., van Dongen, B.F., Röglinger, M., Mendling, J. (eds.) BPM 2019. LNBIP, vol. 360, pp. 127–143. Springer, Cham (2019). https://doi.org/10.1007/978-3-030-26643-1_8

17. Muñoz-Gama, J., Carmona, J.: A fresh look at precision in process conformance. In: Hull, R., Mendling, J., Tai, S. (eds.) BPM 2010. LNCS, vol. 6336, pp. 211–226. Springer, Heidelberg (2010). https://doi.org/10.1007/978-3-642-15618-2_16

18. Polyvyanyy, A., et al.: Entropia: a family of entropy-based conformance checking measures for process mining. CoRR. vol. abs/2008.09558 (2020)

19. Polyvyanyy, A., Kalenkova, A.: Monotone conformance checking for partially matching designed and observed processes. In: ICPM, pp. 81–88. IEEE (2019)

20. Polyvyanyy, A., Moffat, A., García-Bañuelos, L.: An entropic relevance measure for stochastic conformance checking in process mining. In: ICPM. IEEE (2020, in press)

21. Polyvyanyy, A., Solti, A., Weidlich, M., Di Ciccio, C., Mendling, J.: Monotone precision and recall measures for comparing executions and specifications of dynamic systems. ACM Trans. Softw. Eng. Methodol. **29**(3) (2020)

22. Rozinat, A., van der Aalst, W.: Conformance checking of processes based on monitoring real behavior. Inf. Syst. **33**(1), 64–95 (2008)

23. Syring, A.F., Tax, N., van der Aalst, W.M.P.: Evaluating conformance measures in process mining using conformance propositions. In: Koutny, M., Pomello, L., Kristensen, L.M. (eds.) Transactions on Petri Nets and Other Models of Concurrency XIV. LNCS, vol. 11790, pp. 192–221. Springer, Heidelberg (2019). https://doi.org/10.1007/978-3-662-60651-3_8

24. Weijters, A., van der Aalst, W., Alves De Medeiros, A.: Process mining with the heuristics miner algorithm. Technical report, TU/e, Eindhoven (2006)

A Knowledge Graph Based Approach for Mobile Application Recommendation

Mingwei Zhang[1], Jiawei Zhao[1], Hai Dong[2(✉)], Ke Deng[2], and Ying Liu[1]

[1] Software College, Northeastern University, Shenyang, China
{zhangmw,liuy}@swc.neu.edu.cn, zhaojiawei@stumail.neu.edu.cn
[2] School of Science, RMIT University, Melbourne, Australia
{Hai.Dong,Ke.Deng}@rmit.edu.au

Abstract. With the rapid prevalence of mobile devices and the dramatic proliferation of mobile applications (apps), app recommendation becomes an emergent task that would benefit both app users and stockholders. How to effectively organize and make full use of rich side information of users and apps is a key challenge to address the sparsity issue for traditional approaches. To meet this challenge, we proposed a novel end-to-end Knowledge Graph Convolutional Embedding Propagation Model (KGEP) for app recommendation. Specifically, we first designed a knowledge graph construction method to model the user and app side information, then adopted KG embedding techniques to capture the factual triplet-focused semantics of the side information related to the first-order structure of the KG, and finally proposed a relation-weighted convolutional embedding propagation model to capture the recommendation-focused semantics related to high-order structure of the KG. Extensive experiments conducted on a real-world dataset validate the effectiveness of the proposed approach compared to the state-of-the-art recommendation approaches.

Keywords: Mobile app recommendation · Knowledge graph · Knowledge graph embedding · Graph convolutional network · Embedding propagation

1 Introduction

Recent years, people have witnessed a rapid prevalence of smart mobile devices and a dramatic proliferation of mobile applications. The large number and high variety of apps are posing a great challenge for users to choose appropriate ones. As a consequence, app recommendation has attracted more and more attention these years. On the one hand, it can help users find their desired or interested apps more easily and quickly. On the other hand, it will benefit developers and stockholders of apps to get more profits in the mobile app ecosystem.

Supported by National Key Research and Development Project of China (No. 2019YFB1405302).

E. Kafeza et al. (Eds.): ICSOC 2020, LNCS 12571, pp. 355–369, 2020.
https://doi.org/10.1007/978-3-030-65310-1_25

However, sparsity is a typical characteristic of app usage data. For instance, as of May 2020, there are over 2.9 million apps on Google Play [1], but most of billions of users only install at most hundreds of apps. To address the sparsity problem of user-app interactions, researchers usually turn to feature-rich scenarios, where side information of users and apps is used to compensate for the sparsity and improve the performance of recommendation. As detailed in Sect. 5, most of them [2–10] only exploited limited types of side information. In addition, they usually treated different kinds of side information as isolated features of users and apps, and neglected the relations and semantics of them. Consequently, how to effectively organize and make full use of side information of users and apps is a great challenge to make successful app recommendation.

To meet the above challenge, we proposed a KG based app recommendation approach. A KG is a type of directed heterogeneous graph in which nodes correspond to entities and edges correspond to relations [11]. Among various types of side information, the KG contains much more fruitful facts and introduces semantic relatedness among apps, which can help find their latent connections. Beyond that, the KG consists of relations with various types, which is helpful for exploring a user's interests reasonably. To be specific, we proposed a KG convolutional embedding propagation model (KGEP) for app recommendation. First, a KG construction method is designed to organize different kinds of side information effectively. Then, a translation based KG embedding model is adopted to capture the general semantics of side information from the perspective of general KG facts. Finally, a relation-weighted KG convolutional embedding propagation model is designed to further capture the recommendation-focused semantics from the perspective of recommendation. We evaluated the proposed model on a real dataset crawled from Google Play. The experimental results verify the effectiveness of our method for app recommendation when compared to the state-of-the-art methods.

The major contributions of this paper are summarized as follows.

1. It is the first work, to the best of our knowledge, that incorporates a KG to organize and take full advantage of diverse side information for app recommendation.
2. We proposed a novel end-to-end app recommendation model KGEP, which can capture the semantics of rich side information related to both the first-order and high-order structures of the constructed KG, by utilizing KG general embedding techniques and convolutional propagated embedding techniques respectively.
3. We conducted extensive experiments using a real app dataset. The comparative results demonstrate that our approach achieves higher performance compared to the state-of-the-art recommendation methods.

The remainder of this paper is organized as follows. Section 2 formulates the app recommendation problem. Section 3 presents the proposed model in detail. Section 4 discusses the experimental results. Section 5 introduces related works. Finally, we concluded the paper and indicated some future directions in Sect. 6.

2   Notations and Problem Formulation

The app recommendation scenario contains a set of users $\mathcal{U} = \{u_1, u_2, \ldots, u_{|\mathcal{U}|}\}$, a set of apps $\mathcal{A} = \{a_1, a_2, \ldots, a_{|\mathcal{A}|}\}$, and their historical interactions. In addition, we have rich side information for users and apps (e.g., app attributes and description texts). Typically, such auxiliary data consists of real-world entities and relationships among them to profile a user or an app. We organized the side information in the form of KG.

App Recommendation Knowledge Graph (**ARKG**), denoted as $\mathcal{G}$, is a directed graph composed of entity-relation-entity triples (h, r, t), where $h \in \mathcal{E}$, $r \in \mathcal{R}$ and $t \in \mathcal{E}$ are the head, relation, and tail of a knowledge factual triple, and $\mathcal{E}$ and $\mathcal{R}$ are the set of entities and relations in $\mathcal{G}$, respectively. For example, the triple (Facebook, OfferedBy, Facebook) states the fact that the company "Facebook" offers the app "Facebook". According to the side information which we can crawl and their importance for recommendation, we defined the following 13 types of entities for the ARKG.

Definition 1 *(Content-Topic Entity).* Considering *Readme* texts of apps provided by developers contain rich app profiles and are crucial to the efficacy of the ARKG to do recommendation, We used probabilistic topic modeling to incorporate them into the ARKG. A *Content-Topic* entity is a distribution over terms, which can be used to explore users' preference on specific topics. The number of *Content-Topic* entities involved in the ARKG is a hyperparameter and can be configured by recommender service users.

Due to space limitations, the definitions of the other 12 types of entities (i.e., *User, App, Category, Provider, Popularity, Age-Restriction, Ads, Fee, Interactive-Elements, Quality, Updated-Time, Size*) involved in the ARKG are not listed any more. Based on these kinds of entities, 18 relations were defined for the ARKG, the detailed information of which is listed in Table 1.

The relation *INTERACT* denotes historical user-app interactions. The next 11 relations denote that an app has some specific profiles. The last 6 relations denote that one entity is similar to another with the same entity type. Based on the above definitions, how to extract factual triplets and construct the ARKG will be presented in Sect. 3.1.

We formulated the KG-based app recommendation problem as follows. Given the sets of users and apps, and their side information, we aim to construct an ARKG $\mathcal{G}$. Then taking $\mathcal{G}$ as an input, we aimed to predict whether user u has a potential interest in app a with which she has had no interaction before. Our task can be formulated to learn a prediction function $\hat{y}_a^u = \mathcal{F}(u, a | \theta, \mathcal{G})$, where $\hat{y}_a^u$ denotes the probability that user u will engage with app a, and θ denotes the model parameters of function $\mathcal{F}$.

3   Methodology

The framework of our app recommendation model KGEP was presented in Fig. 1, which consists of four main components: 1) ARKG constructing, which aims to

Table 1. Relations involved in the ARKG

Relation	Head entity	Tail entity	Related side information
INTERACT	*User*	*App*	User-app interaction data
HAVINGCT	*App*	*Content-Topic*	Apps' *Readme* texts
HAVINGC	*App*	*Category*	Apps' category data
OFFEREDBY	*App*	*Provider*	Apps' provider data
CONTENTR	*App*	*Age-Restriction*	Apps' content rating data
HAVINGA	*App*	*Ads*	No ads or not of an app
HAVINGF	*App*	*Fee*	Free or not of an app
HAVINGIE	*App*	*Interactive-Elements*	Apps' interactive-elements data
HAVINGQ	*App*	*Quality*	Users' review grades of apps
HAVINGP	*App*	*Popularity*	Apps' install numbers
HAVINGUT	*App*	*Updated-Time*	Apps' updated time
HAVINGS	*App*	*Size*	Apps' size data
USIMILAR	*User*	*User*	User-app rating matrix
CTSIMILAR	*Content-Topic*	*Content-Topic*	*Content-Topic* entity data
QSIMILAR	*Quality*	*Quality*	*Quality* entity data
PSIMILAR	*Popularity*	*Popularity*	*Popularity* entity data
UTSIMILAR	*Updated-Time*	*Updated-Time*	*Updated-Time* entity data
SSIMILAR	*Size*	*Size*	*Size* entity data

construct an ARKG for app recommendation; 2) general KG embedding, which parameterizes each entity or relation as two vectors by preserving the semantic relatedness among the ARKG; 3) recommendation focused convolutional embedding propagation, which recursively propagates embeddings from a node's tail neighbors to update its representation; 4) prediction and learning, which outputs the predicted matching scores by the final representations of users and apps, and learns the model parameters. We presented them in detail in the following subsections respectively.

3.1   ARKG Construction

ARKG construction mainly involves 2 sub-tasks, i.e., entity identification and relation extraction.

Entity Identification. Except *Content-Topic* entities, the other kinds of entities listed in the above section can be explicitly identified from the side information of users and apps. So we just described the identification method of *Content-Topic* entities here.

We adopted an LDA model to identify *Content-Topic* entities. Its basic idea is that documents are represented as random mixtures over latent topics, where each topic is characterized by a distribution over words. The process of *Content-Topic* entity identification can be summarized as follows.

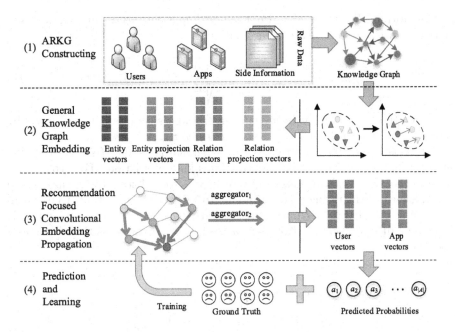

Fig. 1. Framework of the proposed Model KGEP

1. **Text preprocessing and hyperparameter setting**. Taking the *Readme* text of each app as a document, we can get a corpus, i.e., a collection of $|\mathcal{A}|$ documents. We first preprocessed the corpus, i.e., conducting tokenization, stop words removing, stemming, lemmatization and typo corrections. NLTK and Spacy packages of Python were used for these tasks. Then, we set the number of topics and other hyperparameters.

2. **LDA model learning**. Given a preprocessed corpus of documents, we used variational EM algorithm to estimate parameters in LDA model. Then for each app a, let $\mathcal{Z} = z_1, z_2, \ldots, z_K$ be the set of latent topics, we can obtain the parameters $\theta_a = \theta_{a1}, \theta_{a2}, \ldots, \theta_{aK}$ of its Dirichlet distribution over $\mathcal{Z}$.

3. ***Content-Topic* entity identifying**. For each app a, given its inferred Dirichlet distribution parameters $\theta_a = \theta_{a1}, \theta_{a2}, \ldots, \theta_{aK}$ over $\mathcal{Z}$, it is defined that app a has *Content-Topic* z_k if and only if $!\exists \theta_{ai} | \theta_{ai} > \theta_{ak}, (1 \leq i \leq K)$. Namely, an app has one and only *Content-Topic* entity.

Relation Extraction. Due to space limitations, we only detailed the triplet extraction methods for relations *CTSIMILAR* and *USIMILAR*, which are more complex than the methods for other relations.

The relation *CTSIMILAR* represents the similarity among *Content-Topic* entities in the ARKG. Let $\mathcal{W} = \{w_1, w_2, \ldots, w_V\}$ be the set of words and $\mathcal{Z} = \{z_1, z_2, \ldots, z_K\}$ be the set of latent topics, we can get the probability distribution $\Phi_k = \{\phi_{k1}, \phi_{k2}, \ldots, \phi_{kV}\}$ of each topic $z_k (1 \leq k \leq K)$ over $\mathcal{W}$ using variational

EM algorithm. Then, for any two *Content-Topic* entities z_i and z_j, we used Hellinger distance to measure their similarity.

$$similarity\_ct(z_i, z_j) = \frac{1}{\sqrt{2}} \sqrt{\sum_{l=1}^{V} (\sqrt{\phi_{il}} - \sqrt{\phi_{jl}})^2} \tag{1}$$

Given the *Content-Topic-Similarity* threshold $cts(0 < cts < 1)$, there will be a relation $(z_i, CTSIMILAR, z_j)$ if $similarity\_ct(z_i, z_j) \geq cts$.

The relation *USIMILAR* represents the similarity among *User* entities. We used a user-app rating matrix to extract this kind of relations. For typical app recommendation scenario, a user can rate an app from "1 star" to "5 star", where we transformed the rating grades from 0.2 to 1.0, and "none rating" to 0. Then, for each user $u_i(1 \leq i \leq |\mathcal{U}|)$, we can get a rating vector $r_i = \{r_{i1}, r_{i2}, \ldots, r_{i|\mathcal{A}|}\}$. The similarity between any two users u_i and u_j are modeled as their Tanimoto coefficient.

$$
\begin{aligned}
similarity\_u(u_i, u_j) &= \frac{r_i \cdot r_j}{\|r_i\|^2 + \|r_j\|^2 - r_i \cdot r_j} \\
&= \frac{\sum_{l=1}^{|\mathcal{A}|} r_{il} r_{jl}}{\sum_{l=1}^{|\mathcal{A}|} r_{il}^2 + \sum_{l=1}^{|\mathcal{A}|} r_{jl}^2 - \sum_{l=1}^{|\mathcal{A}|} r_{il} r_{jl}}
\end{aligned}
\tag{2}
$$

Given the *User-Similarity* threshold $us(0 < us < 1)$, we can extract a triplet $(u_i, USIMILAR, u_j)$ if $similarity\_u (u_i, u_j) \geq us$ for u_i and u_j.

3.2   General KG Embedding

General KG embedding was then performed on the constructed ARKG to embed its entities and relations into continuous vector spaces, while preserving its inherent structure. For the ARKG mainly consists of N-to-1 and N to N relations, we employed TransD [12], which is suitable for dealing with such complex relations and at the same time has relatively high efficiency, to embed the ARKG.

To be more specific, for each triplet (h, r, t) in the ARKG, it learns two vectors for the head entity h, tail entity t and relation r respectively, denoted as $\mathbf{h}$, $\mathbf{h}_p$, $\mathbf{t}$, $\mathbf{t}_p$, $\mathbf{r}$ and $\mathbf{r}_p$, where $\mathbf{h}, \mathbf{h}_p, \mathbf{t}, \mathbf{t}_p \in \mathbb{R}^m$ and $\mathbf{r}, \mathbf{r}_p \in \mathbb{R}^n$. We set the hyperparameters $m = n = d$ for the convenience of the learned vectors' application in recommendation. The prior vectors $\mathbf{h}$, $\mathbf{t}$ and $\mathbf{r}$ represent the meaning of the entities and relation. The other ones (i.e., $\mathbf{h}_p, \mathbf{t}_p, \mathbf{r}_p$) are called projection vectors representing the way that how to project the entity embeddings $\mathbf{h}$ and $\mathbf{t}$ into the relation vector $\mathbf{r}$'s space. Specifically, they were used to construct mapping matrices, which are defined as follows.

$$
\begin{aligned}
\mathbf{M}_{rh} &= \mathbf{r}_p \mathbf{h}_p^\top + \mathbf{I}^{d \times d} \\
\mathbf{M}_{rt} &= \mathbf{r}_p \mathbf{t}_p^\top + \mathbf{I}^{d \times d}
\end{aligned}
\tag{3}
$$

where $\mathbf{M}_{rh}$, $\mathbf{M}_{rh} \in \mathbb{R}^{d \times d}$ are mapping matrices, and $\mathbf{I}$ denotes the identity matrix of size $d \times d$. With the mapping matrices, the projected vectors of $\mathbf{h}$ and $\mathbf{t}$ are defined as follows.

$$\mathbf{h}_\perp = \mathbf{M}_{rh}\mathbf{h}, \mathbf{t}_\perp = \mathbf{M}_{rt}\mathbf{h} \qquad (4)$$

To learn embeddings of each entity and relation by optimizing the translation principle $\mathbf{h}_\perp + \mathbf{r} \approx \mathbf{t}_\perp$, the plausibility score (aka energy score) of a given triplet (h, r, t) was formulated as follows.

$$g(h, r, t) = -\|\mathbf{h}_\perp + \mathbf{r} - \mathbf{t}_\perp\|_2^2 \qquad (5)$$

where a higher score of $g(h, r, t)$ suggests that the triplet is more likely to be true, and vice versa.

The training of TransD uses the following margin-based ranking loss to encourage discrimination between golden triplets and incorrect ones.

$$\mathcal{L}_{KG} = \sum_{(h,r,t)\in S} \sum_{(h',r,t')\in S'} \max\left(0, \gamma + g(h', r, t') - g(h, r, t)\right) \qquad (6)$$

where $\max(x, y)$ aims to get the maximum between x and y, γ is the margin, $S = \{(h, r, t)\}$ is the set of golden triples contained in the ARKG. Corrupting each golden triplet $(h, r, t) \in S$ by replacing the head entity or the tail entity, the set of negative triples $S' = \{(h', r, t')\}$ can be generated. The process of minimizing the above objective was carried out with stochastic gradient descent (SGD) in mini-batch mode.

This component embeds the entities and relations on the granularity of triples. After getting its outputs, we can use them to make app recommendation directly and roughly by Eq. 5.

3.3   Convolutional Embedding Propagation

Next, focused on app recommendation, we built upon the architecture of graph convolution network to further capture both high-order structure and semantic information in the ARKG to make more precise recommendation. Here we started by describing a single layer, and then discussed how to generalize it to multiple layers. As illustrated in Fig. 2 (a), one single layer mainly involves 2 steps: 1) for each entity, aggregating information from its neighbors to form its neighbors' aggregated vector; 2) integrating with its own current latent vector to update its embedding for the next layer.

Aggregating Information from Neighbours. In the real ARKG, head entities are causally determined by tail entities (e.g. the apps should be profiled by their attributes, and users' preference should be influenced by apps). So information is aggregated from tail entities to head entities in our model. In addition, to characterize both semantic information of the ARKG and users' personalized

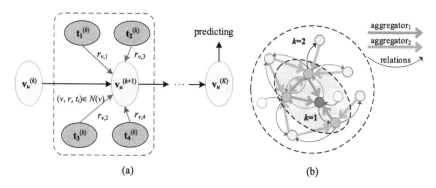

Fig. 2. Illustration of our convolutional embedding propagation approach. (a) an example of how an entity aggregates information from its neighbours. (b) an example of how the model propagates information between two layers. (Color figure online)

interests in relations, neighbours are weighted dependent on the connecting relation and specific user while calculating the neighbours' aggregated vector for a given entity. Specifically, given a user u and a node v in the ARKG ($\mathcal{G}$), we use $\mathcal{N}_v = \{(h, r, t) | (h = v) \wedge (h, r, t) \in \mathcal{G}\}$ to denote the set of triplets where v is the head entity. Then the neighbours' aggregated vector of v specific to u is computed as follows.

$$\mathbf{v}_u^{\mathcal{N}_v} = \sum_{(h,r,t)\in\mathcal{N}_v} w_u^r \mathbf{t} \tag{7}$$

where $\mathbf{t} \in \mathbb{R}^d$ is the vector of tail entity t, and w_u^r is the weight between user u and relation r, which characterizes the importance of relation r to user u and be computed as follows.

$$w_u^r = \frac{\exp(\pi(\mathbf{u}, \mathbf{r}))}{\sum_{(h,r,t)\in\mathcal{N}_v} \exp(\pi(\mathbf{u}, \mathbf{r}))} \tag{8}$$

where $\mathbf{u} \in \mathbb{R}^d$ and $\mathbf{r} \in \mathbb{R}^d$ are the embeddings of user u and relation r. $\pi :$ $\mathbb{R}^d \times \mathbb{R}^d \rightarrow \mathbb{R}^d$ is a weight score function (e.g.., we adopted inner product in this paper).

Generally, $\mathbf{v}_u^{\mathcal{N}_v}$ not only characterizes the local proximity structure of node v, but also exploits the personalized interests of user u in relations.

Updating Embeddings for the Next Layer. To update the embedding of each node v as its representation in the next layer, we concatenated its current representation $\mathbf{v}_u$ with its neighbours' aggregated vector $\mathbf{v}_u^{\mathcal{N}_v}$, and fed this concatenated vector through a fully connected layer with nonlinear activation function σ to transform it to the new representation of v. It can be formulated as:

$$\mathbf{v}_u' = \sigma\big(\mathbf{W} \cdot (\mathbf{v}_u \| \mathbf{v}_u^{\mathcal{N}_v}) + \mathbf{b}\big) \tag{9}$$

where $\mathbf{v}'_u$ (i.e., the output of this layer) is the new representation of node v specific to user u, and $\mathbf{W}$ and $\mathbf{b}$ are transformation weight and bias, respectively. "$\|$" denotes the concatenation operation.

Note that not all entities are updated because some of them in the ARKG have no tail neighbours.

Information Propagating Among Layers. Through a single layer, we can capture 2-order entity connectivity, taking the general KG embedding as the 1-order connectivity. However, exploiting higher-order connectivity is of importance to perform high-quality recommendation. It is intuitive to propagate information between different layers to capture higher-order structural proximity among entities. As illustrated in Fig. 2(b), given the brown entity, its embedding is updated by aggregating information from its neighbours (i.e., the green nodes), while the embeddings of the green nodes are updated by aggregating information from their neighbours (i.e., the blue ones).

More formally, we stacked $K - 1$ propagation layers and used Eq. 9 to propagate embeddings along higher-order connectivity. For notational convenience, we denoted the representation of node v specific to user u at depth $k-1$ as $\mathbf{v}_u^{(k)}$. Generally speaking, $\mathbf{v}_u^{(k)}$ is a mixture of initial representations of node v and its neighbors up to k hops away.

3.4 Model Prediction and Learning

After performing $K - 1$ layers, we obtained the final representation $\mathbf{v}_u^{(K)}$ of node v specific to user u, which characterizes v's high-order entity dependencies up to K hops and captures u's potential long-distance interests. In addition, the outputs of the general KG embedding characterize the distance between head entity h and tail entity t in the space of relation r for a triplet (h, r, t). So for user u and app a, we concatenated the representations of the two components into a single vector to do prediction as follows.

$$\mathbf{u}^* = (\mathbf{u}_\perp + \mathbf{r}_{INTERACT})\|\mathbf{u}^{(K)}, \qquad \mathbf{a}_u^* = \mathbf{a}_\perp\|\mathbf{a}_u^{(K)} \tag{10}$$

where $\mathbf{r}_{INTERACT}$ is the vector of relation "$INTERACT$", $\mathbf{u}_\perp$ and $\mathbf{a}_\perp$ are the vectors of user u and app a in the $\mathbf{r}_{INTERACT}$ space. They are all the outputs of the general KG embedding component, while $\mathbf{u}^{(K)}$ and $\mathbf{a}_u^{(K)}$ are the final outputs of the convolutional embedding propagating component.

Finally, we computed the inner product of user and app representations, so as to predict their matching score:

$$\hat{y}_{u,a} = \mathbf{u}^{*\top}\mathbf{a}_u^* \tag{11}$$

To learn the parameters of our app recommendation model, we adopted negative sampling strategy, and the objective function was defined as binary crossentropy loss with $L2$ norm regularization:

$$\mathcal{L}_{CEP} = \sum_{u\in\mathcal{U}}\sum_{v\in Tm^u}\left(-\log\hat{y}_{u,v} + \sum_{i\in Neg_v^u} -\log(1-\hat{y}_{u,i})\right) + \lambda\|\theta\|_2^2 \tag{12}$$

where $Tm^u = \{v|y_{u,v} = 1\}$ is the set of user u's all training instances. For each training instance (u, v), we randomly sampled x negative apps, denoted as Neg_v^u. λ is coefficient for the regularization and θ denotes all model parameters. The model was trained via Adam optimizer.

4   Empirical Study

In this section, we compared our approach with several state-of-the-art recommendation methods using real-world app usage data and studied the impact of parameters on the performance of our model.

4.1   Dataset Description

We collected our dataset from Google Play. We crawled each app relevant metadata that the ARKG constructing needs. To bypass the cold start, we first omited apps with less than 10 users and then excluded users with less than 10 apps. After this preprocessing step, our dataset contains 12802 users, 4539 apps, and 198077 rating observations. The user app rating matrix has a sparsity as high as 0.341%.

4.2   Comparing Methods

To evaluate the performance of the proposed model, we compared it with the following representative baselines.

1. **UserCF**: A user-user similarity matrix can be obtained while extracting *USIMILAR* relations for the ARKG. Then, we used the classic user-based collaborative filtering as a baseline.
2. **BPR-MF** [13]: The Bayesian Personalized Ranking based matrix factorization, is a representative algorithm designed for implicit feedback, adopting a pairwise ranking loss to optimize the latent factor models.
3. **FISM** [14]: This is representative item-based collaborative filtering Top-N recommendation model, used to verify the effectiveness of our recommendation model.
4. **NFM** [15]: This is a state-of-the-art factorization model, which seamlessly combines FM and neural network in modelling feature interactions.
5. **TransDR**: This is a simplified translation-based recommendation version of our approach, which takes the representation learned by TransD as inputs of a one hidden layer neural network to make recommendation directly.

4.3   Experiment Setup

We divided the preprocessed dataset into three subsets: training, validation, and test. For every user, we randomly selected 70%, 10% and 20% interacted apps into the training set, the validation set and the test set respectively.

For ARKG construction, we set the number of *Content-Topic* entities to 50, the *Content-Topic-Similarity* threshold *cts* to 0.9, and the *User-Similarity* threshold *us* to 0.98, and then we extracted 406044 triplets for the ARKG.

We implemented our KGEP model in Tensorflow. The hyper-parameters were optimized on the validation set, which are listed as follows. The embedding size is 16, the number of propagation layers is 1, dropout is 0, epoch is 80, and learning rate is 0.02. All the experiment results of our model are corresponding to the above hyper-parameter values, except a specific hyper-parameter may vary while preserving the values of the other hyper-parameters when we analyzed our model sensitivity on the given hyper-parameter. For all the baselines, we set respective optimal parameters either according to corresponding references or based on our experiment results. We adopted learner *Adam* for the models: BPR-MF, FISM, NFM and KGEP, and adopt learner *SDG* for TransDR.

We adopted three widely used metrics for performance evaluation: *Recall@K*, *Precision@K* and mean average precision (*MAP@K*), where K indicates recommending top K ranked apps. For all the metrics, the larger the value, the better the performance.

4.4 Performance Comparison with Baseline Methods

The performance comparison results are presented in Table 2. We had the following observations: (1) KGEP consistently yields the best performance on all the metrics and K values. In detail, KGEP improves much more over the strongest baselines on the metric MAP than the other 2 metrics, and when K is smaller; (2) BPR-MF achieves better performance than the other baselines in most cases; (3) TransDR sometimes achieves better performance than all the baselines, indicating that just general KG embedding has efficacy to some extent to make app recommendation.

4.5 Model Analysis and Discussion

To get deep insights on the proposed model KGEP, we investigated its sensitivity on some core hyper-parameters. Figure 3 illustrates the effect of embedding size. Due to the computational cost, we can not train TransD model after the embedding size is larger than 16. So, we used xavier initializer to initialize the propagation embeddings after the dimensionality is larger than 16, and concatenated the 16-dimensional embeddings of TransD to make recommendation. From Fig. 3, we can see, our model KGEP can achieve the best performance when the embedding size is set to 16.

Figure 4 shows the influence of layer numbers. It illustrates that our model achieves the best performance just with one embedding propagation layer on the basis of general ARKG embeddings. We also conducted the experiments to analyze the effects of dropout and learning rate. Due to space limitations, the corresponding figures are not presented any more. The results are that the performance of KGEP would be the best when the learning rate equals to 0.02 among {0.0001, 0.0005, 0.001, 0.05, 0.02, 0.1, 0.5}, and would be better when

Table 2. Performance comparison on the Google Play dataset. The best results are starred, and the second-best results are listed in bold.

Top-K	Metrics	UserCF	BRP-MF	FISM	NFM	TransDR	KGEP
10	Precision (%)	0.155	**0.458**	0.209	0.301	0.315	**1.000***
	Recall (%)	0.254	**1.159**	0.521	0.763	0.567	**2.461***
	MAP (%)	0.361	**1.309**	0.656	0.859	0.871	**3.853***
20	Precision (%)	0.144	**0.440**	0.199	0.277	0.390	**0.600***
	Recall (%)	0.341	**2.187**	0.997	1.352	1.151	**3.061***
	MAP (%)	0.398	**1.516**	0.769	1.001	1.285	**3.996***
30	Precision (%)	0.145	0.426	0.200	0.265	**0.430**	**0.567***
	Recall (%)	0.452	**3.183**	1.491	1.864	1.749	**4.256***
	MAP (%)	0.428	**1.616**	0.821	1.069	1.510	**4.177***
40	Precision (%)	0.145	0.413	0.191	0.258	**0.461**	**0.475***
	Recall (%)	0.550	**4.034**	1.864	2.450	2.385	**4.839***
	MAP (%)	0.450	**1.667**	0.848	1.103	1.599	**4.232***

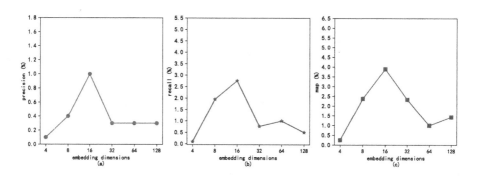

Fig. 3. Effect of embedding size

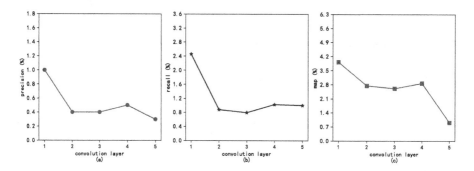

Fig. 4. Effect of embedding propagation layer numbers

the dropout equals to 0 or 0.2 than other values {0.1, 0.3, 0.4, 0.5, 0.6, 0.7, 0.8, 0.9}.

5   Related Work

Knowledge Graph Based Recommendation. Recommender systems are now indispensable in many Web applications, such as App stores. The matrix factorization algorithm BPR-MF [13], the item-based collaborative filtering algorithm FISM [14], and the factorization model algorithm NFM [15] are arguably the most representative among the large number of recommendation algorithms developed. Recently, KG, as one of the most effective data modelling techniques, has been spotlighted in recommender systems. In general, existing KG-aware recommendation can be classified into three categories. The first category is embedding-based methods, such as CKE [16], DKN [17], which preprocess a KG with knowledge graph embedding algorithms and incorporates the learned entity embeddings into a recommendation framework. However, these methods are usually more suitable for in-graph applications such as link prediction than for recommendation. The second category is path-based methods, such as PER [18], KPRN [19], which explore the various patterns of connections among items in KG to provide additional guidance for recommendations. However, they rely heavily on meta-paths, which is hard to optimize in practice, so that has a large impact on the final recommendation performance. The third category is embedding propagation methods, such as RippleNet [20], KGAT [21], KGCN [22], which combine embedding-based and path-based methods in KG-aware recommendation, so as to address the limitations of the above two categories.

Different from the above KG-aware recommendation models, we leverage the general embeddings and the propagated embeddings simultaneously to make app recommendation.

Mobile App Recommendation. Mobile app recommendation has attracted much attention these days. By focusing on different kinds of side information, researchers proposed the following representative app recommendation approaches. Focusing on the privilege data of apps, The studies [2–4] mainly considered privacy leak and security risk issues to perform personalized app recommendations. Focusing on geographical information of users, Zhu et al. [5] proposed a novel location-based probabilistic factor analysis mechanism to help people get an appropriate mobile app. Focusing on version information of apps, Cao et al. [6] proposed a novel version-sensitive mobile app recommendation framework by jointly exploring the version progression and dual-heterogeneous data. Focusing on app usage patterns of users, Xu et al. [7] proposed a neural network based approach to leverage the predictive power of app usage context patterns to do effective app recommendation. Focusing on category information of apps, Guo et al. [8] proposed an app recommendation model based on deep factorization machine, which can make use of categorical and textual information of apps. Further considering the interactions of categories and other side information of apps, Liang et al. [9] utilized a tensor-based framework to effectively integrate app category information and multi-view features of users and apps to do context-aware app recommendation. Focusing on the complex semantics among different kinds of side information, Xie et al. [10] exploited weighted meta-graph and heterogeneous information network for mobile app recommendation, mainly considering user review information. However, it is not an end-to-end method. Meta-graphs are hard to be designed optimally, which will further influence the efficacy of recommendation.

Differed from the above state-of-the-art app recommendation methods, we proposed an end-to-end framework and leveraged KG to recommend apps for users. It can model complex semantics among diverse side information more explicitly to make better recommendation.

6   Conclusion and Future Work

This paper proposed a novel KG based mobile app recommendation approach. We first designed a KG construction method to organize rich side information of users and apps, then adopted a translation based KG embedding method to capture the semantics of side information related to first-order structure of the constructed KG, and proposed a convolutional embedding propagation model to capture the semantics related to high-order structure of the KG. By incorporating KG into app recommendation, our approach can effectively model and take full advantage of rich side information to alleviate the sparsity issue and improve recommendation performance. The comparative experimental results show that our approach outperforms the competing recommendation methods in terms of precision, recall and MAP.

In the future, we will attempt to apply our model to other recommendation application scenarios, such as general Web service recommendation or Web API recommendation for Mashups, to further validate it and find and improve its limitations.

References

1. Number of Android apps on Google Play. https://www.appbrain.com/stats/number-of-android-apps. Accessed 12 May 2020
2. Liu, B., Kong, D., Cen, L., Gong, N.Z., Jin, H., Xiong, H.: Personalized mobile app recommendation: reconciling app functionality and user privacy preference. In: WSDM, pp. 315–324. ACM, New York (2015)
3. Sheng, Q.Z., Stroulia, E., Tata, S., Bhiri, S. (eds.): ICSOC 2016. LNCS, vol. 9936. Springer, Cham (2016). https://doi.org/10.1007/978-3-319-46295-0
4. Yin, H., Chen, L., Wang, W., Du, X., Nguyen, Q.V.H., Zhou, X.: Mobi-SAGE: a sparse additive generative model for mobile app recommendation. In: ICDE, Piscataway, pp. 75–78. IEEE (2017)
5. Zhu, K., Zhang, L., Pattavina, A.: Learning geographical and mobility factors for mobile application recommendation. IEEE Intell. Syst. 32(3), 36–44 (2017)

6. Cao, D., et al.: Version-sensitive mobile app recommendation. Inf. Sci. **381**(1), 161–175 (2017)

7. Xu, Y., Zhu, Y., Shen, Y., Yu, J.: Leveraging app usage contexts for app recommendation: a neural approach. World Wide Web **22**(6), 2721–2745 (2018). https://doi.org/10.1007/s11280-018-0543-8

8. Guo, C., Xu, Y., Hou, X., Dong, N., Xu, J., Ye, Q.: Deep attentive factorization machine for app recommendation service. In: ICWS, Piscataway, pp. 134–138. IEEE (2019)

9. Liang, T., He, L., Lu, C.T., Chen, L., Yu, P.S., Wu, J.: A broad learning approach for context-aware mobile application recommendation. In: ICDM, Piscataway, pp. 955–960. IEEE (2017)

10. Xie, F., Chen, L., Ye, Y., Liu, Y., Zheng, Z., Lin, X.: A weighted meta-graph based approach for mobile application recommendation on heterogeneous information networks. In: Pahl, C., Vukovic, M., Yin, J., Yu, Q. (eds.) ICSOC 2018. LNCS, vol. 11236, pp. 404–420. Springer, Cham (2018). https://doi.org/10.1007/978-3-030-03596-9_29

11. Ji, S., Pan, S., Cambria, E., Marttinen, P., Yu, P. S.: A survey on knowledge graphs: representation, acquisition and applications. arXiv preprint (2020). https://arxiv.org/abs/2002.00388

12. Ji, G., He, S., Xu, L., Liu, K., Zhao, J.: Knowledge graph embedding via dynamic mapping matrix. In: ACL, Stroudsburg, pp. 687–696. The Association for Computer Linguistics (2015)

13. Rendle, S., Freudenthaler, C., Gantner, Z., Schmidt-Thieme, L.: BPR: Bayesian personalized ranking from implicit feedback. In: UAI, Corvallis, Oregon, pp. 452–461. AUAI (2009)

14. Kabbur, S., Ning, X., Karypis, G.: FISM: factored item similarity models for top-N recommender systems. In: SIGKDD, pp. 659–667. ACM, New York (2013)

15. He, X., Chua, T. S.: Neural factorization machines for sparse predictive analytics. In: SIGIR, pp. 355–364. ACM, New York (2017)

16. Zhang, F., Yuan, N.J., Lian, D., Xie, X., Ma, W.Y.: Collaborative knowledge base embedding for recommender systems. In: SIGKDD, pp. 353–362. ACM, New York (2016)

17. Wang, H., Zhang, F., Xie, X., Guo, M.: DKN: deep knowledge-aware network for news recommendation. In: WWW, pp. 1835–1844. ACM, New York (2018)

18. Yu, X., et al.: Personalized entity recommendation: a heterogeneous information network approach. In: WSDM, pp. 283–292. ACM, New York (2014)

19. Wang, X., Wang, D., Xu, C., He, X., Cao, Y., Chua, T.S.: Explainable reasoning over knowledge graphs for recommendation. In: AAAI, pp. 5329–5336. AAAI Press, Menlo Park (2019)

20. Wang, H., et al.: RippleNet: propagating user preferences on the knowledge graph for recommender systems. In: CIKM, pp. 417–426. ACM, New York (2018)

21. Wang, X., He, X., Cao, Y., Liu, M., Chua, T.S.: KGAT: knowledge graph attention network for recommendation. In: SIGKDD, pp. 950–958. ACM, New York (2019)

22. Wang, H., Zhao, M., Xie, X., Li, W., Guo, M.: Knowledge graph convolutional networks for recommender systems. In: WWW, pp. 3307–3313. ACM, New York (2019)

ICS-Assist: Intelligent Customer Inquiry Resolution Recommendation in Online Customer Service for Large E-Commerce Businesses

Min Fu[1,2], Jiwei Guan[2], Xi Zheng[2], Jie Zhou[1(✉)], Jianchao Lu[2], Tianyi Zhang[3], Shoujie Zhuo[1], Lijun Zhan[1], and Jian Yang[2]

[1] Alibaba Group, Hangzhou, China
{hanhao.fm,zj236040,souljoy.zsj,zhanlijun.zlj}@alibaba-inc.com
[2] Macquarie University, Sydney, Australia
{james.zheng,jian.yang}@mq.edu.au, {jiwei.guan,jianchao.lu}@hdr.mq.edu.au
[3] Harvard University, Cambridge, MA, USA
tianyi@seas.harvard.edu

Abstract. Efficient and appropriate online customer service is essential to large e-commerce businesses. Existing solution recommendation methods for online customer service are unable to determine the best solutions at runtime, leading to poor satisfaction of end customers. This paper proposes a novel intelligent framework, called ICS-Assist, to recommend suitable customer service solutions for service staff at runtime. Specifically, we develop a generalizable two-stage machine learning model to identify customer service scenarios and determine customer service solutions based on a scenario-solution mapping table. A novel knowledge distillation network called "Panel-Student" is proposed to derive a small yet efficient distilled learning model. We implement ICS-Assist and evaluate it using an over 6-month field study with Alibaba Group. In our experiment, over 12,000 customer service staff use ICS-Assist to serve for over 230,000 cases per day on average. The experimental results show that ICS-Assist significantly outperforms the traditional manual method, and improves the solution acceptance rate, the solution coverage rate, the average service time, the customer satisfaction rate, and the business domain catering rate by up to 16%, 25%, 6%, 14% and 17% respectively, compared to the state-of-the-art methods.

Keywords: Intelligent customer service · Natural language processing · Deep learning · Distilled learning

1 Introduction

Large e-commerce businesses such as Alibaba and Amazon provide hundreds of thousands of customer services to end customers via conversations every day, and these customer service conversations contain several topics, such as refunds,

© Springer Nature Switzerland AG 2020
E. Kafeza et al. (Eds.): ICSOC 2020, LNCS 12571, pp. 370–385, 2020.
https://doi.org/10.1007/978-3-030-65310-1_26

delivering inquiries, and instructions for using lucky money [23]. When end customers make inquiries through online customer service, they usually demand their requirements and intentions be addressed as fast as possible [14]. These requirements and intentions are usually versatile. As such, customer service solutions should be provided at runtime and should be able to correctly and timely address customers' requirements and intentions. For instance, when a customer calls in to complain about the poor quality of her newly bought shoes, we must recognize her intention of "returning the shoes" and provide her with the solution of how to return the shoes and apply for the refund [14].

Customer service solutions can be determined either manually or automatically. Determining customer service solutions manually is flexible and human-centric, and the representatives need to have enough expert knowledge to handle all types of customer problems [18]. Several existing automated mechanisms have required expert knowledge learned from rich transaction history data to target most customer requirements. However, these approaches are inaccurate, inefficient and unsatisfactory, and most critically they are unable to generalize for diverse business domains [20]. As such, end customers' satisfaction will be significantly affected, and business quality and profits will also be further influenced.

In this paper, we propose a novel machine learning-based approach, called ICS-Assist, to facilitate customer service staff to identify ideal customer service solutions at runtime. ICS-Assist uses a two-stage learning model, coarse-grained learning and fine-grained learning, to identify the proper service scenario of each query made by the end customer. Moreover, ICS-Assist uses multi-aspect features (i.e. multi-round conversations, customer profiles, staff profiles, and order details) as the inputs to train a deep learning model for fine-grained service scenario recognition. Then ICS-Assist further determines the final solutions based on the "scenario-solution" mapping table constructed by business operators. The main differences between our approach and existing methods are: 1) Our approach can achieve accurate customer service scenario recognition at runtime (i.e., while customer service staff are servicing end-customers); 2) We use a novel "Panel-Student" learning scheme to derive a much smaller yet efficient learning model which can recognize service scenario at a finer granularity, a significant improvement over the traditional "Teacher-Student" model [11]; 3) Our approach uses multi-aspect features instead of the commonly used language feature to train the "Panel-Student" learning scheme and recognize service scenarios.

We implement ICS-Assist and evaluate it using a real-world field study with Alibaba Group. The experiments are conducted for over 6 months. On average, over 12,000 customer service staff handle over 230,000 cases per day. We compare the performance of ICS-Assist with existing semantic and relevance matching methods, including HCAN [20], ESIM-seq [2], DAM [30], and DIIN [8]. The experimental results are two-fold: 1) Our method increases the solution acceptance rate by up to 16%, increases solution coverage rate by up to 25%, reduces average service time by up to 6%, increases customer satisfaction rate by up to 14%, and increases business domain catering rate by up to 17%, compared to the state-of-the-art methods; 2) Our method increases the solution acceptance rate by 24%, increases solution coverage rate by 34%, reduces average service time by 8%, increases customer satisfaction rate by 19%, and increases business domain catering rate by 22%, compared to the traditional manual method.

The research contributions of this paper are 1) We propose a novel intelligent framework to recognize customer service scenarios and further determine appropriate customer service solutions at runtime. In this way, we extend the idea of the "Teacher-Student" model to propose a generalizable "Panel-Student" distilled learning method that determines suitable customer service scenarios and solutions for multiple e-commerce business domains. 2) We show a real-world field study to demonstrate the efficacy and validity of our proposed approach.

The remainder of this paper is as follows: Sect. 2 introduces the background; Sect. 3 illustrates our proposed approach; Sect. 4 describes the experimental evaluation; Sect. 5 discusses threats to validity; Sect. 6 provides related work; Sect. 7 provides the conclusion and future work.

2   Background

2.1   Intelligent Customer Service in E-Commerce

E-commerce customer service plays a significant role in business profit-making and customer satisfaction [23]. In contrast to traditional customers' service involving huge human efforts, organizations use intelligent customer service to promote effortless customers experiences and improve productivity. Specifically, the state-of-the-art intelligent customer service is not just multi-channel but omnichannel, which allows the organizations to facilitate effective interactions between them and their customers by unifying the experience across self-assisted and field-service channels [16]. In large e-commerce corporations, such as Alibaba, JD.Com and Amazon, intelligence customer service has been successfully used to save their customer service costs by over 20%. With these successful stories, many small to medium-sized e-commerce companies are starting to develop their intelligent customer service systems [14].

2.2   Business Requirements for Customer Service

As a critical component of the business chain, customer service has been regularized by standardized business requirements, which are formulated by several popular e-commerce corporations based on over 20 years' business exploration [5]. These requirements are 1) Customer service solutions should be correctly determined; 2) The customer service system should cover as many customer service solutions as possible; 3) The time spent on customer service dialogues should be minimized; 4) The satisfaction rate of end customers should be maximized; 5) The Customer service system should be able to cater for as many business domains as possible. Hence, the e-commerce industry uses the following business metrics to evaluate the quality of customer service: 1) Solution Acceptance Rate (SAR), which refers to the percentage of solutions that are accepted by end customers; 2) Solution Coverage Rate (SCR), which refers to the proportion of the solutions that can be recalled from the overall solutions; 3) Average Service Time (AST), which refers to the average time spent on customer service conversations; 4) Customer Satisfaction Rate (CSR), which refers to the percentage of the customers who are satisfied with the customer service; 5) Business Domain Catering Rate (BCR), which refers to how many business domains can be catered for by the customer service system.

3   Our Proposed Method

Our approach is based on the following design decisions: 1) Service solutions should be mapped from recognized service scenarios based on the well-established "scenario to solution" mapping rules defined by the e-commerce business; 2) Customer service scenarios must be determined in a runtime manner; 3) The model can utilize a multi-stage paradigm in order to recognize the optimal customer service scenarios to determine the optimal service solutions. The overview of our proposed approach, named ICS-Assist, is shown in Fig. 1. When a customer inquires, the system selects an available customer service staff to start the conversation. After the customer makes each query, ICS-Assist recognizes the relevant service scenarios based on the two-stage machine learning (coarse-grained learning and fine-grained learning) scenario recognition model proposed by us. If scenarios are not found, the customer service staff responds to the customer on her own expert experience; otherwise, ICS-Assist determines the solutions based on the scenario-solution mapping table maintained by the business itself, and the customer service staff confirms and provides the solutions to the customer. If the problem of the end customer is solved, the customer service ends; otherwise, ICS-Assist waits for the end customer to make another query, and the aforementioned procedure repeats until the problem is solved.

3.1   Data Preparation and Preprocessing

The data processing pipeline for the service scenario recognition in ICS-Assist is shown in Fig. 2. The input data is generated from the historical customer service log, which contains customer utterances and staff operations (e.g. clicking, hovering and querying) in a service session. The service scenarios clicked or searched by the staff are paired with the customer utterances to form the positive samples in the dataset. We also manually check these automatically generated pairs.

However, the training set is imbalanced as some regular service scenarios have millions of cases, such as inquiries about a delivery, refunding, while others may only contain a few thousand. Thus the corpus of customer utterance can be too sparse to learn a well-generalized model. To address this, we apply the data augmentation method of up-sampling on the scarce cases to expand their original size to 100 times. Finally, we combine the augmented rare cases with the regular cases as the positive samples, and also randomly choose an equal number of irrelevant pairs of service scenarios and customer utterances as negative samples.

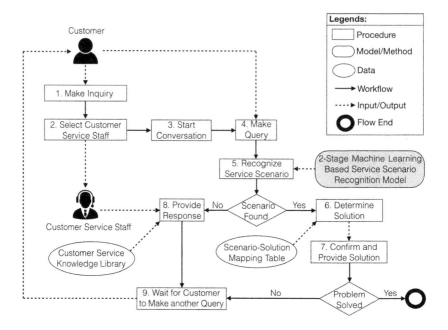

Fig. 1. Overview of ICS-Assist

The data structure for each training sample is a triplet consisting of the customer utterance $\mathcal{U}$, the description of standard service scenario $\mathcal{S}$ and label y, where $y \in \{0,1\}$, both $\mathcal{U}$ and $\mathcal{S}$ are text, $\mathcal{U} = (w_1^u, w_2^u, w_3^u, ...), \mathcal{S} = (w_1^s, w_2^s, w_3^s, ...)$, w_i is the i-th word in the sequence.

The model learning follows a two-stage procedure that contains the coarse-grained ranking and the fine-grained ranking. At the coarse-grained ranking stage, we use a simple approach that narrows down the search range in the candidate set to filter out the irrelevant scenarios. At the fine-grained ranking stage, we propose a Panel-Student knowledge distillation approach to train a lighter model that is able to find out the most suitable service scenarios.

3.2   Coarse-Grained Learning Model

We describe the process for the coarse-grained model. First, we compute the representation **u**, **s** for $\mathcal{U}$, $\mathcal{S}$:

$$\sum_i \text{tf\_idf}(w_i) \times \text{word2vec}(w_i) \tag{1}$$

where $u, s \in \mathbb{R}^{d\_\{wv\}}$, d_{wv} is the dimensionality for Word2Vec [17]. The representation is exactly the weighted average of the word vector for the corresponding words in the text, where the weight we use here is tf-idf.

We get the top-K suitable scenarios by comparing cosine similarity $cos\_sim(\mathbf{u}, \mathbf{s}_k)$, where $\mathbf{s}_k$ is the representation for a scenario in the candidate set. After that, the top-K candidates would be fed into the fine-grained model.

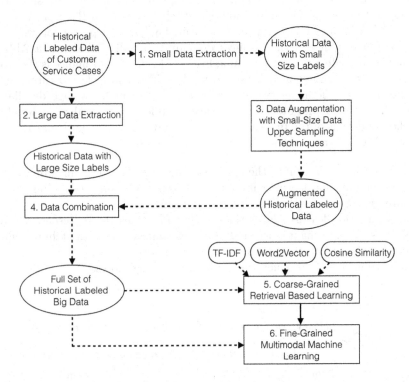

Fig. 2. Training process for service scenario recognition model

3.3   Fine-Grained Learning Model

The fine-grained model learns complicated semantic relationships between customer utterances and service scenario descriptions and finds out the most suitable service scenarios. In our case, the ranking model requires very high precision. To achieve this goal, the simplest way is that we train a model as large as possible with strong fitting capacities, but by doing so the inference time would be slower, which is unfriendly for online recommendation at runtime.

Knowledge distillation [11, 29] is an effective way to distill the knowledge learned from the teacher model and builds an accurate lightweight student model. The teacher model is usually a large neural network or an ensemble of networks containing millions parameters. Hence, the state-of-the-art large-scale pre-trained language models, such as ELMO [19], BERT [4] and XLNet [28], can serve as the teacher network. These models are millstones in natural language processing filed and significantly improve the performance of many downstream tasks such as question answering, textual entailment, and text classification etc.

However, among the aforementioned pre-trained language models, using only one of them as a teacher network seems to be unable to completely train a generalizable student model that can achieve as good performance as the teacher network in diverse business domains. Besides, our empirical studies show that ELMO has the best performance and is slightly better than BERT in the business domain of Alibaba Movie (which is an Alibaba business portal for watching online movies), while in the business domain of Tmall Global (is an Alibaba web portal for selling imported commodities), ELMO's performance is the worst among the three pre-trained language models. Thus, in order to cater for all types of business domains, we explore a Panel-Student knowledge distillation approach that combines all the three *teachers* to form a generalizable *panel*.

The full details of the fine-tuning "Panel-Student" learning scheme are illustrated in Fig. 3, which can be divided into four layers:

1. the input layer that maps the raw text data into the word embeddings;
2. the representation learning layer that encodes the word embeddings into a comprehensive contextualized representation;
3. the interaction learning layer that further processes the representation and extracts both semantic-oriented and relevance-oriented matching signals between the input utterance and service scenario;
4. the output layer that generates the final matching scores.

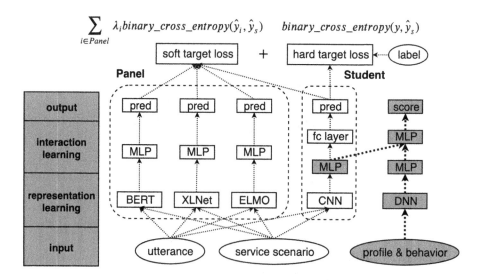

Fig. 3. Fine-grained "Panel-Student" learning model

Panel-Student Framework. We use three high-capacity pre-trained language models in our panel, including ELMO [19], BERT-LARGE [4], and XLNet [28]. As the core task of our ICS-Assist is to match the customer utterance with a suitable service scenario by leveraging semantic-oriented and relevance-oriented matching signals in the text pairs, we follow the fine-tuning setting of the text-entailment task described in each corresponding teacher model (text-entailment can be viewed as a special case of text match [20]). After the fine-tuning stage, we train the student model under the panel's supervision with the soft target loss (shown in Fig. 3) and the hard target loss with ground truth labels. We choose TextCNN [24] as the student model due to its lightweight and fast inference.

The input layer maps the words within $\mathcal{U}$ and $\mathcal{S}$ into the corresponding embeddings $U = [\mathbf{w}_1^u; \mathbf{w}_2^u; \mathbf{w}_2^u; ...\mathbf{w}_N^u]$ and $S = [\mathbf{w}_1^s; \mathbf{w}_2^s; \mathbf{w}_2^s; ...\mathbf{w}_N^s]$, where $\mathbf{w}_i \in \mathbb{R}^d$ is the corresponding embedding given a word w_i, $U, S \in \mathbb{R}^{N \times d}$. We pad the variable length sequence to fixed-length N.

At the representation learning stage, we first apply 1-d convolution over U with k different kernel size:

$$\bar{U}^k = \sigma(W_f^k * U + b^k), \tag{2}$$

where W_f^k is the parameter for k-th convolution kernel, b^k is the bias, σ is the activation function, the output channel number for convolution is d_o, $\bar{U}^k \in \mathbb{R}^{N \times d_o}$. Then we take the maximum and average values over the sequence length dimension and concatenate them to form an overall representative semantic signal. Taking the maximum value can effectively extract the features for the occurrence of some keywords and taking the average can be more robust to the noise in the corpus.

$$\bar{\mathbf{u}}_{max}^k = \max(\bar{U}^k), \tag{3}$$

$$\bar{\mathbf{u}}_{mean}^k = \text{mean}(\bar{U}^k), \tag{4}$$

$$\tilde{\mathbf{u}} = [\bar{\mathbf{u}}_{max}^1; ...; \bar{\mathbf{u}}_{max}^k; \bar{\mathbf{u}}_{mean}^1; ...; \bar{\mathbf{u}}_{mean}^k], \tag{5}$$

where $\bar{\mathbf{u}}_{max}^k, \bar{\mathbf{u}}_{mean}^k \in \mathbb{R}^{d_o}$, $\tilde{\mathbf{u}} \in \mathbb{R}^{2kd_o}$. The representation $\tilde{\mathbf{s}}$ for $\mathcal{S}$ is obtained in a similar way.

At the interaction learning stage, we enhance the interaction between $\mathcal{U}$ and $\mathcal{S}$ by applying more complicated arithmetic operations on the original signal obtained in the previous stage. The original signals $\tilde{\mathbf{u}}, \tilde{\mathbf{s}}$, the element-wise multiplication of the original signals, the element-wise square of the difference between the two signals are concatenated together and fed to an MLP to generate the final matching feature $\mathbf{m}$:

$$\mathbf{x} = [\tilde{\mathbf{u}}; \tilde{\mathbf{s}}; \tilde{\mathbf{u}} \otimes \tilde{\mathbf{s}}; (\tilde{\mathbf{u}} - \tilde{\mathbf{s}})^{\circ 2}], \tag{6}$$

$$\mathbf{m} = \text{MLP}(\mathbf{x}), \tag{7}$$

where $\mathbf{x} \in \mathbb{R}^{8kd_o}$. After the student model is trained, the model can make the following prediction:

$$g^s = \sigma(W\mathbf{m} + b), \tag{8}$$

$$\hat{y}_s = \text{sigmoid}(g^s), \tag{9}$$

where σ is the activation function, and $\hat{y}_s$ is a real number between 0 and 1, which represents the probability of standard service scenario $\mathcal{S}$ matching the given utterance $\mathcal{U}$.

Final Hybrid Model for Service Scenario Recognition. As shown at the rightmost side in Fig. 3, we also use multi-aspect features $\bar{\mathbf{m}}$ learned by a DNN model based on the customer profiles, the log of historical customer behavior and customer service staff. The intermediate multi-aspect feature $\bar{\mathbf{m}}$ will be combined with $\mathbf{m}$ (see Eq. 7) generated by the student TextCNN, and then fed to an MLP to make the final prediction as follows:

$$g^h = \mathrm{MLP}([\mathbf{m}; \bar{\mathbf{m}}]), \tag{10}$$

$$\hat{y}_h = \mathrm{sigmoid}(g^h). \tag{11}$$

The training of the final hybrid model which utilizes the output from our student model has three phases. The first two phases are used for training the student model alone, and the third phase is used for training the hybrid model:

1. Each teacher model in the panel is fine-tuned;
2. The student model (i.e., TextCNN) is trained within the "Panel-Student" scheme using the loss function below:

$$\sum_{i \in Panel} \lambda_i \mathrm{binary\_cross\_entropy}(\hat{y}_i, \hat{y}_s) + \mathrm{binary\_cross\_entropy}(y, \hat{y}_s), \tag{12}$$

The lost function consists of two types of loss: 1) the soft-target loss between the student model's predictions $\hat{y}_s$ and each teacher model's predictions $\hat{y}_i$; 2) the hard target loss between the predictions of the student model $\hat{y}_s$ and the ground truth labels y.
3. All layers within TextCNN up to the MLP are extracted and combined with the output from the MLP layer within the DNN model at the rightmost in Fig. 3 to construct the final hybrid model for scenario prediction. The hybrid model is trained using this loss function:

$$\mathrm{binary\_cross\_entropy}(y, \hat{y}_h), \tag{13}$$

where $\hat{y}_h$ is the prediction for the hybrid model.

3.4   Scenario Recognition and Solution Mapping

Customer service scenarios are determined by our two-stage scenario recognition model, which are represented as the "parameters" for determining solutions. It matches the customer utterance with the best service scenario by solving a pairwise text-match task. Taking the case of "complaining the bought shoes" as an example, the recognized best scenario is "returning the commodities (shoes)".

Given a determined customer service scenario determined by our two-stage scenario recognition framework, the customer service solution can be determined and selected based on the scenario-solution mapping table formulated by the e-commerce company itself according to its business strategies. The customer service solution can be a customized one-to-one mapping from the customer service scenario. Specifically, the solution can be a standard service manual, a road-map, or just a predefined answer. For instance, the above-determined scenario is mapped to the solution of how to apply for the refund of the shoes.

4 Experimental Evaluation

Our experiment was conducted in the real customer service of Alibaba Group. We implemented ICS-Assist as an enterprise-level service system. Over 12,000 customer service staff use ICS-Assist to serve for over 230,000 cases per day on average, and this procedure lasted for over 6 months. In our experimental environment, the queries made by end customers are dispensed to dedicated query processing servers by the query router. Each query processing server encapsulates and passes the query to the service scenario recognition model in our ICS-Assist to predict the service scenarios. The recognized scenarios are then mapped with the service solutions, which are sent to customers by customer service staff.

4.1 Experimental Procedure

The experimental procedure consists of three parts:

1. We apply our proposed "Panel-Student" model and the baseline models [2,8, 20,30] on the public dataset Quora [13], and compare the performance among them. For the baseline models, we reproduce them according to their best hyper-parameter settings. For our proposed model, we set the convolution kernel widths from 2 to 5, and the output channel numbers are all 64. The layer number of the MLP module in Eq. 7 is 3. The dropout rate is 0.2 and the L2 regularization coefficient is 0.05. The activation function for all the layers is ReLu. The optimizer is Adam [15] with a constant learning rate of $1e-4$, decay rate β_1 of 0.9, and β_2 of 0.999.

2. We also conduct similar experiments on our historical dataset. The only difference is that, for our proposed model, we use an additional neural model to handle the handcrafted multi-aspect features to construct the final hybrid model, we adopt a similar architecture like a Wide-Deep model [3], and combine it with the text-based features from the TextCNN model. The training for the final model follows a two-stage paradigm: 1) We freeze the parameters within TextCNN model and train the DNN with a constant learning rate of $1e-3$ until convergence; 2) We make TextCNN's parameters trainable and restart the training phase with an exponential decay learning rate (initial learning rate: $1e-4$; decay rate: 0.95; decay step: 10000).

3. Since the purpose of the two steps above is to demonstrate the superiority of our proposed "Panel-Student" model, we replace this hybrid model in ICS-Assist with each of the state-of-the-art baseline models [2,8,20,30] to create

several variants of ICS-Assist and compare our proposed ICS-Assist (with the "Panel-Student" model) with these ICS-Assist variants as well as the manual method against the 5 business evaluation metrics (SAR, SCR, AST, CSR, and BCR) mentioned in Sect. 2.2.

4.2   Experimental Results

Table 1 shows the comparison between the performance (accuracy, precision, recall, f1-score, and latency) of our proposed Panel-Student model (PS model henceforth) and the other existing models on the Quora dataset. Due to the less execution complexity of our proposed model compared to other models, the accuracy, precision, recall and f1-score of our PS model are slightly less than hcan-hybrid, hcan-only rm [20], dam [30], diin [8] and esim-seq [2], and slightly better than hcan-only sm [20], but our PS model's latency is much lower than these models. We also implement the panel-student model with a single teacher (i.e. BERT, XLNet, and ELMO), and obtain three Teacher-Student models (TS models henceforth). The performance of these three TS models is also worse than our PS model. As such, our model is the best one among all the models.

Table 1. Model performance comparison on quora dataset

Model	Accuracy	Precision	Recall	F1	Latency (ms)
hcan - hybrid	0.831	0.832	0.830	0.831	81
hcan - only sm	0.791	0.791	0.791	0.791	73
hcan - only rm	0.821	0.824	0.817	0.820	21
dam	0.855	0.856	0.854	0.855	109
diin	0.873	0.877	0.867	0.872	151
esim - seq	0.843	0.846	0.839	0.842	95
TS - BERT	0.791	0.783	0.792	0.787	15
TS - XLNet	0.807	0.795	0.809	0.802	15
TS - ELMO	0.781	0.769	0.759	0.764	13
our PS model	0.811	0.807	0.819	0.813	11

Table 2 shows the comparison between the performance of our proposed PS model and the existing state-of-the-art models using our dataset. Again, our PS model outperforms all the baseline models in terms of the overall model performance due to the less execution complexity of our model than others.

Table 3 shows the improvement rate of the business metrics of our proposed ICS-Assist (ICS-Assist (PS)) over the manual method and the variants of ICS-Assist with state-of-the-art models, including the teacher-student model using each single teacher model in our panel. Our ICS-Assist (PS) performs better than all the other variants of ICS-Assist by up to 16%, 25%, 6%, 14%, and 17%, in terms of SAR (Solution Acceptance Rate), SCR (Solution Coverage Rate),

Table 2. Model performance comparison on our dataset

Model	Accuracy	Precision	Recall	F1	Latency (ms)
hcan - hybrid	0.878	0.876	0.879	0.877	198
hcan - only sm	0.845	0.847	0.841	0.844	186
hcan - only rm	0.850	0.848	0.852	0.850	53
dam	0.914	0.914	0.914	0.914	265
diin	0.894	0.899	0.887	0.893	387
esim - seq	0.930	0.932	0.928	0.930	241
TS - BERT	0.871	0.874	0.877	0.875	28
TS - XLNet	0.878	0.884	0.889	0.886	26
TS - ELMO	0.853	0.851	0.861	0.856	25
our PS model	0.894	0.892	0.895	0.893	25

AST (Average Service Time), CSR (Customer Satisfaction Rate) and BCR (Business Domain Catering Rate). Although our PS model's performance (e.g. f1-score) is slightly worse than other models (e.g. dam and esim-seq), our approach still performs better in the business metrics. This is because our PS model has lower latency than other models, and it enables customer service staff to timely utilize the recommended solutions. ICS-Assist (PS) increases SAR by 24%, increases SCR by 34%, decreases AST by 8%, increases CSR by 19%, and increases BCR by 22%, compared to the manual method.

Table 3. Business performance improvement results

ICS-Assist (PS) vs.	SAR	SCR	AST	CSR	BCR
manual	24%	34%	8%	19%	22%
ICS-Assist (dam)	13%	19%	4%	5%	7%
ICS-Assist (hcan)	16%	25%	6%	14%	17%
ICS-Assist (diin)	12%	19%	7%	12%	15%
ICS-Assist (esim)	10%	15%	6%	11%	14%
ICS-Assist (TS-BERT)	3%	2%	3%	3%	5%
ICS-Assist (TS-XLNet)	1%	2%	2%	2%	7%
ICS-Assist (TS-ELMO)	7%	6%	4%	9%	10%

From the experimental results, we can conclude that our approach outperforms other automated state-of-the-art methods as well as the manual method in all the business metrics. The main reasons are as follows: 1) Our method assembles the three pre-trained language models (i.e. BERT, XLNet and ELMO) to distill a more generalizable model that creates better language representations for multiple business domains; 2) Our method takes multi-aspect features as the inputs for the scenario recognition model; 3) Our method employs a two-stage learning approach to maximize the validity of the recommended results, and it makes a reasonable prepossessing on the historical data to address its inevitable drawbacks related to quality, volume, and noise.

5   Threats to Validity

The threats to validity are as follows: 1) The historical customer service data provided by Alibaba Group largely focus on the east Asian and southeast Asian countries, and the countries from other continents are relatively few. 2) The model training parameters with the PS model can be further tuned. The current parameters may not yield an optimized deep learning model because they may cause a local minimum instead of a global minimum. 3) The three representation learning-oriented models (BERT, XLNet, and ELMO) constitute the Panel, but more pre-trained language models could have been investigated.

6   Related Work

6.1   Neural Text Matching Techniques

One line of work related to our system is Neural Text Matching. Text Matching is a core task in many NLP and information retrieval applications, the mainstream of which can be divided into Semantic Matching (SM) and Relevance Matching (RM). Although both SM and RM are modelling similarities between two pieces of texts, SM emphasizes the semantic understanding and reasoning while RM focuses more on keyword matching signals. Typical SM tasks includes question answering [1], paraphrase identification [27], and natural language inference [2,8]. RM models, such as DRMM [9], Co-PACRR [12] and MP-HCNN [21] are frequently used in IR applications like search engines to rank documents by relevance given a user query. In our work, both semantic and relevance matching technologies are involved in our model to enable more comprehensive language understanding and identify suitable service scenarios.

6.2   Collaborative Filtering Techniques

Because our system aims to recommend suitable service scenarios and solutions to the customer service staff, in this way the research work on recommendation Systems is also related to our work. Most recommendation systems are based on collaborative filtering, which learns a representation of user and item based on the rating matrix, and then predict the rating assigned a user given an unseen item. Currently, many recommendation systems adopt neural networks [6,10, 26] to learn a good dense representation and the interaction between the user and item and achieve the state-of-the-art performance. However in our scope, mechanically matching the user and service scenario would ignore the customer's intention and requirement thus impair our service quality.

6.3   Knowledge Distillation Techniques

Researchers from the University of Waterloo try to transfer deep language representation like BERT to a lightweight neural network such as single-layer BiL-STM [25]. But they do not employ multiple teachers' knowledge to distil a simple student model. This experience motivates our multiple knowledge distilling. In addition, The model Fitnets [22] is proposed by A. Romero. This model has extended the model compression idea and introduces the intermediate-level hints techniques to simplify a deeper and thinner student network with fewer parameters and better generalization. The new loss function is imported in hidden layers' feature maps, which helps to reduce parameters in our work. Recently, the IBM researchers have proposed to train the student model from an ensemble of multiple teachers [7]. They implemented different deep neural networks to train convolutional neural network acoustic models on a medium-sized speech corpus. The experimental results highlight that the proposed training techniques could increase a significant amount of knowledge to the student. Hence, our work also follows the idea of distilled learning by proposing a "Panel-Student" model.

7   Conclusion and Future Work

Identifying proper customer service solutions is critical to e-commerce businesses. Existing service solution determination methods are usually unsatisfactory to end customers. This is because they are of low efficiency and unable to achieve runtime solution determination. Hence, this paper proposes an innovative framework, called ICS-Assist, to determine customer service solutions at runtime. We designed a novel two-stage learning model to identify customer service scenarios, which are mapped to end solutions. We implemented ICS-Assist and evaluated it in a 6-month real-world field study at Alibaba Group. The experimental results show that ICS-Assist improves the five business evaluation metrics (solution acceptance rate, solution coverage rate, average service time, customer satisfaction rate and business domain catering rate) by up to 16%, 25%, 6%, 14%, and 17% respectively, compared to the state-of-the-art methods, and it outperforms the manual method by 24%, 34%, 8%, 19%, and 22% respectively, in terms of the five business evaluation metrics. Our future work includes: 1) Explore more representation learning models for determining the members in the panel; 2) Design robust light-weight pre-trained models for customer services; 3) Investigate different customer service application areas such as finance.

References

1. Chen, D., Fisch, A., Weston, J., Bordes, A.: Reading Wikipedia to answer open-domain questions. In: ACL, pp. 1870–1879 (2017)
2. Chen, Q., Zhu, X., Ling, Z.H., Wei, S., Jiang, H., Inkpen, D.: Enhanced LSTM for natural language inference. In: ACL, pp. 1657–1668 (2017)

3. Cheng, H.T., et al.: Wide & deep learning for recommender systems. In: Proceedings of the 1st Workshop on Deep Learning for Recommender Systems, pp. 7–10 (2016)

4. Devlin, J., Chang, M.W., Lee, K., Toutanova, K.: BERT: Pre-training of deep bidirectional transformers for language understanding. In: ACL, pp. 4171–4186 (2019)

5. Eales-Reynolds, L.J., Clarke, C.: Impact of a novel training experience on the development of a customer service culture in a large hospital trust. Int. J. Health Care Qual. Assur. **25**, 483–497 (2012)

6. Ebesu, T., Shen, B., Fang, Y.: Collaborative memory network for recommendation systems. In: SIGIR, pp. 515–524 (2018)

7. Fukuda, T., Suzuki, M., Kurata, G., Thomas, S., Cui, J., Ramabhadran, B.: Efficient knowledge distillation from an ensemble of teachers. In: Interspeech, pp. 3697–3701 (2017)

8. Gong, Y., Luo, H., Zhang, J.: Natural language inference over interaction space. In: ICLR (2018)

9. Guo, J., Fan, Y., Ai, Q., Croft, W.B.: A deep relevance matching model for ad-hoc retrieval. In: CIKM, pp. 55–64 (2016)

10. He, X., Liao, L., Zhang, H., Nie, L., Hu, X., Chua, T.S.: Neural collaborative filtering. In: WWW, pp. 173–182 (2017)

11. Hinton, G., Oriol, V., Jeff, D.: Distilling the knowledge in a neural network. In: NIPS Deep Learning and Representation Learning Workshop (2015)

12. Hui, K., Yates, A., Berberich, K., De Melo, G.: Co-PACRR: a context-aware neural IR model for ad-hoc retrieval. In: WSDM, pp. 279–287, February 2018

13. Iyer, S., Dandekar, N., Csernai, K.: First quora dataset release: Question pairs (2017). https://www.quora.com/q/quoradata/First-Quora-Dataset-Release-Question-Pairs

14. Kaufman, R.: Why your customer service training won't lead to happy customers (or inspired employees). J. Qual. Particip. **37**, 33 (2015)

15. Kingma, D.P., Ba, J.: Adam: a method for stochastic optimization. In: ICLR (2015)

16. Kresch, M.: What is intelligent customer service (2016). https://cloudblogs. microsoft.com/dynamics365/bdm/2016/01/19/what-is-intelligent-customer-service. Accessed 12 May 2020

17. Mikolov, T., Sutskever, I., Chen, K., Corrado, G.S., Dean, J.: Distributed representations of words and phrases and their compositionality. In: NIPS, pp. 3111–3119 (2013)

18. Mirchandani, K.: Learning racial hierarchies: communication skills training in transnational customer service work. J. Workplace Learn. **24**, 338–350 (2012)

19. Peters, M., et al.: Deep contextualized word representations. In: NAACL, pp. 2227–2237 (2018)

20. Rao, J., Liu, L., Tay, Y., Yang, W., Shi, P., Lin, J.: Bridging the gap between relevance matching and semantic matching for short text similarity modeling. In: EMNLP-IJCNLP, pp. 5373–5384 (2019)

21. Rao, J., Yang, W., Zhang, Y., Ture, F., Lin, J.: Multi-perspective relevance matching with hierarchical convnets for social media search. In: AAAI, pp. 232–240 (2019)

22. Romero, A., Ballas, N., Kahou, S.E., Chassang, A., Gatta, C., Bengio, Y.: FitNets: hints for thin deep nets. In: ICLR (2015)

23. Sari, P.K., Alamsyah, A., Wibowo, S.: Measuring e-commerce service quality from online customer review using sentiment analysis. In: Journal of Physics: Conference Series, p. 012053 (2018)

24. Sun, X., Ma, X., Ni, Z., Bian, L.: A new LSTM network model combining TextCNN. In: Cheng, L., Leung, A.C.S., Ozawa, S. (eds.) ICONIP 2018. LNCS, vol. 11301, pp. 416–424. Springer, Cham (2018). https://doi.org/10.1007/978-3-030-04167-0_38

25. Tang, R., Lu, Y., Liu, L., Mou, L., Vechtomova, O., Lin, J.: Distilling task-specific knowledge from Bert into simple neural networks. arXiv preprint arXiv:1903.12136, March 2019

26. Wang, H., Wang, N., Yeung, D.Y.: Collaborative deep learning for recommender systems. In: KDD, pp. 1235–1244 (2015)

27. Wang, Z., Hamza, W., Florian, R.: Bilateral multi-perspective matching for natural language sentences. In: IJCAI, pp. 4144–4150 (2017)

28. Yang, Z., Dai, Z., Yang, Y., Carbonell, J., Salakhutdinov, R.R., Le, Q.V.: XLNet: generalized autoregressive pretraining for language understanding. In: NIPS, pp. 5754–5764 (2019)

29. You, S., Xu, C., Xu, C., Tao, D.: Learning from multiple teacher networks. In: KDD, pp. 1285–1294 (2017)

30. Zhou, X., et al.: Multi-turn response selection for chatbots with deep attention matching network. In: ACL, pp. 1118–1127 (2018)

Detecting User Significant Intention via Sentiment-Preference Correlation Analysis for Continuous App Improvement

Jianmao Xiao[1], Shizhan Chen[1], Qiang He[2(✉)], Hongyue Wu[1], Zhiyong Feng[1], and Xiao Xue[1]

[1] College of Intelligence and Computing, Tianjin University, Tianjin, China
{zt_xjm,shizhan,hongyue.wu,zyfeng,jzxuexiao}@tju.edu.cn
[2] School of Software and Electrical Engineering, Swinburne University of Technology, Hawthorn, VIC 3122, Australia
qhe@swin.edu.au

Abstract. Detecting users' significant intentions (e.g., new features wanted) timely and precisely is crucial for developers to update and maintain their apps in the competitive mobile app market. Sentiment and preference mining from crowd reviews provide an opportunity to proactively collect app users' intentions, e.g., bug fixing and feature refinement. However, users' sentiment and preferences often change over time due to either internal factors (e.g., new bugs) or external factors (e.g., new competitors). This makes it difficult for app developers to grasp users' sentiment and preferences in time. In this paper, we propose a novel and automated framework named DSISP for detecting users' significant intentions effectively via sentiment-preference correlation analysis. DSISP first employs sentiment analysis and NLP (Natural Language Processing) techniques to obtain sentence-level sentiment scores and fine-grained user preference features from app reviews in different time slices. Then, the temporal correlation between user sentiment and preferences is analyzed, which can be used to monitor users' sentiment tendency and preferences in time. Finally, DSISP identifies users' dramatically-changing sentiment (e.g., sentiment valley) to detect users' significant intentions. We evaluate the feasibility and performance of DSISP by using real-world app reviews and app official changelogs. The experimental results show that DSISP can detect users' significant intentions effectively and efficiently, with a precision of 0.962 on average. It can help app developers keep track of how their users' intentions evolve over time so that they can improve their apps correspondingly and continuously.

Keywords: Significant intention · Sentiment analysis · Preference feature · Evolution and maintenance

© Springer Nature Switzerland AG 2020
E. Kafeza et al. (Eds.): ICSOC 2020, LNCS 12571, pp. 386–400, 2020.
https://doi.org/10.1007/978-3-030-65310-1_27

1   Introduction

App stores are digital distribution platforms that allow users to submit ratings, feedback and comments on apps, which explicitly or implicitly expresses their potential sentiment and preferences for apps [1,2], e.g., their satisfaction with particular features, the vulnerabilities encountered or requests for new features. Sentiment represents a user's approval of an app, and preference indicates its intention of the app. Users' preferences can be obtained by mining crowd review features that reflect users' opinions. Keeping track of users' sentiment and preference features timely and precisely can help app developers update and improve their apps, e.g., in terms of fixing bugs, or adding new features, etc. [3,4].

User reviews are direct feedback from users that have experienced the apps. In recent years, researchers have proposed several approaches to extract useful information from crowd reviews for maintaining and evolving mobile apps [3,5]. These approaches are mainly designed for user reviews classification [6,7], clustering [8,9], and summarization [1,3,10]. The extracted information represents crowd-sourced knowledge from the users' perspective and can be used to identify users' intention [11] or detecting app emerging issues [12], etc.

The abovementioned studies are mainly focused on reducing the effort in extracting software aspects or user preferences without considering the changes in users' sentiment and preference over time. In fact, due to app updates or changes in the external environment (e.g., new competitors), users' sentiment and preferences will change dynamically over time. For example, when an app crashes, is injected with ads, or breaches users' privacy, users' complaints will increase immediately. Their sentiment will also turn negative rapidly.

Users' up-to-date sentiment and preferences indicate their instant experiences with apps in use. When the users' sentiment and preferences are not grasped by app providers in time, it may lead to the loss of users and reduce the users' stickiness. For example, Facebook Messenger lost a large number of users in August, 2014 because it was found to contain severe privacy issues (e.g., accessing the photos and contact numbers on users' phones)[1]. Such issues had already been pointed out by users in their reviews a few months ago before that. Therefore, detecting and understanding of users' intentions timely is necessary and critical. However, the problem of how to effectively and timely detect users' significant intentions from app reviews have not been studied systematically.

In this paper, we propose a novel framework named DSISP (Detecting users' Significant Intentions via Sentiment and Preference analysis) for detecting users' sentiment and preferences by analyzing their reviews. DSISP takes user reviews as input and employs sentiment analysis technique [13] to calculate users' sentiment scores within different time slices. Then, it employs NLP and collocation finding technology [14] to mine fine-grained preference features from user reviews. After that, it analyzes the temporal correlation between users' sentiment and preferences. Finally, DSISP uses a SVI (Sentiment Valley Identification algorithm) and

---

[1] http://www.businessinsider.com/facebook-messenger-app-store-reviews-arehumiliating-2014-8.

Twitter-LDA [15] to identify users' significant sentiment and detect their significant intentions, respectively. In summary, the contributions of this paper are as follows.

- We present a method for aggregating crowed users' sentiment for each preference with automated sentiment analysis on app reviews. Then, we analyzed how these preferences are temporal correlation to users' sentiment.
- We propose a framework named DSISP to automatically detect users' significant intentions by analyzing the temporal correlation between users' sentiment and preferences. The source code of DSISP and review data are published on GitHub[2].
- We verify the effectiveness of DSISP based on the changelogs of six apps (include three open-source Android apps) in different app categories.

The remainder of the paper is structured as follows. Section 2 introduces the related work. Section 3 outlines the overall picture of DSISP and details each step involved in its procedure. Section 4 reports the experimental results. Section 5 concludes this paper and points out the future work.

2   Related Work

Currently, a number of approaches have been proposed to mine and analyze app reviews with the goal of deriving important information to help developers update their apps [7,8,16]. For example, Pagano et al. [16] investigated the correlation between app reviews and ratings. Harman et al. [17] proposed the concept of app store mining and identified the correlation between user ratings and app download rankings. These studies provide a basis for developers to understand user behaviors and adjust their app deployment strategies. However, there are several limitations which prevent app developers from using the information in the reviews effectively. For example, an app store generates a lot of app reviews every day - the Facebook app receives more than 10,000 reviews on Google Play every day[3]. Besides, reviews vary in quality. Manual analysis of a large number of such reviews is time-consuming and labor-intensive. To address this issue, automatic feature extraction is proposed to mine user needs [3,8,10].

Chen et al. [18] devised AR-MINER, an approach for filtering and ranking informative reviews using a semi-supervised learning based approach. They demonstrated that, on average, 35% of reviews contain informative contents. Based on AR-MINER, L. Villarroel et al. [7] proposed a method named CLAP, which employs classification and clustering algorithms to automatically prioritize the user reviews to be implemented when planning the subsequent app release. Palomba F et al. [8] proposed a method named CHANGEADVISOR to analyze the structure, semantics and sentiment of sentences in user reviews, extract useful information from user reviews and suggest changes to software components for

---

[2] https://github.com/ztxjm123/DSISP.
[3] App Annie. https://www.appannie.com/en.

developers. Zhou Y et al. [9] proposed an automated method named RISING that supports continuous integration of user feedback through classifying, clustering, and linking user reviews to the source code. Their experimental results show that RISING outperforms CHANGEADVISOR in clustering and positioning accuracy, thus producing more reliable results.

To better understand users' review contents and reduce the information gap between developers and users, most studies tend to artificially customize specific rules or concepts for mining user review features. Guzman E et al. [19] proposed a method for classifying app reviews into several categories related to software maintenance. Specifically, they divided user reviews into bug reports, functional advantages, functional defects, user requests, etc., which can provide developers with a detailed suggestion based on user reviews. Di Sorbo et al. [3,10] proposed a user intention classification method SURF to systematically define specific aspects of an app (such as UI, file download, etc.) that need to be maintained. It can effectively help developers plan app update tasks in the future.

Compared with directly extracting or clustering user review topics, the above-mentioned approaches further refined user review information and partitioned it into specific categories. However, little attention has been paid to how to mine users' significant intentions from app reviews in a timely manner, which are essential for developers to update and maintain their apps. To this end, this paper focuses on extracting users' sentiment and preference features in a continuous period. This will allow app developers or app vendors to track users' behaviors timely, and alert them to users' significant intentions promptly.

3 Methodology

DSISP aims to help developers to keep track of users' significant intentions which may be considered in app maintenance and improvement tasks for developers. It employs data mining and sentiment analysis techniques to automatically analyze users' sentiment and preferences for apps over a period of time. Figure 1 overviews the framework of DSISP. First, DSISP extracts users' sentiment and fine-grained preferences from their reviews through sentiment analysis and NLP, respectively. This obtains the user sentiment and produces a list of fine-grained preference features. Then, the review sentiment and preference evolution are analyzed based on time series. Afterwards, DSISP establishes the temporal correlation between sentiment and preference features. Finally, it employs a sentiment valley identification algorithm to detect users' significant intentions.

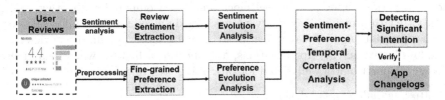

Fig. 1. Overview of the DSISP

3.1   Review Preprocessing

App reviews are generally submitted via mobile terminals and written using mobile keyboards. They often contain lots of noise data, such as misspelled words, non-English words and non-informative words, etc. Such noise data impacts the fine-grained preference feature extraction from user reviews. The review data needs to be preprocessed first.

Multi-language Filtering and Lemmatization. We use the Langid tool[4] to filter non-English comment information from user reviews. Then, we use the Wordnet[5] lemmatizer from NLTK[6] to achieve word stem for reducing the number of features that need to be inspected later.

Noun, Verb, and Adjective Extraction. We use the part of speech (POS) tagging functionality of NLTK to extract the nouns, verbs, and adjectives in the reviews as these parts of a speech are most likely to express the users' fine-grained preference features. We manually inspected 1,040 reviews to validate this assumption.

Noise Word Filtering. This step aims to reduce the non-informative words from user reviews, such as emotional words (e.g., "bad" and "nice"), abbreviations (e.g., "asap"), and useless words (e.g., "someone"), etc. We use wordMapper [20], a dictionary of nearly 300,000 vocabularies related to app reviews, to reduce the impact of non-information words. It contains common spelling errors, abbreviations and abbreviated words in user reviews and their corrections. Based on this dictionary, we add extra words related to app reviews to the dictionary, such as "you're→you are", "app", "developer names", etc., summarized by two researchers from 1,040 user reviews. These predefined stop words are filtered out together with the stop words provided by NLTK.

After the preprocessing, most of the noise data has been removed from the user reviews. However, the preprocessing also shortens the length of the review texts at the same time. Thus, some of the review texts may contain too little information to be useful for extracting preference features. Therefore, in our work, we select reviews with rich vocabulary information - reviews with 4 words or fewer are discarded.

3.2   Review Sentiment Extraction

Sentiment analysis is the process of assigning a positive or negative quantitative value for each review [21]. We use SentiStrength [13], a sentiment analysis tool, to perform user review sentiment analysis. Compared with other tools, SentiStrength provides several advantages: it is designed for short informal texts with abbreviations and slang (features commonly observed in app review). It employs linguistic rules for negations, amplifications, booster words, emotions, which are particularly well suited for processing user reviews.

---

[4] https://github.com/saffsd/langid.py.
[5] https://wordnet.princeton.edu/.
[6] http://nltk.org/.

With SentiStrength, we assign each user review a positive RS^+ and negative RS^- sentimental score, both ranging from 1 (neutral) to 5 (extremely positive or negative). The higher absolute value of the sentence score is taken as the final score of the review sentence, because the larger absolute value can reflect the actual sentiment of the sentence more accurately. In addition, it is worth noting that the emoticons, polarity words, etc., in user reviews would impact their sentiment. For instance, "love" is assigned a score of $[3, -1]$ and "!" a $[1, -1]$ score. Therefore, we analyze the user review sentiment scores directly without data preprocessing discussed in Sect. 3.1.

3.3 Fine-Grained Preference Extraction

Compared with ratings provided by users, user reviews offer finer-grained information and have become a rich source to help detect users' preferences [22]. Most of the reviews contain users' opinions on various aspects of the app (i.e., user preference), such as functional features or app security. For example, let us consider the review sentence "Uploading pictures with the app is necessary!". The functional feature (i.e., user preference feature) "Uploading picture" in this sentence expresses the user's intention directly.

We use the collocation search algorithm of NLTK to extract the fine-grained features in user reviews. Collocation can be expressed as a set of words that often co-occur [23]. It can include two or more words [14], but does not require words that are always adjacent. In user reviews, preference features can often be described as collocation phrases since they usually appear more frequently and represent a specific meaning about the app, e.g., app features or used experience. Given a set of collocation phrases, we use the grammatical relationship collocation extraction algorithm based on n-gram distance to find a collocation of two words in user reviews. Assume a collocation phrase (w_i, w_j), w_i is the base word, and w_j is the collocation word. Both w_i and w_j belong to the review corpus after the preprocessing discussed in Sect. 3.1. We evaluate whether the review collocation phrase is reasonable based on the following three conditions [24]:

$$
\begin{aligned}
\text{strength} &= \frac{\text{freq}_i - \bar{f}}{\sigma} \geq k_0, &&\text{(C1)} \\
\text{spread} &\geq U_0, &&\text{(C2)} \\
p_j^i &\geq \bar{p}_i + \left(k_1 \times \sqrt{U_i}\right), &&\text{(C3)}
\end{aligned}
\tag{1}
$$

where $freq_i$ represents the frequency of collocation phrase (w_i, w_j) appear in user reviews, $\bar{f}$ is the average frequency of all collocation phrases in review corpus. In addition, let us define

$$
spread = U_i = \frac{\sum_{j=1}^{10} \left(p_i^j - \bar{p}_i\right)^2}{10}
\tag{2}
$$

where p_i^j is the appearance times of the collocation phrase (w_i, w_j) in the distance j, the distance range of English words is defined as $[-5, 5]$, similar to [24], $\bar{p}_i = \frac{1}{10} \sum_{j=-5}^{5} p_i^j (j \neq 0)$ is the average appearance times of collocation phrase

(w_i, w_j) in all distances. k_0, k_1, and U_0 are custom thresholds. In our work, we set $k_0 = 1$, $k_1 = 1$, and $U_0 = 10$, similar [24].

In fact, the *strength* in $C1$ of formula (1) is to calculate the $z-score$ of $freq_i$, so as to filter out collocation phrases that appear less frequently in users reviews. The *spread* in $C2$ is the variance of collocation phrases at various distances, the greater the *spread*, the more reasonable the collocation phrase. The $C3$ further filters out collocation phrases that are k_1 times of p_i based on the distance distribution of collocation (w_i, w_j). So as to get the most reasonable collocation phrase.

A large number of collocations can be mined from user reviews, since users might use different words to express the same preference feature, i.e., the collocation phase has a synonym phenomenon. Therefore, we use the synonym dictionary Wordnet to merge different collocations. For example, if we have the following collocation phrases, *<picture view>*, *<view photographs>* and *<see photo>* with a frequency of 20, 10, and 5 respectively, we will select the most frequent occurrence collocation phrase (i.e., *<picture view>*) as the final merged preference feature. After implementing synonym merging, the top 10 collocation phrases with the highest frequency are selected as the final fine-grained preference features.

Preference Feature Score Acquisition. We compute the sentiment score for a preference feature based on the following principles: 1) If preference feature PF_i appears in review sentence j, its sentiment score is equal to the positive or negative score of the sentence in which it is located; 2) If there are both positive Po^+ and negative Ne^- scores in review sentence j, the preference feature sentiment score PFS_i is calculated as:

$$PFS_i = \begin{cases} Po^+, |Po^+| > |Ne^-| \\ Ne^-, \text{else} \end{cases} \tag{3}$$

That is, the largest absolute value is selected as the feature score since it best expresses the user's sentiment toward the preference feature.

3.4   Sentiment and Preference Evolution

Time Series Sentiment Evolution. Assuming the users have made n reviews on an app during time slice T_i. A total of sentiment scores can be obtained, denoted as $RS(\text{ score }) = \{RS_{i1}, RS_{i2}, \ldots, RS_{in}\}$. It is worth noting that at a fixed time, the number of user reviews for the same app is not fixed. Therefore, we take the average sentiment score $ARS(\text{score})$ as the users' sentiment score calculated as follows:

$$ARS(\text{ score }) = \frac{1}{n} \sum_{\substack{j=1 \\ i \in T(T_1, T_2, \ldots, T_m)}}^{n} RS_{i,j} \tag{4}$$

where $T(T_1, T_2, \ldots, T_m)$ represents m consecutive but non-overlapping time slices with equal length. For example, each T_i is 5 days or a week, $RS_{i,j}$ is

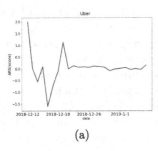 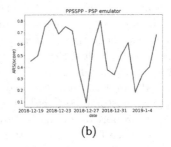

(a)   (b)

Fig. 2. Sentiment evolution of Uber and PPSSPP-PSP

the jth review sentiment score of the app in the T_i, n is the number of reviews within T_i.

Figure 2 shows the sentiment evolution trends of Uber and PPSSPP-PSP. The history of users' sentiment score changes from Dec. 2018 to Jan. 2019 is visualized by line charts. We can see that the users express various changing trends for different apps over time. This phenomenon also validates our assumption above - users' sentiment changes over time. In addition, apart from a stable sentiment trend, users' sentiment often rises or falls rapidly during different time slices, resulting in peaks and valleys, e.g., Uber.

Time Series Preference Evolution. To calculate fine-grained preference feature score during different time slices and grasp the tendency of different preference features over time, for each app, we construct a $TSPFS$ (Time-Series Preference Feature Score) matrix to represent the distribution of fine-grained preference feature scores by all the users on each feature within different time slices.

Table 1. Time-series preference feature score matrix ($TSPFS$)

	T_1	T_2	$\ldots$	T_m
PF_1	$PFS_{1,1}$	$PFS_{1,2}$	$\ldots$	$PFS_{1,m}$
PF_2	$PFS_{2,1}$	$PFS_{2,2}$	$\ldots$	$PFS_{2,m}$
$\ldots$	$\ldots$	$\ldots$	$\ldots$	$\ldots$
PF_n	$PFS_{n,1}$	$PFS_{n,2}$	$\ldots$	$PFS_{n,m}$

Table 1 presents a $TSPFS$ matrix. A row of the matrix indicates that n fine-grained preference features (i.e., $PF_1, PF_2, \ldots, PF_n$), and columns are m consecutive but non-overlapping time slices with equal lengths (i.e., $T_1, T_2, \ldots, T_m$). T_i represents the ith time slice. $PFS_{i,j}$ is the overall score of preference feature j within the ith time slice, and is calculated as follows:

$$PFS_{i,j} = \sum_{\substack{k=1 \\ i \in T(T_1, T_2, \ldots, T_m)}}^{n} FRS_{i,j,k} \tag{5}$$

where n indicates the frequency that feature j appears within the ith time slice, $FRS_{i,j,k}$ is the score of preference feature j in review k in slice T_i.

Figure 3 shows the evolution of users' preference features toward Uber, which includes the preference features and its proportions, feature scores. Take "customer service (-19): 38.45%" in Fig. 3 for example. It is a preference feature, where -19 is the preference feature score, and 38.45% is the proportion of preference features "customer service" of all the preference features at that time. Given a larger proportion of the feature and the absolute value of the feature score, the preference feature can better reflect the user's intention within that time slice.

As we can observe from Fig. 3, users' preferences are constantly changing across different time slices. For example, users' preferences include features "customer service", "waiting time" and "credit card". Their scores are -19, -6 and 4, respectively between December 12, 2018, and December 15, 2018. However, from December 16, 2018, to December 19, 2018, users' preference feature "credit card" disappeared, and the feature scores of "customer service", "waiting time" changed. This means that the degree of preference changed. The similar can be observed in other time slices. Here, we mainly focus on the new features with low feature scores since they are more likely to indicate users' real intention.

Fig. 3. Time series preference feature evolution of Uber

3.5 Sentiment-Preference Feature Correlation Analysis

As discussed before, users' sentiment change over time due to the app updates, security issues, etc. Accordingly, peaks and valleys appear in users' sentiment trend. Figure 4 shows the temporal correlation between users' sentiment and preference features. $(T_1, T_2, T_3, \ldots, T_m)$ represents consecutive but non-overlapping time slices with equal lengths. During different time slices, we can mine users' preference features based on users' sentiment (e.g., valley or peak) and implement sentiment-preference correlation analysis. In this study, we focus on the users' sentiment in valleys since they are more likely to indicate users' preference features. $(t_1, t_2, t_3, \ldots, t_m)$ represents the corresponding sentiment valley time points in each time slice. Through these valley time points, we can mine users' preference features and obtain their significant intentions.

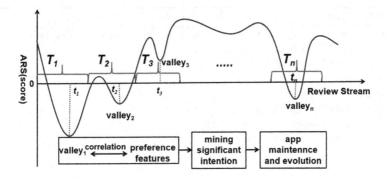

Fig. 4. Temporal correlation between user sentiment and preference features

3.6 User Significant Intention Detection

Users' intentions are in association with their sentiment. In order to detect users' significant intentions, the first step is to identify their significant sentiment (i.e., valley). Given the review sentiment scores and fine-grained preference features obtained with the methods discussed in Sects. 3.2 and 3.3, we partition a fixed time slice v_t, such as 5 or a week, etc., and find the sentiment valleys during that time slice. The specific process for identifying user sentiment valleys is shown in Algorithm 1.

We detect users' significant intentions around sentiment valleys. Similar to twitter texts, user reviews are short texts. Pagano and Maalej [16] found that 80.4% of users' reviews contain 160 characters or fewer, making Twitter-LDA [15] a good candidate for analyzing topics in user reviews. Therefore, we use Twitter-LDA to summarize the fine-grained preference features (i.e., collocation phrases) during the sentiment valley time slice as users' significant intentions (i.e., high-level preference features, referred to as $HLpf$ hereafter). Table 2 shows three most common $HLpf$ topic distribution of Uber app with their sentiments under sentiment valley within the time slices December 12–15, 2018. We can observe that these topics mainly represent the users complain about the worst customer service, credit card and waiting for time problems of Uber. These can well reflect the users' significant intentions.

Table 2. Topic distribution within the sentiment valley of Uber

Topic	$PFS_{i,j}$
customer_service, customer_disgusting, service_sometimes, service_worst, contact_customer	−19
credit_card, credit_cost, card_adding, card_discounted, card_inconvenient	4
waiting_time, waiting_outside, amount_time, driver_waiting, driver_outside	−6

Algorithm 1. User Sentiment Valley Identification (SVI)

Input: D: the set of user reviews which include sentiment score and date
v_t: the number of days in a time slice
Output: $valley\_list$: the list of valleys

1: $initialization : status \leftarrow unknown$
2: **for** each $d \in D$ **do**
3:     **if** $d.status \leftarrow unknown$ **then**
4:         **if** $d.sentiment\_score > d+1$ **then**
5:             $status \leftarrow downhill$
6:         **else**
7:             $status \leftarrow uphill$
8:         **end if**
9:     **end if**
10:    **if** $d.status \leftarrow downhill$ **then**
11:        **if** $d.sentiment\_score < (d+1).sentiment\_score$ **then**
12:            **if** $d.date\_valley\_list[-1].date < v_t$ **then**
13:                **if** $valley\_list[-1].sentiment\_score > d.sentiment\_score$ **then**
14:                    $valley\_list[-1] \leftarrow d$
15:                **else**
16:                    add d to $valley\_list$
17:                **end if**
18:            **end if**
19:        **end if**
20:    **end if**
21: **end for**
22: **return** $valley\_list$

4   Experiments and Results

4.1   Experiment Preparation

Review Dataset. We select the testing apps based on the following three criteria: i) there are adequate user reviews; ii) they are from different categories to ensure the generalization of the testing apps; iii) there are detailed changelogs.

Finally, we select six testing apps from Google Play and collected their changelogs from App Annie. Table 3 lists the testing apps with app name, category, total reviews and review time, etc. Overall, we obtain 48,278 reviews between November, 2018 and April, 2019 for all testing apps. Among them, they are include 3 open-source apps, because we want to verify whether DSISP can detect the users' significant intentions when the app with fewer user reviews but more modifications than closed-source apps. In addition, the review_time is before the app update_time. This can judge whether the user intentions detecting by DSISP are processed by the developer in time, thereby verifying the feasibility and efficiency of DSISP.

Changelogs. We evaluate the performance of DSISP using apps' official changelogs as ground truth. The changelogs reflect the actual modifications made by

Table 3. The subject apps

AppName	Category	Reviews	Review_time	Changelog_version	Update_time
YouTube Music	Music & Audio	5,875	2018.11.9–2019.1.24	2019.04.01	2019.4.1
Uber	Maps & Navigation	7,890	2018.12.12–2019.1.6	3.332.10005	2019.1.9
Facebook	Social	33,288	2018.12.19–2019.1.7	2019.01.08	2019.1.8
PPSSPP-PSP emulator (open)	Action	1,100	2018.12.6–2019.3.17	1.8.0	2019.3.18
AnySoftKeyb oard (open)	Tools	59	2018.12.12–2019.3.21	2019.03.22	2019.03.22
Tutanota (open)	Communication	66	2018.12.22–2019.4.4	3.50.11	2019.4.25

the developer when maintaining and updating an app. Table 4 shows several changelogs of PPSSPP-PSP emulator under version 1.8.0. As we can see that the changelog records include bugs fixing (e.g., Graphics fixes), or new feature added (e.g., Allow putting PSP storage on custom paths like SD cards), etc. Although the changelogs may not cover all the modifications to the releases, they represent a lower bound and the prominent part of the changes [12]. Hence, It is suitable for validating the users' significant intentions detected by DSISP.

Table 4. The Changelog of PPSSPP-PSP emulator under V1.8.0

```
What's New in V 1.8.0:
* Speed improvements in EDF2, FF4
* Graphics fixes in a number of games (lighting, missing geometry, etc)
* Change default Backend to OpenGL (Vulkan still recommended)
* Fix control issue in Sonic Rivals and Rock Band
* Allow putting PSP storage on custom paths like SD cards
  ...
```

Performance Metrics. We employ the following three performance metrics to verify the effectiveness of DSISP. The $Precision_{SI}$ indicates the precision of detecting users' significant intentions. $Recall_{SI}$ indicates whether the detected significant intentions reflect the changes mentioned in the changelogs. F_{hybrid} balances between $Precision_{SI}$ and $Recall_{SI}$.

$$Precision_{SI} = \frac{S(C \cap SI)}{S(C)}, \ Recall_{SI} = \frac{S(C \cap SI)}{S(SI)}$$

$$F_{hybrid} = 2 \times \frac{Precision_{SI} \times Recall_{SI}}{Precision_{SI} + Recall_{SI}} \tag{6}$$

$S(C)$ represents the changelog records, $S(SI)$ is the users' significant intentions detected by DSISP, and $S(C \cap SI)$ represents the number of detected significant intentions which mentioned in changelogs. During our evaluation, we experimentally set the parameters of topic $k = 10$ by empirically, $v_t = 5$. More other v_t values will be discussed in Sect. 4.2.

4.2   User Significant Intention Detection Result

Table 5 reports the results of $Precision_{SI}$, $Recall_{SI}$, and F_{hybrid} achieved by DSISP. We can observe that DSISP has obtained a very high $Precision_{SI}$ with an average value of 0.962, while its $Recall_{SI}$ reaches 0.629 ($F_{hybrid} = 0.755$). For the closed-source apps, the $Precision_{SI}$ has reached 1.0, indicating that the users' significant intentions detected by DSISP cover all changelog information, i.e., the users' preferences in the sentiment valley are genuinely reflect the users' significant intentions.

Furthermore, we also found that except for YouTube Music ($Recall_{SI} = 0.313$) and Uber ($Recall_{SI} = 0.398$) app, the $Recall_{SI}$ of other apps is higher than 0.7. We manually analyzed the reviews of YouTube Music and Uber app, and found that this is due to the fact that there are much more reviews for popular apps under the sentiment valley. As a result, the users' significant intentions mined by DSISP not only cover the changelogs but also include some other modification information which not mentioned in changlogs. Therefore, it led to a lower $Recall_{SI}$. For open-source apps, due to the more frequent modifies and updates by developers, the modify records contained in changlog are also more, so the $Recall_{SI}$ value is higher than the closed-source apps as a whole, which indirectly proves that DSISP can efficiently mine users' significant intentions.

In addition, we also analyzed the effect of different v_t on the efficiency of DSISP. v_t indicates the size of time slice during the sentiment valleys are mined. Table 5 shows the results of DSISP when $v_t = 5$, 10 and 15, we can observe that with v_t increases, the $Precision_{SI}$, $Recall_{SI}$ and F_{hybrid} are showing diversified changes, such as increasing, decreasing, or unchanged, this indicates that different time granularities will have a direct impact on mining users' significant intentions by DSISP. The average optimal $Precision_{SI}$ (i.e., 0.962) and F_{hybrid} (i.e., 0.755) are achieved while $v_t = 5$. This is also the value that we set in our experiment for detecting users' significant intentions mentioned above. More over, the developers can also dynamically set other v_t values as needed.

Table 5. $Precision_{SI}$, $Recall_{SI}$, and F_{hybrid} achieved by DSISP

AppName	$v_t = 5$			$v_t = 10$			$v_t = 15$		
	$Precision_{SI}$	$Recall_{SI}$	F_{hybrid}	$Precision_{SI}$	$Recall_{SI}$	F_{hybrid}	$Precision_{SI}$	$Recall_{SI}$	F_{hybrid}
YouTube Music	1.000	0.313	0.606	1.000	0.333	0.500	1.000	0.338	0.506
Uber	1.000	0.398	0.569	1.000	0.398	0.569	1.000	0.398	0.569
Facebook	1.000	0.717	0.835	1.000	0.717	0.835	1.000	0.717	0.835
PPSSPP-PSP emulator (open)	1.000	0.710	0.830	1.000	0.761	0.864	1.000	0.761	0.864
AnySoftKey-board (open)	1.000	0.785	0.880	0.750	0.750	0.750	0.750	0.750	0.750
Tutanota (open)	0.772	0.850	0.809	0.409	0.818	0.545	0.272	0.857	0.413
Average	0.962	0.629	0.755	0.859	0.629	0.677	0.837	0.637	0.656

Efficient detection performance can provide reliable suggestions for developers to update and maintain their apps in future.

5 Conclusion and Future Work

Timely and effectively detecting users' sentiment and preferences is crucial to capturing users' significant intentions, which is paramount for app developers and app vendors in mobile app maintenance and evolution. In this paper, we proposed DSISP, a framework for automatically detecting users' significant intentions from users' reviews. DSISP produces two summaries at different granularity levels about app reviews. These summaries can help app developers to analyze and quantify users' intentions about individual app features and to use this information to identify new requirements or to plan future releases. Moreover, DSISP can keep track of users' up-to-date sentiment and preferences and analyze how these preference features are temporally correlated with users' intentions. The experimental results show that DSISP can effectively and efficiently detect users' significant intentions, with a precision of 0.962 and a F_{hybrid} of 0.755 on average.

In the future, we will leverage multi-dimensional user feedback information to enhance DSISP, such as email records between users and developers, app reviews on social media, etc. We will also employ the app issues and commits to mining whether users' feedback bugs can be reflected at the source code level with the aim to help app developer maintain and improve their apps.

Acknowledgements. This work is supported by the National Key R&D Program of China grant No.2017YFB1401201, the National Natural Science Key Foundation of China grant No.61832014 and the Shenzhen Science and Technology Foundation (JCYJ20170816093943197).

References

1. Panichella, S., Di Sorbo, A., Guzman, E., Visaggio, C.A., Canfora, G., Gall, H.C.: How can i improve my app? Classifying user reviews for software maintenance and evolution, pp. 281–290 (2015)
2. Dąbrowski, J., Letier, E., Perini, A., Susi, A.: Finding and analyzing app reviews related to specific features: a research preview. In: Knauss, E., Goedicke, M. (eds.) REFSQ 2019. LNCS, vol. 11412, pp. 183–189. Springer, Cham (2019). https://doi.org/10.1007/978-3-030-15538-4_14
3. Di Sorbo, A., et al.: What would users change in my app? Summarizing app reviews for recommending software changes, pp. 499–510 (2016)
4. Palomba, F., et al.: Crowdsourcing user reviews to support the evolution of mobile apps. J. Syst. Softw. **137**, 143–162 (2018)
5. Liu, Y., Liu, L., Liu, H., Wang, X.: Analyzing reviews guided by app descriptions for the software development and evolution. J. Softw. Evol. Process. **30**(12) (2018)
6. Messaoud, M.B., Jenhani, I., Jemaa, N.B., Mkaouer, M.W.: A multi-label active learning approach for mobile app user review classification. In: Douligeris, C., Karagiannis, D., Apostolou, D. (eds.) KSEM 2019. LNCS (LNAI), vol. 11775, pp. 805–816. Springer, Cham (2019). https://doi.org/10.1007/978-3-030-29551-6_71

7. Villarroel, L., Bavota, G., Russo, B., Oliveto, R., Di Penta, M.: Release planning of mobile apps based on user reviews, pp. 14–24 (2016)
8. Palomba, F., et al.: Recommending and localizing change requests for mobile apps based on user reviews, pp. 106–117 (2017)
9. Zhou, Y., Su, Y., Chen, T., Huang, Z., Gall, H.C., Panichella, S.: User review-based change file localization for mobile applications. IEEE Trans. Softw. Eng., 1 (2020)
10. Di Sorbo, A., Panichella, S., Alexandru, C.V., Visaggio, C.A., Canfora, G.: SURF: summarizer of user reviews feedback, pp. 55–58 (2017)
11. Huang, Q., Xia, X., Lo, D., Murphy, G.C. : Automating intention mining. IEEE Trans. Softw. Eng., 1 (2018)
12. King, I.: Online app review analysis for identifying emerging issues. In: The 40th International Conference (2018)
13. Thelwall, M., Buckley, K., Paltoglou, G., Cai, D., Kappas, A.: Sentiment strength detection in short informal text. J. Assoc. Inf. Sci. Technol. **61**, 2544–2558 (2010)
14. Cohen, K.B., Dolbey, A.: Foundations of statistical natural language processing. Language **78**(3), 599 (2002)
15. Zhao, W.X., et al.: Comparing Twitter and traditional media using topic models. In: Clough, P., et al. (eds.) ECIR 2011. LNCS, vol. 6611, pp. 338–349. Springer, Heidelberg (2011). https://doi.org/10.1007/978-3-642-20161-5_34
16. Pagano, D., Maalej, W.: User feedback in the AppStore: an empirical study, pp. 125–134 (2013)
17. Harman, M., Jia, Y., Zhang, Y.: App store mining and analysis: MSR for app stores, pp. 108–111 (2012)
18. Chen, N., Lin, J., Hoi, S.C.H., Xiao, X., Zhang, B.: AR-miner: mining informative reviews for developers from mobile app marketplace, pp. 767–778 (2014)
19. Guzman, E., Elhalaby, M., Bruegge, B.: Ensemble methods for app review classification: an approach for software evolution (N), pp. 771–776 (2015)
20. Vu, P.M., Pham, H.V., Nguyen, T.T.: Mining user opinions in mobile app reviews: a keyword-based approach (2015). arXiv: Information
21. Kucuktunc, O., Cambazoglu, B.B., Weber, I., Ferhatosmanoglu, H.: A large-scale sentiment analysis for yahoo! Answers, pp. 633–642 (2012)
22. Ma, Y., Chen, G., Wei, Q.: Finding users preferences from large-scale online reviews for personalized recommendation. Electron. Commer. Res. **17**(1), 3–29 (2016). https://doi.org/10.1007/s10660-016-9240-9
23. Bird, S., Klein, E., Loper, E.: Natural Language Processing with Python: Analyzing Text with The Natural Language Toolkit. O'Reilly Media, Inc., Sebastopol (2009)
24. Smadja, F.: Retrieving collocations from text: Xtract. Comput. Linguist. **19**(1), 143–177 (1993)

Fine-Grained Task Distribution for Mobile Sensor Networks with Agent Cooperation Relationship

Yang Zhang[1], Ye Tao[1], Shukui Zhang[1]([✉]), Li Zhang[1], and Hao Long[1,2]

[1] School of Computer Science and Technology, Soochow University, Suzhou 215006, China
justin1372008@163.com, 1805023826@qq.com, zhangsk@suda.edu.cn,
greenwuhu@126.com, longhhao@163.com
[2] School of Information and Electrical Engineering, Xuzhou College of Industrial Technology,
Xuzhou 221002, China

Abstract. To enhance the comprehensive research on the distribution sensing tasks in Mobile Sensor Networks (MSNs) nowadays, we proposed Task Distribution algorithm based on Relationships of Agents (TDRA) in this paper. First, the score and feature factors of the mobile agents are considered comprehensively in the direct correlation model, and it constructs the correlation model by combining the direct and indirect correlation samples. Second, we introduce a Mobility Model based on the Exponential Distribution (MMED), and obtain the calculation method of probability parameter λ according to the analysis in this paper. At last, we integrate the constructed correlation model and mobility model; then, we apply to the algorithm of task distribution. By the experiments on the algorithms, it indicates that the proposed algorithm improves the performance of task distribution significantly, and offers a more accurate and reliable service.

Keywords: Mobile Sensor Network · Correlation · Mobile agent · Task distribution

1 Introduction

To make better use of the smart devices' sensing, computing and storing abilities, a new type of sensing computing model called mobile crowdsensing computing [1–3] (MCSC) has emerged. Generally speaking, mobile crowdsensing (MCS) uses the sensing functionality of mobile agents (MAs), to accomplish various sensing tasks by collaboration, which cannot be easily done by one single mobile agent. The function of an agent is explained as follows. First, it is an entity with high autonomy (a system, machine, computer software program, etc.) running in a dynamic environment. Its fundamental goal is to accept the commission from another entity (a user, computer program, system, machine, etc.), and to provide the service or assistance. Second, the agent can make an appropriate reaction by actively learning, communicating and social interaction from the environment. Besides, through collaboration, these intelligent agents can solve the complex problems which are challenging for some traditional ways to accomplish.

© Springer Nature Switzerland AG 2020
E. Kafeza et al. (Eds.): ICSOC 2020, LNCS 12571, pp. 401–415, 2020.
https://doi.org/10.1007/978-3-030-65310-1_28

The various theories and applications [4] of MCS are gradually being enhanced and can be applied to traffic congestion analysis [5], environmental pollution map identification [6], sound pollution monitoring [7], free parking space detection [8], residents' health index measurement [9], etc. In the process of participating in sensing tasks, the collaboration among MAs, or between MA and MCS platforms need to interact through data transmission and communication, so mobile sensor networks (MSNs) is formed. Compared to wireless sensor networks, MSNs in crowdsensing have various remarkable characteristics. In these traditional networks, nodes are typically equipped with the sensors that only have limited functions, and are statically deployed [10]. In contrast, MAs are able to carry sensors with various sensing functions and are therefore able to participate in a variety of complex, difficult sensing tasks [1]. Moreover, the carriers of smart devices are generally mobile users, and MAs have strong capabilities of intelligence, mobility and flexibility; they can offer assistance to people in daily life. Also, MAs can be repeatedly recruited through reward and incentive mechanisms based on collaborative group approaches in MSNs to participate in the sensing task. Therefore, it has excellent reusability and extensibility [4].

In MSNs, the distribution of sensing tasks is a critical part. Task distribution means that allocates the sensing tasks to the qualified MAs, as the requirements of the tasks, and achieves the goals initially set. Therefore, for the MCS, we believe that it is critical to design an efficient task distribution method to facilitate MA's to access to sensing tasks in a low-consumption and fast way.

2   Related Work

Sensing tasks are constrained by the specific space-time, which make MAs to be limited by the task releasing time, the task shortest completion time, and the task completion deadline. Meanwhile, if MAs are not in the task sensing execution area, it may take time to reach there, and a specific amount of resources will be consumed. To address this problem, Xiao et al. [11] have proposed an offline and an online task distribution algorithm, to reduce the additional cost caused by communication. These algorithms use a short-distance connection (i.e. Wi-Fi, Bluetooth) for data transmissions. In online task distribution method, the platform distributes functions according to the sequence in which MAs enter the sensing area until all tasks are distributed to qualified MAs. Furthermore, Xiao et al. studied MAs' historical mobility data to predict their future traces. The sensing tasks are divided into two categories, independent and collaborative types [12]. An online task distribution method based on the maximum completion task time is proposed, it can minimize the maximum task completion time.

In [13], the water filling algorithm is proposed that the latest completion time of the tasks took by multiple agents, is regarded as the quality of service. However, the sequence of the task completion by the agents is neglected. Zhang [14] et al. use the agents' time and space coverage range to represent the service quality of sensing tasks. In [15], a hybrid heuristic algorithm is proposed, which combines the ideas of a genetic and greedy algorithm. This can ensure the quality of service while meeting the conditions of real-time requirements of sensing tasks, and minimizing the delays due to data transmissions. During the task distribution phase, the task quality of service is determined mainly by the MAs.

In MSNs, to minimize an MA's cost while executing a task, or to maximize the social benefits of the MCS platform is the most commonly considered factor of task distribution. In [16], two kinds of task distribution methods, online and offline on polynomial time are designed to ensure the sensing platform provides the maximum social benefit, in the condition that the task completion cost is already determined. It can ensure the sensing platform provides the maximum social benefit. Besides, to ensure stable space-time coverage, [17] proposes a hybrid method based on a greedy algorithm and bee colony algorithm. This algorithm can confirm the quality of service, while minimizing the cost, and maximizing the sensing platforms' profit during task distribution. Messaoud et al. [18] designed a task distribution algorithm based on the tabu search. It can distribute tasks to appropriate MAs, while satisfying information quality and energy constraints. It maximizes the information quality and minimize the MAs' task completion cost. In an in-depth study, [19] adds the principle of fairness to the task distribution. It designed the multi-objective optimization function, which can not only achieve fairness, but is also able to ensure the maximization of service quality and the MSN platform's profit.

Therefore, we believe it is necessary to enhance the research comprehensively when distributing tasks. Take these limitations into account, a new task distribution model is needed. This new model needs to consider a number of factors including the geographical location of MAs, the profit of the platform, time of the task completion, fairness, and the order of task execution progress.

3   Algorithm Design

3.1   Task Distribution

In MSNs, the behavior of MAs can be described as two-factor group (A, T). It shows influence of agent, A, on the task T, and it can be indicated by a bipartite graph. **G** is a bipartite graph of Agent-Task, $G = (V, E)$, V means the vertices, E is the edge. It is an undirected model. The vertices of the graph are divided into two disjoint and independent sets, and the two vertices connected by each edge belong to two different sets. Figure 1 shows the mapping of MAs and sensing tasks, A represents MAs, T represent sensing tasks. A bipartite graph G indicates the relationship between agents and sensing tasks, in the process of dynamic tasks distribution. $V = V_A \cap V_T$, and it represents the nodes set of MAs and tasks. If there is a connection between A and T, an edge, $E(A, T)$, is formed between A and T.

In MSNs, the agent collaborations can be reflected as a collaborative network graph, and the relationship between MAs and sensing tasks can be described as a bipartite graph. To do the further analysis, a new diagram is formed by integrating these two [22]. There is one edge connecting these two agents in the diagram, if they are in a collaboration. According to the above descriptions, the correlation between MAs and sensing tasks can be indicated by a diagram. In other words, the dynamic process of tasks distribution of MAs can also be reflected in the diagram. Through it, we can obtain the evaluation on the correlation between the node V_A of MA and the node V_T of the sensing task, which there is no edge directly connect between them. We believe if the correlation coefficient is high, it is more probable that V_T will be distributed. Therefore, the issue of task distribution is regarded as the issue of correlation between entities. Therefore, the quantification of correlation coefficient and mobility characteristics of MAs plays a significant role in the task distribution research. We introduce the correlation and mobility models, and work out the quantification of correlation coefficient and mobility.

3.2 Correlation Model

The central part of MSNs is MAs, they have a stable correlation coefficient if the MAs are intimately connected. At present, for the correlation coefficient calculation, most studies only consider the immediate, non-directional relationship among MAs. However, this is limited in the real MSNs; only instant, non-directional features cannot obtain the accuracy measure of the correlation coefficient. In this paper, the direct and indirect relationships between MAs are fully considered, and the directivity of the link is measured, a new method of correlation coefficient calculation is given as below.

1) Direct Correlation. When two MAs participate in the same sensing task, they have an intimate relationship due to their interactions. The value of which is the direct correlation coefficient between them, where it reflects one MA's comprehensive behavior evaluation of another MA.

In MSNs, an effective way to compute the direct correlation coefficient is to involve both the target MA and the MA which is waiting for the task to be distributed. The direct correlation coefficient measurement can be based on the number of interactions between them. The initial direct correlation coefficient is as follows:

$$INITDR(i, j) = \frac{Min(N_{ij}, \beta)}{\beta} \tag{1}$$

Where $INIT\_DR$ means the initial direct correlation coefficient, and N_{ij} represents the number of interactions between MA_i and MA_j, and the threshold β indicates the minimum interaction amount between the MAs in the intimate correlation. If the number of interactions between MAs does not reach the set threshold β, the initial direct correlation coefficient is measured by the weight ratio of interactions amount over β. If the number of interactions between the two is greater than the set threshold, then the weight value is 1. If the correlation coefficients among MAs are measured only by the number of interactions, it is not appropriate with the reality. As time goes by, the correlation coefficient changes, which makes it possible for the direct correlation coefficient to become meaningless after a while. Therefore, the logistic function [20] is introduced to describe the phenomenon of the reduced correlations with time. The time attenuation function is as follows:

$$f(ti, j) = \frac{1}{1 + e^{-t_{i,j}}} \tag{2}$$

where, $t_{i, j}$ represents the difference between the time when MA_i interacts with MA_j and the system time, and $f(t)$ is a monotonically increasing function, the value is in the interval (0, 1). To effectively depict the process of correlations varies with time, the value of the logistic function is varying with time, too. Furthermore, the evaluation criteria are added to characterize the weighted difference. The evaluation criteria are as follows:

$$S = \begin{cases} 1, |r_{i,j} \times f(t_{i,j}) - r_{j,i} \times f(t_{j,i})| \leq \varepsilon \\ 0, |ri_{i,j} \times f(t_{i,j}) - r_{j,i} \times f(t_{j,i})| > \varepsilon \end{cases} \tag{3}$$

where ε represents an evaluation factor. $r_{i,j}$ indicates the MA_i's evaluation MA_j, and $r_{j,i}$ indicates the MA_j's evaluation of MA_i. If the time-weighted score difference between the two MAs is less than or equal to the value of ε, then it means the interaction is successful and the number of successful interactions is accumulated. The direct correlation coefficient is calculated as follows:

$$DR(i,j) = INITDR(i,j) \times \frac{SUM_{success}(i,j)}{SUM_{total}(i,j)} \times S \tag{4}$$

where $SUMsuccess(i,j)$ indicates the number of successful interactions between MA_i and MA_j that have occurred, $SUMtotal(i,j)$ indicates the total amount that they have interacted with. However, in Formula (4), the weight assigned to MAs are either 1 or 0, when the interaction is successful or not. In fact, there are always differences in MAs' characteristics of MSNs. Therefore, this article refers to MAs' characteristics to describe the weight. When describing an MA's feature, it varies according to different working duration. Therefore, the influence of its working duration factor on feature also needed to be considered. The working duration (age) weight is calculated as follows,

$$\omega_{age}(i,j) = \begin{cases} 1, & |MA_{time}(i) - MA_{time}(j)| \leq \rho \\ \frac{\rho}{|MA_{time}(i) - MA_{time}(j)|}, & |MA_{time}(i) - MA_{time}(j)| > \rho \end{cases} \tag{5}$$

where, ρ represents a duration benchmark, $MA_{time}(i)$ indicates the work duration of MA_i, and $MA_{time}(j)$ indicates the work duration of MA_j. When the duration difference between two MAs is less than or equal to the benchmark ρ, then these two are not considered to be affected by the working duration, and the weight is 1. Otherwise, work duration (age) weights are calculated as a percentage of the benchmark ρ to the duration difference, therefore it makes an effective portrayal of the features between MAs in different duration. As Formula (5) shows, when the duration difference is greater, the weight of the duration is smaller; conversely, smaller differences results in a greater weight of the duration [21]. An MA's feature is quantified as the following formula:

$$F(i,j) = \frac{\sum\limits_{j \in U} Sim(i,j) \times \omega_{age}(i,j)}{|U|} \tag{6}$$

where U indicates the set of all MAs in the sensing task, i and j represent MA_i and MA_i in U. $Sim(i,j)$ indicates the similarity of MA_i and MA_j. The calculation of similarity is key to the task distribution, it gives a quantification among MAs. Through the calculation, we can obtain the agent set which are similar to this MA, and the result is significant to the accuracy of task distribution. So far, there are various calculation models on the MA similarity, Pearson correlation coefficient is a superior example, and also widely used. It is shown as follows [29],

$$Sim(i,j) = \frac{\sum\limits_{u \in U_{i,j}} (r_{i,u} - \bar{r}_i)(r_{j,u} - \bar{r}_j)}{\sqrt{\sum\limits_{u \in U_{i,j}} (r_{i,u} - \bar{r}_i)^2} \sqrt{\sum\limits_{u \in U_{i,j}} (r_{j,u} - \bar{r}_i)^2}} \tag{7}$$

where, $-1 \leq sim(i, j) \leq 1$, MA_i and MA_j have a higher degree of similarity, if $sim(i, j)$ is larger. $r_{i,u}$ and $r_{j,u}$ represent the evaluation score of the MA on the sensing task i and j. $\bar{r}_i$ and $\bar{r}_j$ represent the mean evaluation score of i and j. $\omega_{age}(i, j)$ represents the work duration weight of the different MAs calculated by Formula (5). Among them, the higher the similarity between MA_i and MA_j in the set $U_{i,j}$, the greater the correlation coefficient between the MAs, and also the duration weight value is higher. Therefore, a direct correlation is constructed according to the difference weight came from different sense tasks. Its calculation method is as follows:

$$DR(i, j) = INITDR(i, j) \bullet \frac{\sum\limits_{s \in SUC} F(i, j)}{\sum\limits_{a \in ALL} F(i, j)} \qquad (8)$$

where, $F(i, j)$ indicates the MA_i's preference on MA_j, SUC indicates the set of successful interactions of MAs in sensing task, and ALL represents a set of the total interactions in sensing tasks.

2) Indirect Correlation. When there is no direct interaction between MAs, an intimate correlation is required through the transmission of several indirect connections among them, and the quantified value is called indirect correlation coefficient. Given a correlation network G among MAs, Fig. 1 illustrates the initial correlation network diagram, the calculation of the indirect correlation coefficient among the current MA_i and other MAs [22] are shown as follows. First, make MA_i as the starting point, all MAs that have a direct intimate relationship with MA_i are arranged around MA_i. Then, the other MAs which has directly intimate between the previous MAs are arranged in the second layer with MA_i as the center, and so on. This forms a series of concentric circles with MA_i as the center. To obtain the shortest path, only the connection edges between different layers of nodes are preserved. The intimate network G' of the target node is obtained as Fig. 2. It illustrates the target node's network, at which point the Layer 1 nodes (MA_1, MA_2, MA_3, MA_4) are the direct intimate nodes of MA_i, and Layer 2 nodes (MA_5, MA_6, MA_7, MA_8) are intimate nods of MA_i's intimate relationship nodes (MA_1, MA_2, MA_3, MA_4) [23]. The following formula obtained by the above analysis is applied to calculate the indirect correlation coefficient between the current MA_i and the second layer agent MA_j of G'.

$$IR(i, j) = \frac{1}{2^{Lj-1}} \times \frac{1}{1+e^{-\frac{n}{2}}} \qquad (9)$$

where $IR(i, j)$ indicates the indirect correlation coefficient between MA_i and MA_j, L_j is the MA_j's layer, and n means that there are n paths from MA_i to MA_j. This approach considers both the length of the path and the multiple combinations of paths. For example, as node MA_7, it is at Layer 2, so $L7 = 2$; there are 2 paths from MA_i to MA_7 ($MA_i \longrightarrow MA_2 \longrightarrow MA_7$ and $MA_i \longrightarrow MA_4 \longrightarrow MA_7$), so that $n = 2$. The indirect correlation coefficient of MA_i to $MA7$ is $(1/2^1)(1/(1 + e^1)) \approx 0.37$.

3) Integrated correlation. The integrated correlation coefficient of MA includes two parts, which are direct and indirect correlation model, respectively. If the correlation coefficient of MA_i to MA_j needs to be calculated. It is necessary to consider not only

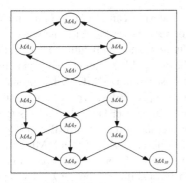

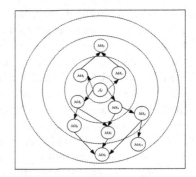

Fig. 1. Initial intimate network

Fig. 2. Schematic diagram of a target node correlation network

the direct correlation coefficient between MA_i and MA_j, but also the indirect correlation coefficient of other MAs in the MSNs with the target MA_j, therefore,

$$RD(i, j) = d \times DR(i, j) + (1 - d) \times IR(i, j) \tag{10}$$

where RD is integrated correlation, the i and j respectively represent MA_i and MA_j. When calculating the correlation coefficient of the target MA_i, it also needs to consider the actual interactions in the MSNs. When the direct interactions between MA_i and MA_j reach a specific benchmark, MA_i mainly depends on its own, and when the interactions of MA_i are less, MA_i relies on the recommended information from other MAs in MSNs. Therefore, it is crucial to use a dynamic weight factor d and $1\text{-}d$ to calculate the correlation of the target MA_i. Dynamic weighting factor d is defined as follows:

$$d = \min\left(1, \frac{|Ni, j|}{Zmin}\right) \tag{11}$$

where, $|N_{i,j}|$ is the number of direct interactions between MA_i and MA_j. If it is able to use only direct interactions to calculate the correlation coefficient, Z_{min} is the amount of minimum direct interactions. Z_{min} has different values for different interactions, and the value is based on the direct correlations' dependence on the indirect correlations.

3.3 Mobility Model

In MSNs, MAs are the main elements. Suppose that MA_i has some specific sensing tasks that must be accomplished. However, the work effort required exceeds its own capability, so another MA's is required to offer collaboration. In order to reduce the communication cost, the communication between them adopts the short-distance wireless communication mode in the progress. This mode of communication mainly depends on MAs' encountering one another, so the essential study of mobility model is to depicts the encountering characteristics. During the progress, MA_i meets MA_j, and MA_i distributes a task to MA_j. Once this is done, MA_i and MA_j work collaboratively to complete the sensing task. MA_i can be called a task publisher and MA_j can be called a task receiver. The meaning of the encounters in this paper is that movement within a close range can be communicated directly through Bluetooth, or the MAs can enter the communication range of some Wi-Fi access and be indirectly connected over the Wi-Fi network.

We assume that when the communication duration and bandwidth are sufficient for each MA to receive tasks, the meeting time of the task publisher and receiver in a model called Mobility Model based on an Exponential Distribution (MMED). The probability parameter of the model is λ. Reports in the literature [24–26] have proven in detail that the encounter time among MAs in MSNs follows the power law, which also supports the exponential distribution approximately. For the above reasons, MMED model has been widely used, and it has been described in the literature [27, 28]. In MMED model, the calculation of the probability parameter λ is critical. Literature [12] proposed that $\int_0^\infty t\lambda_i e^{-\lambda_i t} dt = \frac{1}{\lambda_i}$. Incorporate to this paper, the probability parameter λ calculation is that λ is the reciprocal of the estimated time that the task publisher and receiver encounter one another. This is calculated as follows:

$$\lambda i, j = \frac{m}{\sum\limits_{c \in S} \sum\limits_{(i,j)meet} duration(i, j)} \tag{12}$$

where, m is the number of times that MA_i encounter MA_j during sensing tasks, S is a set of sensing tasks, c is the sensing task for each successful interaction, and the $duration(i, j)$ is the duration of the encounter between MA_i and MA_j. According to the formula, it can be known that when the value of the probability parameters $\lambda_{i,j}$ is smaller, the longer the duration of the meet between MA_i and MA_j, the data transmission and communication between them is better.

4   Task Distribution Algorithms

4.1   Algorithm Description

In order to improve the efficiency and accuracy of task distribution, a correlation model is built to research the collaboration among MAs, and to do the distribution firstly. The calculation on correlation coefficient is divided into two models, direct and indirect ways. Integrate the two models into the comprehensive correlation coefficient. While calculating direct correlation coefficient, the factors of time and preference are considered. Secondly, Mobility Model based on an Exponential Distribution (MMED) is employed for the analysis of MA mobility characteristics, and the calculation of probability parameter λ is already provided in this paper. At last, correlation coefficient and mobility model are integrated to do the tasks distribution in MSNs. The specific steps of the algorithm are described as follows:

(1)   According to Pearson Formula (7), calculate the similarity $Sim(i, j)$ between the target agent MA_i and MA_j;
(2)   Calculate the direct correlation $DR(i, j)$ and the indirect correlation $IR(i, j)$ of MA_i and MA_j according to Eq. (8) and (9);
(3)   Calculate the integrated correlation $RD(i,j)$ of MA_i and MA_j according to Eq. (10) and (11);

(4) Obtain the comprehensive similarity by the integrated correlation and similarity of MA_i and MA_j, and calculate the comprehensive similarity $CSim(i, j)$. The specific calculation method is as follows:

$$CSim(i, j) = \eta RD(i, j) + (1 - \eta)Sim(i, j) \qquad (13)$$

where, η represents the weight of correlation, 1-η represents the weight of MA similarity.

(5) According to Formula (12), calculate MA mobility probability parameter λ. Then, combine the mobility probability parameter λ and the comprehensive similarity into the $Sim\_Mob(i, j)$. The specific calculation method is as follows:

$$Sim\_Mob(i, j) = \varphi CSim(i, j) + (1 - \varphi)\lambda i, j \qquad (14)$$

where φ represents the weight of the comprehensive similarity, and 1-φ represents the weight of the MA mobility encounter probability;

(6) Distribute the sensing tasks that have no MA involved, and calculate the predictive score of agent u on task i, $P(u, i)$. The calculation method is as follows:

$$P(u, i) = \overline{Ru} + \frac{\sum\limits_{n \in NCu} Sim\_Mob(u, n) \times \left(Rn, i - \overline{Rn}\right)}{\sum\limits_{n \in NCu} (|Sim\_Mob(u, n)|)} \qquad (15)$$

where, $Sim\_Mob(u, n)$ represents the comprehensive similarity of MA u and n, $R_{n, i}$ represents the score of the mobile agent n on the sensing task i, $\overline{Ru}$ indicates the average score of the sensing task by the mobile agent u and n;

(7) Calculate MA predictive score according to (6), and continue the task distribution.

4.2 Evaluation Criteria

Evaluating the accuracy of the proposed algorithm on task distribution is very important. This paper uses the mean absolute error (MAE) as one crucial distribution quality measurement [30, 31]. The accuracy of the algorithm is measured by the average error value between the predicted scoring value and the actual scoring value. When the MAE value is smaller, the accuracy of the algorithm in the task distribution is higher. The MAE is calculated as follows:

$$\tau MAE = \frac{\sum\limits_{i \in Utest} |pi - qi|}{n} \qquad (16)$$

where, p_i represents the predictive score for the target task, q_i represents the actual score of the target task, U_{test} represents the MA test set, and n represents the amount of MA test sets. We use *Precision* and *Recall* as the measurement index of the accuracy on task distribution [32]. The data is divided into training set and test set. MAs' behavior prediction model is established on the training set, and the behavior can be estimated. Furthermore, the contact ratio of the predicated results in test set and actual behavior data can be obtained, and we use it as the index of task distribution accuracy. Therefore, Precision and Recall are shown as follows,

$$Precision = \frac{\sum |R(a) \cap T(a)|}{\sum |R(a)|} \tag{17}$$

$$Recall = \frac{\sum |R(a) \cap T(a)|}{\sum |T(a)|} \tag{18}$$

where, $R(a)$ represents the task distribution list of the test set, and $T(a)$ is the task distribution list of the training set.

5 Experimental Analysis

5.1 Experiment Design

In this paper, we use MIT's Reality Mining as an experimental dataset [33]. It contains more than 80,000 records with nearly 100 users' interaction data in Bluetooth network, for approximately 9 months. For some reasons, some user interactions in this dataset produce a relatively small amount of valid data. This part of the user dataset is excluded; we select 80 users with a large amount of data as the experimental object. The data from the experimental dataset for a 12-week period (September 27, 2004 to December 21, 2004) is used. The dataset on the first 8 weeks is used as a training and the data from last 4 weeks are used in the test. The dataset for these 80 users is selected, and the time interval is set as 14 natural days. The data during this period are more active than other time periods. We employ data from the experiment to analyze the correlation among users, and process the task distribution based on the proposed algorithm (TDRA). Six groups of experiment are designed. The first five groups are used to determine five unknown parameters. The last one is used to compare the accuracy of the task distribution algorithms, among the proposed algorithm and others.

5.2 Results and Analysis

1) **Experiment 1.** In Formula (1), set the threshold value β is 30 –100, its effect on the distribution accuracy of the sensing task measurement τ_{MAE} is shown in Fig. 3.

According to Fig. 3, it can be observed that as the value of β becomes larger, the τ_{MAE} initially decreases and subsequently increases gradually. When of $\beta = 80$, τ_{MAE} is the lowest, which means the distribution accuracy has the best behavior.

2) **Experiment 2.** When the evaluation factor ε according to Formula (3) is 1, 2 and 3, the effect τ_{MAE}, reflects the accuracy of the sensing task distribution, is shown

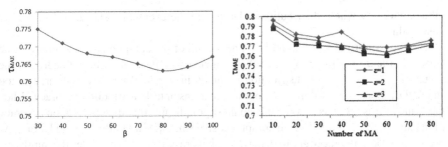

Fig. 3. Effects of different β values on τ_{MAE} **Fig. 4.** Effect of different ε values on τ_{MAE}

in Fig. 4. It can be observed that under the number of collaborators, when ε is 2 (i.e. the score difference on of any two MA interactions is 2), the distribution accuracy of the proposed algorithm is optimal. The reason is that while ε is higher, the successful interactions between MAs is greater, and the opposite is also true. As a result, the correlation coefficient will be very different from the mean value.

3) Experiment 3. When the duration benchmark ρ, obtained from Formula (5) is in the range of 5–15, the effect on the accuracy τ_{MAE} of the task distribution is shown in Fig. 5. It indicates that when the value of ρ is too large or too small, the proposed algorithm does not achieve the best task distribution accuracy. When ρ is 10, the value of τ_{MAE} is the lowest, indicating that the distribution accuracy of the algorithm is optimal when the work duration benchmark is 10. While the work duration benchmark is too low or too high, it makes the deviation of MA's feature becomes large. As a result, the correlation coefficient will be very different from the mean value.

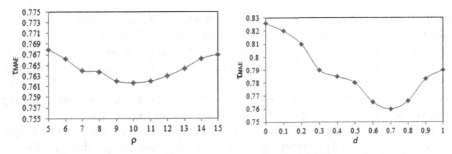

Fig. 5. Effect of different ρ values on τ_{MAE} **Fig. 6.** Effect of different d values for τ_{MAE}

4) Experiment 4. In Formula (9), the value weight factor d is 0–1, and the effect on the accuracy τ_{MAE} of the task distribution is shown in Fig. 6. When the value of d is too large or too small, the proposed algorithm is not optimal in terms of task distribution accuracy. However, when d is 0.7, the τ_{MAE} is minimal, indicating that when the value of correlation weight is 0.7, the distribution accuracy of the algorithm is optimal. If d is 0, the integrated correlation is just indirect, it means the relationship between task publisher and receiver is not intimate, the result deviates the mean value. If d is 1, the integrated correlation is all direct. When there are mistakes occurred in some MAs, the influence on the whole distribution is large, and the eventual result also deviates the mean value.

5) Experiment 5. In Formula (14), the weight of the comprehensive similarity (the correlation and mobility proportional parameter) φ is $0 -1$, and the influence on the accuracy τ_{MAE} of the task distribution is shown in Fig. 7. When φ is too large or too small, the proposed algorithm is not optimal in terms of task distribution accuracy. When the value of φ is 0.6, the τ_{MAE} is the smallest, it indicates that the distribution accuracy of the algorithm is optimal. Both comprehensive similarity and mobility model of MAs need to be taken into account to achieve the best result. If only consider the similarity, neglect the movement, the result will not be satisfied. In the same way, the efficiency and service quality will be affected if only consider the mobility of MAs.

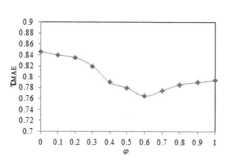

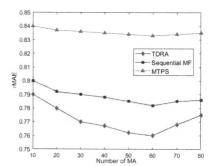

Fig. 7. Effect of different φ values on τ_{MAE} **Fig. 8.** Comparison of different algorithms on τ_{MAE}

6) Experiment 6. In order to verify the accuracy of the proposed task distribution algorithms, some parameters, identified in Experiments 1–5, are set as $\beta = 80$, $\varepsilon = 2$, $\rho = 10$, $d = 0.7$ and $\varphi = 0.6$ in this experiment. The algorithms include Recommendations Based on Collaborative Filtering (Sequential MF) [34], and Fine-grained Multitask Allocation Framework (MTPS) [35]. The experimental results are shown in Fig. 8. We can see that τ_{MAE} decreases and task distribution accuracy increases with an increasing number of MAs with collaborative relationships. However, the task distribution accuracy starts to decrease when the number of MAs with collaborative relationships is too large. When the number of MAs is 60, the accuracy of the proposed algorithm performance task distribution is optimal.

Table 1. Optimal τ_{MAE} values of different algorithms

Task distribution algorithm	Best τ_{MAE}
MTPS	0.833
Sequential MF	0.782
TDRA	0.760

The proposed algorithm (TDRA) is compared with the other two for the optimal τ_{MAE} value. The optimal τ_{MAE} values of each algorithm are shown in Table 1. As it can be seen in this table, compared with the other two task distribution algorithms, the τ_{MAE} value of the algorithm proposed in this paper is the smallest, that is, the accuracy of its task distribution is the best.

According to the experiments above, the correlation among MAs and MAs' preference on the sensing tasks have a huge influence on the algorithms. Furthermore, we believe that the valuable information mining from MSNs through these characteristics, and apply it to the algorithms, brings a positive effect on the sensing tasks distribution.

6 Conclusion

We had taken a research to improve the efficiency and accuracy of the sensing task distribution algorithms. The correlation model and mobility model are constructed, and a new task distribution algorithm is proposed in this paper. Furthermore, several comparative experiments have verified the superiority of the proposed algorithm. By the experiments on three algorithms, It indicates that the proposed algorithm improves the performance of task distribution significantly, and offers a more ac-curate and reliable service. In the future, it is necessary to further study the influencing factors affecting the task distribution, and to improve the efficiency and service quality.

Acknowledgement. This work was supported in part by the National Natural Science Foundation of China (No, 61070169), Pre Research Fund (No, 61403120402), Natural Science Research Project of Jiangsu Higher Education Institution (19KJB520061), the Priority Academic Program Development of Jiangsu Higher Education Institutions (PAPD).

References

1. Ganti, R.K., Ye, F., Lei, H.: Mobile crowdsensing: current state and future challenges. IEEE Commun. Mag. **49**(11), 32–39 (2011)
2. Zhu, H., Zhang, Y., et al.: Exploring deep learning for efficient and reliable mobile sensing. IEEE Network **32**(4), 6–7 (2018)
3. Ma, H., Zhao, D., Yuan, P.: Opportunities in mobile crowd sensing. IEEE Commun. Mag. **52**(8), 29–35 (2014)
4. Jaimes, L.G., Laurens, I.J.V., Raij, A.: A location-based incentive algorithm for consecutive crowd sensing tasks. IEEE Latin Am. Trans. **14**(2), 811–817 (2016)
5. Mohan, P., Padmanabhan, V.N., Ramjee, R.: Nericell: rich monitoring of road and traffic conditions using mobile smartphones. In: Proceedings of the 6th International Conference on Embedded Networked Sensor Systems, pp. 323–336. ACM, Raleigh (2008)
6. Dutta, P., Aoki, P.M., Kumar, N., et al.: Common sense: participatory urban sensing using a network of handheld air quality monitors. In: Proceedings of the 7th ACM Conference on Embedded Networked Sensor Systems, pp. 349–350. ACM, New York (2009)
7. Hachem, S., Mallet, V., Ventura, R., et al.: Monitoring noise pollution using the urban civics middleware. In: 2015 IEEE First International Conference on Big Data Computing Service and Application, pp. 52–61. IEEE, USA (2015)

8. Villanueva, F.J., Villa, D., Santofimia, M.J., et al.: Crowdsensing smart city parking monitoring. In: 2015 IEEE 2nd World Forum on Internet of Things, pp. 751–756. IEEE, USA (2015)

9. Pryss, R., Reichert, M., Herrmann, J., et al.: Mobile crowdsensing in clinical and psychological trials–a case study,2015 IEEE 28th International Symposium on Computer-Based Medical Systems, pp. 23–24. IEEE, Brazil (2015)

10. Guo, B., Liu, Y., Wang, L., et al.: Task allocation in spatial crowdsourcing: current state and future directions. IEEE Internet Things J. **5**(3), 1749–1764 (2018)

11. Xiao, M., Wu, J., Huang, L., et al.: Multi-task assignment for crowdsensing in mobile social networks. In: 2015 IEEE Conference on Computer Communications, pp. 2227–2235. IEEE, Hong Kong (2015)

12. Xiao, M., Wu, J., Huang, L., et al.: Online task assignment for crowdsensing in predictable mobile social networks. IEEE Trans. Mob. Comput. **16**(8), 2306–2320 (2017)

13. Shi, C., Lakafosis, V., Ammar, M.H., et al.: Serendipity: enabling remote computing among intermittently connected mobile devices. In: Proceedings of the Thirteen ACM International Symposium on Mobile Ad Hoc Networking and Computing, pp. 145–154. ACM, USA (2012)

14. Zhang, M., Yang, P., et al.: Quality-aware sensing coverage in budget-constrained mobile crowdsensing networks. IEEE Trans. Veh. Technol. **69**(9), 7698–7707 (2016)

15. Yang, F., Lu, J.L., Zhu, Y., et al.: Heterogeneous task allocation in participatory sensing. In: 2015 IEEE Global Communications Conference (GLOBECOM), pp. 1–6. IEEE, Spain (2015)

16. Han, K., Zhang, C., Luo, J., et al.: Truthful scheduling mechanisms for powering mobile crowdsensing. IEEE Trans. Comput. **65**(1), 294–307 (2016)

17. Wang, Z., Huang, D., Wu, H., et al.: QoS-constrained sensing task assignment for mobile crowd sensing. In: 2014 IEEE Global Communications Conference, Australia, pp. 311–326 (2014)

18. Messaoud, R.B., Ghamri-Doudane, Y.: QEMSS: a selection scheme for participatory sensing tasks. In: 2015 International Conference on Protocol Engineering and International Conference on New Technologies of Distributed Systems, pp. 1–6. IEEE, Dalian (2015)

19. Messaoud, R.B., Ghamri-Doudane, Y.: Fair QoI and energy-aware task allocation in participatory sensing. In: 2016 IEEE Wireless Communications and Networking Conference, India, pp. 1–6 (2016)

20. Kwak, J., Kim, J., Chong, S.: Proximity-aware location based collaborative sensing for energy-efficient mobile devices. IEEE Trans. Mob. Comput. **18**(2), 417–430 (2019)

21. Zhou, Z., Liao, H., Bo, G., et al.: Robust mobile crowd sensing: when deep learning meets edge computing. IEEE Network **32**(4), 54–60 (2018)

22. Wang, R., Jiang, Y., Li, Y., Lou, J.: A collaborative filtering recommendation algorithm based on multiple social trusts. J. Comput. Res. Dev. **53**(6), 1389–1399 (2016)

23. Qiao, X.-Q., Yang, C., Li, X.-F., Chen, J.-L.: A trust calculating algorithm based on social networking service users' context. Chin. J. Comput. **34**(12), 2403–2413 (2011)

24. Hsu, W.J., Spyropoulos, T., Psounis, K., et al.: Modeling time-variant user mobility in wireless mobile networks. In: IEEE INFOCOM 2007-26th IEEE International Conference on Computer Communication, pp. 758–766. IEEE, China (2007)

25. Jeremie, L., Timur, F., Vania, C.: Evaluating mobility pattern space routing for DTNs. In: Processings of the IEEE Conference on Computing and Communication, pp. 1–10. IEEE, China (2006)

26. Cai, H., Eun, D.Y.: Crossing over the bounded domain: from exponential to power-law inter-meeting time in MANET. In: Proceedings of the 13th Annual ACM International Conference on Mobile Computing and Networking, pp. 159–170. ACM, Singapore (2007)

27. Gao, W., Li, Q., Zhao, B., et al.: Multicasting in delay tolerant networks: a social network perspective. In: Proceedings of the Tenth ACM International Symposium on Mobile Ad Hoc Networking and Computing, pp. 299–308. ACM, USA (2009)

28. Wu, J., Xiao, M., Huang, L.: Homing spread: community home-based multi-copy routing in mobile social networks. In: Proceedings IEEE INFOCOM, pp. 2319–2327. IEEE, Italy (2013)

29. Li, S., Li, S.-Q., Liu, B.: Improved collaborative filtering algorithm and its parallel implementation. J. Comput. Eng. Des. **39**(12), 3853–3859 (2018)

30. Wang, H.-Y., Yang, W.-B., et al.: A service recommendation method based on trustworthy community. Chin. J. Comput. **37**(2), 301–311 (2014)

31. Wang, Q., Wang, J.: Collaborative filtering recommendation algorithm combining trust mechanism with user preferences. J. Comput. Eng. Appl. **10**, 261–265, 270 (2015)

32. Mikolajczy, K., Schmid, C.: A performance evaluation of local descriptors. IEEE Trans. Pattern Anal. Mach. Intell. **27**(10), 1615–1630 (2005)

33. http://realitycommons.media.mit.edu/index.html

34. Sun, G.F., Wu, L., Liu, Q., Zhu, C., Chen, E.H.: Recommendations based on collaborative filtering by exploiting sequential behaviors. Ruan Jian Xue Bao/J. Softw. **24**(11), 2721–2733 (2013). (in Chinese). http://www.jos.org.cn/1000-9825/4478.htm

35. Wang, J., Wang, Y., Zhang, D., et al.: Fine-grained multitask allocation for participatory sensing with a shared budge. IEEE Internet Things J. **3**(6), 1395–1405 (2016)

Allocation Priority Policies for Serverless Function-Execution Scheduling Optimisation

Giuseppe De Palma[1], Saverio Giallorenzo[1,2], Jacopo Mauro[3(✉)],
and Gianluigi Zavattaro[1,2]

[1] Università di Bologna, Bologna, Italy
[2] INRIA, Sophia-Antipolis, France
[3] University of Southern Denmark, Odense, Denmark
mauro@imada.sdu.dk

Abstract. Serverless computing is a Cloud development paradigm where developers write and compose stateless functions, abstracting from their deployment and scaling. In this paper, we address the problem of *function-execution scheduling*, i.e., how to schedule the execution of Serverless functions to optimise their performance against some user-defined goals. We introduce a declarative language of *Allocation Priority Policies* (APP) to specify policies that inform the scheduling of function execution. We present a prototypical implementation of APP as an extension of Apache OpenWhisk and we validate it by *i*) implementing a use case combining IoT, Edge, and Cloud Computing and *ii*) by comparing its performance to an alternative implementation that uses vanilla OpenWhisk.

Keywords: Serverless · Function-execution scheduling · Optimisation

1 Introduction

Serverless computing [1], also known as Functions-as-a-Service, is a new development paradigm where programmers write and compose stateless functions, leaving to Serverless infrastructure providers the duty to manage their deployment and scaling. Hence, although a bit of a misnomer—as servers are of course involved—the "less" in Serverless refers to the removal of some server-related concerns, namely, their maintenance, scaling, and expenses deriving from their sub-optimal management (e.g., idle servers). Serverless computing was first proposed as a deployment modality for Cloud architectures [1] that pushed to the extreme the per-usage model of Cloud Computing, letting users pay only for the computing resources used at each function invocation. However, recent industrial and academic proposals, such as platforms to support Serverless development in Edge [2] and Internet-of-Things [3] scenarios, confirm the rising interest of neighbouring communities to adopt the Serverless paradigm.

S. Giallorenzo formerly worked at the University of Southern Denmark, Odense, Denmark.

© Springer Nature Switzerland AG 2020
E. Kafeza et al. (Eds.): ICSOC 2020, LNCS 12571, pp. 416–430, 2020.
https://doi.org/10.1007/978-3-030-65310-1_29

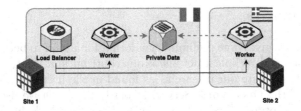

Fig. 1. Example of function-execution scheduling problem.

While Serverless providers have become more and more common [4–10] the technology is still in its infancy and there is much work to do to overcome the many limitations [1,9,11,12] that hinder its wide adoption. One of the main challenges to address is how should Serverless providers schedule the functions on the available computation nodes. To visualise the problem, consider for example Fig. 1 depicting the availability of two **Worker**s—the computation nodes where functions can execute. One **Worker** is in Italy (**Site 1**) and the other in Greece (**Site 2**). Both **Worker**s can execute a function that interacts (represented by the dashed green lines) with the **Private Data** storage located at **Site 1**. When the **Load Balancer** (acting as function scheduler) receives a request to execute the function, it must decide on which **Worker** to execute it. To minimise the response time, the **Load Balancer** should consider the different computational loads of the two **Worker**s, which influence the time they take to execute the function. Also, the latency to access the **Private Data** storage plays an important role in determining the performance of function execution: the **Worker** at **Site 1** is close to the data storage and enjoys a faster interaction with it while the **Worker** at **Site 2** is farther from it and can undergo heavier latencies.

In this paper, we address the problem of *function-execution scheduling optimisation* [9] by proposing a methodology that provides developers with a declarative language, called *Allocation Priority Policies* (APP). Developers can use APP to specify a scheduling policy for their functions that the scheduler later uses to find the worker that, given the current status of the system, best fits the constraints specified by the developer of a given function. To substantiate our proposal, we extended the scheduler of OpenWhisk [5], a well-known open-source distributed Serverless platform, to use APP-defined policies in the scheduling of Serverless functions. In Sect. 3 we detail the APP language and present our prototypical implementation as an extension of Apache OpenWhisk [5]—in Sect. 2 we provide some introductory notions of the Serverless paradigm and an overview of the OpenWhisk platform. To validate our extension, in Sect. 4, we present a use case combining IoT, Edge, and Cloud Computing and we contrast an implementation of the use case using our APP-based prototype with a naïve one using three coexisting installations of the vanilla OpenWhisk stack to achieve the same functional requirements. We present the data on the performance of the two deployments, providing empirical evidence of the performance gains offered by the APP-governed scheduling. We conclude comparing with related work in Sect. 5 and discussing future and concluding remarks in Sect. 6.

2   Preliminaries

In this section, we give some preliminary information useful to better understand the motivations and technical details of our contribution. First, we outline the problems that motivate our research—as found in the literature. Then, we give an overview of the OpenWhisk Serverless platform, which we use in Sect. 3 to implement a prototype of our solution to the function scheduling problem.

Serverless Function Scheduling. The Serverless development cycle is divided in two main parts: *a)* the writing of a function using a programming language supported by the platform (e.g. JavaScript, Python, C#) and *b)* the definition of an event that should trigger the execution of the function. For example, an event is a request to store some data, which triggers a process managing the selection, instantiation, scaling, deployment, fault tolerance, monitoring, and logging of the functions linked to that event. A Serverless provider—like IBM Cloud Functions [10] (using Apache OpenWhisk [5]), AWS Lambda [4], Google Cloud Functions [7] or Microsoft Azure Functions [6]—is responsible to schedule functions on its workers, to control the scaling of the infrastructure by adjusting their available resources, and to bill its users on a per-execution basis.

When instantiating a function, the provider has to create the appropriate execution environment for the function. Containers [13] and Virtual Machines [14] are the main technologies used to implement isolated execution environments for functions. How the provider implements the allocation of resources and the instantiation of execution environments impacts on the performance of the function execution. If the provider allocates a new container for every request, the initialisation overhead of the container would negatively affect both the performance of the single function and heavily increase the load on the worker. A solution to tackle this problem is to maintain a "warm" pool of already-allocated containers. This matter is usually referred to as *code locality* [9]. Resource allocation also includes I/O operations that need to be properly considered. For example, the authors of [15] report that a single function in the Amazon serverless platform can achieve on average 538 Mbps network bandwidth, an order of magnitude slower than single modern hard drives (the authors report similar results from Google and Azure). Those performance result from bad allocations over I/O-bound devices, which can be reduced following the principle of *session locality* [9], i.e., taking advantage of already established user connections to workers. Another important aspect to consider to schedule functions, as underlined by the example in Fig. 1, is that of *data locality*, which comes into play when functions need to intensively access (connection- or payload-wise) some data storage (e.g., databases or message queues). Intuitively, a function that needs to access some data storage and that runs on a worker with high-latency access to that storage (e.g., due to physical distance or thin bandwidth) is more likely to undergo heavier latencies than if run on a worker "closer" to it. Data locality has been subject of research in neighbouring Cloud contexts [16,17].

Apache OpenWhisk. Apache OpenWhisk [5] is an open-source Serverless platform initially developed by IBM—at the core of the company's Serverless offer [10]—and subsequently donated to the Apache Software Foundation. It is a production-ready Serverless platform and it supports the execution of functions written in many programming languages, including JavaScript, Python, Java, Go, and C#.

OpenWhisk is an event-driven system that runs code in response to events (e.g., changes to a database, an HTTP request or IoT sensors readings) or direct invocations. To pick up an event from a source, OpenWhisk defines a feed that activates triggers linked to a set of rules and actions to be executed.

OpenWhisk systems include one *controller* and a pool of *invokers*. The controller is a load balancer that, given an action to be executed, forwards the execution request to one selected invoker. The invokers execute actions using isolated Docker containers. Invokers are the OpenWhisk equivalent of the **Worker**s mentioned in our presentation. Latency-wise, container instantiation is by far the most relevant overhead endured by the invokers. One of the most effective mechanisms to reduce such overhead is to reuse containers, i.e., when a function is invoked multiple times, the system can reuse the container of a terminated invocation of that function rather than creating a fresh one.

The load balancing policy followed by the controller aims at maximising reuse. When the controller needs to schedule the execution of a function, a numeric hash h is calculated using the action name. An invoker is then selected using the remainder of the division between h and the total number of invokers n. The controller checks if the invoker is overloaded. If the chosen invoker is overloaded, the index is incremented by a step-size, which is any of the co-prime numbers smaller than the amount n of available invokers.

When no invoker is available after cycling through the entire invoker pool, the load balancer randomly selects an invoker from those that are considered "healthy"—able to sustain the workload. This happens when there are invokers that are healthy but have no capacity available when the scheduling algorithm was searching for an invoker. When there are no healthy invokers, the load balancer returns an error stating that no invokers are available for executing the function.

Motivation. As discussed, at least three aspects related to function scheduling affect the performances of function execution in Serverless platforms: code, session, and data locality. Load balancing policies adopted by state-of-the-art Serverless platforms like Apache OpenWhisk take advantage only of code locality, but they currently have no way to integrate also information on other types of locality. To take advantage of other forms of locality, the load balancer should have knowledge on the way functions access external resources, like I/O-bound devices or databases, whose usage depends on the implementation of functions.

Our work aims at bridging that information gap, presenting a language that any Serverless platform can use in its scheduling policies to consider those factors. Our approach is conservative: with its default settings (explained in the next section) it can capture the status of current Serverless platforms. Then, more advanced Serverless users and platform providers can use the features offered by our proposal to optimise the execution of functions.

Moreover, optimised scheduling policies could be the outcome of automatic heuristic/inference systems applied to the functions to be executed. Automatic synthesis of optimized scheduling policies is the long-term objective of our research and this paper addresses the first fundamental step, i.e., showing the feasibility of Serverless platforms instructed with customized load balancing rules. Given this objective, we narrow the current exposition to manually-defined configurations and we leave the exploration of automatic configuration to future work.

$$
\begin{array}{ll}
policy\_tag \in & Identifiers \cup \{\texttt{default}\} \qquad worker\_label \in Identifiers \qquad n \in \mathbb{N} \\
app & ::= \overline{tag} \\
tag & ::= policy\_tag : \overline{- \; block \; followup?} \\
block & ::= \texttt{workers} \; [\; "*" \; | \; \overline{- \; worker\_label} \;] \\
& \quad (\texttt{strategy} \; [\; \texttt{random} \; | \; \texttt{platform} \; | \; \texttt{best\_first} \;])? \\
& \quad (\texttt{invalidate} \; [\; \texttt{capacity\_used} : n\% \; | \; \texttt{max\_concurrent\_invocations} : n \; | \; \texttt{overload} \;])? \\
followup & ::= \texttt{followup} : [\; \texttt{default} \; | \; \texttt{fail} \;]
\end{array}
$$

Fig. 2. The APP syntax.

3   The APP Language

Current serverless platforms, like OpenWhisk, come equipped with hard-coded load balancing policies. In this section, we present the *Allocation Priority Policies* (APP) language, intended as a language to specify customised load balancing policies and overcome the inflexibility of the hard-coded load balancing ones. The idea is that both developers and providers can write, besides the functions to be executed by the platform, a policy that instructs the platform what workers each function should be preferably executed on. Function-specific configurations are optional and without them the system can follow a default strategy.

As an extension of the example depicted in Fig. 1, consider some functions that need to access a database. To reduce latency (as per data locality principle), the best option would be to run those functions on the same pool of machines that run the database. If that option is not valid, then running those functions on workers in the proximity (e.g., in the same network domain) is preferable than using workers located further away (e.g., in other networks). We comment below an initial APP script that specifies the scheduling policies only for those workers belonging to the pool of machines running the database.

```
couchdb_query:
  - workers:
    - DB_worker1
    - DB_worker2
    strategy: random
    invalidate: ↵
      capacity_used: 50 followup::
    fail
```

At the first line, we define the *policy tag*, which is couchdb_query. As explained below, tags are used to link policies to functions. Then, the keyword workers indicates a list of *worker labels*, which identify the workers in the proximity of the database, i.e., DB_worker1 and DB_worker2. As explained below, labels are used to identify workers. Finally, we define three parameters: the strategy used by the scheduler to choose among the listed worker labels, the policy that invalidates the selection of a worker label, and the followup policy in case all workers are invalidated. In the example, we select one of the two labels randomly, we invalidate their usage if the workers corresponding to the chosen label are used at more than the 50% of their capacity (capacity_used) and, in case all workers are invalidated (followup), we let the request for function execution fail.

The APP Syntax and Semantics. We report the syntax of APP in Fig. 2. The basic entities considered in the APP language are *a*) scheduling policies, identified by a *policy tag* identifier to which users can associate their functions—the policy-function association is a one-to-many relation—and *b*) workers, identified by a *worker label*—where a label identifies a collection of computation nodes. An APP script is a YAML [18] file specifying a sequence of policies. Given a tag, the corresponding policy includes a list of workers blocks, possibly closed with a followup strategy. A workers block includes three parameters: a collection of worker labels, a possible scheduling strategy, and an invalidate condition. A followup strategy can be either a default policy or the notification of failure.

We discuss the APP semantics, and the possible parameters, by commenting on a more elaborate script extending the previous one, shown in Fig. 3. The APP script starts with the tag default, which is a special tag used to specify the policy for non-tagged functions, or to be adopted when a tagged policy has all its members invalidated, and the followup option is default.

In Fig. 3, the default tag describes the default behaviour of the serverless platform running APP. The wildcard "*" for the workers represent all worker labels. The strategy selected is the platform default (e.g., in our prototype in Sect. 4 the platform strategy corresponds to the selection algorithm described in Sect. 2) and its invalidate strategy considers a worker label non-usable when its workers are overloaded, i.e., none has enough resources to run the function.

Besides the default tag, the couchdb_query tag is used for those functions that access the database. The scheduler considers worker blocks in order of appearance from top to bottom. As mentioned above, in the first block (associated to DB_worker1 and DB_worker2) the scheduler randomly picks one of the two worker labels and considers a label invalid when all corresponding workers reached the 50% of capacity. Here the notion of capacity depends on the implementation (e.g., our OpenWhisk-based APP implementation in Sect. 4 uses information on the CPU usage to determine the load of invokers). When both worker labels are invalid, the scheduler goes to the next workers block, with near_DB_worker1 and near_DB_worker2, chosen following a best_first strategy—where the scheduler considers the ordering of the list of workers, sending invocations to the first until it becomes invalid, to then pass to the next ones in order. The invalidate strategy of the block regards the maximal number of concurrent invocations over the labelled workers—max_concurrent_invocations, which is set to 100. If all the worker labels are invalid, the scheduler applies the followup behaviour, which is to fail.

Summarising, given a policy tag, the scheduler considers the corresponding workers blocks starting from the top. A block includes three parameters:

- workers: contains a non-empty list of worker labels or the "*" wildcard to encompass all of them;

```
default:
  - workers: "*"
    strategy: platform
    invalidate: overload

couchdb_query:
  - workers:
    - DB_worker1
    - DB_worker2
    strategy: random
    invalidate: capacity_used: 50   - workers:::
    - near_DB_worker1
    - near_DB_worker2
    strategy: best_first
    invalidate: max_concurrent_invocations: 100
  followup: fail
```

Fig. 3. Example of an APP script.

- strategy: defines the policy of worker label selection. APP currently supports three strategies:
  - random: labels are selected in a fair random manner;
  - best_first: labels are selected following their order of appearance;
  - platform: labels are selected following the default strategy of the serverless platform—in our prototype (cf. Sect. 4) the platform option corresponds to the algorithm based on identifier hashing with co-prime increments explained in Sect. 2.
- invalidate: specifies when to stop considering a worker label. All invalidate options below include as preliminary condition the unreachability of the corresponding workers. When all labels in a block are invalid, the next block or the followup behaviour is used. Current invalidate options are:
  - overload: the corresponding workers lack enough computational resources to run the function;[1]
  - capacity_used: the corresponding workers reached a threshold percentage of CPU load (although not being overloaded);
  - max_concurrent_invocations: the corresponding workers have reached a threshold number of buffered concurrent invocations.
- followup: specifies the policy applied when all the blocks in a policy tag are considered invalid. The supported followup strategies are:
  - fail: stop the scheduling of the function;
  - default: follow what is defined in the default tag.

---

[1] The kind of computational resources that determine the overload option depends on the APIs provided by a given serverless platform. For example, in our prototype in Sect. 4 we consider a worker label overloaded when the related invokers are declared "unhealthy" by the OpenWhisk APIs, which use memory consumption and CPU load.

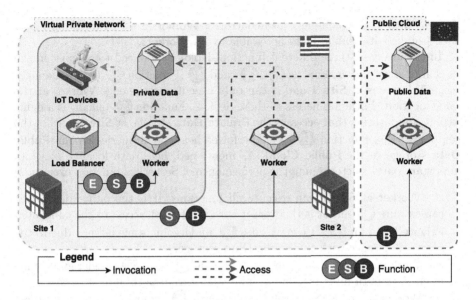

Fig. 4. Use case architecture representation.

4 Implementation in Apache OpenWhisk

We have implemented a serverless platform in which load balancing policies can be customised using the APP language. This implementation (available at https://github.com/giusdp/openwhisk) was obtained by modifying the Open-Whisk code base. Namely, we have replaced the load balancer module in the OpenWhisk controller, with a new one that reads an APP script, parses it, and follows the specified load balancing policies when OpenWhisk invokers should be selected[2].

To test our implementation, we used the Serverless use case depicted in Fig. 4 encompassing three Serverless domains: *i*) a private cloud with a low-power edge-device **Worker** at a first location, called **Site 1**; *ii*) a private cloud with the **Worker** at **Site 1** and a mid-tier server **Worker** at a second location, called **Site 2**; *iii*) a hybrid cloud with the two **Worker**s at **Site 1** and **Site 2** and a third mid-tier server from a **Public Cloud**. **Site 1** and **Site 2** are respectively located in Italy and Greece while the **Public Cloud** is located in northern Europe.

Site 1 is the main branch of a company and it runs both a data storage of **Private Data** and the **IoT Devices** used in their local line of production. **Site 1** also hosts the scheduler of functions, called the **Load Balancer**. The **Worker** at **Site 1** can access all resources within its site. **Site 2** hosts a **Worker** which, belonging to the company virtual private network (VPN), can access the **Private**

---

[2] In this paper we chose to associate one worker label with one invoker. Future developments can use labels to identify pools of resources, following, e.g., recent proposals to change OpenWhisk invokers with Cluster Managers https://bit.ly/3cxYnTB).

Data at **Site 1**. The company also controls a **Worker** in a **Public Cloud** and a data storage with **Public Data** accessible by all **Workers**.

In the use case, three different function deployments need to co-exist in the same infrastructure, marked as Ⓔ , Ⓢ , and Ⓑ . Function Ⓔ (edge) manages the **IoT Devices** at **Site 1** and it can only execute on the edge **Worker** at the same location, which has access to those devices. Function Ⓢ (small) is a lightweight computation that accesses the **Private Data** storage at **Site 1**, within the company VPN. Function Ⓑ (big) performs heavy-load queries on the **Public Data** storage in the **Public Cloud**. As mentioned, here data locality plays an important part in determining the performance of Serverless function execution:

- the **Worker** at **Site 1** can execute all functions. It is the only worker that can execute Ⓔ and it is the worker with the fastest access to the co-located **Private Data** for Ⓢ . It can execute Ⓑ undergoing some latency due to the physical distance with the **Public Data** storage;
- the **Worker** at **Site 2** can execute functions Ⓢ and Ⓑ , undergoing some latency on both functions due to its distance from both data storages;
- the **Worker** at the **Public Cloud** can execute Ⓑ , enjoying the fastest access to the related **Public Data** source.

Finally, besides data locality, the scheduler should also take into account how heavily the functions impact on the load of each **Worker**, considering that the **Worker** in the **Public Cloud** is as powerful as the one at **Site 2**, followed by the **Worker** at **Site 1**, which is a low-power edge device.

Experimental Results. We compare the differences on the architecture and performance of the use case above as implemented using our APP-based Open-Whisk prototype against a naïve implementation using the vanilla OpenWhisk.

Specifically, we implement the use case using a Kubernetes cluster composed of a low-power device—with an Intel Core i7-4510U CPU with 8GB of RAM—in Italy for **Site 1**, a Virtual Machine—comparable to an Amazon EC2 a1.large instance—from the Okeanos Cloud (https://okeanos.grnet.gr) located in Greece for **Site 2**, and a Virtual Machine—comparable to an Amazon EC2 a1.large instance—from the **Public Cloud** of Microsoft Azure located in Northern Europe.

Following the requirements of the use case, we define the APP deployment plan for the use case as follows (we put the three tags in column for compactness):

```
Function_E:            Function_S:            Function_B:
  - workers:             - workers:             - workers:
    - worker_site1         - worker_site2         - worker_public_cloud
  followup: fail          - worker_site1         - worker_site2
                          strategy: random       - worker_site1
                         followup: fail         strategy: best_first
                                                followup: fail
```

Commenting the code above, we have function **E** represented by Function_E, where the only invoker available is the one at **Site 1** (worker_site1). Since we do not allow other invokers to handle **E** , we set the followup value to fail. For **S** we have Function_S, where the invokers available are the ones at **Site 1** and **Site 2** (worker_site2). We let the two invokers split evenly the load of invocations, assigning random as routing strategy. Also here we let the invocation fail since we do not have other invokers able to access the **Private Data** storage within the company VPN. Finally, the policy for **B** (Funcion_B) includes all workers (hence also worker_public_cloud besides the ones at **Site 1** and **Site 2**) selected according to the best_first strategy. As for **S** , also here we let the invocation fail since no other invokers are available.

For the APP-based deployment, we locate the Load Balancer at **Site 1** registering to it the three **Workers**/invokers from **Site 1**, **Site 2** and the **Public Cloud**. For the naïve implementation, we use the same cluster but we install three separate but co-existing vanilla OpenWhisk instances. The three separate instances are needed to implement the functional requirements of limiting the execution of function **E** only on the Italian **Worker**, of **S** only on the Italian and Greek **Workers**, and of **B** on all **Workers**.

To implement the databases (both **Private** and **Public** ones) we used a CouchDB instance deployed at **Site 1** and another in the **Public Cloud**. To simulate the access to IoT devices at **Site 1** (function **E**) we implemented a JavaScript function that, queried, returns some readings after a one-second delay. We followed a similar strategy for **S** and **B** , where two JavaScript functions perform a (respectively lighter and heavier) query for JSON documents.

Architectural Evaluation. An evident problem that arises with the triple-deployment combination is the increased consumption of computational and memory resources to host 3 copies of all the components, most importantly the Controller and the Invoker. A partial solution to this is to deploy separately the Kafka, Redis, and CouchDB components used by OpenWhisk, configuring them to be used by the three different installations simultaneously. However, we did not perform such optimisation to minimise the differences between the two tested architectures.

Quantitative Evaluation. To have statistically relevant figures to compare the two setups (the APP-based and the vanilla one), we fired a sequence of 1000 requests for each function in each setup. We report the results of the tests of the APP-based implementation in Table 1 and those of the vanilla one in Table 2. In both tables, the first column on the left reports the tested function. The three following columns report the number of requests served by the respective **Workers** at **Site 1**, **Site 2**, and in the **Public Cloud**. The last two columns report the time passed from sending a request to the reception of its response: the second-to-last column reports the average time (in ms) and the last one reports the average time (in ms) for the fastest 95th percentile of request-responses.

We comment on the results starting from **E** (first row from the header in both tables). As expected, all requests for **E** are executed at **Site 1**. The slight

Table 1. 1000 invocation for each function in the APP-based OpenWhisk deployment.

	Site 1	Site 2	Public Cloud	Average (ms)	95% Average (ms)
E	1000	0	0	1096.53	1019.03
S	466	534	0	149.18	90.86
B	0	90	910	105.18	64.62

Table 2. 1000 invocations for each function in the vanilla OpenWhisk deployment.

	Site 1	Site 2	Public Cloud	Average (ms)	95% Average (ms)
E	1000	0	0	1159.90	1025.52
S	19	981	0	385.30	302.08
B	185	815	0	265.69	215.793

difference in the two averages (APP ca. 5.6% faster than vanilla) and the two fastest 95th percentile (APP ca. 0.6% faster than vanilla) come from the heavier resource consumption of the vanilla deployment.

As expected, the impact of data locality and the performance increase provided by the data-locality-aware policies in APP become visible for **S** and **B**. In the case of **S** , the Load Balancer of the vanilla deployment elected **Site 2** as the location of the main invoker (passing to it 98.1% of the invocations). We remind that **S** accesses a **Private Data** storage located at **Site 1**. The impact of data locality is visible on the execution of **S** in the vanilla deployment, being 88.35% slower than the APP-based deployment on average and 107.5% slower for the fastest 95th percentile. On the contrary, the APP-based scheduler evenly divided the invocations between **Site 1** (46.6%) and **Site 2** (53.4%) with a slight preference for the latter, thanks to its greater availability of resources. In the case of **B** , the Load Balancer of the vanilla deployment elected again **Site 2** as the location of the main invoker (passing to it 81.5% of all the invocations) and **Site 1** as the second-best (passing the remaining 18.5%). Although available to handle computations, the invoker in the **Public Cloud** is never used. Since **B** accesses a **Public Data** storage located in the **Public Cloud**, also in this case the effect of data locality is strikingly visible, marking a heavy toll on the execution of **B** in the vanilla deployment, which is 86.5% slower than the APP-based deployment on average and 107.8% slower for the fastest 95th percentile. The APP-based scheduler, following the preference on the **Public Cloud**, sends the majority of invocations to the **Public Cloud** (91%) while the invocations that exceed the resource limits of the **Worker** in the **Public Cloud** are routed to **Site 2** (9%), as defined by the Function_E policy.

As a concluding remark over our experiment, we note that these results do not prove that the vanilla implementation of OpenWhisk is generally worse (performance-wise) than the APP-based one. Indeed, what emerged from the experiment is the expected result that, without proper information and software infrastructure to guide the scheduling of functions with respect to some optimisation policies, the Load Balancer of OpenWhisk can perform a suboptimal scheduling of function executions. Hence, there was a chance that the Load Balance of OpenWhisk could have performed some better scheduling strategies in our experiment, however that would have been an occasional occurrence rather than an informed decision. Contrarily, when equipped with the proper information (as it happens with our APP-based prototype) the Load Balancer can reach consistent results, which is the base for execution optimisation.

5   Related Work

While the industrial adoption of Serverless is spreading [19], it is a hot research topic due to its "untapped" potential [1,9,11,12].

Regarding the optimisation of Serverless function scheduling, Kuntsevich et al. [20] present an analysis and benchmarking approach for investigating bottlenecks and limitations of Apache OpenWhisk Serverless platform, while Shahrad et al. [21] report on the performance implications of using a Serverless architecture (over Apache OpenWhisk), showing how its workloads go against the locality-preserving architectural assumptions common in modern processors.

One of the main approaches explored in the literature to improve Serverless performance through function scheduling comes from improving the warm-vs cold-start of functions [1,12]. Those techniques mainly regard containers re-utilisation and function scheduling heuristics to avoid setting up new containers from scratch for every new invocation. However, other techniques have been recently proposed in the literature. Mohan et al. [22] present an approach focused on the pre-allocation of network resources (one of the main bottlenecks of cold starts) which are dynamically associated with new containers. Abad et al. [23] present a package-aware scheduling algorithm that tries to assign functions that require the same package to the same worker. Suresh and Gandhi [24] present a function-level scheduler designed to minimise provider resource costs while meeting customer performance requirements.

Besides resource re-utilisation, other approaches tackle the problem of optimising function scheduling with new balancing algorithms. Steint [25] and Akkus et al. [26] proposed new algorithms for Serverless scheduling, respectively using a non-cooperative game-theoretic load balancing approach for response-time minimisation and a combination of application-level sandboxing with a hierarchical message bus. Sampé et al. [27] present a technique to move computation tasks to storage workers with the aim to exploit data locality with small, stateless functions that intercept and operate on data flows.

Baldini et al. [19] focus on the programming of compositions of Serverless functions. In particular, they demonstrate that Serverless function composition requires a careful evaluation of trade-offs, identifying three competing constraints that form the "Serverless trilemma", i.e., that without specific run-time support, compositions-as-functions must violate at least one of the three constraints. To solve the trilemma, they present a reactive core of OpenWhisk that enables the sequential composition of functions.

Other works explored how to apply the Serverless paradigm to contexts like Fog/Edge and IoT Computing. The work presented in [28] studies the emergence of real-time and data-intensive applications for Edge Computing and proposes a Serverless platform designed for it. The work in [29] introduces instead a framework for supporting Multi-Provider Serverless Edge Computing to schedule executions across different providers.

Hall et al. [30] show how containers introduce an overhead unsuitable for Edge applications (requiring low-latency response or with hardware limitations), proposing a Serverless platform based on WebAssembly as a lighter environment to run Serverless applications in Edge scenarios. In [31] the authors present a variant of Edge Computing called "Deviceless" Edge Computing, where a proto-typical architecture supports the distributed pooling and scheduling of geograph-ically sparse devices with a high tolerance to network disruption and location-aware scheduling of functions.

Besides optimising Serverless scheduling, a common denominator of the works described above is that many extend or experiment with Apache OpenWhisk, which is also the technology we used to implement our prototype. Indeed, a line of future work on APP can test its expressiveness by capturing and implementing the policies presented in those works, so that users can choose to use them in their function deployments. In this context, APP is an encompassing solution i) able to let Serverless providers offer those scheduling strategies as options to their users, who can then choose which of them best suit their needs and ii) able to let different scheduling policies coexist in the same platform, while now researchers and implementors provide them as ad-hoc, incompatible implementations.

Recent work tackled the problem of formally reasoning on Serverless archi-tectures. Gabbrielli et al. [32] present a core calculus for Serverless, combining ideas from both the λ-calculus (for functions, equipped with futures) and the π-calculus (for communication), paired with a repository of function definitions. On a similar research direction, Jangda et al. [33] present a formal model for Serverless architectures, also inspired by the λ-calculus, equipped with two semantics: a more involved one that captures the low-level details of function implementations and a simpler one that omits low-lever details of computation to ease reasoning on the interactions among Serverless functions. These two works offer formalisms that can be used to automatically reason on the properties of APP-defined function deployments. Future works can explore new policies that, through static analyses, capture details of function execution able to optimise their scheduling.

6   Conclusion

We addressed the problem of *function-execution scheduling optimisation*, propos-ing a methodology that provides developers with a declarative language called APP to express scheduling policies for functions. We extended the scheduler of OpenWhisk to use APP-defined policies in the scheduling of Serverless func-tions and empirically tested our extension on a use case that combines IoT,

Edge, and Cloud Computing, contrasting our implementation with a naïve one using the vanilla OpenWhisk stack to achieve the same functional requirements. We believe that APP can be seamlessly integrated in other Serveless platforms.

Besides the future investigations centred around the exploration of locality principles (e.g., code and session locality) as outlined in Sect. 5, an interesting line of work is to evolve APP to be able to express the definition of in-policy elements—such as scheduling strategies (strategy) and invalidation rules (invalidate)—directly in the source APP configuration, next to the ones given as "primitives" by the scheduler (e.g., platform or best_first strategies).

We are also interested in studying heuristics that, based on the monitoring of existing serverless applications, can suggest to its developer optimising scheduling policies. A starting point for this are configurator optimisers such as [34] that can be extended to automatically generate policies based on developer requirements.

Finally, we would like to investigate the separation of concerns between developers and providers, trying to minimise the information that providers has to share to allow developers to schedule functions efficiently, while, at the same time, hide the complexity of their dynamically changing infrastructure.

References

1. Jonas, E., et al.: Cloud programming simplified: a berkeley view on serverless computing. CoRR, vol. abs/1902.03383 (2019)
2. Baresi, L., Mendonça, D.F.: Towards a serverless platform for edge computing. In: IEEE ICFC 2019, pp. 1–10. IEEE (2019)
3. AWS: AWS IoT Greengrass. https://aws.amazon.com/greengrass/. Accessed Apr 2020
4. AWS: Lambda. https://aws.amazon.com/lambda/. Accessed Apr 2020
5. Apache openwhisk (2019). https://openwhisk.apache.org/. Accessed Apr 2020
6. Microsoft: Azure Functions. https://azure.microsoft.com/services/functions. Accessed Apr 2020
7. Google: Cloud Functions. https://cloud.google.com/functions. Accessed Apr 2020
8. Iron.io: IronFunctions. https://open.iron.io. Accessed Apr 2020
9. Hendrickson, S., et al.: Serverless computation with openlambda. Login Usenix Mag. **41**(4) (2016)
10. IBM: Cloud Functions. https://www.ibm.com/cloud/functions. Accessed Apr 2020
11. Baldini, I., et al.: Serverless computing: current trends and open problems. In: Chaudhary, S., Somani, G., Buyya, R. (eds.) Research Advances in Cloud Computing, pp. 1–20. Springer, Singapore (2017). https://doi.org/10.1007/978-981-10-5026-8_1
12. Hellerstein, J.M.: Serverless computing: one step forward, two steps back. In: CIDR (2019). www.cidrdb.org
13. Bernstein, D.: Containers and cloud: from LXC to docker to Kubernetes. IEEE Cloud Comput. **1**(3), 81–84 (2014)
14. Armbrust, M., et al.: Above the clouds: a berkeley view of cloud computing. University of California, Berkeley, Rep. UCB/EECS, vol. 28, no. 13, p. 2009 (2009)

15. Wang, L., Li, M., Zhang, Y. , Ristenpart, T., Swift, M.: Peeking behind the curtains of serverless platforms. In: 2018 USENIX Annual Technical Conference (USENIX/ATC 18), pp. 133–146 (2018)

16. Xie, Q., Pundir, M., Lu, Y., Abad, C.L., Campbell, R.H.: Pandas: robust locality-aware scheduling with stochastic delay optimality. IEEE/ACM Trans. Netw. $25(2)$, 662–675 (2016)

17. Wang, W., Zhu, K., Ying, L., Tan, J., Zhang, L.: Maptask scheduling in MapReduce with data locality: throughput and heavy-traffic optimality. IEEE/ACM Trans. Netw. 24, 190–203 (2016)

18. Ben-Kiki, O., Evans, C., Ingerson, B.: YAML ain't markup language (YAML^{TM}) version 1.1. Working Draft 2008–05, vol. 11 (2009)

19. Baldini, I., et al.: The serverless trilemma: function composition for serverless computing. In: ACM Onward! 2017, pp. 89–103 (2017)

20. Kuntsevich, A., Nasirifard, P., Jacobsen, H.-A.: A distributed analysis and benchmarking framework for apache openwhisk serverless platform. In: Middleware (Posters), pp. 3–4 (2018)

21. Shahrad, M., Balkind, J., Wentzlaff, D.: Architectural implications of function-as-a-service computing. In: MICRO'52, pp. 1063–1075 (2019)

22. Mohan, A., Sane, H., Doshi, K., Edupuganti, S., Nayak, N., Sukhomlinov, V.: Agile cold starts for scalable serverless. In: HotCloud 19 (2019)

23. Abad, C.L., Boza, E.F., Eyk, E.V.: Package-aware scheduling of FaaS functions. In: ACM/SPEC ICPE, pp. 101–106. ACM (2018)

24. Suresh, A., Gandhi, A.: FnSched: an efficient scheduler for serverless functions. In: WOSC@Middleware, pp. 19–24. ACM (2019)

25. Stein, M.: The serverless scheduling problem and NOAH. arXiv preprint arXiv:1809.06100 (2018)

26. Akkus, I.E., et al.: SAND: towards high-performance serverless computing. In: 2018 USENIX Annual Technical Conference (USENIX/ATC 18), pp. 923–935 (2018)

27. Sampé, J., Sánchez-Artigas, M., García-López, P., París, G.: Data-driven serverless functions for object storage. In: Middleware 2017, pp. 121–133. Association for Computing Machinery (2017)

28. Baresi, L., Mendonça, D.F.: Towards a serverless platform for edge computing. In: 2019 IEEE ICFC, pp. 1–10. IEEE (2019)

29. Aske, A., Zhao, X.: Supporting multi-provider serverless computing on the edge. In: ICPP, Workshop Proceedings, pp. 20:1–20:6. ACM (2018)

30. Hall, A., Ramachandran, U.: An execution model for serverless functions at the edge. In: IoTDI 2019, New York, NY, USA, pp. 225–236. ACM (2019)

31. Glikson, A., Nastic, S., Dustdar, S.: Deviceless edge computing: extending serverless computing to the edge of the network. In: SYSTOR 2017. ACM, New York (2017)

32. Gabbrielli, M., Giallorenzo, S., Lanese, I., Montesi, F., Peressotti, M., Zingaro, S.P.: No more, no less. In: Riis Nielson, H., Tuosto, E. (eds.) COORDINATION 2019. LNCS, vol. 11533, pp. 148–157. Springer, Cham (2019). https://doi.org/10.1007/978-3-030-22397-7_9

33. Jangda, A., Pinckney, D., Brun, Y., Guha, A.: Formal foundations of serverless computing. In: Proceedings of the ACM on Programming Languages, vol. 3, no. OOPSLA, pp. 1–26 (2019)

34. Ábrahám, E., Corzilius, F., Johnsen, E.B., Kremer, G., Mauro, J.: Zephyrus2: on the fly deployment optimization using SMT and CP technologies. In: SETTA, pp. 229–245 (2016)

Adaptive Recollected RNN for Workload Forecasting in Database-as-a-Service

Chenzhengyi Liu[1], Weibo Mao[1], Yuanning Gao[1], Xiaofeng Gao[1(✉)], Shifu Li[2], and Guihai Chen[1]

[1] Shanghai Key Laboratory of Scalable Computing and Systems, Department of Computer Science and Engineering, Shanghai Jiao Tong University, Shanghai 200240, China
{liuchenzhengyi,kirino.mao,gyuanning}@sjtu.edu.cn,
{gao-xf,gchen}@cs.sjtu.edu.cn
[2] Huawei Company, Shenzhen, China
lishifu@huawei.com

Abstract. Nowadays, Database-as-a-Service (DBaaS) plays a more and more important role in the era of big data due to its convenience and manageable capacity. However, with increasing complexity of data-driven applications, the management of database systems becomes intractable. To achieve the self-management of resources, forecasting the workload turns out to be essential. In this paper, we propose a novel machine learning based model, named Adaptive Recollected Recurrent Neural Network (AR-RNN) to help DBaaS managers better capture historical information and predict future workload with a recollection mechanism based multi-encoder and an attention mechanism based decoder architecture. Experiments on two real-world datasets show that our model outperforms both traditional and other machine learning methods for workload prediction.

Keywords: Database-as-a-service · Self-driving dbms · Workload forecast · Adaptive Recollected Recurrent Neural Network

1 Introduction

In the era of big data, users' demand for Database-as-a-Service (DBaaS) [9] is soaring sharply since it allows users to easily install their own database software, or manage the database themselves in the clouding without purchasing any hardware. On one hand, DBaaS provides end-users with access to abstract resources and on-demand service. It also ensures the scalability of underlying data so that service providers can manage fluctuations in the workload. However, with increasing complexity of data-driven applications and end-users, the management of database systems becomes more and more intractable. Many database administrators (DBAs) spend about 25% time to tune the database system for better performance [11], which is time-consuming and leads to high manpower costs.

E. Kafeza et al. (Eds.): ICSOC 2020, LNCS 12571, pp. 431–438, 2020.
https://doi.org/10.1007/978-3-030-65310-1_30

In order to achieve self-management of resources, the core step is to accurately forecast system workload, which can be formulated as a time-series analysis problem. Figure 1 shows typical workloads of Alibaba Cluster Workload Traces [1] collected from real-world production. As we can see, the CPU workloads in Fig. 1(a) are non-stationary but relatively periodical. By contrast, the memory workload in Fig. 1(b) is more stationary. In this case, if we find the pattern of users' demand, service providers can provide quality-ensured service with minimal resource redundancy and improve energy utilization. However, it is not a straight-forward problem since non-periodic bursts may occur from time to time, making the curve in Fig. 1 not that smooth.

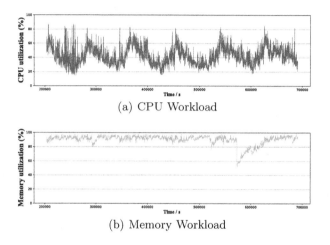

(a) CPU Workload

(b) Memory Workload

Fig. 1. Part of Records From Alibaba Cluster Workload Traces

Many works have been done in designing a model for workload forecasting [10]. Autoregressive Integrated Moving Average model (ARIMA) [2] is one of the most typical traditional schemes. it uses statistical equations to give the explicit predictions but fails short in a number of real world situations. Recent years, with the development of machine learning technologies, some schemes leverage neural network based models to solve this problem, such as Multi-layer Perceptron (MLP) [1], Recurrent Neural Network (RNN), Long Short-term Memory (LSTM) [8], etc. While these models can achieve high performance given enough training data, they also suffer from feature selection and vanishing gradient problems. A novel architecture encoder-decoder network built on double RNNs along with attention mechanism achieves better results in time series, like Encoder-Decoder [4], POS-RNN [5], and STANN [3]. However, these models still fail to express the temporal patterns in some complex situations, since they do not consider the relevant information between inputs.

---

[1] https://github.com/alibaba/clusterdata.

To overcome the above issues, in this paper, we propose *Adaptive Recollected Recurrent Neural Network* (AR-RNN) model to predict future workload in DBaaS. Inspired by human recollection [6], which will first recall and collect the related history information when facing new situations, we design a specific k-dimension tree (k-d tree) to adaptively recollect the information from past periods in AR-RNN, named recollection mechanism. Besides, the AR-RNN system is built on the encoder-decoder framework [4] to get better expression capacity and we deploy the halting units inspired by Adaptive Computation Time (ACT) [7] to control its recollection depth. Compared to other traditional or machine learning methods, the AR-RNN model gets better performance on two real-world workload datasets.

The rest of the paper is organized as follows. In Sect. 2, we introduce some notations and formulate the problem into a time series prediction form. Section 3 and Sect. 4 present our model architecture and provide details for its training phrase. Experimental evaluations will be shown in Sect. 5. At last, We will conclude this paper in Sect. 6.

2 Problem Statement

Given a workload series $(x_1, x_2, \ldots, x_{T-1}) \in \mathbf{R}^{T-1}$ from time 1 to $T - 1$, our goal is to predict the workload at time T, i.e. x_T. Adapting the sliding window algorithm, we use this workload series as the training set to train a network designed to do prediction by using the most recent l workloads as Eq. (1) shows:

$$\hat{x}_t = F(x_{t-l}, x_{t-l+1}, \ldots, x_{t-1}) \tag{1}$$

where F is the network to learn. The total loss can be expressed as Eq. (2).

$$\sum_{i=s}^{T-1} Loss(\hat{x}_i, x_i) \tag{2}$$

where s ($s \gg l$) is the start time of the prediction and *Loss* is the loss function to measure the difference between ground truth and prediction. Parameters in the network will be updated by standard back-propagation algorithm, until the network performs well enough, i.e., until the total loss shown in Eq. (2) is small enough. Then we can use this trained network to predict $\hat{x}_T$ using Eq. (1).

3 Adaptive Recollected RNN

Following the *encoder-decoder* architecture, our proposed Adaptive Recollected Recurrent Neural Network (AR-RNN) contains a k-dimension multi-encoder module and an attention mechanism based decoder module, as shown in Fig. 2. More details will be discussed in following part in this section.

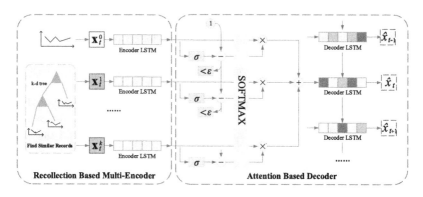

Fig. 2. An overview of AR-RNN

3.1 Recollection Mechanism Based Multi-encoder Module

Inspired by human's recollection [6], similar temporal patterns in historical information can assist us to more accurately forecast future workload series. To better capture the relevant patterns in history, we propose a *k-Recollection Information Retrieval Algorithm* shown in Algorithm 1, whose basic data structure is a *k-d* tree built in time axis. Suppose we are predicting $\hat{x}_t$. Let $\mathbf{x}_t = (x_{t-l}, x_{t-l+1}, \dots, x_{t-1})$ be the sliding window of the most recent l workloads and $\mathcal{H}_t = (x_1, x_2, \dots, x_{t-l-1})$ be the history. Leaves of the *k-d* tree are all sequences of length l in $\mathcal{H}_t$. Our algorithm tries to find k sequences of length l that are most similar to $\mathbf{x}_t$.

Algorithm 1: k Recollection Information Retrieval Algorithm

    Input: history series $\mathcal{H}_t = (x_1, x_2, \dots, x_{t-l-1})$ and $\mathbf{x}_t = (x_{t-l}, x_{t-l+1}, \dots, x_{t-1})$
    Output: k nearest sequences $(\mathbf{x}_t^1, \mathbf{x}_t^2, \dots, \mathbf{x}_t^k)$ in the history series $\mathcal{H}_t$ to $\mathbf{x}_t$

1   $kdTree \leftarrow$ createKDTree($\mathcal{H}_t$);
2   $searchPath \leftarrow$ find the closest path in $kdTree$ that leads to $\mathbf{x}_t$;
3   $kNNList \leftarrow$ find k nodes in $searchPath$ that are closest to $\mathbf{x}_t$;
4   **while** $searchPath$ *is not empty* **do**
5      $backNode \leftarrow searchPath.\text{pop}()$;
6      $maxNode \leftarrow$ farthest node in $kNNList$ from $\mathbf{x}_t$;
7   **if** $|\boldsymbol{x}_t[split] - backNode[split]| < computeDist(maxNode, \boldsymbol{x}_t)$ **then**
8          $tmpNode \leftarrow backNode.fartherChild$;
9   **if** $tmpNode$ **then**
10            $dist \leftarrow$ computeDist($tmpNode, \mathbf{x}_t$);
11   **if** $dist < computeDist(maxNode, \boldsymbol{x}_t)$ **then**
12              $kNNList.\text{swap}(tmpNode, maxNode)$;
13            $searchPath.\text{append}(tmpNode)$;

14 **return** $kNNList$;

For convenience, let $\mathbf{x}_t^0 = (x_{t-l}^0, x_{t-l+1}^0, \ldots, x_{t-1}^0)$ be the original input $\mathbf{x}_t$, and $\mathbf{x}_t^i = (x_{t-l}^i, x_{t-l+1}^i, \ldots, x_{t-1}^i)$ $(i = 1, 2, \ldots, k)$ be its i-th nearest (most similar) sequence. For each i, an encoder LSTM unit will encode $\mathbf{x}_t^i \in \mathbf{R}^l$ into its context vector $\mathbf{c}_t^i \in \mathbf{R}^m$ with computing the state sequence $(\mathbf{s}_{t,0}^i, \mathbf{s}_{t,1}^i, \ldots, \mathbf{s}_{t,l}^i)$ by iterating the following equation from $j = 0$ to $l - 1$:

$$s_{t,j+1}^i = f_e(s_{t,j}^i, x_{t-l+j}^i) \tag{3}$$

where f_e is the encoder LSTM unit and $\mathbf{s}_{t,j}^i \in \mathbf{R}^m$ is the hidden state in LSTM at the j-th iteration. We choose the last state $\mathbf{s}_{t,l}^i$ to be the context vector $\mathbf{c}_t^i$ of input sequence $\mathbf{x}_t^i$. The initial hidden state $\mathbf{s}_{t,0}^i$ can be any random vector in $\mathbf{R}^m$. The reader is referred to [8] for an excellent introduction to LSTM.

The encoder will encode the initial input $\mathbf{x}_t$, together with its k most similar recollection sequences, into a list of context vectors $(\mathbf{c}_t^0, \mathbf{c}_t^1, \ldots, \mathbf{c}_t^k)$.

3.2   Attention Mechanism Based Decoder Module

The attention mechanism based decoder module is inspired by the *ACT algorithm* proposed in [7]. The number of similar sequences k is a hyperparameter which may largely reduce the accuracy without a careful choice. Therefore, we add extra sigmoidal "halting" units h_t^i for each $\mathbf{c}_t^i$ $(i = 0, 1, \cdots, k)$:

$$h_t^i = \sigma(W_h \mathbf{c}_t^i + b_h) \tag{4}$$

where weight matrix $W_h \in \mathbf{R}^{1 \times m}$ and bias $b_h \in \mathbf{R}$ are parameters needed to learn, and σ is the sigmoid function. $h_t^i \in [0, 1]$ shows the importance of $\mathbf{c}_t^i$.

Then we calculate a weighted sum $\mathbf{d}_t = \sum_{i=0}^k w_t^i \mathbf{c}_t^i$, named the hidden vector, where the sum of all weights w_t^i, called the attention weights, is 1.

If $\sum_{i=0}^k h_t^i \geq 1 - \epsilon$, we determine the attention weight w_t^i as follows:

$$w_t^i = \begin{cases} R_t, & \text{if } i = N_t \\ h_t^i, & \text{if } 0 \leq i < N_t \\ 0, & \text{if } N_t < i \leq k \end{cases} \tag{5}$$

where $\epsilon > 0$ is a small constant which allows only using $\mathbf{c}_t^0$ when $h_t^0 \geq 1 - \epsilon$, $N_t = \min\{n : \sum_{i=0}^n h_t^i \geq 1 - \epsilon\}$, and $R_t = 1 - \sum_{i=0}^{N_t-1} h_t^i$. We try to use h_t^i as the weight of $\mathbf{c}_t^i$ until the sum is larger than $1 - \epsilon$, then let the remainder R_t be the weight of the last vector $\mathbf{c}_t^{N_t}$ and abandon vectors with index larger than N_t.

If $\sum_{i=0}^k h_t^i < 1 - \epsilon$, the idea above may lead to a large weight for $\mathbf{c}_t^k$ if all h_t^i are rather small. We turn to use the softmax function in this case, i.e., $w_t^i = \exp(h_t^i) / \sum_{j=0}^k \exp(h_t^j)$. Note that if k is large enough, this case can hardly occur. Here we just handle it for rigor and it is not important in practice.

Once we get the hidden vector $\mathbf{d}_t = (d_1, d_2, \ldots, d_m)$, we send it into the decoder LSTM unit with a new state sequence $(s_0, s_1, \ldots, s_m)$ to decode the hidden vector into the prediction value, by iterating the following equation:

$$s_{j+1} = f_d(s_j, d_{j+1}) \tag{6}$$

where j is an iterator with $j = 0, 1, \ldots, m - 1$, f_d is the decoder LSTM unit. We choose $\hat{x}_t = s_m$ to be the output prediction of the AR-RNN model.

4   Training Procedure

Apart from the halting units, the AR-RNN model is differentiable, whose parameters can be learned by a standard back-propagation algorithm. Let $\mathcal{L}(\hat{x}_t, x_t)$ be the difference between $\hat{x}_t$ and x_t, where $\mathcal{L}$ is a differentiable loss function.

For the loss at the halting unit for x_t, we apply a ponder loss $\mathcal{P}_t$ [7]:

$$\mathcal{P}_t = N_t + R_t \tag{7}$$

where R_t and N_t are defined in Sect. 3.2. The ponder loss $\mathcal{P}_t$ provides an upper bound on total recollection times [7]. It is also what we want to minimize, so the final loss function for x_t is designed as follows:

$$Loss(\hat{x}_t, x_t) = \mathcal{L}(\hat{x}_t, x_t) + \lambda \mathcal{P}_t \tag{8}$$

$$\frac{\partial Loss(\hat{x}_t, x_t)}{\partial h_t^i} = \frac{\partial \mathcal{L}(\hat{x}_t, x_t)}{\partial h_t^i} + \lambda \frac{\partial \mathcal{P}_t}{\partial h_t^i} \tag{9}$$

where λ is a penalty used to consider the ponder loss. Recall that in the training procedure, we need to minimize the total loss, as Eq. (2) shows.

The largest challenge is to calculate the gradients at the halting units. Obviously, if $N_t < i \leq k$, the gradient is 0, because such halting units are not really used. Therefore, we only need to consider $i \leq N_t$. Since the halting units only influence $\mathcal{L}$ via their effect on attention weights, by the chain rule, we have

$$\frac{\partial \mathcal{L}(\hat{x}_t, x_t)}{\partial h_t^i} = \sum_{j=1}^{k} \frac{\partial \mathcal{L}(\hat{x}_t, x_t)}{\partial w_t^j} \frac{\partial w_t^j}{\partial h_t^i} \tag{10}$$

Notice that if $N_t \leq j \leq k$, we have $w_t^j = 0$. By definition of $\mathbf{d}_t$, we get

$$\frac{\partial \mathcal{L}(\hat{x}_t, x_t)}{\partial w_t^j} = \frac{\partial \mathcal{L}(\hat{x}_t, x_t)}{\partial \mathbf{d}_t} \cdot \frac{\partial \mathbf{d}_t}{\partial w_t^j} = \frac{\partial \mathcal{L}(\hat{x}_t, x_t)}{\partial \mathbf{d}_t} \cdot \mathbf{c}_t^j \tag{11}$$

$$\frac{\partial w_t^j}{\partial h_t^i} = \begin{cases} 1, & \text{if } 0 \leq j = i < N_t \\ -1, & \text{if } j = N_t \text{ and } 0 \leq i < N_t \\ 0, & \text{otherwise} \end{cases} \tag{12}$$

Then the gradient at the halting units can be approximated as following:

$$\frac{\partial \mathcal{P}_t}{\partial h_t^i} = \begin{cases} -1, & \text{if } 0 \leq i < N_t \\ 0, & \text{if } i = N_t \end{cases} \tag{13}$$

Finally, by Eqs. (9), (10), (11) and (12), the gradient at the halting units can be shown as:

$$\frac{\partial Loss(\hat{x}_t, x_t)}{\partial h_t^i} = \begin{cases} \frac{\partial \mathcal{L}(\hat{x}_t, x_t)}{\partial \mathbf{d}_t} \cdot (\mathbf{c}_t^i - \mathbf{c}_t^{N_t}) - \lambda, & \text{if } 0 \leq i < N_t \\ 0, & \text{if } N_t \leq i \leq k \end{cases} \tag{14}$$

Now we can use the standard back-propagation algorithm and train the network with gradient descent.

5   Experimental Evaluation

In this section, we will introduce two real-world datasets to experiment with the AR-RNN model and against other 6 baseline methods of different time intervals.

Alibaba Cluster Trace is derived from one of Alibaba Open Cluster Trace Program. It contains batch workloads colocated in every machine in the cluster. **Bus Tracker Trace** is a mobile phone database application for live-tracking of the public transit bus system [11]. We generate our two real world datasets by sampling at random seconds and smoothing with different time intervals.

To demonstrate the effectiveness of the AR-RNN, we compare our model with 6 existing approaches as our baselines: **ARIMA, MLP, LSTM, Encoder-Decoder, POS-RNN**, and **STANN**. To be fair, we set al.l hyperparameters in baselines for the best after a grid search, and we apply RMSE as our metric.

Figure 3 shows the result of all models with different time intervals over two datasets. The ARIMA model has a relative worse performance than machine learning models, since it tries to find a stationary process with differencing steps, which is hard to explain the complex temporal patterns of real-world data. RNN and Encoder-Decoder based models generally perform better due to their inter connection between temporal inputs. We can see that attention based methods outperform other baseline models, and this suggests focusing on more important historical information makes accurate predictions. the AR-RNN gets the best accuracy respectively on two dataset, benefiting from the recollection mechanism extracting the historical workload patterns. Besides, the AR-RNN model performs more robustly with different time intervals than the other methods, since it can adaptively choose the useful information and discard the rest.

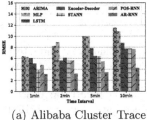
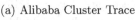
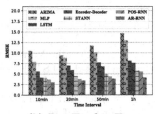

(a) Alibaba Cluster Trace   (b) Bus Tracker Trace

Fig. 3. Models' Comparison of Different Time Intervals Over Two Datasets

6   Conclusion and Future Work

DBaaS plays a more and more important role in the era of big data. In this paper, to help DBaaS better forecast the system workload, we propose a novel machine learning based model, named AR-RNN. It consists of a recollection mechanism based multi-encoder to capture historical information and an attention mechanism based decoder to predict future workload. We evaluate our model on two typical kinds of workloads and the results show it achieves the best performance over both traditional and other machine learning methods.

Acknowledgements. This work was supported by the National Key R&D Program of China [2019YFB2102200]; the National Natural Science Foundation of China [61872238, 61972254], the CCF-Huawei Database System Innovation Research Plan [CCF-Huawei DBIR2019002A], and the CCF-Tencent Open Research Fund [FR202001].

References

1. Assaf, R., Schumann, A.: Explainable deep neural networks for multivariate time series predictions. In: Proceedings of the Twenty-Eighth International Joint Conference on Artificial Intelligence, IJCAI, pp. 6488–6490 (2019)
2. Calheiros, R.N., Masoumi, E., Ranjan, R., Buyya, R.: Workload prediction using ARIMA model and its impact on cloud applications' QoS. IEEE Trans. Cloud Comput. **3**(4), 449–458 (2015)
3. Chatigny, P., Patenaude, J., Wang, S.: Financial time series representation learning. CoRR (2020). https://arxiv.org/abs/2003.12194
4. Cho, K., et al.: Learning phrase representations using RNN encoder-decoder for statistical machine translation. In: Proceedings of the 2014 Conference on Empirical Methods in Natural Language Processing, EMNLP, pp. 1724–1734 (2014)
5. Cinar, Y.G., Mirisaee, H., Goswami, P., Gaussier, E., Aït-Bachir, A., Strijov, V.: Position-based content attention for time series forecasting with sequence-to-sequence RNNs. In: Liu, D., Xie, S., Li, Y., Zhao, D., El-Alfy, E.-S.M. (eds.) ICONIP 2017. LNCS, vol. 10638, pp. 533–544. Springer, Cham (2017). https://doi.org/10.1007/978-3-319-70139-4_54
6. Curran, T.: Brain potentials of recollection and familiarity. Mem. Cogn. **28**, 923–938 (2000)
7. Graves, A.: Adaptive computation time for recurrent neural networks. CoRR (2016)
8. Kong, W., Dong, Z.Y., Jia, Y., Hill, D.J., Xu, Y., Zhang, Y.: Short-term residential load forecasting based on LSTM recurrent neural network. IEEE Trans. Smart Grid **10**(1), 841–851 (2019)
9. Lehner, W., Sattler, K.: Database as a service (DBaaS). In: Proceedings of the 26th International Conference on Data Engineering ICDE, pp. 1216–1217 (2010)
10. Liu, C., Shang, Y., Duan, L., Chen, S., Liu, C., Chen, J.: Optimizing workload category for adaptive workload prediction in service clouds. In: Barros, A., Grigori, D., Narendra, N.C., Dam, H.K. (eds.) ICSOC 2015. LNCS, vol. 9435, pp. 87–104. Springer, Heidelberg (2015). https://doi.org/10.1007/978-3-662-48616-0_6
11. Ma, L., Aken, D.V., Hefny, A., Mezerhane, G., Pavlo, A., Gordon, G.J.: Query-based workload forecasting for self-driving database management systems. In: Proceedings of the 2018 International Conference on Management of Data, SIGMOD, pp. 631–645 (2018)

Exploring Interpretability for Predictive Process Analytics

Renuka Sindhgatta⬤, Chun Ouyang$^{(\boxtimes)}$ ⬤, and Catarina Moreira⬤

Queensland University of Technology, Brisbane, Australia
{renuka.sr,c.ouyang,catarina.pintomoreira}@qut.edu.au

Abstract. In the context of business process management, predictive analytics has been applied to making predictions about the future state of an ongoing business process instance, for example, when will the process instance complete and what will be the outcome upon completion. Machine learning models can be trained on event logs of historical process execution to build the underlying predictive models. Multiple techniques have been proposed so far which encode the information available in an event log and construct input features required to train a predictive model. While accuracy has been a dominant criterion in the choice of various techniques, these techniques are often applied as a black-box in building predictive models. In this paper, we derive explanations using interpretable machine learning techniques to compare the suitability of multiple predictive models of high accuracy. The explanations allow us to gain an understanding of the underlying reasons for a prediction and highlight scenarios where accuracy alone may not be sufficient in assessing the suitability of techniques used to encode event log data to features used by a predictive model. Findings from this study further motivate the need to incorporate interpretability in predictive process analytics.

Keywords: Predictive process analytics · Interpretable machine learning · Prediction explanation

1 Introduction

Modern predictive analytics underpinned by machine learning techniques has become a key enabler to the automation of data-driven decision making. In the context of business process management, predictive process analytics is a relatively new discipline that aims at predicting future observations of a business process by learning from event log data of process execution history. A vast majority of work over the past decade has used supervised machine learning algorithms to construct models for predicting outcomes of a business process instance (or a case) [1], the next activity in a case [2], or the remaining time for a case to complete [3]. Evaluation of a predictive model has so far been assessed in terms of the quality of the model and thus evaluated using conventional metrics in machine learning (such as accuracy, precision, recall, F1 score).

© Springer Nature Switzerland AG 2020
E. Kafeza et al. (Eds.): ICSOC 2020, LNCS 12571, pp. 439–447, 2020.
https://doi.org/10.1007/978-3-030-65310-1_31

As an important branch of state-of-the-art data analytics, predictive process analytics is also faced with a challenge regarding the lack of explanation to the reasoning and outcome of its predictive models. While more and more complex machine learning techniques are used to build advanced predictive capabilities in process analytics, they are often applied and recognised as a 'black-box'. The recent body of literature in machine learning has emphasised the need to understand and trust the predictions (e.g., [4,5]). This has led to an increasing interest in the research community on *interpretable* machine learning [6]. Having an interpretable model is a necessary step towards obtaining a good level of understanding about the rationale of the underlying 'black-box' machinery.

In this paper, we derive interpretation of the predictive models trained with various input features representations of the event logs. We review the techniques that have been evaluated in the benchmark studies on business process monitoring benchmarks for predicting process outcomes and remaining time. By applying interpretable machine learning techniques to two existing benchmarks [1,3], we derive global explanations that present the behaviour of the entire predictive model as well as local explanations describing a particular prediction. Based on these explanations, we are able to analyse the importance and relevance of certain features used by a predictive model in forecasting process behaviour, which may serve as an valuable input for reviewing the suitability of the model. Findings drawn from this work further motivate the need to incorporate interpretability in predictive process analytics. To the best of our knowledge, the closest study to this work is an illustration of the potential of explainable models for a manufacturing business process [7].

2   Background

Two studies [1,3] that evaluate various techniques used in the context of predictive process monitoring are considered in our work. Taking event log data as the input, the benchmark of [1] predicts the outcome of a case defined by using a labelling function, and the one of [3] forecasts the remaining time for a case to complete. A *trace* is a sequence of events of the same case. During the training phase, *prefixes* are generated for each trace and grouped into *buckets* based on their similarities (e.g., trace length or process state) using a *bucketing mechanism*. The prefixes in each bucket are encoded as feature vectors using an *encoding mechanism*. The buckets of feature vectors are then used to train a predictive model underpinned by a *learning algorithm*. During the test phase, the future state for a running trace is predicted by identifying the appropriate bucket, using an appropriate encoding, and finally applying the above trained predictive model. Existing predictive process monitoring methods are built on different combinations of bucketing, encoding and learning algorithms. These methods are evaluated using the following quality measures [1,3]:

- *Accuracy*: for outcome-oriented prediction, this is measured by the *area under the ROC curve* (AUC) metric; and for remaining time prediction, this is measured by the *mean absolute error* (MAE) metric.

– *Earliness*: in both predictions, this is defined as the smallest prefix length with the desired level of accuracy.

Recently, the topic of *interpretable* or *explainable* machine learning has gained attention. To avoid ambiguity, we apply the terms *interpretability* and *explainability* as discussed in the machine learning literature [6,8]. A well adopted approach to address model interpretability is via *post hoc interpretation*. Here, explanations are extracted from a learned model, i.e., *after* the model has been trained. A typical class of techniques, known as *surrogate models*, use the input data and prediction of a black box model (i.e., a trained machine learning model) to emulate the model. In other words, they are approximation models that use interpretable models to approximate the predictions of a black box model, enabling a decision-maker to draw interpretations about the black box [9]. Interpretable machine learning algorithms, such as linear regression and decision trees, are often used to learn a function using the predictions of the black box model. This means that this regression or decision tree will learn both well classified examples and misclassified ones. The explanations derived from the surrogate model reflect a local and linear representation of the black box model.

3   Interpreting Predictive Models for Process Monitoring

With the two existing process monitoring benchmarks, we first derive global and local explanations of selected predictive models using model interpretation techniques, and then conduct several analyses of the derived interpretations about these predictive models. Our detailed analysis and the source code are available at https://git.io/Je186 (for interpreting process outcome prediction) and https://git.io/Je1XZ (for interpreting process remaining time prediction).

3.1   Design and Configuration

Combinations of various bucketing, encoding, and supervised learning algorithms have been evaluated for predicting process outcome [1] and remaining time [3], respectively. In this study, we decide to choose the following techniques, because the methods built upon a combination of these techniques have better performance (i.e. high AUC values or low MAE values) as compared to others.

Bucketing Techniques: i) *single bucket*, where all prefixes of traces are considered in a single bucket, and a single classifier is trained; and ii) *prefix length bucket*, where each bucket contains partial traces of a specific length, and one classifier is trained for each possible prefix length.

Encoding Techniques: i) *aggregation encoding*, where the trace in each bucket is transformed by considering (only) the frequencies of event attributes (e.g., activity, resource) and computing four statistical features for the numeric event attributes (max, mean, sum and standard deviation). This way the order of the events in a trace is ignored; ii) *index encoding*, where each event attribute of an executed event can be represented as a feature, and this way the order of a trace in each bucket can be maintained by encoding each event in the trace at a given index; and iii) *static encoding*, where the trace attributes carrying the same value in a trace is added as a feature. The categorical attributes are one-hot encoded, where each attribute value is represented as a feature (with value 0 or 1).

Machine Learning Algorithms: We choose *Gradient boosted trees* [10] (specifically XGBoost), which is used in both benchmarks and outperformed the other machine learning techniques (e.g., random forest, support vector machines, logistic regression). Note that this study focuses on machine learning algorithms and hence Long Short Term Memory (LSTM) [3], which is used for predicting the remaining time of running cases, is not considered.

Interpretation Techniques: To make sure that the output and performance of a predictive method being studied remain intact, we apply post-hoc interpretation to derive explanations for the predictive methods built upon the above techniques and algorithms in both benchmarks. We choose a representative local surrogate method, known as *Local Interpretable Model-Agnostic Explanations* (LIME) [11], which can explain the predictions of any classification or regression algorithm, by approximating it locally with a linear interpretable model. We use LIME to generate *local* explanations that interpret the prediction for a particular trace. In addition, we also conduct permutation feature importance measurement supported by gradient boosted trees to gain certain *global* explanations about a predictive method. More specifically, the feature importance value generated by XGBoost is used to explain the impact of different features to the overall predictions made by a given predictive method.

3.2 Datasets

We present the results on the following three real-life event logs from the Business Process Intelligence Challenge (BPIC), available in 4TU.ResearchData repository (https://data.4tu.nl/portal). The logs were used for performance evaluation of predictive methods in both process monitoring benchmarks [1,3].

BPIC 2011 contains cases from the Gynaecology department of a Dutch hospital. For interpreting the outcome prediction, the outcome labelling function based on the occurrence of activity *"histological examination - big resectiep"* is used (i.e., *bpic2011_4*). In the log preprocessing, the trace for each case is cut exactly before this event occurs. For interpreting the remaining time prediction, the log is used as-is without any truncation (*bpic2011*).

BPIC 2012 records a loan application process at a Dutch financial institution. For the outcome prediction, each trace in the log is labelled as *"accepted"*, *"declined"*, or *"cancelled"* (based on whether the trace contains the occurrence of activity O_ACCEPTED, O_DECLINED or O_CANCELLED). The log concerned with loan acceptance is considered for generating model explanations (*bpic2012_1*). For the remaining time prediction, three logs are generated depicting loan application, loan offers and loan processing by human workers, respectively. Explanations are presented for the model trained on the loan offers (*bpic2012o*).

BPIC 2015 has five event logs recording the traces of a permit application process at five Dutch municipalities, respectively. For the outcome prediction, the rule stating every occurrence of activity 01_HOOFD_020 is eventually followed by activity 08_AWB45_020_1 is used to label the trace as *positive*. Explanations are derived for one of the municipalities (*bpic2015_5*).

3.3 Interpretations and Analyses

Analysis 1: Data Encoding. In both process outcome and remaining time predictions, the aggregation and index encoding techniques further apply one-hot data encoding to represent the activities, resources and other categorical data from the event log to feature vectors as input for machine learning models. The purpose of this analysis is to understand the impact of one-hot encoding on the predictive methods being studied.

In principle, one-hot data encoding increases the size of a dataset exponentially, because each attribute value of a feature becomes a new feature by itself with the possible value of 0 or 1. For instance, a feature F with three attributes values f_1, f_2 and f_3 will be represented as three new binary features. This data encoding method generates very sparse datasets, which impacts negatively both the performance metrics of the prediction model and the ability to generate interpretations. Below we discuss the findings that were obtained from analysing the explanations derived from applying single bucket and aggregation encoding (*single_agg*) with XGBoost model to process remaining time prediction using *bpic2011* event log as an example.

Figure 1 depicts certain impact of one-hot encoding in the context of *bpic2011* log. The original dataset increased from approximately 20 features to 823 features with this representation (see a snapshot of feature matrix in Fig. 1(a)). Further, a majority of the local explanations can be represented as the follows: *if feature X is absent (value ≤ 0), then it influences the remaining time prediction.* When a dataset is so sparse, it is reasonable to expect such type of explanations. However, the question that may arise from this finding is: *To what extent can this provide a meaningful understanding of why the predictive model made a certain prediction?*

Analysis 2: Feature Relevance. The purpose of this analysis is to reason the relevance of the features identified important for process prediction. Feature importance in global explanations and feature impact to predictions of traces in local explanations are valuable inputs to interpreting feature relevance. To derive such interpretation a good understanding of the business process is often needed. Below, we discuss two examples of applying *single_agg* with XGBoost to remaining time prediction using *bpic2011* and *bpic2012o* event logs, respectively.

For *bpic2011* log, it can be observed that, from the local explanation shown in Fig. 1(c), the predictive model relies on features such as Diagnosis Treatment

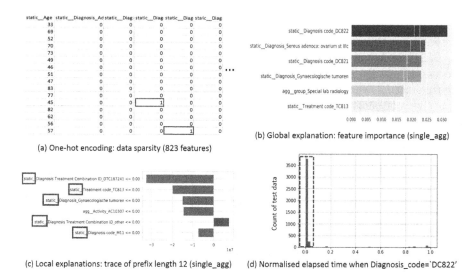

Fig. 1. Interpreting remaining time prediction for *bpic2011* event log using *single_agg* with XGBoost: (a) data sparsity as result of one-hot encoding; (b) global explanation; (c) local explanation for trace of prefix length of 12; and (d) normalised elapse time for a specific diagnosis code.

Combination ID, Treatment code and Diagnosis code in order to determine the remaining time of the case. For a regression problem, like time prediction, this explanation indicates that the model is relying mostly on *static* features, which are the features that do not change throughout the lifetime of a case. The usage of static features for regression suggests that the process execution does not rely on the executions of activities or cases (i.e., sequences of activities following different control-flow logics) and that the model uses attributes that do not change during the case execution when making a prediction. Another interesting observation is from the global explanation shown in Fig. 1(b), which indicates that the most significant feature for remaining time prediction is Diagnosis_code = DC822. By applying statistical analysis on the event log, as depicted in Fig. 1(d), we discovered that 82% of the events associated with this diagnosis code had the feature elapsed time = 0, which means that the corresponding activity starts and ends immediately. To this end, lack of relevant knowledge about the business process limits our ability to derive further insights about the relationship between these static diagnosis codes, with 0-valued elapsed times and its relation with the remaining time of a running case of the process.

For *bpic2012o* log, the analysis leads to different observations. As shown in Fig. 2, the global explanation and the local explanation for trace of prefix length 12 indicate the resource perspective of the business process are the important features used by the predictive model and have a positive impact on the remaining time prediction. The features identified as highly relevant may be case-related (such as agg_opencases), resource-related (such as agg_resource),

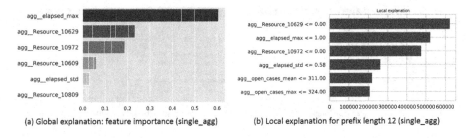

Fig. 2. Interpreting remaining time prediction for *bpic2012o* event log using *single_agg* with XGBoost: (a) global explanation and (b) local explanation for prefix length 12.

or time-dependent (such as `agg_elapsed time`). It is worth noting that the features like `agg_opencases` and `agg_elapsed time`, which have a positive impact on the performance of the predictive model, are not among the data attributes of the original event log and are introduced during feature encoding. These features are known as engineered features. One potential problem with introducing engineered features is that they might contribute to the loss of interpretability of a regression model [8]. However, the features that are engineered in a meaningful way may be aligned with understanding of the business process, in which case, it is likely that they may be interpretable given relevant process knowledge.

Analysis 3: Data Leakage. We investigate the predictive models trained for outcome prediction of *bpic2015_5* event log using *single_agg* and *prefix_agg* (prefix bucket and aggregation encoding), respectively, with XGBoost. Both models have a high accuracy and hence are of interest for deriving interpretations.

Figure 3(a) depicts the global explanation for the model using *single_agg* method, which indicates the occurrences of activities 08_AWB45_010, 08_AWB45_020_2 and 08_AWB45_020_1 are three of the important features for outcome prediction. However, the occurrence of 08_AWB45_020_1 is the outcome to be predicted (as described in Sect. 3.2). Statistical analysis of the event log shows: i) activity 08_AWB45_020_2 is executed after 08_AWB45_020_1 in 68% of the cases, and ii) activity 08_AWB45_010 occurs at the same time as 08_AWB45_020_1 in 50% of the cases. These observations reveal that the predictive model of *single_agg* with XGBoost exhibits a problem of *data leakage* [12], "where information about the label of prediction that should not legitimately be available is present in the input". The features that occur along with or after the activity used as the label influence the model predictions.

Similarly, Fig. 3(b) depicts the global explanation of bucket length 10 when using the model of *prefix_agg* method with XGBoost, from which we observe activity 08_AWB45_020_2 as an important feature used for prediction. This also reveals data leakage as 08_AWB45_020_2 occurs after 08_AWB45_020_1. In both scenarios, model explanations along with the knowledge of the business process can be used to identify potential issues with a predictive model.

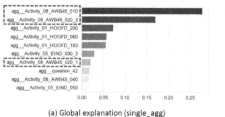
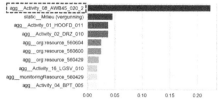

| (a) Global explanation (single_agg) | (b) Global explanation (bucket of prefix length 10; prefix_agg) |

Fig. 3. Interpreting outcome prediction for *bpic2015_5* event log with XGBoost: (a) global explanation when using *single_agg* method; and (b) global explanation for bucket of prefix length 10 when using *prefix_agg* method.

4   Conclusions

In this paper, we have reviewed two existing benchmarks in predictive process monitoring and presented model interpretations as examples to demonstrate that it is not enough to judge predictive methods by solely relying on their performance measures. As learned from our analyses, model interpretations make it possible to reason about the relevance of features used for predictions and help avoid potential issues such as data leakage that may incur to predictive models, and also reveal the use of one-hot data encoding technique can lead to very sparse feature dimensions impacting the explainability of predictive models in the context of process prediction. Hence, we suggest to incorporate interpretability in addition to the evaluation of predictive models using conventional performance measures (such as accuracy). As a first step into future work, it is important to develop a systematic approach for incorporating model interpretability in predictive process analytics.

Acknowledgement. We thank ARC Discovery Grant DP190100314 for supporting part of this research. We also thank the authors of the two process monitoring benchmarks [1,3] for the high quality code they released which allowed us to explore model interpretability for predictive process analytics.

References

1. Teinemaa, I., Dumas, M., Rosa, M.L., Maggi, F.M.: Outcome-oriented predictive process monitoring: Review and benchmark. TKDD **13**(2), 17:1–17:57 (2019)
2. Evermann, J., Rehse, J., Fettke, P.: Predicting process behaviour using deep learning. Decis. Support Syst. **100**, 129–140 (2017)
3. Verenich, I., Dumas, M., Rosa, M.L., Maggi, F.M., Teinemaa, I.: Survey and cross-benchmark comparison of remaining time prediction methods in business process monitoring. ACM TIST **10**(4), 34:1–34:34 (2019)
4. Lakkaraju, H., et al.: Faithful and customizable explanations of black box models. In: Proceedings of the 2019 AAAI Conference on AIES 2019, pp. 131–138 (2019)

5. Rudin, C.: Stop explaining black box machine learning models for high stakes decisions and use interpretable models instead. Nat. Mach. Intell. **1**(5), 206–215 (2019)

6. Guidotti, R., et al.: A survey of methods for explaining black box models. ACM Comput. Surv. **51**(5), 93:1–93:42 (2018)

7. Rehse, J., Mehdiyev, N., Fettke, P.: Towards explainable process predictions for industry 4.0 in the dfki-smart-lego-factory. KI **33**(2), 181–187 (2019)

8. Lipton, Z.C.: The mythos of model interpretability. CACM **61**(10), 36–43 (2018)

9. Molnar, C.: Interpretable Machine Learning: A Guide for Making Black Box Models Explainable. Leanpub (2018)

10. Friedman, J.H.: Greedy function approximation: a gradient boosting machine. Ann. Stat. **29**(5), 1189–1232 (2001)

11. Ribeiro, M.T., Singh, S., Guestrin, C.: "why should I trust you?": explaining the predictions of any classifier. In: Proceedings of the 22nd ACM SIGKDD, pp. 1135–1144 (2016)

12. Kaufman, S., Rosset, S., Perlich, C.: Leakage in data mining: formulation, detection, and avoidance. In: Proceedings of the 17th ACM SIGKDD, pp. 556–563 (2011)

Designing Optimal Robotic Process Automation Architectures

Geeta Mahala[1([⊠])], Renuka Sindhgatta[2], Hoa Khanh Dam[1], and Aditya Ghose[1]

[1] University of Wollongong, Wollongong, Australia
gm168@uowmail.edu.au, hoa@uow.edu.au, aditya.ghose@gmail.com
[2] Queensland University of Technology, Brisbane, Australia
renuka.sr@qut.edu.au

Abstract. The design and implementation of Robotic process automation (RPA) requires an architecture where there is seamless coordination between humans, robotic agents, and intelligent agents automating information acquisition tasks and decision-making tasks. Effective coordination of agents would need to consider the efficiency of different types of resources in completing tasks, the quality when handling complex tasks, and the cost of resources executing the task. In this work, a novel approach for generating an optimal architecture considering distinct types of resources that include human, intelligent and robotic agents is proposed. An optimal architecture is the optimal enactment of process instances executed by a combination of human and automation agents based on their characteristics. The architecture considers resources, resource types, and their characteristics that meet multiple objectives of process execution.

Keywords: Robotic process automation · Multi-objective optimization · Genetic algorithm · Optimal resource architecture

1 Introduction

The idea of Robotic Process Automation, where some (or all) tasks in a business process are automated by deploying software agents, intelligent agents or conversational agents (chatbots) to execute tasks which would have traditionally been executed by human operators, has steadily grown in popularity over the recent past. By various accounts, the size of the global market for RPA products runs into the billions of dollars.

One of the problems that has been highlighted by researchers in this space is that of identifying which tasks to automate [15]. This assumes a simple dichotomy in the available agent types: *human agents* and *robotic agents*. The use of only the former type of agents would represent the old approach to executing processes while the use of the latter would represent an emphasis on automation. More recently, the repertoire of available agent types has expanded to also include *intelligent agents* which are endowed with the ability to learn from past experience and make more complex decisions.

© Springer Nature Switzerland AG 2020
E. Kafeza et al. (Eds.): ICSOC 2020, LNCS 12571, pp. 448–456, 2020.
https://doi.org/10.1007/978-3-030-65310-1_32

This greater variety of resource/agent types also leads to greater diversity in performance characteristics. Human agents tend to be expensive and are typically slower than robotic agents or intelligent agents. Intelligent agents sometimes turn out to be not adept at taking certain decisions (for instance due to limitations in their machine learning routines), necessitating the deployment of human agents to cross-check their decisions. Robotic and intelligent agents take very little time to complete their tasks, relative to human agents. We can also sometimes assume that there is an unlimited supply of robotic and intelligent agents, while we have to contend with a fixed number of expensive-to-deploy human agents. There are clearly, at the very least, three non-functional factors at play: time, cost, and performance (i.e., the extent to which an agent is able to deliver correct outcomes, measured on a numeric scale). We aim to minimize time and cost and maximize performance. It is important to note that all of these factors are measurable and easily monitored. We rate agent *types* on these factors for different *task types* for simplicity in this paper, although our approach could easily be extended to agent *instances*. Rating would involve assessing agents' time, cost, and performance on a comprehensive set of benchmark problems.

This leads us to the problem of identifying an *optimal RPA architecture*. Recall that the traditional notion of a software or system architecture involves the specification of how system components connect and interact to realize overall system functionality. In our setting, an *RPA architecture* specifies how the various agents involved in the execution of a (partially or fully) automated process connect and interact to realize overall process functionality. An RPA architecture specifies, for each process task in each process instance, the agent (type) allocated for executing that task. There is a vast space of possible allocations, each of which leads to different outcomes in terms of overall time taken, overall cost incurred, and performance (or quality of work) achieved in each of the tasks. This suggests a multi-criteria optimization problem where there are at least three distinct (and *incommensurable*) objective functions at play: cost minimization, time minimization, and performance maximization.

In the next section, we provide a background of the over-arching problem. Section 3 provides details of the multi-criteria optimization problem and motives the problem with an example. Section 4 presents related work. We present our conclusions and discuss future work in Sect. 5. It is instructive to take a step back and observe that the solution we have presented also solves the more general problem of devising *process architectures* (i.e., deciding which resource will execute each task in all process instances).

2 Background

An RPA implementation would require human agents and robotic agents working together with suitable coordination. The coordination between agents has been suggested in prior human-automation [12,21] and RPA [19] studies. Such a coordination between the agents can generally be broken down into three broad categories: (i) levels where the task is primarily performed by a human, (ii) levels where the human-agent interaction is high during task execution, and (iii) levels with low human involvement.

Agents executing tasks can be broadly categorised as: (i) *Human Agent (HA)* capable of executing all types of (manual) tasks of the process, (ii) *Robotic Agent (RA)* or specialised software program, that automates *information acquisition* tasks or information gathering tasks, and (iii) *Intelligent Agent (IA)* that automates *information analysis or decision-making* tasks and improves its performance through learning [17].

Agents can have distinct resource characteristics such as performance, experience or suitability when executing different tasks [19]. For example, an IA may have good performance when performing a task to verify the details of the loan application document, but may have low performance in computing the credit risk of the applicant having large number of financial transactions in a different country. In such scenarios, an HA would be required to validate the task done by an IA. Thus, in certain scenarios referred to as a lower level of automation, an HA would often be required to execute the task again after its completion by an IA or RA. At higher levels of automation, HAs exercise a supervisory role intervening only if necessary (failures, errors, or poor execution quality), or further have tasks fully executed by an IA or RA. Human verification tasks may be added dynamically during process execution based on resource characteristics of the IAs or RAs.

The ability of distinct types of resources to automate various tasks of a process leads to increased execution alternatives. The choice of alternatives available needs to account for multiple and often conflicting objectives such as: i) minimizing the *cost* of execution as each of these types of resources have a cost associated with each type of agent executing a task, ii) maximizing the *performance* or quality of the work done by the resource, and iii) minimizing the *makespan* or the shortest possible time for all the process instances to complete execution. For example, an HA can be expensive and may take longer to complete the tasks but will be able to handle any task with minimal errors (or high quality). An IA or RA can take lower time to complete tasks but may execute certain tasks with lower quality. Choosing the right types of resources and the tasks executed by the resources results in a trade-off between different objectives. Hence, selecting an RPA architecture that considers resources, resource types, resource characteristics, and the necessary objectives is complex, time consuming, and crucial to avoid sub-optimal and error prone process executions.

3   Problem Formulation of an Optimal RPA Architecture

In this section we describe the optimization model to enable decisions on the suitability of an RPA solution that meets the required objectives. In this paper, we consider three important objectives. However, our approach is generic and can support multiple and additional objectives. The objectives are to minimize the cost and the overall time taken to execute the process instances (or makespan) while maximizing the performance. The optimization problem is formalized.

The inputs are as follows:

- W, be the maximum number of tasks, $i \in \{1, \ldots, W\}$
- M, be the maximum number of resources $j \in \{1, \ldots, M\}$
- C, be the maximum number of process instances, $k \in \{1, \ldots, C\}$
- ϕ_j, the type of resource j where $\phi_j \in \{HA, IA, RA\}$
- π_j, the cost of a resource of type ϕ_j
- σ_{ij}, is 1 if the the resource of type ϕ_j is *suitable* to perform task i match and zero otherwise
- α_{ij}, the effort on task i by a resource of type ϕ_j
- β_{ij}, the performance of resource of type ϕ_j on task i
- τ_{perf_i}, an acceptable performance threshold for task i
- $d_{ii'}$, is one if there is sequential dependency and tasks i precedes i'

The key inputs to the model are the resources and their characteristics such as suitability, performance, and cost.

Suitability is the inherent quality of a resource j to perform a task i. The suitability of a resource is considered to be a binary value. Suitability can be determined based on agent specification and implementation, or can be determined based on the organization model attributes such as role or department of the resource.

Performance: Automation agents are more susceptible to resource specific errors i.e. errors made by resources when performing a task [16]. Performance measure of an IA can be computed based on the algorithms implemented such as F1-score, root mean square error, precision, or precision@k [20]. These measures can be computed during the training and testing of the algorithms. The performance resource types ϕ_j, on task i can be computed using the measure specific to the implemented algorithms. A threshold τ_{perf_i} indicates an acceptable performance necessary for any agent. If the performance of an agent is below this threshold, the task is either re-executed by an HA or verified by an HA.

Effort: The time taken to complete a task i varies for different resource types. An IA or RA has higher processing power and hence takes significantly lower effort as compared to an HA.

The *process model* provides inputs on the dependencies between the tasks represented by $d_{ii'}$ specifying that to execute task i', the task i needs to be executed before.

The decision variables are as follows:

- x_{ij}, which is true if task i is assigned to resource j, and false otherwise
- e_i, the end date of task i
- s_i, the start date of task i

This leads to the following optimization objectives.

$$\min(\max(e_i) - \min(s_{i'})) \ \forall i, i' \quad \text{(Minimize makespan)}$$

$$\min \sum_{i,j} \pi_j x_{ij} \quad \text{(Minimize cost)}$$

$$\max \sum_{i,j} \beta_{ij} x_{ij} \quad \text{(Maximize performance)}$$

The following constraints are also imposed.

s.t.

$$\sum_j x_{ij} = 1 \ \forall i \text{ where } \beta_{ij} \geq \tau_{perf_i} \quad \text{(ONE TASK TO ONE RESOURCE IF PERFORMANCE IS HIGH)}$$

$$\sum_j x_{ij} x_{ij'} = 1 \ \forall i \text{ where } \beta_{ij} < \tau_{perf_i}, \phi_{j'} = HA$$

$$\text{(ONE TASK IS SUPERVISED BY HA IF PERFORMANCE IS LOW)}$$

$$\sum_j x_{ij}(e_i - s_i) \geq \alpha_{ij} \text{ for all } i \quad \text{(PLANNED END TIME OF TASK CONSIDERS EFFORT)}$$

$$\sum_j (x_{ij} x_{i'j} = 1) \Rightarrow (e_i < s_{i'} \vee s_i > e_{i'}) \text{ for all } i \neq i' \quad \text{(ONE TASK AT A TIME)}$$

$$\sum_{i,j} x_{ij} \sigma_{ij} > 0 \quad \text{(TASK SUITABLE BY RESOURCE)}$$

$$\sum_{ii'jj'} d_{ii'}(x_{ij} x_{i'j'} = 1) \Rightarrow e_i < s_{i'} \quad \text{(SEQUENTIAL DEPENDENCY)}$$

$$x_{ij} \in \{0,1\}$$

Running Example. We illustrate the need for such an optimization architecture with the help of a simple example. Figure 1 (a) presents a business process with 3 tasks to process a claim application. The three types of resources HA, IA, and RA have different resource characteristics on each of these three tasks. An HA has highest performance but requires higher effort and comes with a higher cost. An IA can support the decision making task of evaluating a claim having lower performance than an HA but better cost and effort parameters. An RA can perform the task of notifying the status of the application with high performance but is incapable of performing the first two tasks of the process (namely checking the claim application and evaluating the claim). In this example, we consider all resources of a given resource type with the same resource characteristics. However, our problem formulation does not make any such assumption. The values for effort (α_{ij}), performance(β_{ij}), and cost (π_j) considered for the three tasks and three resource types is presented in Fig. 1 (a).

The allocation of task to resources that meets multiple objectives while satisfying the constraints can result in multiple solutions. One such solution of task allocation with 3 process instances and 6 resources (2 HA, 2 IA, and 2 RA) is shown in Fig. 1 (b). Solutions that meet multiple objectives form a Pareto front of minimum cost, minimum makespan, and maximum performance. A solution on a Pareto front does not dominate another solution on the same front, i.e. by moving along the curve, you could minimize makespan at the expense of reducing performance or maximize performance at the expense of increasing makespan. For example, in Fig. 1 (c) the three solutions on the blue line are non-dominating solutions. The solutions vary with the performance threshold set for the supervisory control of an HA ($\tau_{perf_i} = 5$ for the blue line), i.e. if the performance of an agent is lower than the threshold, it needs to be followed by another task that is performed by an HA to validate or supervise the task executed by an IA or an RA. If the performance threshold is lower (e.g. $\tau_{perf_i} = 3$, orange line), then an IA or RA can do the task without HA supervision. Thus, the makespan reduces, and so does the performance of the entire allocation. Similarly, if the

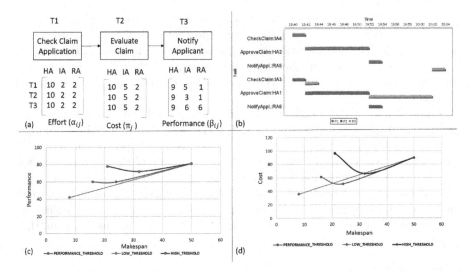

Fig. 1. (a) Example process with resource characteristics, (b) Optimal Solution to execute 3 process instances, (c) Performance vs. Makespan for different performance thresholds (τ_{perf_i}), and (d) Cost Vs. Makespan for different performance thresholds. (Color figure online)

performance threshold is set to a higher value (e.g. $\tau_{perf_i} = 6$), then most tasks performed by IA or RA will be supervised by an HA, resulting in increased performance and increased makespan. Figure 1 (d) presents the makespan and cost for the non-dominating solutions when different performance thresholds are set. The example motivates the need for considering distinct resources, their characteristics, multiple objectives, and constraints for selecting a suitable RPA architecture.

4   Related Work

Prior studies on RPA have focused on the design phase presenting techniques to identify candidate tasks for automation [15]. Studies have explored an increase in the scope of automation by the agents supported by Artificial Intelligence (AI) and Machine learning to do complex tasks [1,18]. Recent work has further distinguished types of resources and their characteristics in terms of suitability for execution of different types of tasks and presented a declarative specification to enable different levels of automation [19]. This work considers such a specifications as input where tasks can be executed by distinct types of resources permitting the generation and selection of an RPA architecture optimizing multiple objectives that are necessary for an effective implementation.

There have been extensive studies focusing on resources and their characteristics [2,7,9,13]. Resource characteristics are used for the allocation of tasks to resources [6,10,11]. The focus of these studies has been human participants and their use for effective resource allocation. The need for robots and human participants to collaboratively work forms an important part of human-automation studies [12,21]. The need for such interactions has been discussed in BPA [1,19]. In this work, we consider distinct types of resources and their characteristics and their interactions with human participants to support effective automation and allocation.

Optimal allocation of tasks to human participants has been widely studied in different domains such as IT service delivery [4,5]. Task allocation to human participants supporting multiple objectives has been an important area of work for flexible business process executions [8,14]. In many of the previous studies, multi-objective optimization uses simulation or conventional constraint based optimization. In this work, we have defined our solution approach to account for the crucial interplay between human and automation agents. Further, we have explored the use of genetic algorithm to support optimization of multiple objectives.

5   Conclusion and Future Work

We offer a solution to the difficult problem of devising an RPA architecture. An approach based on genetic algorithms can be effective in generating useful design alternatives for an RPA architect. Evolutionary search can be employed to find optimal RPA architectures which simultaneously satisfies all objectives and constraints discussed in Sect. 3. Central to genetic algorithms is the representation of the solution. For example, binary representation can be used to constitute an RPA solution as a genotype of bit strings. This string represents a complete RPA setting, including all process instances, tasks in each process instance, and all resources including HA, IA, and RA. Assuming that we use non-dominated sorting algorithm (NSGA-II) [3] as evolutionary search at each generation, NSGA-II would sort the current population into a number of non-dominated fronts. The evolution process would continue until it would arrive at a specified number of generations. In the final generation, NSGA-II would return a set of Pareto optimal solutions as optimal RPA architectures. We also note that our approach is general enough to compute *optimal process architectures* (an allocation of resources to each task in a pool of process instances), but a detailed evaluation requires search through a somewhat different search space. This remains high on our list of priorities for future work.

References

1. van der Aalst, W.M.P., Bichler, M., Heinzl, A.: Robotic process automation. BISE, pp. 269–272 (2018)
2. Arias, M., Munoz-Gama, J., Sepúlveda, M.: Towards a taxonomy of human resource allocation criteria. In: Teniente, E., Weidlich, M. (eds.) BPM 2017. LNBIP, vol. 308, pp. 475–483. Springer, Cham (2018). https://doi.org/10.1007/978-3-319-74030-0_37

3. Deb, K., Pratap, A., Agarwal, S., Meyarivan, T.: A fast and elitist multiobjective genetic algorithm: NSGA-II. IEEE Trans. Evol. Comput. **6**(2), 182–197 (2002)
4. Diao, Y., Heching, A.: Staffing optimization in complex service delivery systems. In: 7th International Conference CNSM 2011, Paris, France, October 24–28, 2011, pp. 1–9. IEEE (2011). http://ieeexplore.ieee.org/document/6104024/
5. Diao, Y., Heching, A.R., Northcutt, D.M., Wallace, R.: Service-delivery modeling and optimization. Interfaces **45**(3), 243–259 (2015)
6. Havur, G., Cabanillas, C., Mendling, J., Polleres, A.: Resource allocation with dependencies in business process management systems. In: La Rosa, M., Loos, P., Pastor, O. (eds.) BPM 2016. LNBIP, vol. 260, pp. 3–19. Springer, Cham (2016). https://doi.org/10.1007/978-3-319-45468-9_1
7. Huang, Z., Lu, X., Duan, H.: Resource behavior measure and application in business process management. Expert Syst. Appl. **39**(7), 6458–6468 (2012)
8. Jiménez-Ramírez, A., Weber, B., Barba, I., Valle, C.D.: Generating optimized configurable business process models in scenarios subject to uncertainty. Inf. Softw. Technol. **57**, 571–594 (2015)
9. Kabicher-Fuchs, S., Mangler, J., Rinderle-Ma, S.: Experience breeding in process-aware information systems. In: Salinesi, C., Norrie, M.C., Pastor, Ó. (eds.) CAiSE 2013. LNCS, vol. 7908, pp. 594–609. Springer, Heidelberg (2013). https://doi.org/10.1007/978-3-642-38709-8_38
10. Kumar, A., Dijkman, R., Song, M.: Optimal resource assignment in workflows for maximizing cooperation. In: Daniel, F., Wang, J., Weber, B. (eds.) BPM 2013. LNCS, vol. 8094, pp. 235–250. Springer, Heidelberg (2013). https://doi.org/10.1007/978-3-642-40176-3_20
11. Kumar, A., et al.: Dynamic work distribution in workflow management systems: How to balance quality and performance. J. Manage. Inf. Syst. **18**(3), 157–194 (2002)
12. Parasuraman, R., Sheridan, T.B., Wickens, C.D.: A model for types and levels of human interaction with automation. IEEE Trans. Syst. Man Cybern. Part A **30**(3), 286–297 (2000)
13. Pika, A., Leyer, M., Wynn, M.T., Fidge, C.J., ter Hofstede, A.H.M., van der Aalst, W.M.P.: Mining resource profiles from event logs. ACM Trans. Management Inf. Syst. **8**(1), 1:1–1:30 (2017)
14. Jiménez-Ramírez, A., Barba, I., del Valle, C., Weber, B.: Generating multiobjective optimized business process enactment plans. In: Salinesi, C., Norrie, M.C., Pastor, Ó. (eds.) CAiSE 2013. LNCS, vol. 7908, pp. 99–115. Springer, Heidelberg (2013). https://doi.org/10.1007/978-3-642-38709-8_7
15. Jimenez-Ramirez, A., Reijers, H.A., Barba, I., Del Valle, C.: A method to improve the early stages of the robotic process automation lifecycle. In: Giorgini, P., Weber, B. (eds.) CAiSE 2019. LNCS, vol. 11483, pp. 446–461. Springer, Cham (2019). https://doi.org/10.1007/978-3-030-21290-2_28
16. Reichert, M., Weber, B.: Enabling Flexibility in Process-Aware Information Systems - Challenges, Methods, Technologies (2012)
17. Russell, S.J., Norvig, P.: Artificial Intelligence - A Modern Approach (3. internat. ed.). Pearson Education (2010)
18. Scheepers, R., Lacity, M.C., Willcocks, L.P.: Cognitive automation as part of deakin university's digital strategy. MIS Q. Executive **17**(2), 89–107 (2018)
19. Sindhgatta, R., ter Hofstede, A.H.M., Ghose, A.: Resource-based adaptive robotic process automation. In: Dustdar, S., Yu, E., Salinesi, C., Rieu, D., Pant, V. (eds.) CAiSE 2020. LNCS, vol. 12127, pp. 451–466. Springer, Cham (2020). https://doi.org/10.1007/978-3-030-49435-3_28

20. Sokolova, M., Japkowicz, N., Szpakowicz, S.: Beyond accuracy, f-score and ROC: a family of discriminant measures for performance evaluation. In: Sattar, A., Kang, B. (eds.) AI 2006. LNCS (LNAI), vol. 4304, pp. 1015–1021. Springer, Heidelberg (2006). https://doi.org/10.1007/11941439_114
21. Vagia, M., Transeth, A.A., Fjerdingen, S.A.: A literature review on the levels of automation during the years. what are the different taxonomies that have been proposed? Appl. Ergon. **53**, 190–202 (2016)

Service Oriented Technology Trends

RESTest: Black-Box Constraint-Based Testing of RESTful Web APIs

Alberto Martin-Lopez$^{(\boxtimes)}$, Sergio Segura, and Antonio Ruiz-Cortés

Smart Computer Systems Research and Engineering Lab (SCORE), Research
Institute of Computer Engineering (I3US), Universidad de Sevilla, Seville, Spain
{alberto.martin,sergiosegura,aruiz}@us.es

Abstract. Automated testing approaches for RESTful web APIs typically follow a black-box strategy, where test cases are derived from the API specification. These techniques show promising results, but they neglect constraints among input parameters (so-called *inter-parameter dependencies*), as these cannot be formally described in current API specification languages. As a result, black-box tools rely on brute force to generate valid test cases, i.e., those satisfying all the input constraints. This is not only extremely inefficient, but it is also unlikely to work for most real-world services, where inter-parameter dependencies are complex and pervasive. In this paper, we present RESTest, a framework for automated black-box testing of RESTful APIs. Among its key features, RESTest supports the specification and automated analysis of inter-parameter dependencies, enabling the use of constraint solvers for the automated generation of valid test cases. This allows to detect more faults, and faster, through a deeper evaluation of valid and invalid input parameters' combinations and the use of novel test oracles. Evaluation results on 6 commercial APIs show that RESTest can efficiently generate up to 99% more valid test cases than random testing techniques, 60% on average. More importantly, RESTest revealed 2K failures undetected by random testing, uncovering bugs in all the services under test.

Keywords: REST · Black-box testing · Constraint-based testing · Web services

1 Introduction

Web APIs allow systems to interact over the network, typically using web services [18]. Modern web APIs typically adhere to the REpresentational State Transfer (REST) architectural style [5], being referred to as RESTful web APIs. RESTful web APIs are comprised of one or more RESTful web services, each of which implements one or more create, read, update, or delete (CRUD) operations to access and manipulate a resource, e.g., a video in the YouTube API. RESTful APIs are commonly described using languages like the OpenAPI Specification (OAS) [15], originally created as a part of the Swagger tool suite [22]. OAS is

© Springer Nature Switzerland AG 2020
E. Kafeza et al. (Eds.): ICSOC 2020, LNCS 12571, pp. 459–475, 2020.
https://doi.org/10.1007/978-3-030-65310-1_33

designed to provide a structured description of a RESTful web API that allows both humans and computers to discover and understand the capabilities of a service without requiring access to the source code or additional documentation.

Web APIs often impose dependency constraints that restrict the way in which two or more input parameters can be combined to form valid calls to the service, these are often called *inter-parameter dependencies* (or simply dependencies henceforth). For example, in the Google Maps API, when searching for places, if the `location` parameter is set, then the `radius` parameter must be set too, otherwise a 400 status code ("bad request") is returned. In a recent study, we reviewed more than 2.5K operations from 40 industrial APIs and found that dependencies are extremely common and pervasive—they appear in 4 out of every 5 APIs across all application domains and types of operations [11]. Unfortunately, current API specification languages like OAS provide no support for the formal description of this type of dependencies, despite being a highly demanded feature by practitioners[1]. Instead, users are encouraged to describe dependencies among input parameters informally, using natural language, which leads to ambiguities and makes it hardly possible to interact with services without human intervention[2]. To address this problem, in previous work we proposed a domain-specific language for the formal specification of dependencies, called Inter-parameter Dependency Language (IDL), and a tool suite for the automated analysis of IDL using constraint programming [12] (c.f. Sect. 2). In this paper, we show the potential of IDL and its tool suite in the context of testing RESTful APIs.

The validation of RESTful web APIs is critical as they play a key role in modern software integration. A faulty API can have a huge impact in the many applications using it. The automated detection of bugs in RESTful web APIs is an active research topic [2–4,9,19,23]. Most contributions in this context follow a black-box strategy, where the specification of the API under test (described using the OAS language) is used to drive the generation of test cases [3,4,9,23]. Essentially, these approaches exercise the API under test using (pseudo) random test data. Test data generation strategies include using default values [4], input data dictionaries [3], test data generators [9] and data observed in previous calls to the API [23]. Failures are detected when the observed output deviates from the specification, e.g., unexpected HTTP status codes.

Problem: Current black-box testing approaches for RESTful web APIs do not support inter-parameter dependencies since, as previously mentioned, these are not formally described in the API specification used as input. As a result, existing approaches simply ignore dependencies and resort to brute force to generate valid test cases, i.e., those satisfying all input constraints. This is not only extremely inefficient, but it is also unlikely to work for most real-world services, where inter-parameter dependencies are complex and pervasive. For example, the search

---

[1] This is reflected in an open feature request in OAS entitled *"Support interdependencies between query parameters"*, with over 290 votes and 55 comments from 33 participants. https://github.com/OAI/OpenAPI-Specification/issues/256.

[2] https://swagger.io/docs/specification/describing-parameters/.

operation in the YouTube API has 31 input parameters, out of which 25 are involved in at least one dependency: trying to generate valid test cases randomly is like hitting a wall. This was confirmed in our evaluation, where 98 out of every 100 random test cases for the YouTube search operation violated one or more inter-parameter dependencies (c.f. Sect. 4.3).

Contribution: In this paper, we present RESTest, an open-source and black-box automated testing framework for RESTful web APIs. RESTest follows a model-based approach enabling its integration with different test case generators and testing frameworks. As its most distinctive feature, RESTest supports the specification and automated analysis of inter-parameter dependencies using the IDL tool suite. This allows to exploit constraint solving as a part of the test generation process, a testing technique generally known as *constraint-based testing* [8]. Constraint-based testing enables a better coverage of the program under test through the systematic generation of valid and invalid input combinations, as well as the use of novel output assertions, i.e., test oracles. For the evaluation of RESTest, we tested 9 operations from 6 commercial APIs, including Tumblr, GitHub and YouTube. Specifically, we compared random testing—state-of-the-art technique for black-box testing of RESTful APIs—and constraint-based testing. As expected, random testing struggled to generate valid test cases: 60% of the generated test cases violated inter-parameter dependencies (about 99% in the APIs of Stripe and YouTube). In contrast, constraint-based testing generated 100% valid test cases for all the services under test, keeping the test case generation time in milliseconds. More importantly, constraint-based testing detected more failures than random testing (4K vs 3K), in more services (9 vs 5), showing the potential of RESTest in practice.

This work includes the following original contributions in the context of automated testing of RESTful web APIs:

1. An open-source and model-based framework for automated black-box test case generation and execution.
2. A new constraint-based approach for improving test case generation techniques, including two novel automated test oracles.
3. Experimental evidence on the limits of using random testing in real-world services with inter-parameter dependencies.
4. A comparison of random testing and constraint-based testing on 6 commercial APIs, showing the potential of both techniques, and especially constraint-based testing, to uncover real bugs.

The remainder of the paper is organised as follows: Sect. 2 introduces the IDL tool suite, used for the automated analysis of inter-parameter dependencies in RESTful web APIs. Section 3 presents RESTest, our testing framework for RESTful APIs. Section 4 explains the evaluation performed and the results obtained. Section 5 outlines threats to validity. Section 6 describes related work. Finally, Sect. 7 draws conclusions and discusses future lines of research.

2 IDL Tool Suite

RESTest relies on the IDL tool suite for the automated management of inter-parameter dependencies in RESTful APIs [12]. *Inter-parameter Dependency Language* (IDL) [21] is a domain-specific language for the specification of inter-parameter dependencies in web APIs. It is based on a thorough study of more than 2.5K operations in 40 real-world APIs [11]. Specifically, it provides support for eight different types of dependencies among input parameters consistently found in practice. Listing 1 shows an example of each type of dependency taken from commercial APIs. The syntax is self-explanatory. For example, the *Requires* dependency in line 1, observed in the API of YouTube, states that, when using the parameter `videoDefinition`, the parameter `type` must be set to `'video'`. IDL specifications can be integrated into OAS documents using the IDL4OAS extension [12]. This allows to enrich API specifications with an accurate, not ambiguous and machine-readable description of the dependencies among input parameters. We refer the reader to the supplementary material of the paper for examples of API specifications using the OAS language and the IDL4OAS extension [21].

```
1  IF videoDefinition THEN type=='video';                   // Requires
2  Or(query, type);                                          // Or
3  ZeroOrOne(radius, rankby=='distance');                    // ZeroOrOne
4  AllOrNone(location, radius);                              // AllOrNone
5  OnlyOne(amount_off, percent_off);                        // OnlyOne
6  publishedAfter >= publishedBefore;                        // Relational
7  limit + offset <= 1000;                                   // Arithmetic
8  IF intent=='browse' THEN OnlyOne(ll AND radius, sw AND ne); // Complex
```

Listing 1. Examples of IDL dependencies from real-world APIs.

IDLReasoner [21] is an open-source Java library for the automated analysis of IDL specifications [12]. Given an OAS specification and a set of IDL dependencies (e.g., using IDL4OAS), the tool translates them into a constraint satisfaction problem (CSP) expressed in MiniZinc [14], a constraint solving language designed for modelling optimisation problems in a high-level, solver-independent way. Then, several analysis operations can be invoked on the resulting CSP, for instance, to know whether a given API request satisfies all the inter-parameter dependencies. Section 3.2 describes the analysis operations used to support test case generation in RESTest.

3 RESTest

In this section, we present RESTest, our framework for automated black-box testing of RESTful web APIs. RESTest follows a model-based approach, where test cases are automatically derived from the specification of the API under test. No access to the source code is required, which makes it possible to test APIs written in any programming language, running in local or remote servers.

Figure 1 shows how RESTest works. It takes as input the OAS specification of the API under test, considered the *system model*. The specification can optionally describe inter-parameter dependencies using the IDL4OAS extension.

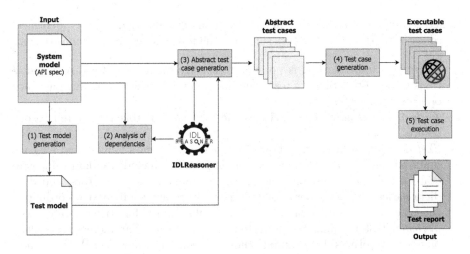

Fig. 1. Test case generation and execution in RESTest.

Then, a so-called *test model* is automatically generated from the system model including test-specific configuration data. The default test model can be manually enriched with fine-grained configuration details such as test data generation settings. Then, both the system and the test models are leveraged for the generation of abstract test cases following user-defined test case generation strategies such as random testing. In parallel, inter-parameter dependencies, if any, are fed into the tool IDLReasoner, providing support for their automated analysis during test case generation, for instance, to check whether an API call satisfies all the inter-parameter dependencies defined in the specification. Finally, abstract test cases are transformed into platform-specific executable test cases and they are executed. In the following sections, we detail the main steps of the process.

3.1   Default Test Model Generation

RESTest takes as input the specification of the API under test, i.e., *system model*. Specifications described using the OAS language—arguably considered the industry-standard and used in related approaches [2–4, 9, 23]—are supported, but other API specification languages could be integrated into the framework using available converters, e.g., RAML to OAS [15]. As a distinctive feature, RESTest supports the specification of inter-parameter dependencies within the OAS document using the IDL4OAS extension [12] (c.f. Sect. 2).

Test case generation in RESTest is driven by the system and the test models. The *test model* includes all test-related configuration settings for the API under test. A default test model, formatted in YAML (i.e., same language used in OAS), is automatically generated from the input API specification (system model). Such test model might be enough to generate effective test cases in some APIs. However, in practice, some manual tuning is often necessary, for example, to generate input values hardly inferred from the specification such as identifiers or codes. In particular, RESTest supports the following configuration settings:

- *Operations under test.* It is possible to specify the subset of the API operations to be tested. Specific test configuration settings can be defined for each operation under test.
- *Authentication data.* This includes the API keys or tokens required to call secured APIs.
- *Test data generators.* This allows to customise the data values used for each input parameter. Test data generators in RESTest include random value generators, regular expression generators, boundary-value generators, and data dictionaries, among others. Default generators are configured according to the type of the input parameters, e.g., English words for string parameters.
- *Weights.* Testers might be interested in testing some parameters more thoroughly than others, for example, those more used in practice. Weights allow to do so. A weight is a real number in the range [0,1]. The higher the weight of a parameter, the more frequently it will be used in test cases. By default, all parameters have a weight of 0.5.

3.2 Automated Analysis of Inter-Parameter Dependencies

API specifications including inter-parameter dependencies in IDL are provided as input to IDLReasoner [12]. This tool transforms the specification into a CSP and automatically checks for inconsistencies in the specification, informing the user about any errors, e.g., parameters that cannot be selected. Once the specification is validated, IDLReasoner provides test case generators with a catalogue of helpful analysis operations. Among these, three analysis operations stand out as particularly helpful during test case generation, namely:

- *isValidRequest.* This operation takes as input an API specification (including inter-parameter dependencies) and a service request (i.e., a list of parameters and their values), and returns a Boolean indicating whether the request is valid or not. A service request is valid if it satisfies all the inter-parameter dependencies defined in the specification.
- *getRandomValidRequest.* This operation receives the API specification of an API operation, and returns a random valid request for the operation, that is, a random assignment of values to input parameters satisfying all the dependencies of the specification.
- *getRandomInvalidRequest.* Contrary to the previous operation, this operation returns a random request violating one or more dependencies.

The use of the IDL tool suite allows to decouple the automated management of dependencies from the specific test case generation approach used. This makes RESTest highly generic and easy to maintain. Furthermore, it eases the use of different CSP solvers and the development of new analysis operations.

3.3   Abstract Test Case Generation

Test cases can be derived from the system and test models using one or more test case generation techniques. These test cases are *abstract* or platform-independent, meaning that they can be later transformed into executable test cases for specific testing frameworks and programming languages. RESTest currently supports random and constraint-based test case generation, but other techniques (e.g., search-based generation) could be easily integrated extending the right interfaces. Abstract test cases comprise test inputs, expected outputs (test oracles), and the required information to build the API request, e.g., the endpoint. RESTest currently supports testing at the operation-level, that is, each test case performs a single API request.

RESTest generates both nominal and faulty test cases. *Nominal test cases* aim to test the API with valid inputs, i.e., those conforming to the API specification. In practice, it is not always possible to guarantee that a nominal test case represents a valid call to the API since it could violate some inter-parameter dependency, for example. Therefore, nominal test cases can be regarded as *potentially valid* test cases aimed at obtaining successful responses from the API (i.e., 2XX status codes). *Faulty test cases* check the ability of the API to handle invalid inputs, and therefore they expect a client error as a response (i.e., 4XX status codes). Faulty test cases are generated by creating faulty variants (i.e., mutants) of nominal test cases. For example, RESTest supports the automated generation of faulty test cases by excluding mandatory parameters, using out-of-range values (e.g., assigning a string to an integer parameter), and violating the JSON schema of the request body, among others. Additionally, as a novel feature of RESTest, the framework supports the automated generation of invalid requests violating inter-parameter dependencies using IDLReasoner.

Test case generation techniques mostly focus on generating test inputs, however, half of the challenge in testing lies on test oracles, that is, how to distinguish correct outputs from incorrect ones. RESTest supports the five test oracles described below, where the last two are novel as they rely on the automated analysis of inter-parameter dependencies.

- *5XX*. The status code must be lower than 500 (server error).
- *OAS*. The response must conform to the OAS schema.
- $2XX_P$. If the request violates the specification of individual parameters (e.g., a mandatory parameter is missing), the status code must not be 2XX (successful response).
- $2XX_D$. If the request violates one or more inter-parameter dependencies, the status code must not be 2XX.
- *4XX*. If the request is valid according to the API specification, the status code must not be 4XX (client error response).

Oracles $2XX_D$ and *4XX* are novel contributions of our work. Both of them reveal failures undetectable by current state-of-the-art test oracles. It is worth noting that oracle *4XX* is particularly helpful as it allows to detect critical bugs: those making the API return a client error response (4XX status code) with a valid API call. Detecting this kind of failures is only possible thanks to the automated analysis of inter-parameter dependencies, which allows to automatically determine whether a request is valid before calling the actual API (assuming that the specification is correct and that the right test data generators are used).

3.4   Test Case Generation and Execution

The last step is concerned with test execution. Abstract test cases are *instantiated* into executable test cases using specific testing frameworks and libraries. RESTest currently supports the generation of executable test cases using REST Assured [17], a Java library for testing RESTful services, developed as a JUnit extension. However, other frameworks and programming languages could be easily supported by implementing specific test writers.

Test execution can be done either offline or online. In *offline testing*, test case generation and execution are independent tasks. This has certain benefits. For example, test cases can be generated once, and then be executed many times as a part of regression testing. Also, test generation and test execution can be performed on different machines and at different times. In *online testing*, test case generation and execution are interleaved. This enables, for example, fully autonomous testing of RESTful web APIs, e.g., generating and executing test cases 24/7 as a part of a Continuous Integration (CI) setup. RESTest supports both offline and online testing. However, more sophisticated techniques for online testing remain to be implemented. For example, the test generation algorithms can react to the actual outputs of the API under test, e.g., to guide search-based test case generation algorithms based on the coverage achieved so far [13].

4   Evaluation

In this section, we assess the ability of RESTest to generate valid test cases (i.e., those satisfying all the input constraints) and to reveal failures in real-world APIs with inter-parameter dependencies. To this end, we compare random testing (RT)—state-of-the-art technique for black-box testing of RESTful APIs—and constraint-based testing (CBT). We address the following research questions:

- **RQ1**: *What is the effectiveness of CBT in generating valid test cases for real-world APIs with inter-parameter dependencies?*
- **RQ2**: *What is the fault-finding capability of CBT in real-world APIs with inter-parameter dependencies?*

4.1   Services Under Test

We tested 9 services from 6 commercial RESTful APIs with millions of users. We selected both read and write operations from those services. In order to assess the potential of CBT, we selected operations containing the eight types of dependencies identified in our study [11], with more than 50% of their parameters

Table 1. RESTful API operations used in the evaluation. P = Number of parameters, D = Number of IDL dependencies, PD = Number and percentage of parameters involved in at least one dependency.

ID	API	Operation	P	D	PD (%)
Foursquare	Foursquare	Search venues	17	8	10 (59%)
GitHub	GitHub	Get user repositories	5	2	3 (60%)
Stripe-CC	Stripe	Create coupon	9	3	5 (56%)
Stripe-CP	Stripe	Create product	18	6	11 (61%)
Tumblr	Tumblr	Get blog likes	5	1	3 (60%)
Yelp	Yelp	Search businesses	14	3	7 (50%)
YouTube-GCT	YouTube	Get comment threads	11	5	8 (73%)
YouTube-GV	YouTube	Get videos	12	5	7 (58%)
YouTube-S	YouTube	Search	31	16	25 (81%)
Mean			13.6	5.4	8.8 (62%)

involved in at least one dependency. Table 1 provides a summary of the services under test (SUTs). For each SUT, the table shows an identifier (used to refer to it within the rest of the paper), API name, description of the operation tested, number of input parameters (P), number of IDL dependencies (D), and number (and percentage) of different parameters involved in at least one dependency (PD). On average, the operations have 14 parameters, 5 dependencies and 9 parameters involved in dependencies.

The OAS specification of each API under test, used as input in RESTest, was taken from the API website or from the APIs.guru repository [1]. When the specification was not available (Foursquare, Tumblr and Yelp), we created it manually based on the online API documentation. Then, we looked for inter-parameter dependencies described in the documentation and included them as a part of the specification using the IDL4OAS extension. The links to the APIs under test and their OAS specifications are available as part of the supplementary material of the paper [21].

4.2 Test Case Generation Techniques

Next, we describe the test case generation techniques used in the evaluation.

Random Testing (RT). This is the state-of-the-art approach used as baseline in our work [4,9,23]. Nominal test cases are generated by randomly selecting a subset of the operation parameters and assigning random values to them within their domain. All parameters are selected with the same probability (i.e., weight = 0.5) except mandatory ones, which are always included in the API request. Notice that this approach neglects inter-parameter dependencies and so the generated test cases may not be valid, i.e., they may generate responses with 4XX status codes (client error). Faulty test cases are generated by mutating nominal test cases as described in Sect. 3.3, e.g., excluding a mandatory parameter from the API call.

Constraint-Based Testing (CBT). Nominal test cases are generated in two steps. First, the domain of each input parameter is discretised and reduced to a fixed number of random values, within their domain, using RESTest test data generators. Then, the analysis operation *getRandomValidRequest* is invoked on IDLReasoner to generate a request that satisfies all inter-parameter dependencies. Analogously to RT, faulty test cases can be generated by mutating nominal test cases. Additionally, faulty test cases can also be generated by invoking the *getRandomInvalidRequest* operation on IDLReasoner to generate an API call violating one or more inter-parameter dependencies.

4.3   Experiment 1: Generation of Valid Test Cases

In this experiment, we aim to answer RQ1 by evaluating the effectiveness of RT and CBT in generating valid test cases, i.e., those satisfying all inter-parameter dependencies. The automated generation of valid test cases has two main benefits. First, these are very helpful during regression testing as a part of Continuous Integration. Second, and more importantly, valid test cases help identify critical bugs: those returning an error (i.e., 4XX or 5XX status code) with an input that should be successfully handled by the service (i.e., 2XX status code). In what follows, we describe the setup and the results of the experiment.

Setup. For each SUT and test generation technique (RT and CBT), we generated 1,000 nominal test cases. Recall that a nominal test case is a potentially valid test case intended to test the API under valid inputs. Then, we ran the test cases on the services under test and counted the number of actual valid test cases based on the 2XX responses obtained. Interestingly, we found that some of the services tested had dependencies not described in the API documentation. This was observed when obtaining 4XX status codes (client errors) with some input combinations that should be valid according to the documentation. For example, when using the `channelType` parameter in the YouTube API, the `type` parameter must be set to `'channel'`, although this dependency is not documented. In order to assess the effect of the missing dependencies, we defined them in the specification and included them in the evaluation as variants of the original SUTs, denoted with * after their name in Table 2. Overall, we added 4 new dependencies and updated 9 dependencies in 4 out of the 9 services under test. The experiments were performed in a standard PC with an Intel i5 processor, 16GB of RAM and an SSD, running on Windows 10 and Java JDK 8.

Results. Table 2 shows the results of the experiment. For each SUT and test generation technique, the table shows the percentage of valid test cases generated (column *Valid*) and the time required to generate the 1,000 test cases in seconds (column *Time*). Note that test case execution times are not included since those are independent of the test case generation approach.

As expected, RT struggled to generate valid test cases in most of the APIs, with the percentage of valid test cases ranging from 1.3% (Stripe) to 89%

Table 2. Percentage of valid test cases and test case generation times.

SUT	RT		CBT	
	Valid (%)	Time (s)	Valid (%)	Time (s)
Foursquare	89.0	1.4	93.6	107.0
Foursquare*	–	–	100	105.4
GitHub	62.1	3.6	100	96.8
Stripe-CC	17.1	0.4	82.0	102.9
Stripe-CC*	–	–	100	105.8
Stripe-CP	1.3	1.7	46.4	109.7
Stripe-CP*	–	–	100	108.8
Tumblr	65.5	0.2	100	100.3
Yelp	54.6	1.7	97.1	102.8
YouTube-GCT	20.5	0.6	99.9	95.9
YouTube-GV	49.2	7.5	100	114.2
YouTube-S	1.6	1.0	49.2	104.3
YouTube-S*	–	–	100	104.0
Mean	40.1	2.0	85.4 (99.7)	104.5

(Foursquare), 40.1% on average. In contrast, CBT successfully managed to generate 100% valid test cases in the API operations of GitHub, Tumblr and YouTube-GV. Similarly, CBT generated 100% valid test cases in the operations of Foursquare, Stripe and YouTube-S once the missing dependencies were included in the specification (rows denoted with *). Some of the test cases generated by CBT did not obtain successful responses in the SUTs of Yelp and YouTube-GCT. Interestingly, we found this was due to actual faults in those services, as discussed in the next section. CBT generated an average of 85.4% valid test cases in the services under test using the dependencies described in their documentation, and 100% (99.7% counting fault-revealing test cases) when considering all the dependencies, including those missing in the API documentation. Overall, out of 1,000 test cases, CBT generated between 11% (FourSquare) and 99% (Stripe-CP) more valid test cases than RT, 59.9% on average.

RT took 2 s on average to generate 1,000 test cases, whereas CBT took 104.5 s (less than 2 min) due to the overhead introduced by the constraint solver. However, the increment in the execution time of CBT is negligible compared to its potential to generate valid test cases and to detect failures. To investigate this further, we measured the time required by both techniques, RT and CBT, to generate and run test cases in the service of Stripe-CP until having 1,000 successful responses. RT took more than 10 h and 73K total generated test cases. CBT took 11 min and 1K test cases.

Based on the results obtained, we can answer RQ1 as follows:

CBT can generate 100% valid test cases for RESTful web services, provided that dependencies are correctly specified. This means an average increment of 60% over RT (99% in highly constrained APIs) at a low price in terms of generation time.

4.4 Experiment 2: Detection of Failures

In this experiment, we aim to answer RQ2 by evaluating the effectiveness of RT and CBT in detecting failures in real-world APIs with inter-parameter dependencies. Next, we explain the experimental setup and the main findings.

Table 3. Failures found by RT and CBT.

SUT	RT				CBT					
	5XX	OAS	$2XX_P$	Total	5XX	OAS	$2XX_P$	$2XX_D$	4XX	Total
Foursquare	0	1,042	127	1,169	1	910	65	424	64	1,464
GitHub	0	0	487	487	0	0	236	0	0	236
Stripe-CC	0	0	0	0	0	0	0	0	180	180
Stripe-CP	0	0	0	0	0	0	0	0	535	535
Tumblr	0	389	806	1,195	0	492	411	160	0	1,063
Yelp	48	19	0	67	50	42	0	68	1	161
YouTube-GCT	0	0	0	0	0	1	0	8	1	10
YouTube-GV	0	0	2	2	0	0	2	114	0	116
YouTube-S	0	0	0	0	0	5	0	0	508	513
Total	48	1,450	1,422	2,920	51	1,450	714	774	1,289	4,278

Setup. For each SUT and test case generation technique, we generated 1,000 nominal test cases and 1,000 faulty test cases, 2,000 test cases in total. Faulty test cases in RT were generated by violating the specification of individual parameters, e.g., omitting a mandatory parameter in the API request. In CBT, however, faulty test cases were divided into two groups: 500 test cases following the same approach as in RT, and 500 test cases violating one or more inter-parameter dependencies. To identify wrong outputs, we used the five test oracles explained in Sect. 3.3, i.e., server errors ($5XX$), conformance to the OAS specification (OAS), faulty requests obtaining successful responses ($2XX_P$ and $2XX_D$) and valid requests obtaining client error responses ($4XX$). Recall that oracles $2XX_D$ and $4XX$ are only applicable in CBT as they rely on checking whether inter-parameter dependencies hold.

Results. Table 3 shows the number of failures detected in the services by each test case generation technique and test oracle. Both techniques succeeded in finding failures, but CBT proved more effective, as it uncovered 4,278 failures in all the services under test, whereas RT revealed 2,920 failures in 5 out of 9.

Regarding test oracles, both techniques uncovered a similar number of failures with oracles *5XX* and *OAS*. RT found twice the failures with test oracle $2XX_P$, but this was expected since it was checked 1,000 times in RT against 500 times in CBT. The true potential of CBT is leveraged with our two novel oracles $2XX_D$ and *4XX*. In fact, they sufficed to reveal 2,063 failures in 8 out of 9 services on their own. It is noteworthy that these failures are undetectable by current state-of-the-art techniques.

Oracle *4XX* uncovered a total of 1,289 failures in 6 services. These failures are specially critical: client errors should not be obtained when requests are well formed. Since we are using a black-box approach, it is difficult to know the exact number of distinct faults causing these failures. However, we analysed the error messages returned by the services and managed to classify the failures in multiple *potential* bugs. Due to space limitations, we describe three of the bugs uncovered with this oracle below, and refer the reader to the supplementary material for a comprehensive list [21]:

- In the Yelp service, when setting the `location` to 'Egypt' and the `locale` to 'fi_FI' (Finnish), the error LOCATION_NOT_FOUND (400 status code) is returned. However, we noticed that changing the locale to Italian, for instance, makes the error disappear and actual results are returned.
- In the YouTube-GCT service, a valid request obtained an error with the following message: *"Check the structure of the commentThread resource in the request body to ensure that it is valid"*. However, no body was included in the request (actually the operation does not allow it), and so this failure becomes hard to debug.
- In the YouTube-S service, there exist two undocumented dependencies: (1) when using the `channelType` parameter, `type` must be set to 'channel'; and (2) when using the `location` parameter, `type` must be set to 'video'. These two unspecified dependencies caused 1 of every 2 requests to be invalid.

As for oracle $2XX_D$, most failures are related to inter-parameter dependencies being wrongly specified in the API documentation, or not correctly implemented in the API itself. For instance, the Yelp service defines the parameters `open_now` and `open_at` as mutually exclusive, nevertheless, a request including both parameters with `open_now` set to 'false' will return a successful response.

In addition to the failures uncovered by our two novel oracles, RESTest successfully found other types of errors such as 500 status codes in Foursquare and Yelp and disconformities with the OAS specification in Tumblr and YouTube, among others. All things considered, we can answer RQ2 as follows:

> *CBT is highly effective at revealing failures having found bugs in the nine services under test. About half of the failures detected by CBT (2K out of 4K) were not detected by RT.*

5   Threats to Validity

The evaluation performed is subject to a number of validity threats.

Internal Validity. *Are there factors that might affect the results of our evaluation?* A possible threat in this regard is the existence of bugs in the tools used, namely, RESTest and IDLReasoner. To mitigate this threat, both tools have been thoroughly tested using standard testing techniques such as equivalence partitioning and combinatorial testing. Furthermore, the tools with their test suites and the results of our experiments are freely available [21], thereby allowing full replication of the evaluation performed. Related to this, we had to manually write the OAS specifications of three services. To minimise bias, we created them solely based on their online documentation, and all specifications were independently revised by at least two authors. Another possible threat is related to the randomness of the testing techniques used (RT and CBT). A thorough evaluation should have included more repetitions per experiment (e.g., 10–30) and statistical analysis. However, due to the strict quota restrictions of the commercial APIs tested, it was not possible to do so (e.g., the YouTube-S service accepts only 100 requests per day). Despite this limitation, the total number of test cases generated (40K) and failures found (7K) make us remain confident about the significance of the results obtained.

External Validity. *To what extent can we generalise the findings?* We tested 9 services from 6 highly popular web APIs, nevertheless, this might not be a sufficiently representative sample. To minimise this threat, we selected API operations of different types (read and create), from different application domains (e.g., financial and social), with different numbers of parameters (from 5 to 31) and containing the eight patterns of dependencies found in our study of real-world APIs [11].

6   Related Work

RESTful API testing approaches can be classified into white-box and black-box. Arcuri [2] is the only author who advocates for white-box testing. He proposed a search-based approach, where test cases are generated aiming to maximise code coverage. Black-box testing approaches do not require access to the source code. Segura et al. [19] proposed to analyse the outputs returned by the service after similar requests. They managed to find bugs when inconsistencies among those outputs were detected, e.g., the API returns more data when using a filter than when no filter is applied. Other approaches achieve a higher degree of automation by leveraging the OAS specification of the API [3,4,9,23]. Ed-douibi et al. [4] tested individual API operations using random, default and example parameter values present in the OAS document. Other authors [3,9,23] tested sequences of operations by inferring dependencies among them (e.g., creating a resource and retrieving it). For the generation of input test values, Karlsson et al. [9] resorted to property-based testing (PBT), while Atlidakis et al. [3] and Viglianisi et al.

[23] used data dictionaries. All these approaches are limited in the oracles they can use, as they can only check the conformance to the OAS document, the absence of 5XX status codes and the correct management of invalid inputs. They cannot be certain about whether a given API call is valid or not, since it may violate some inter-parameter dependency. Neglecting this limitation would lead to false positives for those APIs containing dependencies, as what happened to Ed-douibi et al.: *"four errors were linked to the limitation of OpenAPI to define mutually exclusive required parameters"* [4]. Atlidakis et al. [3] proposed four additional oracles related to operation sequences (e.g., a resource that was deleted must no longer be accessible) but, again, these oracles have no effect if no valid calls to the service are generated in the first place. In contrast to previous approaches, RESTest supports the automated management of inter-parameter dependencies, enabling a deeper and faster evaluation of the SUT through the systematic generation of valid and invalid input combinations.

In the context of constraint-based testing for web services, the most related work is probably that of Sun et al. [20]. They proposed CxWSDL, a WSDL [24] extension to specify six different types of behaviour constraints such as the order in which operations should be invoked. Test cases were automatically derived from the specification using a constraint solver. Inconsistencies in the services tested were found when some constraint was violated. Li et al. [10] presented a constrained combinatorial approach to generate optimal test suites avoiding forbidden combinations of parameters. Xu et al. [25] proposed testing web service robustness by violating constraints, including inter-parameter dependencies, which were extracted from the OWL-S [16] specification of the service. Compared to these papers, we support a wider range of inter-parameter dependencies, including the eight dependency patterns defined in [11], and we focus on RESTful APIs as the current de facto standard for web integration. Further, our approach is integrated into RESTest, an open-source framework that can be easily extended with other test generation strategies as well as testing frameworks and libraries.

7   Conclusion and Future Work

This paper presents RESTest, a framework for automated black-box testing of RESTful web APIs. RESTest implements a novel constraint-based testing approach that leverages the specification of inter-parameter dependencies to automatically generate valid calls to the service, i.e., those satisfying all input constraints. We showed that current random testing techniques can be extremely inefficient in generating valid requests and therefore are unable to exercise the actual functionality of the services, e.g., 98 out of every 100 random test cases violated inter-parameter dependencies in YouTube. In contrast, RESTest can efficiently generate 100% valid test cases when providing the specification of inter-parameter dependencies. More importantly, RESTest implements two novel oracles to evaluate how the API responds to constraint-satisfying and constraint-violating test cases. This allowed us to reveal more than 4K failures uncovering bugs in all the services under test.

Several challenges remain for future work. On the one hand, we plan to implement currently missing features in RESTest, such as testing of sequences of operations and search-based online testing approaches. This will allow us to perform a more extensive evaluation of the framework. On the other hand, we intend to make RESTest SLA-aware with SLA4OAI [6], so that it can be deployed in API gateways such as Governify [7] and perform autonomous functional and non-functional testing of microservices architectures.

Acknowledgements. This work has been partially supported by the European Commission (FEDER) and Junta de Andalucia under projects APOLO (US-1264651) and EKIPMENT-PLUS (P18-FR-2895), by the Spanish Government under project HORATIO (RTI2018-101204-B-C21), and by the FPU scholarship program, granted by the Spanish Ministry of Education and Vocational Training (FPU17/04077). We would also like to thank Ramon Fernandez for his technical support during the development of RESTest.

References

1. APIs.guru. https://apis.guru. Accessed Apr 2020
2. Arcuri, A.: RESTful API automated test case generation with EvoMaster. ACM TOSEM **28**(1), 1–37 (2019)
3. Atlidakis, V., Godefroid, P., Polishchuk, M.: Checking security properties of cloud services REST APIs. In: ICST (2020)
4. Ed-douibi, H., Izquierdo, J.L.C., Cabot, J.: Automatic generation of test cases for REST APIs: a specification-based approach. In: EDOC, pp. 181–190 (2018)
5. Fielding, R.T.: Architectural styles and the design of network-based software architectures. Ph.D. thesis (2000)
6. Gamez-Diaz, A., Fernandez, P., Ruiz-Cortes, A.: Automating SLA-driven API development with SLA4OAI. In: ICSOC, pp. 20–35 (2019)
7. Gamez-Diaz, A., Fernandez, P., Ruiz-Cortés, A.: Governify for APIs: SLA-driven ecosystem for API governance. In: ESEC/FSE, pp. 1120–1123 (2019)
8. Gotlieb, A.: Constraint-based testing: an emerging trend in software testing. In: Advances in Computers, vol. 99, pp. 67–101. Elsevier (2015)
9. Karlsson, S., Causevic, A., Sundmark, D.: QuickREST: property-based test generation of OpenAPI described RESTful APIs. In: ICST (2020)
10. Li, Y., Sun, Z.A., Fang, J.Y.: Generating an automated test suite by variable strength combinatorial testing for web services. CIT **24**(3), 271–282 (2016)
11. Martin-Lopez, A., Segura, S., Ruiz-Cortés, A.: A catalogue of inter-parameter dependencies in RESTful web APIs. In: ICSOC, pp. 399–414 (2019)
12. Martin-Lopez, A., Segura, S., Müller, C., Ruiz-Cortés, A.: Specification and automated analysis of inter-parameter dependencies in web APIs. IEEE Trans. Serv. Comput. (2020, Submitted to). https://bit.ly/2ECr9rc
13. Martin-Lopez, A., Segura, S., Ruiz-Cortés, A.: Test coverage criteria for RESTful web APIs. In: A-TEST, pp. 15–21 (2019)
14. MiniZinc: Constraint Modeling Language. https://www.minizinc.org. Accessed Apr 2020
15. OpenAPI Specification. https://www.openapis.org. Accessed Apr 2020
16. Semantic Markup for Web Services (OWL-S). https://www.w3.org/Submission/OWL-S. Accessed May 2020

17. REST Assured. http://rest-assured.io. Accessed Apr 2020
18. Richardson, L., Amundsen, M., Ruby, S.: RESTful Web APIs. O'Reilly Media Inc., Sebastopol (2013)
19. Segura, S., Parejo, J.A., Troya, J., Ruiz-Cortés, A.: Metamorphic testing of RESTful web APIs. IEEE TSE **44**(11), 1083–1099 (2018)
20. Sun, C.a., Li, M., Jia, J., Han, J.: Constraint-based model-driven testing of web services for behavior conformance. In: ICSOC, pp. 543–559 (2018)
21. Supplementary material of the paper. https://github.com/isa-group/icsoc-2020-supplementary-material
22. Swagger. http://swagger.io. Accessed Apr 2020
23. Viglianisi, E., Dallago, M., Ceccato, M.: RestTestGen: automated black-box testing of RESTful APIs. In: ICST (2020)
24. Web Services Description Language (WSDL) Version 2.0. https://www.w3.org/TR/wsdl20. Accessed May 2020
25. Xu, L., Yuan, Q., Wu, J., Liu, C.: Ontology-based web service robustness test generation. In: WSE, pp. 59–68 (2009)

A Type-Sensitive Service Identification Approach for Legacy-to-SOA Migration

Manel Abdellatif[1,2]([✉]), Rafik Tighilt[2], Naouel Moha[2], Hafedh Mili[2], Ghizlane El Boussaidi[3], Jean Privat[2], and Yann-Gaël Guéhéneuc[4]

[1] Polytechnique Montréal, Montreal, QC, Canada
`manel.abdellatif@polymtl.ca`
[2] Université du Québec à Montréal, Montreal, QC, Canada
[3] École de Technologie Supérieure, Montreal, QC, Canada
[4] Concordia University, Montreal, QC, Canada

Abstract. A common strategy for modernizing legacy systems is to migrate them to *service-oriented architecture* (SOA). A key step in the migration process is the identification of reusable functionalities in the system that qualify as *candidate services* in the target architecture. We propose *ServiceMiner*, a bottom-up service identification approach that relies on source code analysis, because other sources of information may be unavailable or out of sync with the actual code. Our *bottom-up, code-based* approach uses *service-type specific functional-clustering criteria*. We use a categorization of service types that builds on published service taxonomies and describes the code-level patterns characterizing types of services. We evaluate *ServiceMiner* on an open-source, enterprise-scale legacy ERP system and compare our results to those of two state-of-the-art approaches. We show that ServiceMiner automates one of the main labor-intensive steps for migrating legacy systems to SOA. It identifies architecturally-significant services with 77.9% of precision, 66.4% of recall, and 71.7% of F-measure. Also, we show that it could be used to assist practitioners in the identification of candidate services in existing systems and thus to support the migration process of legacy systems to SOA.

Keywords: Service identification · Service types · Legacy migration · Software reuse

1 Introduction

The maintenance and migration of legacy software systems are central IT activities in many organizations in which these systems are mission-critical. These systems embed hidden knowledge that is of significant values. They cannot be simply removed or replaced because they execute effectively and accurately critical and complex business logic. However, legacy software systems are difficult to maintain and scale because their software and hardware become obsolete [1]. They must be modernized to ease their maintenance and evolution.

© Springer Nature Switzerland AG 2020
E. Kafeza et al. (Eds.): ICSOC 2020, LNCS 12571, pp. 476–491, 2020.
https://doi.org/10.1007/978-3-030-65310-1_34

A common strategy for modernizing such systems is their migration to *service-oriented architecture* (SOA), which defines a style where systems are made of services that are reusable, distributed, relatively independent, and often heterogeneous [2]. Service Identification (SI) is considered one of the most challenging steps of the migration process [3]. It consists in identifying reusable groupings—clusters of functionalities in the legacy system that qualify as *candidate services* in the target architecture. Several SI approaches have been proposed in the literature [4–10]. However most of them have limited identification accuracy and usually require several types of inputs (e.g., business process models, use cases, activity diagrams, etc.) that may not be always available especially in the context of legacy systems. We argue that service identification should depend on service types to improve the identification accuracy by narrowing the search space through the types and their associated code-patterns. Service types can be used to classify service candidates according to a hierarchical-layered schema and offers the possibility to prioritize the identification of specific types of services according to the business requirements of the migration process. Also, in our prior work [11], we reported that several practitioners highlighted the importance of identifying service types when migrating legacy systems to SOA. They claimed that type-aware SI provides important information on the nature and business capabilities of the identified services. Besides, existing source-code SI approaches use similar *functional-clustering criteria*—typically *cohesion* and *coupling*, which lead to candidate services that are often architecturally irrelevant for the new SOA-based system.

Consequently, we propose *ServiceMiner*, a type-aware SI approach to support the migration of legacy systems to SOA. We consider a bottom-up approach relying on source code analysis, as other sources of information (e.g., business process models, use cases, activity diagrams, etc.) may be unavailable or out of sync with the actual code. We use a categorization of service types based on previous service taxonomies and describe the code-level patterns characterizing each type of service. We evaluate *ServiceMiner* on an open-source, enterprise-scale legacy ERP system and compare its results to those of two state-of-the-art SI approaches [5,7]. We show that our approach automates the identification of specific types of candidate services, which are architecturally significant for the new SOA-based system.

This paper is structured as follows. Section 2 presents the related work and describes the taxonomy of service types. Section 3 details the service identification approach. Section 4 presents the experimental validation of our approach and details the obtained results. We discuss in Sect. 5 our threats to validity and provide our recommendations. Finally, we conclude in Sect. 6 with future work.

2 Background and Related Work

We describe in this section related work considering service types, their limitations, and the taxonomies on which we build our approach.

2.1   Related Work

Several approaches were presented to identify services from legacy software. However, only five approaches [12–16] considered the types of services.

Marchetto *et al.* [13] proposed a stepwise type-sensitive service identification approach that extracts reusable services from legacy systems based on dynamic analysis of java-based systems. They proposed guidelines to identify Utility, Entity and Task services from legacy systems. They executed several test scenarios and extracted reusable functional groupings that they qualified as candidate services. They identified Utility services by manually mining non-business-centric functionalities and looking at cross-cutting functionalities that can be grouped and exposed as candidate Utility services. They extracted candidate Entity services by analyzing the persistent objects and the classes using them. Finally, they considered each main functionality of the target application as a possible candidate Task service. Although the proposed SI approach is type-sensitive, the identification is still manual and based on executing several test scenarios that may not cover all the functionalities of the system. The approach was validated on small Java systems, limiting its application on real enterprise systems.

Huergo *et al.* [15] proposed a method to identify services based on their types. They rely on UML class diagrams of object-oriented based systems from which they derive state machine diagrams to identify the states of the objects in the system. They start by manually identifying *Master data* that they define as entity classes considered to play a key role in the operation of a business. Each Master data is considered as a candidate Entity service. Next, they derive state machine diagrams that are related to the identified Master data. They analyze the transitions on the state machine diagrams and identify Task and Process services. The identification process is also not fully automated and relies on the manual identification of master data in the system that qualify as Entity services.

Alahmari *et al.* [12] identified services based on analyzing business process models. These business process models are derived from questionnaires, interviews and available documentations that provide atomic business processes and entities on the one hand, and activity diagrams that provide primitive functionalities, on the other hand. Different service granularity are distinguished in relation to atomic business processes and entities. Dependent atomic processes as well as the related entities are grouped together at the same service to maximize the cohesion and minimize the coupling. However the implementation details of the approach is not fully described.

Fuhr *et al.* [14] considered three types of services: Business, Entity, and Utility services, which are identified from legacy code based on a dynamic analysis technique. The authors relied on a business process model to identify related classes. Each activity in the business process model is executed and classes called during the execution of an activity are considered related. The identification of services is based on a clustering technique where the similarity measurement is the number of classes used together in one activity. The identified clusters are then manually mapped into the different service types. A strong assumption of this approach is that business process models are available to execute activities.

Grieger *et al.* [16] presented an approach identifying three service types when analyzing legacy code. The first type refers to initial Design services that implement business values. These occurrences are identified based on refining the existing legacy code related to business values. The second type corresponds to coarse-grained services, e.g, business processes. These are identified based on orchestrating other services related to the same underlying business process (i.e., structural dependent services). The last service type is related to services that implement crosscutting concerns and technical functionalities used across different services (i.e., Utility services). The identification of these services is based on partitioning the functionalities of multiple services to recover individual and common parts. The authors relied on a clone detection algorithm to extract cloned functionalities shared among different services. The identified cloned functionalities are given to software architects to decide if they should to be moved into an existing service or merged into a new one. The proposed approach highly depend on the manual and iterative refinement of the identified candidate services with software architects. The approach also lacks of empirical evidence on its reliability to support software architects during the migration process as there is no information about the quality of the identified services.

We notice that there is a lack of SI approaches that are type-sensitive. These approaches focus on identifying Business, Entity, and Utility services. Most of these approaches are not fully-automated and need other inputs than the source code (e.g., business processes, execution traces, state machine diagrams, etc.) to identify services in legacy systems.

Also, a number of primary studies have been proposed in the literature about SI without taking into account service types. Many of the proposed techniques rely on Business Process Models (BPMs), to identify services within the context of legacy migration [17–19]. These techniques decompose processes into tasks and then map these tasks to legacy source code elements to identify candidate services. Other SI techniques use heuristics based on the *technical properties* of services, as reflected in various metrics [5,7,8,20,21]. Such techniques often use these metrics to drive clustering and machine learning algorithms that identify software artifact clusters as candidate services. Other AI-based techniques use ontologies and Formal Concept Analysis to identify services in legacy systems [9,10,22]. However these techniques are too complex and not ready for industrial applications. There are also wrapping-based SI techniques that put service interfaces around *existing* functional components and subsystems [4,6,23], which solve integration problems but do not solve maintenance issues.

2.2 Taxonomy of Service Types

A number of service type taxonomies exists [2,12–16,24,25] that consider different aspects (e.g., domain specificity, granularity, governance) to distinguish service types. We study and combine these taxonomies and limit ourselves to those services types that are *distinguishable at the code level*. We distinguish between *domain-specific services*, and *domain-neutral services* (cf. Fig. 1). *Domain-specific Services* fall into four major types:

1. **Business services:** They correspond to business processes or use cases. These are services used by users. These services generally compose/use the Enterprise-task, Application-task, and Entity services described in the following.
2. **Enterprise services:** (Also called capabilities [24]) they are of finer granularity than business process services. They implement generic business functionalities reused across different applications.
3. **Application services:** These services provide functionalities specific to one application. They exist to support reuse within one application or to enable business process services [24].
4. **Entity services:** (Also called information or data services) they provide access to and management of the persistent data of legacy software systems. They support actions on data (CRUD) and may have side-effects (i.e., they modify shared data).

Domain-neutral Services are services that provide functionalities to develop, use, and compose domain-specific services:

1. **Utility services:** They provide some cross-cutting functionalities required by domain-specific services. Logging and authentication services are examples of Utility services.
2. **Infrastructure services:** They allow users deploying and running SOA systems. They include services for communication routing, protocol conversion, message processing and transformation. They are sometimes provided by an Enterprise Service Bus (ESB).

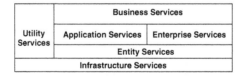

Fig. 1. Taxonomy of service types

In our prior work [11], we validated this taxonomy through an industrial survey with practitioners who participated in real migration projects to SOA. None of them mentioned the identification of other types of services during the migration process. In the following, we will consider the identification of only Utility, Entity and Application services and detail how we can identify such types of services through the analysis of the source code of legacy software systems. In fact, non service-oriented legacy systems are likely not to contain *infrastructure services* and, thus, we do not consider this type of services in our analysis. Second, we do not distinguish between *Application services* and *Enterprise services* because they only differ in terms of scope of reuse: within a single system vs. across systems. Also, we do not consider *Business services* because (1) they orchestrate other services, such as *Enterprise* and *Application services*, and (2) other sources of information, e.g., business process models, are required to detect them.

3   Service Identification by Type: Our Approach

Figure 2 summarizes our SI approach, *ServiceMiner*, which consists of two phases: (1) a *pre-processing phase* in which we build the call graph of the system based on source code analyses, perform an initial clustering of highly connected classes, and compute the code metrics used in the services detection rules and (2) a *processing phase* in which we apply rules on the generated clusters to filtrate, reorganize, and classify them to identify candidate services and their types.

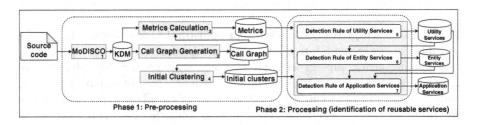

Fig. 2. Overview of *ServiceMiner*

3.1   Pre-processing Phase

Call Graph Generation. Our SI rules in Table 1 use code metrics, such as fanin and fanout, computed on the *call graph* of the legacy system. Thus, in a first step, we parse the source code of the legacy system and build its call graph. Legacy systems come in different languages and may combine several technologies. The OMG *Knowledge Discovery Metamodel* (KDM) [26] was defined to represent (legacy) systems at different levels of abstraction, regardless of languages and technologies. Thus, we use MoDISCO [27], an Eclipse-based open-source implementation of the KDM that provides (1) an extensible parsing framework to obtain KDM models from files in different languages and (2) a framework to navigate the KDM models, which we extend to generate call graphs of legacy systems.

Metrics Calculation. Our rules use class-level and method-level metrics. We use the call graphs obtained in the previous step to compute class-level metrics. For the sake of simplifying the implementation of our SI approach, we use *Understand*[1] to compute method-level metrics. We also analyze the static relationships between the modules of the systems and assign a weight to each of them according to their relative importance. A module may be a procedure, an object, or any other piece of software depending on the programming language. A relationship may be *generalization, aggregation,* or *association,* between classes in object-oriented systems for example. The total relationship strength between a pair of related modules is:

$$Weight(C_i, C_j) = \sum_{t=1}^{T} W_t \times NR_t$$

where C_i and C_j are modules, T is the number of relationships, W_t the weight assigned to a relationship type t, and NR_t the number of type t relationships between C_i and C_j. We study the relationships to ensure that only related modules are grouped together in the following steps.

Initial Clustering: Identification of Functional Groupings. The SI rules in Table 1 apply to candidate clusters that group functionalities in a legacy system. Finding such groupings within a call graph is akin to a call-graph clustering problem. We rely on Kruskal's maximum spanning-tree algorithm [28] to generate our initial set of clusters because (1) it is an efficient polynomial-time algorithm for generating clusters based on a graph structure, (2) it was used by several state-of-the-art SI approaches [7,29], and (3) a free implementation of the algorithm is provided in the open-source Java library *Jgrapht*, which can be easily integrated into our implementation. To enhance the clustering results of the spanning-tree algorithm, we put the modules that are reachable only from certain other modules in the same cluster. For example in case of object-oriented systems, if a class A is only accessible from a class B and the two classes are not in the same cluster then they must be grouped in same one.

3.2   Processing Phase: Identification of Reusable Services

Not all the clusters qualify as candidate services. In this step, we select the functional groupings/clusters to migrate while considering the different types of services. We first discuss service types and their code patterns qualitatively and then express them as rules (see Table 1).

Each type of service is mutually exclusive and their detection is hierarchical: first we detect candidate *Utility services*. Within the remaining groupings, we detect *Entity* and *Application services* as follows:

---

[1] http://www.scitools.com.

1. **Utility services:** They provide highly generic functionalities that are separate from domain-specific business processes and reusable across a range of business functionalities [2]. We detect Utility services by identifying groupings that satisfy the rule described in Table 1: high fanin (groupings that are highly solicited/called) and low fanout (groupings that do not call many other clusters). Utility services are *domain-neutral* so the identified groupings should not be persistent or contain database queries.
2. **Entity services:** They represent and manage *domain-specific* business entities, such as products, invoices. They are *data-centric* and reusable by other *domain-specific* services, such as Application services. We classify a grouping as an Entity service with (1) high fanin, (2) low fanout, (3) persistent modules, (4) access to the infrastructure (e.g., database), and (5) fine grained.
3. **Application services:** They are domain-specific and provide business functionalities specific to one system. They have low fanin compared to Entity and Utility services. They can also compose functionalities provided by Entity services. They generally perform complex computation. We use McCabe complexity metric as well as error handling capabilities to measure complexity computation. We classify a grouping as an Application service if it has (1) a call to at least one Entity service, (2) a high McCabe complexity, and–or (3) an error handling.

Table 1. Detection rules of services according to their types

Service type	Detection rules
Utility services	Very High Fanin **AND** Very Low Fanout **AND** **Not** persistent
Entity services	**Not** Utility service **AND** High Fanin **AND** Low Fanout **AND** Persistent **AND** Access to infrastructure **AND** Fine grained
Application services	**Not** Utility **AND** **Not** Entity **AND** Low Fanin **AND** (Call to Entity ≥ 1 **OR** High McCabe Complexity **OR** Error Handling)

4 Experimental Validation

Our validation divides into (1) a quantitative validation of *ServiceMiner* on a case study in comparison to a ground-truth, (2) a qualitative validation of the identified services that are related to a particular feature of our case study, and (3) a comparison of our identification results with those of two other state-of-the-art approaches [5,7].

4.1 Case Study

As case study, we choose *Compiere* because it is one of the few available, large, and open-source *legacy* system available on the Internet. Compiere is a *legacy system* because it is a large ERP system with a long history, first introduced by *Aptean* in 2003[2]. It provides businesses, government agencies, and non-profit organizations with flexible and low-cost ERP features[3], such as business partners management, monitoring and analysis of business performance, control of manufacturing operations, warehouse management (automating logistics), purchasing (automating procurement to payment), materials management (inventory receipts, shipments, etc.), and sales order management (quotes, book orders, etc.). It supports different databases, such as Oracle and PostgreSQL. We use Compiere v3.3 because (1) it is the first stable release of the system, (2) it was released more than 15 years ago, (3) it includes 2,716 classes for more than 530 KLOC, and (4) it is not service-oriented.

4.2   Ground-Truth Architecture

We need a *ground-truth* service-oriented architecture of Compiere to assess our approach. We asked two independent Ph.D. and Master's students to identify services in Compiere. They relied on several artifacts to build manually the ground-truth architecture by (1) analyzing the system, (2) understanding it, and (3) extracting its reusable parts that could become services. They used *Understand* to recover its design and to visualize class dependencies. They also generated views of its call graph that we make available online[4]. They also reviewed extensively the system documentation as well as its source code to have the best possible understanding and accurately identify services that can be integrated in the targeted SOA-based system. They found 473 services, which they annotated manually according to their type.

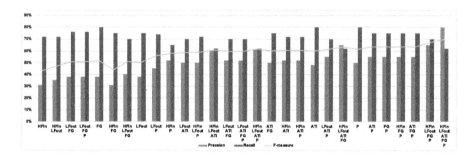

Fig. 3. Evaluation of the detection rules of Entity Services

---

[2] http://www.aptean.com.

[3] http://www.compiere.com/products/capabilities/.

[4] http://si-serviceminer.com.

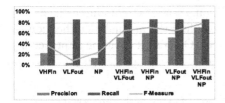

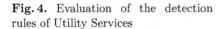

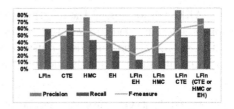

Fig. 4. Evaluation of the detection rules of Utility Services

Fig. 5. Evaluation of the detection rules of Application Services

4.3   Quantitative Validation

We applied *ServiceMiner* on Compiere to show its practical accuracy in identifying services in an existing system by considering, for each service type, several combinations of the criteria related to each rule. We measured precision, recall, and F-measure for each rule and report the results in Figs. 3, 4, and 5.

For example, for Utility services, we considered several possible combinations of the criteria, such as *"very high fanin"*, *"very low fanout"*, and *"Not persistent"*. We tested all possible combinations of these criteria and measured precision, recall, and F-measure for each rule. As shown by Fig. 4, the best F-measure is obtained when considering the three criteria to identify such type of services: considering clusters with only very high fanin or very low fanout or clusters that are only not persistent leads to poor precision values.

We did the same evaluation process to study the effectiveness of the detection rules for Entity and Application services. As shown by Figs. 3, 4, and 5, the best F-measure values were obtained when applying all the detection rules detailed in Sect. 3.2, which we used in *ServiceMiner* to identify in Compiere 403 services: 24 Application services, 278 Entity services, and 101 Utility services. We report in Table 2 the accuracy of *ServiceMiner*: a precision of 77.9%, a recall of 66.4%, and a F-measure of 71.7%.

Table 2 shows that the best accuracy of *ServiceMiner* pertained to Utility services with a precision of 77.9% and a recall of 86%. The identified Utility services relate to logging, Web uploading, printing, etc. For Entity services, we obtained a precision of 80.2%, a recall of 62.3%, and a F-measure of 70.1% with services for products, orders, invoices, etc. We missed some Entity services that have a low fanin/a high fanout because of our choice of metrics and thresholds, which could be refined by the developers when applied to their own systems. We observed a precision of 75%, a recall of 60%, and a F-measure of 66.7% for Application services, which relate to payment processing, tax calculation, and inventory management. The identification of Application services depends on the previous identifications of Entity and Utility services and, thus, false-positive Application services were mainly due to some Entity and Utility services being incorrectly labeled as Application services, such as caching-related services and Web-project deployment services.

Although we missed the identification of some services, we reduced the developers' effort needed to identify services by avoiding the manual identification of at least 66% of the candidate reusable services. Our recall could be improved by setting different thresholds and iterating through the identification process.

Table 2. Overview of service identification accuracy with *ServiceMiner*

Service type	# Services	Precision	Recall	F-measure
Application	24	(18/24) 75.0%	(18/30) 60.0%	66.7%
Entity	278	(223/278) 80.2%	(223/358) 62.3%	70.1%
Utility	101	(73/101) 72.3%	(73/85) 86.0%	78.6%
Total	403	(314/403) 77.9%	(314/473) 66.4%	71.7%

4.4 Qualitative Validation

We apply *ServiceMiner* on Compiere to identify relevant services in the system. We take the example of the sales orders management in Compiere and detail how *ServiceMiner* helps practitioners identify services related to this feature.

Sales orders management entails quotations, sales orders, and invoicing, linked to the shipment of goods to customers. The initial clustering step of our approach builds a set of candidate clusters that we then filtrate with our detection rules to identify candidate services. First, we identify Utility services by applying the first rule in Table 1, which yields Utility services about logging and printing. These services provide cross-cutting functionalities called by multiple other services (e.g., sales) with very low fanout and no persistence.

Second, we identify Entity services, i.e., clusters representing business entities. They refer to the business entities of the system, such as products, invoices, business partners, warehouses, and bank statements. These entities are persistent, have access to the database, and are invoked by other domain-specific services (e.g., Application and Business services).

Third, we apply our last detection rule in Table 1 to identify Application services among the remaining clusters. An example of Application service related to sales orders processing is the payment service responsible for generating payments of the orders based on the information provided by the invoice, business partner, and bank statement Entity services. It is also responsible for handling errors when the payment is unsuccessful.

We obtained architecturally significant candidate services thanks to the application of our type-aware service identification approach on Compiere. We believe that it can assist practitioners in the identification of candidate services because it automates the SI process of Utility, Entity, and Application services with acceptable precision and recall.

4.5 Comparison with State-of-the-Art Approaches

We chose two existing approaches to compare their results against those of *ServiceMiner*: *MOGA-WSI* [7] and *Service Cutter* [5]. These two were the only available approaches. *MOGA-WSI* uses spanning trees and provides candidate services with different levels of inter-service coupling. It relies on genetic and multi-objective optimization algorithms to refine an initial set of services. It also considers a set of managerial goals, such as cost effectiveness, ease of assembly, customization, reusability, and maintainability. *Service Cutter* is a graph-based approach considering 16 coupling criteria and two kinds of clustering algorithms, *Girvan-Newman* (GN) [30] and *Epidemic Label Propagation* (ELP) [31], which differ in terms of their (non-)deterministic behavior.

We assess our approach with respect to a ground-truth architecture and in comparison to the two tools using measures of clustering and information retrieval: MojoFM [32], *Architecture2Architecture* (A2A) [33], precision, and recall. We rely on these metrics to study the identification results of each approach regardless of the types of services.

Table 3 lists the identification results and shows that our approach outperforms *MOGA-WSI* and *Service Cutter* for all the reported metrics. We tried several configurations for both tools but all showed poor results in comparison to our approach. We observed that these approaches generate very unbalanced services. For example, *MOGA-WSI* identified a service of 253 classes and 143 services of one to six classes. Similarly, *Service Cutter* (EPL) identified two coarse-grain services and 393 fine-grained ones. Although service identification using *Service Cutter* with *Girvan-Newman* is deterministic, we were limited to a maximum number of 30 services, which lead to poor identification results.

We argue that our SI approach outperforms the two other approaches because: (1) *ServiceMiner* follows a stepwise process, which identifies Utility services then Entity services and finally Application services, (2) it uses simple, straightforward metrics instead of complex goals, like maintainability, which are subjective and more difficult to define and measure, and (3) the studied state-of-the-art tools are proof of concepts, which may limit their applicability on enterprise-scale systems, such as Compiere.

Table 3. Comparison results of service identification approaches

Approach	#Services	MojoFM	A2A	Precision	Recall	F-measure
MOGA-WSI	396	11.0%	42.0%	14.0%	13.0%	13.5%
Service Cutter (EPL)	395	15.7%	51.0%	12.2%	10.3%	11.2%
Service Cutter (GN)	30	21.6%	41.0%	15.6%	9.7%	14.1%
ServiceMiner	**403**	**65.0%**	**73.0%**	**77.9%**	**66.4%**	**71.7%**

5   Discussion on the Approach

Threats to Validity. Construct validity concerns the accuracy of some observations with respect to a theory. In our validation process, we should have relied
on a real post-migration SOA-based system. However, we could not find any
open-source enterprise-scaled system that was migrated to SOA. Thus, we relied
on a *ground-truth* architecture to validate quantitatively the services identified
by our approach. We are aware that there is no single "correct" SOA for a given
legacy system. However, we relied on several artifacts (e.g., official documentations, source code analysis, etc.) and studied in-depth the system to identify
reusable sets of classes that could be packaged into services. Also, we share our
ground-truth architecture to allow others to confirm/infirm our claims. We put
the original source code as well as the identified services online[5], which also
reduces threats to reliability validity.

Our SI approach as well as its validation depend on several algorithms and
thresholds that threaten the internal validity of our results. To mitigate these
threats, (1) we implemented *MOGA-WSI* based on their original papers to the
best of our understanding and shared it for investigation and replication[6]; (2) we
used the best identification results of these tools to compare our approach; (3)
we explored the use of different metrics and threshold values; and, (4) we chose
the spanning-tree algorithm for its ease of use and available, open-source implementation. Future work should consider comparing with other algorithms to vet
further the reliability of our approach in comparison to other SI approaches.

We know that service detection rules may slightly differ from one system to
another. However, our detection rules are easily customized, being flexible and
extensible. We recommend to consider the same processing steps in the same
order than in our approach to identify the services in existing systems according
to their types. Also, legacy systems most likely embed poor design and coding
practices, e.g., code smells, that reduce the separation of concerns within/be-
tween classes, which reduces the precision/recall of static-based SI approaches.

Our case study may not be representative of all legacy software systems,
which limits the generalizability of our results but *Compiere* is large and complex
enough to validate our approach while we continue our search for other large,
open-source systems. Finally, the identified services may not be representative
of all service types, which may also limit the generalizabiltiy of our results.
Our approach is extensible to new service types. It can also be extended to
identify microservices [34] by mapping each Utility and Entity service identified
by *ServiceMiner* to a microservice and decomposing each identified Application
service into smaller microservices that each have a single responsibility.

Discussions and Recommendations. We believe that our approach is beneficial for both researchers and practitioners interested in migrating legacy systems

---

[5] http://si-serviceminer.com/ICSOC-2020-Replication.
[6] https://github.com/MPoly2018/MOGA-WSI.

to SOA because (1) we automate the SI process, which is one of the most labor-intensive step for migrating such systems to SOA; (2) our SI approach yields to architecturally significant candidate services that can be packaged and integrated in the targeted SOA-based system while identifying their types; (3) our approach offers the possibility to prioritize the identification of specific service types based on their importance and the architectural/business needs of the migration process; and, (4) our approach is extensible to new technologies/languages, thanks to its use of the KDM metamodel as intermediate representation for C, C++, Python, etc.

Finally, we recommend to consider service types to identify services in existing systems to improve accuracy. We also recommend to order the services to be migrated. We suggest to start first with Utility services because they are highly reusable and invoked by other services in the system (e.g., Entity, Application, Business process services, etc.); second, to continue with Entity services because they manage and represent the business entities of the system and are used by the other services; third, to identify Application services as they compose functionalities provided by Entity services; finally, to identify Business services that manage and compose/use the previous types of services.

6   Conclusion and Future Work

In this paper, we proposed *ServiceMiner*, a type-aware service identification (SI) approach for the migration of legacy software systems to SOA. *ServiceMiner* helps during the key step of identifying reusable service candidates using a taxonomy of service types. We evaluated *ServiceMiner* on a real-world legacy ERP system and compared its results with those of two state-of-the-art SI approaches. We showed that, in general, *ServiceMiner* identified relevant, architecturally-significant services with 77.9% of precision, 66.4% of recall, and 71.7% of F-measure. Also, we showed that it outperformed the state-of-the-art SI approaches by providing more architecturally-significant services. We believe that *ServiceMiner* can thus be used to assist practitioners in the identification of candidate services in their systems.

As future work, we will consider the identification of other types of services, such as Enterprise and Business services. We will also perform a qualitative validation of the significance and relevance of the identified services with developers. We will compare other algorithms to further study the reliability of our approach. Finally, we will complete our SOA migration road-map by exploring automatic service packaging techniques to efficiently package and integrate the identified services into the targeted SOA platform.

References

1. Lewis, G., Morris, E., O'Brien, L., Smith, D., Wrage, L.: SMART: the service-oriented migration and reuse technique. Technical report, DTIC Document (2005)
2. Erl, T.: SOA Principles of Service Design. Prentice Hall PTR, Upper Saddle River (2007)
3. Khadka, R., Saeidi, A., Jansen, S., Hage, J.: A structured legacy to SOA migration process and its evaluation in practice. In: MESOCA, pp. 2–11 (2013)
4. Canfora, G., Fasolino, A.R., Frattolillo, G., Tramontana, P.: Migrating interactive legacy systems to web services. In: CSMR, p. 10 (2006)
5. Gysel, M., Kölbener, L., Giersche, W., Zimmermann, O.: Service cutter: a systematic approach to service decomposition. In: Aiello, M., Johnsen, E.B., Dustdar, S., Georgievski, I. (eds.) ESOCC 2016. LNCS, vol. 9846, pp. 185–200. Springer, Cham (2016). https://doi.org/10.1007/978-3-319-44482-6_12
6. Rodríguez-Echeverría, R., Maclas, F., Pavón, V.M., Conejero, J.M., Sánchez-Figueroa, F.: Generating a REST service layer from a legacy system. In: Escalona, M.J., Aragón, G., Linger, H., Lang, M., Barry, C., Schneider, C. (eds.) Information System Development, pp. 433–444. Springer, Cham (2014). https://doi.org/10.1007/978-3-319-07215-9_35
7. Jain, H., Zhao, H., Chinta, N.R.: A spanning tree based approach to identifying web services. Int. J. Web Serv. Res. $\mathbf{1}(1)$, 1 (2004)
8. Adjoyan, S., Seriai, A., Shatnawi, A.: Service identification based on quality metrics object-oriented legacy system migration towards SOA. In: SEKE, pp. 1–6 (2014)
9. Amiri, M.J., Parsa, S., Lajevardi, A.M.: Multifaceted service identification: process, requirement and data. ComSIS $\mathbf{13}$, 335–358 (2016)
10. Zhang, Z., Yang, H., Chu, W.C.: Extracting reusable object-oriented legacy code segments with combined formal concept analysis and slicing techniques for service integration. In: QRS, pp. 385–392 (2006)
11. Abdellatif, M., Hecht, G., Mili, H., Elboussaidi, G., Moha, N., Shatnawi, A., Privat, J., Guéhéneuc, Y.-G.: State of the practice in service identification for SOA migration in industry. In: Pahl, C., Vukovic, M., Yin, J., Yu, Q. (eds.) ICSOC 2018. LNCS, vol. 11236, pp. 634–650. Springer, Cham (2018). https://doi.org/10.1007/978-3-030-03596-9_46
12. Alahmari, S., Zaluska, E., De Roure, D.: A service identification framework for legacy system migration into SOA. In: SCC, pp. 614–617. IEEE (2010)
13. Marchetto, A., Ricca, F.: From objects to services: toward a stepwise migration approach for java applications. STTT $\mathbf{11}(6)$, 427 (2009)
14. Fuhr, A., Horn, T., Riediger, V.: Using dynamic analysis and clustering for implementing services by reusing legacy code. In: WCRE, pp. 275–279. IEEE (2011)
15. Huergo, R.S., Pires, P.F., Delicato, F.C.: MDCSIM: a method and a tool to identify services. IT Converg. Pract. $\mathbf{2}(4)$, 1–27 (2014)
16. Grieger, M., Sauer, S., Klenke, M.: Architectural restructuring by semi-automatic clustering to facilitate migration towards a service-oriented architecture. Softwaretechnik-Trends $\mathbf{34}(2)$ (2014)
17. Souza, E., Moreira, A., De Faveri, C.: An approach to align business and it perspectives during the SOA services identification. In: ICCSA, pp. 1–7 (2017)
18. Sneed, H.M., Verhoef, C., Sneed, S.H.: Reusing existing object-oriented code as web services in a SOA. In: MESOCA. IEEE, pp. 31–39 (2013)
19. Huergo, R.S., Pires, P.F., Delicato, F.C.: A method to identify services using master data and artifact-centric modeling approach. In: ACM SAC, pp. 1225–1230 (2014)

20. Selmadji, A., Seriai, A.-D., Bouziane, H.L., Mahamane, R.O., Zaragoza, P., Dony, C.: From monolithic architecture style to microservice one based on a semi-automatic approach. In: ICSA, pp. 157–168. IEEE (2020)
21. Saidani, I., Ouni, A., Mkaouer, M.W., Saied, A.: Towards automated microservices extraction using muti-objective evolutionary search. In: Yangui, S., Bouassida Rodriguez, I., Drira, K., Tari, Z. (eds.) ICSOC 2019. LNCS, vol. 11895, pp. 58–63. Springer, Cham (2019). https://doi.org/10.1007/978-3-030-33702-5_5
22. Djeloul, M.: Locating services in legacy software: information retrieval techniques, ontology and FCA based approach. In: WSEAS Transactions on Computers (Greece) (2012)
23. Chenghao, G., Min, W., Xiaoming, Z.: A wrapping approach and tool for migrating legacy components to web services. In: ICNDC, pp. 94–98 (2010)
24. Cohen, S.: Ontology and taxonomy of services in a service-oriented architecture. Arch. J. **11**(11), 30–35 (2007)
25. OpenGroup: The open group SOA reference architecture. Accessed 1 June 2020
26. Boussaidi, G.E., Belle, A.B., Vaucher, S., Mili, H.: Reconstructing architectural views from legacy systems. In: WCRE (2012)
27. Bruneliere, H., Cabot, J., Dupé, G., Madiot, F.: MoDisco: a model driven reverse engineering framework. IST **56**(8), 1012–1032 (2014)
28. Kruskal, J.B.: On the shortest spanning subtree of a graph and the traveling salesman problem. Proc. Am. Math. Soc. **7**(1), 48–50 (1956)
29. Mazlami, G., Cito, J., Leitner, P.: Extraction of microservices from monolithic software architectures. In: 2017 IEEE International Conference on Web Services (ICWS), pp. 524–531. IEEE (2017)
30. Newman, M.E., Girvan, M.: Finding and evaluating community structure in networks. Phys. Rev. E **69**(2), 026113 (2004)
31. Raghavan, U.N., Albert, R., Kumara, S.: Near linear time algorithm to detect community structures in large-scale networks. Phys. Rev. E **76**(3), 036106 (2007)
32. Wen, Z., Tzerpos, V.: An effectiveness measure for software clustering algorithms. In: Proceedings. 12th IEEE International Workshop on Program Comprehension, 2004, pp. 194–203. IEEE (2004)
33. Garcia, J., Ivkovic, I., Medvidovic, N.: A comparative analysis of software architecture recovery techniques. In: Proceedings of the 28th IEEE/ACM International Conference on Automated Software Engineering, pp. 486–496. IEEE Press (2013)
34. Newman, S.: Building Microservices: Designing Fine-grained Systems. O'Reilly Media, Inc., Sebastopol (2015)

Automated Quality Assessment of Incident Tickets for Smart Service Continuity

Luciano Baresi[1], Giovanni Quattrocchi[1(✉)], Damian Andrew Tamburri[2,3], and Willem-Jan Van Den Heuvel[3,4]

[1] Politecnico di Milano, Milan, Italy
{luciano.baresi,giovanni.quattrocchi}@polimi.it
[2] Eindhoven University of Technology, Eindhoven, Netherlands
d.a.tamburri@tue.nl
[3] Jheronimus Academy of Data Science, Eindhoven, Netherlands
W.J.A.M.vdnHeuvel@tue.nl
[4] Tilburg University, Tilburg, Netherlands

Abstract. Customer management operations, such as Incident Management (IM), are traditionally performed manually often resulting in time consuming and error-prone activities. Artificial Intelligence (AI) software systems and connected information management can help handle the discontinuities in critical business tasks. AI Incident Management (AIIM) becomes therefore a set of practices and tools to resolve incidents by means of AI-enabled organizational processes and methodologies. The software automation of AIIM could reduce unplanned interruptions of service and let customers resume their work as quick as possible.

While several techniques were presented in the literature to automatically identify the problems described in incident tickets by customers, this paper focuses on the qualitative analysis of the provided descriptions and on using such analysis within the context of an AI-enabled business organizational process. When an incident ticket does not describe properly the problem, the analyst must ask the customer for additional details which could require several long-lasting interactions. This paper overviews *ACQUA*, an AIIM approach that uses machine-learning to automatically assess the quality of ticket descriptions with the goals of removing the need of additional communications and guiding the customers to properly describe the incident.

Keywords: Incident Management · Service continuity · Digital transformation · Artificial intelligence · Natural Language Processing

1 Introduction

Modern companies more and more require data-driven corporate services as drivers for better quality and for saving money: the more data companies can

© Springer Nature Switzerland AG 2020
E. Kafeza et al. (Eds.): ICSOC 2020, LNCS 12571, pp. 492–499, 2020.
https://doi.org/10.1007/978-3-030-65310-1_35

collect, the more "observable" they become. Stakeholders can then exploit these data to carry out dedicated analyses and react in a more appropriate and timely way, with positive effects on the organizational performance of the company. Successful companies, therefore, are those that harness the benefits of automation, data analytics, and connected advanced human-machine interfaces [16].

In this context, service management—and specifically service *incident* management (IM)—is the set operations and processes that manages customer services during their utilization, e.g., through the integration of tools and best-practices [8]. One of the key aspects of IM is to provide *service continuity* [10], that is, the capability of preventing, predicting, and managing service incidents with the goal of maintaining the desired quality of service (QoS) during and after unexpected events. These practices do not only aim to keep users engaged and satisfied of the services they use.

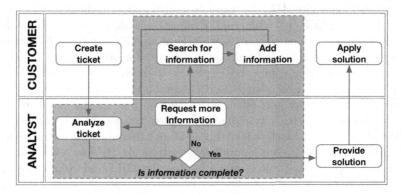

Fig. 1. Customer-Analyst interactions when no automation is in place.

If no automation is in place, IM requires that customers and analysts interact through a workflow similar to the one presented in Fig. 1. Customers describe incidents through (*service incident*) tickets while analysts manually inspect them and provide a solution. Several research efforts have already tried to automate this process [6] but mostly concentrate on the semantic analysis of incident descriptions. These works assume that customer inputs are always sufficiently detailed to perform an analysis, while this in practice could not be true. Users may not interact with the failed component directly and their description of the incident could well be partial or unclear [7]. Consequently, analysts typically interact with customers for extra inputs (as shown in the colored area of Fig. 1), but this slows down ticket resolution—and hence, proper service operations—dramatically.

What is more, although IM approaches have been studied since the seventies [19], the resolution of incident tickets is still mainly done manually by analysts, strongly based on their experience and on interactions with customers [17]. This means that this task is one of the most time consuming and fallible activities [9, 21].

To address the problem, the paper presents *ACQUA* (*Automatic tiCket Quality Assessment*), an approach based on Machine Learning (ML) that aims to reduce—and eventually eliminate—the need of many customer-analyst iterations. *ACQUA* automatically evaluates the quality of incident descriptions and notifies the customer in case additional details are required. *ACQUA* is part of a novel IM family of approaches and techniques that we call AIIM—and that fuses Artificial-Intelligence (AI) with practices from Incident Management.

ACQUA consists of three main activities: i) *feature engineering*, that is, the extraction of meaningful characteristics and metrics from an initial dataset of incident tickets ii) *service ticket modeling*, that is, the creation of different models from the extracted features that are able to evaluate the quality of new, unseen, service tickets, and iii) *service operations validation*, that is, the selection of one of the produced models based on their validated performance over available data as part of conventional Machine-Learning operations.

We plan to evaluate *ACQUA* through comparison with three state-of-the-art approaches: (1) BLEU [18] (BilinguaL Evaluation Understudy) (2) ROUGE [13] (Recall-Oriented Understudy for Gisting Evaluation), and (3) a baseline that uses a simple heuristic for computing the quality of incident tickets. On the one hand, the two reference approaches exploit well-known metrics used in the field of Natural Language Processing (NLP) to evaluate text quality; on the other hand, the baseline approach offers an optimistic take at the problem. To do that we will utilize a real-life industrial implementation and experimentation conducted on a real dataset provided by a large banking corporation (from now on called BANK) in The Netherlands We consider *ACQUA* as a valid first step in the direction of more autonomous large-scale AIIM and connected service governance operations.

The paper is organized as follows. Section 2 discusses some significant related work. Section 3 illustrates the research questions, and methodology used to build *ACQUA*. Section 4 describes the details of *ACQUA* and Sect. 5 concludes the paper.

2   Related Work

Given that downtime causes monetary loss [3], Incident Management became a key activity for businesses, and several works in the literature were presented in order to enhance Service Continuity [7,14]

Shao et al. [20] propose a prioritization algorithm to rank the relevance and severity of tickets according to their descriptions. This way more significant tickets are handled by analysts before the others and service continuity is improved. *ACQUA* and this work are complementary. Our approach can be used as a preliminary step to analyze the quality of the ticket and, when users are able to provide enough details, the ticket can be ranked and processed accordingly.

Gupta et al. [6] analyze the input requests made by analysts to customers to understand how they impact the user experience. When calculating resolution time, the time waiting for user inputs is not counted. Hence, they distinguish

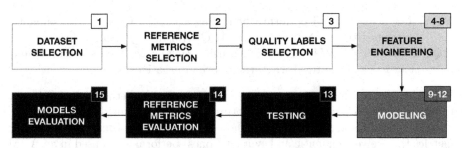

Fig. 2. The *ACQUA* methodology, an overview.eps

between two types of input requests: real and tactical. Real requests are sent to effectively seek for useful additional details, while tactical ones are merely raised to stop the downtime counting. Therefore, they created a system to automatically detect tactical input requests using algorithm TF-IDF [2] for the decision process and Principal Component Analysis [22] to reduce the dimensions composing the feature space. This work does not validate the quality of the user ticket as *ACQUA* does but the working efficiency of analysts during the resolution phase.

3   The *ACQUA* Methodology

This paper addresses the problem of evaluating the quality of service incident tickets in order to speed-up their resolution. Indeed, the research effort concentrates on *how the quality of input text can be measured in the context of Incident Management*. With this goal we present *ACQUA*, a 15-step methodology— tailored from the Cross-Industry Standard Process for Data-Mining (CRISP-DM) [4]—shown in Fig. 2.

The figure illustrates a concrete overview of the *ACQUA* AIIM methodology in a simple box-and-line notation. *ACQUA* is based on machine learning and employs different types of features and classifiers in order to predict the quality of incident tickets. *ACQUA* is composed of four main types of actions. First, preliminary actions (steps 1–3) are depicted in white boxes and are explained in the rest of this section. Second, in feature engineering tasks (steps 4–8, shown in the light gray box) different types of features are extracted and combined in meaningful datasets. Third, in modeling phase (steps 9–12, shown in the dark gray boxes) different classifiers are trained using selected features. Finally, black boxes represent the evaluation actions (steps 13–15) which will reported in our future work.

In order to properly assess *ACQUA* we formulated the following research questions.

RQ1 How do existing state-of-the-art metrics (i.e., *reference metrics*) perform when evaluating the quality of incident tickets?

RQ2 How does *ACQUA* perform when using *reference metrics* as features for ML classifiers in oder to predict the quality of incident tickets?

RQ3 How does *ACQUA* perform when using *deductive features* (i.e., semantic characteristics of the text) w.r.t. *ACQUA* using *reference metrics*?

RQ4 How does *ACQUA* perform when using *embeddings* (i.e., structural characteristics of the text) w.r.t. the above alternatives?

With the first research question we aim to understand whether state-of-the-art textual quality metrics are able to capture the quality of incident descriptions. Subsequently RQs 2, 3, 4 investigate how different types of features (reference metrics themselves, semantic and syntactic ones) perform when used in an AIIM approach.

The data used in this study were obtained (step 1) by exporting the tickets from the IM system (ServiceNow[1]) of BANK. Both customers and analysts of BANK are Dutch speaker therefore the tickets are mostly written in Dutch or a dialect[2]. The 77010 tickets collected in the dataset from September 2016 to April 2019 contain an average of 34 words each and one third of them (23874) required the analyst ask further details to the customer. Reference metrics selection (step 2) refers to the study of the literature in order to find existing metrics that could be used to obtain insights on the quality of text inputs.

Being tickets written by customers in natural language, we identified two metrics, the ones that obtained the highest similarity with the human perception of quality, widely used in the context of Natural-Language Processing: BLEU and ROUGE. These metrics evaluate the quality of *candidate text* (often machine generated) with respect to high-quality reference texts [13].

The original dataset does not contain any indications of the quality of the tickets. Therefore, in step 3 we defined five labels with an associated value between 0 (insufficient details) and 4 (well-described incident). Moreover, we manually labeled each ticket according to the comments left by the analyst and our perception of their quality.

4   Feature Engineering and Modeling

In this section we present the feature engineering and modeling steps (4–12) of *ACQUA*.

The selected dataset contains a large amounts of unstructured data requiring a preliminary processing phase (step 4). Indeed, the customer description of the incident, the comments between analyst and customer and the analyst closing notes are all written in plain text without any structure. For structured columns minor processing was necessary in order to reduce the noise and being able to properly compare values. The preprocessing consists in the following six activities: i) *filtering* to remove missing data, ii) *text transformation* to remove special characters and punctuation, iii) *domain transformation* to eliminate from the ticket text partial or blank parts, iv) *encoding* to transform values and labels

---

[1] https://www.servicenow.com/products/incident-management.html.

[2] A negligible amount of tickets contain also sentences (error messages) written in English.

onto pre-defined numbers, v) *tokenization* to obtain the list of words, and vi) *stemming* to normalized words to a root form.

4.1 Feature Extraction and Selection

ACQUA uses three types of features: reference metrics, deductive and embeddings. In step 5, we computed the value of BLEU and for ROUGE each ticket. These values, in addition to be evaluated as quality metrics in step 14, are then used them as input features for classifiers to understand whether they can provide additional insights during training.

Deductive features are features extracted from the description of an incident and are mainly related to the semantic of what the user describes (step 6). They are a set of boolean features, that indicate if a specific word is mentioned in the text. The intuition is that the occurrence of word like "error" or "warning" prelude to a detailed description of the problem. If incident related keywords (e.g.,"power drain" or 'restart") are included there could be high chances that the incident is explained. In addition to boolean deductive feature, we include also numerical ones that are related to the length of the description such as the number of tokens and the sum of the token length for a total of 13 deductive features.

Embeddings (step 7) are features encoded as sparse vectors obtained from words or documents. They help a machine understand natural language by placing similar text inputs close to one another [12,15]. *ACQUA* uses two embeddings techniques, namely Word2Vec, and Doc2Vec.

Word2Vec is a neural network language model that constructs a log-linear classification network that produces a vector [15] where each word is represented as a point in the space (a vector) and related words are located closely to each other. In *ACQUA* Word2Vec is used to create a machine readable feature from textual, unstructured data that can be used for further (algebraic) calculations.

Doc2Vec is another neural network language model that we used to create embedding features. While Word2Vec computes a feature for every word in a text corpus (e.g., an incident ticket), Doc2Vec computes a feature vector for every document/ticket [12]. This eliminates the need of a vector aggregation step as required by Word2Vec and facilitate the comparison among similar tickets. On the other hand, given that Doc2Vec reasons on a coarse granularity, it is less tolerant to word misspelling compared to Word2Vec. Since a significant amount of ticket description contains misspellings we used both the methods in *ACQUA*.

In the last step of feature engineering (step 8) we generated datasets containing the different types of features in order to answer RQ2, RQ3 and RQ4 in our future evaluation.

4.2 Service Ticket Modeling

The first step of modeling is the selection of classifiers that using the selected features can produce meaningful estimation models for the quality assessment of incident tickets (step 9). Having to deal with different set of features, *ACQUA* does not rely on a single classifier but it uses 5 different types: *random forest* [1], *logistic regression* [2], *k-nearest neighbors* [1], *gradient boost* [5], and a dummy *most frequent* classifier.

Before training the models (step 12), the dataset is split in different parts. 20% of the data are removed and used for testing in step 13. On the remaining 80% *ACQUA* applies the stratified K-Fold [11] algorithm (step 10) to properly tune the classifiers parameters. Data are split into k consecutive partitions (or folds) each of them of approximately the same size. The training and validation sets (i.e., the dataset used to adjust classifiers parameters) are generated in k phase. On each phase one fold, in turn, is used as validation set while the other $k - 1$ as training set. In *ACQUA* we used k equals to 10.

For each of the aforementioned classifiers, hyper-parameter (i.e., classifier parameters) tuning was manually applied in step 11 by taking into account the best practices when dealing with class imbalance and to avoid overfitting. The tuning consisted in an iterative process of training-validation-parameters adjustment-training until reaching satisfactory performance, as envisioned in the CRISP-DM standard process [4]. Finally, in step 12 models are trained with proper tuning parameters to be ready for being evaluated.

In our future work we will present how we tested the models (step 13) and how we compared with reference metrics (step 14) and the performance of the various classifiers (15).

5   Conclusions and Future Work

Incident Management and Service Continuity are key aspects of almost all the businesses to reduce or avoid the costs of downtimes. This paper presented *ACQUA*, a AIIM methodology for assessing the quality of incident tickets in order to minimize the long-lasting communications between customers and analysts. In the feature we plan to carry out an extensive evaluation of the approach.

Acknowledgment. We thank Dr. Jeffrey Vervoort for his valuable contribution to this work carried out during hist master thesis. Finally, some of the authors' work is partially supported by the European Commission grant no. 787061 (H2020), ANITA, European Commission grant no. 825040 (H2020), RADON, European Commission grant no. 825480 (H2020), SODALITE.

References

1. Aggarwal, C.C.: Text classification: basic models. Machine Learning for Text, pp. 113–157. Springer, Cham (2018). https://doi.org/10.1007/978-3-319-73531-3_5
2. Aly, M.: Survey on multiclass classification methods. Technical report (2005)
3. Cao, C., Zhan, Z.: Incident management process for the cloud computing environments. In: 2011 IEEE International Conference on Cloud Computing and Intelligence Systems, pp. 225–229 (2011)

4. Chapman, P., et al.: CRISP-DM 1.0 step-by-step data mining guide. Technical report, The CRISP-DM consortium, August 2000

5. Chen, T., Guestrin, C.: XGBoost: a scalable tree boosting system. In: Proceedings of the 22nd ACM SIGKDD International Conference on Knowledge Discovery and Data Mining, pp. 785–794. Association for Computing Machinery (2016)

6. Gupta, M., Asadullah, A., Padmanabhuni, S., Serebrenik, A.: Reducing user input requests to improve it support ticket resolution process. Empir. Softw. Eng. **23**(3), 1664–1703 (2018)

7. Gupta, R., Prasad, K.H., Luan, L., Rosu, D., Ward, C.: Multi-dimensional knowledge integration for efficient incident management in a services cloud. In: 2009 IEEE International Conference on Services Computing, pp. 57–64 (2009)

8. Iden, J., Eikebrokk, T.R.: Implementing it service management: a systematic literature review. Int. J. Inf. Manag. **33**(3), 512–523 (2013)

9. Janssen, P.: IT-Servicemanagement volgens ITIL, 3rd edn. Pearson Benelux, Gatwickstraat 1, 1043 GK, Amsterdam (2008)

10. Klems, M., Tai, S., Shwartz, L., Grabarnik, G.: Automating the delivery of it service continuity management through cloud service orchestration. In: 2010 IEEE Network Operations and Management Symposium-NOMS 2010, pp. 65–72. IEEE (2010)

11. Kuhn, M., Johnson, K.: Applied Predictive Modeling, p. 1. Springer, New York (2013). https://doi.org/10.1007/978-1-4614-6849-3

12. Le, Q., Mikolov, T.: Distributed representations of sentences and documents. In: International Conference on Machine Learning, pp. 1188–1196 (2014)

13. Lin, C.Y.: ROUGE: a package for automatic evaluation of summaries. In: Text summarization Branches Out, pp. 74–81 (2004)

14. Liu, R., Lee, J.: IT incident management by analyzing incident relations. In: Liu, C., Ludwig, H., Toumani, F., Yu, Q. (eds.) ICSOC 2012. LNCS, vol. 7636, pp. 631–638. Springer, Heidelberg (2012). https://doi.org/10.1007/978-3-642-34321-6_49

15. Mikolov, T., Chen, K., Corrado, G., Dean, J.: Efficient estimation of word representations in vector space. arXiv e-prints, January 2013

16. Mithas, S., Ramasubbu, N., Sambamurthy, V.: How information management capability influences firm performance. MIS Q. **35**(1), 237–256 (2011)

17. Motahari-Nezhad, H.R., Bartolini, C., Graupner, S., Singhal, S., Spence, S.: It support conversation manager: a conversation-centered approach and tool for managing best practice it processes. In: 2010 14th IEEE International Enterprise Distributed Object Computing Conference, pp. 247–256 (2010)

18. Papineni, K., Roukos, S., Ward, T., Zhu, W.J.: BLEU: a method for automatic evaluation of machine translation. In: Proceedings of the 40th Annual Meeting on Association for Computational Linguistics, ACL 2002, Stroudsburg, PA, USA, pp. 311–318. Association for Computational Linguistics (2002)

19. Rowley, D.D.: The fires that created an incident management system (2005)

20. Shao, J., Wei, H., Wang, Q., Mei, H.: A runtime model based monitoring approach for cloud. In: 2010 IEEE 3rd International Conference on Cloud Computing, pp. 313–320 (2010)

21. Wang, Q., Song, J., Liu, L., Luo, X., XinHua, E.: Building it-based incident management platform. In: 5th International Conference on Pervasive Computing and Applications, pp. 359–364, December 2010

22. Wold, S., Esbensen, K., Geladi, P.: Principal component analysis. Chemom. Intell. Lab. Syst. **2**(1–3), 37–52 (1987)

API-Prefer: An API Package Recommender System Based on Composition Feature Learning

Yancen Liu and Jian Cao[✉]

Department of Computer Science and Engineering, Shanghai Jiao Tong University,
Shanghai, China
{LiuYancen,cao-jian}@sjtu.edu.cn

Abstract. With the exponential increase in Web Application Programming Interfaces (APIs), selecting appropriate APIs to construct a mashup is a challenging task. When multiple APIs are put together, their overall function is not just a superposition of their individual functions in many cases. Unfortunately, the approaches proposed to date do not sufficiently model the synthetical functions of the combined APIs. In this paper, an *API Package recommender* system based on composition *feature learning* (API-Prefer) is proposed. API-Prefer tries to learn the composition features of an API pair. Then the composition features can be used to predict whether this API pair can be adopted by a mashup or not. Specifically, a deep neural network is designed for composition feature learning and adoption probability prediction in API-Prefer. Since there is a large amount of API pairs, API-Prefer applies a strategy to select the potential APIs first, then the API packages can be discovered based on the predicted scores over multiple API pairs. Experiments on a real-world dataset show API-Prefer is significantly better than the comparative methods.

Keywords: API package recommendation · Composition feature · Mashup · API · Neural network

1 Introduction

Web services are important components of a modern information system. As a type of Web services, the number of Web Application Programming Interfaces (or APIs, for short) is increasing exponentially on the Web. In order to help developers or non-IT professionals make use of APIs, various tools have been developed. Of them, mashups are becoming a commonly used approach, through which multiple APIs can be combined together to provide more comprehensive functions. Since the number of available APIs on the Web is huge, it is a challenging task to find the APIs we need. To better assist mashup development, we recommend multiple sets of cooperative APIs where each of them can achieve

© Springer Nature Switzerland AG 2020
E. Kafeza et al. (Eds.): ICSOC 2020, LNCS 12571, pp. 500–507, 2020.
https://doi.org/10.1007/978-3-030-65310-1_36

the functions of a mashup as a whole. These sets of cooperative APIs are often referred to as *"API Packages"*.

We propose an *API Package recommender* system based on composition *feature learning* (API-Prefer). API-Prefer extracts the *composition features* of an API pair through a neural network. The contributions of this paper are as follows:

- Based on analyzing the relationships between APIs and mashups, we design a deep learning model to learn the composition features of API pairs to support both *shallow composition relationships* and *deep composition relationships*.
- We propose API-Prefer, an API package recommender system for mashup. API-Prefer is based on composition feature learning. It also includes the strategies to avoid unnecessary calculations and generate the final packages.
- We compare API-Prefer with baselines and state-of-art models and the experimental results show that API-Prefer is significantly better than the counterparts in terms of the recall and precision.

2   Related Work

API (or Web Service) recommendation for mashups has been a popular research topic, and various methods have been proposed in recent years.

When an API is published, its name, description, or tags are often provided. These methods utilize traditional information retrieval ways to select the recommended APIs by matching the description of the mashup with the API description. For example, in [1], a vector space model is used for service retrieval. Recently, researchers began to adopt more advanced technology to extract the semantic relationship between mashups and APIs.

With the continuous development of machine learning and deep neural network in recent years, some methods combining deep learning with service recommendation have emerged. In [2], a method to extract user preference embeddings to personalize and precisely recommend APIs to mashup developers is proposed. Although these approaches try to learn more latent relationships between mashups and APIs through the deep learning model, they don't learn the synthetical functions of composed APIs. Furthermore, these approaches still recommend an API list instead of an API package.

The frequent co-occurrence set-based approach applies some traditional data mining technology to discover frequent API sets. For example, in [3], a method to mine frequent API pairs for recommendation is proposed. An information-retrieval based approach can be combined with the frequent co-occurrence set-based approach. For example, a multi-level relational network is proposed to obtain the comprehensive relationships among topics, tags and APIs [4].

Our model is also a hybrid approach. Different from the other models, our model learns the composition features of API pairs through a deep neural network, which can support both shallow composition and deep composition relationships.

3   API-Prefer: An API Package Recommender System Based on Composition Feature Learning

3.1   Composition Features of APIs

Let us give specific explanation of *composition features* through two real-world examples. The first example is a mashup with the description *"Find lyrics and karaoke videos with this mashup. Record it and publish it also"*. It is based on two APIs, *YouTube API* and *LyricWiki API*. This example represents the case where we can search APIs based on the phrases in the mashup descriptions in a straightforward way, which is called a *shallow composition relationship*. The second example is *RueFind*, whose description is *"RueFind is a travel application which tracks interesting tourist attractions around the world. Users can add, rank or create lists of their favorite attractions"*. *Google Map API* and *Yahoo Weather API* are used in *RueFind*. According to the descriptions, the main function of *RueFind* is to share information on tourist attractions. Although travel relates to maps and weather, it cannot be matched with them directly. This fact indicates that by combining APIs with different functions, synthetical functions can be created. This is called a *deep composition relationship*.

Composition features are context-dependent, i.e., when a set of APIs is applied to mashups with very different functions, their composition features may be different. The approaches to learn composition features are introduced in Sect. 4.

3.2   Overview of API-Prefer

API package recommendation by API-Prefer consists of two stages, i.e., the training stage and the recommendation stage. During the training stage, a deep neural network that can predict whether an API pair can be applied to a mashup or not is trained. Specifically, this network uses a multiple-layer structure to learn the composition features of this API pair for a mashup. During the recommendation stage, given the mashup description, potential API pairs will be inputted to the network and the probability of this API pair being used by this mashup is outputted. Finally, a recommendation algorithm generates multiple API packages in terms of the adoption probability of API pairs and other information.

4   A Deep Neural Network for Predicting the Adoption Probabilities of an API Pair Based on Composition Feature Extraction

The descriptions of mashups and APIs vary in length, so we need to embed these descriptive texts into the uniform vectors. We use the latent Dirichlet allocation topic model to extract the topic feature of the text. After tokenization, the standard steps for text data pre-processing are undertaken, these being

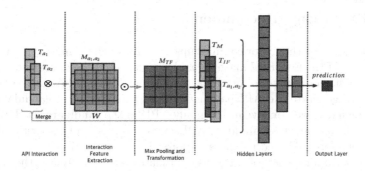

Fig. 1. The deep neural network model for predicting the adoption probability of an API pair

stemming, lemmatization and removing stop words. We transfer the descriptions of the APIs, the historical mashups and the mashup to be developed into 200-dimension LDA topic vectors (Fig. 1).

The LDA topic vector of API_1, API_2, and $mashup$ is denoted by T_{a_1}, T_{a_2} and T_M respectively, which are denoted as: $T = \{t_1, t_2, t_3, ..., t_i, ...\}$.

Since we want to mine the composition features from a pair of APIs, the interactions of the features of two APIs can yield new features. Therefore, we add an interaction layer into the network, through which all the features of two APIs interact in pairs. The results are denoted by a matrix M_{a_1,a_2} as $M_{a_1,a_2} = T_{a_1} \otimes T_{a_2}$ ($M_{i,j} = t_i^{a_1} \cdot t_j^{a_2}$).

However, not all feature interactions are equally useful. Therefore, we add a weight layer W to adjust the interaction features as $M_{TF} = M_{a_1,a_2} \odot W$ ($m_{i,j}^{CF} = (t_i^{a_1} \cdot t_j^{a_2}) \cdot w_{i,j}$). We get the interaction feature matrix M_{TF}. Then we use a 10×10 max polling filter to process the matrix, and this will turn the original matrix into a 20×20 matrix. Then we transform it to a 400×1 vector, which is the interaction feature vector T_{IF}.

We merge the topic information of API_1 and API_2 to a combination feature vector T_{a_1,a_2} as $T_{a_1,a_2} = \{max(t_1^{a_1}, t_1^{a_2}), max(t_2^{a_1}, t_2^{a_2}), ..., max(t_i^{a_1}, t_i^{a_2}), ...\}$. Then we concatenate the combination features, interaction features and mashup features together ($\{T_x = T_{a_1,a_2}, T_{IF}, T_M\}$) as the input to the multiple hidden layers of the network.

After 3 hidden layers, we use a sigmoid function in the output layer to make the prediction score between 0 and 1. The loss function for the network is cross entropy, and we also add a L2 normalization to avoid the overfitting of our model.

Therefore, through a multi-layer neural network, the composition features are actually learned from the combination features, interaction features and mashup features, which are then used to make an adoption probability prediction.

5   API Package Recommendation

We select and sort the historical mashups in terms of the similarity between the descriptions of the historical mashups and the mashup to be developed. After we obtain a sufficient number of mashups, we use the APIs used by these candidate mashups to generate the API packages. As for the number of candidate APIs, on the one hand, we don't want too many APIs in the candidate set, but on the other hand, we want the candidate API set to cover as many potential APIs as it can. Therefore, we need to find an appropriate value for it.

After obtaining a set of APIs as candidates, we can predict the adoption probability $p(API_i, API_j)$ of each API pair. By regarding each API as a node, and the adoption probability of an API pair as the weight of the edge between them, we can draw a relational network of APIs. API packages can be discovered on this network.

In order to discover API packages, we add a restriction on the network, i.e., only when $p(API_i, API_j) > max(p(API_i), p(API_j), \epsilon)$ is true, will an edge appear in this network. To discover all the effective edges for an API, we just get the possibilities between this API with all the other candidate APIs in the candidate set and use the equation above to get all the effective ones. This process is Function $SearchEdges$, which is used in the following Package Discovery Process. Then we try to discover the fully connected sub-graphs and the APIs represented by their nodes can compose packages. As a special case, a single API can also be a package when it is not in any fully connected sub-graph, provided its prediction score is higher than a threshold.

The discovery process starts from an API seed, and makes use of breadth-first search (BFS) to search for other members that are appropriate for a package. The API seeds are chosen based on the their popularity in the mashup candidate set from the largest to the smallest. For an API seed API_{Seed}, after we detect all its effective edges, then:

- If there is no effective edge for it, $p(API_{Seed})$ is compared with a threshold η. If $p(API_{Seed})$ is over the threshold, then API_{Seed} itself can be a package, otherwise, it is skipped.
- If multiple effective edges can be found, we adapt a BFS algorithm to find the fully connected sub-graph for this node. We maintain a *queue* Q_{API} and push the seed node into Q_{API} and the set Pkg first. Then each time we operate on the node API_{head}, which is the head of the Q_{API} until the Q_{API} is empty. For API_{head}, we traverse its effective edges to obtain an API list whose members are sorted in the descending order of their weights. If an API API_i from this list has effective edges with all nodes corresponding to the APIs in the set Pkg, that is, it can form a fully connection graph with these nodes, we then append it to Pkg and Q_{API}. Otherwise, we skip it and fetch the next API_{head}.

We try more API_{Seed}s till the number of packages meets the requirements.

6   Experiments

6.1   Dataset and Experiment Settings

We crawled 12,140 APIs and 6,976 mashups from Programmable Web, which is the largest mashup and API information sharing platform. There are 200 * 200 units in the Interaction Feature Extraction Layer, and we use a 10 * 10 filter for Max-pooling. The configuration of the 3 hidden layers is (200, 100, 20). And the L2 Regularization Strength λ is set to 0.001.

An important parameter in our method is the size of the candidate APIs. When the number reaches around 200, the mean cover rate of the final adopted APIs reaches 0.92, which is an appropriate parameter setting. As for the two thresholds in API package recommendation, after parameter tuning, we finally set $\epsilon = 0.86$ and $\eta = 0.92$.

6.2   Comparison Methods

Some baselines and state-of-the-arts methods are selected as the comparison methods.

- WVSM sorts the APIs by the product of similarity and popularity.
- WJaccard is similar to WVSM. The difference is it uses Jaccard similarity.
- Collaborative Filtering Method (CF) is based on TF-IDF between the mashup description texts is calculated to evaluate whether they are similar or not.
- ERTM [5] recommends the APIs based on an enhanced relational topic model, which leverages the potential Dirichlet distribution of the probabilistic topic model to extract the functional properties of APIs.
- TopicCF [6] combines the topic model with the collaborative filtering approach.
- SASR [7] models multi-dimensional social relationships among potential users, topics, mashups, and APIs using a coupled matrix model.
- MRN [4] captures the deep relationships among APIs on top of the latent topic, tag and API network.

6.3   Evaluation Metrics

We use precision, recall and f1-measure to evaluate our experimental results. $recall = \frac{TP}{(TP+FN)}$, $precision = \frac{TP}{(TP+FP)}$, $f1 - measure = \frac{2 \cdot recall \cdot precision}{(recall+precision)}$.

where precision represents the acceptance degree of users in relation to the recommendation results, recall represents the completeness of the recommendation results, and the f1-measure is the synthesis of the two evaluation indexes.

6.4   Results

Firstly, we compare the performances of all the approaches with the number of recommended APIs and the results are shown in Fig. 2. The performance of

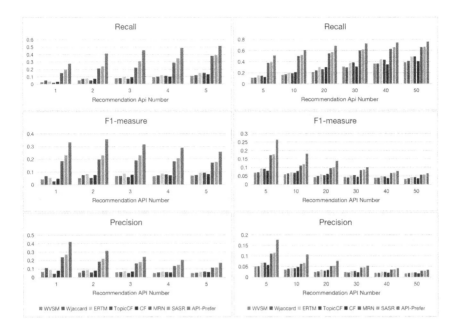

Fig. 2. Performance comparisons of all methods

the baselines is not good when either a small amount $[1, 5]$ or a large amount $[5, 50]$ of APIs are recommended. Which indicates that only considering semantic similarity and few attributes like popularity, cannot get ideal result. MRN and SASR, on the other hand, take all the features into account. Their performances are better than the previous methods. The results show that it is useful to consider multilevel relationships. However, with a recommendation number between $[1, 5]$, the performance of API-Prefer is clearly better than the others. This also reflects the effectiveness of the composition feature learning in API-Prefer.

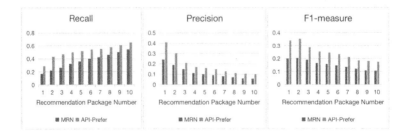

Fig. 3. Performance comparisons of API package recommendation methods

Of all the compared approaches, MRN is the only one that can recommend API packages. We compare the performances of API-Prefer and MRN with the number of API packages to be recommended. Figure 3 shows that performances of API-Prefer are significantly better than the performances of MRN.

7   Conclusions and Future Work

In this paper, we analyze the main deficiency in the current approaches of API recommendations for mashup. Therefore, we propose API-Prefer, an API package recommender system based on composition feature learning. API-Prefer learns the composition features of an API pair based on combination features, interaction features and mashup features through a deep neural network. Then, the adoption probability can be predicted based on the description of the mashup to be developed and the composition features of API pairs. Finally, the API packages can be generated based on the adoption probabilities. The performance of API-Prefer is verified through the experiments.

Our future work will focus on improving the recommendation accuracy by using advanced textual embedding techniques and considering the composition of three or more APIs also have specific features.

Acknowledgement. This work is supported by National Key Research and Development Plan (No. 2018YFB1003800).

References

1. Platzer, C., Dustdar, S.: A vector space search engine for web services. In: Third European Conference on Web Services (ECOWS 2005), pp. 9-pp. IEEE (2005)
2. Fletcher, K.: Regularizing matrix factorization with implicit user preference embeddings for web API recommendation. In: 2019 IEEE International Conference on Services Computing (SCC), pp. 1–8. IEEE (2019)
3. Maaradji, A., Hacid, H., Skraba, R., Vakali, A.: Social web mashups full completion via frequent sequence mining. In: 2011 IEEE World Congress on Services, pp. 9–16. IEEE (2011)
4. Cao, J., Lu, Y., Zhu, N.: Service package recommendation for mashup development based on a multi-level relational network. In: Sheng, Q.Z., Stroulia, E., Tata, S., Bhiri, S. (eds.) ICSOC 2016. LNCS, vol. 9936, pp. 666–674. Springer, Cham (2016). https://doi.org/10.1007/978-3-319-46295-0_46
5. Li, C., Zhang, R., Huai, J., Sun, H.: A novel approach for API recommendation in mashup development. In: 2014 IEEE International Conference on Web Services, pp. 289–296. IEEE (2014)
6. Jain, A., Liu, X., Yu, Q.: Aggregating functionality, use history, and popularity of APIs to recommend mashup creation. In: Barros, A., Grigori, D., Narendra, N.C., Dam, H.K. (eds.) ICSOC 2015. LNCS, vol. 9435, pp. 188–202. Springer, Heidelberg (2015). https://doi.org/10.1007/978-3-662-48616-0_12
7. Xu, W., Cao, J., Hu, L., Wang, J., Li, M.: A social-aware service recommendation approach for mashup creation. In: 2013 IEEE 20th International Conference on Web Services, pp. 107–114. IEEE (2013)

Tail-Latency-Aware Fog Application Replica Placement

Ali J. Fahs$^{(\boxtimes)}$ and Guillaume Pierre

Univ Rennes, Inria, CNRS, IRISA, Rennes, France
ali.fahs@irisa.fr

Abstract. Latency-sensitive applications often use fog computing platforms to place replicas of their services as close as possible to their end users. A good placement should guarantee a low tail network latency between end-user devices and their closest replica while keeping the replicas load balanced. We propose a latency-aware scheduler integrated in Kubernetes which uses simple yet highly-effective heuristics to identify suitable replica placements, and to dynamically update these placements upon any evolution of user-generated traffic.

1 Introduction

Predictable low response time is an essential property for a large range of modern applications such as augmented reality and real-time industrial IoT [1]. When such applications are hosted in Cloud platforms, their response time depends on the provisioned processing capacity and the network characteristics between the end users and the cloud servers. However, users are often dispersed across a broad geographic area far from the cloud data centers. This motivates the need for Fog computing platforms which extend Cloud platforms with additional computing resources located in the vicinity of the end users, where distributed applications may deploy one or more replicated VM or container instances [11].

Choosing the best set of fog servers where an application should deploy its replicas requires one to follow two objectives. First, the chosen placements should minimize the network latencies between end-user devices and their closest application replica. To deliver outstanding Quality-of-Experience to the users it is important that each and every issued request gets processed within tight latency bounds. We therefore follow best practice from commercial content delivery networks [19] and aim to minimize the *tail latency* rather than its mean, for example, defined as the fraction of requests incurring a latency greater than some threshold. Second, a good placement should also allow the different replicas to process reasonably well-balanced workloads. When application providers must pay for resource usage, they usually cannot afford to maintain replicas with low resource utilization, even if this may help in reducing the tail device-to-replica latency.

© Springer Nature Switzerland AG 2020
E. Kafeza et al. (Eds.): ICSOC 2020, LNCS 12571, pp. 508–524, 2020.
https://doi.org/10.1007/978-3-030-65310-1_37

Selecting a set of replica placements within a large-scale fog computing infrastructure remains a difficult problem. We first need to monitor the usage of the concerned applications to accurately identify the sources of traffic and their respective volumes. Then, we must face the computational complexity of the problem of choosing r nodes out of n such that at least $P\%$ of end-user requests can be served in less than L ms by one of the chosen nodes, and the different application replicas remain reasonably load-balanced. Replica placements must then be updated when the characteristics of end-user requests change. Finally, we need to integrate these algorithms in an actual fog orchestration platform.

We propose Hona[1], a tail-latency-aware application replica scheduler which integrates within the Kubernetes container orchestration system [24]. Hona uses Kubernetes to monitor the system resource availability, Vivaldi coordinates to estimate the network latency between nodes [5] and proxy-mity to monitor traffic sources and to route end-user traffic to nearby replicas [7]. Hona uses a variety of heuristics to efficiently explore the space of possible replica placement decisions and select a suitable one upon the initial replica placement. Finally, it automatically takes corrective re-placement actions when the characteristics of the end-user workload changes.

Our evaluations based on a 22-node testbed show that Hona's heuristics can identify placements with a tail latency very close to the theoretic optimal placement, but in a fraction of the computation time. Hona's placements also deliver an acceptable load distribution between replicas. The re-placement algorithm efficiently maintains a very low tail latency despite drastic changes in the request workload or the execution environment. Finally, we demonstrate the scalability of our algorithms with simulations of up to 500 nodes.

2   Background

2.1   Kubernetes

We base this work on the Kubernetes platform which automates the deployment, scaling and management of containerized applications in large-scale computing infrastructures [24]. A Kubernetes cluster consists of a master node which is responsible for scheduling, deploying and monitoring the applications, and a number of worker nodes which actually run the application replicas and constitute the system's computing, network and storage resources.

Application Model: Kubernetes considers an application as a set of *pods*, defined as a set of logically-related containers and data volumes to be deployed on a single machine. Application replication is ensured by deploying multiple identical pods. These pods can be then exposed to external end users as a single entity by creating a *service*, which exposes a single IP address to the end users and acts as a front end which routes requests to one of the corresponding pods.

---

[1] Hona (هنا) means "here" in Arabic.

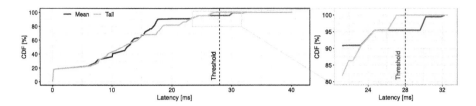

Fig. 1. Optimizing the mean or the tail latency.

Network Traffic Routing: User requests addressed to a Kubernetes service are first routed to a *gateway* node within the Kubernetes system. Every worker node can act as a gateway: the fog computing platform is in charge of routing incoming traffic to any one of them using networking technologies such as WiFi and LTE, possibly in combination with SDN/NFV. Second, the request is further routed internally to the Kubernetes system. Kubernetes services are composed of iptables or IPVS rules installed in every worker node.

Pod Scheduling: When a new set of pods is created, the Kubernetes scheduler is in charge of deciding which worker nodes will be in charge of executing them. The scheduler selects a list of nodes that are capable of executing the new pods, and stores this decision in an object store called *etcd.* In every worker node, a *kubelet* daemon periodically checks *etcd* and deploys the assigned pods.

Kubernetes' Limitations: Kubernetes was designed to manage cluster-based or cloud-based platforms. In consequence, it considers all worker nodes as functionally equivalent to one another, and it does not have any notion of node proximity to the end users. To make it suitable for fog computing scenarios, we aim to modify its scheduling components to proactively place pods in worker nodes located close to the main sources of network traffic. This allows one to considerably reduce the network latencies between the end-user devices and the nodes serving them, while keeping replicas reasonably load-balanced.

2.2   Network Proximity

In fog computing platforms, servers are located close to the end users but necessarily far from each other. Choosing a replica placement in such environment requires an accurate estimation of network latencies across the full system.

Estimating Network Latencies: Hona models network latencies using Vivaldi to accurately predict the latency between hosts without contacting all of them [5]. Hona specifically uses Serf, a mature open-source tool which maintains cluster membership and offers a robust implementation of Vivaldi coordinates [9].

Routing Requests to a Nearby Node: By default, Kubernetes gateways route every incoming request to any node holding a pod of the application regardless of its location. To serve end user requests by nearby replicas, we use `proxy-mity` which redefines the network routing rules to route requests with high probability to a nearby application replica [7]. To avoid overloading certain nodes while others

Table 1. State of the art.

Type	Ref.	Dyn.	Rep.	Obj.	Eval.	Type	Ref.	Dyn.	Rep.	Obj.	Eval.
Data	[18]	✗	✗	RT	Sim	Service	[21]	✗	✗	PX,DT	Sim
	[17]	✗	✗	RT	Sim		[22]	✗	✗	PX,RU	Sim
	[14]	✗	✗	NU	Sim		[12]	✗	✗	RT,RU	Sim
	[2]	✓	✓	RT	Sim		[26]	✗	✗	PX	Sim
	[20]	✓	✓	RT	Sim		[23]	✓	✗	PX,DT	Testbed
VM	[15]	✗	✗	NU	Sim		[10]	✗	✓	DT	Testbed
	[28]	✗	✓	NU	Sim		[16]	✓	✓	PX,RU	Testbed
	[27]	✓	✓	NU	Sim		Hona	✓	✓	PX,LB	Testbed+Sim

are underutilized, `proxy-mity` allows one to define a tradeoff between proximity and load-balancing.

Optimizing the Mean or the Tail Latency: Fog computing platforms were created for scenarios where the network distance between the user devices and the application instances must be minimized. For instance, virtual reality applications usually require a response times under 20 ms. Such applications *"need to consistently meet stringent latency and reliability constraints. Lag spikes and dropouts need to be kept to a minimum, or users will feel detached* [6].*"* Aiming to minimize the mean latency between the user devices and their closest replica does not allow one to satisfy such extremely demanding type of requirements.

To illustrate the difference between placements which optimize the mean or the tail latency, we explore 50 randomly-chosen placements of 4 replicas within a 22-nodes testbed (further described in Sect. 5). We then select the two placements which respectively minimize the mean ("Mean") and the number of requests with device-to-closest-replica latencies greater than a threshold $L = 28$ ms ("Tail"). Figure 1 compares the cumulative distribution functions of the obtained latencies delivered by the two placements. Mean delivers very good latencies overall, and it can process many more requests under 20 ms compared to Tail. However, when zooming at the end of the distribution, we see that roughly 5% of requests incur a latency greater than 28 ms, and up to 32 ms. The users who incur such latencies are disadvantaged compared to the others, and are likely to suffer from a bad user experience.

On the other hand, with the same number of replicas, Tail guarantees that 100% of requests incur latencies under 27 ms. Although the mean latency delivered by this placement is slightly greater than that of the Mean placement, this configuration is likely to provide a much more consistent experience to all the application's users.

In this work, we therefore aim to find replica placements which minimize the tail device-to-closest-replica latency, while maintaining acceptable load balancing between the replicas.

3   State of the Art

The replica placement problem has been extensively studied since the creation of the first geo-distributed environments such as content delivery networks [13], and a very large number of papers have been published on this topic. Table 1 classifies the most relevant recent publications along multiple dimensions:

Type describes *what* is being placed. Data placement [17] focuses on the download delay of cached items by placing caches in specific locations. VM placement aims to reduce network usage [15,27,28] while service placement optimizes mostly network proximity and resource utilization [16,21–23,26].

Dynamicity (Dyn) matters in systems which may experience considerable workload variations over time. Many papers focus on the initial placement problem only, without trying to update the placements upon workload changes.

Replication (Rep) indicates whether the proposed systems aim at placing a single object, or a set of replicas.

Objective (Obj) represents the optimized metrics: Response Time (RT) is the overall response latency including network and processing latency; Network Usage (NU) is the volume of backhaul traffic; Resource Utilization (RU) is the effective use of the available resources; Deployment Time (DT) is the time needed for the algorithm to find and deploy a solution; Proximity (PX) is the latency between end-user and the closest application replica; and Load Balancing (LB) is the equal distribution of load across replicas.

Evaluation (Eval) of placement algorithms is often done using simulators such as CloudSim [4] and iFogsim [8]. However, some authors also use actual prototypes and evaluate them in a real environment or a testbed.

Few papers in Table 1 propose dynamic placement algorithms for replica sets. Yu *et al.* study the placement of replicated VMs to minimize the backhaul network traffic [27]. The algorithm considers the proximity of end users to the fog nodes, but does not take the proximity between distributed fog nodes into account.

Aral *et al.* [2] and Shao *et al.* [20] propose dynamic replica placement algorithms for data services in edge computing. Similarly, Li *et al.* [16] present a replica placement algorithm to enhance data availability. All these papers use the mean latency as their metric for response time evaluation. However, as discussed in Sect. 2.2, optimizing the mean latency does not necessarily imply an improvement in the human-perceived quality of service. These papers also do not consider load balancing between replicas. Finally, only [16] has implemented and tested its proposed algorithms in a real testbed.

In contrast, to our best knowledge, Hona presents the first dynamic replica placement algorithm which aims to maintain the tail latency and the load imbalance within pre-defined bounds. Hona solves the placement problem based on the network routes as well as the origin of traffic, and has been implemented in a mature container orchestration system.

4   System Design

The objective of this work is to dynamically choose the placement of fog application replicas in a fog computing infrastructure to substantially reduce the user-experienced tail latency (thereafter referred to as Proximity) while keeping replicas load-balanced (thereafter referred to as minimizing Imbalance).

4.1   System Model

We define a fog computing infrastructure as a set of n server nodes $\Delta = \{\delta_1, \delta_2, \ldots, \delta_n\}$, where each δ_i is an object of class `Node` which holds information on the status of the node, its Vivaldi coordinates, and its current request workload. Similarly, we define a deployed application as a set of r replicas $\Phi = \{\varphi_1, \varphi_2, \ldots, \varphi_r\}$ (with $r \leq n$). A `Replica` object φ_i holds information on the status of the replica, its hosting node, its current request workload and the locations from which this workload originates.

The replica placement problem can be formulated as the mapping of every replica $\varphi_i \in \Phi$ to a server node $\delta_j \in \Delta$ to optimize some pre-defined utility metrics. It can be solved in principle by exploring the set of all possible placement decisions $\Omega = \{c_1, c_2, \ldots, c_k\}$ where $c_i \subset \Delta$ and $|c_i| = r$. However, the number k of possible placements is extremely large even for modest values of r and n, so the usage of a heuristic is necessary to efficiently identify interesting placement decisions.

We evaluate the quality of a potential replica placement decision according to two metrics. The Proximity metric $P\%$ represents the tail latency experienced by the application users. Specifically, it measures the percentage of network packets which reached their assigned replica with a latency lower than the target L. Greater Proximity values depict a better system. Every replica object φ_i holds two member variables which respectively estimate the total number of packets received by the replica ($\varphi_i.req$) and the number of received packets with a latency greater than the target L ($\varphi_i.sreq$). Using these variables we can compute the Proximity $P\%$:

$$P\% = \left[1 - \frac{\sum\limits_{i=1}^{r} \varphi_i.sreq}{\sum\limits_{i=1}^{r} \varphi_i.req} \right] \times 100\%$$

$$\sigma_{req} = \sqrt{\frac{1}{r} \times \sum_{i=1}^{r} (\varphi_i.req - \mu_{req})^2}$$

$$I\% = \frac{\sigma_{req}}{\sum\limits_{i=1}^{r} \varphi_i.req} \times 100\%$$

Likewise, the Imbalance metric $I\%$ evaluate the load balancing between replicas. Lower Imbalance values depict a better system. We define Imbalance as the standard deviation of the workloads of individual replicas for a given application.

Our heuristics aim to optimize an objective function Θ which is a linear combination of $P\%$ and $I\%$. For each case $c_i \in \Omega$ they evaluate the objective function Θ, and eventually select the evaluated case which maximizes the function:

$$\Theta_\alpha(c_i) = \alpha \frac{c_i.P\%}{P_{max}\%} + (1 - \alpha) \frac{I_{min}\%}{c_i.I\%}$$

The value α represents the desired tradeoff between Proximity and Imbalance, and $P_{max}\%$ and $I_{min}\%$ respectively represent the greatest and lowest observed values of $P\%$ and $I\%$ in the set of evaluated cases. We use $\alpha = 0.95$ to favorize Proximity over Imbalance improvements. This function can easily be extended to integrate other metrics such as financial cost and energy consumption.

4.2   System Monitoring

To evaluate the $P\%$ and $I\%$ metrics, Hona relies on measured data about the sources of traffic addressed to different nodes. The initial replica placement problem must be solved before the application gets deployed, so it cannot rely on information related to this specific application. Instead, we rely on information from other applications, as an approximation of the future traffic of the concerned application. In the replica re-placement problem the application is already deployed so we can rely on the specific traffic addressed to it.

Evaluating the two metrics requires three types of input data:

Cluster information including the nodes, their resources, the pods, and their hosting node is maintained by Kubernetes itself. We can access it with simple calls to its `etcd` service.

Latency information is maintained by Serf. We can obtain an accurate up-to-date estimate of the latency between any pair of worker nodes with a call to the `rtt` interface of Serf's agent at the master node.

Traffic information can be obtained from `proxy-mity` which logs the source and destination of each request transmitted. `proxy-mity` makes this information available to Hona's scheduler via a call to its local Serf agent.

4.3   Initial Replica Placement

When deploying an application for the first time, finding the optimal placement for r replicas among n nodes requires in principle one to explore the full set Ω of possible placements and choose the one which optimizes the objective function Θ. Unfortunately, this space is extremely large even for modest values of r and n, so exploring it in its entirety is not feasible.

We however note that it is not necessary for us to identify the exact optimal placement. In most cases, it is largely sufficient to identify an approximate solution which delivers the expected quality of service to the end users. We can therefore define heuristics which explore only a small fraction of Ω and select the best placement out of the explored solutions. In practice we define a Proximity threshold which represents a sufficiently good solution. Our heuristics stop the search as soon as they find a solution which exceeds the threshold, or when the time quota allocated to the search expires.

We define two heuristics to explore the space of initial replica placements: a random search heuristic, and a heuristic which exploits Vivaldi's geometric model of network latencies.

Random Search Heuristic: This heuristic is presented in Algorithm 1. The *RandomCases* function first computes the load distribution per node (*LPN*) using the information collected from the nodes. It then initializes the set of evaluated cases with a first randomly-selected configuration, and iteratively draws additional randomly-selected configurations until a solution is found or the time quota allocated to the search expires. The *GetBest* function then selects the best studied configuration and the function returns.

In our experience, this heuristic provides good solutions when the Latency threshold is relatively high as many placements can fulfill this QoS requirement. A short random search identifies at least one of them with high probability. However, in more difficult cases with a lower latency threshold, the number of solutions reduces drastically and this heuristic often fails to find a suitable one. We therefore propose a second heuristic which uses Vivaldi's geometric model to drive the search toward more promising solutions.

Vivaldi-Aware Heuristic: Vivaldi models network latencies by assigning each node an 8-dimensional coordinate. The latency between two nodes is then approximated by the Euclidean distance between their coordinates.

Hona introduce an efficient search heuristic which exploits this simple geometric model. As shown in Algorithm 2, the heuristic starts by computing the load distribution per node before grouping the nodes into small groups according to their location in the Vivaldi Euclidean space.

The main idea of this heuristics is to identify groups of nearby nodes and to select a single replica among them to serve the traffic originating from all of them. The grouping of nearby nodes is done using the *CreateGroups* function which randomly selects a first node and creates a group with all nodes in its neighborhood. The size of each group is determined by the *ND (Nodes Density)* variable. This variable is computed as the fraction of total number of system nodes to the desired number of replicas, multiplied by a user-defined variable p. Larger values of p create smaller groups. The algorithm periodically re-generates new groups and group leaders, until a solution is found or the deadline is reached.

Algorithm 1: Random-search initial placement heuristic.

```
Input: Δ, Lat, QoS, Traf, t, r, L
Output: c_sol
1  Function RandomCases(Δ, Lat, QoS, Traf, t, r, L)
2      Δ' ← GetFeasibleNodes(Δ)
3      LPN ← CalculateLoadPerNode(Traf)
4      SN ← GetRandomSet(Δ',r)
5      c_i ← CaseStudy(Δ, Δ', SN, Lat, Traf,
           LPN, L)
6      Cases.append(c_i)
7      while Test(c_i,QoS,t) != True do
8          c_i ← CaseStudy(Nodes, Lat, Traf,
               SN, LPN, L)
9          Cases.append(c_i)
10     c_sol ← GetBest(Cases)
11     return c_sol
```

Algorithm 2: Hona's initial replica placement heuristic.

```
Input: Δ, Lat, r, QoS, t, Traf, tech, p,
       Change, L
Output: c_sol
1  Function CreateGroups(Δ, Lat, r, L, Tech, p)
2      ND ← len(Δ) / (r * p)
3      Temp ← Δ
4      while len(Temp) > 0 do
5          if len(Temp) < ND then
6              Groups.append(group(Temp,
                   Δ, L, Tech))
7          else
8              MainNode ←
                   Random.choice(Temp)
9              Nearby ←
                   GetNearby(MainNode, Temp)
10             GN ← [MainNode] + Nearby
11             Temp.remove(GN)
12             Groups.append(group(GN, Δ,
                   L, Tech))
13 Function group(GN, Δ, L, Tech)
14     group.nodes ← GN
15     if Tech == 0 then
16         group.leader ←
               GetLeaderRequests(GN)
17     if Tech == 1 then
18         group.leader ←
               GetLeaderNeighbors(GN, Δ, L)
19 Function HonaCases(Δ, Lat, r, QoS, t, Traf, Tech,
       p, Change, L)
20     Count = 0
21     LPN ← CalculateLoadPerNode(Traf)
22     Groups ← CreateGroups(Δ, Lat, r, L,
           Tech, p)
23     Leaders ← GetLeaders(Groups)
24     SN ← GetRandomSet(Leaders,n)
25     c_i ← CaseStudy(Δ, Lat, Traf, SN, LPN,
           L)
26     Cases.append(c_i)
27     while Test(c_i,QoS,t) != True do
28         Count++
29         c_i ← CaseStudy(Δ, Lat, Traff, SN,
               LPN, L)
30         Cases.append(c_i)
31         if Count%Change == 0 then
32             Groups ← CreateGroups(Δ,
                   Lat, r, L, Tech, p)
33             Leaders ← GetLeaders(Groups)
34         SN ← GetRandomSet(Leaders,n)
35     c_sol ← GetBest(Cases)
36     return c_sol
```

Algorithm 3: Hona's replica re-placement heuristic.

```
Input: Δ, Φ, QoS, Lat, Reason, Traf
Output: SelectedSolution
1  Function Replace( Δ, Φ, QoS, Lat, Reason, Traff)
2      for ∀φ_i ∈ Φ do
3          Slow[φ_i] ←
               CalculatePercentageSlow(Φ, Traf,
               Lat)
4          ReqPerPod[φ_i] ←
               GetRequestPerPod(Φ, Traf)
5      if Reason=="Proximity" then
6          SortedPods ← Sort(Slow)
7          PotentialNodes ←
               SlowSources(Traf,Φ,Lat)
8      if Reason=="Imbalance" then
9          SortedPods ← ISort(ReqPerPod)
10         PotentialNodes ←
               NearbyTraffic(Traff,Φ,Lat)
11     for φ_i in SortedPods do
12         for δ_i in PotentialNodes do
13             SN ← Nodes(Φ) - Node(φ_i) +
                   δ_i
14             c_i ← CaseStudy(Δ,
                   Lat,Traff,SN,AL)
15             Cases.append(c_i)
16             if c_i is a solution then
17                 solutions.append(c_i)
18                 found ← True
19         if found==True then
20             Return GetBest(solutions)
21     if Solutions==NULL then
22         Return GetBest(Cases)
```

Once a group has been identified, a single node within the group is chosen as the group leader which will receive a replica while the others are excluded as potential replica locations.

We propose two possible criteria for the final selection of the group leader, which result in two variants of this heuristic:

H1 selects the node which generates the greatest number of end-user requests. This increases the number of requests that will be processed by their gateway node, with a gateway-to-replica latency of approximately 0.

H2 selects the node with the greatest number of neighbors. Neighborhood is established as an enclosure of the nodes with a latency lower than the threshold latency L. A replica placed in a node with high number of neighbors will offer a nearby replica for all its neighbors.

Similar to the random placement heuristic, this algorithm randomly chooses r group leaders to produce a replica placement which gets evaluated using function

Θ. The algorithm evaluates as many such placements as possible until a solution is found or the deadline expires, and terminates by returning the best placement.

4.4   Replica Re-placement

Online systems often observe significant variations over time of the characteristics of the traffic they receive [25]. To maintain an efficient replica placement over time, it is important to detect variations when they occur, and to update the replica placement accordingly.

Hona periodically recomputes the Proximity and Imbalance metrics with monitored data collected during the previous cycle. When these metrics deviate too much from their initial values, it triggers the *Replace* function which is in charge of updating the replica placement. To avoid oscillating behavior, and considering that re-placing a replica incurs a cost, Hona re-places at most one replica per application and per cycle.

Algorithm 3 presents the re-placement heuristic. It first sorts the application replicas to identify the least useful ones according to the current conditions, and then tries to find them a better location out of a filtered set of nodes.

The identification of the least useful replica depends on the nature of the performance violation. If the Proximity metric has degraded significantly, then the heuristic will attempt to re-place one of the replicas with the greatest observed tail latency. On the other hand, if the re-placement is triggered by an increase of the Imbalance metric, the heuristic will select one of the replicas which process the lowest amount of load.

Likewise, the set of potential nodes available to host the pod is selected according to the violation type. If the violation was caused by a lack of proximity, the potential nodes will consist of the gateway nodes that are suffering from high tail latency. On the other hand, if the violation was caused by load imbalance, the potential nodes are those located close to the main sources of traffic.

The replacement function then iterates through the list of least useful replicas, and tries to find a better node to hold them. It stops as soon as it finds a suitable solution which improves Θ by at least some pre-defined value. In case no improvement can be obtained by re-placing one replica, the system keeps the current placement unmodified. A potential solution in this case would be to increase the number of replicas. We leave this topic for future work.

5   Evaluation

We evaluate this work using a combination of experimental measurements and simulations. The experimental setup consists of 22 Raspberry Pi (RPi) model 3B+ single-board computers acting as fog computing servers. Such machines are frequently used to prototype fog computing infrastructures [3]. They run the HypriotOS v1.9.0 distribution with Linux kernel 4.14.34, Docker v18.04.0 and Kubernetes v1.9.3. We implemented Hona on top of Serf v0.8.2.dev and the development version of `proxy-mity`.

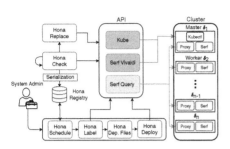

Fig. 2. System architecture.

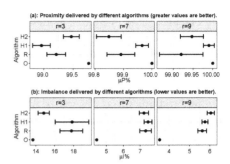

Fig. 3. Initial replica placement analysis (testbed, $n = 21$).

As shown in Fig. 2, Hona is implemented as a daemon running in the Kubernetes master node. It fetches information from Kubernetes and Serf, and expresses its placement decisions by attaching labels to the concerned nodes.

In our cluster, one RPi runs the Kubernetes master and the Hona scheduler, while the remaining RPIs act as worker nodes capable of hosting replicas. Every worker node is also a WiFi hotspot and a Kubernetes gateway so end users can connect to nearby worker nodes and send requests to the service.

We emulate realistic network latencies between the worker nodes using the Linux tc[2] command. We specifically use latency values measured between European cities[3]. Network latencies range from 3 ms to 80 ms and arguably represent a typical situation for a geo-distributed fog computing infrastructure.

The application is a web server which simply returns the IP address of the serving pod. We generate workloads either by equally distributing traffic among all gateway nodes, or by selecting specific gateways as the only sources of traffic. The threshold latency is $L = 28$ ms (the median inter-node latency in our system), the trade-off between Proximity and Imbalance is $\alpha = 0.95$, and the deadline to find a placement is 10 s.

We perform the scalability analysis using a simulator which randomly creates up to 500 virtual nodes in the Vivaldi Euclidean space, and use the same heuristics implementation as in Hona to select replica placements.

5.1 Initial Replica Placement

We first evaluate Hona's initial placement algorithms and compare them with the unmodified Kubernetes scheduler and the optimal solution found using a brute-force approach. In the following graphs, each algorithm is denoted by a letter: **O** for the optimal solution found using brute-force search, **R** for the random heuristic, **H1** and **H2** for the first and second versions of Hona heuristic.

Overall Performance (Testbed Experiments): Figure 3 compares the Proximity and Imbalance of solutions found by the different algorithms for various

---

[2] https://linux.die.net/man/8/tc.
[3] https://wondernetwork.com/.

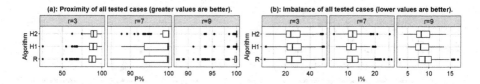

Fig. 4. Individual test cases analysis (testbed, $n = 21$).

numbers of replicas within the 21 worker nodes in the testbed. We run each experiment 100 times, and evaluate 200 configurations per experiment.

Increasing the number of replicas to be placed makes the search easier, and it delivers better results. More replicas can better cover the different regions of the system, and the probability for any node to have a replica nearby increases. Similarly, increasing the number of replicas makes load balancing easier.

The three Hona heuristics perform well in this case with results very close to the brute-force optimal in a fraction of the time (for $r = 9$, O required $\approx$48 min compared to 0.55 s for the heuristics). We however notice that in the relatively difficult case of $r = 3$ the H2 heuristic outperforms the others according to both metrics since it was designed to find solutions when the number of replicas is relatively very small compared to the number of available nodes. This advantage becomes more evident when testing over a large scale cluster.

To better understand the differences between the Random and the Hona heuristics, Fig. 4 depicts the 5th/25th/50th/75th/95th percentiles of *all the tested placements* during the same experiment. In contrast, Fig. 3 shows only the best solutions found by every run of the heuristics. We can clearly see the differences between heuristics; the Random heuristic evaluates placement options across a wide range of quality, whereas the H1 and H2 heuristics better focus their search on promising placement options.

Effect of System Size (Simulator Evaluations): We now explore Hona's placement algorithms in systems up to 300 nodes. Figure 5 depicts the results obtained from 1000 runs of every evaluation. We chose the latencies between nodes by randomly selecting Vivaldi coordinates for every node within a distance of at most 80 ms between nodes. To make the placement problem equally difficult with different system sizes, we also scaled the number of requested replicas accordingly: $r = n/10$. The red lines indicate the target values. We do not plot the brute-force optimal placements which would require extremely long executions.

In Figs. 5a and 5b, we observe greater differences between the three Hona heuristics with larger system sizes. In particular, the H2 heuristic delivers better Proximity for large-scale systems. This is due to the fact that it selects group leaders with respect to the number of neighbors they can serve with low latency.

The H1 and H2 heuristics also outperform the Random heuristic in the number of cases they need to evaluate before finding a solution which meets the user's requirements (Fig. 5c). We observe that H2 finds solutions much quicker than the other heuristics.

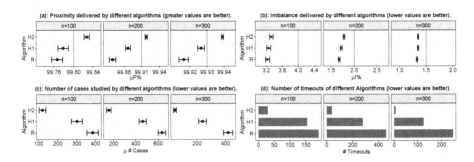

Fig. 5. Initial replica placement with various system sizes (simulator, $r = n/10$).

Finally, Fig. 5d shows the number of heuristic executions which reached the timeout without finding a suitable solution. Here as well, the H2 heuristic significantly outperforms the others because it targets its search to cases which have a greater probability of delivering high-quality results.

We conclude that the H2 heuristic delivers better-quality results than the others, in less time, and with a lower probability of a failed search. In the rest of this paper we therefore use this heuristic for the initial replica placements.

5.2   Replica Re-placement

After the initial deployment of an application, Hona monitors the network traffic it handles and periodically recomputes its performance metrics $P\%$ and $I\%$. When these metrics deviate too much from their expected values, it tries to re-place replicas within the system to address the new situation.

We evaluate the behavior of Hona in our 22-nodes testbed with a variety of scenarios. We define the Proximity target as $P\% = 99.5\%$ of requests with a latency under $L = 28$ ms, with a tolerance of 0.5% before triggering re-placement. Similarly, the Imbalance target is $I\% = 5\%$, with a tolerance of 1% before re-placement. These metrics are evaluated at a periodicity of 30 s.

Figure 6 depicts increasingly difficult re-placement scenarios. We plot the Proximity and Imbalance metrics as calculated at the end of every cycle. The red area depicts the period during which the new situation is introduced, and the vertical red line(s) represents the time(s) at which the re-placement algorithm actually changes the placement of replicas. We do not plot the $P\%$ and $I\%$ metrics in the cycle immediately after a re-placement: these metrics capture the transient state during which a new replica is created while another one is deleted, and therefore do not represent accurate information.

(a) Changing a source of traffic: Figure 6a shows a case where one source of traffic gets replaced with another one. During the first five cycles, no load is issued to the studied application so the Imbalance metric remains at $I\% = 0$. Proximity is calculated according to the background traffic of other applications, which explains its initial value of 90%. Some load is then generated starting from cycle 6. The two metrics reach very good values: almost 100% for $P\%$, and about 2% for $I\%$. At cycle 9, however, we replace one of the main sources of traffic with

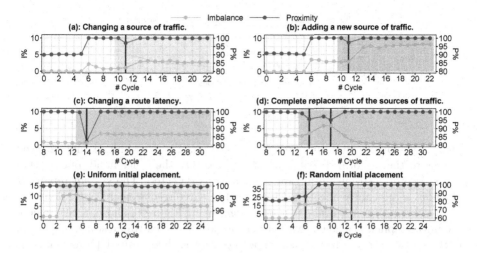

Fig. 6. Replica re-placement analysis (testbed, $n = 21$).

another one located far away from any current replica. This event is detected quickly and, at cycle 11, the system moves the useless replica close to the next source of traffic, which effectively repairs the Proximity degradation.

(b) Adding a new source of traffic: Figure 6b shows a scenario where a new source of traffic is added far away from the current set of replicas. This results in a Proximity violation which is quickly detected by the system. However, in this situation there is no solution that would bring both metrics within their expected bounds. Since we favored Proximity over Imbalance in the objective function Θ, the system moves one replica close to the new source of traffic, which fixes the Proximity violation at the expense of a degraded imbalance. The only solution in this case to solve both QoS violations is scaling up the replica set.

(c) Changing a route latency: Figure 6c shows the case where the load distribution remains unmodified, but the latency between a gateway node and its closest replica changes suddenly from 10 ms to 50 ms. In this case, Serf must first detect the change of network latencies before Hona can react and re-place the concerned replica accordingly. We see in the figure that these two operations take place quickly. One cycle after the latency change, Hona triggers a re-placement operation which brings performance back to normal.

(d) Complete replacement of the sources of traffic: Figure 6d depicts a dramatic situation where the entire workload changes at once: in cycle 11 we stop all the sources of traffic, and replace them with entirely different ones. In this case, the replica re-placement takes place in two steps. A first re-placement is triggered at cycle 14: this operation improves Proximity but at the expense of an increase in the load Imbalance. At cycle 17 a second re-placement is triggered which brings both metrics back within their expected values.

(e) Starting from a uniform replica placement: Figure 6e shows a difficult situation created by a sub-optimal initial replica placement. We initially placed replicas with no information whatsoever about the future workload. In this case

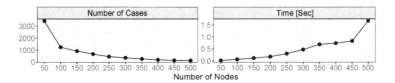

Fig. 7. Complexity of the H2 heuristic (simulator).

replicas get placed uniformly across the system. The Proximity is not affected thanks to the uniform distribution of replicas. On the other hand, once actual traffic is produced, an important Imbalance is detected. The system repairs it (without significantly affecting Proximity) in three re-placement operations.

(f) Starting from a random replica placement: Figure 6f shows a case where the initial replica placement was chosen randomly. When traffic starts in cycle 4, both metrics are far from their expected values. The desired performance is obtained after three re-placement operations.

Hona addresses a wide variety of QoS violations, and provides effective solutions to solve them. In our experiments we never observed oscillating behavior in which the system would not very quickly reach a new stable state.

5.3   Computational Complexity

Figure 7 shows the computation time of the H2 heuristic for placing 10 replicas with QoS bounds of $P\% = 99.5\%$, $L = 25$ ms and $I\% = 4\%$. We used a mid-range machine with a quad-core Intel Core i7-7600U CPU @2.80 GHz. The current implementation is single-threaded, but parallelizing it should in principle be easy as different placements can be evaluated independently from each other.

The left part of the figure depict the number of cases which can be evaluated within 10 s. Clearly, the complexity of evaluating any single case increases with system size as the metric evaluation function needs to iterate through a greater number of potential traffic sources. However, as shown in the right part of the figure, even for large system sizes, the computation time until a satisfactory solution is found remains under 2 s of computation. This comes from the fact that, with larger system sizes, the number of acceptable solutions grows as well, and a solution can be found with a lower number of evaluated cases.

6   Conclusion

Replica placement is an important problem in fog computing infrastructures where one can place computation close to the end-user devices. When many sources can generate traffic it is often not affordable to deploy an application replica close to every traffic source individually. One rather needs to limit the number of replicas, and to choose their location carefully to control the tail latency and the system's load balance. Replica placement decisions must also be updated every time a significant change in the operating conditions degrades the QoS metrics. We have shown that, despite the huge computational complexity of searching for the optimal solution, simple and effective heuristics can identify sufficiently good solutions in reasonable time. We have implemented Hona in Kubernetes, thereby bringing it one step closer to becoming one of the mainstream, general-purpose platforms for future fog computing scenarios.

References

1. Ahmed, A., et al.: Fog computing applications: taxonomy and requirements. arXiv preprint arXiv:1907.11621 (2019)
2. Aral, A., et al.: A decentralized replica placement algorithm for edge computing. IEEE Trans. Netw. Serv. Manage. **15**(2), 516–529 (2018)
3. Bellavista, P., et al.: Feasibility of fog computing deployment based on Docker containerization over RaspberryPi. In: Proceedings of ACM ICDCN (2017)
4. Calheiros, R.N., et al.: CloudSim: a toolkit for modeling and simulation of cloud computing environments and evaluation of resource provisioning algorithms. Softw. Pract. Exp. **41**(1), 23–50 (2011)
5. Dabek, F., et al.: Vivaldi: a decentralized network coordinate system. In: Proceedings of ACM SIGCOMM (2004)
6. Elbamby, M.S., et al.: Toward low-latency and ultra-reliable virtual reality. IEEE Network **32**(2), 78–84 (2018)
7. Fahs, A., et al.: Proximity-aware traffic routing in distributed fog computing platforms. In: Proceedings of ACM/IEEE CCGrid (2019)
8. Gupta, H., et al.: iFogSim: a toolkit for modeling and simulation of resource management techniques in the Internet of Things, edge and fog computing environments. Softw. Pract. Exp. **47**(9), 1275–1296 (2017)
9. HashiCorp: Serf: Decentralized cluster membership (2019). https://www.serf.io/
10. Hong, H.J., et al.: Dynamic module deployment in a fog computing platform. In: Proceedings of IEEE APNOMS (2016)
11. IEEE: IEEE standard for adoption of OpenFog reference architecture for fog computing (2018). https://bit.ly/38sXYjU
12. Jemaa, F.B., et al.: QoS-aware VNF placement optimization in edge-central carrier cloud architecture. In: Proceedings of IEEE GLOBECOM (2016)
13. Karlsson, M., et al.: A framework for evaluating replica placement algorithms. Technical report, HPL-2002-219, HP Labs Palo Alto (2002)
14. Lera, I., et al.: Comparing centrality indices for network usage optimization of data placement policies in fog devices. In: Proceedings of IEEE FMEC (2018)
15. Li, K., et al.: Traffic-aware virtual machine placement in cloudlet mesh with adaptive bandwidth. In: Proceedings of IEEE CloudCom (2017)
16. Li, C., et al.: Flexible replica placement for enhancing the availability in edge computing environment. Comput. Commun. **146**, 1–14 (2019)
17. Liu, J., et al.: Cache placement in Fog-RANs: from centralized to distributed algorithms. IEEE Trans. Wireless Commun. **16**(11), 7039–7051 (2017)
18. Naas, M.I., et al.: iFogStor: an IoT data placement strategy for fog infrastructure. In: Proceedings of IEEE ICFEC (2017)
19. Optimizely: The most misleading measure of response time. White paper (2013). https://bit.ly/3boHgnZ
20. Shao, Y., et al.: A data replica placement strategy for IoT workflows in collaborative edge and cloud environments. Comput. Netw. **148**, 46–59 (2019)

21. Silvestro, A., et al.: MUTE: multi-tier edge networks. In: Proceedings of Cross-Cloud (2018)
22. Skarlat, O., et al.: Towards QoS-aware fog service placement. In: Proceedings of ICFEC (2017)
23. Tang, H., et al.: Dynamic resource allocation strategy for latency-critical and computation-intensive applications in cloud-edge environment. Comput. Commun. **134**, 70–82 (2019)
24. The Kubernetes Authors: Kubernetes. https://kubernetes.io/
25. Urdaneta, G., et al.: Wikipedia workload analysis for decentralized hosting. Comput. Netw. **53**(11), 1830–1845 (2009)
26. Xu, J., et al.: Zenith: utility-aware resource allocation for edge computing. In: Proceedings of IEEE EDGE (2017)
27. Yu, Y.J., et al.: Virtual machine placement for backhaul traffic minimization in fog radio access networks. In: Proceedings of IEEE ICC (2017)
28. Zhao, L., et al.: Optimal placement of virtual machines in mobile edge computing. In: Proceedings of IEEE GLOBECOM (2017)

Two-Sided Matching Scheduling Using Multi-Level Look-Ahead Queue of Supply and Demand

Mincheng Chen[1], Jingling Yuan[1(✉)], Nana Wang[2], Yi Luo[3], and Pei Luo[1]

[1] School of Computer Science and Technology, Wuhan University of Technology, Wuhan, China
wester589@163.com, yuanjingling@126.com, 1123164905@qq.com
[2] School of Civil Engineering and Architecture, Wuhan University of Technology, Wuhan, China
nanawangwhut@163.com
[3] Hubei Key Laboratory of Roadway Bridge and Structure Engineering, Wuhan University of Technology, Wuhan, China
yluo@whut.edu.cn

Abstract. Cloud computing attracts more and more people owing to its compelling advantages in speed, efficiency and cost. The task scheduling as the core in cloud computing affects the quality of service. However, the mapping of tasks to appropriate resources is a complex job. Therefore, a two-sided matching (task-to-resource) scheduling using Multi-Level Look-Ahead Queue of Supply and Demand is proposed. Firstly, we design a Multi-Level Look-Ahead Queue of Supply and Demand (MLLQ-SD) according to the characteristics of cloud task scheduling. Then a task scheduling algorithm using MLLQ-SD (SA-MLLQ-SD) is designed. In addition, a greedy algorithm is used to improve its overall performance. SA-MLLQ-SD helps each task queue be allocated to the appropriate resource queue. Experimental results show that the proposed algorithm reduces the overall execution time and completion time, significantly guarantees the load balance while ensuring the service quality.

Keywords: Cloud computing · Multi-level look-ahead queue · Task scheduling · Quality of service

1 Introduction

In recent years, more and more users submit tasks to the cloud in view of the security, flexibility, and low-cost of cloud computing, which makes the tasks

Supported by the National Natural Science Foundation of China (Grant No: 61303029), National Social Science Foundation of China (Grant No: 15BGL048), Hubei Province Science and Technology Support Project (2015BAA072), the Fund for Creative Research Group of the Key Natural Science Foundation of Hubei Province of China (Grant No. 2017CFA012), the Key Technical Innovation Project of Hubei (Grant No. 2017AAA122).

© Springer Nature Switzerland AG 2020
E. Kafeza et al. (Eds.): ICSOC 2020, LNCS 12571, pp. 525–532, 2020.
https://doi.org/10.1007/978-3-030-65310-1_38

diverse [11]. These tasks need to be allocated to the appropriate computing resources for execution. However, there are many kinds of computing resources in cloud data center. Therefore, cloud computing resources are also heterogeneous, which further increases the complexity of task scheduling. How to reasonably distribute these diversified tasks to heterogeneous resources and ensure the Quality of Service (QoS) has become an increasingly popular research [3,5]. Many efficient methods were proposed in the past several years, such as Hadoop's FIFO scheduling, Yahoo's capacity scheduling, Facebook's fair scheduling, e.g. In addition, some scholars applied genetic algorithm and ant colony algorithm to obtain better scheduling solutions [4,9]. Some scholars narrowed task search space by clustering tasks or resources to reduce scheduling overhead. Piraghaj et al. [8] proposed a novel cloud resource allocation architecture, which maps task groups to the corresponding virtual machines. Zhao et al. [14] combined Bayes theorem with the clustering process to get the optimal clustering set of physical hosts.

However, most of these scheduling algorithms only consider the execution time of tasks, without considering the characteristics of tasks and resources. To optimize the task scheduling in data center, we do the following work:

(1) A Multi-Level Look-Ahead Queue of Supply and Demand (MLLQ-SD) is designed based on the features of cloud task scheduling. MLLQ-SD has two parts: Multi-Level Queue of Task Resource Demand (MLQ-TRD), Multi-Level Look-Ahead Queue of Resource Supply (MLLQ-RS). MLQ-TRD uses Dynamic Priority DP to divide tasks; MLQ-RS uses a Look-Ahead method to adjust the scale of resources in advance, then uses Resource Degree Coefficient RD to divide the available resources.
(2) A two-sided matching scheduling using MLLQ-SD (SA-MLLQ-SD) is designed. We utilize a greedy strategy to further improve its overall performance. SA-MLLQ-SD helps MLQ-TRD to be allocated to matched MLQ-RS. Experimental results reveal that the proposed algorithm not only reduces the overall execution time and completion time, but also significantly ensures the load balance while satisfying the quality of service.

The rest of the paper is organized as follows. Section 2 presents the design of MLLQ-SD. Section 3 proposes a two-sided matching scheduling using MLLQ-SD. Section 4 analyzes the experimental results. Section 5 gives a conclusion.

2   Multi-Level Look-Ahead Queue of Supply and Demand

According to the characteristics of cloud task scheduling, we design a Multi-Level Look-Ahead Queue of Supply and Demand (MLLQ-SD) combined with Multi-Level Feedback Queue. MLLQ-SD is mainly composed of two parts: Multi-Level Queue of Task Resource Demand, Multi-Level Look-Ahead Queue of Resource Supply.

2.1   Multi-Level Queue of Task Resource Demand

Multi-Level Feedback Queue (MLFQ) performs well on terminal tasks, short batch tasks, and long batch tasks of operating system. Each type of tasks can get fair scheduling opportunities and improve system resource utilization. The tasks of cloud data center can be divided into several types, which are similar to the tasks in the operating system. For example, interactive task, short task and long task. Therefore, the similar solutions can be used to process the tasks of cloud data centers. So we design a Multi-Level Queue of Task Resource Demand (MLQ-TRD) based on the thought of MLFQ. A novel dynamic priority is defined, which divides tasks more reasonably and lays a foundation for the reasonable resource allocation of tasks.

Dynamic Priority: MLFQ uses a high response ratio priority algorithm. It can prevent long tasks from occupying resources in the queue for a long time, which reduces the starvation of short tasks. It also can cut down the scheduling time and improve the operational efficiency. We refer to the high response ratio priority algorithm, then propose a novel dynamic priority by comprehensively considering indicators such as the waiting time, execution time, priority and scheduling class of the task. Dynamic Priority DP defined as

$$DP = \frac{r(t_i) \cdot (t_e(t_i) + t_{queue}(t_i))}{t_e(t_i)} \cdot (Pt(t_i) + St(t_i)) \tag{1}$$

where $t_e(t_i)$ and $t_{queue}(t_i)$ denote the expected execution time and waiting time of the task t_i. $Pt(t_i)$ and $St(t_i)$ denote the priority and scheduling class of the task t_i, where the priority represents how important the task is, and the scheduling class represents how latency-sensitive the task is. For example, Google represents the scheduling class by a single number, with 3 as a more latency-sensitive task and 0 as a non-production task [10]. Tasks with higher priority or scheduling class mostly get priority for resources over tasks with lower priority or scheduling class. $r(t_i)$ denotes the resource demand of the task t_i, can be calculated as $r(t_i) = TV_{LEN} \cdot \sqrt{TV_{CPU}^2 + TV_{MEM}^2 + TV_{NET}^2}$, where TV_{LEN}, TV_{CPU}, TV_{MEM} and TV_{NET} are the length, CPU, memory and net required for the task t_i.

We calculate the DP of each independent task in the task waiting queue $QW\{t_0, t_1, \cdots, t_n\}$, and assign tasks to the queues at different levels according to the DP. The pseudocode of algorithm for Multi-Level Queue of Task Resource Demand (MLQ-TRD) is shown in Algorithm 1.

The steps of Algorithm 1 are as follows:

Step 1–2: Initialize MLQ-TRD and DP_LIST. DP_LIST is used to store the DP of every task.

Step 3: Utilize RECEIVE_TASK() to receive the arriving tasks.

Step 4–7: Traverse QW, calculate the DP for every task, and add it to DP_LIST.

Step 8: Utilize SORT() to sort DP_LIST by DP in descending order.

Step 9: Utilize QUEUE_PARTITION to partition the tasks, the top P% tasks are assigned to the first-level queue, the top P%–2P% tasks are assigned to the second-level queue, and so on.

Step 10: Return MLQ-TRD.

ALGORITHM 1: MLQ-TRD	ALGORITHM 2: MLLQ-RS
Input: Arriving tasks;	**Input:** Available resources RS and historical data HD;
Output: MLQ-TRD $\{QS_1, QS_2, \cdots, QS_z\}$;	**Output:** MLLQ-RS $\{QD_1, QD_2, \cdots, QD_z\}$;
1. Initialize MLQ-TRD;	1. Initialize MLLQ-RS;
2. Initialize the DP list of tasks DP_LIST;	2. Initialize the RD list of resources RD_LIST;
3. $QW \leftarrow$ RECEIVE_TASK();	3. $RS \leftarrow$ LOOK_AHEAD(HD);
4. **for** each $t_i \in QW$ **do**	4. **for** each $v_j \in RS$ **do**
5. $DP \leftarrow$ COMPUTE_DP(t_i);	5. $RD \leftarrow$ COMPUTE_RD(v_j);
6. DP_LIST.ADD((t_i, DP));	6. RD_LIST.ADD((v_j, RD));
7. **end for**	7. **end for**
8. $DP\_LIST \leftarrow$ SORT(DP_LIST, DP);	8. $RD\_LIST \leftarrow$ SORT(RD_LIST, RD);
9. MLQ-TRD $\leftarrow$ QUEUE_PARTITION(DP_LIST, P);	9. MLLQ-RS $\leftarrow$ QUEUE_PARTITION(RD_LIST, P);
10. **return** MLQ-TRD;	10. **return** MLLQ-RS;

2.2   Multi-Level Look-Ahead Queue of Resource Supply

Because the traditional scheduling algorithms generally only consider the completion time of the tasks but seldomly consider the resource supply. Sometimes it will lead to mismatches between resource supply and demand, which will directly causes the slow executions to some tasks, and eventually increase the whole completion time. Therefore, we design a Multi-Level Look-Ahead Queue of Resource Supply (MLLQ-RS). MLLQ-RS considers the resource supply situation and classifies the available resources before scheduling. Look-Ahead and Resource Degree Coefficient are the basis of MLLQ-RS.

Look-Ahead: The data center has plenty of computing resources. How to determine the number of virtual machines to handle tasks, has become a problem. Therefore we use a Look-Ahead method to forecast future load demand by the historical task data and determine the number of virtual machines. This Look-Ahead method is our previous work [2], so it will not be described here.

Resource Degree Coefficient: Resource Degree Coefficient RD is utilized to measure the computing power of the resource, can be calculated as

$$RD = \sum \partial_k \cdot R_k, k \in \{CPU, MEM, NET\} \tag{2}$$

where R_k denotes the capability of v_j on one resource; ∂_k denotes the weight of R_k, $\sum \partial_k = 1$.

We calculate the RD of each virtual machine in the available resources $RS\{v_0, v_1, \cdots, v_m\}$, and assign virtual machines to the queues at different levels according to the RD. The pseudocode of algorithm for Multi-Level Look-Ahead Queue of Resource Supply (MLLQ-RS) is shown in Algorithm 2.

The steps of Algorithm 2 are as follows:

Step 1–2: Initialize MLLQ-RS and RD_LIST. RD_LIST is used to store the RD of every virtual machine.

Step 3: Utilize LOOK_AHEAD() to forecast future load demand according to historical data HD and adjust the scale of RS.

Step 4–7: Traverse RS, calculate the RD for every virtual machine, and add it to RD_LIST.

Step 8: Utilize SORT() to sort RD_LIST by RD in descending order.

Step 9: Utilize QUEUE_PARTITION() to partition the virtual machines, the top P% virtual machines are assigned to the first-level queue, the top P%–2P% virtual machines are assigned to the second-level queue, and so on.

Step 10: Return MLLQ-RS.

3   Two-Sided Matching Scheduling

Two-Sided Matching Scheduling Algorithm (TSMSA) traverses QS_k in MLQ-TRD, obtains the QD_k corresponding to QS_k, and then schedules the tasks. For example, assigning the high-priority queue in MLQ-TRD to the high-performance resource queue in MLLQ-RS, and the low-priority queue in MLQ-TRD to the low-performance resource queue in MLLQ-RS. We assign similar tasks to corresponding resources to improve the matching between tasks and computing resources. It narrows down the selection scope of tasks to improve task scheduling efficiency and ensure service quality. We finally use a greedy strategy for task scheduling (GS-QS-QD) between $\{QS_k, QD_k\}$. GS-QS-QD helps the task to find the most optimal virtual machine. Each task should comply with the resource constraints of the virtual machine, and only be executed on one virtual machine during the scheduling process.

Figure 1 illustrates the flowchart of the scheduling algorithm using MLLQ-SD (SA-MLLQ-SD). SA-MLLQ-SD utilizes MLLQ-SD to partition tasks and virtual machine resources. Each task queue is assigned to the matched resource queue by TSMSA. Then GS-QS-QD is used in each $\{QS_k, QD_k\}$ to further improve scheduling efficiency.

4   Experimental Evaluation

Experimental Environment: To guarantee the repeatability of experiments, the CloudSim toolkit is selected as a simulation platform [1]. In the experiment, we assume that the number of hosts is 100, and there is only one virtual machine(VM) on each host. In addition, we simulate random tasks according to Google trace data [10]. Since there is no task length in Google trace data, the task length is randomly generated.

Scheduling Algorithm Evaluation: We not only implement our proposed algorithm SA-MLLQSD, but also implement the Greedy Scheduling Algorithm (Greedy) [7], Ant Colony Scheduling Algorithm (ACO) [6,13], Genetic Scheduling Algorithm (GA) [9] and Task Clustering Scheduling Algorithm(TC) [8,12] as the baseline algorithms. We use the whole execution time of all tasks and the completion time of the tasks as the experimental metrics [15].

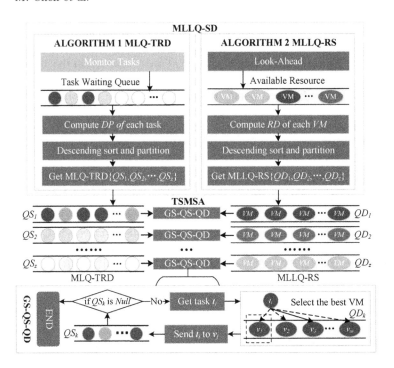

Fig. 1. Two-sided Matching Scheduling using MLLQ-SD

Figure 2(a) shows the results of different algorithms on the whole execution time of different number of tasks. Compared with several other algorithms, the proposed algorithm SA-MLLQ-SD and ACO perform better, but SA-MLLQ-SD is 2.53% longer than TC on the 6th experiment (3000). Figure 2(b) shows the completion time of various algorithms. SA-MLLQ-SD is superior to ACO, GA and TC, but slightly weaker than Greedy. Because Greedy takes the completion time as the optimization goal, so the task completion time is the best. At the same time, to measure the load balance of each virtual machine during the scheduling process, we record the load of each virtual machine. Figure 2(c) shows the number of tasks allocated to each virtual machine (VM) during the execution of various algorithms. Figure 2(c) shows that the number of tasks for each algorithm tends to fluctuate around the average. ACO has the largest fluctuation range, and SA-MLLQ-SD has the smallest fluctuation range. When the total number of tasks increases, this advantage of SA-MLLQ-SD becomes more obvious. SA-MLLQ-SD is far superior to the other algorithms in load balancing. All factors taken into consideration, the division of tasks and resources reduces the scope of task selection, and the matching scheduling of task queues and resource queues ensures the rationality of task selection in resources.

In summary, SA-MLLQ-SD reduces the execution time and completion time, guarantees the load balance of the virtual machines and improve the quality of service.

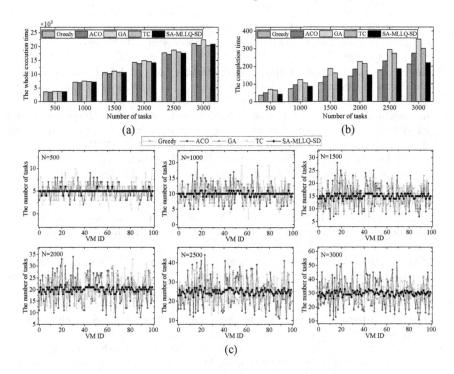

Fig. 2. The number of tasks allocated on each virtual machine

5 Conclusion

This paper has presented a two-sided matching scheduling using Multi-Level Look-Ahead Queue of Supply and Demand (SA-MLLQ-SD). A Multi-Level Look-Ahead Queue of Supply and Demand (MLLQ-SD) we proposed helps each task queue can be allocated to the appropriate resource queue with the matching execution ability. The application of greedy strategy further improved the overall performance. The experiments comprehensively evaluate the performance of the proposed algorithm in comparison to four baseline approaches. SA-MLLQ-SD can reduce the overall execution time and completion time, significantly guarantee the load balance while ensuring the service quality.

In the future research work, we will try to focus on workflow and consider other factors (energy consumption, resource utilization, etc.). It will make the results more comprehensive.

References

1. Calheiros, R.N., Ranjan, R., Beloglazov, A., De Rose, C.A., Buyya, R.: CloudSim: a toolkit for modeling and simulation of cloud computing environments and evaluation of resource provisioning algorithms. Softw. Pract. Exp. **41**(1), 23–50 (2011)

2. Chen, M., Yuan, J., Liu, D., Li, T.: An adaption scheduling based on dynamic weighted random forests for load demand forecasting. J. Supercomput. **76**(3), 1735–1753 (2020)
3. Guo, J., et al.: Who limits the resource efficiency of my datacenter: an analysis of Alibaba datacenter traces. In: Proceedings of the International Symposium on Quality of Service (IWQoS 2019), pp. 1–10 (2019)
4. Keshanchi, B., Souri, A., Navimipour, N.J.: An improved genetic algorithm for task scheduling in the cloud environments using the priority queues: formal verification, simulation, and statistical testing. J. Syst. Softw. **124**, 1–21 (2017)
5. Li, X., Pan, L., Liu, S., Shi, Y., Meng, X.: QoS optimization of service clouds serving pleasingly parallel jobs. In: Pahl, C., Vukovic, M., Yin, J., Yu, Q. (eds.) ICSOC 2018. LNCS, vol. 11236, pp. 560–575. Springer, Cham (2018). https://doi.org/10.1007/978-3-030-03596-9_41
6. Liu, X.F., Zhan, Z.H., Deng, J.D., Li, Y., Gu, T., Zhang, J.: An energy efficient ant colony system for virtual machine placement in cloud computing. IEEE Trans. Evol. Comput. **22**(1), 113–128 (2016)
7. Pathania, A., Venkatramani, V., Shafique, M., Mitra, T., Henkel, J.: Optimal greedy algorithm for many-core scheduling. IEEE Trans. Comput. Aided Des. Integr. Circuits Syst. **36**(6), 1054–1058 (2016)
8. Piraghaj, S.F., Calheiros, R.N., Chan, J., Dastjerdi, A.V., Buyya, R.: Virtual machine customization and task mapping architecture for efficient allocation of cloud data center resources. Comput. J. **59**(2), 208–224 (2016)
9. Rehman, A., Hussain, S.S., ur Rehman, Z., Zia, S., Shamshirband, S.: Multi-objective approach of energy efficient workflow scheduling in cloud environments. Concurrency Comput. Pract. Exp. **31**(8), e4949 (2019)
10. Reiss, C., Wilkes, J., Hellerstein, J.L.: Google cluster-usage traces: format + schema. Google Inc., White Paper, pp. 1–14 (2011)
11. Rosinosky, G., Youcef, S., Charoy, F.: A genetic algorithm for cost-aware business processes execution in the cloud. In: Pahl, C., Vukovic, M., Yin, J., Yu, Q. (eds.) ICSOC 2018. LNCS, vol. 11236, pp. 198–212. Springer, Cham (2018). https://doi.org/10.1007/978-3-030-03596-9_13
12. Sahni, J., Vidyarthi, D.P.: Workflow-and-platform aware task clustering for scientific workflow execution in cloud environment. Future Gener. Comput. Syst. **64**, 61–74 (2016)
13. Wang, T., Wei, X., Tang, C., Fan, J.: Efficient multi-tasks scheduling algorithm in mobile cloud computing with time constraints. Peer-to-Peer Network. Appl. **11**(4), 793–807 (2018)
14. Zhao, J., Yang, K., Wei, X., Ding, Y., Hu, L., Xu, G.: A heuristic clustering-based task deployment approach for load balancing using Bayes theorem in cloud environment. IEEE Trans. Parallel Distrib. Syst. **27**(2), 305–316 (2015)
15. Zhuo, T., Min, Z., Li, Y., Xiaoyong, T., Kenli, L., University, H.: Random task-oriented user utility optimization model in the cloud environment. J. Comput. Res. Dev. **51**(5), 1120–1128 (2014)

A Practice-Oriented, Control-Flow-Based Anomaly Detection Approach for Internal Process Audits

Gerrit Schumann[✉], Felix Kruse, and Jakob Nonnenmacher

University of Oldenburg, 26129 Oldenburg, NI, Germany
{gerrit.schumann,felix.kruse,jakob.nonnenmacher}@uol.de

Abstract. Internal auditing tries to identify anomalies, weaknesses and manipulations in business processes in order to protect the company from risks. Due to the digitalization of processes, auditors also have to check the associated data volumes. Already existing IT-systems focus on process-related data where the control flow, i.e. the actual sequence of process events, is not considered. This paper examines how the control flow and the process-related data can be analyzed in combination to support auditors in process auditing. To realize this, audit requirements were collected in the literature and evaluated by auditors from industry. On this basis, a concept with five indicators was developed, then transferred into a prototype and evaluated using real-life data as well as two auditors. The results show that the requirements can be technically realized and the developed indicators enable auditors to identify and interpret abnormal process executions.

Keywords: Internal auditing · Process mining · Process context · Unsupervised

1 Introduction

Today, business processes can be controlled and monitored by information systems. Many of these systems can store process events such as transactions or machine signals in a structured form. A collection of such digital events is called *event log*. The basic assumption is that the data in the event log represents the sequence of events as they occurred in reality. In this context, one also speaks of the *control flow* of a process [1].

For internal auditing, the control flow is relevant, since auditors could compare the actual control flow of a process with a target control flow in order to detect anomalies. However, a challenge with such an approach is the availability of a reliable reference model. In practice, these models are often designed at the time the process is introduced, while the actual process flows usually change over time. One reason for such a change could be, e.g., new employees who have a slightly different way of working than their predecessors [2]. To overcome this limitation process mining can be used.

Process mining refers to methods and techniques that can generate a structured process model based on event logs [1]. Using such models, process mining provides the basis for a comparison with an existing reference model or an event log. In contrast to sampling, this would allow auditors to check an entire set of process executions.

© Springer Nature Switzerland AG 2020
E. Kafeza et al. (Eds.): ICSOC 2020, LNCS 12571, pp. 533–543, 2020.
https://doi.org/10.1007/978-3-030-65310-1_39

Despite these potentials, process mining is rarely used in auditing. The reasons for this are suspected, e.g., in the high number of cases classified as anomalous [4]. This typically results from the classical approach of control-flow-based anomaly detection. Most approaches use discovery algorithms to determine a reference model from an event log and then use this model in a conformance check to detect anomalies in the log [5]. However, even a single event, which is not provided in the model can lead to a process execution being interpreted as an anomaly. Such a sensitive interpretation can be a challenge for auditors, as a high number of process executions wrongly interpreted as anomalous can lead to unnecessary investigations. Another aspect is the missing alignment of the technical output with the individual interests of the auditors [4]. The concrete challenge is the atomic form in which the process deviations are provided by the methods [6]. I.e., auditors may see that deviations in the control flow have occurred, but an interpretation of the associated markings is not yet mapped to their specific needs.

To make the output of control flow-based anomaly detection manageable for internal auditing in both quantitative and qualitative terms, we propose an approach that extends the control flow with process-related data and also addresses the auditors' requirements.

1.1 Fundamentals

Event Log and Process Related Data. The event log is essential for process mining and is subject to requirements. One is that each *event* must be assigned to a unique *case*. To be able to consider the ordering, the events must also be assigned to a *timestamp* or sort element. The sequence of events in a case is then called a trace [1]. When a process is running, further data can also be generated, which cannot be assigned to a timestamp or event of the log. However, if this data also has a *case* it can be assigned to the corresponding case in the log. In contrast to the log, which describes the process flow over several lines ①, a single line of process information could be provided in this way ② (Fig. 1).

① Event Log			② Process Related Data						
case	event	timestamp	case	amount	class	priority	owner	...	attribute n
312P	90	2020-06-01	312P	16	3	high	doe	...	48
312P	280	2020-06-02							
312P	800	2020-06-03							

Fig. 1. Event log and process related data

Conformance Checking. Conformance checking is a type of process mining and can be used to check whether the real behavior, which is recorded in the log, corresponds to a process model. For the implementation of conformance checks *replays* are used. This term comes from the idea of reproducing or rather "re-playing" the single traces of a log on the process model. As a concrete replay approach, *alignments* have become the standard for conformance checks [1]. Alignments can relate unsuitable events of the log to the process model by a mapping procedure. E.g., let $o = \{90, 265, 160, 280, 467, 492, 413, 496, 730, 769, 810, 820\}$ be a trace of an event log L. If we replay o on the petri net M, this can be visualized in a matrix ①. The bottom row corresponds to the moves of the trace o and the top row to the moves in the petri net M. If a move can be performed both in the trace and in the model, this is called a *synchronous move*. The icon >> indicates a misalignment and appears either when an event recorded in the trace could not be executed in the model (*move-on-log-only*), or when an event that had to be executed by the model did not take place in reality (*move-on-model-only*) [1] (Fig. 2).

Fig. 2. Conformance checking using alignments

During a replay there can be many different alignments between a log and a process model. For the calculation of the replay fitness only the optimal and worst-case alignment is needed. Here, it is necessary to assign costs to the moves. For moves where the log and the model match (synchronous moves), these costs must always be set to 0. If log and model differ and no process knowledge is available, a fixed cost value of 1 can be assigned to all misalignments. To calculate the replay fitness between o and M, the costs of all moves are then summed up for each trace and filled into the formula ② [1].

1.2 Related Work

While most conformance checking methods have focused on the control flow, some studies also considered additional process data. Such data can be used to check whether the control flow also meets the correct process conditions (e.g., correct control flow activity performed by an authorized person). To consider such aspects in the conformance check, in [7] an alignment approach is extended by a heuristic-based procedure. In [8] an approach based on integer linear programming is presented, which, in contrast to [7], is also capable of processing numerical values. In [9] a constraint-based approach for conformance checking of declarative processes is developed. In [10] both the data and the time perspective are linked to the control flow. In [11] a cost function is used to prioritize deviations between a log and a model, considering all process perspectives.

Further studies focused on reducing the high number of control-flow-based alerts or false-positives. E.g., in [12], not every unexpected event is immediately classified as abnormal, but assessed based on the likelihood of its occurrence. In [13] an association rule mining approach is proposed that can be used to determine what behavior might have caused an abnormal process. This can help to differentiate between harmful anomalies and false-positives. Besides the purely technical research, process mining is also investigated in the auditing context [3, 14–17]. These studies stand out from others because they already address concrete tasks and scenarios in the auditing area.

2 Requirements

To determine the requirements for our approach, we conducted a literature research that aimed to identify the criteria according to which an auditor selects anomalous process executions based on their control flow behavior. As a result, only the study by [4] was identified as relevant. This is due to the fact that the known control-flow-related deviation patterns originate from the field of process mining or business process management and until recently these patterns were not checked for consistency with the deviation patterns used by auditors. It was only the study by [4] that provided representative answers by conducting interviews with auditors. According to [4], especially *swapped*, *missing* and *duplicate* events in the control flow are criteria that are relevant for auditors. In order to assess these requirements, the following aspects were discussed with two auditors. A1: Compliance of the collected criteria with those of the own audit department, A2: Suitable way of presenting the criteria in concrete figures/indicators.

After aspect A1 was discussed, it can be stated that the requirements were confirmed by the auditors. They added, that it would be helpful if they could also be informed about the (ab-)normality of the associated process conditions when evaluating the control flow deviations. This could help to interpret whether the deviations may be typical or atypical under certain process circumstances. Aspect A2 showed that, a combination of deviation criteria as numerical indicators would be helpful for the auditors. The concrete proposal was a labeling that consists of four indicators. Three of these would be represented by the fields *missing*, *swapped* and *duplicate* events which provide the rates these deviations types have for each process execution. The fourth indicator should be an overall value, which summarizes the conformance of each process execution.

3   Conceptual Design

Our concept consists of two phases. One for the integration of the control flow and a second one for the process-related data. In the first phase, the upstream task is the process discovery ①, which creates a process model based on the event log and a mining procedure. This model represents the basis for the second task: the conformance check ②, which aims to measure the deviations between the log and the process model by *replaying* the log on the model. The conformance check provides the indicators that show the rates of missing, swapped and duplicate events as well as the overall conformity for each process execution (trace). These indicators will be calculated both for each event of the trace (*event_metrics*) and for the entire trace (*trace_metrics*) ③ (Fig. 3).

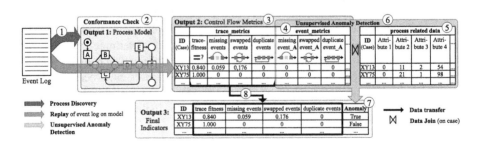

Fig. 3. Concept

In this concept, the process discovery only considers the control flow. The resulting process model thus does not contain *guards*. Guards are rules that explain when process executions have to take a certain path at a decision point in the process model [7]. This means, a process model, which is extended by guards (a data-petri-net [18]), describes not only which process paths are possible, but also under which conditions they may be executed. In our concept, the event log could also be used in combination with the process-related data to create a data-petri-net. However, regardless of the process model type, we propose an additional data combination. This is due to the fact that during a conformance check even guards can only control the behavior that is modeled in the process model. However, a process model can never contain the entire behavior of a real business process without becoming unreadable for a person. Instead, process models are typically created in a more general form. If a conformance check is then performed using such a generalized model, the number of deviating process executions can quickly increase when the log is noisy. In order to identify the legitimate – but not modeled – cases within this set of potential anomalies, the control flow deviations can also be subsequently combined with process context. In our approach, this combination is realized by further processing the previously calculated *event_metrics* ④ together with the process related data ⑤ using an unsupervised anomaly detection ⑥. I.e., the data processed by the anomaly detection contains a row for each process execution with the fields: *case | missing_event_A | swapped_event_A | duplicate_event_A | missing_event_B |...| missing_event_X |...| process_related_attr_1 | process_related_attr_2 |...| process_related_attr_n*. In this way, it is possible to put the control flow behavior of a process execution into a concrete process context, even if this behavior is not provided in the generalized model (e.g., to determine, whether the missing event *A* is typical or untypical, considering the respective process context). In our concept, this results in an additional indicator ⑦ that provides a boolean value, where "*true*" stands for an abnormal and "*false*" for a normal process execution. The approach is unsupervised, as no labels should be used. The final output also includes the aggregated control flow metrics ⑧.

4   Case Study

Setting, Data and Preprocessing. To evaluate our concept, we transferred it into a prototype and conducted a case study in the internal auditing department of an internationally operating automobile manufacturer. In addition to the expertise of two auditors the case study benefited from real-life data from 2058 manufacturing-related permit processes. The event log contains status numbers as events, which were set in the information systems during a permit process. The process-related data provides single-line information on 54 fields about each permit process without referring to events or times in the control flow. The categorical fields of the process-related data set (8% of the data) were converted into numeric values using a frequency-based [19] encoding. A one-hot encoding [20] was omitted because in this data, this would have generated tens of thousands of columns and thus greatly increased the object space dimensionality. Afterwards, a min-max normalization (0, 1) has been performed for all attributes.

Process Discovery. To perform the process discovery and conformance checking, we used *ProM*, an open source framework for process mining algorithms [21]. For the process discovery, the plugin *Inductive Visual Miner* [22] and for the process representation the petri net was used. The Inductive Visual Miner can be adjusted using the *path slider* and the *activities slider*. The latter determines the proportion of events to be considered in the process model. The path slider can be used to control the scope of the noise filtering and ranges, just like the activity slider, from 0 to 1 (0 = maximum noise filtering). In this context "noise" refers to the variation of paths between the events [22].

Since initially no events should be excluded from the log, the activities slider was set to 1 during the entire process discovery. In contrast, the path slider (*ps*) was examined at 21 settings (0.0, 0.05, 0.10,..., 1.0). To simplify the creation of a generalized model, these 21 settings were used for the evaluation of 10 chaotic event filtering [23] and 20 trace filtering [24] iterations. E.g., during the chaotic event filtering, one chaotic event after another was successively filtered out of the log and after each filtering, the 21 *ps*-positions were iterated. Since one process model results from each path slider setting, a total of 630 process models were created in this way (21 *ps* * 10 + 21 *ps* * 20). By replaying the log on each of these process models, the *fitness* and *precision* as well as the *f-score* were calculated. After running all iterations, the model with the maximum f-score was selected for the prototype (f-score: 97.6 | fitness: 96.9 | precision 98.3).

Conformance Check. We used the calculation of alignments in our conformance check. Since the previously created process model is considered as a reference process and the single process executions (traces) should be assessed with regard to their conformity to this reference process, the perspective of *trace fitness* takes effect. To address this perspective through alignments we applied the plugin *Conformance Checking of DPN (XLog)* [11] which used the process model and the log as input. The output is a list of all traces, in which the control flow violations are marked by different coloring. Figure 4 shows two traces of the log: one with 100% trace fitness ① and one with 81.8% ②.

Fig. 4. Conformance checking output

Given the collected requirements to detect missing, swapped, and duplicate events, this output needs additional interpretation. The purple and yellow markings indicate whether the event could be set at the respective position exclusively by the model (move-on-model-only) or by the log (move-on-log-only). For the alignment calculation, these move classifications are performed exclusively for the considered position in the trace and model. However, the fact that, e.g., a move-on-model-only needs to be interpreted as a completely missing event, would only be true if this event was not set at any other position in the trace. Such an actually missing event is shown in ⑤. If, on the other hand, the event would also be set at an earlier or later position in the trace, this should be interpreted as a swapped event ④. The move-on-log-only shows that the event was not intended by the model. Besides a swapped event, this could also be due to a duplicate event ③. Such a global consideration of the entire trace is irrelevant for the fitness calculation and is thus not provided by the plugin. To calculate the *missing*, *swapped* and *duplicate events*, we therefore implemented a script which used the csv-export-file of the plugin as input. In this file, the move type is given by numbers: **0** (*synchronous-move*), **1** (*move-on-log-only*), **2** (*move-on-model-only*). Our script stores these values together with the occurring event names for each trace in three lists (type_0, type_1, type_2). Then it iterates over the lists and derives the deviation categories for each event based on the logic shown in ⑥. In this way, each trace event receives its own deviation categories (*event_metrics*). E.g., for event 730, the columns *730_duplicate, 730_swapped*, and *730_missing* would be created in which the respective frequencies are stored ⑦. In a final aggregation, the values of the *event_metrics* are set in relation to the number of all events occurring in the trace (for trace ② of Fig. 4: 1/14 events = 0.0714 ⑧) (Fig. 5).

⑥ Calculation Logic for the *event_metrics*					Output of the Calculation						
Action	Condition (MT = move type; e = the considered event within the trace)			⑧ trace metrics				⑦ event metrics		
		Case	trace fitness	duplicate events	swapped events	missing events		730_ duplicate	730_ swapped	730_ missing
duplicate+1	A synchronous-move (MT: 0) and a move-on-log-only (MT: 1) was found for e									
swapped+1	A move-on-log-only (MT: 1) and a move-on-model-only (MT: 2) was found for e	XY23	0.8181	0.0714	0.0714	0.0714	...	0	1	0	...
missing+1	Only a move-on-model-only (MT: 2) was found for e									

Fig. 5. Calculation of the control flow indicators

Unsupervised Anomaly Detection. We used two views of the process-related data. In the first view no attributes were filtered out (*data_view*). The second view included, besides the *event_metrics*, only attributes in which our auditors found anomalies (*aud_view*).

For the unsupervised anomaly detection, performance between an iForest [25] and a local outlier factor (lof) [26] was compared. The lof classifies a data point as (ab)normal based on the local density deviation of the data point in relation to its neighbors [26]. The iForest uses a combination of several isolation trees, which isolate outliers from the rest of the data by a recursive, random division of the attribute values [25]. These two methods were implemented using the python library *scikit-learn* which explains the available parameters in [27]. For these parameters, different value intervals were defined and combined with one another. This resulted in 400 iForest and 480 lof parameter settings. Since no process knowledge was assumed in our concept, an internal evaluation of the model quality was necessary. In this way, the influence of the different parameter settings can be measured without using ground truth labels. To do so, we used a classifier performance approach. This assumes that if an anomaly detection method efficiently captures a data set, the abnormal entities identified by this method must be well separated from the normal entities. This separability can in turn be measured by a supervised classification. The goal is to capture the prediction quality of a classifier, which used the previously predicted anomaly classes of the unsupervised anomaly detection as target labels during the training [28]. If the classifier is able to predict the outliers in a test set well, this indicates a good separability. To measure such a classifier performance, we implemented a loop that performed an unsupervised anomaly detection for each of the 400 (iForest) and 480 (lof) parameter settings as well as a subsequent supervised classification on the anomaly detection results. Since the unsupervised anomaly detection did not require training, it was applied to the entire data set. For the subsequent supervised classification, a random forest was applied which used 60% of the data for training and

40% as a test set to measure the prediction quality. To guarantee the same conditions for each iteration, all random variables (in train/test-split, random forest, iForest) were set to 0. As a result of each loop iteration, the classification quality was measured using the f-score and stored in a list. After the loop terminated, the maximum f-score was determined from the list and the corresponding model and parameter setting was used for the final anomaly detection. For both the *data_view* (f-score: 0.936) and *aud_view* (f-score: 0.998) the maximum f-score belongs to the iForest.

4.1 Evaluation

As a first step of this evaluation, the auditors of the partner company converted their audit findings into binary anomaly flags ①. Based on the comparison of these flags with those of the prototype ②, two confusion matrices were calculated. These matrices show differences regarding the hit rate of the actually (ab)normal cases. While in the *data_view* ③ 422 anomaly classifications (20.5%) deviated from the audit report, only 249 (12.1%) deviated in the *aud_view* ④. The results also show that the prediction of actually abnormal cases is more accurate if the set of attributes is limited by auditors (Fig. 6).

Prototype Indicators					②	① Audit Report	
Case	trace fitness	missing events	swapped events	duplicate events	anomaly	anomaly	Case
⑥ XY31	1.0	0.0	0.0	0.0	true	true	XY31
PW24	0.850	0.0	0.166	0.083	true	true	PW24
⑤ RT67	0.944	0.0	0.060	0.0	false	false	RT67
...	...	...	...	...	...	...	...

③ Confusion Matrix – Data View	Audit Report	
Deviations: 422	abnormal	normal
Proto-type abnormal	339	287
normal	135	1297

④ Confusion Matrix – Aud View	Audit Report	
Deviations: 249	abnormal	normal
Proto-type abnormal	446	221
normal	28	1363

Fig. 6. Comparison of the anomaly flags of the prototype with those of the audit report

In a second step, the auditors assessed the indicators in functional terms. As a result, it can be stated that they consider the indicators as a useful audit instrument. This perception is based on the ability to sort and group the process executions by the indicators values. Since the fifth indicator considers every event deviation in its respective process context, auditors can also see when a deviation is relativized by its context. In such a case a control flow deviation would be displayed, but the anomaly flag would be *false* ⑤. The added value of such a relativization becomes clear if auditors would use only the four control flow indicators to select potential audit cases. The auditors would then classify a process execution as relevant for an audit if it deviates from the model (e.g. fitness < 1). If we had used such an exclusively control-flow-based approach for our comparison with the audit report, there would be 7.3% more false-positives. It is also possible to select only those cases that have been classified as abnormal solely because of the process-related data conditions. I.e., no control flow deviation is displayed but the anomaly flag is set to *true* ⑥. The combined view of the four control flow indicators together with the anomaly flag thus allows auditors to better interpret an anomaly.

In a final step, the control flows of the false-positives were examined in detail, as they had a much larger proportion compared to the false-negatives. It was found that the deviations in 76,1% of all false-positives were due to events which, according to the auditors, are known to be chaotic in nature. This includes, e.g., the responses from email distribution lists. In some cases, several departments must provide a statement on a requested permit process. However, the times at which these responses are made can be very arbitrary – which is legitimate. It is only important that all responses are received before proceeding to the next approval step. This implies that some *switched_ events* are legitimate in this case study. If departments do not respond, the requests will be sent again. This is also legitimate and leads to *duplicate_events*. The reason why this behavior was not considered by a loop in the process model is that these cases did not occur often enough to be considered by the process discovery method (when using maximum f-score). Given this legitimate and at the same time negligible process variance, the concerned 76,1% were confirmed as actual false-positives. In the remaining 23,9% alleged false-positives, specific control flow deviations were found which were actually relevant for further audits.

5 Conclusion

In this paper we investigated how a control-flow-based anomaly detection can be used to support auditors in selecting audit-relevant process executions. An important feature of this approach is its intended practical suitability. In addition to the conceptual alignment with the audit-requirements, this claim should also be achieved through a practice-oriented data requirement. Since unlabelled data are common in practice, no labelled data were used during the modeling. The entire procedure was thus realized without process knowledge. The evaluation of the developed indicators confirmed that these can provide auditors with useful assistance in the selection of relevant cases. In addition to the evaluation results, this is also due to the comparison with classical audit methods, which are still characterized by sampling and focusing on process-related data. The practical application of our approach is therefore not only the consideration of a full data population, but also the use of both the control flow and the process related data. In this way it was also shown that control flow deviations can be relativized by their individual context. This in turn can help to reduce the amount of irrelevant cases.

For theoretical application, this paper provides new insights in terms of integrating data-driven methods in internal auditing. Three aspects are crucial in this context: 1) Our approach addresses the current reasons that hinders the establishment of control-flow-based anomaly detection in internal auditing. 2) In addition to a concept, our paper presents an exemplary implementation. 3) The suitability of our approach is evaluated quantitatively using real-life data and qualitatively by two auditors.

A limitation of our approach is that the consideration of process-related data could only reduce the false-positives to a certain extent, but not entirely. I.e., auditors could still be held up examining some irrelevant cases. In future work, we want to overcome this limitation and also test the approach in further real-world auditing scenarios.

References

1. Van der Aalst, W.M.P.: Process Mining: Data Science in Action, 2nd edn. Springer, Heidelberg (2016). https://doi.org/10.1007/978-3-662-49851-4
2. Nolle, T., Seeliger, A., Mühlhäuser, M.: Unsupervised anomaly detection in noisy business process event logs using denoising autoencoders. In: Calders, T., Ceci, M., Malerba, D. (eds.) DS 2016. LNCS (LNAI), vol. 9956, pp. 442–456. Springer, Cham (2016). https://doi.org/10.1007/978-3-319-46307-0_28

3. Jans, M., Alles, M., Vasarhelyi, M.: A field study on the use of process mining of event logs as an analytical procedure in auditing. Account. Rev. **89**(5), 1751–1773 (2014)
4. Hosseinpour, M., Jans, M.: Process deviation categories in an auditing context. Available at SSRN 3280339 (2019)
5. Nolle, T., Luettgen, S., Seeliger, A., Mühlhäuser, M.: Analyzing business process anomalies using autoencoders. Mach. Learn. **107**(11), 1875–1893 (2018). https://doi.org/10.1007/s10994-018-5702-8
6. Hosseinpour, M., Jans, M.: Categorizing identified deviations for auditing. In: SIMPDA 2016, Graz, Austria. pp. 125–129 (2016)
7. de Leoni, M., van der Aalst, W.M.P., van Dongen, B.F.: Data- and resource-aware conformance checking of business processes. In: Abramowicz, W., Kriksciuniene, D., Sakalauskas, V. (eds.) BIS 2012. LNBIP, vol. 117, pp. 48–59. Springer, Heidelberg (2012). https://doi.org/10.1007/978-3-642-30359-3_5
8. de Leoni, M., van der Aalst, W.M.P.: Aligning event logs and process models for multi-perspective conformance checking: an approach based on integer linear programming. In: Daniel, F., Wang, J., Weber, B. (eds.) BPM 2013. LNCS, vol. 8094, pp. 113–129. Springer, Heidelberg (2013). https://doi.org/10.1007/978-3-642-40176-3_10
9. Borrego, D., Barba, I.: Conformance checking and diagnosis for declarative business process models in data-aware scenarios. Expert Syst. Appl. **41**(11), 5340–5352 (2014)
10. Burattin, A., Maggi, F.M., Sperduti, A.: Conformance checking based on multi-perspective declarative process models. Expert Syst. Appl. **65**, 194–211 (2016)
11. Mannhardt, F., de Leoni, M., Reijers, H.A., van der Aalst, W.M.P.: Balanced multi-perspective checking of process conformance. Computing **98**(4), 407–437 (2015). https://doi.org/10.1007/s00607-015-0441-1
12. Böhmer, K., Rinderle-Ma, S.: Multi-perspective anomaly detection in business process execution events. In: Debruyne, C., Panetto, H., Meersman, R., Dillon, T., Kühn, e, O'Sullivan, D., Ardagna, C.A. (eds.) OTM 2016. LNCS, vol. 10033, pp. 80–98. Springer, Cham (2016). https://doi.org/10.1007/978-3-319-48472-3_5
13. Böhmer, K., Rinderle-Ma, S.: Association rules for anomaly detection and root cause analysis in process executions. In: Krogstie, J., Reijers, Hajo A. (eds.) CAiSE 2018. LNCS, vol. 10816, pp. 3–18. Springer, Cham (2018). https://doi.org/10.1007/978-3-319-91563-0_1
14. Alizadeh, M., Lu, X., Fahland, D., Zannone, N., van der Aalst, W.M.P.: Linking data and process perspectives for conformance analysis. Comput. Secur. **73**, 172–193 (2018)
15. Van der Aalst, W.M.P., van Hee, K. M., van Werf, J.M., Verdonk, M.: Auditing 2.0: using process mining to support tomorrow's auditor. Computer **43**(3), 90–93 (2010)
16. Jans, M., Alles, M., Vasarhelyi, M.: Process mining of event logs in internal auditing: a case study. In: 2nd International Symposium on Accounting Information Systems, Rome (2012)
17. Barboza, T.M., Santoro, F.M., Revoredo, K.C., Costa, R.M.M.: A case study of process mining in auditing. In: Proceedings of the XV Brazilian Symposium on Information Systems, pp. 1–8 (2019)
18. De Leoni, M., van der Aalst, W.M.P.: Data-aware process mining: discovering decisions in processes using alignments. In: Proceedings of the 28th Annual ACM Symposium on applied Computing, pp. 1454–1461. ACM Press (2013)
19. Das, S., Cakmak, U.M.: Hands-On Automated Machine Learning: A Beginner's Guide to Building Automated Machine Learning Systems Using AutoML and Python. Packt Publishing, Birmingham (2018)
20. Chollet, F.: Deep Learning with Python. Manning Publications, Shelter Island (2017)
21. ProM. http://www.processmining.org/prom/start. Accessed 19 Apr 2020
22. Leemans, S.: Inductive visual Miner & Directly Follows visual Miner – manual (2019)
23. Tax, N., Sidorova, N., van der Aalst, W.M.P.: Discovering more precise process models from event logs by filtering out chaotic activities. J. Intell. Inf. Syst. **52**(1), 107–139 (2019)

24. Conforti, R., La Rosa, M., ter Hofstede, A.H.M.: Filtering out infrequent behavior from business process event logs. IEEE Trans. Knowl. Data Eng. **29**(2), 300–314 (2017)
25. Liu, F.T., Ting, K.M., Zhou, Z.-H.: Isolation forest. In: Proceedings of the Eighth IEEE International Conference on Data Mining, pp. 413–422. IEEE Computer Society (2008)
26. Breunig, M.M., Kriegel, H.P., Ng, R.T., Sander, J.: LOF: identifying density-based local outliers. ACM Sigmod Rec. **29**(2), 93–104 (2000)
27. Sklearn. https://scikit-learn.org/stable/modules/outlier_detection.html. Accessed 24 Apr 2020
28. Nguyen, T.T., Nguyen, A.T., Nguyen, T.A.H., Vu, L.T., Nguyen, Q.U., Hai, L.D.: Unsupervised anomaly detection in online game. In: Proceedings of the Sixth International Symposium on Information and Communication Technology, pp. 4–10, ACM (2015)

Industry Papers

Latest Image Recommendation Method for Automatic Base Image Update in Dockerfile

Shinya Kitajima[(✉)] and Atsuji Sekiguchi

Software Laboratory, FUJITSU LABORATORIES LTD., 4-1-1 Kamikodanaka,
Nakahara, Kawasaki, Kanagawa 211–8588, Japan
{kitajima.shinya,sekia}@fujitsu.com

Abstract. In recent years, an application deployment method using Docker container has attracted attention by researchers. Docker containers are fast and lightweight, can improve the portability and reproducibility of applications, and are thus often used with CI/CD and DevOps to accelerate the release cycle. However, if a Docker image is not updated, problems such as security risks or a lack of the latest features may occur. Therefore, in this paper, we propose a method for automatically updating the base image to the latest version when the image is considered to be the old version. Our method extracts the information of the base image from the Dockerfile described by the user, and infers the version of the base image that is considered to be certainly used. By applying our method, the user can regularly update the base image. Based on the evaluation result, we confirmed that our method recommends an approximately correct version to the users.

Keywords: Dockerfile · Semantic versioning · Automatic update · PaaS

1 Introduction

In recent years, an application deployment method using a Docker container[1] has been attracting attention from researchers. As the mechanism of a Docker container, the Docker runs an application using a Docker image built based on a Dockerfile based on the container-type virtualization. The time required to start an application is extremely short compared with the server virtualization technology. Therefore, it is compatible with methods such as CI/CD and DevOps that accelerate the release cycle, and the number of cases adopting the Docker container for the application development has significantly increased [4,8]. Container-type virtualization became popular once the portability of the applications was improved using a Docker image and Docker image sharing systems, e.g., Docker Hub[2] [1,10].

---

[1] https://www.docker.com/.
[2] https://hub.docker.com/.

© Springer Nature Switzerland AG 2020
E. Kafeza et al. (Eds.): ICSOC 2020, LNCS 12571, pp. 547–562, 2020.
https://doi.org/10.1007/978-3-030-65310-1_40

```
FROM python:3.5 #Specify base image (python:3.5)

# The processes to add to the base image are listed in the following.
WORKDIR /usr/src/app
COPY requirements.txt ./
RUN pip install --no-cache-dir -r requirements.txt
COPY . .

CMD [ "python", "-u", "./main.py" ]
```

Fig. 1. An example of a Dockerfile.

However, there are some problems when using a Docker container. One such problem is updating the Docker image [1]. In a Dockerfile, which is the source of the Docker image, it is necessary to describe the procedure in a defined format required for building the Docker image. In many cases, version-controlled items such as base images, dependent libraries, and applications are described in a Dockerfile. To reduce security risks, users should use the latest version of these items as much as possible. By regularly updating these items to the latest version, there are advantages in that a large version upgrade can be avoided, making it is easy to roll back and investigate the cause of version update failures. However, when a Docker user manages many different Docker containers, it is extremely complicated to periodically check for updates of the version-controlled items and rewrite the versions in the Dockerfiles when they are updated.

Therefore, in this paper, we propose a method for automatically updating the base image to the latest version when the image is considered to be an old version. The base image can be described without specifying the detailed version in a Dockerfile. Thus, our method infers the version of the base image that is thought to be actually used based on the date of the git commit. When our method infers that a user is applying the old version, it rewrites the Dockerfile to the latest version. A new Docker image is built automatically based on the CI/CD pipeline set by the user when our method rewrites the Dockerfile.

The remainder of this paper is organized as follows. We describe our assumptions in Sect. 2. In Sect. 3, we describe our method for automatically updating the base image. We then evaluate the accuracy of our method in Sect. 4 and describe previous related studies in Sect. 5. Finally, we provide our concluding remarks in Sect. 6.

2 Assumptions

In this section, we describe our assumptions.

2.1 Dockerfile and Docker Registry

A Docker image is built from a Dockerfile. Fig. 1 presents an example of a Dockerfile. In the Dockerfile, the base image is specified by the line starting with "FROM." In the example, the base image is "python:3.5." A user basically selects a base image from Docker images published on public registries, e.g., Docker Hub, and describes it in a Dockerfile.

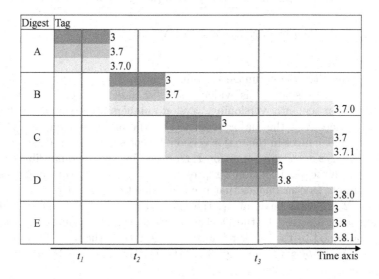

Fig. 2. Relationship between tags and digests.

The Docker images on public registries can be used by anyone. However, there are private registries that are mainly used to store Docker images within an organization, and can be accessed only by a limited number of users.

In the Dockerfile, the user can specify Docker images on these public and private registries. In this study, we assume that users select Docker images on Docker Hub, where most Docker images are published, as the base images. Our method can be applied when the users select Docker images in other Docker registries only if we can obtain a list of tags and digests of the Docker images.

2.2 Tag and Digest

Figure 2 shows the relationship between tags and digests. When a user specifies "python:3.5," it indicates the Docker image with *tag* "3.5" among the Docker images with the *name* "python." In addition, a unique hash value (*digest*) is assigned to each Docker image. If two images are the same Docker images, the digests of these images are equal; otherwise, they are different. Each Docker image has a few tags. A Docker image may have multiple tags, but a tag is attached to only one Docker image. Moreover, a tag may be reassigned to another Docker image, and the tag is untagged from the Docker image that was previously tagged. That is, the tag and digest have a relationship of 1:N.

A tag assigned to a Docker image often represents the version of the application contained in the image. For example, the Docker image "python:3.5.0"

```
FROM [--platform=<platform>] <image> [AS <name>]
```

```
FROM [--platform=<platform>] <image>[:<tag>] [AS <name>]
```

```
FROM [--platform=<platform>] <image>[@<digest>] [AS <name>]
```

Fig. 3. Notation of FROM in Dockerfile.

indicates that the Docker image contains version 3.5.0 of python. A method called semantic versioning[3] is widely used for assigning version numbers to applications. In semantic versioning, version numbers are assigned in the form of $X.Y.Z$, where X is the major version, Y is the minor version, and Z is the patch version. Changes in the major version X represent backward-incompatible changes, changes in the minor version Y represent backward-compatible changes, and changes in the patch version Z represent backward-compatible bug fixes. Our method targets Docker images that use the semantic versioning.

Figure 2 indicates that, at t_1, the three tags "3," "3.7," and "3.7.0" are simultaneously assigned to the Docker image of Digest A. Subsequently, each tag is re-assigned to the Docker image of Digest B. If the user downloads this Docker image at t_2 with the tag "3.7," the Docker image of Digest B will be downloaded.

There are three types of base image notation when describing a Dockerfile[4]. Figure 3 exhibits the three different notations of the base image. Although all of them start with "FROM" followed by the Docker image name in the same way, they are divided into three approaches depending on whether the tag or digest is omitted, the tag is written, or the digest is written. Our analysis of Dockerfiles published on GitHub[5] indicates that, in most cases, users specify the Docker image by name and tag.

It is also assumed that users do not use development-tagged Docker images such as α, β, or release candidate versions. This is because such a development version of the Docker image is mainly released for testing purposes, and is not used in a regular version update.

2.3   Dockerfile Management

Because Dockerfiles are the source code, they are compatible with version control systems, e.g., Git[6]. In particular, when distributing a Docker image of a developed application or an open source software (OSS), Dockerfiles are often stored in the same Git repository with the source code. In addition, when a user creates a new Docker image based on a Docker image published in a public registry, the user often stores the Dockerfile in a Git repository. This is because the

---

[3] https://semver.org/.

[4] https://docs.docker.com/engine/reference/builder/.

[5] https://github.com/.

[6] https://git-scm.com/.

user not only manages the history of the Dockerfiles using the version control system, but also builds Docker images automatically in cooperation with the CI tools when updating the source code or Dockerfiles.

In this study, we assume that a user practices CI/CD and that Dockerfiles are managed on version control systems (Git repositories) such as GitHub or GitLab[7]. When a Dockerfile is updated using our method, a new Docker image is built and tested. The new Docker image is used when it passes a test. There are two types of Git repositories: public repositories that anyone can access, and private repositories that only limited users can access. Our method can be applied regardless of whether the repository where the user places the Dockerfiles is a public repository or a private repository.

3   Automatic Base Image Updating Method

In this section, we propose a method for automatically updating the base image to the latest version when the image is considered to be the old version. Our method infers the version of the base image that is considered to be actually used based on the date of a git commit, and it rewrites the Dockerfile to the latest version when the user uses the old version.

3.1   Extraction of Base Image Information

Our method extracts the information of the base image from the Dockerfile by using regular expressions based on the notations presented in Fig. 3. Here, the information of the base image consists of three pieces of information: Docker image name, tag, and digest. In addition, our method acquires the commit date of the files under the directory containing the Dockerfile to infer the time when the Docker image was built from the Dockerfile.

It is assumed that the user practices CI/CD and builds Docker images whenever the Dockerfile and the source code are updated. Therefore, the Docker image is built immediately after the last update of the files, i.e., the Dockerfile and the source code referenced in the Dockerfile. We cannot obtain the updated dates of the files directly from the Git repository because the Git repository does not store such information. In addition, the build of the Docker image actually starts when the commit result is pushed to the Git repository, not when the file is updated. For these reasons, we use the commit date to infer the version of the base image.

3.2   Inference of the Version of the Base Image

Because the version of the base image may differ depending on the timing of the build, we infer which version of the Docker image was actually used as the base image and check whether the latest Docker image is used. When the user specifies

---

[7] https://about.gitlab.com/.

architecture: arm digest: sha256:ddda089e5533e2c... os: linux size: 309680093	architecture: amd64 digest: sha256:af8fc40f758a1847... os: linux size: 346767745
last_updated: 2020-02-26T20:56:26Z name: 3.7.6	

Fig. 4. Information obtained through Docker Registry HTTP API V2

the base image by the digest, our method should check whether the user specifies the digest of the latest Docker image. However, because there are very few users who specify the digest when using the base image, this study excludes such users.

By contrast when the user specifies the base image by the tag, our method finds the Docker images that have the tag containing the semantic version and that have the same digest as the image specified by the user. Our method the checks whether the user has specified the latest tag.

We describe the relationship between the tag and Docker image actually used by referring to Fig. 2. When the user specifies the tag "3" in the Dockerfile, a Docker image of "3.7.0" is used when building at t_1. However, when the user builds at t_3, a Docker image of "3.8.0" is used. In this way, if we can infer the build timing, we can infer which semantic version of the Docker image was used.

3.3   Acquisition of the Public Information in Docker Hub

The information presented in Fig. 2 consists of a digest, tag, and update date of each Docker image. We can acquire such information from the Docker Hub by using the Docker Registry HTTP API V2[8]. Figure 4 shows an example of some of the information acquired from the Docker Hub through the Docker Registry HTTP API V2. In this example, the last modified date of the Docker image with the tag "3.7.6" is "2020-02-26T20:56:26Z." In addition, the Docker image for each CPU architecture is registered, and the digest of each image is a string starting with "sha256."

However, because the information acquired from this API does not include the past information, it is not possible to later acquire the old digests or the update dates of the Docker images with the same tag but different digests. In other words, to acquire the old information, as in Fig. 2, it is necessary to periodically acquire and store the information of this API.

By rewriting the user's Dockerfile to the latest digest instead of the latest tag, our method can deal with a case in which the Docker image is updated without changing the tag. However, when the tag of the image adopts the semantic versioning, it is difficult to say that specifying the base image by the digest instead of the tag is the best approach. This is because the semantic version is meaningful, as described in Sect. 2.2.

---

[8] https://docs.docker.com/registry/spec/api/.

Table 1. Examples of digests and tags of "python" image acquired through Docker Registry HTTP API V2

Digest	Tag	Digest	Tag
sha256:2f1eb47fe9...	stretch	sha256:b57a7416bf...	alpine3.11
sha256:12dc3e20ed...	slim-stretch	sha256:b57a7416bf...	alpine
sha256:a11a920a22...	slim-buster	sha256:0ca7229fe7...	3.9.0a4-buster
sha256:a11a920a22...	slim	sha256:b76223dfec...	3.9.0a4-alpine3.10
sha256:687124fffb...	rc-stretch	sha256:0ca7229fe7...	3.9.0a4
sha256:e194bc8980...	rc-slim-stretch	sha256:0ca7229fe7...	3.9-rc-buster
sha256:d476b972c3...	rc-slim-buster	sha256:7ddf2b2da7...	3.9-rc-alpine3.10
sha256:d476b972c3...	rc-slim	sha256:b57a7416bf...	3.9-rc-alpine
sha256:5b9baabce7...	rc-alpine3.9	sha256:0ca7229fe7...	3.9-rc
sha256:b76223dfec...	rc-alpine3.10	sha256:a11a920a22...	3.8.2-slim-buster
sha256:7ddf2b2da7...	rc-alpine	sha256:a11a920a22...	3.8.2-slim
sha256:0ca7229fe7...	rc	sha256:d24b098d2b...	3.8.2-buster
sha256:d24b098d2b...	latest	sha256:b57a7416bf...	3.8.2-alpine3.11
sha256:d24b098d2b...	buster	sha256:274e64a8c4...	3.8.2-alpine3.10
sha256:442fe94d3b...	alpine3.9	sha256:d24b098d2b...	3.8.2
sha256:274e64a8c4...	alpine3.10		

Therefore, our method updates the tag only when the version used in the tag is updated. In the future, we will consider an automatic update method for a case in which the Docker image is updated without changing the tag.

Table 1 presents an example of digests and tags of a "python" image acquired using Docker Registry HTTP API V2. The digests are omitted because they are long, and the tags are omitted because there are too many tags. There are several types of tags: only the semantic version, added OS type (e.g. "alpine," "buster," and "stretch"), only the OS type, containing "a" for the α version, "rc" for the release candidate version, 'slim" for Docker images that are lightened by removing unnecessary packages for Python, and "latest" for the latest version.

3.4 Tag Disassembly

In Table 1, the digest of "latest" tag matches the digest of the tags "buster," "3.8.2," and "3.8.2-buster." This indicates that they point to the same Docker image. Therefore, we can infer that the OS of the Docker image of the tag "latest" is "buster," the Python version of which is "3.8.2." In this way, by searching for the Docker images with the same digest, we can infer the semantic version when the tag of the Docker image does not include the semantic version.

Thus, we decompose the tag into two parts: "semantic version" and "additional information such as OS." In this study, we refer to the former as *version* and the latter as *type*. By comparing the versions, we can determine whether a newer version of the Docker image has been published.

Table 2 shows an example of a disassembly of the tags in Table 1 into the version and type. Some versions are the semantic version, such as "3.8.2," but

Table 2. Disassembly of tags into versions and types.

Tag	Version	Type	Tag	Version	Type
stretch	-	stretch	alpine3.11	-	alpine3.11
slim-stretch	-	slim-stretch	alpine	-	alpine
slim-buster	-	slim-buster	3.9.0a4-buster	3.9.0a4	buster
slim	-	slim	3.9.0a4-alpine3.10	3.9.0a4	alpine3.10
rc-stretch	rc	stretch	3.9.0a4	3.9.0a4	-
rc-slim-stretch	rc	slim-stretch	3.9-rc-buster	3.9-rc	buster
rc-slim-buster	rc	slim-buster	3.9-rc-alpine3.10	3.9-rc	alpine3.10
rc-slim	rc	slim	3.9-rc-alpine	3.9-rc	alpine
rc-alpine3.9	rc	alpine3.9	3.9-rc	3.9-rc	-
rc-alpine3.10	rc	alpine3.10	3.8.2-slim-buster	3.8.2	slim-buster
rc-alpine	rc	alpine	3.8.2-slim	3.8.2	slim
rc	rc	-	3.8.2-buster	3.8.2	buster
latest	-	latest	3.8.2-alpine3.11	3.8.2	alpine3.11
buster	-	buster	3.8.2-alpine3.10	3.8.2	alpine3.10
alpine3.9	-	alpine3.9	3.8.2	3.8.2	-
alpine3.10	-	alpine3.10			

others are not, such as "rc" and "3.9.0a4." The types include the OS name such as "alpine," the OS version such as "buster" and "alpine3.11," the property of the Docker image such as "slim," their combination, and a special meaning such as "latest." The "-" part of the version or type indicates that the version or type is not included in the tag.

The user typically updates to the same type as the base image. For example, a user applying a base image of type "alpine" selects a newer version of the Docker image of the same type "alpine" when updating the version of the base image. This is because, if the OS of the Docker image selected for the base image is different from that of the image used, the packages contained in the base image and the commands are different, and the complete Dockerfile needs to be modified. By contrast, to reduce the weight of the Docker image, the user who uses the Docker image of the type "-" as the base image may change to use the Docker image of the type "slim" or "alpine" as the base image. In this study, we consider only the version of the base image, and do not consider changes the type of base image.

3.5   Inference of the Version and Type

The Docker image created by the user depends on the timing when the Dockerfile is built. Therefore, we infer the version and type of the Docker image actually used by the user. We use the name of the base image and the information of the tag acquired in Sect. 3.1 as well as the digest and update date of each tag acquired in Sect. 3.3.

We define the last commit date as t_c, the used tag as tag_u, the time when we started to acquire the information of Docker Hub as t_{start}, the current time as t_{now}, the information of Docker Hub acquired at time t_i as DH_{t_i} and the set of times when we start to acquire the information of Docker Hub to the current time as $T = \{t_i \mid t_{start} \leq t_i \leq t_{now}\}$.

First, to determine when to use the information of the Docker Hub, we use the set $T_a = \{t \in T \mid t_i < t_c\}$ to find t_a according to the following equation:

$$t_a = \begin{cases} max(T_a) & (|T_a| > 0), \\ t_{start} & (|T_a| = 0, |T| > 0), \\ t_{now} & (|T_a| = 0, |T| = 0). \end{cases} \qquad (1)$$

If $DH_{t_i}(t_i < t_c)$ exists, we can use DH_{t_i}. If it does not exist, we use the oldest information DH_{start}. If the past information has yet to be obtained, we use the information of the current time.

Next, we infer the semantic version of the Docker image actually used by using DH_{t_a} acquired at time t_a. We define the digest contained in DH_a as $d_{a,j}(0 \leq j \leq nd_j)$, the tag contained in DH_{t_a} as $tag_{a,j}(0 \leq j \leq nd_j)$, and a mapping function $FT : tag_{a,j} \rightarrow d_{a,j}$ as $d_{a,j} = FT(tag_{a,j})$. In addition, we assume that $tag_{a,j}$ can be decomposed into the version $ver_{a,j}$ and type $typ_{a,j}$, and we define a mapping function $FV : tag_{a,j} \rightarrow ver_{a,j}$ as $ver_{a,j} = FV(tag_{a,j})$ and a mapping function $FP : tag_{a,j} \rightarrow typ_{a,j}$ as $typ_{a,j} = FP(tag_{a,j})$.

In the case of $FS(tag_u) \neq 0$, we infer the version and type of the Docker image actually used as follows. Here, we define a mapping function of the length of the string as len, the version of the inferred result as ver_{eu}, and the type of such result as typ_{eu}.

1. Calculate digest $d_u = FD(tag_u)$ of tag_u.
2. Calculate the set $TU_{a,u} = \{tag_{a,j} \mid d_u = FD(tag_{a,j})\}$ of $tag_{a,j}$, where $d_u = FD(tag_{a,j})$.
3. For $tag_{a,j} \in TU_{a,u}$, calculate $tag_{a,m} \in TU_{a,u}$ where $len(FV(tag_{a,m})) = max(len(FV(tag_{a,j})))$ and $len(FP(tag_{a,m})) = max(len(FP(tag_{a,j})))$.
4. Calculate $ver_{eu} = FV(tag_{a,j})$ and $typ_{eu}FP(tag_{a,j}))$.

We assume that Table 2 represents DH_{t_a} and provide an example for the case in which tag_u is the "latest." In Table 2, the digest of the Docker image with the tag "latest" is "sha256:d24b098d2b..." The tags for the Docker images with the digest of "sha256:d24b098d2b..." are "latest," "buster," "3.8.2-buster," and "3.8.2." Among them, we select the string with the longest notation, that is, the one with the finest granularity of both versions and types, where both the version and type exist. Thus, we select "3.8.2-buster." As a result, we infer that ver_{eu} was "3.8.2" and typ_{eu} was "buster."

3.6   Extracting the Latest Version

Because we assume that the user does not change the type of Docker image when changing the version of the base image, we first enumerate the Docker images from $DH_{t_{now}}$ that have the same type inferred in Sect. 3.5, and extract the most recent version among them. Here, we define a function FS that indicates whether $ver_{now,j}$ is the semantic version as follows:

$$FS(ver_{a,j}) = \begin{cases} 0 & (is\ not\ semantic\ version), \\ 1 & (is\ semantic\ version). \end{cases} \quad (2)$$

The procedure is shown below.

1. Among the tags $tag_{now,j}$ contained in $DH_{t_{now}}$, we calclate the set $TU_{now,eu} = \{tag_{now,j} \mid FP(tag_{now,j}) = typ_{eu}\}$, where $FP(tag_{now,j}) = typ_{eu}$ of $tag_{now,j}$.
2. Calculate the set $TUS_{now,eu} = \{tag_{now,j} \mid tag_{now,j} \in TU_{now,eu}, FS(FV(tag_{now,j})) = 1\}$ of tags whose version is the semantic version among $TU_{now,eu}$.
3. Calculate the tag $tag_{now,latest} \in TUS_{now,eu}$ with the semantic version being the highest among $TUS_{now,eu}$.

Owing to the nature of the semantic version, it is possible to determine which version is higher through the following comparison. The latest version in this study refers to the uppermost semantic version, and the one with a lower semantic version but a newer update date is not considered the latest version. The procedure for comparing the semantic version $sv_1 = X_1.Y_1.Z_1$ with $sv_2 = X_2.Y_2.Z_2$ is as follows. Here, if sv_1 has a semantic version higher than sv_2, we represent as $sv_1 > sv_2$.

1. If $X_1 > X_2$, $sv_1 > sv_2$.
2. If $X_1 < X_2$, $sv_1 < sv_2$.
3. If $X_1 = X_2$,
    (a) If $Y_1 > Y_2$, $sv_1 > sv_2$.
    (b) If $Y_1 < Y_2$, $sv_1 < sv_2$.
    (c) If $Y_1 = Y_2$,
        i. If $Z_1 > Z_2$, $sv_1 > sv_2$.
        ii. If $Z_1 = Z_2$, $sv_1 = sv_2$.
        iii. If $Z_1 < Z_2$, $sv_1 < sv_2$.

We assume that Table 2 represents $DH_{t_{now}}$, and provide an example for the case in which ver_{eu} is "3.8.2" and typ_{eu} is "buster." In Table 2, the tags of the Docker images with the type "buster" are "buster," "3.9.0a4-buster," "3.9-rc-buster," and "3.8.2-buster." Among these tags, only the tag whose version exists and is the semantic version is a "3.8.2-buster." Because the version portion of this tag is "3.8.2" and corresponds with ver_{eu}, we assume that the user is currently using the latest version in this example.

By contrast, if $FV(tag_{now,latest}) > ver_{eu}$, we recommend $tag_{now,latest}$ to the user.

3.7 Automatic Tag Update

In our method, if there are tags with a semantic version higher than the semantic version inferred as described in Sect. 3.6, the tag with the highest semantic version is recommended to the user. There are several possible methods for this as follows.

- With our method the user is notified by e-mail or other means, and the user modifies the Dockerfile.
- With our method the Dockerfile is automatically rewritten into the Git repository and committed, and the Git repository sends a commit notification to the user based on its function.

We assume that the users themselves select one of the methods according to their preferences. In this section, we describe a method used to update the Dockerfile automatically in the latter case.

When managing the source code and Dockerfile in the Git repository, a branch concept is applied. The branch is used from a commit at a certain point and manages multiple changes in a parallel manner. There are several patterns for managing such branches. For example, users prepare two branches, a *master branch* and a *dev branch*, and when users want to make a change, they commit the change to the dev branch and then merge it into the master branch. As described in this example, it is common for users to not directly commit the changes to the master branch. This is because the users want to prevent bugs caused by unverified or unintentional changes in the master branch.

Therefore, we ask the user to select the target branch of our method and apply our approach to the target branch. Our method creates a further branch from the target branch, automatically updates the Dockerfile on the created branch to the latest version of the tag, and commits it. The user receives a commit notification from the Git repository and merges it into the target branch if there are no problems with the change. If the user wants to fully automate the updates, the user should prepare automated tests in advance. When the changed Dockerfile passes the tests, the branch with the changed Dockerfile is merged to the target branch automatically, and the Docker image is created based on the latest base image.

4 Evaluation

In this section, we evaluate whether our method can correctly recommend the latest version. In this evaluation, we describe the results from applying our method to a Dockerfile created by several different users.

4.1 Evaluation Environment

We prepared a system for implementing our method and asked seven users who maintain Dockerfiles in the Git repository to apply the developed system.

Table 3. Tags recommended by our method

Case	Base image name	Tag by user	Recommended tag	User action	Latest version	Reasonable recommend
1	python	3.6	3.8.1-buster	Not changed	Yes	Yes
2	python	3-alpine	3.8.1-alpine3.11	Changed	Yes	Yes
3	maven	3.6.3-jdk-8	3.6.3-jdk-8	–	Yes	Yes
4	python	3-alpine	3.8.1-alpine3.11	Not changed	Yes	Yes
5	python	3.7-slim	3.8.1-slim-buster	Not changed	Yes	Yes
6	node	latest	13.8.0-stretch	Not changed	Yes	Yes
7	maven	3.5.2-jdk-8-alpine	3.6.1-jdk-8-alpine	Not changed	Yes	Yes
8	node	8-alpine	13.8.0-alpine3.11	Not changed	Yes	No
9	nginx	alpine	–	–	–	–
10	jupyter/scipy-notebook	31b807ec9e83	–	–	–	–

In this study, we call this system a "Dockerfile automatic update system." We provided the users with an outline of the system to update the base image of the Dockerfiles automatically, excluding performance of our method, such as what type of Dockerfiles or base images can be updated automatically.

During this evaluation, the public information of the Docker Hub is stored in the database once allowing an investigation into which time information of the Docker Hub was used to recommend the tag. We implemented the tag recommendation by using the data in the database as the latest information, rather than the past information.

We acquire the public information of Docker Hub once a day, and the Docker image name acquired with the information is "python," "golang," "node," "ruby," "openjdk," and "maven," which are thought to be used by many users in our company.

We asked the users to freely register the repository containing the Dockerfile in the Dockerfile automatic update system, and gave permission to the Dockerfile automatic update system to write and read the Dockerfile. The Dockerfile automatic update system accesses the repository registered by the user at any time once per week, reads the Dockerfile, and checks whether the base image used is the latest according to our method. If it is not the latest, it will be updated automatically. When the system reads the Dockerfile, it refers to the master branch of the registered repository. The system creates a new branch from the master branch, commits the automatically updated Dockerfile to the created branch, and pushes it to the repository.

4.2 Evaluation Results

Table 3 provides the Docker image name and tag specified by the user and the tag recommended by our method. There are cases in which multiple Dockerfiles are registered in one repository, and there are 10 items. Each item in the table includes the name of the Docker image, the tags assigned by the user, the tags recommended by our method, whether the user has modified the Dockerfile based on the results of the recommendation, whether our method has recommended the latest version of the tag, and whether we consider the recommendation to be valid.

For cases 9 and 10, no recommendation results were obtained. This is because the evaluation was implemented such that the latest tags can be recommended for only the six types of Docker images for which the Docker Hub information is acquired in advance. In addition, the base image in case 10 is not managed by the semantic versioning, and thus our method cannot be applied as is. It is therefore necessary to improve our method to update the base images that are not managed by the semantic versioning.

In all cases except 9 and 10, our method can correctly recommend the latest version of the tag. Therefore, the results of the recommendation of our method itself are considered to have no problems. However, in practice, the number of users who have adopted the updates of the Dockerfile using our method is limited, and thus we believe that a more detailed analysis is needed.

In case 3, because the user is already using the latest Docker image, the tag assigned by the user matches the tag recommended by our method. Therefore, the recommendation result of our method is considered to be reasonable. In case 2, we can confirm that the user adopted the tag of the recommendation result and updated the Dockerfile. Therefore, the result is considered to be reasonable.

In Cases 1, 4, 5, 6, and 7, it was found that the user did not adopt the tag recommended by our method and did not update the Dockerfile. When we interviewed the users, the following comments were obtained: "I did not realize that a branch was being created because I did not set it to be notified by e-mail," and "I did not think it was a high-priority fix, so I left it as it was." However, the tag recommended by our method is correctly the latest version, and it is considered that the recommendation result itself was valid. In the future, we plan to consider not only a method for recommending the latest version of the tag, but also a method for encouraging an update only when there is a security risk or a fatal bug, a method for changing the recommended tags and the recommended timing based on the user's policy, and a method for quantifying the necessity of an update.

In case 8, the tag recommended by our method was the latest version; however, the user commented that it was difficult to incorporate this change as is because it was a significant upgrade from version 8 to 13. It will therefore be necessary to consider how to deal with such a large increase in the major versions in the future.

5   Related Studies

In this section, we describe previous studies related to Dockerfile and its version control.

Studies related to Dockerfile have dealt with its updates [1,3,7], the Docker image quality [1,10], faster builds of Docker images [4,10], and Docker image retrieval [9].

Schermann et al. structured and collected information regarding the state and transition of the Dockerfile. In addition, Hassan et al. proposed a method called RUDSEA, which analyzes the source code of an application and a Dockerfile managed in the same Git repository to create a Docker image of the application, and recommends updates to the Dockerfile when the source code is changed, based on the relationship between variables in the source code and variables in the Dockerfile [3]. Cito et al. examined Dockerfiles on GitHub and reported that the average Dockerfile update frequency was low, with 62.27% of Dockerfiles having zero or one update per year from the first commit [1]. We believe that the results of these studies suggest that the Dockerfile updates that are originally required may not be applied correctly for particular reasons.

Studies dealing with the quality of Dockerfile are close to our aim. Cito et al. investigated the Dockerfiles on GitHub and actually built Dockerfiles for 560 projects. The authors found that 34% of them failed to be properly built with 28.6% not fixing the version of the base images or dependent components [1]. This result reveals that the management version of the base images and the dependent components in the Dockerfiles are extremely difficult. We propose a method for updating the Dockerfile automatically, focusing on a case in which the version of the base image is managed through semantic versioning.

Zhang et al. investigated the relationship between the quality of Dockerfile and the build time of the Docker image, and concluded that the fewer the layers and the smaller the layer size of the Docker image, the less impact regarding the quality problem and the shorter the build time [10]. In addition, Huang et al. proposed a method called FastBuild to speed up the build of the Docker images by caching externally downloaded files and using the cache transparently [4]. We believe that it is necessary to establish a method to not only automatically update the base image but also automatically convert the image into to a lighter type.

To solve the problem in which it is difficult to select an appropriate Docker image from a Docker repository, Yin et al. proposed a method called STAR that recommends tags for a search based on a Dockerfile [9]. The target is the tag used as metadata in the search, which differs from the tag added to the Docker image we are targeting.

For studies dealing with version updates other than Docker images, we describe research dealing with package managers. Raemaekers et al. surveyed packages distributed in the Maven repository to determine whether changes in the major versions of packages managed by semantic versioning contained significant incompatible changes, and found that 35.8% contained at least one significant change [6]. Dietrich et al. surveyed 17 package managers and concluded that, although a large number of packages have adopted semantic versioning, it is doubtful that all versioning will move to this approach [2]. The results of these studies indicate that semantic versioning itself has not yet penetrated, and it is necessary to consider a method for updating Docker images and libraries that do not adopt the semantic versioning.

Macho et al. proposed a method called BUILDMEDIC, which automatically repairs dependency errors in Maven built files. This method uses the version dependency definitions of the Maven repository to automatically remove unwanted packages and modify the versions of the packages used [5]. In the future, we plan to work on an automatic updating method of dependent packages included in the Docker images.

6 Conclusion

In this paper, we proposed a method for extracting the information of the base image being used from the Dockerfile and to update it automatically to the latest version of the base image. From the results obtained from applying our method to the Dockerfiles used by multiple users, we confirmed that our method recommends approximately correct tags.

Future challenges include the following items.

- Proposal of a method for upgrading the OS of the base image.
- How to handle the updates of the Docker image with the same tags.
- Proposal of a method to recommend tags according to the user policy.

References

1. Cito, J., Schermann, G., Wittern, J.E., Leitner, P., Zumberi, S., Gall, H.C.: An empirical analysis of the docker container ecosystem on GitHub. In: 2017 IEEE/ACM 14th International Conference on Mining Software Repositories (MSR), Buenos Aires, pp. 323–333 (2017)
2. Dietrich, J., Pearce, D., Stringer, J., Tahir, A., Blincoe K.: Dependency versioning in the wild. In: 2019 IEEE/ACM 16th International Conference on Mining Software Repositories (MSR), Montreal, QC, Canada, pp. 349–359 (2019)
3. Hassan, F., Rodriguez, R., Wang, X.: RUDSEA: recommending updates of Dockerfiles via software environment analysis. In: 2018 33rd IEEE/ACM International Conference on Automated Software Engineering (ASE), Montpellier, France, pp. 796–801 (2018)
4. Huang, Z., Wu, S., Jiang, S., Jin, H.: FastBuild: accelerating docker image building for efficient development and deployment of container. In: 35th Symposium on Mass Storage Systems and Technologies (MSST), Santa Clara, CA, USA, pp. 28–37 (2019)
5. Macho, C., McIntosh, S., Pinzger, M.: Automatically repairing dependency-related build breakage. In: IEEE 25th International Conference on Software Analysis, Evolution and Reengineering (SANER), Campobasso, pp. 106–117 (2018)
6. Raemaekers, S., Deursen, A., Visser, J.: Semantic versioning versus breaking changes: a study of the Maven repository. In: IEEE 14th International Working Conference on Source Code Analysis and Manipulation, Victoria, BC, pp. 215–224 (2014)
7. Schermann, G., Zumberi, S., Cito J.: Structured information on state and evolution of Dockerfiles on GitHub. In: IEEE/ACM 15th International Conference on Mining Software Repositories (MSR), Gothenburg, pp. 26–29 (2018)

8. Shah, J., Dubaria, D., Widhalm, J.: A survey of devops tools for networking. In: 9th IEEE Annual Ubiquitous Computing, Electronics & Mobile Communication Conference (UEMCON), New York City, NY, USA, pp. 185–188 (2018)
9. Yin, K., Chen, W., Zhou, J., Wu, G., Wei, J.: STAR: a specialized tagging approach for Docker repositories. In: 25th Asia-Pacific Software Engineering Conference (APSEC), Nara, Japan, pp. 426–435 (2018)
10. Zhang, Y., Yin, G., Wang, T., Yu, Y., Wang, H.: An insight into the impact of Dockerfile Evolutionary trajectories on quality and latency. In: IEEE 42nd Annual Computer Software and Applications Conference (COMPSAC), Tokyo, pp. 138–143 (2018)

Online Topic Modeling for Short Texts

Suman Roy[1]([✉]), Vijay Varma Malladi[1], Ayan Sengupta[1], and Souparna Das[2]

[1] Optum Global Solutions India Pvt. Ltd. (UnitedHealth Group),
Bangalore 560 103, India
{suman.roy,malladi_varma,ayan_sengupta}@optum.com
[2] International Institute of Information Technology (IIIT-H), Hyderabad,
Hyderabad 500 032, India
souparna.das@students.iiit.ac.in

Abstract. Retrieval of knowledge from short texts has attracted a lot of attention these days as topic discovery from them can unearth hidden information. In many applications, such topics are needed to be learned on the fly for streaming short texts. In this work we propose an online topic discovery algorithm (OTDA) for short texts. It overcomes the inability of short texts to capture word co-occurrence information by adopting word-context semantic correlation through the skip-gram view of the corpus, following the approach of semantics-assisted NMF (SeaNMF) model due to Shi *et al.* This OTDA works with one data point or one chunk of data points at a time instead of keeping the entire data in the memory, and also admits the property of memorylessness. We consider a couple of public data sets and an internal data set to conduct experiments using one-pass and multi-pass iterations of the proposed algorithm. The results show encouraging performance of OTDA in terms of average Frobenius loss, Topic Coherence, Normalized Mutual Information (NMI), and emerging topic detection.

Keywords: Data mining · Online topic modeling · Short texts · Non-negative matrix factorization (NMF) · Average frobenius loss · Topic Coherence · NMI · Emerging topic

1 Introduction

Lot of applications involving short texts need to possess the ability to learn topics on the fly as new data points arrive in the context of an evolving system. For example, consider the case when an organization tries to address the issue of understanding customer feedback (which is typically short text) using topic modeling. With the constant churning of feedback from customers it is not very prudent to run the topic modeling algorithm on complete data on every update (whenever a new feedback is collected). Also as an organization introduces new

S. Das—This work was done when the author was an intern with Optum Global Solutions, Hyderabad during May-June'19.

E. Kafeza et al. (Eds.): ICSOC 2020, LNCS 12571, pp. 563–579, 2020.
https://doi.org/10.1007/978-3-030-65310-1_41

services and functionalities on the existing issues in their products/services, the nature of user supplied feedback texts changes over time. To capture the thematic content of evolving feedback materials an online topic modeling algorithm should be in place that can give more importance to the current feedback than the older feedback texts. Motivated by this, we propose an online topic discovery algorithm (OTDA) for streaming short texts which incorporates word-context semantic correlation learnt from the skip-gram view of the corpus much like the semantics-assisted NMF (SeaNMF) model [19], with the adaptivity of forgetting mechanism [5]. The SeaNMF model is solved using a block co-ordinate descent (BCD) algorithm. The well known methods for solving BCD need to hold the entire data matrix in the memory throughout the process of computation which can be prohibitive in case of large amount of data sets. Although various online NMF algorithms like the algorithm [6], have been proposed that can detect latent factors and track their evolution with new data arrival, none of them are suitable to be applied to short texts. To address this issue we incorporate a variant of the online NMF algorithm of [21] in OTDA, grounded in the framework of SeaNMF [19], to discover topics from very large scale/streaming short texts.

The OTDA algorithm works with one data point or one chunk of data points instead of storing the whole data in the memory. Further it updates the topic representation in an underlying space as well as context representation in terms of words on arrival of new data stream, by employing Projected Gradient Descent (PGD) algorithm in both the steps. Admission of context information improves the quality of incremental topic modeling as it can capture the semantics of the short text corpus based on word-document and word-context correlations, thus overcoming the problem of lacking word co-occurrence in short texts. To highlight the adaptivity of our learning algorithm we introduce a decay factor that exponentially reduces the contribution of history data, thereby imposing a forgetting (memorylessness) mechanism on the topic discovery process [5]. We design experiments to investigate the effect of the forgetting mechanism, and the results show that one needs to forget to adapt, that is, in absence of decay parameters the quality of generated topics suffers (NMI values go down) as new data points arrive, and richer topics are generated for streaming data when decay factors are present.

Contribution of This Work. This work has contributed to the body of online topic discovery in several ways. The topic learning incorporates word-context semantic correlation from SeaNMF model, however, it uses the framework of distributed clustering algorithm [22] without an increase in computational overhead and memory requirements. This algorithm has noticeable speed-up as the topic computation is done locally via a reduction in the memory footprint. Also like other online applications, we allow memorylessness with our method by introducing decay factors in the computation which causes the past history to be forgotten at exponential rate and attaches more importance to the current set of data. Extensive experimentation on real-life data sets produce interesting results on metrics, such as average Frobenius loss, Topic Coherence, NMI and emergent topic detection.

Organization: The paper is organized as follows. In the next section (Subsect. 1.1) we discuss the current literature related to this work. In Sect. 2 we review background material on NMF concepts and related matters. We propose our online topic discovery algorithm in Sect. 3. We discuss the data sets and the metrics used for experimentation in Sect. 4 and 5 respectively. The results of the experiments are furnished in Sect. 6. Finally we conclude in Sect. 7.

1.1 Related Work

Two groups of topic models are frequently employed to automatically extract topical contents from the documents, generative probabilistic models such as PLSA [10], LDA [3], and non-negative matrix factorization (NMF) [24]. They normally work well for lengthy documents. However these techniques do not produce meaningful results for short texts as term document matrix is very sparse which produces scarce word co-occurrence information and hence, generates poor quality topics [7, 19]. There are lot of methods proposed in recent times to tackle this problem. These include aggregating short texts into pseudo-documents, and extracting cross document co-occurrence [16, 27] using internal semantic relationship between words. While a pseudo-document generated in the first approach may contain many irrelevant short texts, noise and bias can creep in due to adoption of Wikipedia-centric notions of semantics in the second approach. To alleviate these problems, Shi *et al.* have proposed a novel semantics-assisted NMF (SeaNMF) model for short texts which incorporates word-context semantic correlations learned from the skip-gram view of the corpus [19]. Rest of the discussion on relevant prior art is divided into two parts, online topic discovery and online NMF.

Online Topic Discovery. In one of the earlier work on online topic modeling based on LDA Blei *et al.* [2] develop a family of probabilistic time series models in order to analyze the time evolution of topics in documents. Another LDA-based model is proposed in [23] to model a topic as a continuous distribution over timestamps and the mixture distribution as a function of both word co-occurrences and the document's timestamp. AlSumait *et al.* [1] introduce a topic modeling framework based on the LDA model to make it work in an online fashion such that it incrementally builds an up-to-date model (mixture of topics per document and mixture of words per topic) as a set of documents appear. The authors [11] propose another online topic model for sequentially analyzing time evolution of topic along multi-scales in a large collection of documents. Some online topic models have been also proposed for short texts like tweet data, such as [18] wherein the authors model the generation process of tweets by estimating the ratio between topic words and general words for each user.

Online NMF. We do not come across any work which uses NMF to present online topic model, hence we discuss few pieces of works related to online NMF. Cao *et al.* have proposed an online NMF which finds two factor matrices to approximate the whole data matrix [6]. Although it performs well in practice it cannot be applied to large-scale or streaming data sets due to the memory limitations. Bucak and Gusel have proposed an incremental NMF [5] in which the term topic matrix at $(t+1)$th step is updated on the arrival of $(k+1)$th sample. It has been seen that this works well in practice but, it is time consuming as the updation of rules have slow convergence. Zhou et al. has proposed another variant of incremental NMF with volume constraint [26]. In [8] Guan and Tao propose an efficient online NMF algorithm that learns NMF in an incremental fashion using robust stochastic approximation. In [21] an online NMF algorithm has been proposed for efficient document clustering for very large and streaming data sets. The proposed algorithm in this paper is an improvement of this algorithm in the sense that we consider word context correlation in the model and incorporate decay factors that cause the past history to be forgotten at an exponential rate.

2   Basic NMF Model for Topic Discovery

In this section we discuss basic NMF method, its application to topic modeling and the recently proposed SeaNMF method [19] for short texts.

Notation: Let $\mathbb{R}$ denote the set of real numbers (or reals), $\mathbb{R}_+$ the set of non-negative real numbers and $\mathbb{N}$ the set of natural numbers. $\boldsymbol{x} \in \mathbb{R}^n$ denotes an n-dimensional vector of reals. $\mathbf{1}_K$ denotes a row vector of size 1 whose all elements are 1. Also $\|\boldsymbol{x}\|_1$ and $\|\boldsymbol{x}\|_2$ denote the ℓ_1 and ℓ_2 norms of vector $\boldsymbol{x}$ respectively. We use the notation $\mathbf{X} \in \mathbb{R}^{p \times q}$ to denote a matrix of real numbers having p and q number of rows and columns respectively (or having dimension $p \times q$). We denote the elements of a matrix $\mathbf{X} \in \mathbb{R}_+^{p \times q}$ as $[x_{ij}]_{\{1 \le i \le p, 1 \le j \le q\}}$. We use $\boldsymbol{X}_{i\cdot}$ and $\boldsymbol{X}_{\cdot j}$ to denote the ith row vector and the jth column vector of matrix $\mathbf{X}$. In some cases the column vector $\boldsymbol{X}_{\cdot j}$ will be also denoted as $\boldsymbol{x}_j$ as before. Further $\|\mathbf{X}\|_F^2$ denotes the sum of the squared elements in the matrix $\mathbf{X}$ (also called the Frobenius norm). The zero matrix $\mathbf{0}$ has all zero entries with its dimension to be read off from its context.

Basic NMF Model. The problem of Non-Negative Matrix Factorization (NMF) deals with factoring a given matrix into two non-negative matrices [13,24]. Given an input matrix $\mathbf{X} \in \mathbb{R}_+^{m \times n}$, an integer $K \ll \min(m,n)$, NMF tries to solve a lower-rank approximation, $\mathbf{X} \approx \mathbf{U}\mathbf{V}^T$. where $\mathbf{U} \in \mathbb{R}_+^{m \times K}$ and $\mathbf{V} \in \mathbb{R}_+^{n \times K}$ are factor matrices. This is done by considering the optimization problem that minimizes the following objective function/loss function (also called the error of approximation or the Frobenius loss):

$$\min \mathcal{L}(\mathbf{U}, \mathbf{V}) \left(= \frac{1}{2} \left\| \mathbf{X} - \mathbf{U}\mathbf{V}^T \right\|_F^2 \right), \text{ s.t., } \mathbf{U} \ge 0, \mathbf{V} \ge 0 \qquad (1)$$

Popular algorithms for solving the NMF problem with Frobenius loss as given by Eq. 1 are Multiplicative Update Rule (MUA) [14], Blockwise Co-ordinate Descent (BCD) [12], Projected Gradient Method (PGD) [15] to name a few. We shall mainly adopt PGD [15] which follows alternative minimization principle.

Topic Discovery Using NMF. In topic modeling, $\mathbf{X} \in \mathbb{R}_+^{m \times n}$ is called the term-document matrix where we assume a given corpus with n documents and

m terms. $\boldsymbol{X}_{.l} \in \mathbb{R}^l_+$ represents the l-th column vector of $\mathbf{X}$, which corresponds to the bag-of-words representation of document l with respect to m terms, possibly using TF*IDF weight after some pre-processing, and column-wise ℓ_2 normalization. For solving the minimization problem in Eq. 1 one assumes a pre-determined number of topics K.

Topic Modeling for Short Texts Using NMF. As short texts are sparse and consists of only a few terms many unrelated documents may lead to biased relationship between terms resulting in poor clustering (and topic extraction). Moreover, most of the algorithms for solving NMF fail to appropriately discover the relationship between terms and their contexts. To overcome this problem the authors in [19] propose a novel semantics-assisted NMF (SeaNMF) model to learn topics from short texts.

The SeaNMF approach is based on the idea that terms are dependent on contexts as they appear around them. Towards this the authors define term-context correlation matrix $\mathbf{R}$ [19] using Skip-gram view of the corpus in the presence of an M-dimensional context vector $\boldsymbol{c}$:

$$r_{ij} = \max \left[\log \left(\frac{\#(t_i, c_j)}{\#(t_i) \cdot p(c_j)} \right) - \log \kappa, 0 \right], 1 \leq i \leq m, 1 \leq j \leq M \qquad (2)$$

We use $\mathbb{V}$ to denote the the overall vocabulary of terms and contexts. The notation $\#(t_i, c_i)$ denotes the number of times t_i appears with context c_i in text corpora. Further $\#(t_i) = \sum_{c_j \in \mathbb{V}} \#(t_i, c_j)$ and $\#(c_j) = \sum_{t_i \in \mathbb{V}} \#(t_i, c_j)$ represent the number of times t_i and c_j occur in all possible term-context pairs respectively, and κ is the number of negative samples. Finally, $p(c_j)$ is a unigram distribution for sampling a context c_j defined as $p(c_j) = \frac{\#(c_j)}{\sum_{c_j \in \mathbb{V}} \#(c_j)}$. There are a few techniques to specify the sliding window for a context [19]. For example, each document can be selected as a window of context [19] for a term in short text corpus or it can be a long pseudo-text obtained by aggregating short texts belonging to a cluster. A fixed size window of neighboring words can act as a context for a word, and so on.

Finally, SeaNMF proceeds in two step. In the first step the term-context correlation matrix $\mathbf{R}$ is factored into two matrices, term-topic matrix $\mathbf{U} \in \mathbb{R}_+{}^{m \times K}$ and another newly introduced matrix context topic matrix $\mathbf{U}_c \in \mathbb{R}_+{}^{M \times K}$. In the second step the term document matrix $\mathbf{X} \in \mathbb{R}_+^{m \times n}$ is factored along with the term-topic matrix to obtain the document-topic matrix $\mathbf{V} \in \mathbb{R}_+^{n \times K}$ (some sparsity constraint may be imposed on $\mathbf{X}$ in the process). For details the reader is advised to consult [19].

The computational complexity of SeaNMF for short texts is same as the computational complexity of standard NMF [12] using MUA or BCD method and is equal to $O(nmK)$ for single iteration and $O(TnmK)$ for T iterations (assuming $K \ll \min(n, m)$). However, as $\mathbf{R}$ and $\mathbf{X}$ are sparse matrices the authors conclude that the complexity of the SeaNMF model using BCD is $O(zK)$ ($O(TzK)$) for single (T) iteration(s), where $z = \max(z_{\mathbf{R}}, z_{\mathbf{X}})$, and $z_{\mathbf{R}}$ and $z_{\mathbf{X}}$ are the non-zero elements in the matrices $\mathbf{R}$ and $\mathbf{X}$ respectively, $\max(z_{\mathbf{R}}, z_{\mathbf{X}}) \ll mn$ and

$K \ll \min(m, n)$, which is less expensive than the standard NMF. Further it is required to hold the matrices $\mathbf{X}$ and $\mathbf{R}$ at a storage cost of $O(mn)$ in the SeaNMF model.

3   Proposed Online Topic Modeling for Short Texts

We propose an online Topic Discovery (OTDA) algorithm that updates the matrices $\mathbf{U}, \mathbf{U}_c$ and $\mathbf{V}$ by adding the effects of subsequent samples in an incremental fashion.

3.1   An Incremental Form of NMF

Note the loss function in Eq. 1 can be decomposed as [12]:

$$\mathcal{L}(\mathbf{U}, \mathbf{V}) = \left\| \mathbf{X} - \mathbf{U}\mathbf{V}^T \right\|_F^2 = \sum_{j=1}^{n} \left\| \mathbf{X}_{\cdot j} - \mathbf{U}\mathbf{V}_{\cdot j}^T \right\|_F^2 = \sum_{j=1}^{n} \left\| \boldsymbol{x}_j - \mathbf{U}\boldsymbol{v}_j \right\|_F^2 \quad (3)$$

Consider the problem of generating K topics from the data set. The term topic matrix will look like $\mathbf{U} = [\boldsymbol{u}_1 \cdots \boldsymbol{u}_K]$ which represents each topic as the weighted combination of terms. Further $\boldsymbol{v}_j = [g_{j1} \cdots g_{jK}]^T$ are the reconstruction weights of $\boldsymbol{x}_j$ from these representatives.

When $\mathbf{U}$ is fixed, the minimum value of $\mathcal{L}(\mathbf{U}, \mathbf{V})$ is reached if and only if the cost function $\mathcal{L}(\mathbf{U}, \boldsymbol{v}_j) = \left\| \boldsymbol{x}_j - \mathbf{U}\boldsymbol{v}_j \right\|_F^2$ is minimized for all $j, 1 \leq j \leq n$. Thus, one solves independent Non-negative Least Squares (NNLS) problems of the form,

$$\min_{\boldsymbol{v}_j \geq 0} \left\| \boldsymbol{x}_j - \mathbf{U}\boldsymbol{v}_j \right\|_F^2, j = 1, 2 \ldots n \quad (4)$$

and aggregate the solution as $\mathbf{V} = [\boldsymbol{v}_1 \cdots \boldsymbol{v}_n]$.

3.2   Computing Document Representations

In this step we let the topic representation $\mathbf{U}$ to be fixed. We solve the optimization problem in Eq. 5 to compute $\boldsymbol{v}^{(t)}$:

$$\min \frac{1}{2} \left(\left\| \boldsymbol{x}^{(t)} - \mathbf{U}\boldsymbol{v}^{(t)} \right\|_F^2 + \lambda \left\| \boldsymbol{v}^{(t)} \right\|_1^2 \right) \text{ s.t.}, \boldsymbol{v}^{(t)} \geq 0, \mathbf{U} \text{ is given} \quad (5)$$

where $\lambda > 0$ is a constant. We also impose the sparsity on $\boldsymbol{v}^{(t)}$ by adding a suitable ℓ_1 norm on it. The NNLS problem given by Eq. 5 is the so-called Lasso problem [20] which can be solved using Projected Gradient (PGD) [15] with the gradient computed as: $\frac{\partial \mathcal{L}^{(t)}}{\partial \boldsymbol{v}^{(t)}} = -(\boldsymbol{x}^{(t)})^T \mathbf{U} + (\mathbf{U}\boldsymbol{v}^{(t)})^T \mathbf{U} + \lambda \mathbf{1}_K^T$.

3.3 Solving for Context Representation

In this step we try to compute the context representation of term in an incremental fashion. We assume that the M-dimensional context vector $\boldsymbol{c}^{(t)}$ is available at time instant t, this can be invariant with time or can be learned incrementally as new samples arrive, $e.g.$, it can be learned online as a cluster of data points for streaming data [25]. Thus at time point t we can compute the term context correlation matrix $\mathbf{R}^{(t)}$ with the aid of current context information $\boldsymbol{c}^{(t)}$ using Eq. 2.

Now we solve for the underlying representation of context in the form of context-topic matrix $\mathbf{U}_c^{(t)}$ by minimizing the following cost function in Eq. 6 keeping $\mathbf{U}$ as constant. Also below, we impose the condition that the computed $\mathbf{U}_c^{(t)}$ will be dense by using a ℓ_2-regularization term for it, where $\beta > 0$ is a constant. Again this NNLS can be solved using a standard optimization algorithm.

$$\frac{1}{2}\left\|\mathbf{R}^{(t)} - \mathbf{U}(\mathbf{U}_c^{(t)})^T\right\|_F^2 + \beta\left\|\mathbf{U}_c^{(t)}\right\|_F^2 \quad \text{s.t.,} \ \mathbf{U}_c^{(t)} \geq 0, \ \mathbf{U} \text{ is given} \qquad (6)$$

3.4 Updating Topic Representations

The topic represented in the form of term-topic matrix $\mathbf{U}$ is updated in this step. At time instant t, as $\boldsymbol{x}^{(t)}$ arrives, OTDA first solves for $\boldsymbol{v}^{(t)}$ and $\mathbf{U}_c^{(t)}$ using $\mathbf{U}^{(t-1)}$, and then updates $\mathbf{U}$ by minimizing the following loss function:

$$\mathcal{L}^{(t)}(\mathbf{U}^{(t)}) = \left[\frac{\gamma_0}{2}\sum_{s=1}^t \mu\left\|\mathbf{R}^{(s)} - \mathbf{U}^{(t)}\mathbf{U}_c^{(s)T}\right\|_F^2 + \sum_{s=1}^t \frac{\gamma_s}{2}\left\|\boldsymbol{x}^{(s)} - \mathbf{U}^{(t)}\boldsymbol{v}^{(s)}\right\|_F^2\right] \qquad (7)$$

under the constraints $\mathbf{U}^{(t)} \geq 0$. Further $\boldsymbol{v}^{(s)}$ is obtained as a solution of the minimization problem given in Eq. 5, and $\mathbf{U}_c^{(s)}$ is found by solving Eq. 6.

We introduce decay factors [5] to ensure that the effects of new samples on the representation is higher, while that of old ones wane (memorylessness). That is, $\gamma_0, \gamma_s \ (s = 1, 2 \ldots, t)$ are the decay factors which cause the past history to be forgotten at an exponential rate. We define,

$$\gamma_j = \gamma_0^{(t-2r)}, \quad j \leq 2r$$
$$= \gamma_0^{(t-j)}\gamma_f, \ 2r < j \leq t$$

We assume $\gamma_0 < 1(\gamma_0 \approx 0.5), \gamma_f < 1(\gamma_f \approx 0.9)$ and $r = 1$. The gradient of $\mathcal{L}^{(t)}$ wrt $\mathbf{U}^{(t)}$ is given by

$$\nabla_{\mathbf{U}^{(t)}}\left(\mathcal{L}^{(t)}(\mathbf{U}^{(t)})\right) = -\gamma_0\sum_{s=1}^t \mu[\mathbf{R}^{(s)}\mathbf{U}_c^{(s)} - \mathbf{U}^{(t)}\mathbf{U}_c^{(s)T}\mathbf{U}_c^{(s)}]$$

$$-\sum_{s=1}^t[\gamma_s(\boldsymbol{x}^{(s)}\boldsymbol{v}^{(s)T} - \mathbf{U}^{(t)}\boldsymbol{v}^{(s)}\boldsymbol{v}^{(s)T})] \qquad (8)$$

One can update $\mathbf{U}^{(t)}$ using PGD assuming an initial value of $\mathbf{U}_0^{(t)}$. However, when we implement the first-order PGD we do not get quality results as expected, because there are some known drawbacks for the first-order PGD, for instance, large step size in the update leads to slow convergence etc. Hence we use second order PGD for which we compute the Hessian matrix of $\mathcal{L}^{(t)}$ wrt $\mathbf{U}^{(t)}$,

$$\mathcal{H}_{\mathbf{U}^{(t)}}\left(\mathcal{L}^{(t)}(\mathbf{U}^{(t)})\right) = 2\sum_{s=1}^{t}\left[\mu\cdot\gamma_0\cdot\mathbf{U}_c^{(s)^T}\mathbf{U}_c^{(s)} + \gamma_s\boldsymbol{v}^{(s)}\boldsymbol{v}^{(s)^T}\right] \quad (9)$$

Finally we adopt the following update rule for the second order PGD that can guarantee faster convergence without using any parameter:

$$\mathbf{U}_{k+1}^{(t)} = \mathcal{P}\left[\mathbf{U}_k^{(t)} - \nabla_{\mathbf{U}^{(t)}}\left(\mathcal{L}^{(t)}(\mathbf{U}_k^{(t)})\right)\mathcal{H}_{\mathbf{U}^{(t)}}^{-1}\left(\mathcal{L}^{(t)}(\mathbf{U}_k^{(t)})\right)\right] \quad (10)$$

where $\mathcal{H}^{-1}$ is the inverse of the Hessian matrix $\mathcal{H}$. As the computation of $\mathcal{H}^{-1}$ matrix is time consuming we adopt Conjugate Gradient to calculate it. The second-order PGD has been shown in Algorithm 1. For notational convenience we introduce the following first-order and second-order terms respectively.

$$\mathbf{W}^{(t)} = \sum_{s=1}^{t}\left[\gamma_0\cdot\mu\cdot\boldsymbol{R}^{(s)}\mathbf{U}_c^{(s)} + \gamma_s\cdot\boldsymbol{x}^{(s)}\boldsymbol{v}^{(s)^T}\right] \quad (11)$$

$$\mathbf{H}^{(t)} = \sum_{s=1}^{t}\left[\gamma_0\cdot\mu\cdot\mathbf{U}_c^{(s)^T}\mathbf{U}_c^{(s)} + \gamma_s\cdot\boldsymbol{v}^{(s)}\boldsymbol{v}^{(s)^T})\right] \quad (12)$$

Algorithm 1: 2nd order PGD for updating $\mathbf{U}^{(t)}$

Input   : Number of topics K, Initial term-topic matrix $\mathbf{U}_0^{(t)}$, and document-topic matrix $\mathbf{V}^{(t)}$, and other terms $\mathbf{W}^{(t)}$ and $\mathbf{H}^{(t)}$

/* Using Conjugate Gradient Descent (CGD); k is the index of iterations and Γ is no. of iterations   */

for $k = 1,\ldots,\Gamma$ do

    Compute the gradient $\Delta_k = \mathbf{W}^{(t)} - \mathbf{U}_{k-1}^{(t)}\mathbf{H}^{(t)}$ † ;

    Solve $\mathbf{Q}$ such that $\mathbf{Q}\mathbf{H}^{(t)} = \Delta_k$;

    $\mathbf{U}_k^{(t)} = \max\left(\mathbf{0}, \mathbf{Q} + \mathbf{U}_{k-1}^{(t)}\right)$

end

3.5   Online Topic Discovery

Using second-order PGD we can design an online algorithm for topic discovery for short texts. This algorithm procedure can be performed using one pass and multiple passes. The complete one-pass algorithm is mentioned in Algorithm 2.

This algorithm follows mini-batch implementation [4] which is at the confluence of Stochastic Gradient Descent and the traditional batch descent algorithms. As this algorithm imports p data points at each step, the OTDA algorithm can be expected to converge faster. Consequently the update rules for $\mathbf{W}^{(t)}$ and $\mathbf{H}^{(t)}$ are given by,

$$\mathbf{W}^{(t)} = \mathbf{W}^{(t-1)} + \sum_{i=1}^{p} \left[\gamma_0 \cdot \mu \cdot \boldsymbol{R}^{(t,i)} \mathbf{U}_c^{(t,i)} + \gamma_t \cdot \boldsymbol{x}^{(t,i)} \boldsymbol{v}^{(t,i)^T} \right] \tag{13}$$

$$\mathbf{H}^{(t)} = \mathbf{H}^{(t-1)} + \sum_{i=1}^{p} \left[\gamma_0 \cdot \mu \cdot \mathbf{U}_c^{(t,i)^T} \mathbf{U}_c^{(t,i)} + \gamma_t \cdot \boldsymbol{v}^{(t,i)} \boldsymbol{v}^{(t,i)^T}) \right] \tag{14}$$

Notice that we do not recompute $\mathbf{W}^{(t)}$ and $\mathbf{H}^{(t)}$ afresh each time. Rather we update $\mathbf{W}^{(t)}$ and $\mathbf{H}^{(t)}$ by using Eqs. 13 and 14 respectively. Although only a single pass over the data seems to be feasible in data stream applications, multiple passes can be run in many applications. In the multi-pass OTDA, the document topic assignment matrix $\mathbf{V}$ can be updated using term-topic matrix $\mathbf{U}$. Moreover, the first and second order information $\mathbf{W}$ and $\mathbf{H}$ in the previous pass can be updated and utilized. When multiple passes are feasible one can expect to obtain more accurate results.

Algorithm 2: One-pass OTDA in the mini-batch model (n is the total no of data points

---

Input   : Term-document matrix $\mathbf{X}$, Initial term-topic matrix $\mathbf{U}^{(0)}$, No of data points at each step $= p$, No of steps $S = \left\lceil \frac{n}{p} \right\rceil$, Initial Emerging topic set Etopics(1) $= \emptyset$, Confidence level CL

Initialization: $\mathbf{W}^{(0)} = \mathbf{0}, \mathbf{H}^{(0)} = \mathbf{0}$

for $t = 1, \ldots, S$ do

    Draw $\boldsymbol{X}^{(t)}$ (p data points) from from $\mathbf{X}$;

    Compute $\boldsymbol{v}^{(t)}$ by solving the optimization problem given in Eqn. 5;

    Update $\mathbf{W}^{(t)}$ and $\mathbf{H}^{(t)}$ using Eqns 13 and 14 respectively;

    Update $\mathbf{U}^{(t)}$ by Algorithm 1;

    if $t > 1$ then

      | Etopics(t) = Edetect(CL) using the algorithm in [1]

    end section 3.2

    ;

end

3.6 Computational Savings

As the OTDA proceeds by solving Eqs. 5, 6 and 7 it incurs computational cost of $O(mnK), O(mmK)$ and $O(nmK)$ at each of these steps respectively. However, since $\mathbf{X}$ and $\mathbf{R}$ are sparse matrices, we only need to multiply the non-zero elements with factor matrices. Hence the cost for these operations will be

$O(z_{\mathbf{X}}K), O(z_{\mathbf{R}}K)$ and $O(zK)$, where $z = \max(z_{\mathbf{R}}, z_{\mathbf{X}})$ for single iteration[1]. The proposed OTDA will therefore will have a cost of $O(zK)$ for single iteration. The Frobenius loss of OTDA is frequently very close to the Frobenius loss of the SeaNMF algorithm after $T \leq 2$ iterations as witnessed by our experimentation, which will save computational cost appreciably ($\approx O(zK)$ cost only). Also our one-pass OTDA needs to only load the data matrix once which involves low IO cost. Our experiment results shows that we often do not need many passes to obtain very accurate results.

3.7   Topic Detection and Tracking

Our dynamic topic model enables capturing the topics and their evolution over time. The vector $\mathbf{U}_{\cdot k}^{(t)}$ portrays the evolution of topic k at time t. As each topic is represented in the form of a column vector, represented as a weighted combination of terms the dissimilarity between the representation of a topic k at time point $t+1$ and t, is defined as $\mathrm{Dist}(k,t) = \left\| \mathbf{U}_{\cdot k}^{(t+1)} - \mathbf{U}_{\cdot k}^{(t)} \right\|_2$. We consider a topic to be *emerging* if it is different from its peers in the same stream, or from all the topics seen so far. The identification of emerging topics can be modeled by considering the K topic distances computed at time t using a confidence level CL. Then we use the algorithm in [1] (Sect. 3.2) to compute nominated emerging topics in which the function Edetect(CL) returns the emerging topics Etopics(t) generated in the time slice t and $(t+1)$.

4   Data Sets for Experimentation

We have considered four sets of short text data for experimental purposes, three of which are public datasets and the fourth is an internal data set. Public data sets are Yahoo manner, SearchSnippets and StackOverflow. Yahoo manner data set (Yahoo) is a subset of the Yahoo Answers Manner Questions, version 2.04[2]. The data set SearchSnippets (Snippets) is selected after searching through the transactions on the web using predefined phrases of 8 different domains. StackOverflow (Stack) is the challenge data set published online[3]. The fourth data set (Optum) contains feedback texts that are provided by customers (from an offshore center of Optum) in certain healthcare domains. Three public data sets are labeled with categories, for which we generate the same number of topics. For Optum feedback texts we assume 9 topics by using the standard criterion of selecting optimal number of clusters.

---

[1] We assume a low average number of PGD iterations for updating $\mathbf{U}$ or $\mathbf{V}$ in one round, and also a low average number of trials needed for implementing the Armijo rule [15,21].

[2] https://webscope.sandbox.yahoo.com/catalog.php?datatype=l.

[3] Kaggle.com.

Table 1. Statistics of data sets considered

Some basic statistics of these data sets are shown in Table 1. '#docs' represents the number of documents in each data set,

Data set	# docs	# terms	density(X)	density(R)	doc-length	#cats	#topics generated
Yahoo	24555	14370	0.0482	0.1598	11.1	8	8
Snippets	10060	23031	0.0561	0.513	17.87	8	8
Stack	10000	8162	0.0858	0.354	8.22	8	8
ptum	9999	4372	0.3736	1.896	28.41	NA	9

and '#terms' the number of terms in the vocabulary. The quantity 'density' is defined as $\dfrac{\#\text{non-zero}}{\#\text{docs} \cdot \#\text{terms}}$, where #non-zero is the number of non-zero elements in the matrix. The entities 'density($\mathbf{X}$)' and 'density($\mathbf{R}$)' represent the density of term-document matrix $\mathbf{X}$ and term-context correlation matrix $\mathbf{R}$, respectively. 'doc-length' represents the average length of the documents. '#cats' denotes the number of distinct categories.

5   Evaluation Metrics

We present an evaluation of our approach by comparing the performance of our online topic discovery algorithm with other relevant algorithms on three characteristics, average Frobenius loss [14,21], Topic Coherence (Coherence) [17] and Normalized Mutual Information (NMI) [7]. As a topic can be related to a cluster we use a cluster-related metric Normalized Mutual Information (NMI) to measure the efficacy of our method, especially for labeled data. Due to which, it is not possible to compute NMI values for Optum dataset.

For comparison with our OTDA on average Frobenius loss, we use the work on clustering using online NMF due to Wang *et al.* [21] (ClusterONMF). There is an old work of online NMF for latent factor tracking due to Cao *et al.* [6] (LatentONMF), however it is shown that ClusterNMF performs better than LatentONMF in terms of average Frobenius loss [21], and hence we do not consider LatentONMF in our experimentation. When we compare our OTDA using Coherence and NMI we use three baseline methods other than ClusterONMF, - adaptive Online-LDA (A-OLDA) [1], Online Learning for LDA (L-OLDA) [9] and Dynamic Topic Model (DTM) [2].

6   Experimental Results

We present experimental results on the data sets discussed before. For the benefit of reproducible research we upload all our codes and the baseline methods on https://github.com/varma-ds/OTDA. We have tweaked parameters appearing in loss functions in Sect. 3, but they do not have much effect on the results. So, we use default hyperparameter settings for each of the baselines. We use Scikit-learn's online LDA implementation[4] for L-OLDA and Gensim's LdaSeqModel[5]

---

[4] https://scikit-learn.org/stable/modules/generated/sklearn.decomposition.LatentDirichletAllocation.html.

[5] https://radimrehurek.com/gensim/models/ldaseqmodel.html.

implementation for DTM. For L-OLDA and A-OLDA we use document topic prior value as $1/K$.

6.1   OTDA with Conjugate Gradient

We mainly focus on OTDA with second order methods using conjugate gradient method. The performance of OTDA with first order PGD is not satisfactory, and hence is not presented (for space constraints).

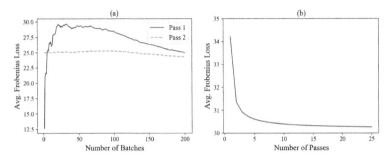

Fig. 1. (a) Average Frobenius loss for one-pass and two-pass with increasing number of batches (b) Average Frobenius loss with increasing number of passes on Yahoo dataset

For the below experiments, we assume that data is divided into different batches of some fixed size. For each batch, both term-document matrix and word context correlation matrix are generated using fixed vocabulary. For computing word-context correlation matrix each short text is considered as a context. Using this information word context correlation matrix is updated for each batch. Other context information like fixed size window of words, streaming text clusters [25] etc. can be also considered.

We present the results for the average Frobenius loss for one-pass and two-pass with increasing number of batches. For the second pass we compute the average Frobenius loss using all the n data points. For the first pass, average Frobenius loss is calculated only for the data points seen so far. From Fig. 1(a), we can see that with only one pass of the algorithm, the average Frobenius loss increases at first and then starts decreasing as the

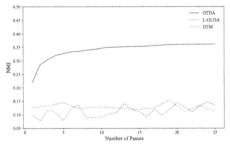

Fig. 2. NMI measured at the end of each pass on Yahoo data

number of batches increases. If two passes are allowed the average Frobenius loss remains almost constant, but it is smaller than the values in the first pass as it learns the topics from the initial batch only. All the data sets show almost similar pattern. Results in Fig. 1(b) indicate that the average Frobenius loss continues to decrease as we increase number of passes with diminishing returns for almost all data sets. Here we reproduce the results for only one initialization and omit results for other initializations for space constraints. We show results for Yahoo data set as other datasets exhibit similar patterns only.

We further compute the NMI values for the labeled data sets using OTDA and plot the results in Fig. 2 for Yahoo dataset. It shows that NMI continues to go up as we increase number of passes to an extent and then stabilizes.

6.2   Comparison with Online Methods

We now compare the performance of OTDA with ClusterONMF [6], A-OLDA [1], L-OLDA [9] and DTM [2] using the metrics topic coherence and NMI. Additionally, we compare Frobenius loss for both OTDA and ClusterNMF during learning. We publish the best score achieved by each of the models for all the datasets in Table 2.

Average Frobenius Loss. We compare our OTDA with ClusterONMF in terms of the average Frobenius loss (using Eq. 4.22 in [6]). We report the result for only one initialization and different batch sizes. Further we produce the results for only one-pass of the algorithm for obvious reasons. We compute the Frobenius loss given using Eq. 4.20 in [6] (at the final iteration) for each batch due to the method of Lee and Seung, which is shown as a dashed line (labeled by L-S) in Fig. 3, wherein which we report the average Frobenius loss for 3 different method on Yahoo dataset only. Similar behavior is observed in other 3 datasets as well, the description

Table 2. Performance of OTDA against baselines. (Best scores across different batch sizes and number of passes are chosen for each model)

Data	Model	Loss at learning	Topic quality	
		Avg. Frobenius loss	Coherence	NMI
Yahoo	OTDA	0.748	**0.485**	**0.390**
	ClusterNMF	0.712	0.449	0.350
	L-OLDA	–	0.302	0.112
	A-OLDA	–	0.269	0.054
	DTM	–	0.340	0.123
Snippets	OTDA	10.114	**0.656**	0.280
	ClusterNMF	9.746	0.411	0.190
	L-OLDA	–	0.491	0.176
	A-OLDA	–	0.271	0.030
	DTM	–	0.560	**0.285**
Stack	OTDA	1.213	**0.327**	**0.186**
	ClusterNMF	1.112	0.084	0.185
	L-OLDA	–	0.295	0.077
	A-OLDA	–	0.190	0.035
	DTM	–	0.322	0.113
Optum	OTDA	1.762	**0.468**	–
	CLusterNMF	1.569	0.430	–
	L-OLDA	–	0.183	–
	A-OLDA	–	0.186	–
	DTM	–	0.191	–

of which is omitted in this paper due to space constraint. In all the cases OTDA produces higher loss than ClusterONMF. It is expected as we minimize the Frobenius loss along with another term involving context information, that acts like a regularization term (see Eq. 7).

Topic Coherence. We compute topic coherence for all the data sets as shown in Table 2. For all of them OTDA performs better than all other baselines. While for Snippets, Stack and Optum datasets appreciable improvement of Coherence is observed for OTDA, Snippets data set shows marginal gain with both OTDA and DTM. Further, in Fig. 4(a) we observe that with increase in batch size, topic coherence values reduce as the models tend to assign more diverse and non-coherent words associated with topics.

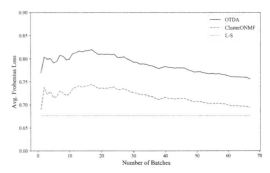

Fig. 3. Comparison of Average Frobenius loss on Yahoo

NMI. Quantitative evaluation using NMI metric is conducted on the three data sets with label information, *e.g.*, Yahoo, Snippets and Stack have the same number of clusters being equal to 8. Table 2 depicts the comparison of clustering for each method on three labeled data sets. Overall, OTDA always outperforms ClusterONMF in terms of NMI values. For Yahoo and Snippets data, OTDA shows an improvement of 5-8% in NMI values in comparison to ClusterONMF. On the other hand, DTM performs slightly better than OTDA on Snippets dataset. Figure 4(b) shows the comparison of different models on Yahoo dataset. We observe a competitive performance between OTDA and ClusterNMF with increasing batch size.

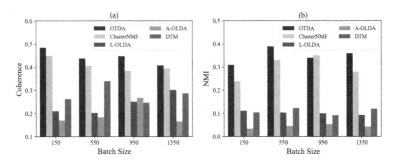

Fig. 4. Comparison of different models *w.r.t.* Topic Coherence and NMI on Yahoo data

6.3 Effect of Decay on Streaming Data

We now examine the effect of decay factors on the streaming data. For that we curate Yahoo data set as follows. We divide the data set into 4 groups and 2 types, characterized by the categories, that is, each type will contain exactly 4 distinct categories of data. Details of this curated data is shown in Table 3.

We assume each group corresponds to one batch and data arrives in batches. Using this curated data we have experimented with and without decay factors in OTDA formulation. The results are presented in Fig. 5. It shows that in absence of decay factors when a new type of data arrives, NMI reduces. But, with the introduction of decay factors in OTDA, the algorithm is able to forget the past topic distributions and learn the new topic distributions.

Table 3. Curated Yahoo data

Group	Data indices	Type	Categories
1	0–3999	1	Family, Maths, Cleaning, Dogs
2	4000–8999	2	Cooking, Finance, Repairs, Diet
3	9000–13999	1	Family, Maths, Cleaning, Dogs
4	14000–18999	2	Cooking, Finance, Repairs, Diet

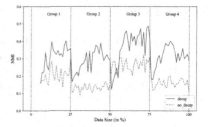

Fig. 5. Decay effect on NMI for Yahoo data

6.4 Emerging Topic Detection

To test the ability of OTDA to detect novel topics as they evolve, we create synthesized data by mixing Yahoo and Stack Overflow data sets from which we take 10 categories (all the categories from Yahoo and only 2 categories from Stack overflow) in the following manner: (1) we add 9 categories in equal proportions (*i.e.p.*) excluding the topic **Maths**; (2) we add all the 10 categories *i.e.p.* including **Maths**; (3) we repeat step 1 and

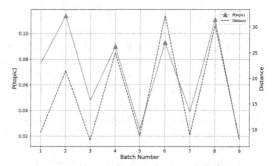

Fig. 6. Probability distribution and Distance of the topic **Maths** across different batch numbers (Trending regions are highlighted)

2 four times; and (4) in the 9th time instant we have added 9 categories *i.e.p.* excluding **Maths**. With this synthesized data, we are able to detect the topic **Maths** as an emerging one at 2nd, 4th, 6th and 8th time instances at 90% confidence level (Fig. 6). The detected Topic probability distribution of **Maths** is also presented in Fig. 6.

7 Conclusion

We have proposed an efficient online NMF algorithm for discovering topics from short texts which processes incoming data incrementally. There are several reasons for choosing NMF over LDA to design this online algorithm.

While our method advocates optimizing loss function directly, other variations of (LDA-based) online topic discovery algorithms using variational inference techniques produce approximations of the actual results. Further, all Markov chain Monte Carlo-based topic extractions (*e.g.*, LDA) are asymptotically exact although computationally expensive. This makes our model a perfect fit for accurate as well as fast, scalable alternative to other topic models.

References

1. AlSumait, L., Barbará, D., Domeniconi, C.: On-line LDA: adaptive topic models for mining text streams with applications to topic detection and tracking. In: Proceedings of ICDM 2008, pp. 3–12 (2008)
2. Blei, D.M., Lafferty, J.D.: Dynamic topic models. In: Proceedings of ICML 2006, pp. 113–120 (2006)
3. Blei, D.M., Ng, A.Y., Jordan, M.I.: Latent Dirichlet allocation. J. Mach. Learn. Res. **3**, 993–1022 (2003)
4. Bottou, L.: Stochastic learning. In: Advanced Lectures on Machine Learning, ML Summer Schools 2003, Canberra, Australia, Revised Lectures, pp. 146–168 (2003)
5. Bucak, S.S., Gunsel, B.: Incremental subspace learning via non-negative matrix factorization. Pattern Recogn. **42**(5), 788–797 (2009)
6. Cao, B., Shen, D., Sun, J.T., Wang, X., Yang, Q., Chen, Z.: Detect and track latent factors with online nonnegative matrix factorization. In: Proceedings of IJCAI 2007, pp. 2689–2694 (2007)
7. Cheng, X., Guo, J., Liu, S., Wang, Y., Yan, X.: Learning topics in short texts by non-negative matrix factorization on term correlation matrix. In: Proceedings of the 13th SIAM International Conference on Data Mining 2013, pp. 749–757 (2013)
8. Guan, N., Tao, D., Luo, Z., Yuan, B.: Online nonnegative matrix factorization with robust stochastic approximation. IEEE Trans. Neural Netw. Learn. Syst. **23**(7), 1087–1099 (2012)
9. Hoffman, M.D., Blei, D.M., Bach, F.R.: Online learning for latent Dirichlet allocation. In: Advances in Neural Information Processing Systems, vol. 23, pp. 856–864 (2010)
10. Hofmann, T.: Probabilistic latent semantic indexing. In: SIGIR 1999, pp. 50–57. ACM (1999)
11. Iwata, T., Yamada, T., Sakurai, Y., Ueda, N.: Online multiscale dynamic topic models. In: Proceedings of the 16th ACM SIGKDD International Conference on Knowledge Discovery and Data Mining, pp. 663–672 (2010)
12. Kim, J., He, Y., Park, H.: Algorithms for nonnegative matrix and tensor factorizations: a unified view based on block coordinate descent framework. J. Global Optim. **58**(2), 285–319 (2013). https://doi.org/10.1007/s10898-013-0035-4
13. Kuang, D., Choo, J., Park, H.: Nonnegative matrix factorization for interactive topic modeling and document clustering. In: Celebi, M.E. (ed.) Partitional Clustering Algorithms, pp. 215–243. Springer, Cham (2015). https://doi.org/10.1007/978-3-319-09259-1_7
14. Lee, D.D., Seung, H.S.: Algorithms for non-negative matrix factorization. In: Leen, T.K., Dietterich, T.G., Tresp, V. (eds.) Advances in Neural Information Processing Systems, vol. 13, pp. 556–562. MIT Press (2001)
15. Lin, C.J.: Projected gradient methods for nonnegative matrix factorization. Neural Comput. **19**(10), 2756–2779 (2007)

16. Quan, X., Kit, C., Ge, Y., Pan, S.J.: Short and sparse text topic modeling via self-aggregation. In: Proceedings of IJCAI 2015, pp. 2270–2276. AAAI Press (2015)

17. Röder, M., Both, A., Hinneburg, A.: Exploring the space of topic coherence measures. In: Proceedings of WSDM 2015, pp. 399–408. ACM (2015)

18. Sasaki, K., Yoshikawa, T., Furuhashi, T.: Online topic model for twitter considering dynamics of user interests and topic trends. In: Moschitti, A., Pang, B., Daelemans, W. (eds.) Proceedings of EMNLP 2014, pp. 1977–1985. ACL (2014)

19. Shi, T., Kang, K., Choo, J., Reddy, C.K.: Short-text topic modeling via non-negative matrix factorization enriched with local word-context correlations. In: Proceedings of WWW 2018, pp. 1105–1114 (2018)

20. Tibshirani, R.: Regression shrinkage and selection via the lasso. J. Roy. Stat. Soc. B **58**, 267–288 (1996)

21. Wang, F., Tan, C., König, A.C., Li, P.: Efficient document clustering via online nonnegative matrix factorizations. In: Eleventh SIAM International Conference on Data Mining. Society for Industrial and Applied Mathematics (2011)

22. Wang, F., Tan, C., Li, P., König, A.C.: Efficient document clustering via online nonnegative matrix factorizations. In: Proceedings of the 11th SIAM International Conference on Data Mining (SDM), pp. 908–919 (2011)

23. Wang, X., McCallum, A.: Topics over time: a non-Markov continuous-time model of topical trends. In: Proceedings of the 12th KDD, pp. 424–433. ACM (2006)

24. Xu, W., Liu, X., Gong, Y.: Document clustering based on non-negative matrix factorization. In: Proceedings of the 26th Annual International ACM SIGIR Conference on Research and Development in Information Retrieval, SIGIR 2003. ACM (2003)

25. Zhong, S.: Efficient streaming text clustering. Neural Netw. **18**(5–6), 790–798 (2005)

26. Zhou, G., Yang, Z., Xie, S., Yang, J.: Online blind source separation using incremental nonnegative matrix factorization with volume constraint. IEEE Trans. Neural Networks **22**(4), 550–560 (2011)

27. Zuo, Y., Wu, J., Zhang, H., Lin, H., Wang, F., Xu, K., Xiong, H.: Topic modeling of short texts: a pseudo-document view. In: KDD 2016, pp. 2105–2114. ACM (2016)

Metrics for Assessing Architecture Conformance to Microservice Architecture Patterns and Practices

Evangelos Ntentos[1]([✉]), Uwe Zdun[1], Konstantinos Plakidas[1],
Sebastian Meixner[2], and Sebastian Geiger[2]

[1] Faculty of Computer Science, Research Group Software Architecture,
University of Vienna, Vienna, Austria
{evangelos.ntentos,uwe.zdun,konstantinos.plakidas}@univie.ac.at
[2] Siemens Corporate Technology, Vienna, Austria
{sebastian.meixner,sebastian.geiger}@siemens.com

Abstract. Many contemporary service-based systems follow the microservice approach, particularly in DevOps or continuous delivery contexts. They share a set of important tenets such as independent development and deployment, high releasability, polyglot technology support, and loose coupling. A number of best practices for microservice architectures have been codified as patterns, which embody those tenets. However, no real-world microservices system can support all patterns and practices well, but rather architectural decisions making trade-offs among them are needed. Conformance to the patterns and practices selected in such decisions is hard to ensure and assess automatically, especially in large-scale, complex, and evolving systems. In this work, we propose a model-based approach based on generic, technology-independent metrics, tied to typical architectural design decisions in the microservice domain. With this approach we can measure conformance to the patterns and related tenets. We demonstrate and assess the validity and appropriateness of these metrics in performing an assessment of a system's conformance to patterns through statistical methods.

1 Introduction

Microservices architectures [10,19] structure an application as a collection of autonomous services, modeled around a domain. They share a set of important *tenets* such as development in independent teams, cloud-native technologies and architectures, polyglot technology stacks including polyglot persistence, lightweight containers, loosely coupled service dependencies, high releasability, end-to-end tracing and monitoring, and continuous delivery [9,10,19]. This work examines ways to ensure architecture conformance to these microservice tenets while applying established patterns and practices. That is, many architectural patterns that reflect recommended "best practices" in a microservices context have already been published in the literature [14,15,20]. Conformance to these

© Springer Nature Switzerland AG 2020
E. Kafeza et al. (Eds.): ICSOC 2020, LNCS 12571, pp. 580–596, 2020.
https://doi.org/10.1007/978-3-030-65310-1_42

patterns impacts how far a microservice system supports the desired microservices tenets.

Unfortunately, as real-world, industrial microservice-based systems are usually highly complex, often highly polyglot, and rapidly changed and released (see, e.g. [2,8]), an automatic or semi-automatic assessment of their pattern conformance is difficult: real-world systems feature various combinations of these patterns and different degrees of violations of the same. Different technologies in various parts of the system implement the patterns in different ways, and these implementations are continuously changing at a high pace. Making matters even more challenging, a high level of automation is required for complex systems. While for small-scale systems of a few services, a manual assessment by an expert is probably as quick and as accurate as an automated one, that is not true for industrial-scale systems of several hundred or more services, which are being developed by different teams or companies, evolving at different paces. In that case, manual assessment is laborious and inaccurate, and a more automated method would vastly improve cost-effectiveness. Another major challenge is that no microservice system can support all microservice tenets well at once. Rather the *architectural decisions* for or against a set of related patterns and practices need to make a trade-off among the desired tenets and important other quality attributes [6,19]. Under these considerations, this paper aims to study the following research questions:

- **RQ1.** How can conformance to the tenets embodied in microservice architecture decision options (i.e. patterns and practices) be automatically assessed?
- **RQ2.** How well do measures for assessing decision options and their associated tenets perform?
- **RQ3.** What is a set of minimal elements needed in a microservice architecture model to compute such measures?

Our approach to address these challenges is to define a set of metrics for each microservice decision associated to the decision's options, i.e. at least one metric per major decision option. Based on a manual assessment of a small set of models and model variants that is representative for the possible decision options and option combinations of the studied decisions, we derive a ground truth. The ground truth is established by objectively assessing whether each decision option is supported. By combining the outcome of all options of a decision, we can then derive an ordinal assessment of how well the decision is supported in each model. We then use the ground truth data to assess how well the hypothesized metrics can possibly predict the ground truth data by performing an ordinal regression analysis. In this paper, we propose an architectural component model based approach which uses only modeling elements that can be derived from the system's source code. For this reason, it is important to be able to work with a minimal set of modeling elements, else it might be difficult to continuously parse them from the source code.

To study the research questions we selected and modeled three major decisions, which represent important aspects in architecting microservices. To illustrate our approach we selected by purpose very different aspects of microservices architecture, in particular: the decision for an external API, message persistence, and end-to-end tracing. For each of these we hypothesized a number of generic, technology-independent metrics to measure conformance to the respective decisions. For the evaluation of these metrics, we modeled 24 architecture models taken from the practitioner literature and assessed each of them manually regarding its support of the patterns and practices contained in each decision. We then compared the results in depth and statistically over the whole evaluation model set. The results show that a subset of each decision related metrics are quite close to the manual, pattern-based assessment.

This paper is structured as follows: Sect. 2 compares to related work. In Sect. 3 we explain the decisions considered in this paper and the related patterns/practices. Next, we describe the research methods and the tools we have applied in our study in Sect. 4. In Sect. 5 we report how the ground truth data for each decision is calculated. Section 6 introduces our hypothesized metrics. Section 7 describes the metrics calculations results for our models and the results of the ordinal regression analysis. Section 8 discusses the RQs regarding the evaluation results and analyses the threats to validity. Finally, in Sect. 9 we draw conclusions and discuss future work.

2   Related Work

Much research has been conducted in collecting and systematizing microservice patterns. For instance, Richardson [14] collected microservice patterns related to major design and architectural practices. Zimmermann et al. [20] introduce microservice API related patterns. Skowronski [15] collected best practices for event-driven microservice architectures. Microservice fundamentals and best practices are also discussed by Fowler and Lewis [9], and are summarized in a mapping study by Pahl and Jamshidi [11]. Taibi and Lenarduzzi [16] study microservice bad smells, i.e. practices that should be avoided (which would correspond to metrics violations in our work).

Many of the works on service metrics today are focused on runtime properties (see e.g. [13]). A number of studies has used metrics to assess microservice-based software architectures, e.g. [1,12,18], but each is focused on narrow sets of architecture-relevant tenets (e.g. loose coupling), and no general approach for an assessment across different microservice tenets exists. Pautasso and Wilde [12] propose a composite, facet-based metric for the assessment of loose coupling in service-oriented systems. Zdun et al. [18] study the independent deployment of microservices by defining metrics to assess architecture conformance to microservice patterns, focused on two aspects: independent deployment and shared dependencies of services. Bogner et al. [1] propose a maintainability quality model which combines eleven easily extracted code metrics into a broader quality assessment. Engel et al. [3] also propose a method of using real-time system communication traces to extract metrics on conformance to recommended microservice design principles such as loose coupling and small service size.

These studies focus on treating microservice architectures as a question of components and connectors, factoring in the technologies used, and producing assessments that combine different assessment parameters (i.e. metrics). Such metrics, if automatically collected, can be utilized as part of larger assessment models/frameworks during design and development time. Our work broadly follows the same approach, but extends it to different architecture tenets relevant to microservice-specific design decisions. Once metrics can be checked automatically, our approach can be classified as a metrics-based, microservice-specific approach for software architecture conformance checking. In general, approaches for architecture conformance checking are often based on automated extraction techniques [5,17]. Techniques that are based on a broad set of microservice-related metrics to cover multiple microservice tenets do not yet exist.

3 Background

External API Decision. One central decision in microservice-based systems is how the external API is offered to clients. This is tightly coupled to the loose coupling, releasability, independent development and deployment, and continuous delivery tenets, as it determines the coupling between client and internal system concerns. In some service-based systems, the *clients can call into system services directly*, meaning high coupling and thus difficulties in releasing, developing, and deploying the clients and system services independently of each other. A better decoupling level might be reached through an *API Gateway* [14], a pattern that describes a common entry point for the system through which all requests are routed. It is a specialized variant of a *Reverse Proxy*, which covers only the routing aspects of an *API Gateway* but not further API abstractions such as authentication, rate limiting, and so on (see [20]). A variant of *API Gateway* for servicing different types of clients (e.g., mobile and desktop clients) is the *Backends for Frontends* pattern [14], which offers a fine-grained API for each specific type of client. A variant where clients can call into system services directly, but are still decoupled is *API Composition* [14], i.e. a service which can invoke other microservices and provides an API for the connected services.

Inter-service Message Persistence Decision. In many business-critical microservice systems, an important concern is that no messages get lost. This concern directly influences the communication between services, and, depending on which option is chosen, the coupling between services, their releasability, their independent development and deployment, as well as their continuous delivery are impacted. Many systems choose communication means that offer *no inter-service message persistence*. Some patterns better support the related aspects of the microservice tenets: The *Messaging* pattern [7] describes service communication, in which persistent message queuing is used to store a producer's messages until the consumer receives them. Many *Stream Processing* [15] components (e.g. Apache Kafka) offer a very similar message persistence level. These solutions offer optimal inter-service message persistence, in the sense that the technology is designed for providing support for it. Some other solutions applied in the microservice field can be used (or adapted) to support it: *Interaction through a*

Shared Database, even though frowned upon with regard to other microservice tenet aspects, supports some level of message persistence as well, but not the automated support of *Messaging*. A more microservice-style technique that supports this level of database-based persistence is the combination of the *Outbox* and the *Transaction Log Tailing* patterns [14] in which each service that sends messages has an outbox database table. As part of the database transaction, the service sends messages by inserting them into the outbox table. A message relay component reads the outbox table and publishes the messages to a message broker. Using the *Event Sourcing* pattern [14] every change to the state of the system should be contained in an event object and stored sequentially in order to be accessible over time. The events are persisted in an event store. This way at least a temporary message persistence is achieved.

End-to-End Tracing Decision. Logging and monitoring are standard practices for creating observability of microservices. As microservice architectures are used for highly distributed and polyglot systems with complex interactions, many of them go one step further and realize end-to-end tracing. It supports tracing and monitoring tenets directly, as well as understandability concerns during independent development and deployment, mastering complexity of highly decoupled services, and thus indirectly releasability and continuous delivery. Like in the other decisions, one option is to offer *No Tracing Support*. In contrast, *Distributed Tracing* [14] is a method used to profile and monitor applications through recording traces on the distributed components. It can either be supported on the microservices of a system, on the gateways of a system, or on both. If both support *Distributed Tracing*, this is optimal, as all relevant traces in ingress, egress, and interservice communication can be recorded. If it is not supported, a lower level of tracing and monitoring can be reached by routing the service communication through a central component, such as a *Publish/Subscribe* or *Message Broker* component [7]. This can also be achieved if all internal inter-service communication is routed through the *API Gateway*, or if *Event Sourcing* or *Event Logging* [14,15] are used, which store all events temporarily. None of the later techniques has the same level of support as *Distributed Tracing*, but all of them can – with some programming or manual effort – be used to reconstruct traces.

4   Research and Modeling Methods

4.1   Model Selection Methods

This study focuses on architecture conformance to microservice patterns and practices. To be able to study this, we first performed an iterative study of a variety of microservice-related knowledge sources, and we refined a metamodel which contains all the required elements to help us reconstruct existing microservice-based systems. For problem investigation and as an evaluation model set for eventually creating a ground truth for our study, we have gathered a number of microservice-based systems, summarized in Table 1. Each of them is either taken directly from a system published by practitioners (on GitHub and/or practitioner blogs) or a system variant adapted according to discussions in the relevant literature. The systems were taken from 9 independent sources. They were developed by practitioners with microservice experience, and they provide a good representation of the microservices best practices summarized in Sect. 3. We performed a fully manual static code analysis for those models where the source code was available (i.e. 7 of our 9 sources; two were modeled based on documentation created by the practitioners). The result is a set of precisely modeled component models of the software systems (modeled using the techniques described below). Variations were modeled to cover the complete design space of our three decisions described in Sect. 3, according to the referenced practitioner sources. Apart from the variations described in Table 1 all other system aspects remained the same as in the base models. This resulted in a total of 24 models summarized in Table 1. We assume that our evaluation models are close to models used in practice and real-world practical needs for microservices. As many of them are open source systems with the purpose of demonstrating practices, they are at most of medium size, though.

Table 1. Selected models: size, details, and sources

Model ID	Model size	Description/Source
BM1	10 components 14 connectors	Banking-related application based on CQRS and event sourcing (from https://github.com/cer/event-sourcing-examples)
BM2	8 components 9 connectors	Variant of BM1 which uses direct RESTful completely synchronous service invocations instead of event-based communication
BM3	8 components 9 connectors	Variant of BM1 which uses direct RESTful completely asynchronous service invocations instead of event-based communication
CO1	8 components 9 connectors	The common component model E-shop application implemented as microservices directly accessed by a Web frontend (from https://github.com/cocome-community-case-study/cocome-cloud-jee-microservices-rest)
CO2	11 components 17 connectors	Variant of CO1 using a SAGA orchestrator on the order service with a message broker. Added support for Open Tracing. Added an API gateway
CO3	9 components 13 connectors	Variant of CO1 where the reports service does not use inter-service communication, but a shared database for accessing product and store data. Added support for Open Tracing
CI1	11 components 12 connectors	Cinema booking application using RESTful HTTP invocations, databases per service, and an API gateway (from https://codeburst.io/build-a-nodejs-cinema-api-gateway-and-deploying-it-to-docker-part-4-703c2b0dd269)
CI2	11 components 12 connectors	Variant of CI1 routing all interservice communication via the API gateway
CI3	10 components 11 connectors	Variant of CI1 using direct client to service invocations instead of the API gateway

(continued)

Table 1. *(continiued)*

Model ID	Model size	Description/Source
CI4	11 components 12 connectors	Variant of CI1 with a subsystem exposing services directly to the client and another subsystem routing all traffic via the API gateway
EC1	10 components 14 connectors	E-commerce application with a Web UI directly accessing microservices and an API gateway for service-based API (from https://microservices.io/patterns/microservices.html)
EC2	11 components 14 connectors	Variant of EC1 using event-based communication and event sourcing internally
EC3	8 components 11 connectors	Variant of EC1 with a shared database used to handle all but one service interactions
ES1	20 components 36 connectors	E-shop application using pub/sub communication for event-based interaction, a middleware-triggered identity service, databases per service (4 SQL DBs, 1 Mongo DB, and 1 Redis DB), and backends for frontends for two Web app types and one mobile app type (from https://github.com/dotnet-architecture/eShopOnContainers)
ES2	14 components 35 connectors	Variant of ES1 using RESTful communication via the API gateway instead of event-based communication and one shared SQL DB for all 6 of the services using DBs. However, no service interaction via the shared database occurs
ES3	16 components 35 connectors	Variant of ES1 using RESTful communication via the API gateway instead of event-based communication and one shared database for all 4 of the services using SQL DB in ES1 However, no service interaction via the shared database occurs
FM1	15 components 24 connectors	Simple food ordering application based on entity services directly linked to a Web UI (from https://github.com/jferrater/Tap-And-Eat-MicroServices)
FM2	14 components 21 connectors	Variant of FM1 which uses the store service as an API composition and asynchronous interservice communication. Added Jaeger-based tracing per service
HM1	13 components 25 connectors	Hipster shop application using GRPC interservice connection and OpenCensus monitoring & Tracing for all but one services as well as on the gateway (from https://github.com/GoogleCloudPlatform/microservices-demo)
HM2	14 components 26 connectors	Variant of HM1 that uses publish/subscribe interaction with event sourcing, except for one service, and realizes the tracing on all services
RM	11 components 18 connectors	Restaurant order management application based on SAGA messaging and domain event interactions. Rudimentary tracing support (from https://github.com/microservices-patterns/ftgo-application)
RS	18 components 29 connectors	Robot shop application with various kinds of service interconnections, data stores, and Instana tracing on most services (from https://github.com/instana/robot-shop)
TH1	14 components 16 connectors	Taxi hailing application with multiple frontends and databases per services from (https://www.nginx.com/blog/introduction-to-microservices/)
TH2	15 components 18 connectors	Variant of TH1 that uses publish/subscribe interaction with event sourcing for all but one service interactions

4.2   Metrics Definition, Ground Truth Calculation, and Statistical Evaluation Methods

To measure conformance to the respective patterns and practices in the design decisions from Sect. 3, we defined a set of metrics for each microservice decision associated to the decision's options, i.e. at least one metric per major decision option. Based on the manual assessment of the models from Table 1, we derived a ground truth for our study (the ground truth and its calculation rules are described in Sect. 5). The ground truth is established by objectively assessing whether each decision option is supported, partially supported, or not supported. By combining the outcome of all options of a decision, we then derived an ordinal assessment on how well the decision is supported in each model, using the scale: [++: very well supported, +: well supported, o: neutral, −: badly supported, −−: very badly supported]. Our scale does not assume equal distances (i.e. it is not a Likert scale), but it assumes the given order. We then used the ground truth data to assess how well the hypothesized metrics can possibly predict the ground truth data by performing an ordinal regression analysis.

Ordinal regression is a widely used method for modeling an ordinal response's dependence on a set of independent predictors. For the ordinal regression analysis we used the *lrm* function from the *rms* package in R [4].

4.3   Methods for Modeling Microservice Component Architectures

From an abstract point of view, a microservice-based system is composed of components and connectors with a set of component types and a set of connector types. Our paper has the goal to automate metrics calculation and assessment based on the component model of a microservice system. That is, if the system is manually modeled or the model can be derived automatically from the source code, our approach is applicable. For modeling microservice architectures we followed the method reported in our previous work [18]. All the code and models used in and produced as part of this study have been made available online for reproducibility[1].

5   Ground Truth Calculations for the Study

In this section, we report for each of the decisions from Sect. 3 how the ground truth data is calculated based on manual assessment whether each of the relevant patterns is either Supported (**S** in Table 2), Partially Supported (**P** in Table 2), or Not-Supported (**N** in Table 2). The ordinal results of those assessments are then reported in the Assessments rows of Table 2.

Following the argumentation, which decision option explained in Sect. 3 has which impact on the *External API Decision* related tenets, we can derive the following scoring scheme for our ground truth assessment of this decision:

---

[1] https://doi.org/10.5281/zenodo.3999477.

Table 2. Ground truth data

External API

	BM1	BM2	BM3	CO1	CO2	CO3	CI1	CI2	CI3	CI4	EC1	EC2	EC3	ES1	ES2	ES3	FM1	FM2	HM1	HM2	RM	RS	TH1	TH2
Reverse Proxy	S	S	S	N	S	N	S	S	N	P	P	P	P	S	S	S	N	N	N	N	S	S	P	P
API Gateway	S	S	S	N	S	N	S	S	N	P	P	P	P	S	S	S	N	N	N	N	S	S	P	P
Backends for Frontends	N	N	N	N	N	N	N	N	N	N	N	N	N	S	S	S	N	N	N	N	N	N	N	N
API Composition	N	N	N	N	N	N	N	N	P	P	N	N	N	N	N	N	N	S	S	S	N	N	P	P
Assessments	++	++	++	--	++	--	++	++	-	o	o	o	o	++	++	++	--	+	+	+	++	++	o	o

Persistent Messaging for Inter-Service Communication

	BM1	BM2	BM3	CO1	CO2	CO3	CI1	CI2	CI3	CI4	EC1	EC2	EC3	ES1	ES2	ES3	FM1	FM2	HM1	HM2	RM	RS	TH1	TH2
Messaging or Persistent PubSub	N	N	N	N	S	N	N	N	N	N	N	N	N	N	N	N	N	N	N	N	N	N	P	N
Shared Database Interaction	N	N	N	N	N	S	N	N	N	N	N	N	S	N	N	N	N	N	N	N	N	N	N	N
Outbox and Trans. Log Tailing	N	N	N	N	N	N	N	N	N	N	N	N	N	N	N	N	N	N	N	N	N	N	N	N
Event Sourcing	S	N	N	N	N	N	N	N	N	N	N	N	S	N	N	N	N	N	N	N	N	N	N	P
All Service Comm. Persistent	S	N	N	N	S	S	N	N	N	N	N	N	N	N	N	N	N	N	N	N	S	N	N	P
Assessments	+	--	--	--	++	+	--	--	--	--	--	+	-	--	--	--	--	--	--	-	++	o	--	o

End-to-End Tracing

	BM1	BM2	BM3	CO1	CO2	CO3	CI1	CI2	CI3	CI4	EC1	EC2	EC3	ES1	ES2	ES3	FM1	FM2	HM1	HM2	RM	RS	TH1	TH2
Distributed Tracing on Services	N	N	N	N	S	S	N	N	N	N	N	N	N	N	N	N	S	P	S	P	P	N	N	N
Distributed Tracing on Gatew.	N	N	N	N	S	N	N	N	N	N	N	N	N	N	N	N	N	S	S	N	N	N	N	N
Pub/Sub, Messaging	S	N	N	S	N	N	N	N	N	N	S	N	P	N	N	N	N	N	P	S	P	N	S	N
Inter-service comm. via Gatew.	N	S	S	N	N	N	P	S	N	P	S	N	N	N	N	P	P	N	N	N	N	N	N	N
Event Sourcing/Logging	S	N	N	N	N	N	N	N	N	N	N	S	N	N	N	N	N	N	N	P	S	N	N	S
Assessments	o	-	-	--	++	++	--	-	--	--	-	o	--	--	--	--	--	+	+	++	o	o	--	o

- ++: All client traffic is routed through an *API Gateway* or *Backends for Frontends*.
- +: All client-connected services provide *API Composition* or only *Reverse Proxy* capabilities.
- o: Some client traffic is routed through *API Gateway* or *Backends for Frontends*.
- -: Some client-connected services provide *API Composition* or only *Reverse Proxy* capabilities.
- --: All client traffic is directly connected to backend services and no *API Composition* happens.

From the argumentation for the *Inter-service Message Persistence Decision*, we can derive the following scoring scheme for our ground truth assessment:

- +: *Message Brokers* or a persistent *Publish/Subscribe* or *Stream Processing* component are used for all inter-service communication.
- +: All interservice communication is persisted by some combination of partial *Message Brokers*, persistent *Publish/Subscribe*, or persistent *Stream Processing* or partial or full coverage with *Shared Database, Event Sourcing, Outbox/Transaction Log Tailing*.
- o: A part of the interservice communication is persisted by partial coverage with *Message Brokers*, persistent *Publish/Subscribe*, or persistent *Stream Processing*.
- -: A part of the interservice communication is persisted by partial coverage with *Shared Database, Event Sourcing, Outbox/Transaction Log Tailing*.

– --: None of the above is supported.

Finally, from the argumentation for the *End-to-end Tracing Decision*, we can derive the following scoring scheme for our ground truth assessment:

- ++: *Distributed Tracing* is fully supported on all services and gateways.
- +: *Distributed Tracing* is fully supported on either the services or the gateways.
- o: *Distributed Tracing* is partially supported or *Event Sourcing/Event Logging* are fully supported.
- -: *Publish/Subscribe*, *Message Broker*, or *Invocations Routed Via API Gateway* are fully supported for service interactions or those patterns are partially supported and at the same time *Event Sourcing/Event Logging* are supported.
- --: None of the above is supported.

6 Metrics

All metrics, unless otherwise noted, are a continuous value with range from 0 to 1, with 1 representing the optimal case where a set of patterns is fully supported, and 0 the worst-case scenario where it is completely absent. For instance, in EC1 client traffic is partially routed through API Gateway resulting $CCF = 0.25$. The metrics results for each model per decision metric are presented in Table 3.

6.1 Metrics for the External API Decisions

Client-side Communication via Facade utilization metric (CCF). This metric returns the number of the connectors from *Clients* to *Facade* components set in relation to the total number of unique *Client* connectors. This way, we can measure how many unique client links are using the External API used by one of the Facade components (i.e. offered through patterns such as *API Gateway, Reverse Proxy, Backends for Frontends*).

$$CCF = \frac{Number\, of\, Client\, to\, Facade\, Links}{Number\, of\, Unique\, Client\, Links}$$

In this metric (and in other metrics below), the number of unique client links is defined as follows:

$$Number\, of\, Unique\, Client\, Links = \\ max\{Number\, of\, Facades\, Linked\, to\, Clients, \\ Number\, of\, Clients\, Linked\, to\, Facades\} \\ + Number\, of\, Client\, to\, Non-Facade/Non-Client\, Links$$

As a result, the only decision option remaining is *API Composition*, for which we formulated the APIC metric.

API Composition utilization metric (APIC). In cases that a client is directly connected to services, it is possible that these services offer an *External API* shielding the interfaces of other services that are connected to them. That is, a client can have access to a system service via other services. To detect such cases, we count the routes from the client to system services via other services and set this number in relation to the total number of system services. That gives us the proportion of services that are accessible by clients via other services. We then divide this number with the unique client links to estimate the proportion of clients connected services which are possibly composing an *External API* using *API Composition.*

$$APIC = \frac{\frac{Number\,of\,Client\,to\,Services\,via\,other\,Services\,Routes}{Total\,Number\,of\,Services}}{Number\,of\,Unique\,Client\,Links}$$

6.2 Metrics for Persistent Messaging for Inter-Service Communication Decision

Service Messaging Persistence utilization metric (SMP). One important aspect in services interconnections is the persistence of the exchanged messages. We defined this metric to measure the proportion of the services interconnections that are made persistent through supporting technology (i.e. *Messaging* or *Stream Processing*).

$$SMP = \frac{Service\,Interconnections\,with\,Messaging\,or\,Stream\,Processing}{Number\,of\,Service\,Interconnections}$$

Shared DataBase utilization metric (SDB). Although a *Shared Database* is considered as an anti-pattern in microservices, there are many systems that use it either partially or completely. The pattern might be beneficial for persistent messaging, but definitely is not the optimal option. To measure its presence in a system, we count the number of interconnections via a *Shared Database* compared to the total number of interconnections. We note that for this metric, our metrics scale is reversed in comparison to the other metrics, because here we detect the presence of an anti-pattern: the optimal result of our metrics is 0, and 1 is the worst-case result.

$$SDB = \frac{Service\,Interconnections\,with\,SharedDB}{Number\,of\,Service\,Interconnections}$$

Outbox/Event Sourcing utilization metric (OES). *Outbox* and *Event Souring* can ensure temporary message persistence. Our metric measures the proportion of the interconnections with *Outbox/Event Sourcing* to the total number of interconnections.

$$OES = \frac{Service\,Interconnection\,with\,Outbox\,or\,Event\,Sourcing}{Number\,of\,Service\,Interconnections}$$

6.3   Metrics for End-to-End Tracing Decision

$$SFT = \frac{Services\ and\ Facades\ Support\ Distributed\ Tracing}{Number\ of\ Services\ and\ Facades}$$

Service Interaction via Central Component utilization metric (SICC) and **Service Interaction with Event Sourcing utilization metric (SIES)**. *Distributed Tracing* can be supported by routing the inter-service communication via a central component (e.g. *Publish/Subscribe, Message Broker* and *API Gateway*). Since *Event Sourcing* also enables tracing by tracking the messages, we distinguish between systems that support *Event Sourcing* (SIES), and systems that do not (SICC).

$$SICC = \frac{Service\ Interaction\ via\ Central\ Component\ w/o\ Event\ Sourcing}{Number\ of\ Service\ Interconnections}$$

Table 3. Metrics calculation results

Metrics	BM1	BM2	BM3	CO1	CO2	CO3	CI1	CI2	CI3	CI4	EC1	EC2
External API												
CCF	1.00	1.00	1.00	0.00	1.00	0.00	1.00	1.00	0.00	0.50	0.25	0.25
APIC	0.00	0.00	0.00	0.00	0.00	0.00	0.00	0.00	0.30	0.10	0.00	0.00
Persistent messaging for inter-service communication												
SMP	0.00	0.00	0.00	0.00	1.00	0.00	0.00	0.00	0.00	0.00	0.00	0.00
SDB	0.00	0.00	0.00	0.00	0.00	1.00	0.00	0.00	0.00	0.00	0.00	0.00
OES	1.00	0.00	0.00	0.00	0.00	0.00	0.00	0.00	0.00	0.00	0.00	1.00
End-to-end tracing												
SFT	0.00	0.00	0.00	0.00	1.00	1.00	0.00	0.00	0.00	0.00	0.00	0.00
SICC	0.00	1.00	1.00	0.00	1.00	1.00	0.14	1.00	0.00	0.60	1.00	0.00
SIES	1.00	0.00	0.00	0.00	0.00	0.00	0.00	0.00	0.00	0.00	0.00	1.00
Metrics	EC3	ES1	ES2	ES3	FM1	FM2	HM1	HM2	RM	RS	TH1	TH2
External API												
CCF	0.25	1.00	1.00	1.00	0.00	0.00	0.00	0.00	1.00	1.00	0.25	0.25
APIC	0.00	0.00	0.00	0.00	0.25	0.50	0.70	0.70	0.00	0.00	0.12	0.04
Persistent messaging for inter-service communication												
SMP	0.00	0.00	0.00	0.00	0.00	0.00	0.00	0.00	0.66	0.11	0.00	0.00
SDB	1.00	0.00	0.00	0.00	0.00	0.00	0.00	0.00	0.00	0.00	0.00	0.00
OES	0.00	0.00	0.00	0.00	0.00	0.00	0.00	0.08	0.00	0.00	0.00	0.66
End-to-end tracing												
SFT	0.00	0.00	0.00	0.00	0.00	1.00	0.90	0.90	0.14	0.62	0.00	0.00
SICC	0.00	0.60	0.45	0.45	0.00	0.00	0.00	0.00	1.00	0.11	0.00	0.00
SIES	0.00	0.00	0.00	0.00	0.00	0.00	0.00	0.80	0.00	0.00	0.00	0.66

$$SIES = \frac{Service\ Interaction\ via\ Central\ Component\ with\ Event\ Sourcing}{Number\ of\ Service\ Interconnections}$$

7 Ordinal Regression Analysis Results

The metrics calculations for each model per each decision metric are presented in Table 3. The dependent outcome variables are the ground truth assessments for each decision, as described in Sect. 5 and summarized in Table 2. The metrics defined in Sect. 6 are used as the independent predictor variables. The ground truth assessments are ordinal variables, while all the independent variables are measured on a scale from 0.0 to 1.0. The aim of the analysis is to predict the

Table 4. Regression analysis results

Intercepts/Coefficients	Value	Model p-value
External API		
Intercept (≥Badly Supported)	*−3.5690*	*4.423828e−11*
Intercept (≥Neutral)	*−4.5042*	
Intercept (≥Well Supported)	*−10.2692*	
Intercept (≥Very Well Supported)	*−15.7271*	
Metric Coefficient (CCF)	*20.3552*	
Metric Coefficient (APIC)	*18.1419*	
Persistent messaging for inter-service communication		
Intercept (≥Badly Supported)	*−5.6344*	*2.002198e−09*
Intercept (≥Neutral)	*−9.5937*	
Intercept (≥Well Supported)	*−11.2074*	
Intercept (≥Very Well Supported)	*−21.0398*	
Metric Coefficient (SMP)	*94.5503*	
Metric Coefficient (SDB)	*10.4199*	
Metric Coefficient (OES)	*13.3840*	
End-to-end tracing		
Intercept (≥Badly Supported)	*−35.4940*	*4.440892e−15*
Intercept (≥Neutral)	*−53.7947*	
Intercept (≥Well Supported)	*−103.6085*	
Intercept (≥Very Well Supported)	*−135.5906*	
Metric Coefficient (SFT)	*44.6971*	
Metric Coefficient (SICC)	*94.1809*	
Metric Coefficient (SIES)	*125.5634*	

likelihood of the dependent outcome variable for each of the decisions by using the relevant metrics.

Each resulting regression model consists of a *baseline intercept* and the independent variables multiplied by *coefficients*. There are different intercepts for each of the value transitions of the dependent variable ($\geq$*Badly Supported*, $\geq$*Neutral*, $\geq$*Well Supported*, $\geq$*Very Well Supported*), while the coefficients reflect the impact of each independent variable on the outcome. For example, a positive coefficient, such as $+5$, indicates a corresponding five-fold increase in the dependent variable for each unit of increase in the independent variable; conversely, a coefficient of -30 would indicate a thirty-fold decrease.

In Table 4, we report the p-values for the resulting models, which in all cases are very low, indicating that the sets of metrics we have defined are able to predict the ground truth assessment for each decision with a high level of accuracy.

8 Discussion

8.1 Discussion of Research Questions

For answering **RQ1** and **RQ2**, we suggested a set of generic, technology-independent metrics for each microservice decision, and we associated at least one metric to each major decision option. The ground truth is established by objectively assessing how well a pattern and/or practice is supported in each model, and extrapolating this to how well the broader decision is supported. We formulated metrics to assess a pattern's implementation in each model, and performed an ordinal regression analysis using these metrics as independent variables to predict the ground truth assessment. Our results show that every set of decision-related metrics can predict with high accuracy our objectively evaluated assessment. This suggests that automatic metrics-based assessment of a system's conformance to the tenets embodied in each design decision is possible with a high degree of confidence.

Regarding **RQ3**, we can assess that our microservice meta-model has no need for major extensions and is easy to map to existing modeling practices. More specifically, in order to fully model our evaluation model set, we needed to introduce 25 component types and 38 connector types, ranging from general notions such as the *Service* component type, to very technology-specific classes such as the *RESTful HTTP* connector, which is a subclass of *Service Connector*. Our study shows that for each pattern and practice embodied in each decision and the proposed metrics, only a small subset of the meta-model is required. The decision *External API* requires to model at least the *Service, Client,* and the *Facade* component types and the technology-related connector types (e.g. *RESTful HTTP, Synchronous Connector, HTTP, HTTPS*). The *Persistent Messaging for Inter-Service Communication* and *End-to-End Tracing* decisions need a number of additional components (e.g. *Event Sourcing, Stream Processing, Messaging, PubSub*) and the respective connectors (e.g. *Publisher, Subscriber, Message Consumer* and *Messages Producer*) to be modeled.

8.2   Threats to Validity

We deliberately relied on third-party systems as the basis for our study to increase internal validity, thus avoiding bias in system composition and structure. It is possible that our search procedures introduced some kind of unconscious exclusion of certain sources; we mitigated this by assembling an author team with many years of experience in the field, and performing very general and broad searches. Given that our search was not exhaustive, and that most of the systems we found were made for demonstration purposes, i.e. relatively modestly sized, this means that some potential architecture elements were not included in our meta-model. In addition, this raises a possible threat to external validity of generalization to other, and more complex, systems. We nevertheless feel confident that the systems documented are a representative cross-cut of current practices in the field, as the points of variance between them were limited and well attested in the literature. Another potential threat is the fact that the variant systems were derived by the author team. However, this was done according to best practices documented in literature. We made sure only to change specific aspects in a variant and keep all other aspects stable.

Another potential source of internal validity threat is the modeling process itself. The author team has considerable experience in similar methods, and the models of the systems were repeatedly and independently cross-checked, but the possibility of some interpretative bias remains: other researchers might have coded or modeled differently, leading to different models. As our goal was only to find one model that is able to specify all observed phenomena, and this was achieved, we consider this threat not to be a major issue for our study. The ground truth assessment might also be subject to different interpretations by different practitioners. For this purpose, we deliberately chose only a three-step ordinal scale, and given that the ground truth evaluation for each decision is fairly straightforward and based on best practices, we do not consider our interpretation controversial. Likewise, the individual metrics used to evaluate the presence of each pattern were deliberately kept as simple as possible, so as to avoid false positives and enable a technology-independent assessment. As stated previously, generalization to more complex systems might not be possible without modification. But we consider that the basic approach taken when defining the metrics is validated by the success of the regression models.

9   Conclusions and Future Work

In this work we have hypothesized that it is possible to develop a method to automatically assess microservices tenets in microservice decisions based on a microservice system's component model. We have shown that this is possible for microservice decision models comprising patterns and practices as decision options. Our approach first modeled the key aspects of the decision options using a minimal set of component model elements (which could be automatically extracted from the source code). Then we derived at least one metric per decision option and used a small reference model set as a ground truth. We then used ordinal regression analysis for deriving a predictor model for the ordinal variable. Our statistical analysis shows a high level of accuracy.

While so far many studies on metrics for component model and other architectures exist, the specifics of microservice architectures and their particular tenets have not been studied. As discussed in Sect. 2, only using general metrics does not help much in assessing microservice architectures. Our approach is one of the first that studies a metrics-based assessment of multiple, very different microservice tenets. Our main goal is a continuous assessment, i.e. we envision an impact on continuous delivery practices, in which the metrics are assessed with each delivery pipeline run, indicating improvements, stability, or deteriorations in microservice architecture conformance. With small changes, our approach could also be applied, during early architecture assessment.

As future work, we plan to study more decisions, tenets, and related metrics. We also plan to create a larger data set, thus better supporting tasks such as early architecture assessment in a project.

Acknowledgments. This work was supported by: FFG (Austrian Research Promotion Agency) project DECO, no. 846707; FWF (Austrian Science Fund) project API-ACE: I 4268.

References

1. Bogner, J., Wagner, S., Zimmermann, A.: Towards a practical maintainability quality model for service-and microservice-based systems, pp. 195–198 (2017). https://doi.org/10.1145/3129790.3129816

2. Chen, L.: Microservices: architecting for continuous delivery and DevOps. In: 2018 IEEE International Conference on Software Architecture (ICSA), pp. 39–397, April 2018. https://doi.org/10.1109/ICSA.2018.00013

3. Engel, T., Langermeier, M., Bauer, B., Hofmann, A.: Evaluation of microservice architectures: a metric and tool-based approach. In: Mendling, J., Mouratidis, H. (eds.) CAiSE 2018. LNBIP, vol. 317, pp. 74–89. Springer, Cham (2018). https://doi.org/10.1007/978-3-319-92901-9_8

4. Harrell, F.E.: Regression Modeling Strategies. SSS. Springer, Cham (2015). https://doi.org/10.1007/978-3-319-19425-7

5. Guo, G.Y., Atlee, J.M., Kazman, R.: A software architecture reconstruction method. In: Donohoe, P. (ed.) Software Architecture. ITIFIP, vol. 12, pp. 15–33. Springer, Boston, MA (1999). https://doi.org/10.1007/978-0-387-35563-4_2

6. Haselböck, S., Weinreich, R., Buchgeher, G.: Decision models for microservices: design areas, stakeholders, use cases, and requirements. In: Lopes, A., de Lemos, R. (eds.) ECSA 2017. LNCS, vol. 10475, pp. 155–170. Springer, Cham (2017). https://doi.org/10.1007/978-3-319-65831-5_11

7. Hohpe, G., Woolf, B.: Enterprise Integration Patterns. Addison-Wesley, Boston (2003)

8. Knoche, H., Hasselbring, W.: Drivers and barriers for microservice adoption - a survey among professionals in Germany. Enterp. Model. Inf. Syst. Archit. (EMISAJ) Int. J. Conceptual Model. **14**(1), 1–35 (2019). https://doi.org/10.18417/emisa.14.1

9. Lewis, J., Fowler, M.: Microservices: a definition of this new architectural term, March 2004. http://martinfowler.com/articles/microservices.html
10. Newman, S.: Building Microservices: Designing Fine-Grained Systems. O'Reilly, Sebastopol (2015)
11. Pahl, C., Jamshidi, P.: Microservices: a systematic mapping study. In: 6th International Conference on Cloud Computing and Services Science, pp. 137–146 (2016)
12. Pautasso, C., Wilde, E.: Why is the web loosely coupled?: a multi-faceted metric for service design. In: 18th International Conference on World Wide Web, pp. 911–920. ACM (2009)
13. Pietrantuono, R., Russo, S., Guerriero, A.: Run-time reliability estimation of microservice architectures. In: 2018 IEEE 29th International Symposium on Software Reliability Engineering (ISSRE), pp. 25–35, October 2018. https://doi.org/10.1109/ISSRE.2018.00014
14. Richardson, C.: A pattern language for microservices (2017). http://microservices.io/patterns/index.html
15. Skowronski, J.: Best practices for event-driven microservice architecture (2019). https://hackernoon.com/best-practices-for-event-driven-microservice-architecture-e034p21lk
16. Taibi, D., Lenarduzzi, V.: On the definition of microservice bad smells. IEEE Softw. **35**(3), 56–62 (2018). https://doi.org/10.1109/MS.2018.2141031
17. Van Deursen, A., Hofmeister, C., Koschke, R., Moonen, L., Riva, C.: Symphony: view-driven software architecture reconstruction. In: 4th Working IEEE/IFIP Conference on Software Architecture (WICSA 2004), pp. 122–132. IEEE (2004)
18. Zdun, U., Navarro, E., Leymann, F.: Ensuring and assessing architecture conformance to microservice decomposition patterns. In: Maximilien, M., Vallecillo, A., Wang, J., Oriol, M. (eds.) ICSOC 2017. LNCS, vol. 10601, pp. 411–429. Springer, Cham (2017). https://doi.org/10.1007/978-3-319-69035-3_29
19. Zimmermann, O.: Microservices tenets. Comput. Sci. Res. Dev. 301–310 (2016). https://doi.org/10.1007/s00450-016-0337-0
20. Zimmermann, O., Stocker, M., Zdun, U., Luebke, D., Pautasso, C.: Microservice API patterns (2019). https://microservice-api-patterns.org

Author Index